# EXPERIMENTAL PSYCHOLOGY Second Edition

UNDERSTANDING PSYCHOLOGICAL RESEARCH

# EXPERIMENTAL
# PSYCHOLOGY Second Edition

## UNDERSTANDING PSYCHOLOGICAL RESEARCH

**Barry H. Kantowitz**
Purdue University

**Henry L. Roediger, III**
Purdue University

**WEST PUBLISHING COMPANY**
St. Paul   New York   Los Angeles   San Francisco

**Library of Congress Cataloging in Publication Data**

Kantowitz, Barry H.
  Experimental psychology.

  Bibliography: p.
  Includes index.
    1. Psychology, Experimental.    2. Psychology—
Research.    I. Roediger, Henry L.    II. Title.
BF181.K35    1984    150′.724    83-23497
ISBN 0-314-78017-3

to/Figure Credits

*il Abstract.* Copyright © 1983 by Photographer D. Van Blair.
the permission of the Image Bank, Inc.

**Fig. 2–1.** From The *Intelligent Eye* by R. L. Gregory. Copyright © 1970 R. L. Gregory. Used with permission of McGraw-Hill Book Company. **Fig. 2–2.** From L. C. Drickamer and S. H. Vessey, *Animal Behavior: Concepts, Processes, and Methods,* copyright © 1982 by PWS Publishers. Used with permission of Willard Grant Press. All rights reserved. **Fig. 5–1.** Photo © by Barbara Van Cleve; courtesy Fronteras Imports. **Fig. 5–2.** Reprinted with the permission of Historical Pictures Service, Inc. **Fig. 6–1.** "Waterfall" by M. C. Escher is reprinted courtesy of the Escher Foundation, Haags Gemeentemuseum, The Hague. **Fig. 6–2.** © 1983 B. Kantowitz, Text-Eye. **Fig. 6–4.** © B. Kantowitz, Text-Eye. **Figs. 6–5, 6–7, and 6–8.** From Ittelson and Kilpatrick, 'Experiments in Perception.' Copyright © 1951 by Scientific American, Inc. All rights reserved. **Fig. 8–1.** Reprinted with the permission of The Bettmann Archive, Inc. **Fig. 8–3.** Courtesy of the Neuropsychology Laboratory, Northeastern University. Photo by Shelley Gordon-Unnerstull. **Fig. 8–3a.** Copyright © Rex Jeschke. **p. 252 Excerpt:** From N. H. Azrin, W. Holz, R. Ulrich, and I. Goldiamond, "The control of the content of conversation through reinforcement." *Journal of the Experimental Analysis of Behavior,* 1961, 4, 25–30. Copyright © 1961 by the Society for the Experimental Analysis of Behavior, Inc. **Fig. 9–4.** From W. S. Verplank. *Journal of Abnormal and Social Psychology.* 1955, 51, 668–676. Copyright © 1955 by the American Psychological Association. Reprinted by permission. **Fig. 10–1.** Reprinted with the permission of the Bettmann Archive, Inc. **Fig. 11–2.** From Wolfgang Köhler, *The Mentality*

*Continued following Index*

# CONTENTS

## Part II: INTRODUCTION 109

## 5
## Psychophysics 114

| Experimental Topics | 5 | 6 | 7 | 8 | 9 | 10 | 11 | 12 | 13 | 14 |
|---|---|---|---|---|---|---|---|---|---|---|
| Confounding | | | X | | X | | | | | |
| Converging operations | | X | | | | | | | | X |
| Counterbalancing | | | | X | | | | | | |
| Demand characteristics | | | | | | | | | X | |
| Ethical issues | | | | | | | | | | X |
| Experimental control/ extraneous variables | | | | | | | X | | X | |
| Experimenter effects | | | | | X | | | | X | |
| Field research | | | | | X | | | | X | |
| Generalization of results | | | | | | X | | | | X |
| Interaction effects | | | X | | | X | | | | |
| Measurement scales | X | | | | | | | | | |
| Operational definition | X | | | | | | | X | | |
| Phenomenological report | | X | | | | | X | | | |
| Regression artifacts | | | | | | | | X | | |
| Reliability of measures | | | | | | | | X | | |
| Replication | | | | | | | X | | | |
| Scale attenuation | | | | | | X | | | | |
| Selection of dependent variable | | | X | | | | | | | |
| Small *n* design | X | | | | X | | | | | |
| Within- and between- subjects designs | | | | X | | | | | | |

We have chosen to organize our book topically, for reasons described in the Preface. However, the subjects discussed in a topi-

**ORGANIZATION OF THE BOOK**

cally organized book are included in our text. The table above lists important methodological topics covered in Chapters 5–14 and the specific chapters in which they are discussed. (Many of these same concepts are introduced briefly in Part I of the book, the first four chapters). The table should be useful for those who prefer an alternate organization to the one we have used in writing the text.

# PREFACE

As authors and teachers, we are pleased that the acceptance of this text has justified preparation of a second edition. We are indebted to the many users of the first edition who contacted us to share their experience and to offer constructive criticism that allowed us to improve the text. These suggestions have all been most carefully considered, and we hope that both teachers and students will find the second edition to be an improvement. We encourage teachers to keep us informed of their needs so that the third edition may benefit from the voices of experience.

## Text Organization

The philosophy of the text remains unchanged. As with the first edition, we have striven to achieve an integrated treatment of experimental psychology with a seamless link binding methodology and content. The book includes two main parts. The first four chapters constitute Part 1 and discuss some basic methodological preliminaries that students need. In these chapters we describe some general aspects of science and theory construction; features of and differences among observational, correlational, and experimental methods (with an emphasis on the latter); and how to read and write research reports.

In Part 2, the remaining ten chapters, we flesh out the bare bones provided in Part 1 by illustrating experimental topics in the context of actual research problems. The chapters are provided with content titles (for example, Perception) and some content is covered in its own right, but the main purpose of the chapters is to present methodological topics in the context of actual research. This organization reflects our belief that the best way to provide students with an understanding of methodology is to imbed such methodology in the context of real problems that occur in conducting research. Methodology does not exist in a vacuum, but is devised to solve concrete research problems. In our opinion, presenting methods devoid of context, as occurs in many books on research methods and experimental psychology, leads students to think of methodology as rather sterile and uninteresting. We hope that presenting methods in the context of important content issues will overcome this problem.

## Chapter Format

The chapters in Part 2 all share a common format. This parallel structure should help orient students to important features of the text that facilitate learning.

- *Chapter opening.* The chapters begin with an outline and preview (as well as a quote). Following a brief orientation to the content area explored in the chapter, the student will come across the first of several boxed inserts that readers of the first edition found to be helpful, and which have thus been carried over to the second edition.

- *Introducing the Variables* quickly orients the student to those independent, dependent, and control variables commonly used in particular research areas. Of course, coverage of these variables does not exhaust the possibilities, but includes some of the most common ones.

- *Experimental Topics and Research Illustrations.* This section represents the main part of the chapter in which two or three methodological issues are presented in the context of an actual research problem. Thus, for example, in Chapter 10 we discuss the difficulty of ceiling and floor effects in the context of a memory experiment in which this problem actually arose. Many of these experimental topics were introduced in Part 1 and are now covered in more detail in Part 2. Some crucial topics are even covered more than once in Part 2, to insure better comprehension. The content topics were chosen to be good vehicles for discussing the particular methodological point under consideration. Thus the content may not represent the most important topics in the subject under discussion, nor do we intend our chapters to represent anything like a complete summary of contemporary work in the area. To reiterate, our intent is to illustrate issues of method in the context of actual research problems that are of interest. Two other unique features appear toward the end of each chapter in Part 2.

- *From Problem to Experiment: The Nuts and Bolts* presents the rationale behind experimental-design decisions—how many subjects should be used, why variable *X* was selected instead of variable *Y*, and so on—when hypotheses are taken from a general form to the specifics of an experiment. These decisions are the "nuts and bolts" of experimental research. They are second nature to practicing experimenters, and hence seldom articulated in journal articles, but may be mysterious puzzles to the uninitiated student who does not understand, for example, why rats in a particular experiment weighed only 80 percent of their normal weight.

- *Psychology in Action* suggests safe and simple experimental demonstrations, requiring little or no equipment, that can be used in or out of class. For example, Chapter 7 includes a demonstration of the Stroop effect, Chapter 11 contains examples of designs to induce mental "blocks" in thinking, and Chapter 14 presents methods to measure one's personal territory or "space bubble."

- *End-of-Chapter Features*. Finally, each chapter contains a *Summary* in which the main points of the chapter are reviewed, a set of *Key Terms* for review and study, and several *Discussion Questions*.

## Chapter Sequence

Although students will be best served by reading Part 1 in correct serial order, those professors and students more interested in methodology than in content can ignore the chapter numbering of Part 2. The table that cross lists chapter numbers and experimental topics (to be found at the end of the Table of Contents) can be used to determine the order that chapters in Part 2 are to be assigned. Thus, the teacher has the option of following a more or less traditional order, or creating a unique ordering better suited to his or her educational goals. Two lesser used, but still quite necessary chapters for some, have been relocated to appendixes, as suggested by several readers. Appendix A contains a review of basic statistics, and Appendix B provides a very brief sketch of the history of experimental psychology.

## Major Changes
## from the First Edition

Users of the first edition will discover many changes in the text. As already mentioned, we have altered the ordering of the chapters and created new appendixes. The Previews, Summaries with numbered points, Key Terms, and Discussion Questions in the chapters of Part 2 are also new. These changes are easily noticed, but the main difference between the editions is the reworking of chapters in response to reviewers' criticism, users' comments, and our own added experience. In many places we substituted better content examples to illustrate some methodological point in order to increase clarity. Other changes include more detail on how to write journal articles, including suggestions of the 1983 *Publication Manual* of the American Psychological Association. Also, the Appendix of Statistics now includes material on misuses of statistics.

### Ancillaries

As a result of suggestions from readers, an accompanying workbook is available for this edition. David Payne and Teresa Blaxton prepared this volume, which is keyed to the text and offers extra review and study opportunities that can be pursued independently by students. We believe that this workbook will prove valuable for students, and we urge you to consider using it.

Teresa Blaxton and David Payne have also prepared an instructor's manual that contains many aids for teaching a course on experimental psychology and research methods. Included are a selection of test questions for each chapter (both multiple choice and essay) and suggestions for lectures and demonstrations. The manual, free from the publisher on adoption of the text, contains a number of pointers that should help instructors.

### Acknowledgments

It takes many more people than authors to create a text and we are pleased to acknowledge with gratitude the assistance of numerous others. Our first debt is to the users of the first edition who created the justification for revision. Without their suggestions, this new edition would not exist. We thank our editor, Mary Schiller, for her enthusiasm in this project and for impressive organizational skills that greatly facilitated the revision. While many psychologists offered suggestions for revision, we would be remiss not to specifically thank John Jahnke, James Pomerantz, Jerome Friedman, David del Castillo, Richard Haude, Gary Meunier, and Kenneth McIntire for cogent reviews and sage advice. In addition, we also appreciate the valuable suggestions of Robert Baron, Robert Crowder, David Elmes, Harold Hawkins, Peter Herman, Don Homa, Susan Kantowitz, Janet Polivy, Mark Sanders, and Charles Snyder, who saw the manuscript at an earlier stage. We also thank Janet Payne, who prepared the indexes for the book. The staff at West Publishing offered expert professional aid and turned a manuscript into a book with remarkable speed and efficiency. John Orr, our

Production Editor, deserves special praise for his masterful efforts on our behalf. Finally, our deepest gratitude and affection goes to our families, who provided desperately needed succor during the times of stress that inevitably accompany the creation of a text.

Barry H. Kantowitz  
Henry L. Roediger, III

# About the Authors

**Barry H. Kantowitz** is Professor of Psychology at Purdue University. He received a B.A. and M.A. from Queen's College of the City University of New York and a Ph.D. from the University of Wisconsin in 1969. He directs the Human Information Processing Laboratory at Purdue, and has spent a year on a National Institutes of Mental Health Post-doctoral Fellowship at the University of Oregon and has also served as a senior Lecturer at the University of Trondheim in Norway. Dr. Kantowitz's research interests are in attention and reaction time and he has published numerous articles on these topics, which appeared in the *Journal of Experimental Psychology, Memory & Cognition*, and *Acta Psychologica*, among others. He is coauthor of several textbooks, including *Psychology: Understanding Behavior* (with R. A. Baron and D. Byrne), *Human Factors: Understanding People-System Relationships* (with R. D. Sorkin), and *Research Methods in Psychology* (with D. G. Elmes and H. L. Roediger). In addition, Dr. Kantowitz edited and contributed a chapter to *Human Information Processing: Tutorials in Performance and Cognition*. In 1974 he was elected a Fellow of the American Psychological Association.

**Henry L. Roediger, III** received a B.A. degree in psychology from Washington & Lee University in 1969 and a Ph.D. from Yale University in 1973. He has been on the faculty of Purdue University since 1973, except for three years spent at the University of Toronto as a visiting professor. His research interests lie within the field of cognitive psychology, particularly human learning and memory. He has published over 30 articles and reviews, most of which appeared in the *Journal of Experimental Psychology: Learning, Memory, and Cognition*, the *Journal of Verbal Learning and Verbal Behavior*, and *Memory & Cognition*. He has coauthored two other texts, *Psychology* (with J. P. Rushton, E. D. Capaldi, and S. G. Paris) and *Research Methods in Psychology* (with D. G. Elmes and B. H. Kantowitz). In addition, Dr. Roediger has served as Consulting Editor of *Memory & Cognition* since 1978 and has been Associate Editor of the *Journal of Experimental Psychology: Learning, Memory, and Cognition* since 1981. He has recently been named Editor of the *Journal of Experimental Psychology: Learning, Memory, and Cognition*.

# PART I

## PART OUTLINE

# INTRODUCTION

As was stated in the preface, this text presents an integrated approach, blending content and methodology. Part 1 builds the foundation by explaining fundamental concepts that are required for an understanding of the meld of content and methodology presented in part 2.

We first discuss some general issues pertinent to all the sciences and then show how these general issues apply in particular to the science of psychology. As with any science, psychology centers about two crucial concepts: theory and data. Acquiring data keeps most experimental psychologists very busy. Thus, there is extensive discussion of the research techniques that psychologists use to acquire meaningful data. We divide these techniques into two broad classifications: (1) observation and correlation, and (2) experiments. Part 1 provides an introduction to these topics, and part 2 elaborates and provides many concrete illustrations.

Once experiments are finished, they must be written and read. The journals of experimental psychology are often difficult for beginners to understand. So we provide a set of guidelines that will help you to read articles in psychology journals. After you have become an accomplished reader of research, you will be ready to write summaries of your own research efforts, most probably in the form of lab reports. We show you how the skills you acquired in reading journal articles can be put to good use in writing research reports.

We hope you find part 1 interesting. Although it will take you more than one reading to grasp all the concepts, we advise that you spend the time necessary to understand part 1, because this will make part 2 much easier for you. Welcome to the fascinating world of experimental psychology.

**INTRODUCTION TO PART ONE**

# CHAPTER 1 ▬▬▬▬▬▬▬▬▬▬▬▬

## Preview

Science is perhaps the most successful enterprise attempted by the human race. The current state of civilization, for better or worse, can be traced to the gifts of science. In this chapter we discuss some fundamental aspects of the scientific process, ones that are necessary for considering the more concrete topics covered later in the book. We also discuss various methods by which beliefs are established, including the scientific method. We then turn to various types of theory construction in science.

## Chapter Outline

# EXPLANATION IN SCIENTIFIC PSYCHOLOGY

Ask any scientist what he conceives the scientific method to be, and he will adopt an expression that is at once solemn and shifty-eyed; solemn, because he feels he ought to declare an opinion, shifty-eyed because he is wondering how to conceal the fact that he has no opinion to declare. If taunted he would probably mumble something about "Induction" and "Establishing the Laws of Nature," but if anyone working in a laboratory professed to be trying to establish Laws of Nature by induction we should begin to think he was overdue for leave.

P. B. Medawar

The basic motive behind science is curiosity, to learn how and why things work as they do. Psychologists attempt to study and explain behavior. As one example of this process, let us consider the following case history of the research process. A common observation—one you probably have made yourself on many occasions—is that people working in a group often seem to slack off in their effort. Many people in groups seem willing to let a few do the work. Bibb Latané, a social psychologist, noticed this tendency and decided to study it experimentally. The relevant comparison is whether people work harder at a task when they work as individuals than when they work in a group. First he examined the research literature to see if there was any evidence for this phenomenon of people working less hard in groups, which he named *social loafing*. The earliest study of social loafing was conducted by a German psychologist named Ringelmann (reported in Moede, 1927), who asked people to pull on a rope as hard as they could. The subjects pulled by themselves, or with one, two, or seven others. A sensitive gauge was used to measure how much pressure they exerted. If people exert as much effort in groups as when alone, then the group performance should be the sum of all the individual output. But Ringelmann discovered that groups of two pulled at only 95 percent of their capacity, and groups of four and eight sank to 85 percent and 49 percent, respectively. Thus evidence exists for the phenomenon of social loafing; it is probably not just our imaginations when we work in groups and notice others (and ourselves?) seeming to slough off.

Latané and his colleagues went on to perform a systematic series of experiments on the phenomenon of social loafing (Latané, Williams, and Harkins, 1979; Latané, Harkins, and Williams, 1980). They first showed that the phenomenon could be obtained in other experimental situations besides rope pulling. They have also demonstrated that social loafing occurs in several different cultures (including the Japanese, who are supposed to be so work-oriented), and even holds for young children. Thus social loafing seems a pervasive and important characteristic of working in groups.

The evidence from Latané's experimental studies points to *diffusion of responsibility* as a possible reason for social loafing. People working by themselves feel responsible for completing the task, but when they work in groups this feeling of responsibility diffuses to others. The same phenomenon occurs in other group situations: if one of your professors asked a question in a class of only two other people, you would probably feel responsible for trying to think up an answer. However, if there were two hundred other people in the class, you would likely feel much less responsible for answering.

One possible benefit of such basic research into a phenomenon is that the findings may be applied later to solve some practical problem. One great problem in American society is the declining productivity of the work force. Although social loafing is, at best, only one factor involved in this complicated issue, Marriott (1949) showed that factory workers in large groups produce less per individual than do those working in small groups. Thus, basic research that would show a way to overcome the problem of social loafing may be of great practical import. In fact, Latané, Harkins, and Williams (1980) did find conditions that eliminated the effect of social loafing in their experimental situation. When individual performance could be monitored within the group situation (rather than just performance of the entire group), the individuals worked just as hard as when they worked alone. Although more research must be done, it may be that simply measuring individual performance in group situations could help eliminate social loafing and increase productivity. The proposed solution may seem simple, but in many jobs only group performance is measured and individual performance is ignored.

We have taken the trouble to discuss Latané's studies of social loafing as an example of psychological research to illustrate how an interesting problem can be brought into a laboratory setting and studied in a controlled manner. The experiments performed will, when carefully conducted, promote a better understanding of the phenomenon of interest than will simple observation of events and reflection about them. This book is largely about the proper conduct of such experimental studies—how to develop hypotheses, arrange experimental conditions to test the hypotheses, collect observations (data) within an experiment, and then how to analyze and interpret the data collected. In short, in this book we try to cover the fundamentals of scientific inquiry as applied to psychology.

Before we can discuss the specifics of experiments, we must discuss some larger issues in this chapter. We describe here various ways in which people come to believe things to be true about the world, and the benefit of a scientific approach. We then discuss two different, but interwoven, methods of science, and describe several types of scientific theory. The aim of science is to provide a theoretical understanding of the world about us. Sometimes practical benefits may flow from this knowledge, as is likely to be the case in the recent studies of social loafing, but often the scientist is satisfied to have understood some interesting phenomenon better, whether or not there are immediate practical gains to be had. The basic aim of science is to satisfy the quest for knowledge, as we describe below.

## CURIOSITY: THE WELLSPRING OF SCIENCE

Scientists want to discover how and why things work. In this desire they are no different from a child or anyone else who also is curious about the world we inhabit. While the casual observer may not feel terribly frustrated if some observation (for example, that water always goes down a sink drain counterclockwise) cannot be explained, the professional scientist has a strong desire to pursue an observation until an explanation is at hand. It is not so much that scientists are different from other people but just that they are willing to go to much greater lengths to satisfy their curiosity than nonscientists. This unwillingness to tolerate unanswered questions has led science to develop several techniques for obtaining relief from curiosity. It is the careful application of these techniques that distinguishes scientific curiosity from everyday curiosity.

### The Fixation of Belief: Mommy Told Me

Each of us has certain beliefs about the world we live in. You probably believe that the earth is round and that it revolves about the sun and not vice versa. Such beliefs were not, of course, held by all people at all times. Four hundred years ago people believed that the sun revolved about the earth. Five hundred years ago the world was considered to be flat. Why are these beliefs not held today? Before we can answer this question, we must first look at some of the ways people form their beliefs. Scientific method is only one means by which beliefs are formed.

The simplest way of fixing belief is to take someone else's word on faith. Some trusted authority tells you what is true and what is false. Young children usually believe what their parents tell them simply because Mommy and Daddy are always right. As they get older they may discover unhappily that Mommy and Daddy may be unlearned when it comes to a subject like astrophysics, macroeconomics, or differential calculus. While this may cause them to doubt some of their parents' earlier proclamations (for example, that premarital sex is bad for you), it may not result in utter rejection of this method of fixing belief. Instead, some higher authority than Mom or Dad may be sought. Religious beliefs are formed in this way. Long after you have rejected your parents as the ultimate source of knowledge, you may still believe much of what they told you about heaven, hell, and sin. Believing the evening news means accepting the news commentator as an authority. You believe your professors because they are authorities. Since we lack the resources to investigate everything we learn, much of our knowledge and beliefs have been fixed by this *method of authority*. Provided nothing happens to raise doubts about the competence of the authority setting your beliefs, this method offers the great advantages of comfort and security with minimum effort. It is most pleasant in a troubled world to have complete faith in beliefs handed down to you.

Another way of fixing belief is the *a priori method*. Here, propositions that seem reasonable are believed. The belief that the world is flat, which we know at one time was widely held, was fixed a priori. Indeed, it still looks flat if you are not in a spacecraft.

There are at least two serious drawbacks to the methods just discussed. First, neither of them relies upon facts obtained by systematic investigation. Stating this objection slightly differently, we would say that there is no *empirical* basis for fixing belief. Having one's beliefs fixed by authority carries no guarantee that the authority obtained data before forming an opinion.

The second major disadvantage of these methods appears when two persons holding different beliefs try to reconcile their opinions. Neither method offers any procedure for establishing the superiority of one belief over another.

The method of science corrects these two disadvantages. First, science relies upon systematic observation. The most abstract and esoteric scientific theory will be judged useless or incorrect unless it is consistent with data, that is, systematically collected facts about the world. Second, science is self-correcting. Procedures exist to compare new beliefs to old beliefs, and old beliefs are discarded if they are lacking. This does not imply that each and every scientist instantaneously drops outmoded beliefs in favor of new opinions. Changing scientific beliefs is usually a slow process. But eventually incorrect beliefs are weeded out. They are gradually replaced by newer beliefs that provide a better account of those facts of interest. These advantages of scientific method make it the preferred technique for satisfying curiosity. The remainder of this chapter introduces scientific method.

Certain basic elements are shared by all approaches to science. The most important of these are *data* (observations) and *theory* (explanation). Science needs and uses both data and theory. However, individual scientists often differ about which is more important and which comes first. Trying to decide this is a little like trying to decide whether the chicken or the egg came first. We shall not try to foist our own prejudices in this matter upon you. Important scientific achievements have been obtained by scientists who stress data and by scientists who stress theory. We shall call the scientist who starts with data and works up to theory an *inductive* scientist and one who starts with theory and works down to data a *deductive* scientist. Although we shall pretend that these two approaches are black and white with no shades of gray in order to emphasize their differences, it is easy to combine them, and many psychologists have used both approaches.

**TWO METHODS OF SCIENCE: INDUCTIVE AND DEDUCTIVE**

### The Inductive Scientist: Good Data Never Die

The inductive scientist is primarily concerned with data. But what are data and where do they come from? What does the scientist do with data once they are obtained? Data (more than one) or a datum (singular) are technical terms that correspond to what the nonscientist means by the terms facts or fact. Thus, a datum is a piece of information resulting from a systematic observation. The

Drawing by C. Schulz. Copyright 1976 United Features Syndicate, Inc.

difference between a fact (nontechnical term) and a datum (technical term) can be illustrated through the casual or systematic observation of a cow. Let's say you are driving by a farm and you see a solitary cow grazing. You might state that you know for a fact that the cow is black. However, a scientist would object to your statement on the grounds that your observation has not been systematic. In particular, you have only seen one side of the cow. Before the scientist would accept your fact as a datum he or she would insist upon viewing the other side of the cow to see if it also were black. Without this observation your fact would be only a plausible guess to the scientist. Perhaps you feel that this example is a bit farfetched, like quibbling over how many angels can crowd onto the head of a pin. But if you substitute the moon for the cow, the argument jumps into proper perspective. Until spacecraft actually made observations of the far side of the moon, no one really knew what was there. While it was plausible to assume that the far side of the moon was just like the visible side, no one knew for sure. There were no data. Useful data are thus obtained by systematic, rather than by haphazard or casual, observation. There are many systematic ways to make observations and these are discussed in the next chapter. For now, merely note that observations must be made in some orderly (and usually predetermined) way before they can lead to data.

Data have many characteristics—variance, reliability, replicability, to name a few you will encounter later on—that are of great importance to the scientist, and these facets of data are treated throughout this text. Before the scientist can do much with data, they must be checked to assure that they meet current standards. This is often accomplished by the use of statistics (see the appendix A), although statistics by themselves do not guarantee that data will be useful. A large part of the craft of experimental psychology is establishing situations for obtaining data in such a manner as to make it quite likely that these data meet all necessary requirements. Thus it is essential that the scientist demonstrate that data exhibit proper characteristics; discussion of how this can be accomplished is deferred until following chapters.

After the scientist is satisfied that his or her data are in order and can be sensibly interpreted, the final step is communication. The data are published in a suitable journal for other scientists to read. Then the inductive scientist goes back to the laboratory to obtain additional data. It is here that the most dramatic distinction between inductive and deductive scientists occurs. The inductive scientist believes that if enough data are gathered, patterns of explanation will become obvious. For example, if I ask you to complete the series "2, 4, . . . ," you might say "6" or "8," or you might reply "16." You do not have enough data for a pattern to emerge. If I give you an additional datum, say "16," you can now predict that the next number in the series should be 256. The pattern calls for squaring each number (multiplying it by itself) to obtain the next number. With sufficient data, the pattern became obvious. The inductive scientist is guided mostly by past data that tell what questions should be asked next. But the deductive scientist questions the value of this approach, claiming that data by themselves will never turn into explanation, regardless of how much data may be gathered.

### The Deductive Scientist: Looking Down at Data

The deductive scientist emphasizes the importance of explanation. Data are useful only insofar as they directly bear upon the validity of some proposed explanation. In particular, data may permit the deductive scientist to decide which of two or more alternate explanations is correct. If, however, no explanations of some effect or phenomenon have been offered, then the deductive scientist has little interest in obtaining data. Instead, the scientist would devote her or his time and energy to creating some explanation. The deductive scientist believes that data cannot be collected intelligently without the guiding framework of some explanation, even if this attempted explanation is far from complete. Many deductive scientists would have little interest in obtaining data if only one explanation were available. These scientists argue that explanations are discarded only when better explanations emerge. Data are most valuable when they can distinguish among competing explanations. While data that are inconsistent with a single explanation may eventually motivate new and better explanations, the deductive scientist would rather spend time thinking about explanations than gather more data. The deductive scientist becomes enthusiastic about data only after the many details of some explanation have been worked out beforehand. Even then, the pure deductive scientist may not gather data if existing data, possibly obtained by an inductive scientist, can be located and borrowed.

It should be clear, then, that the deductive scientist is concerned primarily with ideas. He or she devotes the most effort into formulating theoretical explanation. Once the explanation has been completed, the scientist deduces what should occur in some particular situation. She or he is able to generate a prediction even though no other scientist may have studied this particular situation. You may never have seen a raw egg thrown into a rotating electric fan. Nevertheless, you probably can make an excellent prediction about the outcome of this particular situation. To do so you are making a deduction based upon your intuitive theoretical understanding of biology and physics. A physicist and a biologist could probably make more exact predictions than you, such as the precise dispersion pattern depending upon the size of the egg, the speed of the fan, and so on. But even without this knowledge, you can still generate a reasonably accurate, although undetailed, prediction.

### Comparing Inductive and Deductive Scientists

Portraits of inductive and deductive scientists have been constructed by Mitroff and Kilmann (1975). Their descriptions are as follows:

> Type A [what we would call the inductive scientist] is the kind of scientist who first and foremost regards himself as a Hard Experimentalist. He takes extreme pride in his carefully designed and detailed experimental work. In general, he prefers hard data gathering to abstract theorizing. . . . He feels that one really doesn't understand something until he has collected some hard data on it. He feels that abstract theorists have a tendency to get lost in their abstractions for their own sake and hence to mistake them for reality. . . . He feels that theorizing and speculating are only warranted when the data are available that clearly support such activities. He is quick to master complicated and sophisticated experimental techniques.

> Type B [what we would call the deductive scientist] is the kind of scientist who first and foremost regards himself as an Abstract Theorizer. He takes extreme pride in his ability to construct formal, analytical models. . . . In general, he prefers building abstract theoretical models to experimental data gathering. He feels that one really doesn't understand something until he has built a general theory of it. He feels that hard data gatherers have a tendency to become so engrossed in collecting data for its own sake that they never get around to putting it all together in some systematic conceptual sense.

These portraits should give you some insight into the personalities of the two different types of scientists. We have been very careful to avoid stating which type of science is "better" because both are necessary. In the long run, both types of scientist have the same goal. They differ about the best tactics for reaching this goal. The inductive scientist starts with data and works up to (or induces) explanation. The deductive scientist starts with explanation and then uses data to verify or correct the abstract model. It is important to realize that neither the inductive nor deductive approach is an automatic formula for scientific success. Intuition and creativity play an important role that has only begun to be documented (Medawar, 1969).

Before concluding this section, we should remind you of the warning that preceded it. In order to distinguish clearly between inductive and deductive approaches to science, we have pretended that they are black and white. In psychology, this is seldom the case. While well-established sciences like physics and astronomy can divide practitioners into those concerned almost entirely with explanation and theory and those concerned with data acquisition, the dividing line in psychology is much more blurred. A psychologist can often act like a deductive scientist one moment and an inductive scientist the next.

Being familiar with observation and data, you may have found it easier to understand the deductive scientist than the inductive scientist. Detailed discussion of the distinctions between types of common observation and scientific observation is left for chapter 2. Now we focus upon theory and explanation. The concept of a theory is more difficult than the concept of an observation. There is more than one type of theorizing in science, and even a specific science, such as psychology, contains more than one kind of theoretical statement.

**THEORY
CONSTRUCTION
IN PSYCHOLOGY**

### What Is a Theory?

A theory can be crudely defined as a set of related statements that explain a variety of occurrences. The more the occurrences, and the fewer the statements, the better the theory. The law of gravity explains falling apples, the behavior of roller coasters, and the position of bodies within the solar system. With a small number of statements about the mutual attraction of bodies, it explains a large number of events. It is therefore a powerful theory. (This does not necessarily mean it is a correct theory, since there are some events it cannot explain.)

Theory in psychology performs two major functions. First, it provides a framework for the systematic and orderly display of data—that is, it serves as a convenient way for the scientist to *organize* data. Even the most dedicated inductive scientist will eventually have difficulty remembering the outcomes of dozens of experiments. Theory can be used as a kind of filing system to help experimenters organize results. Second, it allows the scientist to generate *predictions* for situations where no data have been obtained. The greater the degree of agreement about these predictions, the better the theory. With the best of intentions, scientists who claim to be testing the same theory often derive from the theory different predictions about the same situation. This unfortunate circumstance is relatively more common in psychology, where many theories are stated in a loose verbal fashion, than in physics, where theories are more formal and better quantified through the use of mathematics. Although psychologists are rapidly stating their theories more precisely through formal mechanisms like mathematics and computer simulations, it is still true that the typical psychological theory has nowhere near the elegance of theories in more established, older sciences.

Sometimes these two functions of theory—organization and prediction—are called *description* and *explanation*, respectively. Unfortunately, formulating the roles of theory in this manner often leads to an argument about the relative superiority of deductive or inductive approaches to science—a discussion we have already dismissed as fruitless. According to the deductive scientist, the inductive scientist is concerned only with description. The inductive scientist defends against this charge by retorting that description is explanation—if we could correctly predict and control all behavior by referring to properly organized sets of results, then we are indeed also explaining behavior. The argument is futile because both types of scientist are correct. *If* we already had all the data we needed properly organized, we could make predictions without recourse to a formal body of theoretical statements. Since we don't have all the data properly organized as yet, and perhaps never will, theories are required to bridge the gap between knowledge and ignorance. Remember, however, that our theories will never be complete because all the data will never be in. So, we have merely recast the argument between inductive and deductive scientists about which technique will more quickly and surely lead to truth. Ultimately, description and explanation will be equivalent. The two terms describe the path taken more than the eventual theoretical outcome. So, to avoid this pitfall, we shall steadfastly refer to the two major functions of theory as *organization* and *prediction* rather than description and explanation.

### Four Kinds of Psychological Theory Construction

Just as there is more than one way to build a house, there also are several ways to build a theory. If we start with the foundation and work our way up to the roof, we have an *inductive* theory. If we alternate where we can between foundation and roof, putting in a wall here or there, than a basement window, then a chimney, we have a *functional* theory. If we build the roof first and have a crane hold it up while we insert the foundation under it, we have a *deductive* theory, once the crane is removed. If, on the other hand, we always need a crane to hold up the roof, we have a *model*.

These fanciful analogies with house construction are far from exact descriptions of the kinds of theory. Marx (1963) has more formally described these four modes of theory construction. They are illustrated in figure 1-1. Two of them correspond quite closely to the style of the inductive and deductive scientists previously discussed. An *inductive theory* starts from the data base and organizes empirical relationships into theoretical principles. In psychology this type of theory construction is most often identified with the work of Skinner (1956) on reinforcement and learning.[1]

The *deductive theory* starts with explanation and then consults data to test predictions of (deductions from) the theory. If the data are not in agreement with predictions, the theory is modified and new predictions are generated. This process is continued repeat-

1. One researcher in this tradition, Murray Sidman, has written an impressive volume called *Tactics of Scientific Research*, which is highly recommended for anyone wishing to understand the detailed arguments in favor of this type of theorization.

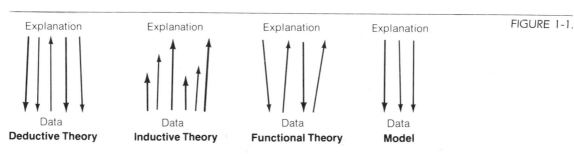

FIGURE 1-1.

Four modes of theory construction in psychology. While all theories use both data and explanation, they differ in their emphases upon each and in how each modifies the other (adapted from Marx, 1963).

edly until either the modifications to the theory become so unwieldly that a newer, more compact theory replaces it, or most psychologists lose interest in the issues the theory explains. The deductive theory is often referred to as the classical type of theory construction because it offers the greatest degree of formality and has been quite successfully employed in older sciences like physics and chemistry. Psychologists who favor the deductive theory argue that these past successes in other sciences make it the best choice. Clark Hull is the psychologist most often associated with deductive theory construction in the area of learning and motivation. Hull's theory (1943) was an ambitious attempt to formally characterize a wide span of knowledge. It dominated work in this area for over a decade. Yet now it is considered outmoded, if not incorrect, by most psychologists in the area of learning, although psychologists in other areas such as social psychology still use constructs derived from Hull's theory.

The *functional theory* is a hybrid creature combining both inductive and deductive elements. It stresses data and explanation about equally. The name *functional theory* is derived from a school of psychology discussed in appendix B. As a compromise position it was, and still is, more typical of American psychological research than either the pure inductive or deductive mode. Some noted psychologists associated with functional theory are Arthur Melton and Benton Underwood (in the area of memory) and Leon Festinger (for his cognitive-dissonance theory of attitude change in social psychology).

The *model* has become the theory of choice in recent times, particularly in cognitive psychology. The great popularity of information processing approaches to psychology (see chapter 17 especially) with their accompanying "black box" diagrams has much to do with this change in the theoretical style of American psychology. The model has several unique features, not all of which can be schematically represented in figure 1-1, that account for its current popularity. The model can tolerate large differences between its predictions and actual data. Figure 1-1 represents this by *not* showing any arrows leading from data back to model. This unusual theoretical feature arises because a model is really an *analogy*. Analogies in psychology are generally based upon physical, electronic, chemical, and computer technologies. Right now, computer analogies are most popular, but psychology has a long history of borrowing concepts from other sciences and adapting them to handle psychological issues. For example, Freud's model of the mind can be considered to derive from the hydraulic (fluid-flow) analogy, with the ego and superego acting like a valve controlling fluid pressure and flow (the force of the id).

Do not confuse this use of the term *model* with its use in phrases like "mathematical model" or "computer model." These are really formal deductive theories and not models in the technical sense of one of the four kinds of theory construction. Models are used to guide data collection and to serve as frameworks for more formal subsequent theoretical efforts. These latter efforts often are of the deductive type. From this perspective models are initial stages of theoretical development rather than ultimate ends. As models are modified by data collection they become more and more like functional or deductive theories.

Never forget that a model is just an analogy. No one expects an analogy to be 100 percent accurate. A model can tolerate discrepancies that would be fatal to a formal deductive theory. Why then are models useful if they can be so inaccurate? The model serves mainly to meet the organizational requirements of theory. It is less useful when precise predictions are made, although models do make predictions.

Another unique feature of the model as used in psychology is its limited scope. While classical theories like Hull's tried to encompass many different kinds of situations and events, current models are most typically tied to only a few specific types of situations. That is why models are sometimes referred to as "pocket theories." These limitations make it easier to make theoretical statements, since only a small amount of ground needs to be covered. However, the disadvantage of models is that it is difficult to tie several models together to explain several situations. Many psychologists feel that the extensive use of models has resulted in a patchwork theoretical structure and has caused the various subspecialties within experimental psychology to draw apart from each other. For better or worse, there is nothing on the theoretical horizon that will soon replace the model.

### Evaluating Theories: When Explanations Collide

The sophisticated scientist does not try to determine if a particular theory is true or false in an absolute sense. There is no black and white approach to theory evaluation. A theory may be known to be incorrect in some portion and yet continue to be used. In modern physics, light is represented, according to the theory chosen, as either discrete particles called quanta, or continuous waves. Logically, light cannot be both at the same time. Thus, you might think that at least one of these two theoretical views must necessarily be false. The physicist tolerates this ambiguity, perhaps not cheerfully, and uses whichever representation—quanta or wave—is more appropriate. Instead of flatly stating that a theory is true, the scientist is much more likely to state that it is supported substantially by data, thereby leaving open the possibility that new data may not support the theory. A theory can never be proved but only disproved. Data that are inconsistent with a theory can lead to its eventual rejection. Data that are only partially consistent with a theory cause it to be modified and to evolve. But data that support a theory only postpone its ultimate rejection. Although scientists do not state that a theory is true, they must often decide which of several theories is best. Although none of them may be true—that is, ultimately all may be rejected and replaced by others—the scientist still needs to decide which theory is best for now. In order to do so, there must be explicit criteria for evaluating a theory.

We have already hinted at one important criterion when we earlier stated that the fewer the statements in a theory, the better the theory. This criterion is called *parsimony* or sometimes Occam's razor, after William of Occam. If a theory needs a separate statement for every result it must explain, clearly no economy has been gained by the theory. Theories gain power when they can explain many results with fewer explanatory concepts. Thus, if two theories have the same number of concepts, the one that can explain more results is a better theory. If two theories can explain the same number of results, the one with fewer explanatory concepts is to be preferred.

*Precision* is another important criterion, especially in psychology where it is often lacking. Theories that involve mathematical equations or computer programs are generally more precise, and hence better, than those which use loose verbal statements (all other things being equal, of course). Unless a theory is sufficiently precise so that different investigators can agree about its predictions, it is for all intents and purposes useless.

*Testability* goes beyond precision. A theory can be very precise and yet not able to be tested. For example, when Einstein proposed the equivalence of matter and energy ($E = MC^2$), nuclear technology was not able to directly test this relationship. Since theories can never be proved, but only disproved, the scientist places a very high value on the criterion of testability. A theory that cannot be tested can never be disproved. At first you might think this would be a good quality since it would be impossible to demonstrate that such a theory was incorrect. The scientist takes the opposite view. For example, let's take ESP (extrasensory perception). Some believers in ESP claim that the presence of a disbeliever is sufficient to prevent a person gifted with ESP from performing, since the disbeliever puts out bad vibes that disrupt ESP. This means that ESP cannot be disproved, because only believers can be present when it is demonstrated. The scientist takes a dim view of this logic, and most scientists, especially psychologists, are skeptical about ESP. Unless a theory can potentially be disproved, it is not testable. Our belief in a theory increases as it survives tests that could reject it. Since it is logically possible that some future test may find a flaw, our belief in a theory is never absolute. If it is not logically possible to test a theory, it cannot be evaluated and hence is useless to the scientist. If it is logically possible but not yet technically feasible, as was once the case with Einstein's theory, then evaluation of a theory is deferred.

## THE SCIENCE OF PSYCHOLOGY

Some students find it difficult to think of psychology as a science in the same sense that physics and chemistry are sciences. They believe that there are aspects of human experience, such as the arts, literature, and religion, that defy scientific analysis. How can the beauty of a Klee lithograph, a Beethoven sonata, a Cartier-Bresson photograph be reduced to cold scientific equations? How can the tender feelings of a first romance, the thrill of driving a sports car at 100 miles per hour, and the agony of a defeated football team be captured in the objective, disinterested fashion required by science?

Some psychologists, known as humanists, would answer these questions in the negative. These humanists, most often clinical and counseling psychologists, claim that it is impossible objectively to evaluate and test much of human feelings and experience by traditional scientific methods. Even tough, "brass-instrument" experimental psychologists concur that the domain of science is limited. We cannot establish or refute the existence of God by scientific means any more than we could test gravity by theological methods. Science operates where its tools are appropriate (see chapter 14). This does not imply that knowledge cannot be gained wherever science fears to tread—that is, by nonscientific means. Many important fields of human endeavor have yet to benefit from extensive scientific analysis—ethics, morals, law, to name but a few.

However, most scientists would hold out the hope that scientific analysis eventually might be usefully applied to many such areas. Much of contemporary psychology was regarded as the sole property of philosophy at one time. As psychological techniques improved, these aspects of human expertise and behavior moved into the realm of science. And now most psychologists believe that virtually all facets of human experience are fair game for the science of psychology. Deriding scientific progress in psychology, as did one United States senator who criticized the National Science Foundation for supporting research on romantic love, will not halt efforts to expand psychological knowledge. While concern for the proper and ethical use of such knowledge is valid and important, ignorance is no solution.

### Soft-shelled and Hard-boiled Psychology

Psychologists can be arranged along a continuum according to how well they think physics and chemistry serve as a model for psychology to emulate. The "hard-boiled" psychologists think these older sciences are perfect models while the "soft-shelled" psychologists believe that social sciences must find another model. Humanistic psychologists are at the extreme end of this continuum and do not believe in any shells at all. (Humanists believe in bare experience.) As authors we have tried to be as eclectic as possible, sampling from along this continuum while trying to avoid the danger of having our feet firmly planted in mid-air. Since we are experimental psychologists by trade, and since this book is intended as an experimental-psychology text, we tend to sample more from the hard-boiled end of the continuum.

All science has data and theory. What distinguishes among the different sciences, and among the subspecialties within a science like psychology, is the different techniques used. Astronomers don't need Skinner boxes any more than animal-learning psychologists need telescopes. Yet both practice science. A learning theorist's memory drum is not intrinsically superior to a social psychologist's "aggression machine" (see chapter 13). Even the modern microcomputer of an information-processing psychologist does not guarantee better science, although it may improve the odds. Most of this text is devoted to explaining the techniques needed in psychological research today. While the hard-shelled psychologist does have more refined techniques, this is in part because of selection of problems that are amenable to sophisticated analysis. As psychology subjects more and more of human experience and behavior to scientific analysis, it is only natural that initial techniques may be crude. At one time this was true of hard-shelled psychology too. Having a hard shell should not preclude one from having an open mind.

### Psychology and the Real World

Scientists in general, and psychologists in particular, have many reasons for pursuing their profession. While we think it rather easy to prove that psychological research does serve mankind, we would like to stress that we do not find this the only, or necessarily the major, justification for a career as a research psychologist. Many scientists investigate certain problems simply because they find them interesting. We have complete sympathy with a colleague who might state that he or she studies gerbils just because gerbils provoke his or her curiosity. It is true that certain studies are performed on animals because they are unethical or impractical to perform on humans—for example, studies of long-term crowding, punishment, drugs, and so on—but it is equally true that the behavior of animals is interesting in its own right.

Scientific research is often divided into two categories: basic and applied. Applied research aims at solving a specific problem—like how to cure bedwetting—whereas basic research has no immediate practical goal. Basic research establishes a reservoir of data, theoretical explanations, and concepts that can be tapped by the applied researcher. Without this source, applied research would soon dry up and sputter to a halt, unless applied researchers became of necessity basic researchers. It takes quite a while for a concept developed by basic research to find some useful application in society. Adams (1972) discusses a study that traced five socially important products to discover the impact, if any, of basic research. Although basic research accounted for 70 percent of the significant events, these events occurred twenty to thirty years before the ultimate use of the product. This long time lag obscures the crucial role of basic research so that many persons incorrectly believe that basic research is not very useful to society. It is quite difficult to tell what basic research being done today will have an impact thirty years from now. But this inability to predict hardly means that we should stop doing basic research.

While the division of research into basic and applied categories is common, a far more important distinction is between good and bad research. The principles and practices covered in this text apply with equal force to basic and applied research. You can and should use them to evaluate all the psychological research you encounter, whether as a student, a professional psychologist, or an educated person reading the daily newspaper.

***Are experiments too far from real life?*** Students of psychology typically demand a higher level of relevance in their psychology courses than they expect from other sciences. Students who are not at all dismayed that their course in introductory physics did not enable them to repair their automobile are often disturbed that their course in introductory psychology did not give them a better insight into their own motivations, did not cure their neuroses, and failed to show them how to gain eternal happiness. If you did not find such information in introductory psychology, we doubt that you will find it in this text either. If this seems unfair, read on.

The data that psychologists gather may at first seem unimportant, since you may not find an immediate relationship between basic psychological research and pressing social or personal problems. It is natural for you to then doubt the importance of this research and to wonder why the federal government, through agencies like the National Institute of Mental Health, is funding researchers to watch rats press bars or run through mazes.

The difficulty, however, is not with the research but with your expectations as to how "useful" research should be conducted. As has been noted by Sidman (1960), you expect progress to occur when researchers establish laboratory situations that are analogous to real-life situations: "In order to study psychosis in animals we must learn how to make animals psychotic." This is off the mark. The psychologist tries to understand the underlying *processes* rather than the physical situations that produce these processes. The physical situations in the real world and the laboratory need not be at all similar provided that the same processes are occurring. Let's say we would like to know why airplane accidents occur. A basic researcher might approach this problem by having college sophomores sit in front of several lights that turn on in rapid succession. The sophomore has to press a key as each light is illuminated. This probably seems somewhat removed from mid-air collisions of aircraft. Yet although the physical situations are quite different, the processes are similar. Pressing a key is an index of attention (see chapter 7). Psychologists can overload the human operator by presenting lights faster than he or she can respond. Thus, this simple physical situation in a laboratory allows the psychologist to study failure of attention in a carefully controlled environment. In addition to the obvious safety benefits of studying attention without having to crash airplanes, there are many scientific advantages to the laboratory environment (see chapter 3). Since failures of attention are responsible for many kinds of industrial accidents (DeGreene, 1970, chapters 7 and 16), studying attention with lights and buttons can lead to improvements outside the laboratory.

By the same token, establishing similar physical situations does not guarantee similarity of processes. We can easily train a rat to pick up coins in its mouth and bury them in its cage. But this does not necessarily mean that the "miserly" rat and the miserly human who keeps coins under his mattress both do so because the same psychological processes are controlling their behaviors.

The psychologist confronts this issue directly when dealing with generalization of results (see chapters 10 and 14). Experimenters take great pains to ensure broad conclusions can be drawn from their results. And experiments need not be performed only in laboratories. Especially in social psychology, field studies and observations in natural surroundings are becoming more and more popular (see chapters 2, 13, and 14). So look carefully before you conclude that an experiment has nothing to do with real life.

**SUMMARY**

**1.** Science is concerned with the methods and techniques for resolving curiosity. Our beliefs can be established by the *method of authority* and the *a priori method*. The *scientific method* offers advantages over these other methods. Science relies upon systematic observation and is self-correcting.

**2.** Scientists operate *inductively* and *deductively*. The inductive scientist stresses the importance of data. He or she carefully arranges situations that make it likely that collected data will meet all requisite scientific criteria. The deductive scientist is primarily concerned with theory and explanation. He or she uses data to test theory. Both data and theory are necessary in science. The inductive and deductive scientists differ only about the tactics of science; their ultimate goal is the same.

**3.** A theory is a set of related statements which explain a variety of occurrences. Theory serves as a framework for the organization of data. Theory also generates predictions for new situations where data have not yet been obtained. A *deductive theory* starts with explanation and is later modified after its predictions are compared with data. An *inductive theory* starts from data and organizes empirical relationships. A *functional theory* stresses induction and deduction about equally. A *model* is an analogy. It is the dominant mode of theory construction in psychology.

**4.** Models guide data collection and serve as starting points for subsequent formal theoretical efforts. Current psychological models tend to be of limited scope, covering only a small subarea of explanation. Theories are evaluated according to criteria of parsimony, precision, and testability.

**5.** More and more aspects of human experience are becoming amenable to analysis by the scientific tools of psychology. While a minority of humanistic psychologists see this as dangerous, most psychologists view it as the natural progression of a young and growing science.

**6.** Basic research creates the knowledge that applied research eventually draws upon. Psychologists are concerned with understanding the processes that govern behavior. Although the physical settings in a laboratory seldom mimic those of the real world, the same psychological processes can occur in both. Knowledge of these processes gained through basic research can help improve utilization of these processes outside the laboratory.

a priori method
curiosity
data
deductive
description
diffusion of responsibility
explanation
functional

inductive
method of authority
model
parsimony
precision
social loafing
testability
theory

**DISCUSSION
QUESTIONS**

**1.** Make a list of five statements that might be considered true. Include some controversial statements, (for example, Blacks have lower IQs than Whites), as well as some you are sure are correct. Survey some of your friends by asking if they agree with these statements and the justification for their opinion. Classify their justifications into one of the methods of fixing belief discussed in this chapter.

**2.** Compare and contrast inductive and deductive approaches to science. Clarify your answers by referring to at least one branch of science outside of experimental psychology.

**3.** The two major goals of theory are *organization* and *prediction*. Evaluate the relative utility of the four types of theory in figure 1–1 in realizing these two goals.

**4.** Is it necessary (or even desirable) for experimental psychologists to justify their research in terms of applied benefits to society?

# CHAPTER 2

## Preview

This chapter is about three research techniques. First, systematic observation of a phenomenon is described as the first step in the scientific process of understanding it. In a second technique, the correlational, two sets of observations are examined together to determine if they are related to one another. The third technique, that of using ex post facto experimental designs, attempts to find firmer evidence for a relation between two factors. All these techniques are employed to make scientific observations and inferences as error-free as possible.

## Chapter Outline

# RESEARCH TECHNIQUES: OBSERVATION AND CORRELATION

*Scientific observation does not differ from everyday observation by being infallible although it is quantitatively less fallible than ordinary observation. Rather, it differs from everyday observation in that the scientist gradually uncovers his previous errors and corrects them. . . . Indeed, the history of psychology as a science has been the development of procedural and instrumental aids that gradually eliminate or correct for biases and distortions in making observations.*

*Ray Hyman*

Scientists have several different popular images that correspond to the various activities in which they are engaged (Hyman, 1964). First, the scientist is sometimes portrayed as the brilliant, if eccentric, creative genius who formulates novel theories about the way the world is structured, and changes forever the way some aspect of nature is viewed. Names such as Galileo, Newton, Darwin, Freud, and Einstein come to mind in this context. A second image of a scientist is as a careful, systematic collector of facts, who spends most of his or her time scrutinizing pointer dials or other varieties of scientific technology. This view of the scientist emphasizes the hard work and occasional tediousness of scientific research, as the scientist's nose is firmly pressed to the grindstone. A third image of the scientist is as one who then turns from the laboratory to reveal to the world what the facts collected may mean. Thus we receive pronouncements that new drugs can combat disease, or that cigarette smoking causes cancer, or that the brain produces substances similar to morphine to combat pain. A fourth image has the scientist as a hopelessly obscure person, perhaps brilliant, but unable to communicate with anyone who does not speak the same jargon.

These stereotypes, while greatly oversimplified, contain a recognizable element of fact. The creative aspects of the scientist are poorly understood, but we will try to provide you with some understanding of the other aspects of science. We will be dealing with how observations are made, analyzed, interpreted, and communicated, since these aspects of scientific activity can be learned in part from textbooks. In this chapter and the next we will be concerned with fundamentals of research techniques; in chapter 4 we will be concerned with the reading and writing of articles for scientific journals, and in appendix A with statistical analysis and interpretation of observations. In the last ten chapters we integrate these topics by considering how they are used to study different problem areas in psychology. As with most complex skills, however, the intricacies of psychological research can be learned only in part by reading about them; one must participate to acquire the inarticulate, tacit knowledge of research.

## OBSERVATION

Science is perhaps the only intellectual enterprise that builds cumulatively. Because of science we know more about the world today than at any other time in history. On the other hand, literature, art, and philosophy may be in a different state today than in ancient Greece, but we probably cannot say these disciplines are in a better state or more accurately represent the world. The mark of psychology's scientific immaturity is how little it has, in certain respects, advanced beyond the philosophical speculations of its inception.

One primary reason that science cumulates is that scientists strive for the most accurate observation of the world possible. Science is self-correcting in that theories and hypotheses are put forward that allow prediction about what should happen under specified conditions, and then these ideas are tested by comparing the predictions to carefully collected observations. When the facts differ consistently and drastically from the predictions, it is necessary to modify or abandon our theoretical conception. Much of the scientific enterprise is concerned with observation, the collection of data on some particular aspect of the world.

In this chapter we consider several different types of observation. The simplest case is *descriptive observation*, where one simply observes natural phenomena and records numerous facts about them. Such simple observation may be useful in the early stages of inquiry, but it is soon necessary to go beyond this. It is more important to relate observations to one another than simply to collect them willy-nilly. Scientists want to know what goes with what. For this reason scientists want to relate observations to one another (to correlate them) to see what does go with what, so that future events can be predicted with some certainty. The mere *correlation* of observations, however, is also of limited usefulness to scientists. It may tell us what quantities are related, but it gives little indication as to *how* or *why*. The scientific method that provides the best observation and understanding of events is the experimental method, and this is dealt with in chapter 3. The crux of the experimental method is that some factor is manipulated in a controlled setting where all other relevant factors are held constant. Thus, one can measure the contribution of this factor on whatever behavior (of animate or inanimate objects) is of interest. With the experimental method we find out not only whether or not two observations are related, but also what *leads to* (produces, causes) what. This will become clearer later in this chapter and the next. At the end of this chapter we consider several procedures that might be labeled *quasi-experiments*. They do not allow the control that a true experiment has, yet they can lead to somewhat more powerful inferences than simple correlations that only tell us to what extent two factors are related.

As we all know, observers are fallible. Seeing might be believing, but it should not be, at least not always. Often our perceptions fool us, as in the optical illusions in figure 2–1. We have all seen magicians perform seemingly impossible feats before our eyes, but we knew that we were being tricked by natural means. Even this demonstrates that direct perceptions can fool us if we are not careful, and sometimes even if we are. Scientists, being human, are also subject to errors of observation. Essentially the research techniques employed by scientists—including logic, complicated apparatus, controlled conditions, and so on—are there to guard against errors of perception and to ensure that observations more accurately reflect the state of nature. Even with our best methods and most careful techniques of observation, we can only approximate this ideal.

## Naturalistic Observation

One of the most useful ways to go about exploring an unknown phenomenon, at least initially, is simply to watch it and describe it in as much detail as possible. If you stumble across an aardvark one day and decide you want to know more about it, one of the best ways is to follow it day and night and record your observations. You will discover a great deal this way, but certainly not everything you want to know.

There are two primary characteristics typically associated with naturalistic observation. One is that it is concerned with naturally occurring phenomena. The second is that the observer usually stays out of the way and does not intervene. In fact, the observer in most

FIGURE 2–1.

(a)

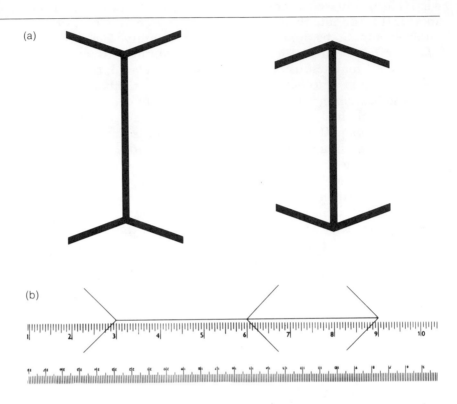

(b)

(c)

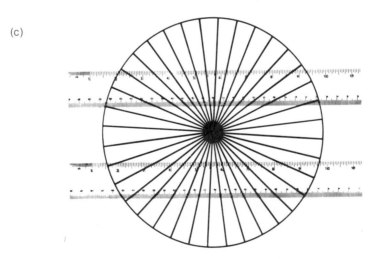

Visual illusions. (a) The Müller-Lyer illusion. The vertical lines are the same length, but appear unequal due to the different direction of the fins in the two cases. (b) The illusion apparently distorts even an objective measuring device, the ruler. But close examination indicates that the ruler is not really distorted and that the lines are of equal length. (c) The rulers now appear bent due to the influence of the circle. These illusions are maintained even though we "know," as in (b), they cannot be so. Our observations can suffer distortions no matter how careful we are (examples taken from R. L. Gregory, 1970, pp. 80-81).

cases does everything possible to keep her or his presence from being known, since this might affect the ongoing phenomenon. Thus the attempt is made for the observer to be as unobtrusive as possible in naturalistic observation. When the researcher's presence is obvious, the observations are said to be *reactive*. That is, the observation of the natural phenomenon, say the behavior of the aardvark, is likely to be in part a reaction to the detected presence of the observer. This is especially true in studies of certain aspects of human behavior, where people know how they are supposed to behave and, if they know they are observed, will simply behave as they should. So studies of shoplifting or speeding are likely to uncover little of interest if the participants know they are observed. Since the researcher's interest is in naturally occurring behavior, efforts in naturalistic research must be taken to make the measures nonreactive and unobtrusive. An interesting book by Webb, Campbell, Schwartz, and Sechrest (1966) describes many unobtrusive measures that may be taken in naturalistic research on human behavior.

Naturalistic research of interest to psychologists is perhaps most prevalent in the area of ethology, the study of animal behavior (often in the wild). Simply observing the behavior of animals or humans allows one to gain a global impression of the characteristics and range of behavior, but one may soon desire more systematic observation. One way ethologists make more systematic observations is by identifying different categories of experience for the organism under study and then recording the number of times the organism engages in each behavior. These behaviors can be divided into large units such as mating, grooming, sleeping, fighting, eating, and so on, or into much smaller units. For example, an *ethogram* of the various behaviors involved in the courtship pattern of a fish, the orange chromide, is shown in figure 2–2. (An ethogram is a relatively complete inventory of the specific behaviors performed by one species of animal.) By counting up the number of times that any specific behavior occurs, ethologists can begin to get some idea of the significance of the behavior.

Often it is difficult to obtain accurate records of an animal's behavior in the wild. It may be hard to keep the animal in view in its natural habitat, researchers cannot remain forever vigilant, and the presence of human observers may make the measures reactive, to mention only some of the greatest problems. Applying similar techniques to human behavior is even more difficult, for people do not appreciate having their every action noted by curious scientists. Barker and his associates (for example, Barker and Wright, 1951; Barker, 1968) have attempted to apply methods of naturalistic observation to humans in a number of settings, although a variety of sensitive behaviors, such as sex, have not been studied. Other variants of the naturalistic approach have been used to study more sensitive aspects of human behavior. Some are briefly described here.

FIGURE 2–2.

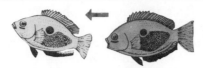

a. *Charging:* An accelerated swim of one fish toward another.

b. *Tail Beating:* An emphatic beating of the tail toward another fish.

c. *Quivering:* A rapid, lateral, shivering movement that starts at the head and dies out as it passes posteriorly through the body.

d. *Nipping:* An O-shaped mouth action that cleans out the (presumptive) spawning site.

e. *Skimming:* The actual spawning movement whereby the fish places its ventral surface against the spawning site and meanders along it for a few seconds.

Ethogram showing courtship pattern in orange chromide. An ethogram can be compiled for all behaviors of a species or for only selected aspects of behavior. (From Drickamer, L. C., and Vesey, S. H. *Animal Behavior: Concepts, Processes, and Methods.* Boston: Willard Grant Press, 1982, p. 28)

***The case study.*** One of the most venerable forms of inquiry in psychology is the case study. Freud's psychoanalytic theory arose from his observations and reflections on individual cases. In general, a case study is the intensive investigation of a single case of some sort, whether of a neurotic patient, a spiritual medium, or a group awaiting the end of the world. An interesting case study of this last instance was provided by Festinger, Riecken, and Schachter (1956) who infiltrated a small group of persons who were indeed awaiting the end of the world. The members thought themselves in contact with beings from another planet who communicated to one member that the destruction of the earth was near. The group was expecting to be rescued by spacecraft before the catastrophe. Festinger and his colleagues were especially interested in the reactions of the group when (if?) the calamity did not occur. They observed that for many of the members of the group the belief in its delusional system actually increased rather than decreased after the predicted date of catastrophe had passed.

The case study is a type of naturalistic observation and is subject to all the disadvantages and the few advantages (to be discussed shortly) of that method. One chief disadvantage is that case studies allow no firm inferences to be made about what causes what. All one can do is describe the course of events. The type of case study that best attempts to minimize this problem of inference is the *deviant-case analysis*. Here the researcher considers two cases that bear a number of similarities and yet differ in outcome. For example, one twin brother might become schizophrenic and the other not. The researcher attempts to pinpoint, through a careful comparison of the two cases, the factors that are responsible for the difference in outcome. But, of course, any conclusions even from this method cannot really be considered firm or well established, because the researcher can never be certain that he or she identified the critical causes in the differing outcomes.

*Phenomenological report.* Another historically important naturalistic method in psychology is the subjective, or phenomenological, report of subjects. The method of *introspection* was of great importance early in the history of psychology, as described in appendix B, but in many other cases subjects' reports have also been used as evidence. Much of the "evidence" for Freud's psychoanalytic theory is based on his interpretations of his patients' reports of dreams or free associations. Even today in some areas of psychology it is common to take reports by subjects as a type of evidence, though these reports are rarely used as the primary data of investigations.

*Survey research.* Case studies and phenomenological reports usually involve only a few subjects, and often these individuals are not at all representative of the population at large. Freud's theory, for example, is based mostly on the cases of neurotic Viennese housewives. It is often of interest to obtain information on a large random sample of people in a large geographic area (such as the United States), even though the amount of information obtained from any one person is necessarily quite limited. This technique is little used in most areas of psychology, though it is familiar to most of you through its use in predicting elections and the like. With the precise sampling techniques now available, relatively few people can be queried and the results will nonetheless generalize well to the population at large. It is difficult to imagine that this method will ever become popular with many psychologists because of the generally descriptive nature of the results obtained. Nonetheless, clever use of the method may allow contributions to some areas of psychology (for example, a developmental psychologist may sample Americans' beliefs about effective child-rearing practices).

One problem common to case studies, phenomenological reports, and surveys is that all three are reactive methods, since subjects know they are being investigated. Although this problem limits these methods in the investigation of some topics, it is certainly not a fatal flaw in and of itself. Most experimental investigations are also reactive.

**Advantages and disadvantages of naturalistic observations.** Naturalistic observation is extremely useful in the early stages of research, when one desires simply to gain some idea as to the breadth and range of the problem of interest (Miller, 1977). It is primarily descriptive, however, and does not allow one to infer how factors may be related. In some cases there is no way to employ more controlled methods of observation, so only naturalistic ones are available. If you want to know how penguins behave in their natural habitat, you simply have to observe them there. Still, for most psychological problems, naturalistic observation is useful primarily in defining the problem area and raising interesting questions for more controlled study by other means, especially experimental ones. For example, the case study by Festinger and his colleagues of the group predicting the end of the earth helped lead to Festinger's (1957) cognitive dissonance theory of attitude change, which has been quite important in guiding social psychological research. Once again, the primary problem unique to naturalistic observation is that it is simply descriptive in nature and does not allow us to assess relationships among events. An investigator might note that grooming behavior in free-ranging monkeys occurs at certain times following five different prior conditions (such as eating). If one is interested in finding out which antecedent conditions are necessary to produce grooming, naturalistic observation cannot provide an answer, since it is not possible to manipulate these antecedent conditions. For this, one needs an experiment.

Naturalistic observation typically produces data that are deficient in other ways, too. Scientific data should be easy to reproduce by others using standardized procedures, if these others doubt the observations or are interested in repeating them. Many naturalistic methods such as the case study do not allow reproducibility and are thus open to question by other investigators. Another problem in naturalistic approaches is maintaining as strictly as possible a descriptive rather than interpretive level of observation. In the study of animals the problem is often one of *anthropomorphizing*, or attributing human characteristics to animals. When you come home and your dog wags its tail and moves about excitedly, it seems perfectly natural to say that it is happy to see you. But this would be anthropomorphizing if one were engaged in naturalistic observation of the scene. Instead, one should record the overt behaviors of the dog with the least possible attribution of underlying motives, such as being happy, sad, or hungry. Of course, the case studies of Freud are based entirely on just such interpretation of the facts. Besides being nonreproducible, such cases then suffer from the possibility that if we are allowed to (a) select our data from case studies and answers people give to the questions we ask, and then (b) weave these "facts" into a previous conceptual system of our own devising, case studies could probably be used to "prove" any theory. (This is not to detract from the creative flair and genius which are evident in Freud's system, but he is certainly open to criticism in terms of the evidence on which it is based.)

Another instance of this interpretive problem closer to scientific psychology is one reported by Pavlov in his early researches on the conditioned reflex (see chapter 8). He and his co-workers discovered they had a problem when they began to study the dog's psychological processes, a problem that had not been apparent when they had previously been concerned only with the digestive system. The problem was severe, for they could not agree on the observations they were making. Pavlov describes the problem of studying conditioned reflexes:

> But how is this to be studied? Taking the dog when he eats rapidly snatches something in his mouth, chews for a long time, it seems clear that at such a time the animal strongly desires to eat, and so rushes to the food, seizes it, and falls to eating. He longs to eat . . . When he eats, you see the work of the muscles alone, striving in every way to seize the food in the mouth, to chew and to swallow it. From all this we can say that he derives pleasure from it     Now when we proceeded to explain and analyze this, we readily adopted this trite point of view. We had to deal with the feelings, wishes, conceptions, etc., of our animal. The results were astounding, extraordinary; I and one of my colleagues came to irreconcilable opinions. We could not agree, could not prove to one another which was right. . . . After this we had to deliberate carefully. It seemed probable we were not on the right track. The more we thought about the matter, the greater grew our conviction that it was necessary to choose another exit. The first steps were very difficult, but along the way of persistent, intense, concentrated thinking I finally reached the firm ground of pure objectivity. We absolutely prohibited ourselves (in the laboratory there was an actual fine imposed) the use of such psychological expressions as the dog guessed, wanted, wished, etc. (Pavlov, reprinted 1963, pp. 263–264)

One further problem will be discussed here, though it is relevant to all types of observation in all types of research. This is the issue of how much our conceptual schemes determine and bias what we "see" as the facts. Pavlov's statement is eloquent testimony of how difficult it is to establish objective methods so that we all see the facts in the same way. He had found it initially "astounding" and "extraordinary" that this was not the case, and was surprised at the elaborate precautions needed to ensure objectivity. Philosophers of science have pointed out that our observations are always likely to be influenced by our conceptions of the world, if in no other way at least by the particular observations we make (see, for example, Hanson, 1958, chapter 2). "Pure objectivity" to use Pavlov's phrase, may be quite elusive. One illustration Hanson uses is two trained microbiologists viewing a stained and prepared slide through a microscope and "seeing" different things. (As is well known, the primary thing a novice typically reports seeing in a microscope is his or her own eyeball.) The problem of objective and reliable observation in science is an ideal to be approximated, but we may never be completely confident that we have obtained it. Certainly, however, we must make every possible step toward this ideal, which is what much of the technical paraphernalia of science is concerned with.

The problem of observations being unduly influenced by expectations is not automatically overcome with the use of the technical equipment of hard science, however, as is evident in an illustration cited by Hyman (1964, p. 38). In 1902, shortly after X rays were discovered, the eminent French physicist Blondlot reported the discovery of "N rays." Other French scientists quickly repeated and confirmed Blondlot's discovery and in 1904 no fewer than 77 publications appeared on the topic. However, the discovery became controversial when American, German, and Italian scientists failed to replicate Blondlot's findings. The Americn physicist R. W. Wood, failing to find N rays in his own lab at Johns Hopkins University, visited Blondlot. Blondlot displayed a card to Wood with luminous circles painted on it. Then he turned down the room light, fixed N rays on the card, and pointed out to Wood how the circles increased in luminosity. When Wood said he could see no change, Blondlot argued that this must be because his (Wood's) eyes were too insensitive. Next Wood asked if he could perform some simple tests, to which Blondlot consented. In one case Wood moved a lead screen repeatedly between the N rays and the cards while Blondlot was to report the corresponding changes in luminosity of the circles on the card. (The lead shield was to prevent passage of the N rays.) Blondlot was consistently in error, and often reported a change in luminosity when the screen was not moved! This and other tests clearly indicated that there was no evidence for the existence of N rays, despite their "confirmation" by other French scientists. After 1909 there were no further publications on N rays. The mistake was too much for Blondlot. He never recovered and died in disgrace some years later. Even with the sophisticated apparatus of physicists, errors of observation are possible, and must be guarded against.

## THE CORRELATIONAL APPROACH

Scientists are not long contented with the type of descriptive information that is derived from observational studies. Of much greater interest is how two *variables* are related to one another. (A variable is something that can be measured or manipulated. More on this in the next chapter.) The use of correlational techniques permits us to assess and specify the degree of relationship between two variables of interest. The assessment is usually made *ex post facto*, or from after the fact. All this means is that the observations of interest are collected and then one computes a *correlation coefficient,* which indicates the degree of relation between the two variables or measures.

You are probably all familiar with the concept of a correlation, whether or not you recognized it when it was disguised in the abstract statement of the preceding paragraph. One typical example of the correlational approach is the relationship between cigarette smoking and lung cancer. Studies in the 1950s and early 1960s consistently found a moderately high positive correlation between cigarette smoking and lung cancer: the greater the number of cigarettes a person smoked, the more likely was that person to have lung cancer. Knowledge of this relationship allows predictions to be made. From the knowledge of how much one smokes, we can predict (though not perfectly) how likely that person is to contract cancer, and vice versa. The Surgeon General's report in 1964, which concluded that smoking was dangerous to health, was based almost entirely on correlational evidence. We shall consider some problems in interpreting correlational evidence, but first, let us consider the properties and calculation of the correlation coefficient itself.

### The Correlation Coefficient

There are several different types of correlation coefficients, but almost all have in common the property that they can vary from $-1.00$ through 0.00 to $+1.00$. Commonly they will not be one of these three figures, but something in between, such as $+.72$ or $-.39$. The magnitude of the correlation coefficient indicates the degree of relationship (larger numbers reflecting greater relationships), while the sign indicates the direction of relationship, positive or negative. It is important to put the appropriate sign in front of the correlation coefficient, since otherwise one cannot know which way the two variables are related, positively or negatively. It is common practice, though, to omit the plus sign before positive correlations, so that a correlation of .55 would be interpreted as positive. It is a better practice always to include the sign. An example of a *positive* correlation is the relationship between lung cancer and smoking. As one variable increases, so does the other (though not perfectly, that is, the correlation coefficient is less than $+1.00$). There is also a documented *negative* correlation between smoking and another variable, namely grades in college. People who smoke a lot have tended to have lower grades than those who smoke less (Huff, 1954, p. 87).

As mentioned, there are actually several different types of correlation coefficients, and which is used depends on the characteristics of the variables being correlated. However, as an example of calculation of a correlation coefficient, we shall consider one commonly used by psychologists, *Pearson's product-moment correlation coefficient,* or Pearson *r.* You should remember that this is only one of several and if you actually need to compute a correlation on some data, you should consult a statistics text to determine which is appropriate for your particular case.

Let us imagine that we are one of the bevy of psychologists who devote their careers to the study of human memory. One of these psychologists hits upon a simple, intuitive idea concerning head size and memory, which goes like this. Information from the outside world enters the head through the senses and is stored there. An analogy can be made between the head (where information is stored) and other physical vessels, such as boxes, where all kinds of things can be stored. On the basis of such analogical reasoning, which is common in science, one can make the following prediction from our knowledge of the properties of physical containers: as head size of a person increases, so should the person's memory. More things can be stored in bigger boxes than smaller, and similarly more information should be stored in larger heads than smaller ones.

This "theory" proposes a simple relationship, that as head size increases so should memory. A positive correlation between these two variables is predicted. A random sample of the population could be taken and the persons chosen could be measured on two dimensions, head size and how many words they can recall from a list of thirty presented to them once at the rate of one word every three seconds. Three hypothetical sets of results from ten subjects are presented in table 2–1. Notice that for each individual there are two measures, one of head size and the other of number of words recalled. Also notice that the two types of measures need not be similar in any way to be correlated. They do not have to be on the same scale. Just as one can correlate head size with number

---

TABLE 2–1

Three hypothetical examples of data taken on head size and recall representing (a) a positive correlation, (b) a low (near zero) correlation, and (c) a negative correlation.

| Sub-ject | (a) Head size (cm.) | Recall (words) | Sub-ject | (b) Head size (cm.) | Recall (words) | Sub-ject | (c) Head size (cm.) | Recall (words) |
|---|---|---|---|---|---|---|---|---|
| 1 | 50.8 | 17 | 1 | 50.8 | 23 | 1 | 50.8 | 12 |
| 2 | 63.5 | 21 | 2 | 63.5 | 12 | 2 | 63.5 | 9 |
| 3 | 45.7 | 16 | 3 | 45.7 | 13 | 3 | 45.7 | 13 |
| 4 | 25.4 | 11 | 4 | 25.4 | 21 | 4 | 25.4 | 23 |
| 5 | 29.2 | 9 | 5 | 29.2 | 9 | 5 | 29.2 | 21 |
| 6 | 49.5 | 15 | 6 | 49.5 | 14 | 6 | 49.5 | 16 |
| 7 | 38.1 | 13 | 7 | 38.1 | 16 | 7 | 38.1 | 14 |
| 8 | 30.5 | 12 | 8 | 30.5 | 15 | 8 | 30.5 | 17 |
| 9 | 35.6 | 14 | 9 | 35.6 | 11 | 9 | 35.6 | 15 |
| 10 | 58.4 | 23 | 10 | 58.4 | 16 | 10 | 58.4 | 11 |
| | $r = +.93$ | | | $r = -.07$ | | | $r = -.89$ | |

of words recalled, one could also correlate I.Q. with street-address number, or any two sets of numbers at all. Box 2–1 shows how Pearson $r$ is actually computed. (You need not work through this example to understand the rest of the discussion of correlation.)

In order to give you a better idea of the graphical representation of correlations, the data in the three panels of table 2–1 are presented in the three panels of figure 2–3, where head size is plotted along the horizontal $X$-axis (the abscissa) and number of words recalled is plotted along the vertical $Y$-axis (the ordinate). Notice that the high positive correlation between head size and number of words recalled in the (a) panel in table 2–1 is translated into a visual representation that tilts upward to the right, while the negative correlation in panel (c) is depicted as sloping downward to the right. Thus you can see how knowing a person's score on one variable helps predict (though not perfectly in these cases) the level of performance on the other. So knowing a person's head size in the hypothetical data in the (a) and (c) panels helps predict recall, and vice versa. This is the primary reason correlations are useful: they specify the amount of relationship and allow predictions to be made. Notice that this last statement cannot be made about the data in panel (b) where there is essentially a zero correlation. The points are just scattered about and there is no consistent relationship, which is just what a low Pearson $r$ reflects. Even in the cases where the size of the correlation is rather large, it should be noted that it will not be possible to predict perfectly an individual's score on one variable given his or her position on the other. Even with $r = +.75$ between head size and number of words recalled, it is still quite possible for a person with a large head size to recall few words and vice versa. Unless the correlation is perfect ($+1.00$ or $-1.00$), prediction of one score when given the other will not be perfect, either.

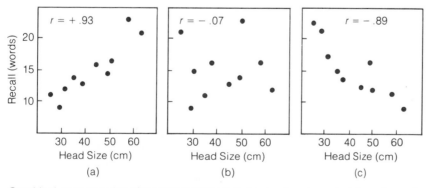

FIGURE 2–3.

Graphical representation of the data in Table 2-3 showing the characteristic pattern of (a) a high positive correlation, (b) an essentially zero correlation, and (c) a strong negative correlation.

**Box 2–1** Computing Pearson *r*

Let us call one set of numbers in table 2–2 *X* scores and the other set *Y* scores. For example, head sizes might be *X* scores and words recalled *Y* scores. The formula for computing Pearson *r* from the raw scores in panels (a), (b), or (c) of table 2–1 is as follows:

$$(2\text{–}1) \qquad r = \frac{n\,\Sigma XY - (\Sigma X)(\Sigma Y)}{\sqrt{[n\,\Sigma X^2 - (\Sigma X)^2][n\,\Sigma Y^2 - (\Sigma Y)^2]}}$$

Then *n* refers to the number of subjects on which observations are taken (10 here); the terms $\Sigma X$ and $\Sigma Y$ are the totals of the *X* and *Y* scores, respectively; $\Sigma X^2$ and $\Sigma Y^2$ are the sum of all the *X* (or *Y*) values after each is squared; and the $(\Sigma X)^2$ and $(\Sigma Y)^2$ are the total of all the *X* or *Y* values with the entire total or sum squared. This leaves the value $\Sigma XY$, or the sum of the crossproducts. This is obtained very simply by multiplying each *X*-value by its corresponding *Y* and then summing these products. You may see other formulas for calculation of Pearson *r* besides the raw-score formula in equation 2–1, but these will be equivalent (in general) to the one presented here. An illustration of how Pearson *r* is calculated using this raw-score formula is presented in table 2–2 using the data from the (a) column of table 2–1. You should try to work out the values for Pearson *r* for the (b) and (c) panels yourself to make certain you understand how to calculate the values and to gain an intuitive feel for the concept of correlation. The values of *r* are given below the appropriate columns in table 2–1.

What do you think the real correlation would be between head size and recall of a random sample of the population at large? Although we have not actually done such a study, we think it quite likely that it would be rather large and positive (perhaps +.60 to +.70), in support of the theory of memory storage based on head size. What can we conclude from this? How can correlation coefficients be interpreted? We turn to this issue next.

*Interpreting correlation coefficients.* An important warning is always given in any discussion of correlation: The existence of even a sizable correlation implies nothing about the existence of a causal relationship between the two variables under consideration. On the basis of just a correlation, one cannot say whether factor *X* causes factor *Y*, factor *Y* causes factor *X*, some underlying third factor causes both, or the two are completely unrelated. Let us consider some examples. Suppose we have found a correlation of +.70 between head size and recall of words. This is in general agreement with our theory that larger heads hold more informa-

TABLE 2–2 Calculation of Pearson $r$ for the data in the first (a) column of table 2–1 by the raw-score formula (equation 2–1).

| Subject number | X Head size (cm.) | $X^2$ | Y Words recalled | $Y^2$ | $X \cdot Y$ |
|---|---|---|---|---|---|
| 1 | 50.8 | 2580.64 | 17 | 289 | 863.60 |
| 2 | 63.5 | 4032.25 | 21 | 441 | 1330.50 |
| 3 | 45.7 | 2088.49 | 16 | 256 | 731.20 |
| 4 | 25.4 | 645.16 | 11 | 121 | 279.40 |
| 5 | 29.2 | 852.64 | 9 | 81 | 262.80 |
| 6 | 49.5 | 2450.25 | 15 | 225 | 742.50 |
| 7 | 38.1 | 1451.61 | 13 | 169 | 495.30 |
| 8 | 30.5 | 930.25 | 12 | 144 | 366.00 |
| 9 | 35.6 | 1267.36 | 14 | 196 | 498.40 |
| 10 | 58.4 | 3410.56 | 23 | 529 | 1343.20 |
| $n =$ 10 | $\Sigma X =$ 426.70 | $\Sigma X^2 =$ 19,709.21 | $\Sigma Y =$ 151 | $\Sigma Y^2 =$ 2451 | $\Sigma XY =$ 6915.90 |

$$r = \frac{n\Sigma XY - (\Sigma X)(\Sigma Y)}{\sqrt{[n\Sigma X^2 - (\Sigma X)^2][n\Sigma Y^2 - (\Sigma Y)^2]}}$$

$$r = \frac{10(6915.90) - (426.70)(151)}{\sqrt{[(10)(19,709.21) - (426.70)^2][(10)(2451) - (151)^2]}}$$

$$r = \frac{69,159.00 - 64,431.70}{\sqrt{[197,092.10 - 182,072.89][24,510 - 22,801]}}$$

$$r = \frac{4727.30}{\sqrt{[15,019.21][1709]}} = \frac{4727.30}{\sqrt{25,667,829.89}}$$

$$r = \frac{4727.30}{5066.34}$$

$$r = +.93$$

tion, but certainly there are other interpretations of this relationship. It could be argued that the high positive correlation between head size and recall is *mediated* or produced by some third factor underlying both, such as age. We know that people's heads grow as they age and that recall also improves with age. Therefore age (or one of its correlates) might actually be responsible for the large positive correlation we have found between head size and number of words recalled.

In correlational studies we cannot conclude that any one factor produced or caused another since there are likely to have been a number of factors which varied simultaneously with those of interest. In an experiment one attempts to avoid this problem by directly manipulating one factor while holding all the others constant. Then the influence of the manipulated factor on whatever it is we are measuring can be directly attributed to the factor of interest. When two factors (or more) are varied at the same time so that we cannot know whether one factor, the other factor, or both operating together produce some effect, we say that the factors are confounded. *Confounding* is inherent in correlational research and leads to the interpretational difficulties with such research. In the example of the correlation between head size and recall, we cannot say that variations in head size produced or caused differences in recall since head size was confounded with at least one other factor, age.

In other cases the relationship between two factors may seem to allow a causal interpretation, but again this is not strictly permitted. Some studies have shown a positive correlation between the number of handguns in a geographic area and the number of murders in that area. Proponents of gun control might use this evidence to support the contention that an increased number of guns leads to (causes, produces) more murders, but again this is not the only plausible interpretation. It may be that people in high crime neighborhoods buy handguns to protect themselves, or that some third factor, such as socioeconomic class, actually mediates both. So no conclusion is justified simply on the basis of a moderate or even high correlation.

Since correlations can be calculated between any two sets of scores, it is apparent that often even very high correlations are accidental and not linked to one another at all. There may be a very high correlation between the number of preachers and the number of pornographic movies produced each year since 1950, with both being on the increase. But it would take an unusual theory to relate these two in a causal manner.

A high degree of correlation is given greater weight in cases where obvious competing explanations (from confounding factors) seem less plausible. We have already mentioned that most of the early evidence linking cigarette smoking to lung cancer was correlational, yet the conclusion was drawn (over the protests of the cigarette manufacturers) by the 1964 Surgeon General's report that cigarettes were likely to lead to or cause cancer. This eventually led to warnings on cigarette packages and a ban of advertising for cigarettes on television, among other things. So the correlation was taken as indicative of a causative relationship, probably because competing hypotheses seemed implausible. It seems unlikely, for example, that having lung cancer causes one to smoke more cigarettes (to soothe the lungs?). More plausible, perhaps, is that some underlying third factor (such as anxiety) produces the relationship or that it is accidental. In fact, Eysenck and Eaves (1981) have recently argued that the correlation between lung cancer and smoking in humans is produced by personality differences. Certain personality types, according to Eysenck and Eaves, are more likely to smoke and to get lung cancer. Thus they argue that the smoking-cancer correlation does not imply causation. We should mention, though, that the link between cigarette smoking and lung cancer has now been established by experimental studies with nonhuman animals, typically beagles. Most authorities disagree with the view of Eysenck and Eaves.

As a final example of the pitfalls of the correlational approach, consider the negative relationship mentioned previously between cigarette smoking and grades. More smoking has been related to poorer grades. But does smoking cause poorer grades? It seems unlikely, and certainly there are ready alternative interpretations. Students with poor grades may be more anxious and thus smoke more. Or more sociable students may smoke more and study less. And so on. Once again, no firm conclusions on the causal direction of a relationship between two variables can be established simply because the variables are correlated, even if the correlation is perfect. Like the observational method, the correlational method is very useful for suggesting possible relationships and directing further inquiry, but it is not useful for establishing direct causal relationships. The correlational method is superior to the observational method because the degree of relation between two variables can be precisely stated and thus predictions can be made about the (approximate) value of one variable if the value of the other is known. Once again, the greater the correlation (nearer +1.00 or −1.00), the better is the prediction.

*Low correlations: A caution.* If high correlations cannot be interpreted as evidence for some sort of causal relationship, one might think it should at least be possible to rule out a causative relationship between two variables if their correlation is very low, approaching zero. If the correlation between head size and recall had been −.02, would this have ruled out our theory that greater head size leads to better recall? Or if the correlation between smoking and lung cancer had been +.08, should we have abandoned the idea that they are causally related? The answer: sometimes, under certain conditions. But other factors can cause low or zero correlations and may mask an actual relationship.

One common problem is that of *truncated range*. In order to calculate a meaningful correlation coefficient, there must be rather great differences among the scores in each of the variables of interest; there must be a certain amount of spread or variability in the numbers. If all the head sizes were the same in the panels of table 2–1 and the recall scores varied, the correlation between the two would be zero. (You can work it out yourself using Equation 2–1 in Box 2–1.) If we only looked at the correlation between head size and recall in college students, it might be quite low because the differences in head size and recall among college students may not be very great compared with the population at large. This could happen even though there might be a positive (or negative) correlation between the two variables if head size were sampled over a wider range. So the problem of restricted range can produce a low correlation even when there is an actual correlation present between two variables.

You might think that everyone would recognize this problem and avoid it, but it is often more subtle. Consider the problem of trying to predict success in college from Scholastic Aptitude Test (SAT) scores at a school with very high admission standards. The scores on the verbal and quantitative subtests can range from 200 to 800, with average (mean) performance of just below 500. Imagine that mean scores at our hypothetical college are 700 on each subtest. The admissions officer at this college computes a correlation between combined SAT scores and freshman grades and finds it to be +.10, very small indeed. Her conclusion: SAT scores cannot be used to predict grades in college. The problem, however, is that the only scores considered were ones from a very restricted range, specifically very high ones. People with low scores were not admitted to the college. So the truncated-range problem is very likely to be a factor here. If the college had randomly admitted people and then after the fact the correlation had been determined between SAT scores and grades, it would probably have been much higher. Since psychologists often use homogeneous populations such as college students, the restricted-range problem must be carefully considered in interpreting correlations.

A final problem in interpreting low correlations is that one must be certain that the assumptions underlying the use of a particular correlation coefficient have been met. Otherwise its use may well be inappropriate and lead to spuriously low estimates of relationship. These have not been discussed here, but we have said to check on these assumptions in a statistics book before employing Pearson $r$ or any other correlation coefficient. For example, one assumption underlying Pearson $r$ is that the relationship between the two variables is linear (can be described by a straight line) rather than curvilinear, as in the hypothetical (but plausible) relationship in figure 2–4 between age and long-term memory. At very young ages

FIGURE 2–4.

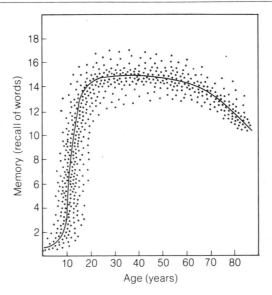

A hypothetical figure depicting a curvilinear relationship between long term memory and age. Although memory is related to age in a systematic fashion and one could predict recall by knowing age, Pearson $r$ would be quite low since the relationship is not linear.

the line is flat, then it increases between ages 3 and 16, where it again levels off until late middle age, where it drops slightly, until very old age, where it decreases at a greater rate (Craik, 1977). Thus one can predict recall of words from age fairly well, but Pearson $r$ will be rather low since the relationship is not linear between the two variables. This could, of course, always be checked by plotting a scatter diagram as in figure 2–4. Low correlations, then, may not reflect an absence of relationship, but only that the assumptions of the particular coefficient employed were not met.

## EX POST FACTO DESIGNS

The crux of experimental method is to vary some factor of interest and observe its effect while all other relevant variables are held constant. In this way we can observe the direct effect of the variable unconfounded with other factors. Correlations, on the other hand, measure a relationship between two variables but allow no statement as to whether the relationship between the two is direct, mediated by a confounded third variable, completely accidental, et cetera. Experiments differ from correlations because the experimenter has control over the experimental variables so that she or he can manipulate the ones of interest and hold constant the others. Experiments thus allow stronger conclusions about the relation between two variables than do correlations because of the control that can be employed over extraneous factors. For this reason it is the preferred method of scientists for determining relations among variables. Most of this book is concerned with application of experimental methods, and we shall see that even with experiments there are numerous problems of interpretation to consider.

There are a number of procedures used by scientists, especially in the social sciences, which are intermediate between correlations and true experiments. These procedures are carried out after the fact (after some natural occurrence) and are thus called *ex post facto research designs*. They are sometimes called quasi-experiments. As in experiments, subjects may be separated into different groups and different treatments may be administered. But unlike true experiments, these procedures do not allow the researcher to have control over assignment of subjects to treatments, or (often) to manipulate the variables involved. The research is after the fact because the investigator must attempt to make what inferences he or she can from "manipulations" which have occurred naturally and over which the investigator had little or no control. Therefore the main problem in such quasi-experimental research concerns confounding produced because the researcher lacked control over the extraneous variables.

There are several statistical procedures commonly invoked to gain a better understanding of the direction of relationship in correlational research. One interesting technique is the *cross-lagged correlation procedure* (Rozelle and Campbell, 1969), which is used to examine patterns of correlations over time. One very interesting recent use of this technique was by Eron, Huesmann, Lefkowitz, and Walder (1972), who were interested in seeing whether or not watching violent television programs leads to (helps cause) aggressive behavior. They measured children's preference for violent television in the third grade and how aggressive the children were as rated by their peers. They found a moderate positive correlation, $r = +.21$, indicating that more aggressive children tended to watch more violent TV (and vice versa). Of course there is nothing in this fact to suggest that watching violent TV programs causes aggressiveness. But Eron and his co-workers conducted a ten-year follow-up study of these children in the thirteenth grade and the results are summarized in figure 2–5. The correlation between a preference for violent TV and aggression was essentially zero ($r = \pm.05$) in the thirteenth grade. Similarly the relation between preference for violent TV in the third and thirteenth grade was negligible ($r = +.05$), but there was a moderate relationship between aggressiveness in the two grades ($r = +.38$), indicating that it is a somewhat stable trait. Of more interest are the cross-lagged correlations—the diagonals—in assessing the direction of the relationship. Do aggressive people watch violent TV, or does watching violent TV produce aggressiveness? There is no relation between aggressiveness in the third grade and watching violent TV in the thirteenth ($r = +.01$), but there is a fairly substantial relation between a preference for watching violent TV in the third grade and aggressiveness in the thirteenth ($r = +.31$). In fact, the relation is even greater than between these two variables in the third grade.

FIGURE 2–5.

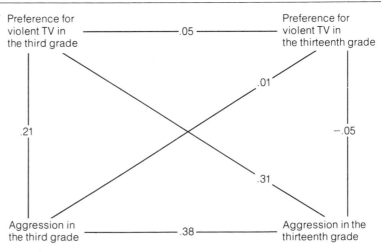

Correlations between a preference for violent television programs and aggression as rated by peers for 211 males over a 10 year period. The important cross-lagged correlations are on the diagonals (after Eron, Huesman, Lefkowitz, and Walder, 1972).

Thus the direction of relationship seems to be that watching violent TV programs in the third grade may produce aggressiveness later. The underlying assumption is that if one variable causes another, measurement of the first variable (watching violent TV programs) at one point in time should be more strongly related to the second variable (aggressiveness) at a later point in time than when the two variables are related initially. That is, causes should take time to produce their effects.

Using these cross-lagged correlations and other complex analyses, Eron and his colleagues concluded that watching violent TV early in life probably causes, in part, aggressive behavior at later times (see also Huesmann et al., 1973). Of course many other factors contribute to aggressiveness, but this is an excellent example of how cross-lagged correlations can contribute to determining cause-and-effect relationships (Cook and Campbell, 1977).

## Designs Employing Subject Variables

Much research in psychology is concerned with differences among classes of people in the way they behave. A *subject variable* is some characteristic of people that can be measured. Examples are numerous and include intelligence (I.Q.), weight, anxiety, sex, age, need for achievement, attractiveness, race, ability to recall dreams, as well as many types of pathological conditions (schizophrenia, neurosis, et cetera). Subject variables are often used in psychological research, but their use demands special consideration since their investigation is after the fact. Thus experiments employing subject variables are one type of quasi-experiment.

In experiments an investigator has control over manipulation of the experimental variable, so that it can be manipulated while all else is held constant. So if we are interested in the effect of pornographic movies upon physiological arousal and later sexual excitement, we can take two statistically equivalent groups of people (or the same people at different times), show them a movie with pornographic scenes included or omitted (holding other variables constant), and measure their responses. One can then have confidence (but never certainty) that the difference between the movies produced any observed differential effect in arousal.

The case is very different with subject variables, though. An experimenter cannot manipulate a subject variable while holding other factors constant; she or he can only select subjects who already have the characteristic in some varying degree, and then compare them on the behavior of interest. If the subjects in the different groups (say, high, medium, and low I.Q.) differ on the behavior, we cannot conclude that the subject-variable difference produced or is responsible for the difference in behavior. The reason is that other factors may covary with the subject variable and thus be confounded with it. So if high I.Q. subjects perform some task better than low I.Q. subjects, we cannot say that I.Q. produced or caused the difference because the different groups of subjects are likely to vary on other relevant dimensions such as motivation, education, and the like. When subject variables are investigated we cannot safely attribute differences in behavior to this variable as we can with true experimental variables. Such designs then essentially produce correlations between variables. We can say that the variables are related, but we cannot say that one variable produced or caused the effect in the other variable.

This is a very important point, so let us consider an example. Suppose an investigator is interested in the intellectual functioning (or lack thereof) of people suffering from schizophrenia. People diagnosed as belonging to this group are given numerous tests that are meant to measure various mental abilities. The researcher also gives these tests to another group of people, so-called normals. He or she discovers that schizophrenics do especially poorly relative to normals in tests involving semantic aspects of language, such as those which involve understanding the meaning of words or comprehending prose passages. The investigator concludes that the schizophrenics perform these tests more poorly *because* they are schizophrenics and that their inability to use language well in communication is a likely contributing cause of schizophrenia.

Studies like this are common in some areas of psychology. Despite the fact that conclusions similar to this are often drawn from such studies, they are completely unwarranted. Both conclusions are based on correlations, and other factors could well be the critical ones. Schizophrenics may do more poorly than normals for any number of reasons. They may not be as intelligent, as motivated, as educated, or as wise at taking tests. It may simply be that they have been institutionalized for a long time with resulting poverty of social and intellectual intercourse. So we cannot conclude that the reason that the two groups differ on verbal tests is schizophrenia or its absence in the two groups. Even if we could conclude this, it would certainly not imply the other conclusion, that language problems are involved in causing schizophrenia. Again, all we would have is a correlation between these two variables, with no idea of whether or how the two are causally related.

Use of subject variables is very common in all psychological research, but it is absolutely crucial in some areas such as clinical and developmental psychology, so the problems with making inferences from such research should be carefully considered. A primary variable in developmental psychology is age, a subject variable, which means that much research in this field is correlational in nature. In general, the problem of individual differences among subjects in psychology is one that is often ignored, though there are often appeals to consider this problem as crucial (see Underwood, 1975). We devote a chapter later in the book to individual differences (chapter 12), but let us consider here one way of attempting more sound inferences from experiments employing subject variables.

***Matching.*** The basic problem in the investigation of subject variables, and in other ex post facto research, is that whatever differences are observed in behavior may be caused by other confounded variables. One way to try to avoid this problem is by *matching* subjects on the other relevant variables. In the comparison of schizophrenics and normals we noted that the two groups were also likely to differ on other characteristics such as I.Q., education, motivation, institutionalization, and perhaps even age. Rather than simply comparing the schizophrenics to normals, we might try to compare them to another group more closely matched on these other dimensions so that, we hope, the main difference between the groups is in the presence or absence of schizophrenia. For example, we might use a group of patients who, on the average, are similar to the schizophrenics in terms of age, I.Q., length of time institutionalized, sex, and some measure of motivation. When the two groups have been matched on all these characteristics, then we can more confidently attribute any difference in performance between them to the factor of interest, namely, schizophrenia. By matching, investigators attempt to introduce the crucial characteristic of experimentation—being able to hold constant extraneous factors to avoid confoundings—into what is essentially a correlational observation. The desire is to allow one to infer that the variable of interest (schizophrenia) produced the observed effect.

There are several rather severe problems associated with matching. For one thing it often requires a great deal of effort because some of the relevant variables may be quite difficult to measure. Even when one goes to the trouble of taking the needed additional measures, it may still be impossible to match the groups, especially if few subjects are involved before matching is attempted. Even when matching is successful, it often greatly reduces the size of the sample on which the observations are made. Thus we then have less confidence in the reliability of our observations (that is, that they are stable and repeatable).

Another problem with matching involves the introduction of the dreaded *regression artifact*. This is discussed in chapter 12, but we will explain it briefly here. Under certain conditions in many types of measurements a statistical phenomenon occurs known as *regression to the mean*. The mean of a group of scores is what most people think of as the average, the total of all observations divided by the number of observations. For example, mean height in a sample of sixty people is the sum of all their heights divided by sixty. Typically, if people who received extreme scores (that is, very high or very low) on some characteristic are retested, their second scores will be closer to the mean of the entire group than were their original scores. Consider an example. We give two hundred people a standard test of mathematical reasoning for which there are two equivalent forms, or two versions of the test that we know to be equivalent. The average (mean) score on the test is 60 of 100 possible points. We take the 15 people who score highest and the 15 who score lowest. The mean of these groups is, say, 95 and 30, respectively. Then we test them again on the other version of the test. Now we might find that the means of the two groups are 87 and 35. On the second test the scores of these two extreme groups regressed toward the mean; the high-scoring group scored more poorly while the low-scoring group did somewhat better. Basically it happens for the high-scoring group because some people whose "true scores" are somewhat lower than actually tested lucked out and scored higher than they should have on the test. When retested, people with extremely high scores tend to score lower, nearer their true score. The situation is reversed for the low-scoring group. That is, some of them scored below their "true" score on the first test and thus retesting lends to their scoring higher or nearer the true score.

This regression toward the mean is always observed under such conditions when there is a less than perfect correlation between the two measures, and the more extreme the selection of scores, the greater the regression toward the mean. It also occurs in all types of measurement situations. If abnormally tall or short parents have a child, it will likely be closer to the population mean than the height of the parents. As with most statistical phenomena, regression to the mean is true of groups of observations and is probabilistic (that is, it may not occur every time). For example, a few individual subjects may move away from the mean in the second test of mathematical reasoning, but the group tendency will be toward the mean.

How does regression toward the mean affect ex post facto research where subjects have been matched on some variable? Again, consider an example. This one, like much ex post facto research done on applied societal problems, has important implications. Let us assume we have an educational program that we believe will be especially advantageous for increasing the reading scores of black children. This is especially important because black children's scores are typically lower than those of whites, presumably because of different cultural environments. We take two groups of children, one black and one white, and match them on several criteria including age, sex, and most important, initial reading ability. We give both groups of children the reading improvement program and then test their reading ability after the program. We find, much to our surprise, that the black children actually perform *worse* after the reading program than before it, while the white children improve. We conclude, of course, that the program helped white children but actually hurt black children, despite the fact that it was especially designed for the latter.

This conclusion, even though it may seem resonable to you, is almost surely erroneous in this case because of regression artifacts. Consider what happened when the black and white children were matched on initial reading scores. Since the populations differed initially with blacks scoring lower than whites, in order to match two samples it was necessary to select the black students having higher scores than the mean for their group and the white students having lower scores than their group mean. Having picked these extreme groups, we could predict (because of regression to the mean) that when retested, the black children would have poorer scores and the white children would have better ones, on the average, even if the reading improvement program had no effect at all! The exceptionally-high-scoring black children would tend to regress toward the mean of their group, while the low-scoring whites would regress toward the mean for their group. The same thing would have happened even if there were no program and the children were simply retested.

The same outcome would likely have been obtained if children were matched on I.Q.s instead of reading scores, since the two are probably positively correlated. So simply finding another matching variable may be no solution. One solution would be to match very large samples of black and white children and then split each group, giving the reading program to one subgroup but not the other. All would be retested at the end of the one subgroup's participation in the program. (Assignment of subjects to the subgroups of black and white children should, of course, be random.) Regression to the mean would be expected in both subgroups, but the effect of the reading program could be evaluated against the group that had no program. Perhaps black children with the reading program would show much less drop (regression to the mean) than those without, indicating that the program really did have a positive effect.

Ex post facto research with subject variables is conducted quite often to evaluate educational programs, so its practitioners need to be aware of the many thorny problems associated with its use. Without matching, one may not be able to say much with regard to the results, or draw important conclusions, because of confoundings. Matching helps alleviate this problem in some cases where its use is possible, but then one introduces the possibility of regression artifacts. And many researchers seem unaware of this problem. One famous blooper in such evaluational research, very similar to the hypothetical study outlined here, is discussed in chapter 12.

When matching is a practical possibility, and when regression artifacts are evaluated, we can feel somewhat more confident of conclusions from our results. But we should remember that what we have is still only a correlation, albeit a very carefully controlled one. Matching is useful, but it is not a cure-all. In our earlier example comparing schizophrenics to others on mental test performance, if the schizophrenics still perform worse than the new matched control group, can we then conclude that schizophrenia *produces* inferiority in language usage? No, we cannot. It could still be something else, some other difference between the two groups. We can never be absolutely sure we matched on the relevant variables.

### Other Ex Post Facto Designs

Subject variables are, of course, not the only ones that are identified after the fact. There are other natural "treatments" that are of interest to investigators. For example, we might be interested in the psychological effects that a tornado (or some other natural disaster) has when it sweeps through a community. Obviously we cannot randomly assign communities to the tornado and no-tornado conditions to evaluate the mental health of communities that have been struck and those which have not, so the research must proceed after the fact. What one might try to do in this case is to find a town similar to the one hit by the tornado on a number of characteristics and compare the mental health of the citizens in the two cases to try to see what effect the tornado had. This is about as close as one could ever get to a true experiment in ex post facto research, since a tornado is no more likely to strike one town than a similar one close by. Even with the best of controls, though, the conclusions will still be based on correlational results. It may be quite likely that the tornado produced whatever differences exist in mental health, but such conclusions will not be as certain as those would be from experiments where there is true random assignment before some variable is manipulated.

Ex post facto studies are conducted in situations where true experiments are impossible or impractical. Yet the situations involved are often of great intrinsic interest, so a great deal of such research is conducted. It must also be noted that much of this research is of poor quality. For this reason an understanding of the issues and problems one confronts in ex post facto research is critical for many disciplines in the behavioral sciences. The experimental method is widely employed in most areas of psychology and our book is therefore mostly concerned with it. But most other behavioral sciences such as sociology and political science rely much more heavily on ex post facto research. These research designs, as well as other quasi-experimental designs, are discussed in books by Campbell and Stanley (1963), Cook and Campbell (1977) and Kerlinger (1973, chapter 22). Let us end this discussion with a word of advice from Kerlinger: "Always treat the results and interpretations of ex post facto investigations with great care and caution. Where one must be careful with experimental results and interpretations, one must be doubly careful with ex post facto results and interpretations" (1973, p. 392).

It has become unpopular among scientists of late, owing to the influence of some philosophers of science, to use the term *cause* because the philosophical implications become frightfully complicated. Thinking too long about the cause of even a very simple event leads to an infinite regress of causes for that event. For this and other reasons the term *cause* has dropped out of use in some circles (see Kerlinger, 1973, pp. 392–393). In this book we muddle through, using the term *cause*, since its meaning is always limited; experiments lead to causal inferences because one factor is varied while all others are, in the ideal case, held constant. Thus we can say that whatever effect occurs in such cases was caused by the factor that varied. We limit ourselves to this usage, but others prefer various circumlocutions. Instead of saying that there is evidence that cigarette smoking causes cancer, we can say that it leads to, produces, is an antecedent condition of, determines, or directly affects cancer. We use these terms interchangeably with *cause*.

A more interesting point is that many factors that are experimentally varied are themselves quite complicated sets of independent events, any one of which could be the cause of an experimental effect. Time is a good example of such a variable. If we are interested in the effects of how long one studies a persuasive communication on how much a person's attitude changes toward the communication, we vary the amount of time people spend studying the message. Now suppose we find an increase in attitude change with increases in study time, with other factors held constant. Can we say that time caused an increase in attitude change? In a sense this is true, but in a more fundamental sense it is not. Presumably it is some psychological process acting over time that causes the attitude change. It is something correlated with time, but not time itself, since time is not a causative agent. If we leave a bicycle outdoors in the rain and it rusts we do not say that time caused the rust, but chemical processes acting over time.

It is often the case that a manipulated variable is actually composed of a number of complex and interacting parts, any one or set of which may actually cause some effect. For this reason it is sometimes said that experiments are only controlled correlations, since the variable manipulated is actually composed of a number of confounded parts. This is certainly an accurate characterization in at least some cases, but even so we are far ahead of having a simple correlation because we know the direction of effect. Take the example of how amount of time studying a persuasive communication affects attitude change. We could simply give the message to a number of people and let them read it for as long as they desired. We could time this for each person and then see how much the person's attitude changed. If we found a positive correlation we would not know whether the time people spent studying the passage caused more attitude change, or whether the more people decided to change their attitudes, the more they studied the passage to make sure they knew the facts. There are other possible reasons for the relationship, too. But in the experiment where time is varied while other factors are held constant, we can say that more study time leads to (determines, produces, causes) more attitude change. Experiments allow us to know the direction of the relation and this is their overwhelming advantage to correlations. They also provide us with the information (which a correlation does not) that the causal factor is at least embedded in the independent variable, and not some third outside factor. It is in this sense that they tell us about causes. We turn to this important scientific tool—the experiment—in the next chapter.

**SUMMARY**

**1.** Much of science is concerned with the careful observation and study of the natural world. Two basic techniques discussed in this chapter are naturalistic observation and the correlational approach. Both of these are fairly weak scientific methods relative to the experiment, since they do not allow us to make statements about what factors cause what effects. But they are very useful in early stages of exploration of a topic and in studying topics that cannot practically or ethically be studied by experimental means.

**2.** Naturalistic observation typically involves the unobtrusive (nonreactive) observation of events naturally occurring in the environment. Of more use to psychologists are three reactive variants of naturalistic observation: case studies, phenomenological reports, and surveys. However, all these methods of simple observation have the disadvantage of being descriptive and not allowing statements about how factors are related to one another.

**3.** The correlational approach allows statements of relationship, of what goes with what. Correlations can vary from $-1.00$ to $+1.00$ with the magnitude of the number reflecting the strength of the relationship and the sign indicating the direction. As examples, height is positively correlated with weight, and mean yearly temperature is negatively correlated with distance of location from the equator. There are several measures of correlation, but the one most commonly used by psychologists is the Pearson product-moment correlation coefficient, or Pearson $r$.

**4.** The correlational approach allows one to establish the amount of relationship between two variables, which is useful for prediction. However, its primary drawback is that it cannot establish the direction of relationship. Even if two variables, $X$ and $Y$, are strongly related, we cannot say whether the relationship is accidental, or $X$ caused $Y$, or $Y$ caused $X$, or some third factor caused both.

**5.** In correlational studies a number of factors usually vary together so that the results are confounded. But correlational research is quite appropriate in situations where it is impossible to perform experiments, for example, as in studying conditions related to race riots.

**6.** When researchers discover that the correlation between two measures is near zero, they will often conclude that there is no relation between the measures. Before drawing such a conclusion, even though it often is correct, researchers must determine if assumptions underlying the use of the correlational measure have been met. One common problem is that of truncated range, or a lack of variation in the distribution of one set of scores. If all the measures on one variable are about the same, the correlation coefficient will approach zero even if there is a true relation between the measures when a wider sampling of scores is taken.

**7.** Quasi-experimental research is that which attempts to introduce a measure of control into correlational studies to better determine cause-and-effect relations. Such research often is done after the fact (that is, after some natural event has occurred) and is thus called ex post facto research. In some cases statistical techniques, such as the cross-lagged correlational procedure, can be used to determine causes in correlational studies.

**8.** *Ex post facto* studies in psychology often employ subject variables. These variables are measures such as age, I.Q., mental health, height, hair color, and sex, as well as the myriad other characteristics that differ from one person to the next. Such variables are determined after the fact, since they are often inherited dispositions (or at least people come to the psychological study with the variable already determined). Because it is not possible to randomly assign people to the conditions of interest, studies that use subject variables are inherently correlational in nature.

**9.** In order to attempt cause-and-effect statements from manipulation of subject variables, researchers often match subjects on other variables. Thus if a researcher were interested in the effects of hair color on performance in some task or the reaction from others in some situation, he or she would attempt to control as many other variables as possible to ensure that hair color was the only aspect on which people in the various conditions differed. Matching is often a useful tool for these purposes, but one must be certain that the possibility of regression artifacts does not cloud the conclusions.

**10.** Regression to the mean refers to the fact that when a subgroup with extreme scores is taken from a larger group and retested, they will tend to score nearer the mean of the whole group on the second test. If in matching two groups on the basis of a first test the researcher is taking high scorers from a group that generally does poorly and low scorers from a group that generally does well, then even if the groups are not treated differently in an experiment, the researcher can expect them to score differently on a second test simply because of regression to the mean. This problem is referred to as a regression artifact.

**KEY TERMS**

anthropomorphize
case study
cause
confounding
correlation
correlation coefficient
cross-lagged correlation
  procedure
descriptive observation
deviant-case analysis
ethogram
ethology
ex post facto research
introspection

matching
naturalistic observation
Pearson *r*
phenomenological report
quasi-experiment
reactive measures
regression artifact
regression to the mean
subject variables
survey research
truncated range
variable

**DISCUSSION QUESTIONS**

**1.** Imagine that you are a researcher just beginning a study of how mothers interact with their babies. You want to gain some idea as to the frequency (1) that the mother performs some act regarding the baby that is relatively independent of the baby's immediate needs, (2) the baby acts in various ways when the mother is not attending to it, and (3) of the mother's and child's actions when they are interacting. Make a list of all the behaviors that you think might occur with relatively great frequency in the three categories. This would be a type of ethogram, as discussed in this chapter. If you observed mothers and babies for five hours a day over a period of weeks, what kinds of conclusions could you draw? What kinds of information would you want to know, but not be able to obtain, from this sort of naturalistic observation?

**2.** One of the first pieces of evidence that linked lung cancer with cigarette smoking was published by Doll (1955). He tabulated the average number of cigarettes consumed by the people of eleven countries in 1930 and the number of deaths from lung cancer among men in 1950. The measure of deaths was taken twenty years after the measure of cigarette consumption, since it seems natural that it would take years for a cause-and-effect relation to be seen, if one was there. Since very few women smoked in 1930, it also seemed best to relate the smoking rates to male deaths. The following table is an adaptation of Doll's important results.

| Country | 1930 Cigarette consumption | 1950 Deaths per million |
|---|---|---|
| Australia | 480 | 180 |
| Canada | 500 | 150 |
| Denmark | 380 | 170 |
| Finland | 1,100 | 350 |
| Great Britain | 1,100 | 460 |
| Holland | 490 | 240 |
| Iceland | 230 | 60 |
| Norway | 250 | 90 |
| Sweden | 300 | 110 |
| Switzerland | 510 | 250 |
| United States of America | 1,300 | 200 |

(a) Examine the results. What do the two columns of numbers seem to show?

(b) Plot a graph relating the two measures, such as the one in figure 2–3. What does it show?

(o) Now calculate the exact relation between the two variables by using the formula for Pearson $r$ given in box 2–1 (and illustrated in table 2–2). What is the exact magnitude and sign of the correlation coefficient you obtained?

**3.** Do the analyses you performed in 2(c) permit the conclusion that smoking causes lung cancer? If the correlation coefficient were higher, say +.95, would you be more certain of the cause-and-effect relation? If you think these data do not argue that smoking causes lung cancer, how else might you explain the results?

**4.** Make a list of pairs of variables that you feel sure are highly correlated (either positively or negatively) but between which you think there is little chance of a causal connection. How could you determine whether the correlation does indicate a cause-and-effect relation?

**5.** Suppose you wanted to determine whether people with long noses have a better sense of humor than people with shorter noses. Nose length is, of course, a subject variable. You decide to give two groups of people with different-sized noses a series of twenty jokes (which experts have rated as excellent) to see if the people with long noses like them better than those with short noses. What steps would you take to insure that some other variable was not confounded with nose length in your two groups of people? How would you go about selecting people for the study, assuming that you had two hundred people for whom you had measures of nose length and many other characteristics?

# CHAPTER 3

## Preview

Did you know that—

Males take longer to begin urination when the adjacent urinal is occupied than when it is vacant? (Middlemist, Knowles, and Matter, 1976)

Prolonged visual deprivation changes your senses of smell and taste? (Schutte and Zubek, 1967)

Creating mental images can triple the number of unrelated words you can remember from a long list? (Bower, 1972)

Blind children can position a marker more accurately than blindfolded sighted children? (Jones, 1972)

All of these interesting findings were established by *experiments.* Experiments are the most powerful research technique available to psychologists. You cannot understand psychological research without detailed knowledge about experiments—procedures, common pitfalls, advantages over other research techniques, and so on. This chapter will provide you with these basic details and should be read (and reread) very carefully.

## Chapter Outline

# RESEARCH TECHNIQUES: EXPERIMENTS

*No one believes an hypothesis except its originator, but everyone believes an experiment except the experimenter.*

W. I. B. Beveridge

Imagine you are a student in a class in environmental psychology and have received the following assignment: Go to the library and "defend" a table by preventing anyone else from sitting down for as long as you can. You must use only nonverbal means to accomplish this. To carry out this task you might wait in the crowded library until a table was vacant, quickly sit down and proceed to strew your books, clothing, and other belongings all over the table in hopes that this disarray might keep others away. After some time, say fifteen minutes or so, someone finally does sit down at your table, ending your assignment. Have you performed an experiment?

Before answering this question, let us sketch out the major criterion for an experiment as was briefly discussed in the preceding chapter. An experiment occurs when the environment is systematically manipulated so that the effect of this manipulation on some behavior can be observed. Aspects of the environment that are not of interest, and hence not manipulated, are held constant so as not to influence the outcome of the experiment. We must introduce two special terms—*independent* and *dependent variables*—to describe how the environment is manipulated and how behavior is observed.

Many students are surprised to discover that the actions described do not constitute an experiment. All experiments require at least two special features called independent and dependent variables. The dependent variable is the behavior recorded by the experimenter, in this case the time until someone else sat down at your table. The independent variable is a manipulation of the environment controlled by the experimenter, in this case strewing articles on the table. But an experimenter must have at least two ways, or *levels*, of manipulating the environment. Sometimes these two levels might be just the presence or absence of manipulation. The library example fails to meet this criterion, since there was only one level of the independent variable. How might we change the procedure to obtain an experiment? The simplest answer would be to have the experimenter repeat her or his actions by sitting down again, this time without scattering anything. Then our independent variable would have the necessary two levels: items strewn about and no items strewn about the table. Now we have something to compare with the first condition. The possible outcomes of this experiment are three: (1) strewing articles on the table results in a longer time before the table is invaded by another person; (2) the time until invasion is the same whether or not articles are strewn about; (3) scattering articles results in a shorter time until invasion. Without the second level of the independent variable (no articles strewn about), these three outcomes cannot be formulated. Indeed it is impossible to say anything about how effective articles are in defending library tables until there are two levels of the independent variable. When this library experiment is performed, the first possible outcome is obtained. A table can be better protected by a person plus assorted articles than by only a person.

Thus, experiments must have at least independent and dependent variables. The research techniques discussed in the preceding chapter did not allow or require manipulation of the environment, but before an experiment can be established, independent variables with at least two levels are necessary.

### Advantages of Experiments

The main advantage of experiments over the techniques discussed in chapter 2 is better control of extraneous variation. In the ideal experiment, all factors (variables) except the one being studied are not permitted to influence the outcome—in the jargon of experimental psychology we say that these other factors are *controlled*. If, as in the ideal experiment, all factors but one (that under investigation) are held constant, we can logically conclude that any differences in outcome must be caused by manipulation of that one independent variable. As the levels of the independent variable are changed, the resulting differences in the dependent variable can occur only because the independent variable changed. In other words, changes in the independent variable *caused* the observed changes in the dependent variable. Whereas nonexperimental research techniques are limited to statements about correlation (that is, variable *A* and variable *B* are related), experiments permit statements about causation—that is, independent variable *A* causes dependent variable *B* to change.

This does not mean that scientists never misinterpret experimental results. Scott and Wertheimer (1962) relate the story of a researcher working with fleas. The flea was trained to jump when the experimenter said "Jump." Then the researcher removed two of the flea's legs and said "Jump" again. The flea jumped. Finally the researcher removed all the flea's legs and said "Jump." The flea sat unmoving. The investigator, so they say, concluded that removing all of a flea's legs causes it to become deaf.

Thus, in principle, experiments lead to statements about causation. In practice, these statements are not always true. No experiment is 100 percent successful in eliminating or holding constant all other sources of variation but the one being studied. However, experiments eliminate more extraneous variation than other research techniques. Later in this chapter we will discuss specific ways in which experiments limit extraneous variation.

Another advantage of experiments is economy. Using the technique of naturalistic observation requires that the scientist wait patiently until the conditions of interest occur. If you lived in Trondheim, Norway—near the Arctic Circle—and wanted to study how heat affects aggression, relying on the sun to produce high temperatures would require great patience and lots of time. The experimenter controls the situation by creating the conditions of interest, thus obtaining data quickly and efficiently.

In a study of crowding in a men's room, Middlemist, Knowles, and Matter (1976) controlled the spacing of males at a row of urinals by placing a bucket of water and a "Don't Use" sign inside a urinal. A confederate was stationed at an end urinal. The experimenters controlled the distance between the subject and the confederate by putting the bucket either adjacent to the confederate or one urinal away. If they merely observed naturalistically they would have had to wait until two men simultaneously used the urinals, and hope that the pairs of men would stand apart or adjacently enough times so the experimenters could obtain reliable data for both conditions. Since men normally prefer to stand apart at urinals wherever possible, this might have taken some time. Furthermore, there might have been subject differences (of the kind discussed in chapter 2) between those men who chose to stand next to another man versus those who stood apart. So this experiment offered advantages of economy and avoidance of subject differences over naturalistic observation.

***Why experiments are conducted.*** The same general reasons that apply to the conduct of any research also explain why psychologists perform experiments. In basic research, experiments are performed to test theories and to provide the data base for explanations of behavior. These kinds of experiments are typically well planned, with the investigator having a clear idea of the anticipated outcome. So-called *critical experiments* try to pit against each other two theories that make different predictions. One outcome favors Theory A and the other Theory B. Thus, in principle, the experiment will determine which theory to reject and which to keep. In practice, these critical experiments do not work out so well, since supporters of the rejected theory are ingenious in thinking up explanations to discredit the unfavorable interpretation of the experiment. For example, two major explanations of forgetting are that (1) items decay or fade out over time just the way an incandescent light bulb fades when the electricity is turned off; this explanation is called "trace decay," or (2) items never fade, but because of this they interfere with each other, causing confusion. A simple "critical" experiment would vary the time between successive items, holding the number of items constant (Waugh and Norman, 1965). Memory should be worse with longer times, according to trace-decay theorists, since there is more time for items to fade out. However, since the number of items is the same for all conditions, interference theory predicts no differences in forgetting. When this experiment is performed there is no difference, which would seem to nullify the trace-decay explanation. However, trace-decay theorists argue that the extra time between items allows people to rehearse—that is, repeat the item to themselves—which prevents forgetting.

Less often, researchers perform an experiment just to see what happens; we can call this a *"what-if experiment*. Students often come up with what-if experiments since these experiments require no knowledge of theory or the existing data base and can be formulated on the basis of one's own experience and observations. Some scientists frown on what-if experiments; the main objection to them is their inefficiency. If, as is often the case, nothing much happens in a what-if experiment—say, the independent variable has no effect—nothing is gained from the experiment. But if nothing much happens in a careful experiment where a theory predicts that something will happen, the null result can still be useful. We must admit to having tried what-if experiments. Most of them did not work, but they were fun. Our advice is to check with your instructor before trying a what-if experiment. He or she probably can give you an estimate of the odds of your coming up with anything, or may even know the results of a similar experiment that has already been performed.

This brings us to the last major reason for doing experiments in basic research. This is to repeat or replicate a previous finding. A single experiment by itself is far less convincing than a series of related experiments. The simplest replication is the direct repetition of an existing experiment, with no change in procedures.

Although this is a useful exercise for the student, the scientist finds this boring and inefficient, unless the original experiment was quite novel. Instead, a better way to replicate is to *extend* the previous procedure by adding something new while retaining something old. Thus, part of the replication is a literal repetition, but the additional part adds to scientific knowledge. This kind of repetition demonstrates the generality of a result by showing how it is (or is not) maintained over different independent variables.

Let us illustrate this point by an example from the area of attention. In a dichotic listening task, separate words are presented to each ear simultaneously and subjects are asked to repeat or to remember the words heard in one ear. After the words have been presented, the subject is tested by being asked to recall them either one ear at a time (say, all the words from the left ear first, then those from the right ear), or pair by pair (that is, the first word from the left ear, then the first word from the right ear—the first pair—and so forth). When the dichotic list is presented slowly (about one pair per second), pair by pair recall is as efficient as ear by ear. A good way to replicate this finding would be to include two presentation rates; slow (one pair per second) and fast (two pair per second). When this is done, we find that at the fast rate, pair by pair recall is less efficient, although the slow rate still allows equally efficient recall either way (figure 3-1b). This difference between fast and slow rates was very important in formulating early models of attention (Broadbent, 1958). When this research was first done, models of attention were not sufficiently well developed to predict presentation-rate differences. Effects of this variable were discovered by the systematic replication of the basic dichotic finding. Replication allows us to increase our data base, even if theory is lacking, so that eventually good explanations may be invented.

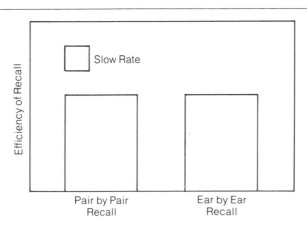

FIGURE 3-1a.

At a slow presentation rate, recall in a dichotic listening task is equally efficient whether items are recalled pair by pair or ear by ear.

FIGURE 3-1b.

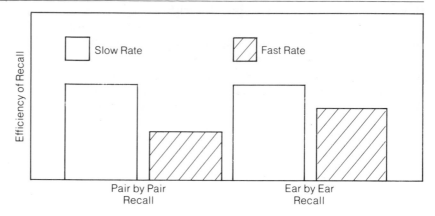

Replication and extension of results in Figure 3-1(a). At the slow presentation rate recall is still equal for both modes of recall; this replicates the prior finding. At the fast presentation rate the two modes of recall are no longer equivalent; this extends the prior finding.

## VARIABLES

Variables are the gears and cogs that make experiments run. Effective selection and manipulation of variables makes the difference between a good experiment and a poor one. This section covers the three kinds of variables that must be carefully considered before starting an experiment: *independent*, *dependent*, and *control* variables. We conclude by discussing experiments that have more than one independent or dependent variable.

### Independent Variables

*Independent variables* are those *manipulated* by the experimenter. The brightness of a lamp, the loudness of a tone, the number of food pellets given to a rat all are independent variables, since the experimenter determines their amount. Independent variables are selected because an experimenter thinks they will cause changes in behavior. Increasing the intensity of a tone should increase the speed with which people respond to the tone. Increasing the number of pellets given to a rat for pressing a bar should increase the number of times the bar is pressed. When a change in the level (amount) of an independent variable causes a change in behavior, we say that the behavior is under control of the independent variable. Failure of an independent variable to control behavior, often called *null results*, can have more than one interpretation. First, the experimenter may have guessed incorrectly that the independent variable was important and the null results may be correct. Most scientists will accept this interpretation only reluctantly and so the following alternate explanations of null results are common. The experimenter may not have created a valid manipulation of the independent variable. Let us say you are conducting an experiment on second-grade children, and your independent variable is the number of small candies (M&Ms, peanuts, et cetera) they get after each correct response. Some children get only one while others get two. You find no difference in behavior. Perhaps if your independent variable had involved a greater range—that is, it went from one piece of candy to ten pieces of candy—you would have obtained a difference. Your manipulation was not sufficient to reveal an effect of the independent variable. Or perhaps, unknown to you, the class had a birthday party just before the experiment started and their little tummies were filled with ice cream and birthday cake. In this case maybe even ten pieces of candy would not show any effect. This is why, in studies of animal learning with food as a reward, the animals are deprived of food before the experiment starts. Thus, experimenters must be careful to produce a strong manipulation of the independent variable. Failure to do so is a common cause of null results. Other common causes of null results are related to dependent and control variables, to which we now turn.

## Dependent Variables

The *dependent variable* is that *observed* and *recorded* by the experimenter. It *depends* on the behavior of the subject. The time to press a switch, the speed of a worm crawling through a maze, the number of times a rat presses a bar all are dependent variables, since they are observed and recorded by the experimenter.

One criterion for a good dependent variable is reliability. When an experiment is repeated exactly—same subject, same levels of independent variable, and so on—the dependent variable should yield the same score as it did previously. Unreliability can occur because of some deficit in the way we measure some dependent variable. Assume we wish to measure the weight in grams of an object, say, a candle before and after it is lit for fifteen minutes. We use a scale that works by having a spring move a pointer. The spring contracts when it is cold and expands when it is hot. As long as our weight measurements are taken at constant temperatures, they will be reliable. But if temperature varies while objects are being weighed, the same object will yield different readings. Our dependent variable is then unreliable.

Null results can often be caused by deficits in the dependent variable even if it is reliable. The most common cause is a restricted or limited range of the dependent variable so that it gets "stuck" at the top or bottom of its scale. Imagine you are teaching a rather uncoordinated friend how to bowl for the first time. Since you know from introductory psychology that reward improves performance, you offer to buy your friend a beer every time he or she gets a strike. Your friend gets all gutter balls, so you drink the beer yourself. Thus you can no longer offer a reward and you expect a decrement in performance. But since it is impossible to do any worse than all gutter balls, you cannot observe any decrement. Your friend is already at the bottom of the scale. This is called a *floor effect*. The opposite problem, getting 100 percent correct, is called a *ceiling effect*. Ceiling and floor effects (see chapter 10) prevent the influence of an independent variable from being accurately reflected in a dependent variable.

## Control Variables

A *control variable* is a potential independent variable that is held constant during an experiment. It is a variable that does not vary because it is *controlled* by the experimenter. For any one experiment, the list of desirable control variables is quite large, far larger than can ever be accomplished in practice. In even a relatively simple experiment, for example, requiring people to memorize three-letter syllables, many variables should be controlled. Time of day (diurnal cycle) changes your efficiency and ideally this should be controlled. Temperature could be important since you might fall asleep if the testing room were too warm. Time since your last meal might also affect memory performance. Intelligence is also related. The list could be extended. In practice an experimenter tries to control as many salient variables as possible, hoping that the effect of uncontrolled factors will be small relative to the effect of the independent variable. The smaller the size of the effect produced by the independent variable, the more important it is to carefully control other extraneous factors. Holding a variable constant is not the only way to remove extraneous variation. Statistical techniques (discussed later in the chapter) also control extraneous variables. However, holding a variable constant is the most direct experimental technique for controlling extraneous factors, and so we shall limit our definition of control variables to only this technique. Null results often occur in an experiment because there is insufficient control of these other factors—that is, they have been left to vary unsystematically. This is especially true in studies outside of laboratories, where the ability to hold control variables constant is greatly decreased.

INDEPENDENT variable is MANIPULATED
DEPENDENT variable is OBSERVED
CONTROL variable is held CONSTANT

### Name the Variables

Because understanding *independent*, *dependent*, and *control* variables is so important, we have included some examples for you to check your own understanding. For each situation name the three kinds of variables. Answers are provided at the end of this section. No peeking!

**1.** An automobile manufacturer wants to know how bright brake lights should be in order to minimize the time required for the driver of a following car to realize that the car in front is stopping. An experiment is conducted to answer this. Name the variables.

**2.** A pigeon is trained to peck a key if a green light is illuminated, but not if a red light is on. Correct pecks get rewarded by access to grain. Name the variables.

**3.** A therapist tries to improve a patient's image of himself. Every time the patient says something positive about himself the therapist rewards this by nodding, smiling, and being extra attentive. Name the variables.

**4.** A social psychologist does an experiment to discover if men or women give lower ratings of discomfort when six people are crowded into a telephone booth. Name the variables.

*Answers*

**1.** *Independent (manipulated) variable:* Intensity (brightness) of brake lights.

*Dependent (observed) variable:* Time from onset of brake lights until depression of brake pedal by following driver.

*Control (constant) variables:* Color of brake lights, shape of brake pedal, force needed to depress brake pedal, external illumination, et cetera.

**2.** *Independent variable:* Color of light (red or green)

*Dependent variable:* Number of key pecks

*Control variables:* Hours of food deprivation, size of key, intensity of red and green lights, et cetera.

**3.** *Independent variable:* Actually, this is not an experiment because there is only one level of the independent variable. To make this an experiment we need another level, say rewarding positive statements about the patient's mother-in-law. Then the independent variable would be: Kind of statement rewarded.

*Dependent variable:* Number (or frequency) of statements

*Control variables:* None. This is a poor experiment.

4. *Independent variable:*    Sex of participant
   *Dependent variable:*    Rating of discomfort
   *Control variables:*    Size of telephone booth, number
           of persons (6) crowded into
           booth, et cetera.

## More Than One Independent Variable

It is unusual to find an experiment reported in a psychological journal in which only one independent (manipulated) variable was used. The typical experiment manipulates from two to four independent variables simultaneously. There are several advantages to this procedure. First, it is often more efficient to conduct one experiment with, say, three independent variables than to conduct three separate experiments. Second, experimental control is often better, since with a single experiment some control variables— time of day, temperature, humidity, and so on—are more likely to be held constant than with three separate experiments. Third, and most important, results generalized—that is, shown to be valid in several situations—across several independent variables are more valuable than data that have yet to be generalized. Just as it is important to establish generality of results across different types of experimental subjects (see chapter 12), we also need to discover if some result is valid across levels of independent variables. For example, let us say we wish to find out which of two kinds of rewards facilitate learning geometry by high school students. The first reward is an outright cash payment for problems correctly solved and the second reward is early dismissal from class—that is, each correct solution entitles the student to leave class five minutes early. Assume that the results of this (hypothetical) experiment showed early dismissal to be better. Before we made early dismissal a universal rule in high school we should first establish its generality by comparing the two kinds of reward in other classes such as history, biology, et cetera. Here subject matter of the class would be a second independent variable. It would be better to put these two variables into a single experiment than to conduct two successive experiments. This would avoid problems of control, such as one class being tested the week of the big football game (when no reward would improve learning), while the other class was tested the week after the game was won (when students felt better about learning).

When the effects produced by one independent variable are not the same at each level of a second independent variable, we have an *interaction*. The search for interactions is a major reason for using more than one independent variable per experiment. This can be best demonstrated by example.

Piliavin, Piliavin, and Rodin (1975) were interested in discovering under what conditions an innocent bystander would help someone in an emergency. The emergency was faked on a New York City subway car (the F train, appropriately enough). A white male carrying a cane stumbled and fell to the floor. Would other passengers aid this "victim?"

There were two independent variables. For half of the trials, victims had an ugly red birthmark placed on their face with theatrical makeup. The presence or absence of this birthmark was the first independent variable. For half of the trials, an observer wearing a white medical jacket (identifying him as a doctor or at least as some kind of medical personnel) was present. The same observer was present without the white jacket for the remaining half of the trials. So the presence or absence of a medical intern was the second independent variable. The dependent variable was the percentage of trials in which passengers came to the aid of the victim by either touching the victim or asking him if he needed help.

Results of this experiment are shown in figure 3–2, with each independent variable plotted alone. People were more willing to help victims who lacked an ugly birthmark. They were also more willing to help when no intern was present.

Figure 3–3 shows, however, that this interpretation of the results can be misleading. If, as figure 3–2 implies, both independent var-

FIGURE 3–2.

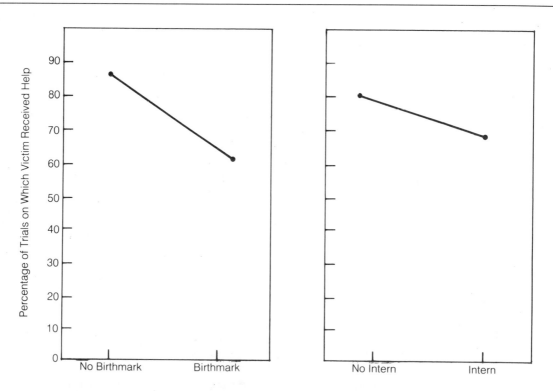

Effects of two independent variables on helping behavior. Each variable is plotted separately. (Data from Piliavin et al., 1975)

FIGURE 3–3.

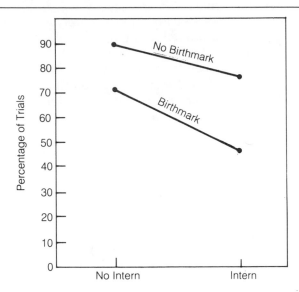

Effect of two independent variables on helping behavior. (Data from Piliavin et al., 1975)

FIGURE 3–4.

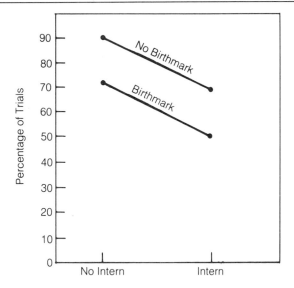

Fictitious data showing no interaction between the two independent variables.

iables have their own effect, the results should look like the two parallel lines plotted in figure 3–4. Instead, the lines in figure 3–3 are not parallel. This indicates an interaction between the two independent variables. The percentage of trials in which help was given depends on the levels of both independent variables. If the victim had no birthmark, then the presence or absence of an intern had little effect on helping. But when the victim had a birthmark, passengers were far less willing to help when an intern was present.

Now let us imagine that this experiment was performed in two separate parts. In the first part only the birthmark was manipulated. The experimenter would not have known that the presence of an intern would have reduced helping. In the second part, only the presence of the intern would vary. Results would have been quite different, depending on whether the victim had a birthmark. You can see that by doing the experiment in two parts, we would have lost a great deal of information.

Figure 3–3, which contains the actual results, shows an interaction. The effects of one independent variable depend on the level of the other independent variable. The least amount of help was given when the victim had a birthmark and an intern was present.

In summary, an interaction occurs when the levels of one independent variable are differentially affected by the levels of other independent variables. When interactions are present, it does not make sense to discuss the effects of each independent variable separately. Because the effects of one variable also depend on the levels of the other variables, we are forced to discuss interacting variables together.

## More Than One Dependent Variable

The dependent (observed) variable is used as an index of behavior. The experimenter must decide which aspects of behavior are relevant to the experiment at hand. Although some variables are traditional, this does not mean that they are the only, or even the best, index of behavior. Take, for example, the behavior of a rat pressing a bar or a pigeon pecking a key. The most common dependent variable is the number of presses or pecks observed. But the force with which a key is pecked can also lead to interesting findings (see Notterman and Mintz, 1965), as can the latency or time to respond. Researchers can usually come up with several dependent variables that may be appropriate. Let us say we wish to study the legibility of the typeface that you are now reading. We cannot observe "legibility," of course. What dependent variables might we observe? Here are some that have been used in the past: retention of meaningful information after reading text, time needed to read a fixed number of words, number of errors in recognizing single letters, speed in transcribing or retyping text, heart rate during reading, and muscular tension during reading. And this list is far from exhaustive.

Reasons of economy argue for obtaining as many dependent measures at the same time as is feasible. Despite this, the typical experiment uses only one or at most two dependent variables simultaneously. This is unfortunate since just as the generality of an experiment is expanded by having more than one independent variable, it is also expanded with several dependent variables. The reason more dependent variables are not used probably is that it is statistically difficult to analyze several dependent variables at once. Although modern computer techniques make the calculations quite feasible, many experimental psychologists have not been well trained in these multivariate statistical procedures and thus hesitate to use them. Although separate analysis could be conducted for each dependent variable by itself, this loses information in much the same way that separate analysis of independent variables ignores interactions. Because multivariate analysis is complex, we will not treat it here. Nevertheless, you should be aware that it is often advantageous to use more than one dependent variable in an experiment.

## EXPERIMENTAL DESIGN

The purpose of experimental design is to minimize extraneous or uncontrolled variation, thereby increasing the likelihood that an experiment will produce reliable results. Entire books have been written about experimental design. Here we will cover only a sample of some common techniques used to improve the design of experiments. Although this treatment is necessarily less complete than that of an entire text devoted to the subject, it should give you an understanding of the aims of the psychologist designing an experiment, even though it will not give you all the techniques that could be used.

### Within- and Between-subjects Designs

One of the first design decisions an experimenter must make is how to assign subjects to the various levels of independent variables. The two main possibilities are to assign only some subjects to each level, or to assign each subject to every level. The first possibility is called a *between-subjects design* and the second a *within-subjects design*. This can be shown with a simple example. Thirty students in introductory psychology have signed up for an experiment that you are conducting to test ability to remember nonsense words. Your independent variable is the number of times you will say each item, one time or five times. You expect that an item presented five times will be learned better than an item presented only once. The between-subjects design calls for you to divide your subjects in half—that is, into two groups of fifteen students each—with one group receiving five repetitions and the other, one repetition. (How to select which subjects to put in each group will be discussed shortly.) The within-subjects design has all thirty subjects learning with both levels of the independent variable—that is, each is tested with one repetition and again with five repetitions. (How to determine the order in which each subject gets these two treatments will also be discussed later.) Which design should you use?

The between-subjects (two groups) design is conservative. There is no chance of one treatment contaminating the other, since the same person never receives both treatments. Nevertheless, most experimental psychologists would prefer the within-subjects (one group) design. It is more efficient, since each subject is compared with herself or himself. Any differences resulting from one versus five repetitions cannot be the result of differences between the people in the two groups, as would be the case for the between-subjects design, since the same people get all treatments. However, the between-subjects design must deal with differences among people and this decreases its efficiency—that is, its ability to detect real differences between one and five repetitions of the memory items. But there is a risk in the more efficient within-subjects design. Imagine that all thirty subjects first learned items with five repetitions and then learned with one repetition. As a result of their earlier experience with five repetitions they might decide to repeat to themselves four more times the item that was only presented once. This would destroy any differences between the two levels of the independent variable. The danger is that an early part of the experiment might change behavior in a later part of the experiment. This, of course, ruins the experiment. We can minimize this danger by *counterbalancing* (discussed shortly), but cannot eliminate it entirely. So if an experimenter suspects that the effects of one treatment may linger on to alter a later treatment, the between-subjects design should be used. Because it is less efficient it will require that a much greater number of subjects be tested, but this is preferable to a within-subjects design in which effects have been carried over or transferred from one part of the experiment to another.

***Randomization and matching.*** In any between-subjects design the experimenter must somehow guarantee that there are no differences among the subjects in the two or more treatment groups. Clearly, if we took the five best memorizers and deliberately placed them in the one-repetition group, and put the five worst in the five-repetition group, we might wind up with no difference in results or even, perhaps, with the one-repetition group doing better. To prevent this outcome, the experimenter must ensure that both groups are equivalent at the start of the experiment. One way to do this would be to administer a memory test to all thirty subjects before the regular experiment started. Then pairs of subjects could be formed from those subjects who had equal or very similar scores. One member of each pair would be randomly assigned to one group, and the other member to the second group. This technique is called *matching*. One difficulty with matching is that an experimenter cannot match for everything. Thus, there is always the possibility that the groups, even though matched on some characteristic(s), differ on some other characteristic that may be relevant (see chapter 2).

A more common technique to ensure that equivalent groups are formed is *randomization*. In our repetition experiment, one way to form two groups by randomization would be to draw names out of a hat. Or we could ask each person to step forward, and then throw a die. Even throws would be assigned to one group and odd throws to the other. Or if we did not have any dice, a table of random numbers could be used to generate even and odd digits. This method of assigning subjects to experimental conditions has no bias since it ignores all characteristics of the subjects; so we expect that groups so created would be equivalent on any and all relevant dimensions. However, randomization does not guarantee that the groups will always be equal. By chance, a greater number of better memorizers might have been assigned to one of the groups. The odds of this rare occurrence can be calculated by the methods of statistics. This is why experimental design and statistics are often treated as the same topic. However, design is concerned with the logic of arranging experiments whereas statistics deals with calculating odds, probabilities, and other mathematical quantities. So if we are sure that all relevant dimensions have been dealt with, matching is preferable to randomization. Since we seldom are sure, randomization is used more often.

*Counterbalancing.* Although the within-subjects (one group) design avoids problems of forming equivalent groups since there is only one group, it has the analogous difficulty of determining the order in which treatments should be given to subjects. Again, one solution is to use randomization by drawing the treatment titles out of a hat, by using a random-number table or computer. The logic behind this is the same as just discussed. However, although randomization produces equivalent orders in the long run, it is less likely to be suitable when there are only a small number of treatments. In most experiments the number of subjects exceeds the number of treatments, so randomization is a good technique for assigning subjects to treatments.

Complete counterbalancing makes sure that all possible treatment orders are used. In the repetition experiment, this is easy since there are only two orders: one and five repetitions, five and one repetition. So half the subjects would receive one repetition followed by five repetitions while the other half would get the opposite order. As the number of treatments increases, the number of orders gets large indeed. Three treatments have six different orders, four treatments have twenty-four different orders, five treatments have one-hundred-and-twenty different orders, and so on. As the levels of an independent variable increase, complete counterbalancing soon becomes impractical.

Counterbalancing does not eliminate the effects of order. It does allow experimenters to evaluate possible order effects. If such effects are present, and especially if they form interactions with other more important independent variables, steps need to be taken to correct the design. For example, the experimenter might decide to repeat the experiment using a between-subjects design to avoid order effects.

*Mixed designs.* Experiments need not be exclusively of within-subjects or between-subjects design. It is often convenient and prudent to have some independent variables treated as between-subjects and others as within-subjects in the same experiment (assuming the experiment has more than one independent variable, of course). If one variable seems likely to affect others—for example, the administration of a drug—it can be made a between-subjects variable while the rest of the variables are within-subjects. This compromise design (*mixed design*) is not as efficient as a pure within-subjects design, but it often is safer.

## Control Conditions.

Independent variables must be varied (or manipulated) by the experimenter. This implies that each and every independent variable must have at least two settings or values within the experiment. For example, if intensity of an electric shock given to a rat is an independent variable, the settings chosen by the experimenter might be 10 and 20 microamperes of electric current. The technical term for the setting of an independent variable is *level*. So we would state that the levels of the independent variable were 10 and 20 microamperes.

Most experiments contain, in addition to independent variables, some control group (between-subjects design) or *control condition* (within-subjects design). In its simplest form the control group does not receive the levels of interest of the independent variable. In the electric-shock example just described, a control group of rats would receive no shock (0 microamperes). Or an experimenter might be interested in the effect of noise on studying. Using a between-subjects design, the experimenter would expose one group of subjects to loud noise for half an hour while they were studying; this is the level of interest of the independent variable. A control group would study the same material for half an hour in a quiet setting. Then both groups would be tested on the material. Any obtained difference on the test between the two groups would be attributed to the effect of noise.

The control group sometimes does receive treatment. In the helping experiment discussed previously (figure 3–3), the observer was either dressed as a medical intern or dressed normally. The normal dress could be considered a control condition. It allows us to determine how much less help is given when an intern is present. The important characteristic of a control condition is that it provides a *baseline* against which some variable of interest can be compared. Sometimes the best baseline is no treatment, but often the best baseline requires some activity. A frequent example occurs in memory research where a group of subjects is required to learn two different lists of words; the experimenter is interested in how learning one list interferes with learning the other. The experimental group (receiving the level of interest of the independent variable) first learns list A, then learns list B, and then is tested again on list A. The experimenter would like to show that learning list B interferes with learning list A. But before any conclusion of this sort can be reached, a comparison control condition is required. Merely comparing the final test of list A with the first test is insufficient, since subjects might do worse on the last list-A test simply because they were tired, or do better because they had extra practice. A control condition with no treatment would have a control group learn list A, then sit around for the time it took the experimental group to learn list B, and then be tested again on list A. But this would be a poor control condition because subjects might practice or rehearse list A while they were sitting around. This would improve their final performance on the last list-A test, and incorrectly make it appear that in the experimental group, list B interfered more than it really did with list A. A proper baseline condition would occupy the control group during the time the experimental group was learning list B—perhaps the experimenter would have them do arithmetic or some other "busy work" that would prevent rehearsal. (See figure 3–5).

Sometimes the control condition is contained implicitly within the experiment. Recall the memory experiment discussed earlier where the independent variable was the number of repetitions of an item, one or five. No experimenter would bother to include a control group or condition with zero repetitions, since no learning could occur under this odd circumstance. The control condition is implicit, in that five repetitions can be compared with one, and vice versa. Since the experimenter might well be as interested in effects of a single repetition as in five repetitions, we probably would not explicitly call the one-repetition level a control condition. But it does provide a baseline for comparison—and so for that matter does the five-repetition condition, since the one-repetition results can be compared with it.

| FIGURE 3–5. | Examples of experimental and control groups for list learning. | | |
|---|---|---|---|
| Experimental Group | Learn List A | Learn List B | Test List A |
| Control Group | Learn List A | Do arithmetic | Test List A |

### Pitfalls

It is quite easy to formulate an inadequate experimental design, and most experimental psychologists have hidden away, either in a dusty file cabinet or in a journal article, mistakes of this kind. In this section we discuss only a small sample of errors in design, ones that are so common you should be aware of them. You should not let this discussion of error fool you into believing that any experiment that is free from error is guaranteed to produce results that merit publication.

***Demand characteristics.*** Laboratory experiments attempt to capture behavior as it really exists outside the laboratory. Sometimes the laboratory setting itself, or the knowledge that an experiment is under way, may alter patterns of behavior. Try this simple demonstration to convince yourself that such effects occur. Tell five of your friends that you are conducting an experiment for your psychology class and would like their cooperation as subjects. If they agree, ask them to hold three ice cubes in their bare hands. Note how many hold the cubes until they melt. Now ask five other friends to hold the ice cubes, without mentioning anything about an experiment. Instead of holding the ice cubes until they melt, they probably will consider your request somewhat strange and soon so inform you. So there is something unusual about the ready compliance of those friends who knew they were participating in an experiment, since more of them were willing to hold the ice cubes for a longer period of time. Psychologists call the influence of an experimenter's expectations or the subject's knowledge that an experiment is under way *demand characteristics*. To the extent that the behavior of research participants is controlled by demand characteristics instead of independent variables, experiments are invalid and cannot be generalized beyond the test situation.

A well-known example of a demand characteristic is the *Hawthorne effect*, named after the Western Electric Company plant

Drawing by C. Schulz. Copyright © 1967 United Features Syndicate, Inc. Used by permission.

Even the best designed experiments are not always successful. Careful attention to principles of experimental design improves the odds of success, but does not guarantee it.

where it was first observed. The company was interested in improving worker morale and productivity, and conducted several experiments to better the workers' environment (such as improving lighting). No matter what experimental manipulation was tried, worker productivity improved. The workers knew they were in a "special" group and therefore tried to do their best at all times. (See Parsons, 1974, and Bramel and Friend, 1981, for alternate interpretations of these results.) Thus, the demand characteristics were more important in determining the workers' productivity than the experimental manipulations.

*Experimenter effects.* A closely related pitfall, similar to demand characteristics, is allowing the experimenter to influence the outcome accidentally by providing participants with slight clues as to his or her expectations. For example, an experimenter might not be aware that he nods approvingly when a correct response is given, and frowns after errors. These effects are not limited to experiments with humans. For example, a horse named Hans was trained to count to any number of stamping his foot. If the trainer said, "Count to three," the horse would stamp three times. Observers assumed that the horse picked up some signal from that trainer that told it when to stop. They were amazed to discover that Hans could perform this trick even when the trainer was not present. In fact, Hans had been trained to pick up minute changes in observers' facial expressions, which "gave away" the answer.

The *experimenter effect* can also occur in seemingly objective experiments with animal subjects. Rosenthal and Fode (1963) told student experimenters that the rats they were to test in a maze were special strains: either maze-bright or maze-dull. Actually the rats came from the same population. Nevertheless, the rats that were labeled maze-bright had fewer errors than those labeled maze-dull, and this difference was statistically reliable. The student experimenters were observed while they tested the rats and did not cheat or do anything overt to bias the results. It seems reasonable that the lucky students who got bright rats were more motivated to perform the experiment than those unfortunates who had to teach stupid rats to go through the maze. Somehow this affected the results of the experiment, perhaps because experimenters handled the two groups of rats differently.

The best way to eliminate this kind of experimenter effect is to hide the experimental condition from the experimenter, on the premise that experimenters cannot communicate what they do know. Such a procedure was, for instance, used in a study of the behavioral effects of air pollution. Subjects breathed either pure air or air taken from a busy roadway. The air was contained in tanks, and the experimenter did not know which tank held pure air and which tank held polluted air. The subjects' poorer performance in polluted air cannot be attributed to the experimenter's giving away the independent variable.

Experimenter effects are not always this subtle. One of the authors was once involved in an experiment concerning the human eye blink response. Several experimenters helped conduct the same experiment, and it was soon noticed that one of them obtained results that were quite different from the rest of us. His subjects started out experimental sessions with massive flurries of frenzied blinking. The cause of this odd behavior was easily discovered. In order to record eye blinks the experimenter must attach a tiny metal rod to the subject's eyelid with special tape, which is ordinarily a painless procedure. However, the experimenter in question had a very heavy thumb and was unable to attach the rod without irritating the eye, causing the strange flurries of blinking.

**Automation of experiments.** Experimenter effects can be eliminated or greatly reduced by having computers or other equipment conduct the experiment, so that the subject is untouched by human hands. In many laboratories, a subject enters a testing booth and sees a message on a screen that tells her or him to push a button in order to begin. Pushing the button causes instructions for the experiment to appear on the screen. The entire experiment is then conducted by a computer. The experimenter appears at the end of the data collection to debrief the participant, explaining the aims of the study and how the subject has helped advance science. Until then the experimenter simply monitors the equipment and the subject to ensure that the subject is following instructions and that nothing untoward happens. Since you probably will not have such sophisticated experimental equipment, it is especially important for you to watch out for experimenter effects in your own research efforts.

---

**Problem:** Author's supply

**FROM PROBLEM TO EXPERIMENT: THE NUTS AND BOLTS**

Many of the decisions that go into creating an experiment are not clearly explained in journal reports of research. Although some of this brevity can be attributed to the economy imposed by journal editors who like short articles, a larger part is based on the assumption that experimental psychologists, or indeed psychologists researching any specialty, share a common background knowledge. This is true in all branches of science. For example, a physicist writing in a journal assumes that the readers already know that a dyne is a unit of force, and will not bother to explain that term. Similarly, psychologists usually assume the reader knows what the terms *stimulus* and *response* mean, although these may be defined anyway. So one purpose of this text is to give you some of the vocabulary necessary if you wish to read (or write) psychological research.

Another problem for the new researcher is related to the "lore of the laboratory." "Everybody" knows there are certain "obvious" ways to perform certain kinds of research. These ways differ from area to area but are well known within each category. They are so well known that researchers seldom bother to explain them and indeed are quite surprised when new researchers are ignorant of these "obvious" tricks and techniques. Animal researchers often deprive animals of food for many hours before the experiment, or keep their pigeons at a certain percentage of the weight the pigeons would attain if they had food continuously available. Although the reasons for this are obvious to the researcher, they may not be obvious to you. How does an experimenter know how many items to use in a memory experiment? How long should an experiment take? Why was one dependent variable selected from a set of what appear to be equally valid dependent variables? How many subjects should be used in an experiment? This section in the chapters of Part Two will answer "obvious" questions like these.

## From Problem to Experiment

All research aims at solving a problem. This problem can be abstract and theoretical or concrete and applied. The problem may arise from an observation made more or less casually, such as that people seem to be more aggressive during the summer. Here the problem can be stated as "Why does summer heat cause aggression?" or even more skeptically as "Does high temperature cause aggression?" A problem may arise from an accidental discovery in a laboratory, such as the finding of mold on a piece of bread. Solving this problem—why is the mold growing here?—led to the discovery of penicillin. Finally, a problem may arise directly from a theoretical model, as when we ask, "Why does reinforcement increase the probability of the occurrence of the behavior that preceeded it?"

The first step the experimenter must take is to translate the problem into a testable hypothesis. Then the hypothesis must be transformed into an experiment with independent, dependent, and control variables.

*From problem to hypothesis.* A problem is, more or less, a vague statement that must be verified or a question that must be answered. Unless either is made specific and precise, it cannot be experimentally tested. Any hypothesis is a particular prediction, derived from a problem, often stated in the form: if A, then B. The crucial distinction between a problem and a hypothesis is that a hypothesis is directly testable whereas a problem is not.

The purpose of any experiment is to obtain data. Once obtained, these data must be analyzed. Once analyzed, data must be reported. We briefly discuss these aspects in turn.

**DATA**

## Obtaining Data

Fixing an experimental design does not establish all the conditions needed for data acquisition. Although the design tells you how to assign subjects to experiments, it does not tell you how to get the subjects. Without subjects, there are no data.

Psychologists who investigate animal behavior have much more control over subject selection than those who study humans. Although animal psychologists must bear the additional expense of obtaining, housing, and feeding their subjects, they can select the strain they wish to purchase and always have subjects available, barring some catastrophe.

Research with humans most often uses college students enrolled in introductory psychology as subjects. Provided that this participation is used as a learning experience for the student, it is considered ethical and proper (APA, 1973). If the experiment is not used as a learning experience, the experimenter should pay subjects. Since college students are a select population, experimenters need to be careful about generalizing results to other subject populations. For example, techniques from a programmed learning system designed to teach inorganic chemistry might not prove successful in the teaching of plumbing.

The technique of selecting subjects from some population is called *sampling*. Sampling is necessary because it is usually impossible to test the entire population, say, all college sophomores in the United States. *Random sampling* means that any member of a population has an equal chance of being selected as a subject. Furthermore, each selection is independent of other selections, so that choosing one person does not affect the chances of selecting anyone else. Statistical implications of sampling are discussed in appendix A.

After your sample has been selected and your design is fixed, one major decision remains. Should you test your subjects one at a time or in a group? Both procedures have advantages and disadvantages. The biggest advantage of group testing is economy. It takes only one hour to test thirty subjects for an hour as a group, whereas it takes thirty hours to test them singly. So, all other things being equal, it is faster, and therefore better, to test subjects in groups. But there are many instances where all other things are far from equal. For example, take a listening experiment in which separate words are presented to left and right ears. One hurried doctoral student decided to save time and test her subjects in a group. She forgot that, unless subjects were positioned exactly between the two loudspeakers, one message would reach one ear before the other message reached the other ear. This invalidated the independent variable. Of course, it would have been fine to test subjects in a group if each subject wore earphones, thus avoiding this difficulty. The other problem in group testing is the possibility that subjects will influence each other, thus influencing the data. Perhaps a subject may cheat and copy answers from another, or the sexual composition of the group may alter motivation. Sometimes these problems can be prevented by placing subjects in individual booths that prohibit social interaction.

### Analyzing Data

The immediate result of an experiment is a large series of numbers that represent behavior under different conditions. As Sidman (1960) humorously describes it, scientists believe that all data are tainted at birth. Data belong to Chance or to Science but never to both. Before the psychologist can be sure that data belong to Science, the demon Chance must be exorcised. This is done by a ritual called statistical analysis.

Once statistical analysis tells you which data are reliable, you still have to decide which data are important. No mathematical calculation can guess what hypotheses are being tested, what is predicted by the theories, et cetera. Statistics are never a substitute for thought. Statistical analysis is a theoretically neutral procedure that serves theory and hypothesis testing. Except in the case of a what-if experiment, the theories and hypotheses precede the statistics.

Since it is virtually impossible to grasp the meaning of the large set of numbers an experiment produces, data are usually condensed by *descriptive statistics*. The most common are the mean and the standard deviation. As part of the data analysis, means are calculated for each level of each independent variable, as well as for combinations of independent variables to show interactions.

### Reporting Data

Data are presented in tables or figures. Usually figures are easier to understand. Figure 3–3 is a typical example of how results of an experiment are reported. The dependent variable is plotted on the *ordinate*—the vertical scale. The independent variable is graphed on the *abscissa*—the horizontal scale. More than one independent variable can be shown in the same graph by using solid and dotted lines and/or different shaped symbols for each independent variable.

Raw (unanalyzed) data are hardly ever reported. Instead, some descriptive statistic, like the mean, is used to summarize data. Other statistics often accompany data to tell the reader about the reliability of these data.

Many different styles and formats can be used to report data. We recommend the format given in the *Publication Manual* of the American Psychological Association. This little booklet will tell you more than you would like to know about every aspect of preparing the report of an experiment. If it is not in the library or bookstore you can purchase it by sending to Publication Sales, American Psychological Association, 1200 Seventeenth Street, N.W., Washington, D.C. 20036.

**1.** An experiment is a controlled procedure for investigating the effects of one or more independent variables upon one or more dependent variables. The *independent variable* is manipulated by the experimenter whereas the *dependent variable* is observed and recorded. Experiments offer the investigator the best chance of eliminating or minimizing extraneous variation. Experiments are performed to test theories, to show that a published experiment is in some way deficient, and to replicate and expand previous findings. Only rarely are experiments performed just to see what might happen.

**2.** Independent variables are chosen because an experimenter thinks they will control behavior. If they do not, this may mean that the manipulation was inadequate or that the experimenter was wrong. Dependent variables must be *reliable*—that is, they must consistently produce the same results under the same conditions. *Ceiling* and *floor effects* result from inadequate range of the dependent variable. *Control variables* are potential independent variables that are not manipulated during an experiment.

**3.** Most experiments test more than one independent variable at a time. In addition to economy, this allows the experimenter to gain important information about interactions. *Interactions* occur when the effects of one independent variable are not the same for different levels of another independent variable. Occasionally experiments use more than one dependent variable.

**4.** Experimental design assigns subjects to different conditions in ways that are expected to minimize extraneous variation. In a *between-subjects design* different groups of subjects experience different treatments. In a *within-subjects design*, the same subjects go through all treatments. The between-subjects design is safer, but the within-subjects design is more efficient. *Mixed designs* have some independent variables that are between-subjects and others that are within-subjects. In between-subject designs equivalent groups are formed by *matching* and by *randomization*. Order effects in within-subjects designs are evaluated, but not eliminated, by *counterbalancing*. Control conditions provide a clear baseline against which the condition(s) of interest can be compared.

**SUMMARY**

**5.** There are many pitfalls in experimental design. *Demand characteristics* result from the subject's knowledge that he or she is participating in an experiment. *Experimenter effects* are artifacts introduced accidentally when the experimenter provides clues to the subject or influences the subject unsystematically. The latter can be minimized by using machinery to conduct the experiment.

**6.** Selecting subjects from some population is called *sampling*. *Random sampling* means that each member of the population has an equal chance of being selected. It is more efficient to test subjects in groups, but care must be taken to avoid contaminating the experiment.

**KEY TERMS**

abscissa
baseline
between-subjects design
control conditions
control variable
counterbalancing
critical experiment
data
demand characteristics
dependent variable
experiment
experimenter effects

Hawthorne effect
independent variable
interaction
level
matching
mixed designs
randomization
random sampling
sampling
what-if experiment
within-subjects design

**DISCUSSION QUESTIONS**

**1.** Design an experiment to discover why plumbers get paid more than college professors. Take a random sample of plumbers and professors. Have half of each group perform the job of the other occupation, while the other occupation either (a) observes quietly or (b) offers advice. Name the dependent, independent and control variables you would select for this experiment. What are some of the design problems associated with such an experiment?

**2.** Transform each of the following problems or statements into at least two testable hypotheses:

(A) You can't teach an old dog new tricks.

(B) Eating junk food lowers your grade point average.

(C) A penny saved is a penny earned.

(D) The best way to study is cramming the night before an exam.

**3.** Create a fictitious experiment with two independent variables. Draw hypothetical results that illustrate interaction and lack of interaction. Label your graphs carefully.

**4.** Explain the quotation by Beveridge at the head of this chapter.

# CHAPTER 4

## Preview

Trying to read a psychology journal article for the first time can be a frightening experience for the unprepared. Even professional psychologists sometimes have difficulty deciphering the communications of their colleagues. Frequent use of jargon and terse descriptions are obstacles that appear in most, if not all, journals. While the experienced psychologist manages without extra hints and cues, the new reader can easily get confused somewhere between the introduction and conclusion of an article. This chapter should prepare you for your first encounter with the literature of experimental psychology in two ways. First, we will explain the format and style most often used so that you will know what to expect in each section of an article. Second, we will provide hints to help you become a critical reader so you can objectively evaluate an article. We want you to do better than the Mock Turtle and not have to "reel and writhe" your way through every psychology article you must read. The chapter ends with some advice for writing a research report.

## Chapter Outline

**The Parts of an Article**
  Title and Authors
  Abstract
  References
  Introduction
  Method
  Results
  Discussion
  Determining the Order of Sections
**Checklist for the Critical Reader**
  Introduction

  Method
  Results
  Discussion
  Checklist Summary
**Two Sample Journal Articles**
**Writing a Research Report**
  Format
  Style
  Publishing an Article
**Summary**
**Key Terms**

# HOW TO READ AND WRITE RESEARCH REPORTS

*"I couldn't afford to learn it," said the Mock Turtle with a sigh. "I only took the regular course." "What was that?" inquired Alice. "Reeling and Writhing, of course. . . ."*

Lewis Carroll

The basic psychology article consists of seven parts: title and author(s), abstract, introduction, method, results, discussion, references. Each part has an important function and is a necessary component of the article.

**THE PARTS OF AN ARTICLE**

## Title and Author(s)

The title is supposed to give you some idea of the contents of an article. Since titles must be short, the most common title states only the dependent and independent variables—for example, "Reverse Peristalsis as a Function of Chloride Concentration in an Isotonic Solution." This is not too exciting, but remember that without titles the front pages of journals would contain only the names of the editors, and be even less exciting (except, perhaps, for the editors). Some psychologists, realizing that the titles convey little information, have opted for catchy or clever titles.

The experienced researcher pays more attention to the names of the authors than to the titles. A reader who has read several articles published by the same author soon gets to appreciate that writer's viewpoints and whether or not they coincide with his or her own biases. So most of us first read those authors with whom we are likely to agree, except for the minority who cannot resist first reading those authors with whom they disagree, especially if these authors cite the reader's work in their disagreement. This is a little like worrying a cavity in a tooth: it is slightly painful but hard to resist.

There are so many psychology articles published each month that no one, even if she or he were to read during meals and in the bathroom, has the time to read all of them. The table of contents is a first step in filtering out articles irrelevant to your own interests. But a better decision can be made by consulting the abstract and the references of an article.

## Abstract

The abstract is a short paragraph (about a hundred words) that summarizes the key points of an article. According to the *Publication Manual* of the American Psychological Association, it should be "succinct, accurate, quickly comprehended, and informative." Some abstracts actually approach these criteria. The abstract is your best way to discover quickly what the article is about, if you are not an experienced researcher. The student new to an area can use the abstract to decide if a particular article merits reading. The experienced researcher will not make this decision without also consulting the references.

## References

These are found at the end of the article. Psychology journals list full titles of referenced articles, since the title helps us to remember what the article was about, in case we have already read it. Other journals, such as *Science*, overtly admit that titles are useless baggage and do not waste journal space by printing them in the references.

For the student, the references are primarily valuable as a guide to related information. The experienced researcher uses references as an index of merit for the article. Articles lose points when the references are not recent or when the reference section omits important publications.

## Introduction

The introduction specifies the problem to be studied and tells why it is important. A good introduction also specifies the hypotheses to be tested and gives the rationale behind any predictions. The introduction can also set up the "straw men" that the experiment is about to demolish. Many authors strive to create the impression that the introduction was written even before the results were obtained. For every experiment where the hypotheses (the real hypotheses, before results were in) are confirmed, there are several where the hypotheses were rejected and scores where no firm conclusion one way or the other could be reached. These latter do not usually appear in journals and so the sample of published articles you may read does not represent the population of experiments that have been performed. Most experiments do not live up to the researcher's hopes and expectations. In the words of Beveridge (1957):

> Unfortunately research has more frustrations than successes and the scientist is more often up against what appears to be an impenetrable barrier than making progress. Only those who have sought know how rare and hard to find are those little diamonds of truth which, when mined and polished, will endure hard and bright. Lord Kelvin wrote: "One word characterises the most strenuous of the efforts for the advancement of science that I have made preseveringly during fifty-five years; that word is failure."

## Method

The method section describes in detail the operations performed by the experimenter. It is usually printed in smaller type to conserve space, but this should not mislead you into believing it is an unimportant part of the article to be quickly skimmed over. The method section should contain enough information for another experimenter to replicate the study.

It is customary to divide the method section into subsections that cover subjects, apparatus, and procedure. The subject section tells how many subjects there were, how they were selected (randomly, haphazardly, only the investigator's relatives, et cetera) and who they were (college undergraduates taking introductory psychology, paid volunteers obtained by an ad in a newspaper, a particular strain of rats purchased from a supply house). The procedure explains what happened to the subjects and includes instructions (for human subjects), statistical design features, and so forth. If an uncommon statistical technique was used—that is, one that cannot be looked up directly in an advanced statistics text and cited—an extra design subsection is often included. Sometimes even a standard statistical technique is described in a design subsection.

## Results

This section tells what happened in the experiment. Descriptive statistics summarize the data, and it is unusual to find raw data or individual scores reported. Inferential statistics are presented so that the reader can decide whether or not to believe the data.

Beware of statements like "although the data just barely missed reaching the level of significance by a teensy-weensy bit, it is clear that a trend in the predicted direction did occur."

This kind of statement is dangerous for several reasons. First, the word "trend" is a technical term and existence of a trend can be determined only by an appropriate statistical test. (See any statistics text for a discussion of trend analysis.) Second, it implies that results that are significant go beyond a trend—that is, they are true and utterly reliable—and that failure to reach a prescribed level of significance only means that "truth" is latent rather than explicit. This implication is false because even significant results are reliable only in a probabilistic sense, for example, five times in a hundred. This is discussed in appendix A in some detail. There is no fixed rule for setting an appropriate level of significance, and statistics will never replace thought as a technique for evaluating results. So when you read a statement like "$F(4,60) = 2.93, p < .05$," all this means is that the odds for obtaining an F-statistic at least as large as 2.93 by chance if the experiment were repeated would be 5 percent.

It is up to you to decide if these odds are just right, too high, or too low. Depending on the import of your conclusions, you may require more or less certainty that what happened did not happen by chance. For example, imagine the problem of a graduate-student admissions officer who must decide whether or not to discriminate against admitting women because they are less likely to finish the program than are men. She commissions a statistical analysis to test this hypothesis. Here, odds of 5 in 100 are too high. Before considering such a drastic step, the admissions officer needs to be extremely sure that the hypothesis is correct. (Never mind that discrimination may or may not be befitting regardless of whether the hypothesis is correct.) So a level of significance of 1 in 1,000 would be more appropriate. Or take the case of a breakfast-cereal company that wishes to include a "prize" inside the box. It performs a statistical analysis to decide which of five potential prizes, all costing the same, is preferred by consumers. If there is any difference among prizes, the company wants to be sure to find the best one. If the firm is wrong and incorrectly selects one, when in fact all are equally attractive, no great harm is done since each prize costs the same. Here odds of 5 in 100 are too low. So a level of significance of 50 in 100 might be more appropriate. The situation determines what the level of significance should be. So our third objection to the statement about data just barely missing the level of significance is that it might imply (incorrectly, of course) that a fixed level (usually .05) is always appropriate.

Either tables or graphs may be used to summarize data. It is often helpful to draw a rough graph for yourself from tabular data. If an article contains several figures, check that the scales are comparable so that effects can be easily compared across different figures. The way a graph is drawn can be misleading, as the following example illustrates.

Imagine that a psychologist is interested in the sexual arousal of college students viewing movies. She measures arousal by attaching electrodes to the participants, and then recording voltage. She shows the participants two films: *Deep Throat*, a very explicit adult X-rated film in which a variety of sexual acts are depicted, and *Bambi*, a Walt Disney family film and childhood favorite. We would expect *Deep Throat* to be the more arousing film. However, when (fictitious) results are plotted as in figure 4-1a, there appears to be virtually no difference between the two films. Now look at figure 4-1b. Here there is a clear difference, as we expected. Is this figure from a better experiment? Not at all. Actually the data plotted in both figures are exactly the same. At first glance even the vertical scales may appear similar. The trick is that the first figure

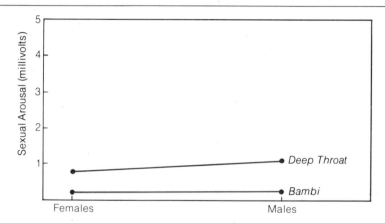

FIGURE 4-1(a)

Amount of sexual arousal in male and female college students watching movies (fictitious data).

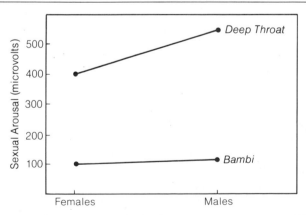

FIGURE 4-1(b)

Amount of sexual arousal in male and female college students watching movies (fictitious data).

measures arousal in millivolts whereas the second figure uses microvolts. One millivolt equals 1,000 microvolts. Furthermore, figure 4-1a stretches out the distance between males and females, causing the lines to appear flatter. But when we look at figure 4-1b, we see an interaction, with *Deep Throat* having a greater arousing effect for males than for females. This interaction is equally present in figure 4-1a, but the scale makes it difficult to notice. So the way a graph is drawn can emphasize or conceal obtained results.

### Discussion

The discussion is the most creative part of an article, where an author is permitted to gild the data and evoke deep theoretical conclusions. Most editors have firm standards for both method and result sections, but the author is given enough rope to hang herself or himself in the discussion. Hence, although any article should be approached with caution, an extra degree of skepticism is required for discussion sections. In the words of the *Publication Manual:* "In the discussion section, you are free to examine, interpret, and qualify your results, as well as to draw inferences from them." Freedom for the authors requires caution from the readers.

### Determining the Order of Sections

Most readers start at the front of an article and dutifully plod their way to the references, except perhaps those who cut their teeth on mystery novels and so reverse this process. But as you become more and more familiar with a research area it becomes less necessary to follow the order printed in journals. For example, if you are truly an expert in some area, merely reading the results section may be enough for you to infer the rest of the article. After you have read a few articles, do not be afraid to depart from the traditional order of things.

**CHECKLIST FOR THE CRITICAL READER**

In this section we offer some hints that have helped us to become better consumers of the information presented in psychological journals. The major suggestion is for you to avoid rushing through the article. Instead, you might deliberately stop after each section and write down the answers to the questions we shall list here. This will be difficult at first—thinking is always harder than reading—but with practice this process becomes automatic and requires little extra time.

## Introduction

**1.** *What is the author selling?* Skeptics should regard the introduction as a sales pitch for the article. While an experienced reader can also figure out *why* the author is selling some point of view, beginners can be satisfied with only discovering *what* the author is selling.

**2.** *What hypotheses will be tested in the experiment?* The answer to this should be obvious and stated directly within the introduction section.

**3.** *If I had to design an experiment to test this hypothesis, what would I do?* This is the key question for the introduction. It is essential that you answer this *before* you continue on to the method section of the article. If the author has any skill as a wordsmith, once you have finished the next section you are likely to agree with the method that the author has advocated in the article. In fact, a really clever author will plant the seeds to this answer in the introduction itself, and this makes it a great deal harder for the reader to answer it independently by himself or herself. Write down the major ideas for your method of testing the hypothesis.

## Method

Compare your answer to question 3 with that of the author of the article. They probably will differ, if you have not peeked. Now answer question 4a.

**4a.** *Is my proposed method better than the author's?* Regardless of who had the better method, you or the author, this forced comparison will make you think about the method section critically, instead of passively accepting it.

**4b.** *Does the method actually test the hypothesis?* The hypothesis is sometimes the first casuality, disappearing between the introduction and method sections. Always check that the method used is adequate and relevant to the hypothesis at hand.

**4c.** *What are the independent, dependent, and control variables?* This is an obvious question and can be answered quickly. Listing the variables helps you avoid passive reading of the method section. After you have resolved differences between your proposed method and the author's, answer the next question.

**5.** *Using the subjects, apparatus, and procedures described by the author, what results would I predict for this experiment?* It is essential that you answer this before reading the results section. You may find it impossible to predict a single outcome. This is not really a problem, since the author probably had more than one prediction also, and then went back and "polished" the introduction once results were in. Draw a rough sketch illustrating the most likely outcomes.

### Results

Compare the results with your predictions. If they are the same, go on to question 7. If not, answer question 6.

**6.** *Did the author get the "wrong" results?* After some thought, you will reach one of two conclusions. Either your prediction was wrong or the results are hard to believe. Perhaps the method was inappropriate or perhaps these results would not be obtained again if the experiment were repeated. You might even try your own experiment.

**7.** *How would I interpret these results?* You should answer this before reading the discussion.

### Discussion

Compare your interpretation with the author's. Answer question 8a or 8b, whichever is appropriate.

**8a.** *Why didn't I think of that?* (Author wins)

**8b.** *Why didn't the author think of that?* (You win) The discussion section is the most difficult to evaluate. Often only future research can decide if it is correct. Some authors often have already done some of this future research but have not gotten around to reporting it yet. In such cases the discussion often sets up this "new" research.

### Checklist Summary

If you have read your first article carefully, writing down the answers to all eight questions, by now you should be pleasantly exhausted. To help you recover, we will take typical psychology articles and analyze them according to the checklist summarized in table 4–1.

## TWO SAMPLE JOURNAL ARTICLES

In this section we reprint two short articles from the *Bulletin of the Psychonomic Society* (formerly called *Psychonomic Science*) and use them to illustrate the checklist of table 4–1. The purpose of this exercise is not to decide which article is better, but only to help you practice reading articles. The answers to the checklist

| Questions for Critical Readers | TABLE 4–1 |
| --- | --- |

*Introduction*
   1. What is the author selling?
   2. What hypotheses will be tested in the experiment?
   3. If I had to design an experiment to test this hypothesis, what would I do?

*Method*
   4a. Is my proposed method better than the author's?
   4b. Does the method actually test the hypotheses?
   4c. What are the independent, dependent, and control values?
   5. Using the subjects, apparatus, and procedures described by the author, what results would I predict for this experiment?

*Results*
   6. Did the author get the "wrong" results?
   7. How would I interpret these results?

*Discussion*
   8. Is my interpretation better than the author's?

questions (interspersed between the sections of the articles) are those which might be given by an alert, intelligent, and careful reader with only an elementary knowledge of psychology.

## Trick or Treat: A Field Study of Social Class Differences in Altruism

Glenn E. Littlepage and Harold D. Whiteside
Middle Tennessee State University, Murfreesboro, Tennessee 37132

(1) From the *Bulletin of the Psychonomic Society, 1976, vol. 7(6), 491–492.* Copyright 1976 by the Psychonomic Society

*Previous research has demonstrated social class differences in altruism; specifically, middle-class members are more sensitive to reciprocity norms than lower-class members. The present study investigated social class differences in altruism in a situation in which reciprocity norms were not particularly salient. Children trick or treated and received candy from 63 houses representing upper-, middle-, and lower-middle-class neighborhoods. Candy from each house was rated for subjective quality; results revealed that quality of candy was not related to social class. Contrary to studies of altruism in other settings, the relative cost of giving had no effect. This suggests that cost factors may not be related to altruism in all conditions.*

Recent evidence suggests that altruistic behavior is less likely if the costs of helping are high. Sechrest and Flores (1974) have noted that the extent to which prison inmates shared cigarettes with other prisoners was a function of the number of cigarettes available. This suggests that the quantity of a commodity might influence a person's generosity with respect to that commodity. Therefore, persons of a higher social class, being more affluent, might be expected to be more generous in situations involving financial altruism than members of lower classes. While Rosenhan (cited in Sechrest & Flores, 1974) found no social class differences in contributions to charity, a survey by the Commission on Foundations and Private Philanthropy (1970) suggests that the wealthy do contribute more per capita. Nevertheless, the motivational base for such donations has not been specified and the generality has not been demonstrated. The present study attempts to shed some light on these issues by examining social class differences in altruism in a naturally occurring context.

Although previous research has shown that social class affects altruistic behavior (Berkowitz & Friedman, 1967; Dreman & Greenbaum, 1973), these effects have been demonstrated only for altruistic behavior motivated by reciprocity norms. If, a Sechrest and Flores (1974) suggest, those with a greater surplus are more willing to share, then social class should be positively related to altruistic behavior, even in situations in which the reciprocity norm is not salient.

The present study was designed to investigate altruistic behavior in such a situation. Halloween provided an appropriate setting. Most trick or treaters are not identifiable to the donors, and many households do not have children who solicit candy from others. Thus, reciprocity norms or notions of exchange should not be particularly salient.

The authors are grateful to Jeff Haynes, Cindy Ingram, Linda Haley, and Nick Littlepage for their assistance. Address reprint requests to Glenn Littlepage, Psychology Department, Middle Tennessee State University, Murfreesboro, Tennessee 37132. This paper is sponsored by Robert E. Prytula, who takes full editorial responsibility for its contents.

*Question 1.* The author is selling the idea that altruistic behavior (for example, giving to charity) has been shown to be related to social class only when there are "reciprocity norms" (for example, you scratch my back and I'll scratch yours). The contribution of the experiment is an investigation of altruism and social class in a situation where there are no reciprocity norms.

*Question 2.* Although this experiment does have a hypothesis, you may have missed it since it was not clearly labeled as such. It is that social class should be positively related to altruistic behavior—that is, those who have more will give more—even when the reciprocity norm is absent. It should be noted that the authors never operationally define what they mean by a reciprocity norm.

*Question 3.* The introduction has already anticipated the method by specifying a trick-or-treat situation, so it may be difficult for you to think of other situations to test the hypothesis where reciprocity norms also may be absent. This same type of situation could be established in a laboratory where subjects are allowed to win either cash or tokens and then are asked to donate. According to the hypothesis, those who win more should give more. Or if a field setting is preferred, another possibility might be studying organ donors—for example, those who specify that their eyes should be donated to an eye bank after death. The field setting used in this experiment is quite reasonable.

## Method

**Subjects** Subjects consisted of residents of selected areas of a relatively small community (population about 30,000). Only residents who opened their doors and provided candy to "trick or treaters" were included.

**Procedure** Nine areas of town were selected to represent three distinct economic categories. Three areas consisted of mostly two-bedroom frame houses, selected to represent lower-middle-class dwellings. Three other areas, consisting primarily of three-bedroom brick houses, were designated as middle-class dwellings; and three additional areas, containing mostly spacious brick dwellings in prestigious areas, were selected to represent the upper class.

The study involved children trick or treating at houses in the selected areas. Three children between the ages of 6 and 9 years served as data collectors. Each received candy from seven houses in each area; each trick or treated in three areas, one from each social class. They all began trick or treating around 5:00 p.m. and concluded about 8:00 p.m.; data collection was arranged so that social class was counterbalanced with time of night. The candy received from each house was collected and identified.

Following data collection, the children were paid and were given candy to replace the study candy. The study candy was rated for quality by 13 college students, using a 7-point scale ranging from "terrible—the child would be very disappointed with this candy" (coded 1) to "excellent—the child would be very pleased with this candy" (coded 7).

*Question 4a.* The token or cash experiment might be better than the trick-or-treat situation because laboratory settings are more controlled (see Chapter 3). The organ-donor study might be more difficult to carry out.

*Question 4b.* Yes, the method does test the hypothesis, although the trick-or-treat situation only examines altruism where a very low cost is involved for the donor. This is not necessarily a defect in the study, since one experiment cannot do everything. However, we must be cautious about generalizing the results of the study to other altruistic situations, where the cost and inconvenience are considerably greater. The manipulation of social class, although crude since no numbers (mean income, education level, and so forth) to represent class are generated, is adequate for the study. The dependent variable (ratings by college students of candy quality) again is adequate but could be improved upon, for example, by scoring the amount of candy given at each house.

*Question 4c.* Independent variables: area of town, time of collection. Dependent variable: rated quality of candy. Control variable: same children in all conditions.

*Question 5.* We would predict that no differences between areas of town would be found if only quality were rated, on the grounds that candy is so cheap that even low-class families could afford high-quality candy. However, we would also predict that more candy would be given by high-class families, although the experiments did not obtain the data to test this prediction.

### Results

The ratings showed considerable variability, but were positively correlated (mean r = +.57). Ratings of the candy collected from each house were used as an index of the quality of the candy and served as data. These data were analyzed using a 3 by 3 by 13 analysis of variance design, with repeated measures on the last factor to assess the effects of Social Class, Time of Night, and Rater, respectively. This analysis revealed that neither Social Class, Time of Night, nor their interaction significantly influenced the quality of candy given to trick or treaters, but that the Raters differed in their overall evaluation of the candy, $F(13,634) = 53.36$, $p < .001$. Ratings for the candy collected in the nine areas are presented in Table 1.

***Question 6.*** The results are in agreement with our prediction. Perhaps the experimenters used the wrong dependent variable and would have obtained better results by scoring quantity of candy and/or actual cost of the candy.

***Question 7.*** These results are inconclusive.

### Discussion

These results, contrary to the hypothesis, suggest that Halloween giving is not related to social class. Apparently, the social norms which influenced this traditional form of altruism are followed equally closely regardless of social class.

These findings are inconsistent with Sechrest and Flores' (1974) results showing that a large surplus leads to more altruism. It is not entirely clear why helping was related to size of surplus in their study but not in the present one. However, these are several differences between these two studies. First, in their study, subjects were prisoners and may have felt some pressures toward group solidarity. Similarly, because many prisoners may not have had access to cigarettes, other prisoners may have perceived them to be in need. Also, it is possible that, although Sechrest and Flores (1974) tried to eliminate threat, it was perceived by the prisoners. It is unlikely that subjects in the present study felt great solidarity with the trick or treaters, perceived a threat, or felt the children were in great need. In addition, Sechrest and Flores' (1974) subjects received a commodity and were immediately

| TABLE 1 | Mean Candy Ratings by Social Class and Time of Night | | |
|---|---|---|---|
| Approximate Time | Lower-Middle Class | Middle Class | Upper Class |
| 5:00–6:00 | 3.46 | 3.76 | 3.99 |
| 6:00–7:00 | 3.90 | 3.95 | 4.05 |
| 7:00–8:00 | 4.12 | 3.28 | 3.88 |

asked to respond altruistically with the same commodity; thus, the surplus was very salient to the request. Perhaps a trick-or-treat request does not cause residents to pay much attention to their own income level, and thus their ability to buy candy. Finally, Halloween candy may represent such a small portion of income that it represents a minimal cost to even the poorest subjects in this study.

Thus, there are many differences between this study and the Sechrest and Flores (1974) study that may have accounted for the differing results. Although it is not possible to pinpoint the critical differences, it is apparent that cost factors are not related to altruism in all situations. Further research is needed to document the relationship between a surplus and altruism and to specify the conditions under which the relationship holds.

### References
Berkowitz, L., & Friedman, P. Some social class differences in helping behavior. *Journal of Personality and Social Psychology*, 1967, **5**, 217–225.

Commission on Foundations and Private Philanthropy. *Foundations, private giving, and public policy.* Chicago: University of Chicago Press, 1970.

Dreman, S. D., & Greenbaum, D. Altruism and reciprocity: Sharing behavior in Israeli kindergarten children. *Child Development*, 1973, **44**, 61–68.

Sechrest, L., & Flores, L. Surplus and sharing in a prison sample, *Journal of Social Psychology*, 1974, **94**, 33–44.

***Question 8.*** The authors also realized that their results were inconclusive, although they disguise this conclusion in gobs of jargon and potential explanations. However, it is unrealistic for a reader to expect any author to state explicitly that results of an experiment were meaningless. It is certainly possible that our proposed experiment with a quantity dependent variable would also have null results. It is quite proper and useful, especially in a short paper such as this, to report null results. This experiment has the virtue of drawing our attention to other factors, such as the cost of giving, which also play a role in altruism.

### When Is Recall Higher than Recognition?
Endel Tulving
University of Toronto

(2) From *Psychonomic Science*, 1968, vol. 10 (2). Copyright 1968 by the Psychonomic Society

*Sixteen Ss learned a list of 48 paired words (A-B pairs) to a criterion of two perfect trials and were then tested for the recognition of B-members of all pairs. Approximately 10% of the learned words were not correctly identified in the recognition test. These data show that recall is higher than recognition when retrieval cues present at the recall test are more effective in providing access to stored information than are retrieval clues present at the recognition test.*

Recognition tests of memory usually yield higher scores of retention than do recall tests. Such superiority of recognition over recall is explained in terms of two factors: (1) the differences in the number of alternatives from among which correct responses are to be selected (Brown, 1965; Davis, Sutherland, & Judd, 1961; Slamecka, 1967), and (2) the differences in the amount and nature of retained information necessary for the identification and for the unaided reproduction of learned items (McNulty, 1965). If the two factors are equated in recall and in recognition, then the two measures should, and sometimes do, yield identical estimates of retention.

No extant theoretical formulation of recall and recognition specifies any conditions under which recall might be superior to recognition, even though some experiments demonstrating this relationship have been reported (e.g., Bahrick & Bahrick, 1964; Lachman & Field, 1965). In these experiments, however, recognition tests of individual items were paced by E, and S's failure to correctly identify items learned earlier may have been related to lack of time for considering the alternatives available to S on the basis of unaided recall. The present paper reports a simple experiment showing that Ss sometimes fail to recognize items they can reproduce even if they have unlimited time in the recognition test. An explanation of this phenomenon is also proposed.

*Question 1.* The author is selling the idea that recall can be better than recognition, contrary to much of public opinion. (Would you rather take a multiple-choice recognition test or an essay recall test as a final exam?)

*Question 2.* Subjects (Ss) can sometimes fail to recognize words they can recall correctly.

*Question 3.* One possibility for a design to verify the hypothesis would be to arrange a test where the recognition alternatives (multiple choices) were either quite similar (BEAR-BARE) or highly associated (BREAD-BUTTER). These confusing alternatives might lower recognition to the point where recall would be better.

**Method**

Sixteen Ss, undergraduate and graduate psychology students of both sexes, participated in the experiment. Each S learned a single list of 48 paired words (A-B pairs), under the typical paired-associate anticipation conditions, and was then tested for the recognition of B members of the pairs.

Two different lists were used, each with eight Ss. In both lists, A and B members of all pairs were common monosyllabic English words. To eliminate the massive amount of experimental practice necessary for the mastery of a 48-pair list, A-B pairs were made up of words meaningfully relaetd to each other. In List 1, for instance, pairs such as the following were used: TOOTH-ACHE, AIR-PORT, FLOOR-SHOW, HOME-STEAD. The A members of pairs in List 2 were identical with the A members of List 1, but B members were all different. Thus, the pairs in List 2 corresponding to the examples given from List 1 were: TOOTH-PICK, AIR-CRAFT, FLOOR-CLOTH, HOME-SICK.

Each S was tested individually. On the first trial the prompting method was used. Each pair of words, hand-printed on a 3 × 5 card, was shown to S, followed by a card bearing only the A member of the pair. The S was asked to call out the B member of the pair when presented with the A member. No S made any errors on this trial. Beginning with the second trial, the standard paired-associate method was used. A given A member was shown, the S asked to name the B member and then, regardless of the S's response, both A and B members of the same pair were presented. One trial consisted of the test and presentation of all 48 pairs. The presentation of cards bearing A members and pairs was paced by S and thus the rate varied from S to S. On the average, Ss took approximately 5 min to go through the list on the second trial (first anticipation trial), but they speeded up in the course of practice, and on the fifth trial the average time per trial had been reduced to approximately 3 min. Two different orders of presentation of pairs were used with each S, but these orders were different for different Ss.

Paired-associate training was continued with each S until the S had anticipated all 48 B members correctly on two consecutive trials. The S was then given a sheet of paper on which were printed, in alphabetical order, the 96 B members of Lists 1 and 2, and he was asked to check off all the words he had just learned. Thus, all 16 Ss took the same recognition test, with one-half of the items "old" for one group and the other half old for the other group. This procedure eliminated any possible effects of response bias or guessing on the recognition scores. Unlimited time was allowed for this test.

*Question 4a.* The author's method is at least as good as ours, if not better.

*Question 4b.* Yes, the method should test the hypothesis, if it works. There is a problem of equating dependent variables for recall and recognition. Percentage or number correct may not be equivalent in both tasks because guessing may be more effective in the recognition task. Since, however, this effect works in the opposite direction predicted by the hypothesis—that is, it tends to make recognition look better compared to recall—it is not a problem if recall turns out to be better. (There are, of course, a host of other problems as well.)

*Question 4c.* Independent variables: words in lists, orders of presentation of pairs. (These independent variables are not of primary interest and are therefore not carefully examined; the focus is on the two dependent variables.) Dependent variables: number of items correctly recalled and also recognized. Control variable: subjects must be correct on two consecutive trials, number of pairs (48) in each list.

*Question 5.* We would predict that no difference would be found between recall and recognition.

### Results

The data were pooled over both groups (i.e., both lists), since there were no apparent differences in the results of the two groups. The number of trials required to reach the criterion (excluding the first prompting trial, but including the two criterion trials) ranged from 5 to 9, the mean for 16 Ss being 7.2. Every S reached the criterion of two perfect trials immediately following his first perfect trial. It is a safe conclusion, therefore, that had the Ss been given another paced paired-associate test trial, their performance would have been perfect on that trial.

The numbers of correct identifications of old items as old ranged from 36 to 47, with a mean of 43.4. Thus, on the average, Ss failed to recognize 4.6 items among the 48 that they had been able to recall in the presence of A words. The mean number of incorrect identifications of new items as old was .87, and the median was zero.

***Question 6.*** This time our prediction is incorrect. It appears that recall can be better than recognition.

***Question 7.*** Learning a compound word, such as *airport*, makes it more difficult to remember only half of that word. This is especially true when it is the second half of the word that must be recognized (in this case, *port*). Memory is directional and is organized from left to right as we read. In a compound word, the connection between the first and second half (*air-port*) is much stronger than the (reverse) connection between the second and first half (*port-air*). Words contained within compound words are not perceived as words in their own right, but only as segments of the larger word. So a segment presented alone is not likely to be recognized. This is similar to the Einstellung effect (discussed in chapter 11), where doing a problem over and over the same way blinds you to alternative solutions. You can see this in the following word game played by young children. Ask a friend to pronounce the following words as you spell them out: MAC (pause) ARTHUR; MAC (pause) DON-ALD; MAC (pause) HINE. Was the last word pronounced to rhyme with *dine* or *green* (as in *machine*)?

**Discussion**
The results of this experiment clearly show that it is possible for Ss to recall—that is, to reproduce from memory—learned verbal units even if they cannot identify these units as old items in a recognition test. Thus, under the conditions of the present experiment, recall is superior to recognition. While the generality of these results—with respect to factors such as the nature of the material, length of the list, amount of practice given prior to the recognition and recall tests, and the like—remains to be determined, some relevant features of the conditions of the experiment must be identified for the purpose of the interpretation of the results.

The recall test was one involving aided or cued recall. The Ss reproduced each B item in the presence of a specific retrieval cue, the corresponding A item. Noncued recall of B items certainly would have been considerably lower than the obtained cued recall (cf., Tulving & Pearlstone, 1965), and also lower than the observed recognition performance. On the other hand, it is an equally safe conclusion that aided or cued recognition—recognition of a B item in the presence of its corresponding A item—would have been at least as high as cued recall. Recall cannot be higher than recognition as long as retrieval cues are identical, but it can be higher if retrieval cues are different in the two test situations.

The results of the present experiment suggest that in some cases the A item was a more effective retrieval cue in providing access to the stored information about the related B item than was the B item in providing access to the stored information about its own "copy." This apparent paradox is resolved if we draw a distinction between nominal and functional memory units (Tulving, 1968). Although the stored B item is nominally identical with the B item in the recognition test, the two need not represent identical subjective units. For instance, CRAFT in the recognition test may be coded differently from CRAFT in the higher-order unit of AIRCRAFT in the input list and may thus fail to provide access to desired information available in the memory store. Effectiveness of retrieval cues is critically dependent upon the extent to which they coincide with additional information stored about each to-be-remembered item at the time of input (Tulving & Osler, 1968). It is thus not surprising that some other item can be a more efficient cue for the retrieval of a given item than that item itself.

An important implication of the present results has to do with claims sometimes made that recognition "does not require retrieval" (Schonfield & Robertson, 1966) or that "recognition eliminates the search or retrieval problem" (Murdock, 1968). If recognition performance depends not only on the amount and organization of information in the memory store, but also on the number and nature of retrieval cues present at the time of the recognition test—as present data clearly indicate it does—then it becomes as necessary for students of memory to worry about retrieval problems in recognition tests as it is necessary in situations when memory is tested with different kinds of recall tests. Consideration of the role of retrieval cues in both recall and recognition does at least make it possible to provide one answer to the question: "When is recall higher than recognition?" Recall is higher than recognition whenever retrieval cues present at the recall test are more effective in providing access to stored information than are retrieval cues present at the recognition test.

## References

Bahrich, H. P. & Bahrick, P. O. re-examination of the interrelations among measures of retention. *Quart. J. exp. Psychol.*, 1964, 16, 318–324.

Brown, J. A. comparison of recognition and recall by a multiple-response method. *J. verbal Learn. verbal Behav.*, 1965, 4, 401–408.

Davis, R., Sutherland, N. S., & Judd, B. R. Information content in recognition and recall. *J. exp. Psychol.*, 1961, 61, 422–429.

Lachman, R., & Field, W. H. Recognition and recall of verbal material as a function of degree of training. *Psychon. Sci.*, 1965, 2, 225–226.

McNulty, J. A. An analysis of recall and recognition processes in verbal learning. *J. verbal Learn, verbal, Behav.*, 4, 430–436.

Murdock, B. B., Jr. Modality effects in short-term memory: Storage.or retrieval; *J. exp. Psychol.*, 1968, 77, 79–86.

Slamecka, N. J. Recall and recognition in list-discrimination tasks as a function of the number of alternatives. J. exp. Psychol. 1967, 74, 187–192.

Schonfield, D., & Robertson, B. Memory storage and aging. *Canad. J. Psychol.*, 1966, 20, 228–236.

Tulving, E. Theoretical issues in free recall. In T. R. Dixon and D. L. Horton (Eds.) *Verbal behavior and general behavior theory*. Englewood Cliffs, N.J.: Prentice-Hall, 1968.

Tulving, E., & Osler, S. Effectiveness of retrieval cues in memory for words. *J. exp. Psychol.*, 1968, 77, 593–601.

Tulving, E., & Pearlstone, Z. Availability versus accessibility of information in memory for words. *J. verbal Learn. verbal Behav.*, 1966, 5, 381–391.

Note

1. This research was supported by the National Research Council Grant APB-39 and the National Science Foundation Grant GB 3710. The author is indebted to Miss Laurian King for collecting the data.

*Question 8.* Both interpretations are similar, although they emphasize slightly different aspects of memory. Both explanations could be tested by further experiments. This short article has inspired a great deal of research on this topic. For more information about the approach suggested in the article, see Tulving and Thompson (1973).

## WRITING A RESEARCH REPORT

You have gotten an idea, reviewed the pertinent literature, designed a procedure, collected your data, and analyzed the results. Now you may have to report your results. Your course may require a written record of your research. Even if it does not demand a report, you are obligated to publicize the results of a carefully done project. In order to maintain the self-correcting nature of science, we believe that it is important to publish good data. However, this does not mean that journals should be cluttered with information derived from every undergraduate project. If your research is promising, you will receive encouragement from your instructor. In this section we will review the format of a typical report and discuss some of the stylistic considerations that make up a comprehensible paper.

If you follow our suggestions for reading articles, then you will have a pretty good idea about the format of a research report, and you will probably have a good feel for technical writing style. Some aspects of technical writing are not too obvious, so we will discuss them here. What we present are general guidelines. If you need additional information, you should examine R. J. Sternberg's book, *Writing the Psychology Paper*. The *Publication Manual of the American Psychological Association* (this organization is called the APA, for short) will also help, because it is the official arbiter of style for many journals.

## Format

Since you already know about the major content sections of a journal article from your active reading of research reports, the outline of a typical report in figure 4–2 emphasizes the sequence of pages you will have to put together in your APA-style report. A run through that sequence will give you an idea of what you are supposed to include. Your cover page has the title of your project, your name, and your affiliation (your institution or place of business). If you were submitting your article for publication, you would also include a short title (running head) that would be used at the top

FIGURE 4–2.

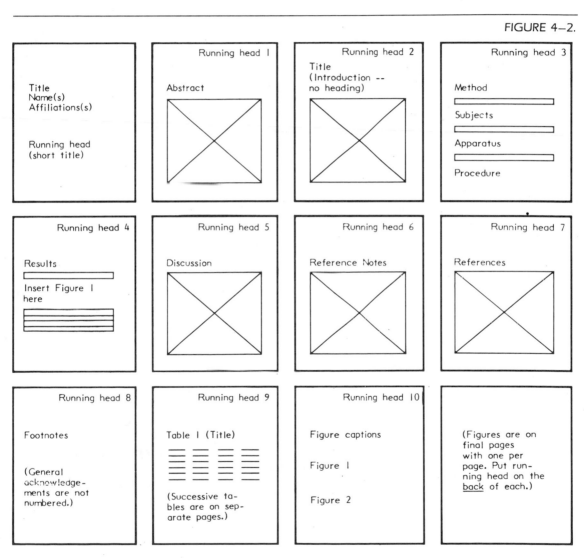

Page sequence for a report in APA format.

of the pages of your published article. Usually the title page is not numbered. The next page, page 1, contains the heading *Abstract* and the abstract itself. On this page and on all subsequent ones except the figures, you should have an abbreviated title and the page number in the top right-hand corner of the page. Page 2 repeats the whole title and includes your introductory material. Ordinarily, you do not have a heading for the introduction. After your introduction is finished, the method section begins. Note the format shown for the headings on page 3 in figure 4–2. The side headings, like *Subjects* and *Apparatus*, help point the reader to pertinent information. The results section immediately follows the method. You do not include your figures and tables in the body of this section (they come at the end of the report). Instead, you indicate their approximate location as shown on page 4 of figure 4–2. Next comes the discussion, which ends the major textual portion of your report.

Reference notes appear on a separate page after the discussion. Reference notes refer to unpublished works, papers presented at conferences, and personal communications from other researchers. They occur in the reference-note list in the order in which they are mentioned in the text (Note 1, Note 2, et cetera.) If your report is a follow-up of one of your previous projects that has not been published, then you would cite your previous work as a reference note. The regular references begin on a separate page. The format for presenting references is complex, and you should use care in preparing them. You might also study the APA manual and recent journal articles. Any footnotes are on a separate page after the references, and are listed in numerical order. For most college laboratory reports, footnotes are not necessary. When you prepare something for publication, you may acknowledge financial and intellectual support that would appear on the footnote page. General acknowledgments are not numbered. Other, perhaps peripheral, information would appear as numbered footnotes, but such footnotes are generally discouraged.

Following the footnotes are your data tables mentioned in the results section. Each table should be on a separate page and numbered consecutively, according to its appearance in the results section. Make the titles of your tables short but communicative. Captions for your figures are numbered consecutively and appear on a separate page following the data tables. Finally, you have your figures, each on a separate piece of paper. Put your name (or the short title) and the number of the figure on the back.

## Style

Now that you have some idea of the format, let us consider style. After you have suffered through some obscurely written article, we are sure you recognize the advantage of clear, unambiguous writing. The APA format helps standardize the order and general content. However, making sure that the reader understands what you are saying is up to you. We have read many research reports prepared for our classes—some good, some awful, most of them in between—and we have found that the biggest problem is transition, or flow, from one section to the next. Deliberately or not, many students write as if they were composing a surprise-ending short story, but their report should be as straightforward as possible.

Your abstract should include your variables (independent, dependent, and important control variables), number and type of subjects, major results, and important conclusions. The body of your report should then expand upon the abstract. (This is why most abstracts are written last, by the way, even though the report might be clearer if it were written first as an outline for the main part of the report.) You should remember the following: in your introduction you state why you are interested in particular variables and what other investigators have found; in your method you state how you examined those variables; in the results you state what happened when you examined the variables; and in your discussion you state what the effects of the variables mean. Thus the body of your report should represent a tight "package," not a disjointed essay containing sections that seem independent of each other. You have to tell your readers what you were trying to do, over and over again.

Perhaps the best way to think about your report is as follows: do not be afraid to be somewhat redundant by having each section build on the previous one. If you repeat the purpose of your research often enough as you go through each section of the report, even the dullest reader will have gotten something from your report by the time he or she gets to the reference list. Shown in table 4–2 is a summary of the information that should be included in each section of your report.

The APA publication manual outlines style problems as follows: use the precise word, avoid ambiguity, order presentation of ideas, and consider the reader. These warrant some discussion.

Scientific writing demands clarity, so each word has to be chosen carefully. Consider these sentences that regularly appear in undergraduate research reports: "I ran the subjects individually." "The white, albino rat was introduced to the Skinner box." Actually, none of the subjects in the study from which the first sentence was pulled did any running during the course of the project. What the author meant to say was, "I tested the subjects individually," or "The subjects were tested individually." From reading about rats introduced to Skinner boxes, you might conclude that the researcher had very clever rats. The rat did not shake hands with a box; all that happened was that the rat was put into the operant conditioning chamber. Furthermore, "white, albino" is redundant. All albino rats are white. The lesson here is that in

| TABLE 4–2 | A Summary of the Information in Each Section of a Research Report |
|---|---|

| Section | Content |
|---|---|
| Title | Experiments state independent and dependent variables— "The effects of X on Y." Other studies state the relationships examined— "The relation between X and Y." |
| Abstract | In less than 150 words, state what was done to whom and summarize the most important results. |
| Introduction | State what you plan to do and why (you may have to review results from related research). Predicted results may be appropriate. |
| Method | Present enough information to allow someone else to repeat your study exactly the way you did it. For clarity use subheadings (*Subjects, Apparatus*, etc.), and make sure that dependent, independent, subject, and control variables are specified. |
| Results | Summarize important results in tables or figures. Direct the reader to data that seem most relevant to the purpose of the research. |
| Discussion | State how the results relate to the hypotheses or predictions stated in the introduction. Inferences and theoretical statements are appropriate. |
| References | In APA format, list only those references which were cited in your report. |

scientific writing you must be careful to choose the correct word or phrase and avoid ambiguity. You should also remember to be careful with pronouns like *which, this, that, these* and *those*. Many students find it irresistible to begin a paragraph with one of these pronouns, and more often than not the referent for the pronoun is not very easy to determine. You can usually avoid any ambiguity by including the referent of the pronoun each time it is used.

After you have decided on your words and phrases, you have to put them together carefully. A common problem is to shift tenses of verbs abruptly. In general, you should use the past tense in the review of other studies in your introduction (Smith *found* . . .) and in your method (The subjects *were* . . .). When you are describing and discussing your data, the present tense is usually appropriate (The data *show* that . . ., which *means* that . . .).

Make sure that collective and plural nouns agree with their verbs and pronouns. Plural words that end in *a* are troublesome, such as *data, criteria,* and *phenomena*. Each of those nouns is plural, so they each require plural verbs and pronouns. "These data *are*" is correct, but "this phenomena *is*" is not correct. The singular forms for those nouns are: *datum, criterion,* and *phenomenon* ("This phenomenon *is*").

Many scientific writers overuse the passive voice in their reports. Consider this statement: "It is thought that forgetting is caused by interference." Although that statement is fairly concise and it is precise, it is also stuffy and less direct than, "We think that interference causes forgetting," which is really what was meant in the first statement. In general, you should be careful about using either the active or passive voice too much. If you overuse the passive voice, you become stuffy. If you overuse the active voice, you may take interest away from what you did and place too much emphasis on yourself (I think . . ., I did . . ., et cetera). If you want to emphasize what was done and not who did it and why, use the passive construction. On the other hand, if you think that the agent of the activity is also important, or if the reason for the action is important, then you should use the active voice.

## Publishing an Article

Assume that your report has been written, proofread, corrected, and the last page has just emerged from a steaming typewriter. Now what? Although it is unlikely that your first student effort will produce an article of professional quality, you may nevertheless find it interesting to discover what happens when an article is submitted to a journal by a professional psychologist.

The first step is to send copies of the manuscript (the technical term for an unpublished work) to a small number of trusted associates who can check it over to make sure that it has no obvious or elementary flaws and that it is written clearly. Once the comments come back, the indicated corrections are made and, with some trepidation, the author commits the manuscript to the mails, addressed to the editor of the most appropriate journal. After this it is necessary to forget about it entirely for the next few months, or otherwise to exhibit great patience. The reviewing process is slow. The editor who receives the manuscript is a harried, over-worked, tired individual who often regrets accepting the editorship. Editors of journals, like elected politicians, serve a fixed term of office, usually four to six years. About two or three weeks after submitting the potential article, the author will receive a form letter thanking him for interest in the journal and acknowledging receipt of the manuscript. The manuscript gets a number (like 84–867) and if an associate editor has been assigned to handle it the author is instructed to direct all future correspondence to that editor.

The editor then sends copies of the manuscript to one or two reviewers. It is unlikely that both of them will be good friends of the author. Blind reviewing, where an author conceals his or her identity, can be used with some journals for those who do not believe in the impartiality of reviewers. The reviewer, who may also review for several other journals, puts the manuscript in the pile on his or her desk with a muttered curse. A conscientious reviewer may take up to a day or two to carefully read and evaluate a manuscript. When each reviewer gets around to it, a summary statement is sent to the editor. When the reviewers are in agreement, the editor's decision is easy. Should the reviewers disagree, the editor must carefully read the manuscript and sometimes may request a third opinion. Finally, an editorial decision is reached and the author receives a letter stating either (1) why the manuscript cannot be published, (2) what kind of revisions are needed to make the manuscript acceptable, or (3) that the journal is happy to publish the article. Since rejection rates are quite high in most journals (above 80%), editors spend a great deal of time devising tactful letters of rejection.

Whether or not the article was accepted, the comments of the reviewers are most valuable. The best psychologists in the area have provided, free of charge, their careful opinions about the research. Of course, reviewers can also make mistakes. Anyone who disagrees with a review has the privilege, even the responsibility, of writing a reply to the editor. This usually will not get the article accepted, but it is important that rejected authors have the right to appeal or protest. Anyway, there are always other journals.

If the article was perchance accepted for publication, the author is not yet finished. Some revision may be required. The copyright for the article is signed over to the publisher. Some months later the author receives galley or page proofs from the publisher. These must be carefully checked to ensure that the words and tables set in type by the printer match the original manuscript. After making corrections (and authors are charged for excessive corrections that do not result from printer's errors), the article is returned. Some months after this the article finally appears in print in the journal. The entire process, from submitting the manuscript until final publication, takes a year or more. Authors do not get paid for articles in journals, but on the other hand neither do they get charged for the privilege of appearing in print.

As you might expect, it is a great thrill to see your name in print, especially for the first time. An even greater thrill, however, is the knowledge that you may have added some small amount to our understanding of why people think and act as they do.

**SUMMARY**

When you read a research report, it is important that you read actively and critically, so you can derive maximum benefit from other people's research. The checklist for critical readers is designed to get you into the habit of actively asking questions about the reports you read: What hypotheses are being tested, how are they being tested? Does the method test the hypotheses? Do the results apply to the hypotheses? How does the author relate the results to the purposes of the research? What interpretations and inferences are made by the author? You should also consider these questions when you write your own report. The APA format provides a framework for your report, but it is up to you to write clearly. Writing and (possibly) publishing the results of a project may be a tedious process. However, remember that the purpose of psychological research is to find out why people think and act as they do. In order for psychological science to be self-correcting, reports must be published and knowledgeable consumers must read them.

abscissa
abstract
APA format
apparatus
author
checklist for critical readers
discussion
figures

introduction
method
ordinates
references
report contents
results
subjects
tables
title

**KEY TERMS**

# PART II

## PART OUTLINE

# INTRODUCTION

In each chapter of part 2 we will discuss two or three topics that are important in psychological research. The discussion does not pretend to supply a comprehensive survey of each research area, but is intended to illustrate the topics in a concrete way. Of course, the various topics have application beyond the particular content area chosen to illustrate them. We will bring methodology—the special techniques employed to make data useful and appropriate—into play only to solve problems related to specific content areas. Both the principles and topics, as well as the specific content areas used to illustrate them, will be listed at the head of each chapter. You can also locate specific topics by looking them up in the Table of Contents, which shows which chapters discuss each topic. Very important topics are covered in more than one chapter.

The introduction to each chapter will tell you what these topics are and why they are important in the context of the particular subject discussed in the chapter. You can tell that the introduction has ended when you encounter the first heading. It looks like this:

## THIS IS THE FIRST HEADING

Headings in this kind of type mark off major sections. This first section is designed to orient you toward the chapter contents. In it we will discuss some general problems that psychologists are trying to understand in this area. We may, in this section, talk about some of the people who were important in establishing the area of inquiry, or we may use the section to explain how a general issue in science applies to some specific psychological problem area.

Smaller headings are often used within each major section to help you organize the chapter. The next kind of heading you will encounter looks like this:

### This Is a Secondary Heading

This kind of heading refers to a more specific topic within the general issue indicated by its preceding major heading. Sometimes this is further divided with a minor head.

***This is a minor heading.*** It is run into the text, like this. If you find yourself getting lost in the details of a chapter look back at the preceding headings. Find the minor heading and then see how it relates to the headings above it. If you are not sure about this relation, back up to the next highest heading and reread from there. No good explorer continues into the unknown without a landmark, and you shouldn't either. The three different kinds of headings have been carefully constructed to guide you through the chapter. Use them to keep on the right path.

## INTRODUCING THE VARIABLES

Next you will find a section set in type like this. This section introduces you to some of the independent, dependent, and control variables you will find in the chapter. It is not an exhaustive list of all the variables you would likely read about by venturing into the depths of psychology journals. Instead, it illustrates a few key variables that are important in the context of the chapter.

Independent, dependent, and control variables are the most important components of psychological research. Without them, there would be no research. The independent variable is the variable manipulated by the experimenter. The dependent variable is the variable observed or recorded by the experimenter. The control variable is a potential independent variable that is not varied in some particular experiment. Instead, it is held at a constant value or level. If these crucial concepts are not entirely clear to you, go back to chapter 3, where several examples can be found.

Later on in the chapters you will discover summaries of real experiments. Make sure you know the independent, dependent, and control variables used in these studies.

## EXPERIMENTAL TOPICS AND RESEARCH ILLUSTRATIONS

Topic:

Illustration:

This section is the meat of the chapter. Principles that guide psychological research will first be defined and discussed. Then specific studies will be used to illustrate how these principles were used (or not used, as the case may be) to ensure sound research.

The first experimental topic discussed in each chapter will be illustrated by two or more studies. You should try to compare these studies and see not only how they differ but also what they have in common that relates them to the same principle. Then check your comparison against that given in the chapter. The second (and third, if included) topic will most often be illustrated by a single study.

When you design your own research project, take these topics and principles into account. They will help you avoid the most common types of errors in psychological research. The Table of Contents will help you locate these principles when you need them.

**Problem:**

## FROM PROBLEM TO EXPERIMENT: THE NUTS AND BOLTS

This section takes you behind the scenes in research and answers these hidden questions. You may be surprised to discover that many answers are quite arbitrary. An experiment is designed to last one hour because it is more convenient for the students who will serve as participants. The number of items might be determined by how many slides fit in a slide-projector tray. Although not every detail will be covered in each experimental design, after reading several "Nuts and Bolts" sections you should have a good understanding of some hidden factors that are not made explicit in journal reports.

The general format of each "Nuts and Bolts" section is simple. We look at a psychological problem and work out the nuts and bolts details to come up with an answer. First, we formulate a hypothesis, and then we design an experiment to test that hypothesis.

## CHAPTER AIDS: SUMMARY, KEY TERMS, AND DISCUSSION QUESTIONS

The summary, key terms, and discussion questions allow you to check your understanding of each chapter in part 2. The summary is a brief reminder of the highlights of a chapter. It is not a substitute for reading the chapter. The numbered statements are short reviews of important chapter sections. If you do not understand one of them, go back and reread that part of the chapter. You can also review the chapter by looking over the headings listed at the start of each chapter.

The key terms are another form of review. You probably will not be able to define all the key terms after just one reading of the chapter. Go back and find the key terms you missed. An even better way to review is to write down your own definition for each key term. Then go back and check your definition against the text.

The discussion questions give you one more way to check your understanding. Questions range from very specific mathematical calculations with only one correct answer, to broad, and even far out, topics relating philosophy to experimental design. There is no unique correct answer to these broad questions and they are included to promote discussion and thought (not in that order, we hope). Even if your instructor does not go over these in class, you should spend some time thinking about possible answers. The wide range of questions is intended to demonstrate that experimental psychologists encourage (or at least tolerate) many different viewpoints. There is no single approach to experimental psychology that has a monopoly on truth.

# CHAPTER 5

## Preview

This chapter covers some fundamental psychophysical methods—techniques used by psychologists to map attributes of the physical world into their mental or psychological values. Psychophysics got its start as a solution to the famous mind-body problem of philosophy. Developments in psychophysics are used to explain the concepts of operational definitions, measurement scales and Fechner's law. A third topic, the use of experimental designs based upon small numbers of subjects, is illustrated by psychophysical methods.

## Chapter Outline

# PSYCHOPHYSICS

*Observation is a passive science, experimentation an active science.*

Claude Bernard

We live in an era where all sorts of marvelous machines are taken for granted. Telephones, automobiles, household appliances, televisions, and so on, all efficiently serve our needs. We accept such devices not only because they are helpful but also because we feel in control of them. No one would want a machine if it were the boss, and indeed some have complained that there is in our computer age a disturbing tendency in this direction. Nevertheless, most, if not all, of us are content in our knowledge that machines operate by natural and physical laws that are well understood by their designers, so that in principle the behavior of these machines is entirely predictable and controllable. Yet, the most marvelous machine of all is the human mind and body. Is it also entirely predictable and controllable?

Many persons would strongly disagree that a human mind is in principle no different from, say, an elevator or an electric typewriter. They would argue that the natural laws that govern the behavior of physical devices are not sufficient to explain the poetic majesty of the human mind. People, they would claim, are more than an assemblage of cogs and gears (or neurons and such). The human spirit transcends natural physical laws. Most experimental psychologists do not accept this position. Psychologists believe that human behavior is in principle identical to the behavior of any physical system, since both are entirely predictable and controllable once the appropriate natural laws are discovered. The *mind-body problem*—whether mental systems (mind) and physical systems (body) are governed by the same kinds of natural laws—has concerned philosophers for ages.

As we shall see, the mind-body problem is closely linked to the psychological problem of *measurement*. If the world exists outside of the mind, then things or objects in the world must exist in various quantities. If things exist in varying quantities, then the amount of "thingness" should be amenable to measurement. Thus, we should be able to state that object *A* has more of a certain attribute (such as size, weight, pleasantness, and so forth) than object *B*. Under certain circumstances we may even be able to state this relationship more precisely, for example, object *A* has twice as much as object *B*. So by measurement we mean the ability to assign numerical values to objects in a systematic way.

One common way to measure is based on comparisons of similar objects. You may be able to easily tell the difference between a 1977 Triumph Spitfire and a 1978 Triumph Spitfire, whereas your parents may not be able to distinguish between a Triumph Spitfire and an MG Midget. By determining how dissimilar objects must be before a person can reliably tell them apart, we can obtain a scale of measurement. These scales can be different for different people. You may be able to tell that two sport cars are different just by comparing tail lights, whereas your parents may not be able to distinguish among any sport cars that have two seats and a convertible top (see figure 5–1).

*Psychophysical methods* are techniques used by psychologists to measure attributes of the physical world in terms of their mental or psychological values. At first, this may seem to be an unnecessary enterprise. Why not just measure the physical values and leave it at that? It is easy to decide than an object is 45 centimeters long or weighs 200 kilograms. However, it turns out that there often is not a direct one-to-one relationship between physical values and mental values. For example, if a rock band in a discotheque turned up its amplifiers to obtain twice as much sound energy as before (a change in physical units), this doubling of energy would not result in your experiencing a sound that appeared to be twice as loud as before. In fact, for you to feel that the sound was twice as loud, the energy would have to be increased roughly ten times. So knowing about changes in physical units does not always directly tell us about changes in psychological units.

In this chapter, psychophysical methods are used to illustrate three experimental principles or topics. *Operational definitions* let us communicate the steps that are necessary to define a scientific process. They ensure that scientists use technical terms in similar ways. *Measurement scales* refer to the degree of precision with which we can assign numbers to objects. Different psychophysical methods result in different types of scales. Last we shall discuss why it

FIGURE 5–1.
Can you tell if these cars are the same model and year? (They are not.)

ıs often appropriate to formulate psychophysical laws based on very *small numbers of observers* instead of the large numbers of subjects typically used in many psychology experiments.

**THE MIND OR THE BODY: IS ONE DOMINANT?**

The mind-body problem, although dating back at least to Plato, is still an unresolved issue in philosophy. Psychologists, however, have a more pressing need to reach some workable solution so that they can continue studying the relationship between mind and body. Our brief discussion will touch only lightly on the more abstract philosophical issues and instead will focus more on the pragmatic implications of the mind-body problem for the working psychologist. This approach is highly justified, since, as we shall discover, psychophysical techniques were originally developed by Fechner as part of his solution to the mind-body problem.

If you were asked to take sides in proposing solutions to the mind-body problem, you would soon see that such solutions could be classified into two main types. One type would claim that either mind or body is dominant so that either (1) mind controls matter, or (2) matter controls mind. This philosophical viewpoint is called *monism*. Monism is often misinterpreted as stating that only one category (mind or body) really exists and that the other does not. Although such an extreme position has occasionally been held, most supporters of monism would be satisfied to convince you that one of the two categories is irrelevant even if it does exist. Another type of solution, called *dualism*, claims that both mind and body exist as separate entities, but that these two entities may be related in some way. We shall now discuss each solution in turn.

### Monism: Mind or Body

As a practicing monist, you can select either mind or matter, but not both, as the dominant entity. The dominance of mind is most associated with the writings of George Berkeley (1685–1753), also known as the Bishop of Cloyne in County Cork, Ireland. The dominance of body is most associated with John Watson (1878–1958), known in psychological circles as the founder of behaviorism. (Appendix B).

***Bishop Berkeley: Mind triumphs over matter.*** Berkeley (1710) argued that object and sensation were the same thing, so that one could not be abstracted from the other. Seeing is believing and perception is reality. Although the external world may exist, it is only the sum of our individual sensations. Take away the redness of the lips, the soft caress of gentle hands, the pine-scented smell of auburn hair, and your lover is gone. Without sensation the mind cannot unite these elements to create your lover; that is, your lover is but a conglomeration of assorted sensations joined in your mind. Thus the world is never the same for any two people, since their minds will unite sensations differently.

One logical difficulty faced by Berkeley was how to account for the high degree of similarity that people report about objects in the world. Berkeley found the necessary continuity in God and in the soul. (Remember, he was a bishop.) A famous limerick (Knox, quoted by Bertrand Russell, 1951) expressed this problem and Berkeley's solution:

> There was a young man who said, "God
> Must think it exceedingly odd
>    If he finds that this tree
>    Continues to be
> When there's no one about in the Quad."

> Dear Sir:
>    Your astonishment's odd:
> I am always about in the Quad.
>    And that's why the tree
>    Will continue to be,
> Since observed by
>                Yours faithfully,
>                   God.

Berkeley's views were sensational, but they were not popular even among philosophers. Although a trace of this philosophy can be found in phenomonology—the use of conscious experience as a datum in psychology—Watson's opposing monistic view had a far greater influence on the development of modern psychology.

***John Watson: Psychology loses its mind.***   Watson's belief in the dominance of body and behavior was a reaction to the preceding fifty years, during which experimental psychology concerned itself with the study of conscious experience (see appendix B). According to Watson, insofar as psychology was concerned with the scientific, objective study of humans, mind was a trivial and irrelevant topic. Psychology as the science of mind had reached a dead end. It was time for psychology to discard the "yoke of consciousness" (Watson, 1913). Psychology as the science of behavior had an unlimited future.

As a relative newcomer to the science of psychology, you may find Watson's position rather extreme, since, after all, you know that you have a mind. Indeed, although most psychologists would agree that Watson's radical behaviorism was helpful to psychology then, now the pendulum has swung back at least partway toward allowing conscious experience to be a legitimate topic in experimental psychology. Even so, Watson had a lot going for his philosophical position. You can discover this for yourself by trying to prove to another person that you have a mind. For example, you might argue that you have a mind because you can think. But how can another person know what you think? You could continue your argument by stating that the discussion about whether or not you think proves that you do indeed think. However, the other person could reply that the discussion only proves you can talk. No matter what example you eventually come up with to prove that you have a mind, the other person can always reply that the only direct evidence you have offered depends on your behavior. Without behavior, there is no direct way to prove you have a mind. So, if mind cannot be studied directly, but can only be inferred from behavior, why not eliminate the middleman and only study behavior?

Watson's monistic position had the great advantage of being a very workable solution to the mind-body problem. Although a philosopher might be reluctant to accept it, psychology forged ahead by studying behavior and ignoring mind. Even today Watson's influence is indelibly branded on contemporary psychology.

### Dualism: Mind and Body

The dualistic position that mind and body are separate entities goes back as far as Plato, who maintained that mind was more important since ideas remained long after flesh decayed. Dualism is most strongly associated with Descartes, who believed that mind and body interacted at the pineal gland located at the base of the brain. Although medical science does not currently attribute this function to the pineal gland, Descartes's philosophical position nevertheless remains strong. The psychologist Titchener maintained a version of dualism called *parallelism*. Consciousness was held to parallel activity in the central nervous system but neither consciousness nor brain activity was the cause of the other. They both just move along in a parallel fashion.

The contemporary philosopher Gilbert Ryle (1949) has argued that dualism is nothing but a logical mistake. Since the action of bodies can be well described by mechanical principles, there is a natural desire to assume that some coherent system of principles also describes the action of minds. Of course, each of us can only potentially know the workings of our own mind, with the minds of others being a privileged sanctuary. Yet we can accurately comment that another person "hopes" or "expects" or "fears" something, suggesting that we do have some access to the minds of others. This dilemma caused philosophers to take dualistic positions. Ryle argues that dualism, which he calls "the dogma of the Ghost in the Machine" is a category mistake. Such a mistake occurs when a concept is misused. Let us pretend that a rather naïve friend is visiting you. You show your friend the football stadium, the library, the psychology building, and so on. After seeing all this, your friend states, "This is all very nice, but I really wanted to see the University." Your friend has mistakenly regarded the University as a member of the same class of buildings that you have displayed, and so you must explain that the University is a superordinate category to which all the buildings belong. There is no single building that itself is the University. Similarly, there is no man who really is the Average Taxpayer and anyone who mistakenly searches for such a person will find only a confusing myth. The dualistic distinction between mind and body is exactly the same kind of category mistake that occurs when you try to find the University or the Average Taxpayer. Mind and body cannot be contrasted.

Although the philosophical implications of the mind-body problem could be discussed at even greater length, our purpose has been only to introduce this issue to you. As psychologists, we are concerned more with the psychophysical aspects of this problem than with the philosophical ones. And so we proceed to a solution of the mind-body problem, called the *identity hypothesis*, which has greatly influenced psychophysics.

### Fechner Meets the Mind-Body Problem

Gustav Fechner (see figure 5–2) believed that everything has a soul. The soul and the body are related in the same way as the inside and outside of a circle, which are opposite sides of the same line. This solution to the mind-body problem is called the identity hy-

FIGURE 5–2.
Gustav Fechner (1801–
1887), the father of
psychophysics.

pothesis, since inside and outside refer to the same identical circle. As we shall see later in this chapter, Fechner found a mathematical relationship between the magnitude of a stimulus and the psychological sensation produced by that stimulus. *Fechner's law*, as it is now called, states that psychological sensation is proportional to the logarithm of the magnitude of the physical stimulus. Fechner believed that this proved the identity hypothesis. Mind was the logarithm of body! Although this relationship was gratefully accepted by psychology, Fechner did not have much influence in philosophy, and the identity hypothesis is not now highly regarded as a solution to the mind-body problem. But Fechner's contribution held an important place in the beginnings of experimental psychology.

## INTRODUCING THE VARIABLES IN PSYCHOPHYSICAL RESEARCH

### Dependent Variables

Observers in psychophysical studies are asked to make one of two kinds of judgment about stimuli that were presented. If only one stimulus had been presented on a particular trial, an absolute judgment is required. Absolute judgments can be simple statements about the presence or absence of a signal (Yes, I saw it, or No, I didn't) or

*(continued on next page)*

*Variables—continued*

direct estimates about some property of the stimulus (How many grams does this weigh?). If two stimuli must be compared on a particular trial, a relative judgment is required. Again, simple statements, like stimulus *A* is a larger than (or smaller than) stimulus *B*, can be made; or direct estimates, like stimulus *A* is twice as large as stimulus *B*, can be given.

### Independent Variables

The major independent variables manipulated in psychophysical studies are either the magnitude or quality of stimuli. Changing the intensity—the physical correlate of loudness—of a tone would be a manipulation of stimulus magnitude, as would be changing the weight of an object or the concentration of an odor. The frequency—the physical correlate of pitch— of a tone would be manipulated to produce a qualitative change in the stimulus. Other qualitative judgments could require that observers compare various foods (do you prefer spinach or turnips?) or the styles of different musical groups (Cat Stevens versus the Beatles).

### Control Variables

The main thing to be controlled in a psychophysical experiment is the observer's frame of mind about his or her judgment. It is important that this attitude remain constant from trial to trial. An observer who is very willing to make a positive judgment (Yes, I saw it) should maintain this same willingness over the course of an experiment. Classical or traditional psychophysics assumed that observers could accomplish this without too much difficulty. Once an observer was trained, attitude was supposedly controlled. Modern psychophysical theories, such as the theory of signal detection (to be discussed later), do not accept this assumption. They assume that the observer makes a response based on a decision that depends both on the stimulus and on psychological factors involved, such as the relative costs and benefits of the decision. So, as will be detailed later, modern psychophysical methods incorporate special techniques to guarantee (or at least to test) the assumption that the observer maintains a constant strategy.

---

## 5.1

### EXPERIMENTAL TOPICS AND RESEARCH ILLUSTRATIONS

**Topic:** Operational Definition

**Illustration:** Thresholds

---

No serious discussion, scientific, or otherwise, can progress very far unless the participants agree to define the terms they are using. Imagine that you and your date are having a friendly argument about who is the best athlete of the year. How do you define athlete? You both would agree about such common sports as tennis, swimming, and gymnastics. But what about more esoteric sports like frisbee throwing, hang-gliding, and hopping cross-country on a pogo stick? Should practitioners of these activities be considered for your athlete-of-the-year award? Until this question of definition is answered, your discussion may just go around in circles.

Similar problems can arise in scientific discussions. Let us imagine that scientists in psychophysical laboratories in West Lafayette, Indiana and Clayton Corners, Arkansas are studying tail-flicking responses to flashes of light in the horseshoe crab. One laboratory finds that its crabs give tremendous tail flicks, while another lab finds that its crabs hardly move their tails at all. The scientists are very concerned and exchange terse letters and autographed pictures of their respective crabs. Eventually the reason for the discrepancy is discovered. They were each defining the flash of light differently, since their flashes were of different durations, even though the brightness of the two flashes was similar. When they adjusted their flashes to be the same, both labs obtained the same results. This example is a little farfetched since, as we all know, crabs cannot autograph their pictures. Furthermore, all good psychophysicists know the importance of defining the stimulus exactly, so this confusion would probably not have occurred in the first place. But this example does show what *could* happen if scientists were not very careful about defining their terms.

Although social conversation and scientific discourse both require definitions, the requirements for scientific definition are more stringent. Terms that are perfectly adequate for ordinary conversation are most often too vague for scientific purposes. When you state that someone has a pleasant personality, other people have a good enough idea of what you mean so that a need for better definition does not arise. But when a psychologist uses the term *personality* in a technical sense, a great deal of precision is necessary. This important distinction between *technical* usage and *common* usage occurs frequently in psychology. It is all too easy to slip and use technical language imprecisely. Words like information, anxiety, and threshold have broad everyday meanings that must be precisely limited when they are used in a technical sense. The most common way of providing such technical meaning is by way of an *operational definition*.

An operational definition is a formula for building a construct in a way that other scientists can duplicate. "Take the eye of a newt, the leg of a frog, three oyster shells and shake twice" is an operational definition, although it is not entirely clear what is being defined. However, this recipe can be duplicated and so meets the major criterion for an operational definition. You can tell from this example that an operational definition does not have to make any sense, as long as it is clear and can be copied. For instance, we might operationally define a construct called *centigrams* as the product of your height in centimeters and your weight in grams. Since any scientist can easily determine the centigram score, this is a valid operational definition. Of couse, it probably could not be used for any important scientific purpose, but the potential utility of an operational definition is an issue separate from its validity.

The major virtue of operational definitions is that they help prevent us from confusing technical concepts with their equivalents in common language. We can illustrate this by referring to an experiment where participants were faced with two rows of ten lights and one row of ten buttons (Morin and Grant, 1955), as shown in figure 5–3. A stimulus lamp went on and a correct button press would extinguish it and present the next stimulus lamp, and so forth. This would be a simple task if each light were connected to the button directly underneath it. However, lights and buttons were haphazardly joined. This was why the top row of feedback lights was used. Pressing any button lit up a feedback light showing which stimulus light (that is, the one directly below the feedback light) was controlled by that button. After several days of practice, participants were tested to see if they had learned the light-button relationships. All participants could correctly draw a diagram linking lights and buttons, so the experimenters disconnected the feedback lights. The time taken to press the buttons went up dramatically. A similar effect occurs when you learn to operate a typewriter. It does not take long before you are able to diagram the relationship between keys and letters. But even though you know where each letter can be found on the keyboard, it takes a fair amount of practice until you can type equally well with eyes open or closed. This seems like a contradiction. On the one hand, being able to draw the diagram correctly is evidence that the light-button relationships had been learned. On the other hand, the increase in time is evidence that the relationships were not learned.

This apparent contradiction stems from using the term *learning* in its common-language sense. But technically, learning can never be observed directly. Instead, it is inferred from a change in behavior—that is, we need at least two measures of behavior before we can state that learning occurred. In the light-button experiment, one measure of learning was the decrease in time needed to press the buttons with succeeding days of practice. However, these data occurred with the row of feedback light connected, so that a reversal (an increase in time required) when conditions are changed by removing feedback lights is not really astonishing. The other measure of learning—drawing a diagram—assumes that no one

FIGURE 5–3.

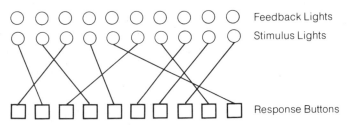

Stimulus lights and response buttons are not connected in any obvious relationship. For example, pressing the leftmost response button does not control the leftmost light, but instead turns off the third light from the left (after Morin & Grant, 1955).

could do this before the start of the experiment, since participants would have had no experience with the arbitrary connections between lights and buttons. So there was no need to obtain two drawings (before and after) and only one (after) was requested. This showed learning. Note that the two operational definitions of learning are quite different. The first uses time as a measure, whereas the second uses ability to draw a diagram. Since these definitions differ, it should not be odd that the results of two different measures of learning also differ. Our confusion arises from the common-language habit of calling both of these measures indices of learning. Since they have separate operational definitions, it would be better to call them by different names, for example, learning (time) and learning (drawing). Thus, measurement of any process that cannot be directly observed, but must instead be inferred, should be tied to operational definitions.

The difficulty with having a few dozen varieties of learning, each with its own operational definition, is that so many definitions can make it difficult to get any kind of theoretical integration. There is considerable economy or parsimony in having to discuss only one kind of learning. Psychology, like any science, strives for general concepts that unify data. From this viewpoint, undue preoccupation with operational definition might seem to be pushing us in the wrong direction. The solution is to seek operational definitions that come together upon common theoretical constructs. This notion of converging operations is so important that it is covered as a topic in its own right (see chapter 14). Since giving up operational definition entirely, as some philosophers of science have suggested, is too risky—it would lead to difficulties as in the earlier example of the light flashes and horseshoe crabs—we must instead aim for a theoretical framework that pulls our operational definitions together.

In the following sections we will discuss the operational definition of a theoretical construct called a *threshold*. First we will give the common-language meaning of this term and then see how attempts at increasing the precision of definition have led to rather sophisticated methodological techniques to improve the operational definitions of a threshold.

***Thresholds: Classical psychophysics.*** In common language a threshold is the part of a doorway you step through or over to enter a room. Classical psychophysicists believed that stimuli had to cross such a (hypothetical) barrier to enter the brain or the mind. If a stimulus were strong it could easily jump over the threshold. A crude analogy that may be helpful is to think of the stimulus as a pole vaulter. The bar corresponds to the threshold. A good jump will put you over the bar (across the threshold), whereas a feeble jump will not. The obvious question, then, is how strong a stimulus was necessary for a signal to cross the threshold. Answering this question was a major concern of classical psychophysics.

At first, the answer may seem obvious. All we have to do is slowly increase the intensity of a stimulus, such as a tone or a dim light, until the observer responds, "Yes, there it is." Unfortunately, if we try to repeat this process, the point at which an observer suddenly detects the stimulus changes from trial to trial. To deal with this variability, classical psychophysicists developed statistical methods to estimate the best value for the threshold. We will briefly discuss only one such method, invented by Fechner, known as the *method of limits.*

If we performed an experiment using the method of limits to determine the threshold for a tone, results would look like those shown in table 5–1. Each column represents data from one block of trials. The first block starts with a clearly audible tone to which the observer responds Yes. The tone intensity is lowered in successive steps until the observer reports No, thus ending that trial block. The next block of trials starts with an intensity so low that the observer cannot hear the tone and responds No. On successive trials the intensity is gradually increased until the observer reports hearing the tone. This process of alternating trial blocks continues until table 5–1 is complete. Each block is started at a different intensity to avoid extra cues that might mislead the observer.

If the observer were a perfect stimulus detector, the point at which responses switch from Yes to No (or vice versa) should always be the same. This ideal point would be the threshold. Stimuli less intense than this value would never be detected and stimuli that were greater

---

**TABLE 5–1**     Using the Method of Limits to Determine an Absolute Threshold

| Stimulus Intensity | Response | | | | |
|---|---|---|---|---|---|
| | ↓ | | ↓ | | |
| 200 | | | Yes | | |
| 180 | Yes | | Yes | | |
| 160 | Yes | | Yes | | |
| 140 | Yes | Yes | Yes | | |
| 120 | Yes | No | No | Yes | |
| 100 | Yes | No | | No | |
| 80 | No | No | | No | |
| 60 | | No | | No | |
| 40 | | No | | ↑ | |
| 20 | | No | | | |
| | | ↑ | | | Mean |
| Threshold | 90 | 130 | 130 | 110 | 115 |

Note: In the first series of trials the experimenter starts with a strong stimulus and decreases its intensity until the observer can no longer detect it. The threshold is the mean of the stimulus intensities that yielded the first "no" response and the last "yes" response. In the next series of trials a weak stimulus was increased in intensity until it was detected. It is customary to start each series at a different stimulus intensity to make it less likely that the observer's responses will be influenced by the length of a series. Stimuli are in arbitrary units—that is, the intensities ranging from 20 to 200 could represent weight or anything else that might vary in intensity.

or equal to this ideal threshold would always be detected. Unfortunately, real data from real people do not have this ideal characteristic and instead look like the data in table 5–1.

Observers are influenced by their expectations as to when it is time to change their response from Yes to No, or vice versa. For example, if a series requires several Yes responses before the threshold is reached, some observers may decide that they are giving too many Yes responses and prematurely respond No. Other observers may be very cautious about changing their responses and so may delay too long. Indeed, the same observer at different times may commit both of these kinds of errors. So the threshold is operationally defined as the mean (average) of the points in each trial block where the observer switches from Yes to No (or No to Yes). This is, of course, a statistical definition. A threshold defined this way, based on an observer's ability to detect a signal, is called an *absolute threshold* since the Yes-No judgments are not based on a comparison of two stimuli, but instead are absolute judgments about a single stimulus.

Since the absolute threshold is a statistical concept, much like the Average Taxpayer, it has other statistical properties in addition to the mean. These will now be illustrated by computing a *difference threshold* in table 5–2. Difference thresholds are based on

Using the Method of Limits to Determine a Difference Threshold — TABLE 5–2

| | Comparison Stimulus (grams) | Response | | | | |
|---|---|---|---|---|---|---|
| | | ↓ | | ↓ | | |
| | 400 | | | | | |
| | 380 | | | Heavier | | |
| | 360 | Heavier | | Heavier | | |
| | 340 | Heavier | | Heavier | | |
| | 320 | Heavier | | Equal | Heavier | |
| Standard stimulus } | 300 | Equal | Heavier | Equal | Equal | |
| | 280 | Equal | Equal | Equal | Equal | |
| | 260 | Lighter | Equal | Lighter | Lighter | |
| | 240 | | Equal | | Lighter | |
| | 220 | | Ligher | | | |
| | 200 | | Lighter | | | |
| | | ↑ | | ↑ | | Mean |
| Upper Threshold | | 310 | 290 | 330 | 310 | 310 |
| Lower Threshold | | 270 | 230 | 270 | 270 | 260 |
| | Interval of Uncertainty = 310 − 260 = 50 grams | | | | | |

Note: For descending series, the upper threshold is the mean of stimulus values corresponding to the last "Heavier" response and the first "Equal" response. The lower threshold is the mean of the last "Equal" response and the first "Lighter" response. The standard stimulus is always 300 grams.

relative judgments, where a constant unchanging comparison stimulus is judged relative to a series of changing stimuli. The question being asked by the experimenter is how different must two stimuli be before they can be reliably distinguished?

The traditional example of a difference threshold requires the observer to lift pairs of weights, one of which is always the same, and to judge if the new weight is heavier, lighter, or equal to the standard weight. Several series of ascending and descending trials are given. The upper threshold is the average point at which the observer changes from "Heavier" responses to "Equal" responses. The lower threshold is the point where "Equal" responses give way to "Lighter" responses. The difference between these two values is called the *interval of uncertainty*. The difference threshold is operationally defined as half the interval of uncertainty. In table 5–2 this equals 25 grams. The mean of upper and lower thresholds is called the *point of subjective equality* (285 grams in table 5–2).

You may feel that the method of limits is quite inefficient, since each column in table 5–1 contains many successive responses (either Yes or No) that do not change. A newer version of the method of limits, called the *staircase method*, (Cornsweet, 1962) concentrates responses around the threshold. For the first trial, it is similar to the method of limits. However, once an estimate of the threshold is obtained, the staircase method never presents stimuli that are far from this estimate. This is shown in table 5–3. As soon as the threshold estimate is crossed, the direction of stimulus intensity reverses. This improves the efficiency of the method by keeping the stimuli much closer to the threshold than is the case for the method of limits. The threshold is calculated as the mean value of all stimuli presented, starting with the second trial (column 2 in table 5–3).

From the time of Fechner until about twenty years ago, the method of limits was a major psychophysical technique. But a new development, called the *theory of signal detection*, has now become the dominant psychophysical method. In an exciting contradiction

| TABLE 5–3 | Using the Staircase Method to Determine an Absolute Threshold | | | | |
|---|---|---|---|---|---|
| *Stimulus Intensity* | | | | | *Response* |
| | ↓ | | | | |
| 180 | Yes | | | | |
| 160 | Yes | | | | |
| 140 | Yes | Yes | ↓ | Yes | |
| 120 | Yes | No | No | ↑ | |
| 100 | Yes | No | | | |
| 80 | No | ↑ | | | |
| | Threshold = 124 | | | | |

to earlier work, signal-detection theory denies the very concept of a threshold.

***No thresholds: The theory of signal detection.*** According to signal-detection theory, perception in general is controlled by two basic internal processes. Arrival of a signal or stimulus at a receptor creates a (hypothetical) sensory impression that on the average is dependent on the intensity of the signal. But this impression is not sufficient to cause a Yes response even for strong signals. Instead, the magnitude of this sensory impression is evaluated by a subsequent decision process. In order for an observer to report sensing a signal, both sensory and decision processes must be involved. We will first discuss the decision process since it is easier to understand.

Any decision you make is dependent on the costs and benefits associated with it. Imagine that a friend has set up a blind date for you. The costs (a wasted evening) are probably less than the possible benefits (an exciting evening now and more exciting evenings in the future), so many of us would accept a blind date even though we know nothing about the person we will be dating. So we are likely to respond Yes, and this decision is based mostly on costs and benefits, since we lack information about the stimulus (the person who is our date). Now let us imagine a situation where costs are high: accepting or offering a proposal of marriage. Even those of us who are eager to accept a blind date would not get married if we were offered only information needed to help us decide whether to go on a blind date. The costs of an unsatisfactory marriage are much greater than of a blind date that does not pan out. In terms of decision theory, we are conservative decision makers when considering marriage, but liberal decision makers when considering a blind date. This decision bias does not depend on the stimulus, indeed the same person could be involved in both instances, but only on the costs and benefits of our decision.

Now we can return to the sensory end (beginning) of signal detection. The sensory process transmits a value to the decision process. If this value is high, the decision process is more likely to yield a Yes response, once costs and benefits have been considered. If this value is low, the decision process is more likely to yield a No response, even if costs and benefits favor a Yes decision. How does the sensory process find a value to send?

Signal-detection theory assumes that *noise*, a random disturbance that can be confused with signals, is always present inside the human. (Just to make sure this assumption holds a typical signal-detection experiment will present white noise—a hissing sound you can hear by turning your television to an unoccupied channel—along with the signal.) Noise can be auditory or visual (see figure 5–4) or indeed can occur in any modality, but we will consider only the auditory system for now. Imagine you are sitting in a soundproof booth wearing headphones. On each trial you must

FIGURE 5–4.

Noise can make it difficult to detect a signal.

decide whether you heard a faint tone combined with white noise or only the noise by itself. Signal-detection theory assumes that any stimulus, even noise, produces a distribution of sensory impressions. Of course, the sensory impression on each trial is only one point and the distributions are built up from many sensory impressions, each occurring at a different point in time (see discussion of distributions in the appendix A). Since sensory impressions cannot be directly observed, the distributions for stimulus trials and for noise trials are hypothetical. The sensory impression arising from a trial for which only noise occurred will tend to be small, so that over many trials a (hypothetical) distribution with a small mean will be established. When a signal plus noise is presented, the sensory impression will be larger, so that a distribution with a greater mean will be formed over many trials.

Repeated trials generate two distributions—one for noise only and one for the signal plus noise—like those shown in figure 5–5. Since the two distributions overlap in the middle, some values of sensory impression are ambiguous, because they could have occurred as a result of noise or the signal. Of course, if the two distributions were far enough apart, this problem would be minimized, but even in the laboratory life is usually not that simple. A criterion, shown as a vertical line in figure 5–5, must be set to determine whether a response will be Yes or No. The position of this criterion is set by the decision process. If costs and benefits favor a liberal decision policy, the criterion will be set far to the left so that most responses will be Yes. If a conservative policy is used, the criterion moves to the right so that most responses will be No. In either case, some errors will be made.

Correctly detecting a signal when it is presented is called a *hit*. Incorrectly responding Yes when only noise is presented is called a *false alarm*. With a liberal decision strategy—criterion set to the left—hits will be high, but so will false alarms. With a conservative

FIGURE 5–5.

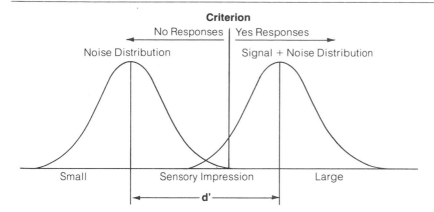

Hypothetical distributions along a sensory continuum. Once a particular sensory impression occurs, the criterion determines if a Yes or No response will be made. Large impressions to the right of the criterion lead to Yes responses, while small impressions lead to No responses. The distance between the means of the two distributions is called *d*'.

decision strategy, false alarms will be low but so will hits. If we plot hits as a function of false alarms, as the criterion moves from conservative to liberal we get the representation depicted in figure 5–6. This figure is called a *receiver-operating characteristic* (or ROC) function. Both hits and false alarms are infrequent (conservative criterion) at the lower left of the curve. As the criterion becomes more liberal, hits and false alarms become more likely and the ROC curve moves upward to the right. The slope of (a tangent drawn to) the ROC function tells us the criterion. Flat slopes reveal a liberal-decision criterion and steep slopes a conservative criterion. The distance from the diagonal to the ROC curve tells us how far apart the noise and signal-plus-noise distributions of figure 5–5 lie. When they are far apart, the ROC function moves upward to the left, away from the diagonal. When they are close together, it moves toward the diagonal. So the ROC functions tells us about both the sensory process (distance between signal-plus-noise and noise-only distributions) and the decision process (slope). Of course any experimental condition only generates a single point on the ROC function, so that many trials are required to map out the entire curve.

By now you may be wondering what all this has to do with thresholds. Nowhere does the ROC function have a label saying this is the threshold. And this is the point of signal-detection theory. Whether an observer will respond Yes or No depends on the sensory impression *and* the decision criterion. There is no operational definition of a threshold. Instead, two quantities are operationally defined.

The sensitivity of the observer is called d' and is defined as the distance between signal and noise distributions in figure 5–5. The

FIGURE 5–6.

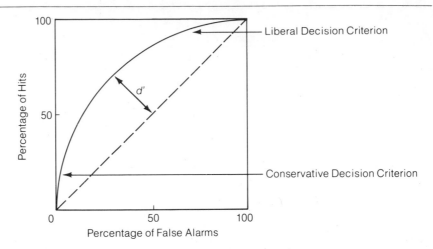

A Receiver Operating Characteristic. The distance from the diagonal to the center of the curve is proportional to d'. The diagonal represents chance performance with the observer guessing about the presence or absence of a signal. Thus, the percentage of hits equals the percentage of false alarms along this "guessing" diagonal.

FIGURE 5–7.

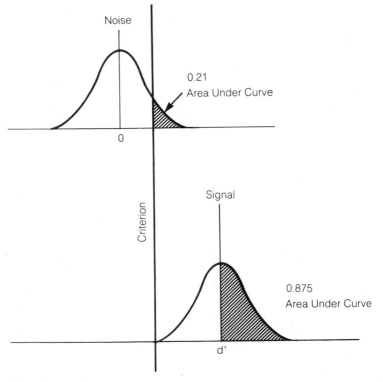

Calculating d'.

criterion of the decision process is called *beta* and is the slope of the ROC function at the point of interest, for example, a hit rate of 55 percent. Together these *two* quantities determine what a classical psychophysicist would call a threshold.

***Calculating d'.*** Given a set of data, we can easily calculate $d'$ by using tables based on the area under the normal curve. Suppose you know that the hit rate is .875 and the false-alarm rate is .21. What is $d'$? First, draw the noise distribution as in figure 5–7. Since the false-alarm rate represents the area under the curve from the criterion to plus infinity on the right, it equals .21. Since the normal curve is symmetrical, half of its area (.5) lies between zero and plus infinity. Therefore, the area between zero and the criterion must be .5 − .21, which equals .29. Now look up .29 in the normal table (table 5–4). You will find that $t = .8$. This is the normalized distance of the criterion from zero.

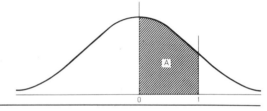

Tabled Values of the Normal Curve                                          TABLE 5–4

| t | Area (from 0 to t) |
| --- | --- |
| 0 | 0 |
| 0.1 | .039 |
| 0.2 | .079 |
| 0.3 | .118 |
| 0.4 | .155 |
| 0.5 | .192 |
| 0.6 | .226 |
| 0.7 | .258 |
| 0.8 | .288 |
| 0.9 | .316 |
| 1.0 | .341 |
| 1.1 | .364 |
| 1.2 | .385 |
| 1.3 | .403 |
| 1.4 | .419 |
| 1.5 | .433 |
| 1.6 | .445 |
| 1.7 | .455 |
| 1.8 | .464 |
| 1.9 | .471 |
| 2.0 | .477 |
| 2.1 | .482 |
| 2.2 | .486 |
| 2.3 | .489 |
| 2.4 | .492 |
| 2.5 | .494 |

(From Kantowitz and Sorkin, 1983)

FIGURE 5–8.

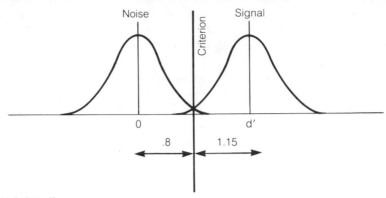

Calculating d'.

Second, we repeat this process for the signal distribution shown in the bottom of figure 5–7. Since the hit rate is .875, this is the area under the curve from the criterion to plus infinity. Again, because of symmetry half the area under the curve (.5) is between $d'$ and plus infinity. Therefore, the area between the criterion and $d'$ is .875 − .5, which equals .375. Consulting table 5–4, we find that an area of .375 corresponds to a $t$ of about 1.15.

We can now put these two $t$ values together to find $d'$ (see figure 5–8). Since the mean of the noise distribution is given the value of zero, $d'$ is the sum of the two $t$ values: 0.8 + 1.15 = 1.95. Our calculation of $d'$ is now complete.

## 5.2
### EXPERIMENTAL TOPICS AND RESEARCH ILLUSTRATIONS

**Topic:** Measurement Scales

**Illustration:** Fechner's Law

It is a dictum in psychophysics that anything that exists, be it jelly beans or your attitude toward spinach, exists in some amount. And anything that exists in some amount can be measured. Measurement is a systematic way of assigning numbers to objects. But not all measurement systems are equivalent. In particular, different scale types result from different measurement operations. A scale type is mathematically defined (Suppes and Zinnes, 1963) by its uniqueness—that is, the kinds of transformations, such as adding a constant or multiplying by a constant and so forth, that can be performed without altering the unique mathematical properties of the scale. Psychologists are most concerned with four types of scales called *nominal, ordinal, interval,* and *ratio,* although other types also exist. These four scale types have been listed according to increasing power of measurement, with each successive scale type having the properties of preceding types plus other new ones. This means, for example, that data obtained using a ratio scale of measurement could be analyzed by methods appropriate to any of the three lesser scales. However, methods of analysis appropriate only for a ratio scale would not fit the other scales.

It is interesting that the simplest measurement operation (counting) produces the highest scale type (ratio). A *ratio scale* remains unique if all the scale numbers are multiplied by a constant. Any other arithmetic operation destroys the ratio properties of the scale. The easiest way for you to tell whether a scale has ratio properties is to look for two characteristics. First, the scale has a real zero corresponding to no objects or none of the scale property. A physical scale that satisfies this condition is weight in grams. Zero grams truly means no weight. The second characteristic of the ratio scale, from which its name derives, is that ratios of scale values make sense. Thus, a ten-gram weight has the same relationship to a five-gram weight as a twenty-four-gram weight has to a twelve-gram weight, since the ratio of two weights is 2.0 in both cases.

An *interval scale* is unchanged if a constant is added or if scale values are multiplied by a constant. In an interval scale there is no real zero, and although distances between adjacent scale numbers are equal, the actual size of the interval is not very important. Ratios of pairs of scale values are not meaningful. Fahrenheit and Centigrade are interval scales. Although the zero value will change depending on whether Fahrenheit or Centigrade scale units are chosen, the distance between adjacent units is equal. A temperature increase from 34° to 35° produces the same change as an increase from 35° to 36° (on either scale).

An *ordinal scale* is unchanged by any monotonic (steadily increasing or decreasing) operation, such as taking the square root, adding or multiplying by a constant, or taking a logarithm. It lacks an absolute zero, and the distances between adjacent scale values are unequal. This scale type is achieved most often by asking people to rank order a set of objects, for example, to list all their friends of the opposite sex according to attractiveness. If $Person_1$ is the most attractive, $Person_2$ the next most, and so on, the difference in attractiveness between adjacent persons changes as we go down the list.

A *nominal scale* is the weakest type of measurement, since it merely sorts objects into different categories. Just about any arithmetic transformation can be used without changing the scale properties, as long as objects are not pulled out of one bin and pushed into another. Numbers on an athlete's jersey represent nominal measurement since all they do is identify particular individuals without telling you anything about them. (For that you need a scorecard.) It would be silly to add the numbers that two athletes are wearing and expect the result to be meaningful. Sex is also a nominal measurement, since all individuals can be classified into one of two categories: male or female.

***Fechner's law: Defining an interval scale.*** According to *Weber's law*, the difference threshold is a constant (see Psychology in Action section at end of chapter). Fechner took this as his starting point and by adding one crucial assumption was able to formulate a law that he thought uncovered the fundamental relationship between mind and body. Fechner assumed that all *just-noticeable differences* (difference thresholds) represented equal intervals along an internal psychological scale (figure 5–9). The zero point of the psychological scale corresponds to the absolute threshold. The next step on the scale corresponds to the physical stimulus that is one just-noticeable difference above the absolute threshold. The following point will be one just-noticeable difference above that, or two just-noticeable differences above the absolute threshold. This process can be continued to build a psychological scale. Once this is done there is a fixed mathematical relationship between the value of the physical scale corresponding to some point on the psychological scale and the physical value corresponding to the preceding point on the internal psychological scale. In order to find the physical-scale value that corresponds to the next highest phychological value, we must first take the physical size of the last step on the external scale (*x* in figure 5–9) and multiply it by the Weber fraction. Then we add this product to our original value (*x* plus *x* times Weber fraction in figure 5–9). This sum gives us the physical value that corresponds to the next just-noticeable difference on the internal psychological scale. When this relationship is expanded and solved mathematically, we find that the psychological-scale value (ψ) is proportional to the logarithm of the physical-stimulus value. This equation (ψ = *K* log stimulus) is called Fechner's law.

***Steven's power law: Direct scaling methods.*** Fechner's law uses an *indirect* scaling method because the psychological scale is built up by putting successive just-noticeable differences in a row. Thus, the psychological-scale values are derived—and therefore are in-

FIGURE 5–9.

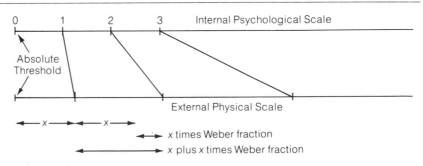

Fechner's Law. Equal units on an internal psychological scale correspond to progressively greater units on an external physical scale. Each psychological scale division corresponds to one just noticeable difference on the physical scale.

direct—from measures of discrimination. A *direct* scaling technique has the observer respond in psychological-scale units in the first place, so that scale values need not be calculated from something else.

The method of *magnitude estimation* requires that the observer state a number which represents the intensity of a stimulus. The first stimulus that the experimenter presents is arbitrarily assigned some convenient number, say, 100. Then other stimuli get their numbers, depending on how close the perceived intensity is to the first stimulus. For example, the experimenter could present a tone of moderate intensity and tell you it has a value of 100. Then a weaker tone might be presented. So you would give it a lower number, say 87. These numbers reported by the observer represent perceived psychological values directly. When data are gathered in this way, the equation relating psychological value to physical value differs from the logarithmic relationship of Fechner's law. Instead, the equation obtained by Stevens (1961) is $\psi = k$ (Stimulus)$^n$, where $n$ is an exponent. This equation is called *Steven's power law* (power is another term for exponent).

The method of magnitude estimation is not limited to psychological scales that have a physical correlate. Essay exams are often graded by this method. Similarly, legal penalties, severity of crimes, works of art, and so forth, can be scaled by magnitude estimation.

There is some debate as to what the observer is really reporting in the method of magnitude estimation. This is part of a larger debate about the nature of phenomenological reports in general (see chapter 6). The controversy centers on whether observers report the intensity of sensation as claimed by Stevens, or instead report a learned association based on a correlation with a physical attribute linked to the stimulus—such that, for example, judgments of loudness reflect your experience that softer sounds are further away from you (Warren, 1963).

---

**5.3**
**EXPERIMENTAL TOPICS AND RESEARCH OF ILLUSTRATIONS**

**Topic:** *Small n Design*

**Illustration:** *Psychophysical Methods*

---

Unlike in most other areas of psychology, in psychophysical research only small numbers of observers (subjects) are used. Experimental control replaces statistical control as a method for reducing error variance and for increasing the reliability of data. When an experiment is complicated with many uncontrolled sources of variance as in, say, a field experiment in social or environmental psychology (see Chapters 13 and 14), it is unlikely that the same results will be obtained when the experiment is repeated, even with the same subject. But psychophysical techniques are characterized by extremely fine control of the experimental situation.

The same results can be obtained again and again. For example, if an observer returns to the laboratory and the experimenter uses the same conditions in a repeat experiment, the same ROC function should be obtained. Because the ROC function is so precisely replicated, there is little need for the more complex statistical operations, like analysis of variance. It is simpler and more elegant to manipulate independent variables directly and to replicate previous data precisely.

An example of the precise control possible in psychophysical experiments is shown in figures 5–10 and 5–11. The same observer has generated both ROC functions. In figure 5–10 the probability that a stimulus, rather than noise only, would be presented was varied from low to high. When signal probability is low, the observer acts like a conservative decision maker, since it is not likely that on any given trial a signal had been presented. As signal probability increases, the observer becomes more liberal, since the odds in favor of a signal trial are better. This change in the decision criterion—from conservative to liberal—sweeps out the ROC function in figure 5–10, starting from the lower left and moving along the curve to the upper right.

To generate the ROC function of figure 5–11, the experimenter kept the signal probability constant and varied the pay off. This manipulation also affects the decision process. When the cost of false alarms is high relative to the cost of hits, the observer is conservative. As the relative cost of false alarms decreases, the

FIGURE 5–10.

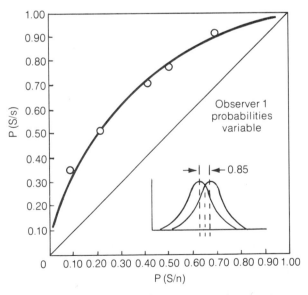

ROC graph obtained by varying signal probability. The insert shows hypothetical noise and signal plus noise distributions (data from Green & Swets, 1966).

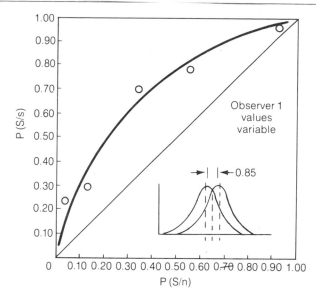

ROC graph from the same observer as above but obtained by varying the values of the
decision outcomes and holding signal probability constant at 0.5. Notice how closely the
two functions agree (data from Green & Swets, 1966).

FIGURE 5–11.

observer becomes more willing to respond "signal" and adopts a
liberal-decision criterion.

The insert in both figures shows the hypothetical noise and signal-plus-noise distributions. Both curves are well fitted by a $d'$
equal to .85—that is, the solid curve passes close to the actual data
points. This exact fit is even more impressive when we stop to
realize that the two ROC functions were generated in slightly different ways: two different operations were used to vary the decision
criterion. The extreme similarity of the two ROC functions shows
a high degree of experimental control.

Psychophysical experiments needs thousands of trials even though
a small number of observers is used. The total effort—number of
trials times number of observers—in psychophysical experiments
often exceeds that of less controlled experiments, so that using a
small number (n) of subjects is not an economy to lessen overall
experimental effort, or a cheap way to avoid the terrors of statistics.
Indeed, the psychophysicist does use very refined statistical techniques based on fitting psychophysical models rather than analysis
of variance.

By now you may be wondering whether it is better to use large
numbers of subjects and analysis of variance or small numbers
with lots of trials. There is no absolute answer to this question.
But most psychologists prefer experimental control to after-the-
fact statistical control. The greater the degree of experimental control, the less the need for analysis of variance. Instead, other sta-

tistics (like parameter estimation) are used to fit exact theoretical models. (Sorry, but you cannot avoid some kind of statistics in psychology.) Most of the time, though, experimental control is not as good as we would wish, so that we are forced to use inferential statistics. Whenever precise replication cannot be achieved at will, inferential statistics will be needed. When a finding can be consistently repeated with the same subject by returning to a given setting of an independent variable (after a different setting has intervened), the need for standard inferential statistics (described in appendix A) is not great.

---

**FROM PROBLEM TO EXPERIMENT: THE NUTS AND BOLTS**          **Problem:** Do pigeon's have visual thresholds?

**Problem:** How can we measure a pigeon's visual threshold?

Since this problem is based more on methodology than content, we do not require much in the way of a formal hypothesis. Content issues would arise once the feasibility of measuring a pigeon's visual threshold was first established. Primarily for the sake of completeness we offer the following hypothesis.

**Hypothesis:** As wavelength (color) of light is varied, the pigeon's visual thresholds will change in a manner similar to the human's.

The first problem we must overcome is obvious: pigeons cannot talk. So we give our pigeon-observer two response keys to peck at: one for "Yes, I see it" and the other for "No, I don't." Our dependent variable is the absolute threshold defined as it was for humans earlier in the chapter. Our independent variable is light color, and control variables will be the reinforcement schedules used to maintain pecking behavior. This deserves discussion. We want to reward the Yes key when the stimulus is visible, and the No key when it is not. But we have no way of determining just from looking at the stimulus whether it is visible to the pigeon.

One solution (Blough, 1961) hinges on the certainty that the stimulus will be invisible when it is turned off. Pecking the No key was rewarded when the stimulus was off. The disappearance of the light spot signaled the pigeon to peck the No key. According to principles of conditioning, this makes the disappearance a secondary reinforcer just like the click of a food dispenser. When the stimulus really is present the pigeon will peck the Yes key in order to turn off the light. Then it pecks the No key and gets rewarded. This solves our problem and makes it possible to determine visual thresholds for the pigeon.

**SUMMARY**

**1.** The relationship between mind and body has puzzled philosophers for ages. Monism claims that one is predominant, whereas dualism claims that both are important. Gustav Fechner produced psychophysics in an attempt to resolve the mind-body problem by showing that mental representation is the logarithm of physical experience.

**2.** Operational definitions are required in science both to make experiments more public and to increase the precision of technical terms beyond their use in ordinary conversation. The method of limits gives an operational definition for the concept of threshold. Classical psychophysics was largely aimed at evaluating thresholds. The more modern theory of signal detection denies the threshold concept and replaces it with two other operationally defined constructs: $d'$ and beta. Beta is a measure of the decision-making process and $d'$ an index of a sensory process. Both $d'$ and beta can be computed from ROC (receiver-operating characteristics) functions that plot hits against false alarms.

**3.** Measurement scales result when numbers are assigned systematically to objects. Psychologists deal most often with nominal, ordinal, interval, and ratio scale types. Only certain kinds of data analysis and scale transformations are appropriate for each scale type. Fechner's law is based on the assumption of interval scaling along an internal psychological continuum.

**4.** Psychophysical experiments often use only small numbers of observers, in contrast to most areas of psychology, where large numbers are typical. This procedure is highly acceptable, or even preferred, because of the high degree of experimental control in psychophysical experiments, which greatly reduces error variance. Even with a single subject, the psychophysicist can manipulate an independent variable to replicate earlier results quite precisely.

**KEY TERMS**

**absolute threshold**
**beta**
**criterion**
*d'*
**difference threshold**
**dualism**
**false alarm**
**Fechner's law**
**hit**
**identity hypothesis**
**interval of uncertainty**
**interval scale**
**just-noticeable difference**
**magnitude estimation**
**measurement**
**measurement scales**

**method of limits**
**mind-body problem**
**monism**
**noise**
**nominal scale**
**operational definition**
**ordinal scale**
**point of subjective equality**
**psychophysical methods**
**ratio scale**
**receiver-operating**
  **characteristic (ROC)**
**signal-detection theory**
**staircase method**
**Stevens's law**
**threshold**
**Weber's law**

**1.** The identity hypothesis of Fechner was his solution to the mind-body problem. This philosophical approach led to Fechner's law. Contemporary psychologists prefer the theory of signal detection to classical threshold models. What philosophy of the mind-body problem is most consistent with the theory of signal detection? (Hint: Relate $d'$ and beta to the mind-body problem.)

**2.** Does the method of limits or the staircase method offer a better operational definition of the concept of a threshold, or are the two methods equivalent insofar as operational definition is concerned?

**3.** Calculate $d'$ for the following pairs of hit and false-alarm rates: (.90, .10), (.90, .25), (.90, .50), (.90, .90).

**4.** Give two examples of each kind of measurement scale.

**5.** Contrast the following experimental-design approaches: (1) use large numbers of subjects and analysis of variance, (2) use small numbers of subjects with large numbers of trials.

# Psychology in Action

## Weber's Law

For this demonstration you will need several empty cardboard milk containers, a supply of sand, gravel, lead shot, or similar material to partially fill them, and a scale. Fill one of the containers about one-eighth full and add slightly more to another container. Ask a friend to lift them and tell you which weighs more. At first your subject will teach you they are equal in weight. Keep adding material to the heavier container until your subject can tell which is heavier (Of course, you do not permit your subject to see you filling the heavier container and you randomly place the containers so that the heavier one is not always picked up with the same hand.)

Once the heavier container is determined, it becomes the new standard stimulus. Add material to a new container until it is just noticeably heavier than the standard container. Keep on repeating this procedure until the last container is almost completely filled. Now weigh each of the containers, making careful notes of the differences in weight between adjacent containers. You will find that adding a constant amount of material is not enough to produce a noticeable difference. Imagine you are holding a three-pound package. You certainly would notice if someone quietly tiptoed up and added another pound. But if you were carrying a hundred-pound load, adding another pound would go unobserved. Although $x$ amount is sufficient to distinguish the first two containers, amounts greater than $x$ are required to tell apart containers later in the series. If you have done your experiment carefully, you will find that a constant percentage of the weight of a container is required before the next container seems heavier. This percentage is called the Weber fraction. Mathematically, Weber's law can be stated as follows: the difference threshold divided by the stimulus magnitude equals a constant (the Weber fraction). Weber's law does not hold for extreme values of stimulus magnitude. Thus, if you repeated your experiment with barbells or paper clips instead of milk containers, you would not get this result. The Weber fraction also differs for different individuals and for different tasks, such as judging line length instead of weight.

# CHAPTER 6 ▬▬▬▬▬▬

## Preview

In this chapter, we shall be concerned with two topics. A *phenomenological report* occurs when an observer describes his or her perception of the environment. What safeguards are needed before the psychologist can accept a phenomenological report and rest assured that it meets the requirements of reliability, replicability, and so forth, imposed by science? *Converging operations* attempt to bolster a conclusion about a perceptual process by deliberately choosing different pathways in the hope that they all eventually lead to the same point. Imagine that you are part of a group of Scouts on a map-reading exercise. Your instructor starts each of you out in a different direction. If you arrived at the goal alone, you might doubt that you correctly followed map and compass. But if several of your companions independently arrived at the same place, you would feel more confident that "This is the place!"

## Chapter Outline

# PERCEPTION

*Discovery consists of seeing what everybody has seen and thinking what nobody has thought.*

Albert Szent-Györqyi

Perception is the psychological process whereby events in the external world are noticed and interpreted. It is the way you, the observer, bring the world outside into focus inside your head. We all tend to take perception for granted since we are so good at it. But, as we shall see, perception is a very complicated psychological process and presents special problems for those who study it.

You will recall that in chapter 1 we discussed how important it is for a scientist to remain objective and to dispassionately observe, record, and interpret data. A physicist noting the amount of deflection of a meter usually has little difficulty in accurately recording this datum without being influenced by his or her feelings or prejudices about meters in general. Not only is there no emotional involvement with the data, but the physicist also is sufficiently removed from the situation in a psychological sense so that the meter reading can be easily recorded.

This psychological distance vanishes when you are asked to report your own sensations and perceptions of the world as data in their own right. Your reaction to what looks like a purple blotch or a rotating square depends a great deal on your experience with similar kinds of perceptual objects. The interpretation you place on some set of stimuli is your own, and may or may not be shared by others. Although this may be obvious when you are considering esthetic or emotional reactions to stimuli such as works of art, it

**145**

is equally the case when you make intellectual evaluations of stimuli (Is that a tilted square or a trapezoid?). So the psychologist interested in studying perception must somehow get inside your head to share your perceptual interpretation of objects placed in the external world. This is a difficult task, but not an impossible one, and we shall examine some of the ways psychologists try to accomplish this.

Before you can appreciate the difficulties faced by the psychologist in studying perception, you must first realize how complicated your perception really is. Perception is like solving a puzzle. To create a percept you must put together many clues about the outside world. Most of the time you assemble these clues correctly, and quickly solve the puzzle. This is why you think perception is so easy. But sometimes, especially when tricky psychologists have manipulated these cues, your puzzle is assembled incorrectly, so that you perceive an inner reality that does not mirror the external stimuli. Once you understand that the arrangement of stimuli in the outside world need not correspond to the arrangement of perceived stimuli inside your head (and, of course, vice versa) you can begin to appreciate the dilemma faced by those who study perception: How can the psychologist know when your reported perception corresponds to mental impressions that have been uninfluenced by your knowledge of the world, as compared to those that have already been neatly sorted and arranged after having been filtered through the net of experience?

## ILLUSIONS: PROVING PERCEPTION CAN BE UNRELIABLE

The aim of this section is to convince you that perception is not easy, automatic, and always correct. Rather, perception is an attempt to assemble cues based on probabilities, and *not* certainties, that particular configurations of cues should belong together. Our emphasis is thus on the potential unreliability of perception, rather than on detailed psychological explanations for the illusions to be presented.

### Impossible Figures

Look at the waterfall in figure 6–1. At first, it seems to be quite ordinary. Each component of the picture is perfectly all right by itself. But as you stare at it, you soon notice that something is amiss. The parts of the figure do not go together properly. There is no start or finish to this waterfall. This illusion succeeds—that is, it causes an inaccurate perception—because of ambiguous and inconsistent cues about depth. There are many cues to depth that we have learned from experience. Relative size is one of them. All other things being equal, smaller objects are perceived as further away than larger objects. Haze is another cue to depth. Loss of

FIGURE 6–1.
A perpetual-motion
waterfall. M. C. Escher's
*Waterfall*, Escher
Foundation, Haags
Gemeentemuseum, The
Hague)

detail occurs under natural conditions when objects are far away. Photographs taken with a telephoto lens restore this missing detail and thus appear more novel than pictures taken with standard lenses (see figure 6–2).

*Size constancy* occurs when we use depth cues to allow us to take into account the distance between us and an object being perceived. An automobile you are standing next to appears about the same size as one parked down the block. Thus if you reported your perception that both cars looked about the same size, this would be an example of size constancy. This phenomenon creates serious problems for the psychologists studying perception. The image formed on the retina of your eye is far smaller for the distant car than for the nearby car. Nevertheless, your perceptual report that they look the same implies that the image on the retina should be the same for both cars. Your knowledge of the world has acted on your perception. Psychologists would prefer people to report what they see, but often people instead report what they know. We shall return to this important distinction often in this chapter, but for now we shall continue to show you that perception can be fooled.

FIGURE 6–2.

(a) A view of the town of Ålesund, Norway, taken with a wide-angle lens. This illustrates several depth cues. Haze and lack of detail become more pronounced as your gaze shifts from the foreground to the background. Perspective gives the appearance of two converging lines that come together at the two low peaks in the background. (b) The same view taken with a telephoto lens. Depth cues are minimized relative to the wide-angle photo. There is more detail and less perspective. The telephoto lens also compresses the picture, as you can see by estimating the distance from the warehouses in the foreground to the hills in the background. This distance seems greater in panel (a). © B. Kantowitz, Text-Eye)

Our last set of impossible figures includes the Freemish crate for shipping optical illusions and the endless staircase (see figure 6–3). As you study these illusions, the contradictions that result from conflicting depth cues become obvious.

Although you may feel there is something artificial about the illusions shown so far, it is important to realize that any situations where cues are ambiguous will produce errors of perception. For example, illusions have been responsible for airplane crashes (Kantowitz and Sorkin, 1983, p. 132). Examine figure 6–4. Most people lack the experience to quickly interpret this scene. It is not an illusion, but an accurate representation of a real-world scene with no trick photography. But this scene happens to be fifty feet underwater off the island of Bonnaire. It is a closeup photo of a Christmas-tree worm embedded in a coral reef. Although the illusions that psychologists study in the laboratory are specially created to highlight perceptual unreliability, it is important for you to realize that these laboratory illusions merely abstract essential components of everyday perception to help us understand how perception works outside the laboratory.

### Illusions of Perspective

Another important depth cue is perspective. A railroad track that disappears into the distance gives the impression that the two rails converge. Of course, we know that the rails remain the same distance apart—it would make it rather difficult for trains if rails did

FIGURE 6–3.

Impossible figures. The lower right hand figure is the Freemish crate, designed by Cochran. The other figures were constructed by Penrose and Penrose. The upper right-hand figure has proved so popular that it has a well-known name in psychology: it is called the endless staircase. (From Baron, Byrne, and Kantowitz, 1980).

converge—but even so the appearance of convergence remains. Artists use this depth cue of perspective to create the illusion of distance in their paintings, photographs, and other visual arts.

Psychologists have manipulated perspective to yield misleading illusions, as shown in figure 6–5. There are two possible interpretations of this figure. The face at the left is smaller, and ordinarily you would conclude that this person is farther away from you than is the larger person. But this first interpretation does not seem to hold because of constraints imposed by the wall of the room. You know that rooms are rectangular and so the two windows must be equally distant from you. Hence the second interpretation—that the person on the left must be a midget and the one on the right a giant. This is an implausible interpretation and may seem odd to you, but how else can figure 6–5 be explained?

The conflict between these two explanations can be resolved by looking at figure 6–6. The room is trapezoidal, and not rectangular as you expected. Thus the person on the left really is farther away,

FIGURE 6—4.

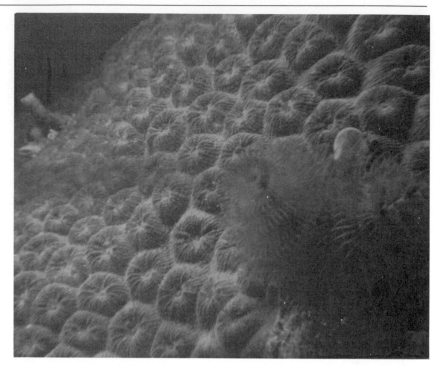

Underwater photo of a Christmas-tree worm. The body of the worm is hidden in a tube bored into the coral. The plumes of the worm gather food and oxygen. The cratered surface is a piece of coral. (© B. Kantowitz, TEXT-EYE)

FIGURE 6—5
The two men appear to be of quite different size, even though the same distance from the viewer. (From Ittelson and Kilpatrick, 1952)

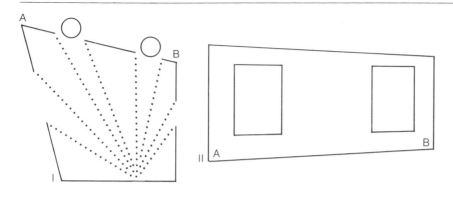

FIGURE 6–6.

Top (I) and frontal (II) views of the distorted room shown in the preceding figure.
The man on the left is really further away from the viewer and hence appears smaller
(after Bartley, 1958).

and the first interpretation is correct. Since midgets, giants, and trapezoidal rooms all are rare, figure 6–5 was difficult to interpret. But since you probably have seen more midgets and giants than trapezoidal rooms, you misinterpreted the figure by letting your knowledge govern your perception. Now that you know the room is not rectangular, look again at figure 6–5. This time imagine the wall tilting away from you, as shown in figure 6–6, with the left side much farther back than the right side. The illusion is gone— or at least weaker—because your new knowledge allows a correct, although unusual, perception of the scene.

Similar principles explain the card illusion of figure 6–7. It seems obvious that in each row the cards on the left are closest to you and the cards on the right farthest away. Even though the card on the right is largest in each row, the depth cue of overlap is more important than relative size. We know from experience that something that blocks another object must be in front of that object. Now look at figure 6–8. The cards on the right are really the closest. Once again you have been tricked because you relied on your knowledge of the world to interpret a set of stimuli. But if you go back to figure 6–7, your new knowledge is less helpful than it was in the previous example. It may still look as if the card on the right

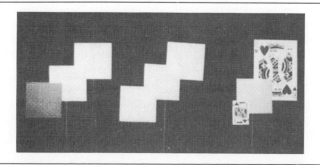

FIGURE 6–7.
Which of the three cards
in each set appears
closest? (From Ittelson
and Kilpatrick, 1952)

FIGURE 6–8.
The cards on the right are closest. Misleading cues for depth (size and overlap) have fooled you in the preceding figure (From Ittelson and Kilpatrick, 1952)

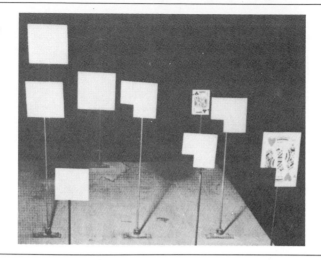

is farthest away from you. It is difficult to undo your habits of perception, even when you know for sure that you are seeing an illusion.

There are two reasons for presenting these illusions. First, you should now be convinced that seeing and believing do not necessarily coincide. Perception can be inaccurate. Second, your knowledge of the true state of the external world does not always improve perception, as was the case when you reexamined figure 6–7, and may cause misperceptions in unusual circumstances. If you yourself have difficulty deciding what you are perceiving, imagine how much trouble a psychologist might have trying to decide how to interpret your perceptual report. Are you reporting what you know should be there, what is there even if it contradicts your preconceptions about the world (for example, rooms are rectangular), or something in between? The rest of this chapter is devoted to techniques used by the experimental psychologist to unravel the puzzle of perception.

## INTRODUCING THE VARIABLES IN PERCEPTION RESEARCH

### Dependent Variables

The simplest dependent variable is the verbal description given by an observer. Although this is the easiest measure to obtain, it often has several disadvantages. An untrained observer seldom is able to give a precise report. Although this can be corrected by proper training, there is always the possibility that the training, rather than the stimulus, is controlling the observer's report. We shall return to properties of subjective reports in a later section.

More objective measures of perception include reaction time and reports that can be verified directly by the experimenter. For example, if a string of six letters is presented in a tachistoscope (a device for controlling illumination and duration of stimuli) for 50 milliseconds and the observer is asked to report the letters, the experimenter can easily determine whether this report was correct or not. Observers are often asked to rate their confidence that their report is correct. Such rating measures, although not objective, can provide converging operations when used with other objective measures such as reaction time.

As you can see, the major dimension for classifying dependent variables in perception is verifiability. Of course, all dependent variables must be verifiable and consistent. But some dependent variables can be verified directly, whereas others require subtle statistical methods, like scaling, before verification can be achieved. So we will divide dependent variables into those which can be *immediately* verified (judged as correct or incorrect) by the experimenter, and those which cannot.

### Independent Variables

As you might expect, the independent variables that are most common in studies of perception are those which alter the physical characteristics of stimuli. Psychologists change the size, shape, backgrounds, perspective, and angle of view of visual stimuli. Auditory stimuli can be varied according to frequency (pitch), intensity (loudness), waveform (timbre), and complexity (number of separate waveforms and their relationship to one another). The time course of perception is studied by presenting parts of a stimulus separated by short time intervals, or by limiting the presentation time of the entire stimulus to tens or hundreds of milliseconds.

Another class of perceptual independent variables is more qualitative than quantitative. Animals and people have been placed in abnormal circumstances where the usual perceptual inputs are either absent or grossly distorted. Some examples of this type of manipulation would be raising animals in the dark, having people wear special goggles that distort their vision, allowing normal perception but preventing motor movements, and having a uniform visual field with no patterns or lines. Many such studies try to determine whether perception is learned like other behavior or is innate and instinctive. At one time the distinction between innate and learned perception was a major controversy in psychology. Now, however, most psychologists admit there are both innate and learned components in perception.

### Control Variables

This chapter is concerned with what might be termed the intellectual aspects of perception; however, it cannot be denied that perception has emotional and motivational aspects as well. Thus when people are asked to report "taboo" four-letter words, these words require a greater display duration than do innocent control words. Similarly when hungry people observe an out-of-focus image, they report seeing food-related objects more often than people who have eaten recently. Although these phenomena are interesting in their own right, when we focus on the stimulus as the most important determinant of perception, these other effects become artifacts and must be controlled. In terms of signal-detection theory (see chapter 5), the decision aspects of perception must be held constant. Reporting a taboo word requires a greater display duration, not because the word is harder to perceive, but because observers are more reluctant to say a taboo word to the experimenter and hence after their decision criterion.

Physical aspects of the stimulus that are not being investigated must also be controlled. Stimulus duration, intensity, illumination, contrast, and so on need to be held constant when they are not manipulated as independent variables.

## 6.1

**EXPERIMENTAL TOPICS AND RESEARCH ILLUSTRATIONS**

**Topic:** Phenomenological Report

**Illustration:** Perceptual Moment versus Moving Window

A *phenomenological report* can occur when an observer describes his or her perceptual experience. In order to understand when such a description is a useful dependent variable, as opposed to a description that cannot be verified, we must distinguish between *reports* and *responses*. Responses are the more general category. All reports are also responses. However, any response is not necessarily a report.

When a psychologist records a response, she or he is interested in some particular characteristic of that response: its latency, its duration, its force, and so on. Observing and recording the response is an end in itself. This is only partly true when the psychologist seeks a report. The report itself is not of primary interest. Rather, the report is useful only to the extent that it illuminates a perceptual event that is hidden from direct observation by the experimenter. If the magical meter could be inserted painlessly into your head so that it measured your perceptual experience, the psychologist would have no need for phenomenological reports. The experience could be tapped directly. Since psychologists will never have this kind of meter, a perceptual experience will be filtered through the report of the observer before the psychologist can lay eager hands on it. The report is valuable only to the extent that it makes a hidden perceptual experience (among others—see chapter 11) available to the psychologist.

How does the psychologist know when the response of the observer qualifies as a report? The answer is deceptively simple: It qualifies only when a verifiable relationship between the response and a previous perceptual event can be directly inferred. Natsoulas (1967, p. 250) defined a report as:

> a presumed or confirmed relationship between some preceding or synchronous event ($e_i$) and the response. This relationship must be such as to make possible direct inferences from knowledge of the response to $e_i$.

This definition is purposely abstract and will make more sense once we find some concrete examples.

In the preceding chapter we discussed how a pigeon could be trained to tell us its absolute visual threshold (Blough, 1958). You will recall that the pigeon pecked one key when it saw the stimulus and a different key when it did not. Appropriate reinforcement contingencies were used to ensure that the pigeon's behavior was controlled by the stimulus. According to the definition just given, do the pigeon's pecking responses qualify as reports?

In this instance, the preceding event ($e_i$) is the stimulus with particular reference to its intensity. A peck on one key indicated that the stimulus was below the threshold, whereas a peck on the other showed that the pigeon could see the stimulus. This relationship is the direct inference called for in the definition. Knowing the response—that is, which key was pecked—allows a direct inference as to whether or not the pigeon was able to see the stimulus. So we must conclude that the pecking responses do indeed qualify as reports.

If you think of a phenomenological report as being equivalent to the method of introspection (see appendix B) used early in the history of psychology, you may very well find this conclusion shocking and distasteful. How could any self-respecting scientist be interested in the introspections of a pigeon? There is something odd about nonverbal introspection. The way out of this difficulty is for you to realize that a phenomenological report is not the same as introspection. The goal of the method of introspection was to break down and analyze mental events into their basic component pieces. Just as a chemist can break down water into hydrogen and oxygen, so was an introspectionist expected to produce the elements of experience. The phenomenological report is not analytic. It describes a whole experience without attempting to isolate basic elements.

It is important for you to realize that the essential characteristic of a phenomenological report is the relationship between it and the preceding perceptual event. To the extent that alternate relationships or inferences can be proposed, the report is weakened. For example, had Blough not been careful to eliminate the possibility that the pigeon learned only to switch between keys after a long string of pecks on a single key, this alternate relationship could have also explained the pecking behavior. In that case, the pecking could not have been correctly interpreted as a perceptual report.

The pecking example also illustrates that the qualitative nature of the report is relatively unimportant. A key press is every bit as good as a verbal statement that the stimulus was or was not seen. Verbal statements can be responses rather than reports. It is only the relationship between the preceding event and the report that needs to be considered in order to establish whether a response is also a report. And just because a statement is verbal does not guarantee that it is also a report.

Before leaving the definition of a report, we will tackle one more concrete example. Imagine you are at a party—either as a detached scientific observer or as a participant, depending on your likes— and one of the revelers starts ripping off his or her clothing and screaming, "There are little green bugs crawling all over me!" Is this verbal utterance a phenomenological report? On the one hand the collateral motor behavior of tearing off clothing is consistent with the verbal description of the perceptual experience. If you had little green bugs crawling all over you, it would not be unreasonable for you to remove your clothing as quickly as possible. But what is the relationship between the (alleged) report and a preceding perceptual event? Are there any alternate inferences that could be drawn? In this case, the alternate inference is quite obvious—the reveler is stoned out of his or her mind. We can confirm this alternate explanation by the converging operation of asking other people if they can see any green bugs. If they cannot see the little bugs, our faith in the alternate explanation is increased. Thus, we must reject the phenomenological report because an alternate relationship exists that is either more plausible or better supported by related lines of evidence.

***Does perception take only a moment?***  How is external information perceived over time? There have been two major opposing views on this subject. The first states that perception is accomplished in a series of successive brief units of time, much like a series of snapshots with blanks during the time it takes to advance the film. This view is called the *perceptual moment* hypothesis (Stroud, 1956), and it assumes that any events that occur during the same snapshot are perceived as simultaneous.

The opposing viewpoint, which we shall call the *moving window* hypothesis, states that perception is a continuous process with no gaps. A simple analogy (Allport, 1968) will help us understand the distinction between these two opposing viewpoints. Imagine that you are on a railroad platform peering into the compartments of a train that is just pulling out of the station. You can see inside the train only when a window passes in front of you. Therefore your view of the world inside the train is made up from successive but separate inputs. This is analogous to the perceptual-moment hypothesis. Now imagine that you are inside the train looking out at the railroad platform. The passing scene, although always changing, moves smoothly and continuously past the window. This corresponds to the moving-window hypothesis, although we are really concerned with movement in time rather than in space.

A clever experiment aimed at determining which of these opposing hypotheses is correct was conducted in England by Allport (1968). He displayed a series of twelve parallel horizontal lines on a cathode-ray tube, a device closely related to a television screen. Each line was displayed for a very small fraction of a second, one right after the other. The visual effect, when this was done fast enough, was that all the lines appeared to be continuously present, just as fan blades look like a solid, transparent ring when they are spinning very rapidly. When Allport slightly slowed the display time of the lines, not all of them appeared to be displayed at once—there seemed to be a constantly moving gap, so that only eleven lines appeared to be present at the same time. Which way should the missing line or gap move, from top to bottom, as the lines are really being drawn, or from bottom to top?

The prediction of the perceptual-moment hypothesis is illustrated in figure 6–9. Panel A shows all the lines when the presentation rate is fast. Although the lines are drawn sequentially from top to bottom, they look as though they appear simultaneously. Panel B shows what is perceived when the presentation rate is slowed. Now one line is missing. This missing line is represented as the dotted line in panel B. According to the perceptual-moment hypothesis, the line is missing because at the slower presentation rate it is not included in the same perceptual moment as the preceding upper lines that were presented before the (missing) bottom line. At the slower presentation rate, the perceptual moment can now contain only five lines. (In panel A, the perceptual moment contains all six lines because the faster presentation rate means that less time is needed for the computer to draw all six lines. In panel B, the slower presentation rate means that more time is needed for the equipment to draw the five lines in this panel than to draw all the lines in panel A.) However, the bottom line (line 6) will be contained in the next perceptual moment. This is shown in panel C. Since the perceptual moment can contain only five lines, only line 6 and the next four lines to be displayed will be seen on the screen. Since the lines are drawn from top to bottom, line 1 is drawn after line 6. After line 1 comes lines 2, 3, and 4. This makes a total of five lines and fills the perceptual moment. Thus, line 5 is missing. It must go in the next perceptual moment. This is shown in panel D. When the panels are compared, it is obvious that the missing line appears to move up. The perceptual-moment hypothesis predicts that the apparent motion will be in the opposite direction from where the lines are actually drawn. The lines are drawn from top to bottom, whereas the apparent motion of the missing line is from bottom to top.

The prediction of the moving-window hypothesis can be seen in figure 6–10. Panel A again shows all the lines together. In panel B the bottom line is missing because it does not fit into the window. The window next moves down as illustrated in panel C. Because the size of the window is fixed, in order for the previously missing

FIGURE 6–9.

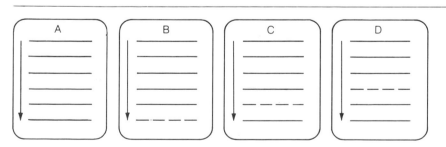

Prediction of the perceptual moment hypothesis. Only six lines are shown to simplify the figure. The dotted missing line moves up.

FIGURE 6–10.

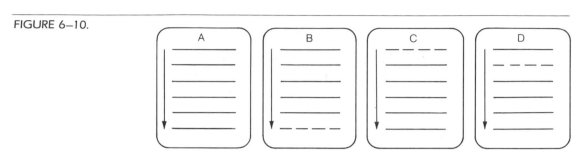

Prediction of the moving window hypothesis. Only six lines are shown to simplify the figure. The dotted missing line moves down.

bottom line to fit in, the previous top line must be left out. As the window continues to move smoothly downward, successive lines are omitted. As each previously missing line is enclosed, another must be ejected. So the missing line moves from top to bottom, that is, in the same direction as the real presentation, according to the moving-window hypothesis.

Now we are almost ready to talk about results of Allport's experiments. But first we must decide whether the observer's response (that the missing line moves up or down) qualifies as a phenomenological report. In this case, there is a presumed relationship between the report and the preceding perceptual event. The direction of this relationship depends on which hypothesis—perceptual moment or moving window—is held, but in either case the relationship is clear. Are there any alternate inferences that could be drawn? This depends on the specific details of procedure used. It might be that some observers always tend to see lines moving upward regardless of the true direction of motion. But Allport took this possibility into account by randomizing the direction of real motion from trial to trial—that is, in half the trials the true motion was up and in the other half the true motion was down. So the observer's response can be accepted as a report.

The actual results of this experiment were clear. All observers reported that the missing line moved in the same direction as the true motion. Thus, the moving-window hypothesis was supported while the perceptual-moment hypothesis was not.

**Stabilized images and visual-analyzing systems.** Ordinarily your eye is in constant motion, even when you think your gaze is fixed on one single spot. This constant oscillation of the eye is called *nystagmus* and prevents a gap in your vision caused by light rays falling on the blind spot—the place inside your eye where the optic nerve joins the retina. Nystagmus prevents any single spot on the retina from being stimulated continuously. Using special optical techniques, psychologists have been able to circumvent nystagmus to keep particular points inside the eye constantly stimulated. An image so formed is called a *stabilized image*.

In a series of studies, Brown and his students (Schmidt et al., 1971; Cosgrove et al., 1974) have used the stabilized-image technique to demonstrate the existence of specific visual-analyzing systems. Although there has been psychophysiological evidence of receptor cells that respond only to certain kinds of stimuli, for example, tilted lines, Brown tried to use only behavioral techniques to reach this same conclusion. The usual finding is that a stabilized image soon fades away. But it seldom fades away as a single unit. Instead, fragments of the stimulus fade in and out together. For example, if the stimulus were the letter *R*, an observer might see the top loop disappear (figure 6–11).

The rate at which parts of a figure (such as lines) faded out was the dependent variable used by Brown and his co-workers. In the first study (Schmidt et al., 1971), the independent variable was the shape and orientation of simple lines or pairs of lines. The fade rate was controlled by this independent variable with, for example, right angles being more stable (having a lower fade rate) than other angles. We shall focus on the Cosgrove et al. (1971) study, which

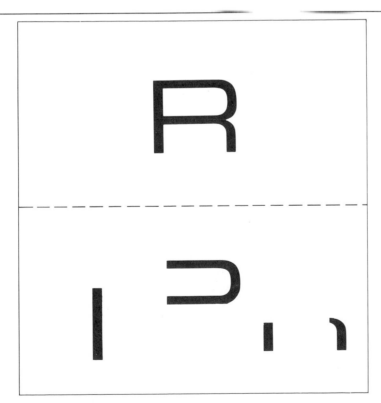

FIGURE 6–11.

Stimulus is a stabilized-image experiment (A) and fragments perceived by an observer (B).

used this same technique with colored stabilized lines. A vertical bar grating (having parallel lines close together) was first presented. This was followed by a colored stabilized line, also vertical. The bar grating has been found to increase the fade rate for non-colored lines. On seeing the colored line disappear, the observer pressed a button. Then a different colored line appeared in the same position as the missing line. The observer pressed a button to indicate when the new line appeared. It turned out that changing the color of the new line made it easier (faster) for the new line to appear than if the same color had been maintained. These results were interpreted as supporting the existence of specific visual systems that analyze color. If exactly the same system had been used, changing the color should not have altered the fade rate.

Was pressing a button in this experiment to indicate the disappearance or the reappearance of a line a phenomenological report? Yes, it was. The presumed relationship between fade rate and stabilized image, although not previously tested with colored lines, had received some empirical confirmation in the earlier studies. The button press was clearly related to a prior perceptual event. However, this study is not nearly as elegant as the Allport moving-line experiment previously discussed. Recall our earlier distinction between dependent variables that can be immediately verified and those which cannot. Although the subject may correctly perceive the reappearance of a colored line, this cannot be immediately verified by the experimenter. Although the internal consistency of the data suggests that the observer is reporting perceptual events that are controlled by the color of the stimuli, the experimenter may well be uncomfortable because there is no independent check of these results. This is a common problem in perceptual research, since only the observer has direct access to the perceptual experience. How might this experiment be improved to add such a check?

Think back to the pigeon-threshold experiment. The experimenter could not directly know when the pigeon detected the stimulus, and also had to rely on a phenomenological report. But there was one important additional check that was lacking in the Brown experiment. The experimenter could be sure that if no stimulus was presented, the pigeon could not see it. So immediate verification of the observer's report was possible for trials in which no stimulus occurred and this was used to establish appropriate reinforcement contingencies for the pigeon. In general, deleting the stimulus entirely is termed a "catch" trial, and catch trials are often used in psychophysical research. So Brown could have not replaced the colored line on some proportion of trials to see whether the observer then incorrectly reported the reappearance of the line. However, inserting catch trials often changes the decision costs associated with perception, and some investigators prefer to hold these constant. (To check for such a change would complicate the experiment, since it requires that performance on a block of trials where no catch trial is used be compared with stimulus-presented trials in a different block that did contain catch trials.)

There is still another way to make the dependent variable instantly verifiable by the experimenter, without using catch trials. Recall that the disappearing line was immediately replaced by another line of either the same or different color. It would have been easy for Brown to require that his observers state the color of the line when it reappeared. Had this been done, we could expect (given his interpretation of results) that observers would report lines that come back faster to be the different color, and lines that take longer to be the original color. Such an outcome would greatly strengthen the conclusions of the study.

It is important to realize that immediate verification of a dependent variable, although certainly desirable, does not in itself determine whether a response qualifies as a phenomenological report. There can be valid reports that cannot be immediately verified by the experimenter, especially when illusions are studied. But the property of immediate verification greatly improves experiments in perception by adding confirming data, as in the Brown experiment discussed previously. These extra data can be viewed as a very weak form of converging operation, and we now turn to that as our next topic.

---

**Topic:** Converging Operations

**Illustration:** Stroop Effect

**6.2**

**EXPERIMENTAL
TOPICS AND
RESEARCH
ILLUSTRATIONS**

---

The distinction between perceiving and responding, discussed in the preceding section, was a major impetus for applying the ideas of the physicist Bridgman to the psychological concept of perception. In a classic article entitled "Operationism and the Concept of Perception," Garner, Hake, and Eriksen (1956) showed that perception was more than just a response. This may seem obvious to you after reading the preceding section, so we must take a step backward in time.

Twenty years ago experimental psychology was barely starting to recover from the throes of a rigidly applied framework of Watsonian behaviorism. Observers made responses that discriminated one stimulus pattern from another, and so for many psychologists such responses were equivalent to perception. We now realize, largely owing to Garner, Hake, and Eriksen, that such a limited concept of perception arises from a very literal and incomplete interpretation of operationism. You will recall that, according to operationism, concepts are defined by the operations used to measure them. If weight was defined as the movement of a meter located in a small rectangular box on your bathroom floor, then the response indicated on the scale dial defined weight. If perception was defined as an observer saying one stimulus looks different from another, then that response was perception.

Garner, Hake, and Eriksen pointed out this was only part of operationism. Equally important was the need for a *set* of operations to define each concept. They cited Bridgman (1945, p. 248) to emphasize this neglected aspect:

> Operational definitions, in spite of their precision, are in application without significance unless the situations to which they are applied are sufficiently developed so that *at least two* methods are known of getting to the terminus. Definition of a phenomenon by the operations which produced it, taken naked and without further qualification, has an entirely specious precision, because it is a description of a single isolated event. (emphasis added)

So, operationally defining perception as a discrimination response—that is, *A* or *B*—is not enough. At least two operations are required. When only a single operation is used, it is impossible to distinguish between limitations of the perceptual system versus those of the response system. Since perceptual and response systems are to some extent independent, two or more operations are required to separate the limitations of each system.

*Converging operations* are a set of two or more operations that eliminate alternate concepts that might explain a set of experimental results. This abstract definition is best understood through several examples. We start with an example used by Garner, Hake and Eriksen (1956).

Let us take the so-called perceptual defense experiment mentioned earlier in which taboo or vulgar words are presented to an observer. Garner and his co-workers suggested using four words—two ordinary and two vulgar—and the exposure time needed for an observer to report these words by pronouncing them to the experimenter turns out to be greater for the vulgar words. Does this mean that perception of vulgar words takes longer? Without any converging operations, it is impossible to tell. The alternate explanation, that the response system inhibits overt vocalization of vulgar words, cannot be eliminated. The results could be owing to either the perceptual system or the response system.

What converging operation might allow us to conclude which system is responsible for this effect? Garner and his colleagues suggested keeping the stimuli the same, but switching the responses so that ordinary words would be pronounced when vulgar words were the stimuli, and vice versa. So when the observer saw a vulgar word, the correct response would be an ordinary word. Vulgar words would have to be pronounced only when ordinary words were the stimuli. If vulgar responses still required more exposure time when paired with ordinary stimuli, we could conclude from both experiments that the response system, and not the perceptual system, was responsible for the effect.

Such an experiment was performed by Zajonc (1962). He used a paired-associate technique where taboo words could be paired either with neutral words or vulgar words. Results showed no perceptual effects. Greater exposure time was required when the response was a taboo word, not when the stimulus was vulgar. This converging operation supported the response system as the locus for "perceptual defense."

It is very important to understand that this second experiment by itself no more provides converging operations than did the first experiment alone. Only the combination of *both* experiments yields converging operations. If only the results of the second experiment were known, it would be logically possible to argue that ordinary-word stimuli need longer exposure times when vulgar responses are used because (1) ordinary stimuli take longer to be perceived than vulgar stimuli—that is, vulgar stimuli are somehow more potent, or (2) vulgar responses are inhibited. So, as was the case with the first experiment considered by itself, it would be impossible to choose between perceptual and response systems as the cause of the effect. However, when results of both experiments are jointly considered, only one conclusion can be drawn.

Another example of the need for converging operations arises in conjunction with the well-known Stroop effect. In its traditional version, observers are asked to name the color of the ink in which words are printed. (see figure 6–12) The words can be either color names themselves or neutral, noncolor nouns like "bird." The basic result is that the time required to name the ink increases when the word is the name of a color other than the ink—for example, the word GREEN spelled out in blue ink. The correct response would

FIGURE 6–12.

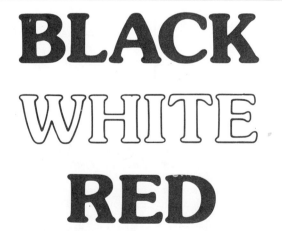

Stimuli rised in Stroop test. The correct responses from top to bottom would be "black," "white," "black."

be blue. The time required to say "blue" is greater for the stimulus GREEN than for a neutral stimulus also printed in blue ink.

The Stroop effect is a highly reliable one; the question is, what causes it? One possibility is that it is caused by the input or perceptual aspects of the task. Stroop and others have found that reading is usually faster than naming; therefore, the perceptual argument is that reading color words inhibits the perception of the ink color. An alternative hypothesis is that output (the subject's responses) is affected and not perception. The output notion goes like this: after the subject has perceived both the ink color and the color word, there is response competition when two different color names are elicited—one by the ink and another by the word. On the basis of Stroop's original work, we have no way of deciding between these two hypotheses. Which is important—the perceptual system or the response system?

A simple but clever experiment was conducted by Egeth, Blecker, and Kamlet (1969) to answer this question by using converging operations. Three important conditions from one of their studies are shown in figure 6–13. The control or baseline conditions is shown at the top of this figure (Neutral Condition). Subjects saw

FIGURE 6–13.

| | Response | Symbols in Colors | | Color of Patches |
|---|---|---|---|---|
| **Neutral Condition** | Same | XXXX | XXXX | Both patches red |
| | Different | XXXX | XXXX | One patch red, one blue |
| **Perceptual Inhibition Condition** | Same | RED | RED | Both patches red |
| | Different | RED | RED | One patch red, one blue |
| **Response Competition Condition** | Same | SAME | SAME | Both patches red |
| | Different | SAME | SAME | One patch red, one blue |

3. An outline of some of the conditions in the work by Egeth, Blecker, and Kamlet (1969). In all three conditions, subjects responded SAME when there was agreement among the stimuli and DIFFERENT when there was a mismatch. Subjects saw two colored patches on each trial and responded on the basis of the colors. The Neutral Condition served as a control by having neutral symbols (XXXX) imbedded in colored patches. Color names were in the patches in the Perceptual Inhibition Condition—the color names should inhibit the perception of the colors SAME or DIFFERENT appeared in the patches in the Response Competition Condition—reading the response SAME in different colored patches should inhibit the correct response of DIFFERENT. The Stroop effect occurred in the Response Competition Condition but not in the Perceptual Inhibition Condition.

two color patches with a neutral symbol (XXXX) imbedded in them. The two color patches were either the same color or different colors. An important factor in this study is that instead of responding with color names, the subjects responded SAME when the two patches matched, and DIFFERENT when the colors of the two patches were different.

The crucial conditions of the experiment are illustrated in the next rows. As in the baseline condition, the subjects responded SAME or DIFFERENT on the basis of the colors of the two patches. In the Perceptual Inhibition Condition, color words appeared in the color patches, and on a given trial the same color word appeared in both boxes. Both color patches could be the same and match the color word (a SAME trial) or the color patches could be different, with only one patch matching the names (a DIFFERENT trial). Egeth and his co-workers reasoned that there should not be any response competition in the Perceptual Inhibition Condition because the responses SAME and DIFFERENT should not compete with the various responses to the color names. The prediction is that if the Perceptual Inhibition Condition leads to slower responding than the neutral condition, then the Stroop Effect is caused by perceptual inhibition, not by response competition. In the Perceptual Inhibition Condition, Egeth and his colleagues found that the Stroop effect disappeared: responding was about as fast as in the control condition.

So far so good. We seem to have eliminated one alternative as an explanation of the Stroop effect. Now for a converging operation that will bring back the Stroop effect and identify the processes involved. To accomplish this, Egeth and his co-workers used the condition outlined at the bottom of figure 6–13. As was true of the other two conditions, the subjects responded SAME and DIFFERENT in the Response Competition Condition. However, in the Response Competition Condition the words SAME or DIFFERENT appeared in the color patches rather than neutral symbols or color names. The experimenters reasoned that if response competition is important, then mismatches between SAME or DIFFERENT and the stimulus information should result in slower responding than in the Neutral Condition. That is, if conflict among responses causes the Stroop effect, then responding should be slower in the Response Competition Condition than in the Neutral Condition. This is exactly what they found. The Stroop effect returned: now the responses SAME and DIFFERENT took longer when they conflicted with the response in the stimulus. Recall that the identical response words did not produce a Stroop effect in the Perceptual Inhibition Condition. Thus, the converging operations removed the perceptual process as an alternative explanation for the results, leaving us to conclude that a response process accounts for the Stroop effect. Other studies on the Stroop phenomenon also lead to the conclusion that response competition is an important contributing factor to Stroop interference.

The two examples of converging operations just discussed are relatively simple in that only two experiments were required to obtain converging operations. Quite often there are more than two competing alternative explanations, so that a set of two experiments will not be sufficient to eliminate all but one. In this more typical case the experimenter has little choice but to try to establish several converging operations in hopes of being left with only one viable explanation for all the experimental results.

| | |
|---|---|
| **FROM PROBLEM TO EXPERIMENT: THE NUTS AND BOLTS** | **Problem:** The color-distance illusion |

It is well known in the visual arts that warm colors (yellow, orange, red, and transitions between these colors) give the appearance of moving toward the viewer whereas cool colors (blue, green) seem to recede away from the viewer. So a two-dimensional picture can be made to look three-dimensional by artistic devices like having blue backgrounds and warm-colored foregrounds. This illusion can be quite convincing. One of us remembers viewing an exhibition of stained glass where one work of art had several deep blue panes of glass surrounding a red circle. The illusion of three dimensions was so strong that the circle looked as if it floated about ten centimeters in front of the blue background. The author had to go up and touch the glass to convince himself that the red and blue pieces of glass were in the same plane.

Let us imagine that an experimental psychologist wishes to investigate this warm–cool color illusion. The problem can be simply stated.

**Problem:** Why do warm colors appear to come forward and cool colors appear to recede?

Before trying to answer this question in any detail, a careful experimental psychologist would first attempt to demonstrate the phenomenon in controlled laboratory circumstances. He or she would want to rule out the possibility that the illusion occurs because of other artistic devices (such as perspective) or variations in brightness, both of which can create an appearance of distance. So a general hypothesis that color serves as a cue to depth would first be advanced. As is always true, several more specific testable versions of this general hypothesis can be formulated.

**Hypothesis:** When pairs of color patches are presented in the same plane, the warmer color will be judged closer by a person viewing these stimuli with one eye (monocularly).

The major independent variable is, of course, the color (or, more technically, the hue) of the visual test patches. Another independent variable that would probably be manipulated at the same time is the distance between the eye and the stimuli. This variable would be included because the experimenter had no prior reason to select some particular viewing distance. Since there is nothing special about the viewing distance, you might think that this independent variable is unnecessary. Any distance selected at random would do. Although this reasoning is correct if the assumption that distance does not matter is true, this is only the experimenter's best guess. Since it is easy and inexpensive to use three or four viewing distances instead of only one, most experimenters would go ahead and manipulate distance. Data showing that viewing distance has no effect on the depth cue of color, although a null finding, still is of interest, since it would allow ruling out certain explanations of the illusion. Finally, the experimenter's guess might be wrong, and the two independent variables (hue and viewing distance) might interact.

How many hues should be tested in this experiment? If all possible pairs of hues are to be presented to the observer, we find that the number of stimuli (a stimulus is one pair of color patches) increases dramatically with the number of hues to be tested. The minimum experiment would have three hues: one warm, one cool, and one neutral gray. This would require a total of three stimuli to present all possible pairs. Although this total is most reasonable in terms of demanding experimental effort, three stimuli (and only two real colors) are too few to establish the generality of the effect. The next number of hues is five: two warm colors, two cool colors, and one gray. This would require ten stimuli. Seven colors would require twenty-one stimuli and nine colors thirty-six stimuli. In order to keep the experiment to a reasonable time, we might select five colors and four viewing distances.

The dependent variable is a forced-choice judgment, with the observer being required to state which of the two color patches appears closer. (Actually they are both the same distance from the observer.) This would be scored by creating a matrix, with all the hues listed down the columns and also across the rows. Each cell in the matrix specifies a combination of two colors. The main diagonal would not have any entries, since the same color would not be presented twice within a stimulus. Cell entries would be the number of times (or the percentages) that color $X$ was judged to be closer than color $Y$.

As with any perceptual experiment, many control variables are required. What the person in the street calls color is actually composed of three independent attributes: hue, saturation, and brightness. *Hue* is the frequency of the light and corresponds to shade of color—red, green, et cetera. *Saturation* corresponds to the strength of color—that is, whether it is pale and washed out or deep and strong. *Brightness* refers to the amount of light reflected from a surface. Since our experiment has hue as its major independent variable, both saturation and brightness must be controlled. Brightness especially is an important cue to depth, with brighter objects being perceived as closer to the viewer, all other things being equal. So we must be extremely sure that all our stimuli are of equal brightness. Another of the control variables has already been given in the hypothesis, which specified monocular (one eye) viewing conditions. Because each eye sees external objects from a slightly different location, binocular vision (both eyes) is an important cue for depth perception. Since we are primarily interested in color as a possible depth cue, all other cues to distance must be eliminated from the experiment.

We do not know what the results of this experiment would be. However, for purposes of further discussion let us pretend that warm colors were judged as closer. We would then formulate another hypothesis, trying to provide a converging operation to bolster the results and interpretation of this first experiment.

**Hypothesis:** When an observer is asked to move an adjustable colored stimulus so that it appears in the same plane as a fixed colored stimulus, the distance between the two stimuli will be set so that the adjustable stimulus will be closer to the observer if it is a cool color and the fixed stimulus is a warm color, and vice versa.

This hypothesis is more complicated than the first, so let us explain it in more detail. Imagine two colored circles in front of you with one of them sitting on a pully so that it can move forward and backward. The other circle cannot be moved. Your task is to adjust this pully until both stimuli appear equally distant from you. The hypothesis predicts that, since warm colors will appear closer to you, a cool color (which appears further away) placed on the pully must be moved closer in order to appear even with the fixed warm color. Similarly, if the fixed color is cool it will appear further away so that a warm color (which will appear closer) on the pulley must be moved further away from you than the fixed color.

The independent and control variables are as before. The dependent variable is now the distance between the observer and the adjustable stimulus. However, in scoring this distance, we probably would take the position of the fixed stimulus as zero and record a negative number if the adjustable stimulus is closer to the viewer, and a positive number if it is further away. Whereas the first experiment yielded a qualitative assessment of the warm–cool illusion, this experiment gives a number based on perceived distance. Thus, it provides an indication of how strong or weak the illusion might be for different combinations of colors. If we were bold enough, this hypothesis could be made even more specific by predicting that the size of the illusion would depend on the difference in frequency between the hues of each pair of stimuli. As stimuli were further apart in the visual spectrum, greater distance settings would result.

So far our two experiments have been aimed more at establishing the replicability and reliability of the (hypothetical) finding that warm colors move forward and cool colors recede than at explaining why this happens. The converging operations provided by the two experiments are weak, since they are quite similar and differ only in the precision with which the dependent variable is measured. In particular, the judgments made by the viewer are relative judgments concerning two colors viewed simultaneously. One next step toward explaining our (hypothetical) result would be to provide a stronger converging operation by requiring an absolute judgment about a single stimulus.

**Hypothesis:** *When an observer, using both eyes, is required to estimate the distance of a single colored stimulus chip, warm colors will be judged closer than cool colors.*

Our independent variable is unchanged as are the control variables. The dependent variable is a direct estimate of distance. There are several scaling techniques that could be used, but for the sake of simplicity we shall let our observer make a judgment in distance units that are familiar to him, such as inches or centimeters. Of course, it is unlikely that, even for a neutral-gray stimulus, such estimates will be highly accurate, but that is not the issue we wish to investigate. All we care about in this experiment are the relative values of the distance estimates for warm versus cool colors. If results agree with those hypothesized for the first two experiments, we have learned that there is some absolute property of color that serves as a cue for distance. If no differences are found—that is, if distance estimates are the same for all colors— there remain two possibilities. You noticed, we hope, that the hypothesis stated normal binocular vision (both eyes) was to be tested. This was another converging operation. If results were negative, a careful experimenter would replicate this third experiment using monocular vision as before. If results still were negative with monocular vision, then we would be forced to conclude that the warm– cool distance illusion was a property of relative judgments and that a contrast between two stimuli was necessary to produce it. This would be a major step in explaining the effect, but still only a beginning. The remaining steps are left as exercises for future experimenters. (If you want to find out more about this, look up *chromatic aberration* in a perception text, for example, see Kaufman, 1974).

**1.** Perception is the psychological process whereby events in the external world are noticed and interpreted. Perception is not always accurate (verifiable).

**SUMMARY**

**2.** Illusions illustrate how perception is not always verifiable (accurate). Impossible figures and illusions of perspective show how perception depends on your past experience. You try to interpret perceptual data in a meaningful way, even if the actual stimulus contains ambiguities. Thus, you can be tricked by certain stimuli because of your expectations about the way the world is organized.

**3.** Phenomenological reports allow the psychologist to study another person's perceptual experiences. However, care is needed to distinguish between reports and responses. Examples of perceptual issues that have been studied by phenomenological reports are selecting whether the perceptual-moment or moving-window hypothesis is correct, and the study of stabilized images.

**4.** Converging operations allow inferences about perceptual operations that are stronger than inferences from a single experiment or experimental condition. Converging operations allowed psychologists to distinguish between perceptual-inhibition and response-competition explanations of the Stroop effect.

**KEY TERMS**

**converging operation**          **phenomenological report**
**illusion**                      **response**
**impossible figure**             **size constancy**
**moving window**                 **stabilized image**
**perceptual moment**             **Stroop effect**
**perspective**

**DISCUSSION QUESTIONS**

**1.** Is an autobiography a phenomenological report?

**2.** Consult Garner (1974) and discuss how converging operations are used to bolster the concepts of dimensional integrality and separability.

**3.** Design your own experiment to further investigate the warm–cool color distance illusion.

**4.** Consult a perception text (such as Coren and Girgus, 1978; Kaufman, 1979) and discuss additional examples of illusions and phenomenological reports. The rotating trapezoid is one of many relevant illusions you will find appropriate for discussion.

# Psychology in Action

## The Stroop Effect

You can easily try the Stroop test for yourself. All you need are some index cards, colored markers, and a watch with a second hand or, even better, a stop watch. Take sixteen index cards and, using your markers, write the name of the color in its color—that is, with a green marker write GREEN, et cetera. If you have eight markers, each color will be repeated twice. If you only have four markers, repeat each color four times. Take another sixteen index cards and write color names that do not correspond to the ink—that is with a green marker write RED, et cetera. Your stimuli are now completed. Pick one of your two decks and, for each card, name the color of the ink. Time how long it takes you to go through all sixteen cards. Do the same for the other deck. Were you faster for the deck that had compatible color names and inks?

You can also replicate the experiment by Egeth and co-workers by making up a deck of stimulus cards based on figure 6–13. Have some friends serve as experimental subjects and require that they respond SAME or DIFFERENT. Record the time needed for them to go through an entire deck of cards.

For your last experiment, crumple up some cellophane or plastic wrap to make a viewer. Make a large frame out of cardboard and tape the crumpled cellophane to it. Have your subjects view the cards through the crumpled cellophane. This will make the words appear blurry and less distinct. What happens to the magnitude of the Stroop effect? Why?

# CHAPTER 7 ═══════════════

## Preview

Three experimental principles will be discussed in this chapter. *Confounding*, you will remember, occurs when an uncontrolled factor covaries (changes) together with an independent variable. It is a serious flaw in any experiment, since it prevents us from making a firm statement about causation—the very purpose of an experiment in the first place. *Interaction* occurs when more than one independent variable is manipulated in the same experiment and results depend on the combination of independent variables. The concept of interaction is covered in chapter 3. Here we discuss how changes in measurement scales can create or eliminate interaction. The last topic, *selection of dependent variables*, relates to how well the dependent variable serves as an index of the kind of behavior being investigated. As was noted in chapter 3, the dependent variable used in any experiment has no doubt been selected from a wide range of possible dependent variables. Here we will discuss the dangers of an inappropriate selection.

## Chapter Outline

# ATTENTION AND REACTION TIME

*The great tragedy of Science—the slaying of a beautiful hypothesis by an ugly fact.*

T. H. Huxley

There are many instances in life in which a small amount of time has a crucial effect. A jet airplane traveling at seven hundred miles per hour will cover almost two miles in ten seconds. The few seconds it takes the pilot to notice another plane on a collision course and make an appropriate correction can mean the difference between life and death. The time it takes a driver of an automobile to notice that the car he or she is following is stopping and step on the brake pedal determines whether an accident or a safe stop will occur. The time required for a child to pull down its pants could spell the difference between a big mess and reaching the potty quickly enough to prevent a minor disaster. The familiar adage "time is money" shows how important a role time plays in American life.

Psychologists, too, are much concerned with the time needed to accomplish different mental operations. By measuring this time they are able to make inferences about the structure and organization of mental events—events that by their nature cannot directly be observed. Studying reaction time—that is, the time between the occurrence of a particular stimulus and a response to that stimulus—gives psychologists a window into the mind. As we shall see, this window is often streaked and clouded, but use of good methodology and experimental principles can clean up the window and improve our view of mental operations.

**173**

A topic closely related to reaction time is that of attention. Paying attention to something can often speed up your reaction time. If you expect the car in front of you to stop, you will react more quickly than if you were not ready. Attention also plays a role in how many different things you can do at the same time. A drummer in a rock band can keep playing in rhythm while having a conversation, perhaps with an attractive listener, at the same time. But does the conversation force her to play more poorly (or the drumming force her to converse more poorly) than if only one task were being performed at a time?

## THE ABC OF REACTION TIME

The psychologist's interest in reaction time began in the eighteenth century when an assistant at the Royal Observatory was fired because his reaction times did not agree with his employer's reaction times. Today, of course, labor unions would prevent such misfortune, but back in those days employees did not have much in the way of job security. Although history has duly noted the mistake of the Royal Observatory, experimental psychology came too late to help the poor assistant. Here is how it happened.

Astronomers in those days recorded the time and position of astral events by observing when some celestial body crossed a hairline in the eyepiece of their telescope. A nearby clock ticked every second and the observer was expected to note the crossing time to the nearest tenth of a second. When Kinnebrook, the unfortunate assistant at the Royal Observatory, had his crossing times checked by his boss, they were always too great. Kinnebrook was warned, but was unable to shorten his observation times and so was booted out of the Observatory.

This would have been the end of the tale except that the astronomer Bessel heard of the incident from some of his friends and began to wonder whether the systematic difference between Kinnebrook and his boss was caused by something other than incompetence. He suspected that each person might observe the same crossing with slightly different reaction times. Indeed, when astronomers began to compare their measurements of crossing times, systematic differences among astronomers were found consistently. This phenomenon was named the *personal equation*, and one can imagine astronomers of the day busily comparing personal equations at the annual meeting of the Royal Astronomical Society.

The personal equation remained only a problem in astronomy until the Dutch physiologist Donders realized he could use it to calibrate the time required for various mental operations. Donders established three kinds of reaction-time situations that are still known as Donders *A*, *B*, and *C* reactions. In the *A* reaction shown in figure 7–1, sometimes called *simple reaction*, a light goes on and the observer responds by pressing a key or button. There is only one stimulus and one response. When you step on your brake pedal

FIGURE 7–1.

Stimulus

Response

The Donders *A* (or simple) reaction task. One stimulus is linked to one response.

in response to the sudden illumination of the brake lights of the car in front of you, the time between the onset of the lights and your depression of the brake pedal is called simple reaction time. Donders believed that simple (or *A*) reaction time was a baseline that took into account factors (such as speed of nerve conduction) that were components of more complex reaction times. These more complicated reaction situations he called *B* and *C* reactions. In a *B* or *choice reaction* situation as shown in figure 7–2, there is more than one stimulus and more than one response. Each stimulus has its own unique response. When your car is at a traffic light you are faced with a choice (or *B*) reaction. If the light is green, you step on the accelerator and if it is red, on the brake pedal. What mental operations are necessary for such a choice reaction? First, you must identify which light, red or green, has been illuminated. Then you must select which pedal, accelerator or brake, you should press down. So a choice reaction involves the mental operations of stimulus identification and response selection. In order to estimate the time required for these two mental operations, we must study yet a third kind of reaction—the Donders *C* reaction shown in figure 7–3. Here, as in the *B* reaction, there are several stimuli. However, unlike the *B* reaction, only one stimulus is linked with a response. If any other stimulus occurs, the correct behavior is to withhold responding and to do nothing. Waiting in line at a takeout restaurant would be an example of a *C* reaction. Until your number

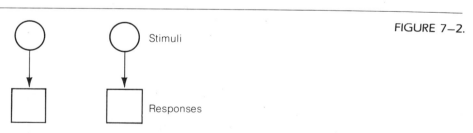

FIGURE 7–2.

Stimuli

Responses

The Donders *B* (or choice) reaction task. Two stimuli are linked to two responses.

FIGURE 7–3.

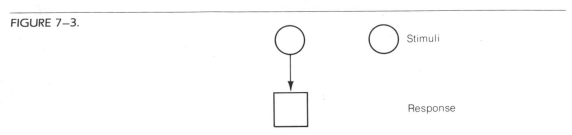

The Donders *C* reaction task. There are two stimuli but only one of them is linked to a response.

is called you should not respond. What mental operations are necessary to perform a *C* reaction? As in the *B* reaction, you must identify your number when it is called. However, once this is accomplished there is no need to select a response, since only one response is appropriate. So the *C* reaction requires stimulus identification, but no response selection.

We can now estimate the time required for the mental operations of identification and selection by subtracting appropriate pairs of reaction times. The *C* reaction measures identification plus assorted baseline times (nerve-conduction time, et cetera). So subtracting the *A* reaction time from the *C* reaction time tells us how long identification takes. Similarly, subtracting the *C* reaction time from the *B* reaction time estimates selection time, since the *B* reaction includes identification, selection, and baseline times, while the *C* reaction includes only identification and baseline times. These relationships are shown in figure 7–4.

You would think that such an important discovery—the ability to measure mental events—would have made Donders a famous man in his time, that he would have received many awards and perhaps even the nineteenth-century equivalent of a ticker-tape parade down Wall Street. At first, Donders's method was considered very promising and when Wundt (see appendix B) opened his psychology laboratory in 1879, his students devoted much effort to studying reaction time. But they were not able to obtain firm estimates of the times needed to perform different mental processes. Early in the next century, introspectionists mounted a fierce attack on the subtractive method and it was discredited.

Donders's subtractive method predicted that when the three kinds of reactions are ordered, the *B* reaction should take the longest, then the *C* reaction, then the *A* reaction. This prediction comes about because the *A* reaction has only basic mental components (baseline time), the *C* reaction two components (baseline and identification), and the *B* reaction three components (baseline, identification, and selection). Indeed, when data are acquired, this prediction is completely confirmed. Nevertheless, despite a promising beginning, Donders's subtractive method was scorned for much of

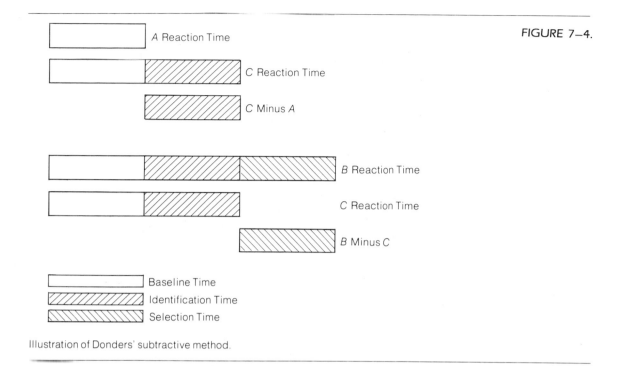

FIGURE 7–4.

Illustration of Donders' subtractive method.

the last century. In order to understand this rejection of method and supporting data, we must realize that the dominant mode of psychological inquiry in the early twentieth century was the method of introspection (see appendix B). Although psychology later rejected this method, at that time it was all-powerful. Trained introspectionists performed *A*, *B*, and *C* reactions and reported that a *C* reaction did not feel like an *A* reaction plus something else, nor did a *B* reaction feel like a *C* reaction plus something else. Instead, the three reactions all felt completely different. Strange as it may seem now, at that time this was enough to discredit Donders's subtractive method. It did not feel right and so, much like the hapless assistant Kinnebrook, it was booted out.

Today, of course, Donders holds a respected position in experimental psychology, and his method (and more sophisticated extensions of it) are widely used. Indeed, even now Donders's method has "never been discredited on any basis other than introspective report" (Taylor, 1976, p. 179).

The most popular extension of Donders's subtractive method is the *additive factors* method proposed by Sternberg (1969). The mathematics of this new method is beyond the scope of this text, but we can give an approximate verbal description. The method of additive factors takes a total reaction time and breaks this down into successive stages of information processing. The definition of a stage was left vague, but it roughly corresponded to one complete subunit of processing. There are two important differences between the subtractive method and the additive-factors method (Taylor, 1976). First, Sternberg used experimental manipulations to alter the durations of stages. The experimental independent variables used to accomplish this were called *factors*. Second, Sternberg provided a way to infer a relationship between factors and stages. Factors that influenced different stages would cause additive (non-interacting) influences on reaction time. Factors that influenced the same stage (or stages) would interact. So by doing factorial experiments and looking for patterns of interaction and additivity, psychologists could discover how processing stages were related. It is important to realize that the method of additive factors does not estimate the time required by a processing stage. It only tells us how to discover these stages. Donders was a hundred years ahead of his time and it is only recently that the rest of psychology has caught up with him.

## INTRODUCING THE VARIABLES IN ATTENTION RESEARCH

### Dependent Variables

The range of dependent variables is considerably more restricted than that of independent variables in studies of attention. Reaction time is by far the preferred variable and is extensively used. Percentage of correct responses is also used, especially in studies of attention where memory plays a role. When an experiment is framed within the context of a particular model, such as the theory of signal detection (see chapter 5), derived statistics like $d'$ and beta are also used as dependent variables. Another common statistic is amount of information in bits, where one bit is the information present in the toss of a fair coin that can come up either heads or tails. These derived statistics may be combined with reaction time to yield measures of the rate of performance, such as bits/sec or $d'$/sec.

### Independent Variables

Although studies of attention and reaction time have used an impressive variety of independent variables, these variables center around the need for the human to make decisions and the rate at which such decisions can be made. Thus, varying the number of alternatives in a choice reaction task increases the number of decisions that must be made to identify the correct stimulus and select its associated response. Varying the presentation rate of a series of stimuli limits the amount of attention that can be devoted to processing each stimulus and is a common technique used to study the upper bounds of attention. Another way of increasing the attention demanded by some task is to increase its complexity; thus, a simple version of a task may require naming a visually presented digit, whereas a more complex decision may require subtracting the digit from nine.

The key point in manipulating attention is to gradually increase task demands until the person is hard pressed to keep up with them. The use of *overload* as a diagnostic device has been borrowed from engineering, where it is quite common. For example, the strength of materials is tested by placing them in a hydraulic press and gradually increasing the pressure until the material fails. This gives the metallurgical engineer information about the material that could not be easily gained from the intact structure. Although a far gentler method of imposing overload is required for the study of human attention, the underlying goals and techniques are similar to those of the engineer. By discovering how the human system reacts to overloads of information, the psychologist gains an insight into human performance and information processing with more reasonable attentive loads.

**Control Variables**

Research in attention and reaction time is usually quite carefully controlled. Perceptual factors like the intensity and duration of stimuli are often under the control of a computer or other automated equipment that conducts the experiment. Even speech sounds can be presented exactly the same way trial after trial by using a "talking computer." This precise control is necessary if psychologists are to interpret small changes in reaction time on the order of tens of milliseconds (one millisecond being equal to one one-thousandth of a second).

---

**7.1**

**Topic:** Confounding

**Illustration:** Dichotic Listening

**EXPERIMENTAL TOPICS AND RESEARCH ILLUSTRATIONS**

---

One of the most frequently used tasks in the study of attention was derived from the difficulties encountered by air traffic controllers who must direct several airplanes at once. Radio communication between controllers and airplane pilots occurs often as the controllers give directions and the pilots acknowledge their instructions. This is a trying and stressful task for the controller, and indeed the Federal Aviation Administration has instituted a special early-retirement plan because the job is so demanding. Psychologists studying this task wondered if it could be made easier by having spatially separated loudspeakers so that the voices of different pilots would appear in different locations. This research has continued and now there is a large body of data concerning attention and listening.

In a *dichotic listening* task two separate and independent messages are presented, with each message heard in a different ear. This differs from stereo high-fidelity, where both ears hear both messages, although with different intensities. Dichotic stimuli are usually arranged so that each word arrives simultaneously in both ears. For example, the right ear might receive the message "One, Red, Jump" while the left ear hears "Quick, Tango, Fox." The words in each pair "One-Quick," "Red-Tango," "Jump-Fox" would occur at the same time. This task is illustrated in figure 7–5. The difficulty of the dichotic-listening task depends on the rate at which word pairs are presented. At a very slow rate, say, one pair every two seconds, it is easy to attend to both words. Of course, if the list of words is even moderately long there may be problems in remembering all the words. Psychologists studying attention try to separate difficulties resulting from inability to pay attention from difficulties caused by excess memory load. One way to accomplish this goal is to use extremely short lists, for example, only one word pair presented at a time. Most people have little difficulty remembering only two words so that problems can usually be traced to deficits in attention rather than memory. If, however, longer lists are used, then it becomes quite possible (and even likely for lists of more than four or five pairs) that attention and memory can be mixed up together. In more technical terms, the processes of attention are *confounded* with those of memory.

This use of the term *confounding* differs slightly from our earlier use where confounding referred to independent variables rather than psychological processes. But we shall see that saying processes are confounded really means that independent variables have been confounded. Since certain variables are theoretically associated more with memory than with attention—for example, delay of recall—it is a small step to speak of confounding processes when in actuality variables were confounded. Operationally, confounding must always be traced back to independent or uncontrolled variables, but it is often more convenient to speak of confounded processes in addition to confounded variables. When experimental procedures are inadequate so that more than one independent variable (or more than one psychological process) can account for obtained results, we say that the variables (or processes) have been confounded.

FIGURE 7–5.

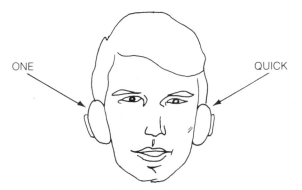

The dichotic listening task. Separate words are presented in each ear at the same time.

***A monitoring experiment.*** An example of confounded memory and attentional processes is provided by an experiment performed by Broadbent and Gregory (1963). They used a dichotic-listening task in which digits were presented to one ear and a signal-detection task was presented to the other ear. The signal-detection task consisted of a burst of white noise that might or might not contain a pure tone. The tone was present in half of the noise bursts and absent in the remaining half. Of course, the sequence of tones was randomized so that on any one trial the listener did not know in advance whether the tone was present. So listeners in this experiment had to perform two tasks simultaneously: they had to try to detect a tone if one occurred and they had to try to hear the digits. Listeners were asked to perform (at different times, of course) under two sets of instructions. In the Concentrated Attention condition they were asked to devote all their attention to detecting the tone. In the Divided Attention condition they were required to detect the tone and to report the digits after they occurred. So in the Concentrated Attention condition, subjects ignored the digits and reported the presence or absence of the tone at the end of each trial. In the Divided Attention condition they first reported as many digits as they could remember from the original list of six digits and then reported the presence or absence of the tone.

The results of this experiment can be found in figure 7–6. Tone detection was better in the Concentrated Attention condition, that is, $d'$ (see chapter 5) was greater. Therefore Broadbent and Gregory concluded that paying attention to only one task is more effective and causes better performance than paying attention to two tasks.

But this conclusion may be in error, since the procedures used by Broadbent and Gregory confounded memory and attention. Did you notice the defect in experimental design? In the Concentrated Attention condition, listeners reported the presence or absence of the tone immediately. But in the Divided Attention condition, they first reported the digits. This meant that the tone report was delayed until they had finished naming all the digits they could remember. Since delay affects memory, the possibility exists that listeners could have correctly reported the presence or absence of the tone in the Divided Attention condition if the report was immediate, as was the case in the Concentrated Attention condition, but simply forgot whether the tone was heard while they were busy reporting digits. The Concentrated and Divided Attention conditions were intended to be alike in every respect except the requirement to pay attention to one versus two ears. If this had been accomplished, any different results, like those in figure 7–6, could be reasonably assigned to differences in attention. But the two conditions also differed in the amount of time from the end of a trial until the tone report was made. So it is equally possible that the observed differences in figure 7–6 could be caused by this unequal delay across experimental conditions. In short, it is im-

FIGURE 7–6.

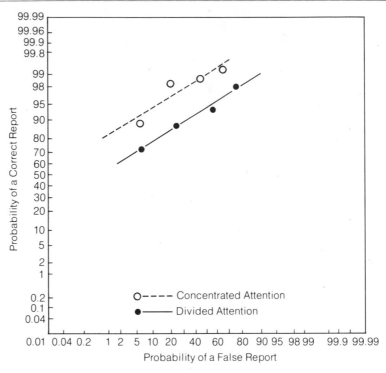

Effects of concentrated and divided attention upon signal detection. Better performance (higher $d'$) is indicated when the line is closer to the upper left-hand corner of the graph. Thus the figure shows that the Concentrated Attention condition is superior to the Divided Attention condition (data from Broadbent & Gregory, 1963).

possible to conclude which of these two factors, attentional instructions or delay of report, is responsible for the results, because these two factors have been confounded in the experiment.

How could we alter the experimental procedures to remove this unpleasant confounding? This could be accomplished quite simply by requiring listeners in the Divided Attention condition to first make the tone report and then report the digits. With this slight alteration in procedure, both conditions have the tone report occurring at the same time. When the experiment is done this way (Kantowitz, 1974, p. 121), results are the same as those of figure 7–6. Broadbent and Gregory were lucky, since their confounding did not alter the correct conclusion. But science cannot depend on good fortune as a substitute for good experimental design. Different results might have occurred, and until the experiment was repeated without confounding memory and attention, it was impossible to interpret the results obtained by Broadbent and Gregory.

*A shadowing experiment.* The Broadbent and Gregory experiment required listeners to monitor messages, that is, to listen and make no attempt at repeating the message until it had ended. One problem with this procedure is that the experimenter has no direct way of checking that the listeners are indeed monitoring and not thinking about something completely unrelated to the experiment. A more common procedure in studies of dichotic listening is to require that the listener repeat aloud each word in one of the ears as it occurs. As in monitoring experiments, the listener is then required to recall as much of the message as possible at the end of the list. However, because the experimenter has heard the listener repeat each word, the experimenter knows that attention has been devoted to at least one ear. This procedure is called *shadowing* a message, and the ear that is shadowed is called the attended ear. You might expect that listeners do relatively well at recalling the words from the attended ear, and so may wonder why psychologists bother to test them at all. The main purpose of shadowing experiments relates to the fate of the message in the unattended ear. Since the shadowing procedure guarantees that attention is devoted to the attended ear, theoretical questions focus on the listener's ability to attend to messages in the other ear. The usual finding is that the unattended message is recalled poorly compared with the shadowed or attended message. This may seem obvious to you, but the interesting point for psychologists is that the unattended message can be recalled at all. Although we shall not go into any theoretical detail (see, for example, Broadbent, 1971, chapter 5), the bare fact of any correct recall from the unattended channel forces psychologists to postulate attentional mechanisms like a filter that can rapidly switch back and forth between the two ears, or an attenuator that weakens but does not completely eliminate the unattended message, or one of several other alternate models.

Although the shadowing technique has been widely used since the early 1950s, it was almost fifteen years before the possibility of a basic confounding in the paradigm was suggested and tested. Norman (1969) believed that the relatively poorer performance on the unattended message was not caused by the listener's inability to attend to the message, but instead could be attributed to the interference produced by the overt vocalization of the attended message during shadowing. It is well known that any overt vocalization—for example, counting backward by threes—will interfere with memory and rehearsal (see chapter 10). So Norman argued that the unshadowed message could be attended as well as the shadowed message but that its poor recall was caused by prevention of rehearsal. Thus, memory, and not attention, would be the proper locus of this deficit. Norman hypothesized that rehearsal—a memory process—was blocked by the overt vocalization of the shadowed message.

In order to test his hypothesis, Norman had to create a situation where vocalization of the shadowed message stopped. This would remove the source of interference blocking rehersal of the unshadowed message and should result in greatly increased recall of the unshadowed message. The main experimental conditions required that listeners shadow a verbal message and memorize a list of digits simultaneously presented in the other ear (Condition MS— Memorize and Shadow). The test of memory for these digits was either immediate—as soon as the digit list ended—or delayed for twenty seconds. The memory task was also tested by itself with no concurrent shadowing (Condition *M*). A memory interference condition (*MI*) required shadowing only after the digit list had been presented. Results for the tests of digit memory are shown in figure 7–7.

In the immediate-recall conditions, memory was always better than in delayed recall, indicating that if listeners stopped shadowing, the digit list was available in short-term memory. But the digit list was not maintained (or transferred to long-term memory) if recall was delayed and shadowing continued. So even though the digit list was available immediately, continued shadowing wiped it out.

FIGURE 7–7.

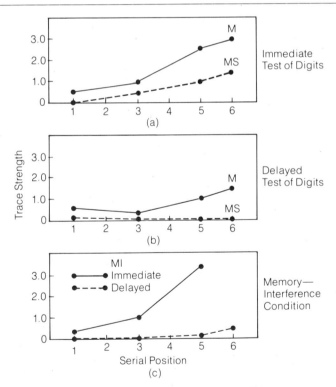

Memory performance for immediate and delayed tests with (*MS*) and without (*M*)shadowing. Trace strength is a derived dependent variable similar to *d'*. The top and middle panels show that memory is better when shadowing is not required (*M*),regardless of whether the test is immediate (top panel) or delayed (middle panel). Memory is better when tested immediately. The bottom panel for condition *MI* shows a similar finding even though no shadowing was required during the presentation of the digit list in this condition (from Norman, 1969).

Memory was always better when no shadowing was required. In the delayed-recall conditions, memory was poor. This was equally true in the *MI* condition, where *no shadowing was required* during the presentation of the digit list. Here, any memory decrement must be caused by interference, and not attention, just as counting backward interferes with memory. So Norman concluded that the decrement in memory that occurred when listeners were required to shadow was *not* caused by their inability to attend to two messages (digit list and verbal message) simultaneously.[1]

This type of confounding is more subtle and difficult to spot than the direct confounding of independent variables. However, confounding of psychological processes is a more serious (and more likely) error in psychological research because it can go unnoticed, at least for a while. In attention research it is difficult to separate effects caused by limitations on the listener's ability to attend to more than one stimulus at a time from an inability to remember more than one item at a time.

---

**Topic:** Interaction

**Illustration:** Dichotic Listening

---

An interaction occurs when the effects of one independent variable are not identical over different levels of other independent variables. As we explained in chapter 3, the search for interaction is a major reason for including more than one independent variable in an experiment.

Interactions depend very much on the measurement scale (see chapter 5) used by the dependent variable. It is easy to create or eliminate interactions (other than a cross-over interaction which can be plotted to look like an *X*) by applying mathematical or statistical transformations to data, for example, by taking the square root or logarithm or reciprocal of each data point. Indeed, many statistical packages that analyze data on computers offer the user a variety of possible transformations. However, as figure 7–8 shows, such a transformation can drastically alter an interaction. The top panel in figure 7–8 shows fictitious data for number of emitted vocal responses in a given time depending on whether your mouth is full of marbles or is in its normal state. The two curves clearly diverge as time increases, showing a strong interaction. In the

---

1 It could be argued that listeners might have shifted attention to the memory task at the expense of shadowing, thereby improving memory performance and decreasing shadowing performance. However, memory was still better when no shadowing was required. Furthermore, Norman properly included a shadowing-only condition to test this possibility and shadowing performance was, for the most part, the same whether or not listeners were required to remember digits.

FIGURE 7–8.

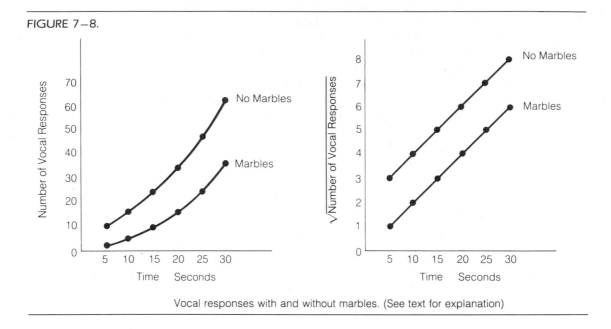

Vocal responses with and without marbles. (See text for explanation)

right panel, the same data are plotted, except we have used the transformation of taking the square root of each data point. Now the curves are obviously parallel, showing no interaction. The mathematical operation of taking a square root has eliminated the interaction shown in the untransformed data in the left of figure 7–8. This kind of alteration is well known, and psychologists are duly suspicious when arbitrary transformations of data are reported in journal articles. However, the same kind of transformation can occur in more subtle ways, depending on how the dependent variable is measured, even when no explicit mathematical transformations of data are performed. The following study of dichotic listening shows how this can happen.

Knight and Kantowitz (1975) presented five pairs of dichotic words to listeners. These pairs were presented either at a fast rate (2 pairs/sec) or a slow rate (1 pair/sec). The dichotic list was immediately followed by a probe word—that is, one of the words previously contained in the list. The listener was to respond with the word that followed the probe word in the same ear as the probe word. This procedure may at first seem rather more complicated than the usual procedure of asking the listener to recall as many words as possible, but it has the distinct advantage of minimizing interference among words during output, since only a single item must be recalled. Knight and Kantowitz were interested in (among other things) the relationship between rate of presentation (slow or fast) and the serial position of the probe. If the probe came from the first dichotic word-pair, it had serial position one, if from the second pair, serial position two, and so on. However, the probe word could never come from the last (fifth) dichotic word pair, since it would then be impossible for the listener to report the following word—that is, there were no more words after the last word. So probe serial position could only assume the values one through four as an independent variable. Serial position is a very common independent variable, especially in memory research (see chapter 10) and it has become customary to plot dependent variables as a function of serial position. Figure 7–9 shows the number of correct responses in this experiment as a function of serial position of the probe word and also presentation rate.

It is clear from figure 7–9 that the two curves are far from parallel and that a strong interaction between serial position and presentation rate has occurred. Without going into any details about theoretical models of attention, let us merely state that this sort of interaction suggests a joint effect of attentional and memory processes. Indeed, because the interaction is so strong—it is a so-called cross-over interaction—researchers would have great faith in the conclusion that slow and fast items are either represented in, or retrieved from, memory differently. In general, as was stated earlier in this chapter, interactions indicate shared or common stages of information processing, whereas additivities (no interactions) indicate separate processing of information.

Now look at figure 7–10, where the same data are presented, except that the scale has been changed for the independent variable. Instead of probe serial position being plotted, recall delay has been calculated for each serial position. Recall delay is the time between presentation of an item within a dichotic pair and presentation of the probe word. So the lower the serial position of

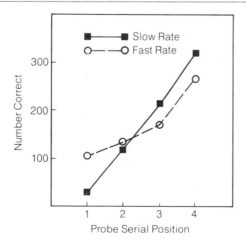

FIGURE 7–9.

Number of words correctly recalled as a function of presentation rate and serial position of probe word. The crossing lines indicate a strong interaction (Knight & Kantowitz, 1974).

an item—that is, the earlier it was presented—the greater the recall delay. As figure 7–10 clearly shows, measuring recall delay instead of serial position completely eliminates the interaction with presentation rate: the two curves are parallel. The interpretation of figure 7–10 is rather different from our interpretation of figure 7–9. Using recall delay as the dependent variable we would say that, regardless of presentation rate, all items are affected the same way in memory. We might even go so far as to suggest that the rate of loss or decay in memory (related to the slope of the parallel lines in figure 7–10) is the same for items presented both at the fast rate and at the slow rate.

Which of these two interpretations is correct? Or, in other words, which of the two figures is the right way to plot the relationship between the two independent variables? Figure 7–9 shows the traditional method of plotting these data and so has history on its side. However, serial position is scaled only on an ordinal metric (see chapter 5). In figure 7–10 recall delay is measured on a ratio scale (see chapter 5). Since ratio scales represent a higher order of measurement, this suggests that figure 7–10 should be preferred. The main point to remember is not so much that one figure is better, but that interactions cannot be interpreted without first giving considerable thought to the measurement scale used for variables.

Interactions can be misleading even when the dependent variable is scaled correctly. The following fictitious example shows how this could happen in a dichotic-listening experiment. Paying

FIGURE 7–10.

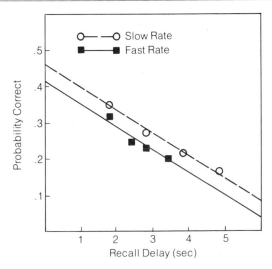

Probability of correct recall as a function of presentation rate and recall delay. These data are the same as in the preceding figure. (Plotting probability correct instead of number correct does not change the shape of the data). The parallel lines show no interaction (Knight & Kantowitz, 1975).

people more money to perform a task usually helps them do better. This result is attributed to motivational processes—that is, the worker tries harder and is more attentive to the task. So an industrial psychologist who knows something about dichotic listening designs an experiment to discover whether paying more attention and improving motivation by a monetary reward are related. One independent variable is the amount of money paid for each correct recall of a dichotic word: either one cent or fifty cents. The other independent variable is the number of dichotic word-pairs presented in each auditory list: either five or ten pairs. The results of this hypothetical experiment are shown in figure 7–11. As expected, paying listeners more money improved their performance. Also people did better on the shorter word list, recalling a higher percentage of words. But most important of all the two independent variables show a clear interaction, since the lines are far from parallel. Increasing the payoff caused a large improvement in recall for the long ten-word list, but very little improvement for the short five-word list. This interaction would suggest that what experimental psychologists call attention and what industrial psychologists call motivation are closely related.

But there is a serious flaw that prevents this experiment from supporting such a conclusion. Recall of the short list was quite good even when the payoff was only one cent per word. In order for recall of the short list to improve as much as recall for the long list—that is, for the two lines in figure 7–11 to be parallel—recall would have to exceed 100 percent. This is, of course, impossible. Recall of the shorter list has bumped into the top of the measurement scale for the dependent variable and this may be the expla-

FIGURE 7–11.

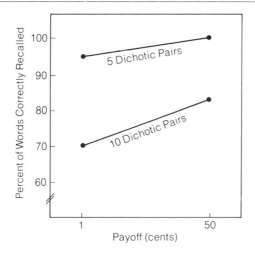

Percent of words correctly recalled in dichotic listening as a function of payoff and list length. Increasing payoff has a greater effect upon the longer list (fictitious data).

nation for the interaction. This type of problem is called scale attenuation (ceiling and floor effects) and is discussed in detail in chapter 10. For now, merely note that it is another instance where an interaction cannot be trusted. This experiment would have to be repeated with longer lists—say, ten and fifteen dichotic pairs— to avoid the ceiling effect in figure 7–11.

The search for interactions is an important part of psychological research and explains much of the popularity of analysis of variance as the major statistical technique used by psychologists. But a graph showing nonparallel lines does not always mean that a legitimate interaction is portrayed. The scale of measurement used in the dependent variable must be carefully examined before any conclusion about the presence or absence of an interaction can be reached. Transformations of the scale can create or eliminate interactions. Scale attenuation also can alter patterns of interaction.

## 7.3

**EXPERIMENTAL TOPICS AND RESEARCH ILLUSTRATIONS**

**Topic:** Selection of Dependent Variable.

**Illustration:** Speed-accuracy Tradeoff

As discussed in chapter 3, the experimenter must select one dependent variable from a host of possible dependent variables. An extremely popular dependent variable used in research on attention and information processing is reaction time. Indeed this variable is so popular that the study of reaction time has become virtually a content area in itself. When experimental psychologists get together, it would be quite likely for some of them to identify their research interests by stating "I'm in reaction time." This may sound odd to you, since a psychologist studying memory would not say "I'm in percent correct," but it does indicate that a dependent variable may become so important that it is studied not only as a means of investigating specific content areas but also as an object of study in its own right.

At first one might think that reaction time would be a poor topic to illustrate selection of a dependent variable, since by naming reaction time we have already made the selection. It is true that some psychologists routinely measure reaction time with little thought about the implications of this selection decision. Right now, reaction time is "in." The speed with which a task can be performed is often taken as an indication of the attentional requirements of the task. Things that can be done quickly are interpreted as having small attentional requirements. This logic is not always correct, since attention can be operationally defined in ways that need not involve reaction time. In this section we shall see how an even simpler use of reaction time, in which no assumptions about attention are made, can be misleading because not enough thought was given to selection of the dependent variable.

There is an inverse (backward) relationship between the speed and accuracy of performance. When you try to do something very fast, you make more mistakes than if you do it slowly. Conversely, if you try to do something very accurately, say typing a term paper, you must go more slowly to achieve the desired accuracy. Psychologists call this relationship the *speed-accuracy tradeoff*. It has important implications for studies that measure reaction time as the dependent variable.

This can be illustrated by an experiment conducted by Theios (1975) in which the task of the participant was quite simple. A digit was presented visually and the participant only had to name the digit. The independent variable was the probability (relative frequency) of the digits, which varied from .2 (a particular digit was presented 20 percent of the time) to .8. Reaction-time data from this experiment are shown in figure 7–12. Theios concluded that stimulus probability had no effect on reaction time.

This conclusion appears quite reasonable when errors are ignored. But when the error data also shown in figure 7–12 are considered, another interpretation emerges (Pachella, 1974). The average error rate of 3 percent may not seem very high to you, but stop and think about how simple the task was. All that was required was to name a digit, hardly a mind-blowing task for college students. Even worse, the error rate varied systematically according to stimulus probability, the independent variable. The highest error rate (6 percent) occurred with the lowest stimulus probability, and as the probability increased, error rate decreased. What would the reaction times have been if the error rates were equal for all levels of stimulus probability? According to the speed-accuracy tradeoff, reaction times in the low stimulus-probability conditions would have to increase in order to decrease the error rate. Pachella (1974) has suggested that in order to lower error rates to 2 percent, reaction time in the .2 stimulus-probability condition might have to be increased as much as 100 milliseconds. So the conclusion that stimulus probability does not affect reaction time must be questioned, once error rates are considered.

The basic problem here lies with the selection of reaction time as the *only* important dependent variable. Since reaction time depends in part on the error rate, we must consider both speed and accuracy as dependent variables. In short, reaction time is not a univariate dependent variable, but instead is a multivariate variable. Although it may reduce to a single dependent variable in some cases where error rate is constant across all levels of the independent variables, in general, two dependent variables—reaction time and error rate—must be jointly considered.

This point will be illustrated one more time by reference to an attention experiment conducted by Knight and Kantowitz (1974). They presented two stimuli separated by a very short time period

FIGURE 7–12.

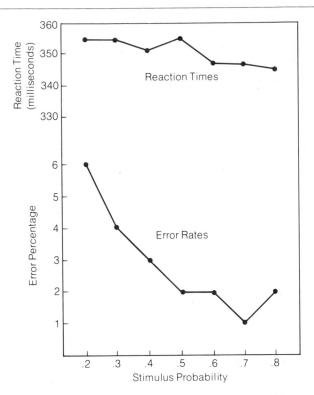

Reaction time and error rate as a function of stimulus probability. While reaction time is fairly constant, error rate declines as stimulus probability increases (data from Theios, 1975).

called the interstimulus interval. This was the independent variable. The dependent variables were reaction time and error rate. Previous research had shown that under conditions similar to that investigated by Knight and Kantowitz, reaction time was constant for different interstimulus intervals. Such a finding is similar to that of Theios, where stimulus probability was held to have no influence on reaction time. But when Knight and Kantowitz plotted error data as a function of interstimulus interval (see figure 7–13), a definite relationship was found. Error rates were higher at shorter interstimulus intervals. Again we could ask: what would the reaction times have been if error rates were equal at all interstimulus intervals? According to the speed-accuracy tradeoff, reaction times at shorter interstimulus intervals would have been greater. So the earlier conclusion of previous investigators that reaction time was not influenced by interstimulus interval was shown to be misleading. Correctly selecting two dependent variables would have allowed them to reach a more accurate conclusion.

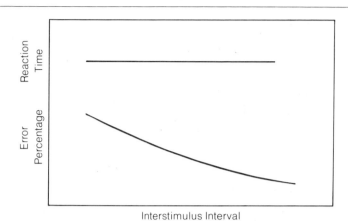

FIGURE 7–13.

Reaction time and error rate as a function of interstimulus interval. While reaction time is constant, error rate decreases for longer interstimulus intervals (adapted from Knight & Kantowitz, 1974).

---

**Problem:** Measuring Attention

**FROM PROBLEM TO EXPERIMENT: THE NUTS AND BOLTS**

Some of the things we do seem to proceed fairly automatically, and others seem to require great concentration. Motor skills like walking do not require much mental effort, whereas doing mental arithmetic can be quite taxing. In order to study the attentional requirements of various tasks, we must have some way to measure attention.

**Problem:** How can we determine the amount of attention or mental effort that any arbitrary task might require?

As is usually the case, this problem must be refined further and some hypotheses must be formulated before any meaningful solution can be attempted.

**Hypothesis:** Increased attentional demands will be accompanied by increased stress, which will show up as a change in some physiological measure of body function.

This hypothesis is a little vague because it fails to specify the dependent variable precisely. There are many physiological correlates of behavior, and it is not clear from the hypothesis whether the experimenter should record heart rate, galvanic skin response, or brain waves, or perform a chemical analysis of breathing exhalations. This difficulty could be bypassed by deciding to record every physiological measure that could be conveniently instrumented. Use of several dependent measures is indeed quite common in studies that investigate physiological correlates of attention, and this approach, although not terribly efficient, would strike some psychologists as a reasonable one. Although some of the dependent variables might prove to be useless, presumably they could be thrown out and only the "good" physiological measures retained.

Let us arbitrarily select three dependent variables: heart rate, brain wave (EEG), and pupil (a part of the eye, not a student) diameter. We hope that one or more of these will be correlated with attention. Now we must choose an independent variable. In order to do this we need to first select a task where we are fairly certain that (a) attention is required, and (b) the amount of attention required can be varied by changing task difficulty. This is not as easy as it first appears, and to do this properly we must search the available literature to find converging operations (see chapter 6 or 14), where the same task has been used in different situations. Without going into the details of how this can be accomplished, let us assume that one task that meets this requirement is the dichotic-listening task discussed earlier in this chapter. We will further assume that attentional requirements of dichotic listening can be controlled by varying the presentation rate of dichotic lists, with faster rates calling for more attention. So our independent variable will be the presentation rate of a series of dichotic lists that are to be shadowed (repeated aloud). How many different presentation rates should be used? Clearly at least two, since we cannot manipulate attention required with only a single presentation rate. The actual number selected would be a compromise between having as many different presentation rates as possible and the limitations of time, money, and so forth. Let us say that four presentation rates will be used; 1 word-pair every 4 seconds, every 2 seconds, and every 1 second, and 2 pairs every 1 second.

What about control variables? First we need to make sure that the only difference among the various dichotic lists is the blank interval between successive pairs of words, and that the duration of the words does not change with presentation rate. This means that we cannot simply use a tape recorder with someone speaking in time with a metronome, since, as people speak more quickly to generate faster presentation rates, the word durations also change. So we use a computer to generate our dichotic lists. We will also need to control for variables that are likely to influence heart rate, EEG, and pupil diameter. This list of variables is quite extensive, and our present discussion will illustrate control on only two dependent variables. Heart rate is known to change with respiration (breathing) rate. It is difficult to control someone's breathing rate without resorting to unpleasant chemical and mechanical treatments. Most experimenters would not take this kind of risk and would simply monitor breathing rates. Technically this kind of control adds another dependent variable. The control achieved is statistical rather than experimental—in this case, by correlating heart and breathing rates. Pupil diameter is very sensitive to amount of illumination, with bright light causing the pupil to contract. So the experimenter would take care to keep the level of illumination constant throughout the study. Control would then be experimental rather than statistical, unlike the case for control of heart rate.

If we actually did this kind of experiment, you probably would expect only EEG to be related to attention. However, there are data (see Kahneman, 1973) suggesting that all three of our dependent variables are related to attention and amount of mental effort.

**Hypothesis:** *The amount of attention required by some task can be measured by reaction time to a simultaneous Donders B reaction task.*

Here the dependent variable is specified precisely. It is choice reaction time. The logic behind this hypothesis is that the choice reaction task requires attention, so that attention devoted to the other task (usually called the primary task) must be diverted away from the reaction task, leading to increased reaction time. A further assumption is that both the primary task and the choice reaction task draw on a common source of attention or capacity.

Let us use the same independent variable as in the previous example—dichotic presentation rate. Our listener must shadow a dichotic list and at the same time respond to a choice reaction signal. Since the dichotic list occupies the auditory modality, a visual reaction signal should be used. Similarly, a motor reaction response like a keypress should be used, since the speech mechanism is occupied by shadowing. If the hypothesis is correct, longer reaction times will occur when faster presentation rates are used.

Control variables would be computer control of the dichotic list, control of the intensity of the visual signals, and the timing of the visual signals. The most important control would be instructions (or payoff) to guarantee that performance on the dichotic lists was not changed by adding the reaction task. So we would have a control condition (not a control variable) where only one task was required, and an experimental condition where both tasks had to be done together. Unless performance on the primary task was the same in both control and experimental conditions, we could not reach any conclusions about the attention demands of shadowing. For example, if listeners did much better when no reaction task was required, this could indicate a shift of attention from shadowing to reaction task, when both were performed together. The logic of the hypothesis demands that the same amount of attention always be devoted to the listening task within any one presentation rate. The reaction-time task measures the surplus attention left over from shadowing. If the listener voluntarily diverts attention away from the shadowing task to do the reaction task, the experiment is spoiled.

**SUMMARY**

**1.** Interest in reaction time began with the personal equation, a systematic difference in reaction times found among eighteenth-century astronomers. This phenomenon led Donders to formulate his *subtractive method.*

**2.** The Donders *A* reaction time, when subtracted from the C reaction time, yields identification time. Similarly, Donders *B* reaction time minus *C* reaction time yields an estimate of selection time.

**3.** The current descendant of Donders's efforts is the *method of additive factors.* It uses factorial combinations of independent variables to reveal internal processing stages.

**4.** In *dichotic listening* experiments, two independent messages are presented simultaneously, one to each ear. The *shadowing* technique requires that a listener repeat one of the messages aloud, whereas the *monitoring* task requires that a subject only listen and not vocalize.

**5.** *Confounding* occurs when a factor that covaries with an independent variable may account for observed changes in behavior. Both the shadowing and monitoring tasks in dichotic listening can be misused to confound factors related to attention and memory.

**6.** *Interactions* occur when the effect of one independent variable differs for levels of other independent variables manipulated in the same experiment. Mathematical transformations of data can remove (or create) interactions. Altering the way a dependent variable is scaled or measured can also change interactions.

**7.** Dependent variables must be carefully selected. Studies that measure reaction time must also record error rate. Speed can be traded off for accuracy, as when a task is completed more rapidly but at the expense of a higher error rate. Thus, reaction time is only one component of a multivariate dependent variable. Error rate is the other component.

**KEY TERMS**

| | |
|---|---|
| additive factors | interaction |
| attention | monitoring |
| choice reaction | personal equation |
| confounding | reaction time |
| dichotic listening | shadowing |
| Donders *A* reaction | simple reaction |
| Donders *B* reaction | speed-accuracy tradeoff |
| Donders *C* reaction | subtractive method |
| error rate | transformation |

**1.** What arguments could Kinnebrook have used to keep his job at the Royal Observatory?

**2.** Read the articles by Sternberg and by Taylor cited in this chapter. What are the critical differences between the subtractive method and the method of additive factors? What are some of the problems with the method of additive factors?

**3.** What variables are confounded in the following experiment? An experimenter who believes that women talk much more than men suspects that women will do better in a shadowing task than men, especially at faster presentation rates. Two groups of subjects, one consisting of ten men and the other of ten women, are formed. The women shadow dichotic messages at a rate of 10 pairs per second for 20 trials. Each trial consists of one minute of dichotic messages. Then the women listen to 20 additional trials at a rate of 5 pairs per second. So that the effects of presentation rate are counterbalanced, the men start with the slower rate (5 pairs per second) and then shadow the faster dichotic messages. How would you improve this experimental design?

**4.** List five samples of speed-accuracy tradeoff that occur in everyday life outside the laboratory. Select two of your examples and design a laboratory experiment that will measure speed-accuracy tradeoff. Plot graphs of hypothetical results for each experiment.

# Psychology in Action

## Speed-accuracy Tradeoff

The following demonstration requires a pencil, a newspaper, and a watch with a second hand. It helps if you have a friend to time you, but a photographic timer with a buzzer can be used instead. Set your timer (or your friend) to thirty seconds. Now, going at a comfortable speed, work your way through a newspaper article crossing out every letter *e* that occurs. Stop after thirty seconds and count the number of lines that you have completed. This number is your baseline figure. (Enter it in table 7–1.) Now keep the time constant at thirty seconds, but try to increase the number of lines that have crossed-out letter *e*'s by 10 percent. Then repeat this process with 10 percent fewer lines than your baseline—that is, go slower this time. Then repeat with 15 percent more lines (go faster), and 15 percent fewer. Now take a well-deserved rest. When you have recovered, go back over each of the five passages you have crossed out and count the number of letter *e*'s you should have crossed out and the number you actually crossed out. Dividing the number crossed out by the total number gives you your error rate or percentage. Did you systematically make more errors as you tried to go faster and include more lines, thus revealing a tradeoff between speed and accuracy?

TABLE 7–1        Empirical Determination of Speed-Accuracy Tradeoff

| | Number of Lines | Number e's Crossed Out Correctly (1) | Number e's Missed (2) | Total e's (1) + (2) | Percent (2) ÷ [(1) + (2)] |
|---|---|---|---|---|---|
| Baseline (B) | | | | | |
| B + 10% | | | | | |
| B − 10% | | | | | |
| B + 15% | | | | | |
| B − 15% | | | | | |

# CHAPTER 8 ═══════════════

## Preview

This chapter is concerned with two crucial methodological issues, which are discussed in the context of experiments on conditioning and learning in animals. The first is the use of between-subjects and within-subjects designs, which occurs when different groups of subjects are assigned to experimental conditions (between-subjects) and when the same group of subjects participates in all conditions (within-subjects). We discuss the advantages and disadvantages of each, and note that in some cases the outcome of an experiment may hinge on the type of design used. In within-subjects designs the researcher must pay careful attention to the order in which the conditions are administered to the subjects. In order not to confound conditions with other factors (such as practice at the task), the experimenter must balance the conditions against these factors. Thus counterbalancing is the second major topic considered in this chapter.

## Chapter Outline

# CONDITIONING
# AND LEARNING

*We should be careful to get out of an experience only the wisdom that is in it—and stop there; lest we be like the cat that sits down on a hot stove-lid. She will never sit down on a hot stove-lid again—and that is well; but also she will never sit down on a cold one anymore.*

Mark Twain

In the early 1900s the German public was introduced to the feats of Clever Hans, a remarkable horse that belonged to Herr von Osten, a mathematics teacher. Von Osten would read arithmetic problems to Clever Hans and the horse would tap out the correct answer with his forefoot. When asked to add "eight plus three" Hans tapped his foot eleven times. The horse was about equally adept at addition, subtraction, multiplication, and division; he was also able to answer simple questions about spelling, reading, and musical harmony.

Needless to say, many Germans found Clever Hans's talents hard to believe. Yet von Osten seemed earnest, and he did not try to profit from his horse's notoriety. So that the skeptics would be satisfied, the horse was tested in the absence of von Osten. Surprisingly, Hans performed his tasks about as well as ever.

Could Hans really understand language and do arithmetic? Two psychologists, Pfungst and Stumpf, performed a series of experiments that finally convinced everyone that although Hans was in some ways a very clever horse, his talents did not extend to mathematics. Pfungst (1911) reported that Hans actually accomplished his feats by detecting subtle nonverbal signals that the questioners provided unconsciously. The researchers noted that when Hans tapped he would go quickly at first, then slow down, then stop at the right place (or sometimes miss by a number or two). They discovered that the questioners tended to incline their heads as they gave Hans a problem, then straighten up as he neared the correct answer. Hans also seemed to be sensitive to each questioner's eyebrow movements, dilation of nostrils, and tone of voice. When prevented from seeing or hearing his questioners while he tapped, Hans was no longer able to perform. The horse had simply learned covert signals from von Osten indicating when he should stop tapping.

Although Hans could not understand mathematics, he at least had the horse sense to outwit his human observers for a long while. Actually, the process by which Hans learned his trick is as interesting as the trick itself. Today psychologists refer to this process as instrumental learning, a topic that we will describe in this chapter. From a cue, Hans learned to perform a response that was rewarded with attention and food. The same learning techniques are used by animal trainers to teach animals marvelous acts. Elephants stand on their front paws, dolphins caper about performing a long series of tricks, and killer whales can even "kiss" their trainers. In these cases animals are explicitly trained to perform, whereas Hans mastered his trick on his own.

In this chapter we consider two fundamental types of learning, classical and instrumental conditioning, in order to illustrate several methodological issues. Before discussing these issues we will describe briefly the two fundamental types of conditioning.

## DOES THE NAME PAVLOV RING A BELL?

Early in this century some fundamental psychological discoveries were made by Ivan P. Pavlov (1849–1936). The basic discovery that he made—which is now called Pavlovian or *classical conditioning*—is well known today even by those outside psychology, but the fascinating story of how it came about is not. Pavlov was not at all trained as a psychologist (there were no psychologists in Russia, or elsewhere, when he received his education), but as a physiologist. He made great contributions in physiology concerning the measurement and analysis of stomach secretions accompanying the digestive process. He was able to carefully measure the fluids produced by different sorts of food, and he regarded the secretion of the stomach juices as a physiological reflex. For his important work on the gastric juices in the digestive process he was awarded the Nobel prize for medicine in 1904.

It was only after he had won the Nobel prize that Pavlov turned to some more or less incidental discoveries made in the course of his work, which led to the ones for which he is so well known today. In one type of physiological experiment, Pavlov cut a dog's esophagus so that it would no longer carry food to the stomach (see figure 8–1). But he discovered that when he placed food in the dog's mouth, the stomach secreted almost as much gastric juice as when the food went to the stomach. Thus the reflexive action of the stomach seemed to depend on stimuli located in other places besides those in direct contact with the stomach lining. But then Pavlov made an even more remarkable discovery. He found that it was not even necessary to place food in contact with the mouth to obtain salivary and gastric secretions. The mere sight of food would produce the secretions, or even the sight of the food dish without the food, or even the sight of the person who usually fed the animal! Obviously, then, secretion of the gastric juices must be caused by more than an automatic physiological reflex produced when a substance comes into direct contact with the stomach lining. A physiological reflex is one that is shown by all animals of a certain species; it is "wired" into the nervous system. Pavlov had discovered a new type of reflex, one that he sometimes called a psychic reflec and sometimes a conditioned reflex. The standard paradigm for studying Pavlovian conditioning in the laboratory is outlined in figure 8–2.

The importance of Pavlov's discovery is that any stimulus in the environment that normally is neutral (that is, has no specific effect on behavior) can be made to control certain responses by pairing it with other stimuli that produce an automatic physical reaction. For example, if a person is subjected to a stressful event in a particular situation (say, one's office or room), then the body will respond with defensive reactions—the heart may race, blood pressure increase, adrenalin flow, and so on. These responses might become conditioned to the situation, so that even without a stressful event a person may show all these physiological changes in the

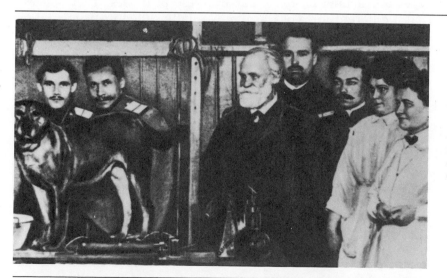

FIGURE 8–1.
Ivan Pavlov and his staff are shown here with one of the dogs used in his experiments. The dog was harnessed to the wooden frame shown in the picture. Saliva was conducted by a tube to a measuring device that could record the rate and quantity of salivation.

FIGURE 8–2.

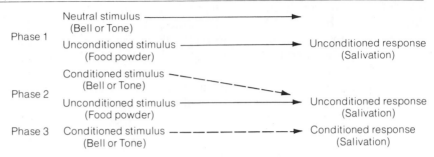

An outline of the stages in classical conditioning. A neutral stimulus such as a bell or a tone that elicits no response when presented by itself is delivered to the organism slightly before an unconditioned stimulus *(US)*, such as food powder, that produces an unconditioned response *(UR)*, salivation. After a number of such pairings (Phase 1) the neutral stimulus becomes associated with the *UR*, as indicated by the broken line in Phase 2. The response becomes conditioned to the neutral stimulus, which is now called the conditioned stimulus *(CS)*. Eventually (Phase 3), the *CS* will elicit salivation (now called the conditioned response, *CR*, in absence of the *US*. If the *CS* is repeatedly presented without the *US*, the *CR* will grow weaker and eventually extinguish altogether.

situation. Some researchers in the field of behavioral medicine have argued that many disorders so prevalent today—hypertension, gastric ulcers, headaches—may be caused by conditioned reactions that occur when people are in situations where they have repeatedly experienced stress. Pavlovian conditioning also seems to play a role in the development of other important human behaviors, including phobias (irrational fears).

Although processes of classical conditioning are of importance, other psychologists (particularly B. F. Skinner) argue that many types of learning do not occur by these processes. They suggest that a different form of learning—usually called instrumental or operant conditioning—is the prototype for much learning.

### Instrumental (Operant) Conditioning

The earliest examples of the second type of conditioning were experiments by E. L. Thorndike at Columbia University, who put cats in puzzle boxes from which they sought to escape. These experiments were performed at about the same time as Pavlov's. They are described in detail in chapter 11, but briefly, the primary point is that the experiment concerned learning from the consequences of some action. Thorndike's cats performed some response that allowed then to escape from the puzzle box and then, when they were replaced in the box, they tended to perform the same response again. Thus the consequences of a behavior affected how it was learned. Since the behavior was instrumental in producing the consequence (the reward), this form of learning was called *instru-*

*mental conditioning.* It was seen as obeying different principles than Pavlovian conditioning (what is the US?, the UR?, the CS?, the CR?), and was also viewed as a more general type of learning.

Over the years a great number of American psychologists have devoted much effort to understanding instrumental conditioning. In fact, this was perhaps the central topic in experimental psychology from 1930 to 1960, with the involvement of such famous psychologists as Clark Hull, Edward Tolman, and Kenneth Spence. But perhaps the most famous investigator and popularizer of the study of this type of conditioning is B. F. Skinner, whose importance is unparalleled in psychology today.

Skinner calls this type of conditioning *operant conditioning,* because the response operates on the environment. This is distinguished from *respondent conditioning* studied by Pavlovians, where the organism simply responds to environmental stimulation. The primary datum of interest in the study of operant conditioning is the frequency with which some response occurs. The primary responses that have been studied are those of lever pressing by rats and button pecking by pigeons in operant-conditioning apparatuses, or, more colloquially, in Skinner boxes. These are simply small, well-lit, little boxes with a lever or button that can be depressed and a place for dispensing food (see figure 8–3).

In operant conditioning, the experimenter waits until the animal makes the desired response and then rewards it, say, with food. If the entire response is not performed, the experimenter must reinforce successive approximations to it until the desired response occurs. So, for example, if you want to teach a pigeon to walk around in figure-eights you must first reward quarter-circle turns, then half-turns, and so on. This procedure of reinforcing greater and greater approximations to the desired behavior is called shaping the behavior. Operant conditioning works on the principle of the law of effect: If an operant response is made and followed by a reinforcing stimulus, the probability that the response will occur again is increased. What will serve as a *reinforcing stimulus* is not specified ahead of time, but must be discovered for each situation. Using this straightforward principle, Skinner and many others have undertaken the experimental analysis of numerous behaviors.

The role of stimuli other than the reinforcing stimulus is also important in the study of operant conditioning. A *discriminative stimulus* is one that informs the organism when a behavior will be followed by a reward. For example, a pigeon might be trained to peck a button for food only in the presence of a red light. If any other light is on, pecking will not be followed by food. Animals learn such contingencies between stimuli and responses quite readily. A discriminative stimulus (or $S^D$) may be said to "set the stage" or "provide the occasion" for some response. One of the primary tasks of operant conditioning is to bring some response "under stimulus control." An organism is said to be under stimulus control when it responds correctly and consistently in the presence of a discriminative stimulus and not in its absence.

FIGURE 8–3.

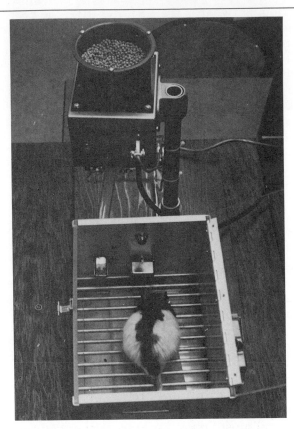

Typical Skinner box with a lever (middle) and light above and food cup to the left. The top of the picture shows the pellet dispenser with 0.45 mg precision food pellets. When the animal makes a correct response a pellet of food rolls down the clear tube between the dispenser and the box and falls into the cup. Ten to twelve pellets can be seen in the food cup. All of this machinery is controlled by programming equipment which allows the experimenter to set different tasks for the animal.

FIGURE 8–3a.

Both operant- and classical-conditioning procedures are actively investigated by contemporary psychologists interested in learning. We will be discussing both procedures in the context of specific experimental issues later in the chapter.

## INTRODUCING THE VARIABLES IN CONDITIONING AND LEARNING

### Dependent Variables

One important dependent variable in animal-learning research is the frequency of responding, often plotted over time. Another important dependent variable commonly used in classical conditioning is the amplitude of the response. Rather than just noting whether or not a dog salivates to a conditioned stimulus, we can measure the amplitude of the response by seeing how much saliva is produced. Another commonly measured characteristic of responses is their latency, or the time it takes the animal to accomplish the response. This measure is widely used in maze-learning experiments, where the time it takes an animal to complete the maze is recorded. Often results are plotted in terms of speed rather than latency, speed being the reciprocal of latency (1/latency).

A derived measure of learning is resistance to extinction. After a response has been learned, if the experimenter no longer applies reinforcement when the animal executes the response, the response gradually grows weaker or extinguishes. Resistance to extinction, then, can be used as an index of how well the response was learned in the first place. It is considered a derived, rather than basic, measure because what is still being measured is frequency, amplitude, or speed of response. These all decline during extinction, but they may decline at different rates after different manipulations of the independent variable. Thus resistance to extinction is a derived measure of the effectiveness of some independent variable on learning.

### Independent Variables

A great many independent variables may be manipulated in studies of animal learning and conditioning. Many have to do with the nature of reinforcement. Experimenters can vary the magnitude of reinforcement in Pavlovian and instrumental conditioning. Experimenters can also vary the schedule by which reinforcement is administered. They can also vary the delay after the response, before they present the reinforcing stimulus to the subject. (Typically, longer delays produce less learning.) Another popular variable is the drive level of the animal (how motivated it is). This can be manipulated by varying the amount of time the organism has been deprived of the reinforcing stimulus (say, food or water) before the experiment. These are, of course, a small sample of the possible independent variables.

### Control Variables

Control of extraneous variation is typically quite sophisticated in basic animal learning research, but even here there are subtle problems. One of these is the problem of pseudoconditioning in classical conditioning experiments. Pseudoconditioning refers to a temporary elevation in the amplitude of the conditioned response that is not caused by the association between the CS and US. Thus it is not true conditioning, but only mimics conditioning. It is recognized by being relatively short-lived and variable in nature, and is usually caused by the general excitement of the experimental situation for

(continued on next page)

the animal, including the presentation of the CS and US. The appropriate control for pseudoconditioning is to have one group of animals in the experiment exposed to the same number of CS and US presentations as the animals in the conditioning group, but to have the presentations unpaired and presented randomly. Thus both the experimental and pseudoconditioning control groups should be affected by the general excitement induced by the experimental situation, and any difference between the two groups should be due to the learning produced by the CS–US pairings in the case of the experimental group (Rescorla, 1967).

## 8.1

**EXPERIMENTAL TOPICS AND RESEARCH ILLUSTRATIONS**

**Topic:** Within- and Between-subjects Designs

**Illustration:** Stimulus Intensity

One fundamental question about classical conditioning is how the intensity of a neutral stimulus affects the conditioning process. For example, if a tone is paired with food given to dogs, will the intensity of the tone affect how quickly the dog becomes conditioned so that the tone alone (now called the conditioned stimulus) produces salivation? A reasonable hypothesis is that the stronger the stimulus, the more quickly conditioning will occur. It seems reasonable that animals will notice more salient stimuli and thus better associate them with the unconditioned stimulus. Thus we might predict that the stronger the conditioned stimulus, the faster and stronger conditioning will occur.

Many researchers have investigated this question over the years, and the surprising finding from most of the early research was that stimulus intensity did not seem to have much effect on Pavlovian conditioning. Relatively weak stimuli seemed to produce just as good conditioning as did strong stimuli (Carter, 1941; Grant and Schneider, 1948). Since most theories of the time predicted that conditioning should be affected by the intensity of the stimulus (Hull, 1949), the failure to find the effect constituted something of a puzzle. The researchers who did these experiments on stimulus-intensity effects in conditioning typically used between-subjects designs, so that different groups of subjects received different stimulus intensities. Before discussing the reason for their doing this, let us consider some of the general advantages and disadvantages of between-subjects and within-subjects experimental designs.

***Between-subjects versus within-subjects designs.*** Perhaps the simplest sort of experimental design is the case where there are two conditions, an experimental and control, and different groups of subjects are assigned to each. In a *between-subjects design* a different group of subjects is usually assigned to each level of each independent variable. One potential problem is using a between-subject design is that a difference obtained on the dependent variable might be caused by the fact that different groups of subjects were used in the two conditions. That is, subjects may be confounded with the independent variable of interest. In order to overcome this potential problem, experimenters randomly assign subjects to conditions in between-subjects designs. Thus, *on the average,* the groups should be of equal ability in the two conditions. In all between-subjects designs, then, the subjects should be randomly assigned to the different conditions to ensure that the groups are equivalent prior to the manipulation of the independent variable. This is absolutely crucial, since otherwise any difference observed between the groups on the dependent variable might be merely because subjects in the different groups differed in ability. If subjects are randomly assigned to groups, then we can minimize the possibility of this sort of confounding and be more confident that any difference we find on the dependent variable is actually owing to the independent-variable manipulation. When subjects are randomly assigned to conditions in a between-subjects design, this is referred to as a *random-groups design.*

There are two primary drawbacks to between-subjects or random-groups designs. One is that they are wasteful in terms of the number of subjects required. When a different group of subjects is assigned to each condition, the number of subjects required for an experiment can quickly become quite large, if the experimental design is at all complex. Thus between-subjects designs are impractical when, as is often the case, there is a shortage of subjects available for an experiment.

The second problem is more serious and has to do with the variability introduced by using different groups of subjects. One basic fact of all psychological research is that subjects differ greatly in their abilities to perform almost any task (or on any dependent variable). When numerous subjects are used in between-subjects designs, some of the differences in behavior in the experimental conditions will be owing to differences among subjects. In between-subjects designs this variability caused by subject differences cannot be estimated statistically and taken into account.

The problem of between-subjects variability is typically greater in experimental work with humans than with other subjects such as pigeons or rats. The "lower" animals do not seem to vary as much in performing tasks as do humans, so this difficulty is not as great in research with animal subjects where between-subjects designs are employed.

Both the problems with between-subjects designs can be reduced by using *within-subjects designs*, where all subjects are given treatments at every level of the independent variable. But new problems are introduced by within-subjects designs. On the positive side, within-subjects designs use fewer subjects than between-subjects designs because each subject serves in all conditions. Also, there are statistical techniques for taking into account the variance that is produced by the differences between subjects. Thus a within-subjects design is usually more effective than a between-subjects design in detecting differences between conditions on the dependent variable because this variance can be estimated statistically and taken into account. The exact statistical techniques for analyzing within-subjects experiments will not be discussed here, but in general the within-subjects design is more powerful—more likely to allow detection of a difference between conditions if there really is one—than is the between-subjects design. This advantage makes the within-subjects design preferred by many investigators whenever it is possible to use it.

Unfortunately, within-subjects designs simply cannot be used in investigating some types of experimental problems, and even when they can be used they have requirements that between-subjects designs do not. It is not possible to use within-subjects designs in cases where performing in one condition is likely to completely change performance in another condition. This problem is usually called *asymmetrical transfer* or a *carry-over effect.* If we want to know how rats differ in learning a maze with and without their hippocampuses, we cannot use a within-subjects design since we cannot replace a hippocampus once it is removed. But the same problem occurs any time the independent variable may provide a change in behavior that will carry over until the subject is tested under the other condition.

If we want to test people on a task either with or without some specific training, it is impossible to test them first with training and then with no training. And we cannot test them always in the reverse order (no training and then training) because then we have confounded conditions with practice on the task. For example, if we want to see if a specific memory-training program is effective, we cannot teach people the program (the training phase), test them, and then test them again with no training. Once a person has had the training we cannot take it away; it will carry over to the next part of the experiment. We cannot test people in the other direction, either, with a memory test, a training phase, and then a second memory test. The reason is that if people improved on the second test we would not know whether or not the improvement was a result of training or merely practice at taking memory tests. In other words, training and practice would be confounded. A between-subjects design is appropriate in this case. One group of subjects would have their memories tested with no training, the other group would be tested after being trained with the memory program.

Within-subjects designs are also inappropriate in cases where subjects may figure out what is expected of them in the experiment and then try to cooperate with the experimenter and produce the desired results. This is more likely to happen with within- than between-subjects designs because the subjects participate in each condition in the former case. This problem makes within-subjects designs all but nonexistent in certain types of social psychological research.

Even when these problems do not eliminate the possibility of using a within-subjects design in some situation, there are additional problems to be considered. In within-subjects designs the subjects are always tested at two or more points in time and thus the experimenter must be on guard for factors related to time affecting the experimental results.

The two primary factors that must be considered are *practice effects* and *fatigue effects*, which tend to offset one another. Practice effects refer to subjects performing better in the experimental task simply because of practice and not the manipulation of the independent variable (as in the memory experiment just discussed), and fatigue effects refer to decreases in performance over the course of the experiment, especially if the experimental task is long, difficult, or boring. The effects of practice and fatigue may be taken into account and minimized by systematically arranging the order in which the experimental conditions are presented to subjects. This is referred to as *counterbalancing* of conditions and is discussed later in the chapter.

As we have said, when appropriate, within-subjects designs are generally preferred to between-subjects designs, despite the fact that they involve a number of additional considerations. The primary advantage, once again, is that within-subjects designs are typically more powerful or more sensitive because the possibility of error resulting from subject variability is reduced relative to that in between-subjects designs.

A third sort of design, the *matched-groups design*, attempts to introduce some of the advantages of a within-subjects design to a between-subjects comparison. The matched-groups design attempts to reduce subject variability among groups by matching the subjects in the different groups on other variables. Thus, in a human memory experiment, subjects might be matched on the basis of I.Q. before they are randomly assigned to conditions. (Each subgroup of matched subjects is randomly assigned.) Matching on relevant variables can help reduce the variability caused by randomly assigning subjects to each group (the random-groups design). Also, it is very important that assignment to conditions still be random within matched sets of subjects; otherwise there is the possibility of confounding and other problems, especially regression artifacts (see chapters 2 and 12). Matching in many situations tends to involve much work, since subjects must be measured separately on the matching variable. One matching technique used in animal research is the *split-litter technique*. This involves taking animals from the same litter and then randomly assigning them to groups. Since the animals in the different groups are genetically similar, this helps reduce variability resulting from subject differences that occurs in random-groups designs.

***Stimulus intensity in classical conditioning.*** Let us now return to the problem we considered earlier. How does the intensity of the conditioned stimulus affect acquisition of a conditioned response? Common sense, as well as some theories, led to the prediction that more-intense stimuli should lead to faster conditioning than less-intense stimuli. However, as mentioned earlier, the first research on this topic failed to find such effects. For example, Grant and Schneider (1948) varied the intensity of a light as a conditioned stimulus in an eyelid-conditioning experiment. In such experiments, people are attached to an apparatus that delivers puffs of air to the eye and records responses (eye blinks). Thus the unconditioned stimulus is the air puff, the unconditioned response is the blinking, and the conditioned stimulus is a light that precedes the air puff. Originally the light does not cause a subject to blink, but after it is repeatedly paired with the air puff, eventually the light by itself causes the blinking, which then is the conditioned response. Grant and Schneider asked simply whether more-intense lights would cause faster conditioning. Would a bright light cause subjects to develop a conditioned response faster than a dim light? They tested different groups of subjects in the two cases, one with each intensity of light, and discovered that conditioning was just as fast in the condition with the dim light as it was in the condition with the bright light, contrary to expectations. Other researchers obtained similar results when they examined the effects of stimulus intensity on conditioning in between-subjects designs, even when they used different stimuli (such as tones instead of lights).

The use of between- or within-subjects designs is usually determined by the nature of the problem studied, the independent variables manipulated, the number of subjects available to the researcher, and other considerations described in the preceding section. Rarely do researchers consider the possibility that the very outcome of their research could depend on the type of design they choose. However, this is exactly the case in the issue of the effects of stimulus intensity on conditioning, as was discovered after Grant and Schneider's (1948) research.

Years later Beck (1963) again asked the question of whether the intensity of the stimulus affected eyelid conditioning. She was also interested in other variables, including the intensity of the unconditioned stimulus (the air puff) and the anxiety level of her subjects. But for our purposes we will consider only the effect of the intensity level of the conditioned stimulus, which was varied within-subjects as one factor in a complex experimental design. Beck used two intensity levels and presented them in an irregular order across 100 conditioning trials in her experiment. She found a large and statistically reliable effect of stimulus intensity on development of the conditioned response, contrary to what other researchers had found.

Grice and Hunter (1964) noticed Beck's effect and wondered if she had found an effect where others had found none because she had used a within-subjects design whereas most others had used between-subjects designs. To discover this they tested three groups of subjects: in two groups the variable of intensity of the conditioned stimulus was varied between-subjects, and for the remaining group it was varied within-subjects. They used a soft tone (50 decibels) or a loud tone (100 decibels) as the conditioned stimuli in an eyelid-conditioning experiment. Subjects in each group participated in 100 trials. On each trial subjects heard a buzzer which alerted them that a trial was beginning. Two seconds later they heard a tone (soft or loud) that lasted .5 seconds, and then after another half-second they received a puff of air to the eye. The tone was the conditioned stimulus, the air puff the unconditioned stimulus. The Loud Group received the 100-decibel tone on all 100 trials, whereas the Soft Group received the 50-decibel tone on all 100 trials. These two groups represent a between-subjects comparison of stimulus-intensity level in eyelid conditioning. Subjects in the third group (the Loud/Soft Group) received 50 trials with the loud tone (*L*) and 50 trials with the soft tone (*S*). The trials occurred in one of two irregular orders, such that one order was the mirror image of the other. In other words, if the order of the first ten trials was *L, S, S, L, S, L, L, L, S, L*, the other order would be *S, L, L, S, L, S, S, S, L, S*. In the Loud/Soft Group, half the subjects received each order.

Grice and Hunter reported the results of their experiment in two ways. One was the percentage of the last 60 trials on which subjects showed a conditioned response, that is, blinking to the tone before the air puff came. These results are shown in figure 8–4. One line represents the between-subjects comparison in which each subject had experience with only the loud stimulus or the soft stimulus. As you can see, the percentage of trials on which subjects responded did not vary as a function of stimulus intensity in the one stimulus, between-subjects case. (The slight difference seen is not statistically reliable.) On the other hand, when stimulus intensity was varied within-subjects in the Loud/Soft Group, a large effect of stimulus intensity was found. Subjects responded just slightly more than 20 percent of the time to the soft stimulus, but almost 70 percent of the time to the loud stimulus, a difference that proved reliable.

The conditioning performance is plotted somewhat differently in figure 8–5, where the percentage of conditioned responses to the stimuli is shown for each successive block of 20 trials so that you can see how quickly the conditioned response was acquired. (Recall that performance in figure 8–4 showed the percentages for only the last 60 trials.) In figure 8–5 you can see that the difference

FIGURE 8–4.

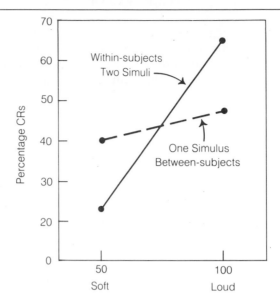

Results of Grice and Hunter's (1964) experiment. When stimulus intensity was varied between-subjects so that every subject had experience only with the loud or soft stimulus, no reliable effect of stimulus intensity was found. However, when there was a within-subjects manipulation of stimulus intensity so that every subject experienced both intensities, a large effect was obtained. (The measure was the percentage of the last 60 trials on which a conditioned response occurred.) The results show that the type of experimental design can affect the results obtained in an experiment.

between the loud and soft stimulus occurs in the very first block of trials for the Loud/Soft Group, and it holds over all five blocks of 20 trials. However, for the between-subjects comparison, there is not even a hint of a difference between the loud and soft stimuli in producing conditioned responses on the first 40 trials, and only a slight (and not statistically significant) difference after that.

The results of Grice and Hunter's experiment show that the choice of a between-subjects or within-subjects design can have far-reaching effects. In this case, the actual outcome of experiments designed to examine the effects of stimulus intensity was determined by the choice of design. When subjects experienced both stimuli they reacted to them differently, but when they experienced only one stimulus or the other, they showed no difference in responding. Grice (1966) reports other situations in which a similar pattern of results occurs. In many experimental situations, researchers cannot tell whether or not their findings would be changed by switching from a between-subjects to a within-subjects design (or vice versa) because it is impossible to ask the experimental question with the other design, for reasons discussed earlier. However, Grice and Hunter's (1964) research reminds us that the choice of an experimental design can have ramifications beyond

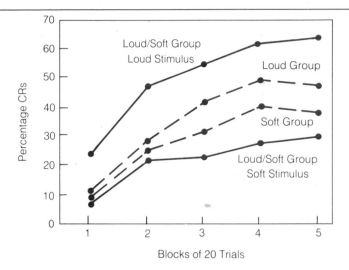

FIGURE 8–5.

Learning of the conditioned response in Grice and Hunter's (1964) experiment. The graph shows the percentage of trials in which subjects produced a conditioned response, in blocks of 20 trials. In the between-subjects manipulation (the comparison between the Loud and Soft groups), there was no difference over the first 40 trials in responding to the loud and soft tones, and only a slight difference on the last 60 trials. However, when the same comparison between tones was made within-subjects (the Loud/Soft Group), a large difference was revealed on the first 20 trials, and then it increased throughout the 100 conditioning trials.

mundane considerations of the number of subjects used and the like. The actual outcome of the research may be affected.

**Topic:** Counterbalancing

**Illustration:** Simultaneous Contrast

**8.2**

**EXPERIMENTAL TOPICS AND RESEARCH ILLUSTRATIONS**

Whenever a within-subjects design is used, one needs to decide with care the order in which the conditions should be presented to the subjects. The arrangement must be such that on the average the conditions are presented at the same stage of practice, so that there can be no confounding between the experimental conditions and stage of practice. Counterbalancing is also necessary to minimize the effect of other variables besides time that might affect the experiment. Often it is necessary to counterbalance across variables in which the experimenter is not interested, even in between-subjects designs, so that these extraneous variables do not affect the conditions of interest. An example of this problem should make it clearer.

In learning an instrumental response, the particular magnitude of the reward used greatly influences performance. Typically, performance is greater as the magnitude of reward is increased. However, the particular magnitude of reward used does not have an invariable effect on performance, but depends on the experience that the organism has had with other reinforcement conditions. One example of this effect is provided by an experiment done by Bower (1961) on simultaneous contrast.

In Bower's experiment there were 3 groups of 10 rats, each of which received 4 trials a day in a straight-alley maze for 32 days, or a total of 128 trials. The independent variable was the magnitude of reward used. One group of rats received eight food pellets in the goal box on their four trials. Since they received a constant eight pellets on each trial, this condition is referred to as Constant 8. Another group received only one pellet after each trial (Constant 1). These two groups can be considered as controls for the third (Contrast) group. Subjects in this group received two trials each day in two different straight alleys. The two alleys were quite discriminable, one being black and one being white. In one alley they always received a one-pellet reward, whereas in the other alley they always received eight pellets. Bower was interested in seeing how the exposure to both levels of reinforcement would affect running speed as compared with exposure to only one level all the time. Will rats run at a different speed for a one (or eight) pellet reward if they have experienced another level of reward, rather than having had constant training at one particular level?

Before examining the results, let us consider some design features that Bower had to face for the contrast subjects. Since magnitude of reward was varied within-subjects in this condition, there are two problems to consider. First, it is important to ensure that not all subjects receive the greater or lesser reinforcement in either the black or white alley, since then alley color would be confounded with reward magnitude, and rats may simply run faster in black alleys than white (or vice versa). This is easily accomplished by having half the animals receive eight pellets in the black alley and one pellet in the white, and having the other half of the animals receive the reverse arrangement. For the control subjects which receive only one reward magnitude, half would be tested in a white alley and half in a black alley. The second problem is in what order the rats should be given the two conditions on the four trials each day. Obviously they should not first be given the two large-reward trials followed by the two small-reward trials (or vice versa), since time of testing would be confounded with reward magnitude. Perhaps a random order could be used for the 128 trials. But random orders are not preferred in such cases, since there can be, even in random orders, long runs in which the same occurrence appears. So it would not be surprising to find cases where there are two trials in a row of the same type (large or small magnitude of reward), although across all subjects there would be no confounding with practice. It is preferable in cases such as this to counterbalance the conditions rather than vary them randomly. *Counterbalancing*, you will remember, refers to any technique used to systematically vary the order of conditions in an experiment to distribute the effects of time of testing (such as practice and fatigue), so that they are not confounded with conditions.

When there are two conditions to be tested in blocks of four trials, there are six possible orders in which the conditions can occur within trials. In the present case, if $S$ stands for a small (one pellet) and $L$ for a large (eight pellet) reward, then the six orders are *SSLL, SLSL, SLLS, LLSS, LSLS, LSSL*. Bower's solution to the counterbalancing problem was to use each of these orders equally often. On a particular day of testing he would pick a particular order for the trials for half the subjects (for example, *LSSL*), and then simply test the other half of the subjects using the other order (*SLLS*). On the next day he would pick another order for half the rats, while the others received the reverse order, and so on. Thus there was no confounding between order and conditions, and all the orders were used equally often, so the experiment did not depend on just one order. We shall return to this point in a moment.

Bower's results are presented in figure 8–6, where the mean running speed for each of the four conditions is plotted across blocks of two days (eight trials). First notice that for the rats that received constant reward, those rewarded with eight pellets performed better after the first few days than those rewarded with

FIGURE 8–6.

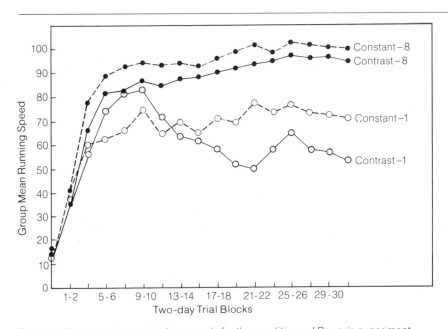

These are the group mean running speeds for the conditions of Bower's experiment, averaged over blocks of 8 trials (2 days). The rats that received both one pellet and eight pellet trials ran more slowly for the one pellet reward than rats that always received one pellet. This is referred to as a negative contrast effect (after Bower, 1961, Fig. 1).

only one. It was not exactly big news, of course, that rats ran faster for more, rather than for less, food. The real interest was in how fast rats in the contrast conditions ran for one- and eight-pellet rewards. Although there was no statistically reliable effect between speeds of the Constant-8 and Contrast-8 conditions in figure 8–6, the Contrast-1 rats ran reliably more slowly for the reward than did the Constant-1 rats, at least toward the end of training. This is referred to as a *negative contrast effect*, since the contrast subjects ran more slowly for the small reward than did the rats that always received the small reward. One interpretation of this phenomenon considers emotional states induced in the contrast rats owing to their experience in the situation. Since the contrast rats are familiar with both levels of reward, when placed in the distinctive alley that tells them that they will receive a small reward, they are annoyed or frustrated at having to run down the alley for only one crummy pellet.

It is an interesting question as to why Bower did not find a *positive contrast effect*, or faster running for the Contrast-8 subjects relative to the Constant-8 subjects. Why weren't the Contrast-8 rats happy or elated to learn, when placed in the distinctive alley signaling a large reward, that they would get eight pellets rather than only one? One possibility is that they *were* more elated, but that a ceiling effect prevented this from being reflected in their running speeds. Perhaps performance was already so good in the Constant-8 condition because of the large reward that there was no room for improvement in the Contrast-8 condition. The rats in the control (Constant-8) condition were already running as fast as their little legs would carry them, so no matter how much more elated the Contrast rats might be, this could not be reflected in their performance. This ceiling-effect interpretation of the present data is bolstered somewhat by other reports of positive contrast effects (Padilla, 1971), although it remains the case that negative contrast effects seem more easily obtained than positive ones. The problem of ceiling effects in data analysis is discussed more fully in chapter 10.

The results of Bower's experiment should remind you of the lesson of the previous section contrasting between- and within-subjects designs. As in Grice and Hunter's experiments on stimulus-intensity effects, Bower found that the effect of a reward of a particular magnitude depended on the type of design used. In a within-subjects design in which the animals had experience with both reward magnitudes, the effect on behavior was greater than in the between-subjects comparison in which a different group of animals received constant rewards over the series of trials. Once again, the nature of the design used can affect the conclusion reached about how strong an effect is produced by the independent variable.

**Further considerations in counterbalancing.** There is a great variety of counterbalancing schemes that can be used in various situations. Some of these become very complex. Here we discuss only some of the simpler counterbalancing designs to provide you with a few tricks of the trade.

The case represented by Bower's (1961) contrast group is in many ways typical of the counterbalancing problem as it usually arises. There were two conditions to be tested within-subjects, and thus they must be counterbalanced so as not to be confounded with stage of practice. One solution to this problem, and the one most psychologists would pick, would be to use an *ABBA* design, where *A* stands for one condition and *B* stands for the other. This would unconfound particular conditions with time of testing, since each condition would be tested at the same time on the average (1 + 4 = 5 for *A*, and 2 + 3 = 5 for *B*, where the numbers refer to the order of test). But perhaps the specific order of testing might also matter. For example, let us assume there is a very large practice effect on the dependent variable but that it occurs very early in training, on the first *A* trial. Then it would contribute to the *A* condition but not the *B* condition so that the *ABBA* design would not eliminate the confounding of conditions with practice.

Two solutions to this problem of large effects of practice early in training can be suggested. One is to give a number of practice trials in the experimental situation before the experiment proper begins. Thus the subjects are given practice, and performance on the dependent variable is allowed to stabilize before the experimental conditions of interest are introduced. Another solution is to employ more than one counterbalancing scheme. For example, half the subjects might get the reverse of the scheme that the other half receives. So half the subjects would get *ABBA* and the other half would get *BAAB*. Bower's solution to the counterbalancing problem was the ideal extension of this logic, since he used every possible counterbalancing scheme equally often, But when more than two conditions are involved, this becomes unwieldy. In most situations an adequate solution to the problem of practice effects at the beginning of a testing session would be to give subjects practice and then use two counterbalancing schemes, one of which is the reverse of the other. Grice and Hunter (1964), in the experiment on stimulus intensity described earlier, did just this.

For situations in which there are more than two conditions, there is one particular scheme for counterbalancing that we would like to recommend as being generally desirable. This is the *balanced Latin square design*. Suppose there were six conditions in a particular experiment and you wanted subjects to receive all six conditions in a counterbalanced order, so that practice effects would not confound the results. For example, in a simultaneous contrast experiment such as Bower's, six different reward magnitudes could be used rather than only two. A balanced Latin square design would ensure that, when each condition was tested, it would be preceded and followed equally often by every other condition. This last feature is very useful in minimizing carry-over effects among

TABLE 8–1

Balanced Latin square for six experimental conditions (1–6) presented to each subject. Rows indicate the order in which subjects *a* through *f* receive the experimental conditions.

| | Order of Testing Conditions | | | | | |
|---|---|---|---|---|---|---|
| *Subjects* | *1st* | *2nd* | *3rd* | *4th* | *5th* | *6th* |
| *a* | 1 | 2 | 6 | 3 | 5 | 4 |
| *b* | 2 | 3 | 1 | 4 | 6 | 5 |
| *c* | 3 | 4 | 2 | 5 | 1 | 6 |
| *d* | 4 | 5 | 3 | 6 | 2 | 1 |
| *e* | 5 | 6 | 4 | 1 | 3 | 2 |
| *f* | 6 | 1 | 5 | 2 | 4 | 3 |

conditions, and makes the balanced Latin square preferred to other counterbalancing schemes.

Constructing a balanced Latin square is easy, especially if there is an even number of conditions in the experiment. Let us number the six conditions in an experiment from one to six. A balanced Latin square can be thought of as a two-dimensional matrix where the columns (extending vertically) represent conditions tested, and the rows represent the subjects. A balanced Latin square for six conditions is presented in table 8–1. The subjects are labeled *a* through *f*, and the order in which they receive the conditions is indicated by reading across the row. So subject *a* receives the conditions in the order 1, 2, 6, 3, 5, 4. The general formula for constructing the first row of a balanced Latin square is 1, 2, $n$, 3, $n - 1$, 4, $n - 2$, and so on, where $n$ stands for the total number of conditions. After the first row is in place, then just number down the columns with higher numbers, starting over when you get to $n$ (as in table 8–1). When a balanced Latin square is used, subjects must be run in multiples of $n$, in this case six, in order to appropriately counterbalance conditions against practice.

When an experimental design has an odd number of conditions, it becomes a bit more complicated to use a balanced Latin square. In fact two squares must be used, the second of which is the reverse of the first, as can be seen in table 8–2, where once again letters

TABLE 8–2

Balanced Latin square for five experimental conditions (1–5) presented to each subject. Rows indicate the order in which subjects *a* through *e* receive the experimental conditions. When there is an odd number of subjects, each condition must be given to each subject twice for a balanced Latin square.

| | Square 1 | | | | | Square 2 | | | | |
|---|---|---|---|---|---|---|---|---|---|---|
| *Subjects* | | | | | *Order of Testing* | | | | | |
| | *1st* | *2nd* | *3rd* | *4th* | *5th* | *1st* | *2nd* | *3rd* | *4th* | *5th* |
| *a* | 1 | 2 | 5 | 3 | 4 | 4 | 3 | 5 | 2 | 1 |
| *b* | 2 | 3 | 1 | 4 | 5 | 5 | 4 | 1 | 3 | 2 |
| *c* | 3 | 4 | 2 | 5 | 1 | 1 | 5 | 2 | 4 | 3 |
| *d* | 4 | 5 | 3 | 1 | 2 | 2 | 1 | 3 | 5 | 4 |
| *e* | 5 | 1 | 4 | 2 | 3 | 3 | 2 | 4 | 1 | 5 |

indicate subjects and numbers stand for conditions in the experiment. When a balanced Latin square is used with an unequal number of conditions, each subject must be tested in each condition twice. The case represented in table 8–2 is for five conditions. In general, the first square is constructed in exactly the same manner as when there is an even number of conditions, and then the second square is an exact reversal of the first.

The balanced Latin square is an optimal counterbalancing system for many purposes, since each condition occurs, on the average, at the same stage of practice, and each condition precedes and follows every other equally often. This latter feature is not true of other counterbalancing schemes, and thus there is more concern that testing in one condition may affect testing in another condition.

---

**Problem:** The Partial Reinforcement Extinction Effect

**FROM PROBLEM TO EXPERIMENT: THE NUTS AND BOLTS**

In order to produce instrumental learning (operant conditioning), we follow the behavior that we are interested in having the animal learn with a reinforcement stimulus. The animal soon learns that the reward is forthcoming in thc situation if the appropriate response is emitted. For example, suppose we want to teach an animal to learn a maze. The simplest sort of maze is the straight alley, which is composed of a start box where the animal is placed, an alley through which the animal runs when the start box door is opened, and the goal box where the animal is reinforced. The reinforcement is typically food, and usually the animal has been deprived of food prior to the experiment. The dependent variable is running speed or time to run the straight-alley maze. Often the animal's speed in each section of the runway is measured, so that the experimenter finds a speed for its leaving the start box, traversing the alley, and approaching the goal. Learning is indicated by the fact that after a number of trials the rat's speed increases (the latency decreases). At first the rat dawdles along, but on later trials it really hustles.

Suppose we now wanted to ask a straightforward question about learning in this situation: How is learning affected by the amount of reinforcement? Intuitively, you might expect that learning would increase as the amount of reinforcement increases. But if you read the first part of this chapter carefully, you should realize that this depends on how "amount of reinforcement" and "learning" are defined. We could vary the amount of reinforcement by varying the percentage of trials on which subjects receive reward, or by varying the magnitude of reward after each trial. We could also measure learning in at least two ways—one might be running speed, the other resistance to extinction. The latter measure is found by seeing how long after training an animal will continue running a maze when it no longer receives reinforcement. Let us confine our interest to the case where we vary the percentage of rewarded trials. Our experiment has now become more manageable. We vary the percentage of trials on which the animals receive rewards for running the maze (the independent variable), and we measure the time it takes the animals to run the maze and their resistance to extinction (or running speeds during extinction training).

In many experiments such as these, researchers have found that resistance to extinction is generally greater the *smaller* the percentage of trials during which the animal received reinforcement during training. If an animal receives continuous reinforcement (that is, is reinforced after every trial), its running behavior will extinguish much more rapidly when reinforcement is withdrawn than will animals that received reinforcement on only some percentage of the acquisition trials. In general, the smaller the percentage of reinforced trials, the greater will be the resistance to extinction (that is, the faster the animal will run when reinforcement is withdrawn). This fact, that infrequent reinforcement will lead to greater persistence in responding than continuous reinforcement, is called the *partial reinforcement extinction effect*, and several explanations of it have been proposed (Amsel, 1962, 1971; Capaldi, 1966, 1971).

A number of variables may contribute to the typical partial reinforcement extinction effect. When rats are rewarded on only some proportion of trials, a number of factors may vary simultaneously. One factor is the number of nonrewarded trials (or $N$ trials) that precede a rewarded (or $R$) trial. Another factor is the number of transitions from nonrewarded to rewarded trials (or $N$-$R$ transitions) during the course of partial reinforcement training. A third factor is the number of different $N$-lengths (or number of different sequences of nonrewarded trials preceding a rewarded trial) during partial reinforcement. All these variables could be (and have been) examined, but let us consider the first by way of an experiment in animal-learning research.

Basically we want to design an experiment in which the number of nonrewarded trials would be varied before a rewarded trial. There could be three $N$-lengths of one, two, and three nonrewarded trials before a rewarded trial, with the hypothesis being that resistance to extinction should increase with $N$-length. The greater the number of nonrewarded trials, the faster the rats should run during extinction.

A simple straight alley is used as the training apparatus, and the time for the rat to run the maze is the dependent variable. Do we want to use a within-subjects or between-subjects design? If we use a within-subjects design, we have to counterbalance the three schedules of reinforcement. But even if we do this there is a serious problem of carry-over effects, or the effect that training rats under one schedule has on training them on the next. It is probably wiser to use a between-subjects design, especially since with animal subjects there is less problem of variability resulting from individual differences. Stable results in the partial reinforcement situation could probably be achieved with only fifteen subjects in each of three groups.

Before the experiment is begun, it is usual to pretrain the animals to get them used to the experimental situation. This reduces the amount of within-subjects variability caused by extraneous factors, such as fear of being handled by the experimenter. Thus for several days the animals are handled for an hour or so each day by the experimenter, who of course should wear special gloves, since rats sometimes bite. The rats should also be placed in the goal box with food pellets in the food dish to ensure that they will eat the pellets. Otherwise, as you might readily suppose, the pellets are unlikely to serve as a reinforcer. Finally, the rats should be placed in the straight alley and allowed to explore it for a few minutes on each of several days before actual testing. This is so it will not be frightening when they are placed in it for testing.

On each trial of the experiment proper, the experimenter takes the rat from its home cage and places it in the start box. The start-box door is opened, which starts a timer, and the rat moves down the alley to the goal box. Near the goal box, the rat passes through a photoelectric beam, which stops the timer. When the rat enters the goal box, the goal-box door is closed so that the rat cannot return to the alley. Typically the rat is confined to the goal box for a constant period of time in all conditions, say thirty seconds. Then the rat is placed in a separate cage to await the next trial.

In this experiment, the independent variable is the number of nonrewarded or $N$-trials (1, 2, or 3) preceding a rewarded or $R$-trial. This is straightforward since it is easy either to provide or to not provide food when the rat runs the maze. The only tricky aspect is that the experimental procedure confounds the number of nonrewarded trials with the amount of reward that the rats receive during a series of tests. The rats with greater $N$-lengths get less reward. One way to correct this confounding is to provide subjects in conditions with $N$-lengths of two and three with intertrial reinforcements. These are simply periods when rats are given rewards between trials in the neutral cage. The rewards are not dependent on the instrumental response.

The rats should be given a number of days of training, perhaps ten, to ensure that they are quite familiar with their particular schedule of reinforcement. Twelve trials per day would be an appropriate number. After ten days of learning, extinction training is introduced. This consists of simply running the rats at twelve trials per day for perhaps four days with no reward at all, and measuring the time taken for the rats to run the maze. This phase of the experiment is critical since we want to ascertain the effect of the training schedules on resistance to extinction, but a problem enters here. It is common during extinction for at least some rats to simply stop running. Either they refuse to leave the start box, or they stop halfway down the alley. What happens to our dependent measure in cases such as this? The convention adopted to avoid this problem is to allow the rats a fixed amount of time to traverse the alley and then remove them and begin the next trial if they fail to beat the cutoff. A limit of 90 seconds is often used; if a rat has not made it a few feet down the maze in 90 seconds, it is unlikely that it will make it at all. Thus the experimenter simply removes the animal, records its time as 90 seconds, and places it in the netural cage in preparation for the next trial. Since different schedules of training sometimes produce lopsided or skewed distributions of running times, it is often necessary to use the median time for each animal rather than the mean to eliminate the effect of a few extremely long times (see appendix A for a discussion of medians).

The basic purpose of the experiment is to see whether the number of nonrewarded trials produces greater resistance to extinction. Or, if subjects receive greater N-lengths, will they run faster when given no reward during extinction? In an experiment very similar to the one described here, Capaldi (1964) found that greater N-lengths were associated with greater resistance to extinction.

## SUMMARY

**1.** The study of animal learning and behavior has identified two basic types of conditioning. In classical (or Pavlovian or respondent) conditioning, a neutral stimulus such as a light or tone precedes an unconditioned stimulus which produces an automatic or unconditioned response. After a number of such pairings, the originally neutral stimulus produces the response. The stimulus is then referred to as the conditioned stimulus and the response is called the conditioned response. In instrumental or operant conditioning, a particular behavior that occurs in some setting is rewarded and thereafter the response tends to recur more frequently than it would have otherwise.

**2.** In all experimental research, whether with humans or other organisms, a fundamental question is whether to use the same organisms in each condition of the experiment (a within-subjects design) or whether to use different organisms in the different conditions (a between-subjects design).

**3.** Within-subjects designs are preferred when they can be used because they minimize the amount of variability caused by differences among subjects. Also, within-subjects designs employ fewer subjects than between-subjects designs, though of course it is necessary to test each individual for longer periods of time.

**4.** The primary danger in within-subjects designs is that of carry-over effects, the relatively permanent effect that testing subjects in one condition might have on their later behavior in another condition. In such cases it is necessary to use between-subjects designs, even though more subjects will be needed and there is less control of subject variability.

**5.** The choice of an experimental design may in some instances strongly affect the outcome of an experiment. For example, stimulus intensity appears to play little role in classical conditioning when manipulated between-subjects, but a great role when manipulated within-subjects. Thus the type of experimental design chosen can sometimes be critical.

**6.** In within-subjects designs it is necessary to counterbalance conditions, or to vary the conditions in a systematic way so that they are not confounded with time of testing. If conditions are not counterbalanced, then time-related effects such as fatigue or practice may account for the results rather than manipulation of the independent variable. It is also necessary to counterbalance in between-subjects designs across variables that are not of central interest, such as black or white arms in an experiment using a T-maze. One quite useful counterbalancing scheme is the balanced Latin square design, where each condition precedes and follows every other equally often.

**KEY TERMS**

*ABBA* design
balanced Latin square design
between-subjects design
classical conditioning
conditioned response (CR)
conditioned stimulus (CS)
counterbalancing
discriminative stimulus
fatigue effect
instrumental conditioning
matched-groups design
negative contrast effect
operant conditioning
partial reinforcement
 extinction effect
positive contrast effect
practice effect
random-groups design
reinforcing stimulus
simultaneous contrast
split-litter technique
unconditioned response (UR)
unconditioned stimulus (US)
within-subjects design

**DISCUSSION QUESTIONS**

**1.** Discuss the advantages of within-subjects designs. What complications and problems are entailed by using a within-subjects design?

**2.** Discuss the advantages and disadvantages of using a between-subjects design.

**3.** In each of the following cases, tell whether it would be best to examine the independent variable in a within-subjects or between-subjects design. Justify your answer in each case.

(*a*) a social psychological study of helping, in which the researchers are interested in how group size affects whether or not an individual will help someone else in the group
(*b*) a study of the effect of varying loudness of a tone in measuring how quickly people can respond to the tone
(*c*) an experiment designed to answer the question of whether the color of a woman's hair affects the likelihood that she will be asked out for dates
(*d*) a study in which three different training techniques are compared as to their effectiveness in teaching animals tricks

**4.** Tell what a balanced Latin square is and tell why it is a preferred counterbalancing scheme in many situations. Draw up two balanced Latin squares similar to those in tables 8–1 and 8–2 for cases in which there are (a) three conditions, and (b) four conditions.

**5.** The results of two experiments described in this chapter showed different effects of an independent variable when it was manipulated between-and within-subjects. Make a list of three variables for which you think between- and within-subjects designs would show the same effects, and provide two further instances in which you think the two types of designs would produce different results. Justify your reasoning in each case.

## Training Your Pet

Many people have dogs as pets and these dogs vary greatly in their education. Some know a vast repertoire of tricks, others few or none. This probably reflects more on the owner, of course, than the pet. Some owners know how to teach their pets, others do not. The study of conditioning and learning has allowed "discovery" of a number of principles that have been implicitly used by animal trainers for years. Since these principles have now been made explicit, anyone can become a successful teacher. In most cases when animals learn tricks or useful functions (such as fetching, or bringing in the newspaper), a form of instrumental or operant conditioning is used. Let us consider how you might teach your dog to roll over.

First, it is best to have the dog rather hungry, so you might withhold food from it for 10 to 24 hours or so. Then take a number of small pieces of the dog's favorite food to serve as reinforcers. A dog that one of us once owned learned tricks readily for bits of green pepper, so the particular stimulus that will serve as a reinforcer may differ quite a bit for different dogs, and especially for animals of different species. Next it is best to perform some action, such as snapping your fingers, that the dog will associate with the knowledge that it is about to receive a reward. Just get the dog's attention, then snap your fingers, then give it a reward. Repeat this several times until the dog knows that whenever you snap your fingers it means a reward is forthcoming. You will be able to tell by the dog's behavior when this has been established, perhaps by its coming close and salivating. This is a form of classical conditioning and the analogy in operant conditioning in a Skinner box is called magazine training. When the animal performs a correct response and receives a reward, the magazine that holds the food pellets makes a distinctive sound, a click, as the food pellets are placed into the food dish for the animal. Thus the animal associates the click with the reward and knows that a reward is forthcoming whenever that sound occurs. This is very useful because then the animal can be rewarded immediately for some activity, even when it is not near the food box or is oriented in some other direction. Similarly, when you snap your fingers, it will signal imminent reward to your dog, even if the dog is turned away from you and not paying attention.

Once you have given your dog the equivalent of magazine training, you are ready to begin the conditioning. You want to snap your fingers and reward the dog whenever it behaves appropriately. Since it is unlikely that the dog will simply roll over on its own, it is not a good strategy to wait for the entire behavior to appear before you reinforce the dog. Rather, as discussed earlier in the chapter, you should reward it for approximations to the appropriate behavior and gradually shape its behavior. You might first reward the dog when it sits down, which it is likely to do while waiting for the food it sees you are holding. After receiving a reward or two, the dog will then sit readily in anticipation of food. (You have already taught your dog to sit!) Then withhold food until the animal approximates more closely the desired behavior, perhaps until it lies down. A hungry animal will often be quite active and thus perform many actions. This is good, because then it will sooner perform one that approximates the one you want. When the dog lies down, reward it again. (Sometimes it may be necessary to actually push the dog down gently, then reward it. Hungry dogs tend to want to jump up rather than lie down.) After the dog has learned to lie down for a reward, wait until it turns slightly to one side or the other before rewarding it again. The process may be hastened if you give it a little shove onto its side and reward it. You then reward it for turning further and further, until you have trained it to turn all the way over. It may be necessary to flip the dog yourself the first time, but in very short order (probably in 10 to 15 minutes) you will have taught it to roll over, or do whatever you want.

You may want, toward the end of the process, to give the dog a verbal command and hand motion to signal it to what you want it to do. You might say "Roll over, Corky!" and then move your hand in a circular motion that indicates (only to you at the moment) a turning motion. When the dog has learned the behavior, the command and hand signal will then serve as a discriminative stimulus for the behavior. It will set the occasion for performing it, so the dog knows that whenever you utter the command it will be rewarded for performing the behavior.

The principles underlying operant conditioning can be used to powerfully control many types of animal behavior, including that of humans, as we shall see in the next chapter. It is, of course, easier to train certain animals for some particular behaviors than others. It is much easier to train a dog to roll over than a cat. Much current interest in the field of animal learning and conditioning is concerned with the biological boundaries of learning, or the spe-

cies-specific learning abilities of animals (Seligman, 1970). None-theless, the principles of operant conditioning are quite useful in training in a wide variety of species. The limits are probably determined as much by the ingenuity of the trainer in applying the principles as by the limits of the organism that is being taught. B. F. Skinner once trained two pigeons to play ping-pong (see Skinner, 1960). A good introduction to the principles of operant conditioning is that of Reynolds (1975) and a more applied approach is contained in Maller and Fenman's (1979) *Twenty-One Days to a Trained Dog.* As figure 8–7 reminds you, though, the conditioner also becomes the conditioned. If you snap your fingers in the presence of your dog after the conditioning, it may well expect a reward.

FIGURE 8–7.

"Boy, have I got this guy conditioned! Everytime I press down on the bar he drops in a piece of food" (Columbia *Jester*).

# CHAPTER 9

## Preview

In this chapter we consider research problems that often occur when one attempts to do applied research. We use as our examples attempts that have been made to extrapolate the learning principles discussed in the previous chapter to wider situations. First we consider research techniques when applied to single cases, or the topic of research designs with small numbers of subjects. Research conducted outside the laboratory is called field research. Although such research is important in terms of the attempt to apply principles derived from basic research more broadly, often experimental control in natural settings is difficult. One final problem discussed is the issue of experimenter effects in research, or the influence that the experimenter may exert—either consciously or unconsciously—on the results of the experiment being conducted.

## Chapter Outline

# APPLICATIONS OF LEARNING THEORY: METHODOLOGY OUTSIDE THE LABORATORY

When our sciences of human nature and human relations are anything like as developed as are our sciences of physical nature, their chief concern will be with the problem of how human nature is more effectively modified. The question will not be whether it is capable of change, but how it is to be changed under what conditions.

John Dewey

The major justification for laboratory research is its ability to provide precise statements about causality. Once some effect or phenomenon is understood from laboratory research, the applied psychologist then can use this information to improve some aspect of the world outside the laboratory. This applied enterprise serves a scientific function in addition to solving some practical difficulty. If an important effect has been correctly identified inside the laboratory, then the behavioral laws and relationships that describe or explain this effect should also operate outside the lab. Indeed, if they do not, serious doubts about the validity of the original laboratory research can be raised. To be useful, knowledge must be applied, and laboratory research is thus a beginning, not an end.

In this chapter we show how some findings, originally discovered and refined in the laboratory, can be applied usefully and meaningfully outside the lab. Our emphasis is on how these results work when taken from the laboratory. We do not intend these few specific applications to be interpreted as the ultimate justification for the laboratory research, since it is far too early to tell to what extent these basic research findings will shape our lives in the future. The lesson to be learned here is the generalization of experimental principles—the specific applications that we discuss are important only as illustrations of this point.

## IS CONTROLLING BEHAVIOR ETHICAL?

Applications of psychology hit closer to home than applications of any other science. For some, the spectre of a cadre of applied psychologists controlling behavior conjures up Orwellian images of a Big Brother watching over us. Of course, people have always attempted to control your behavior, ever since you were an infant. Your parents wanted you to eat good food instead of ice cream and candy, wanted you to become toilet trained, and may well be responsible for your present occupation as a student. Since this control lies in the bosom of the family, society has raised no objection. But society also tolerates control of your behavior by complete strangers. Corporate giants solicit your trade by expensive advertising on television, radio, and in print. Although society occasionally objects to the poor taste exhibited by some of these commercial messages, or to their high frequency of occurrence, few have objected to the principle of advertising that is generally seen as a First Amendment Constitutional right in the United States. The university controls your behavior by giving grades and demanding your physical presence in class. Business controls your behavior at work by specifying hours of employment and pay schedules. You would have to be a hermit isolated from all other people before none would attempt to control your behavior; indeed, even then society might try to demand payment of a property tax on your cave. With all these examples of behavior control, why then do people get so uptight whenever psychologists attempt to control behavior?

One answer might be that psychologists are better at controlling behavior than are the various social institutions, whose control is seen as hit or miss and so it is less resented. You have the option of turning off your television if a commercial offends you, driving faster than 55 miles per hour if you wish to violate the law, and cutting class if it's a nice spring day. Although you probably do not violate these rules often, it still is comforting to believe that you can ignore them if you so wish. In short, you have freedom of action and can do whatever you want to do regardless of the rules.

The control of behavior that is technically possible through psychology is seen by many as a gross limitation of this freedom. Indeed for many it appears directly counter to the most treasured principles of our democratic society. In a well-known article entitled "Freedom and the Control of Men," B. F. Skinner (1955) has addressed this issue directly. He argues that it is the end, not the means, that is of primary importance. If control of behavior is used to achieve ends we all admire and consider praiseworthy, then it should be used. Skinner cites T. H. Huxley on the automatic attainment of virtue:

> If some great power would agree to make me always think what is true and what is right, on condition of being a sort of clock and wound up every morning before I got out of bed, I should close instantly with the offer.

Doubtless, some of you do not agree with Huxley and Skinner. The price of being an automatic clock may seem too high to justify the end. But you do not object to an airplane being bound by the laws of physics or to a moth being attracted by a flame. That humans are subject to behavioral laws in the same way that machines are governed by physical laws has been discussed in chapter 1 and now reappears in a slightly different guise. All of us already are a "sort of clock" whether we like it or not. If this is accepted, Skinner's point that control should be used to further good ends becomes more palatable. It would be unfortunate not to use behavioral control to increase the quality of life for everyone and to further the aims of humanitarian action.

The danger, not discussed much by Skinner, is that control of behavior can be used to achieve evil ends as well as good ends. In this regard psychology is in the same position as any other science. Should nuclear energy be used for war or peace or not used at all? Scientists in every discipline have recently become far more sensitive to the possible applications of their findings, and psychology is no exception (Bevan, 1976). While psychologists surely have moral and ethical obligations to ensure that their science is used to improve life, you as an educated consumer of psychological research share this obligation. But in order for you to bear this responsibility wisely, you must first know how psychology can be applied and the methodological problems that such applications involve. The rest of this chapter is directed to this aim.

### Clinical Applications of Psychology

Interest in the applications of psychology is hardly new. More than fifty years ago John Watson, the founder of behaviorism, showed that a normal child could be conditioned to show fear. Watson and Rayner (1920) trained little Albert—an eleven-month-old infant—to fear a white rat. Prior to the experiment Albert showed no emotional response to the rat. Conditioning was accomplished by striking a steel bar to produce a loud sound when Albert reached to pet the rat. After little training the sight of the rat alone caused the baby to cry and to crawl rapidly away from the rat. This conditioned emotional response transferred to other furry objects such as a rabbit and a fur coat. Although Watson and Rayner had intended to subsequently extinguish this fear response, little Albert was removed from the hospital before that could be attempted. While the scientific value of this experiment was substantial, it is doubtful that any contemporary investigator would consider this research ethical and proper, especially since the fear response was never extinguished. The applied implications of this experiment are obvious. Watson was reacting against Freudian psychotherapy and added a caustic note to that effect:

> The Freudians twenty years from now, unless their hypotheses change, when they come to analyze Albert's fear of a seal skin coat—assuming that he comes to analysis at that age—will probably tease from him the recital of a dream which upon their analysis will show that Albert at three years of age attempted to play with the pubic hair of the mother and was scolded violently for it. (Watson and Rayner, p. 140)

Watson and Rayner demonstrated that many phobias, like fear of furry objects, could have been produced by conditioned emotional reactions.

Clinical psychology is the dominant mode of applied psychology today. There are more clinical psychologists in the American Psychological Association than any other kind of psychologist. Although Watson was an experimental psychologist, his findings have had important implications for practicing clinical psychologists, and an entire school of therapy—behavior modification—bases its therapeutic techniques on principles of conditioning and learning discovered by Watson and many others.

Since clinical psychologists must alter patterns of behavior every working day, they directly confront the kinds of ethical issues raised earlier. What right does a clinical psychologist have to impose his or her own value system on a patient? Some clinicians claim that this is an unfair and misleading question, since they do not impose any value system and take great pains to remain morally neutral during therapy.

Other clinical psychologists (Krasner, 1962; London, 1964) do not accept this waiver of moral responsibility and instead claim that therapists must view themselves as moral agents. London explains how easy it is for therapists to be unaware of their moral philosophy by using the example of "normality." As a statistical term the word *normal* describes the shape of a distribution and is a characteristic of a set of measurements and not an aspect of human personality. In its statistical and scientific usage the term has no moral implications. But when the term *normal* is used by most therapists, it often means optimal or best, or at the very least not bad. Normal behavior is seen as desirable behavior. This transcends scientific neutrality and becomes a moral position. This is not necessarily evil, but therapists should acknowledge that they hold moral positions that in part determine their professional dispensation of therapy.

If it is agreed that therapists hold moral positions, the question of who will guard the guardians immediately arises. Whose morality should be imposed on patients? Is it desirable for a therapist to "cure" a patient of homosexuality to enable him or her to enjoy "normal" sexual relationships, or is it presumptuous of the therapist to consider homosexuality as a disease that needs to be cured? The unhappiness that drives a homosexual to seek clinical help could perhaps be relieved more readily by counseling the patient to accept his or her homosexuality than by trying to get the patient to conform to traditional sexual roles. Any practitioner who applies psychological principles to control behavior must consider the moral implication of such actions.

## INTRODUCING THE VARIABLES

### Dependent Variables

Dependent variables are usually quite similar to those discussed in the preceding chapter. The frequency of occurrence of some behavior is almost always the major dependent variable. Cumulative response functions in which the number of responses is plotted over time, are often computed. The time between successive responses is also of interest.

### Independent Variables

The most common independent variables in studies of behavior modification are kinds of reward or reinforcement and the contingencies that control delivery of reinforcement. A common reward system used with humans in mental or penal institutions is called the token economy. Correct behavior is reinforced with tokens, often circular disks, that can be exchanged for various privileges or even for food.

Reinforcement programs are quite varied and ingenious—often they are based on animal research—and these are generally types of partial reinforcement. An example of one such contingency that could be used to help a person cut down on smoking is a DRL reinforcement schedule that differentially reinforces low rates of responding. The smoker places his or her supply of cigarettes in a special case that has a timer. At first, the timer is set for short intervals, perhaps five minutes or so. Each day the timer setting is increased. If the smoker tries to get a cigarette from the case before the time limit has expired, the timer automatically resets and the smoker must wait the entire interval, and not just the time remaining to the limit. This schedule punishes early attempts to obtain cigarettes so that the smoker soon learns to wait the full time limit. As is the case with most reinforcement contingencies, it is of great importance that the subject's environment be rigidly controlled. If the smoker is able to mooch cigarettes from friends, the timer is of no use.

### Control Variables

Although not altogether absent, control variables are sadly lacking in much of applied research. The field settings in which most of this research is conducted prevent the kind of experimental control we would demand inside the laboratory. The success of applied psychology is even more impressive when we stop to consider the lack of control in the typical applied setting.

## 9.1

**Topic:** Small *n* Design

**Illustration:** Behavior Problems in Children

A child, seemingly quite happy while playing by herself, begins to whine and cry. At first the whines are rather soft and are ignored by the parent, who continues to talk on the telephone. Soon the whines accelerate to cries and the parent must discontinue the conversation to look after the unhappy child. Some time later the parent is once again talking to a neighbor who is present in the home. The child at first plays quietly in another part of the house, but soon begins whining. Once more the whines accelerate to cries and the parent must eventually interrupt the conversation again to deal with the child. The next day the parent is involved with housework and again the child begins to whine and cry. This time the parent is determined to ignore it; after all, it is obviously a mistake to encourage this type of behavior. The child continues crying and then suddenly begins shrieking and wailing. The parent ignores this for as long as possible, but this is none too long, being concerned about the child and worried that something serious might be the matter.

Months later the parents decide to seek psychological help for their child. She is now having temper tantrums quite frequently and often also banging her head on the floor. Sometimes her head even bleeds. The parents are, of course, quite concerned with these problem behaviors exhibited by their child. They have been worried for months.

The psychological therapist, perhaps a clinical psychologist, now sees the child for the first time. What conclusions is he or she to draw? What caused this behavior and what can the therapist do to remove it and return the child to a more normal existence? The parents describe the child's problem the best they can, but of course they have forgotten the original mild crying episodes. The interpretation and proposed cure for the child's psychological malady will depend critically on the psychologist's interpretation of the problem. A Freudian therapist might seek an explanation in terms of an unresolved Electra complex; the child is in love with her father and regards the mother as a threat. This is better resolved in most children, but appears to be the source of this child's difficulty. Or perhaps the therapist decides that the problem behavior is owing to frustration from the little girl's penis envy. This is the alleged malady suffered by young girls when they discover from observing their brothers or fathers that they have no penis. Supposedly this discovery produces an adverse psychological reaction and may be responsible for the child's abnormal behavior. Other therapists would look for different causes, depending on their training. And the therapy would depend on the supposed cause, though traditional psychoanalytic therapies have not been too effective with children.

Behavior therapists would look in a different direction. They would seek to discover the learning history of the child which has produced such seemingly maladaptive behavior. In a sense, this is what the psychoanalytic therapist does, but the behavior therapist attempts to be much more specific and provide empirical tests for the interpretation. In particular the behavior therapist would attempt to discover the contingencies of reinforcement that produced and maintain the child's crying, tantrums, and head-banging. What is reinforcing the child's behavior? The proposed therapy would be designed to change the contingencies of reinforcement so that the child is rewarded for appropriate, and not maladaptive, behavior.

One potent source of reinforcement for all children is parental attention. Young children will go to great lengths to attract the attention of parents occupied with some other activity. The behavior therapist's interpretation might go something like this. Once when the child was feeling alone and neglected, she began to whine and cry. The parent dropped what he or she was doing, attended to her, and thus reinforced the behavior. The next time the child felt neglected she again tried the crying gambit and was again reinforced. Before long the child found that she had to cry more loudly for attention, both because the parents were becoming somewhat used to it and also because they were consciously trying to ignore it in hopes the child would stop. The parents realized that they should not reward the crying with attention, but every time the child increased the extremity of the behavior, the parents would once again start paying attention, at least for a while. Thus the problem behavior increased in intensity and frequency through this vicious cycle until the parents were forced to see the therapist. In a very real sense the parents unwittingly shaped the child's behavior by reinforcing increases in intensity. Just as a pigeon can be trained to walk around in figure-eights, as discussed in the last chapter, by first rewarding approximations to the figure-eight, so can a child be reinforced for head-banging and temper tantrums by rewarding successive steps along the way.

At this point the behavior therapist's interpretation of the child's behavior has the same status as that of the psychoanalyst's belief that it is a result of penis envy. However, the behavior therapist has a much more straightforward test of his or her interpretation. If the child's behavior is sustained by an unfortunate set of reinforcement contingencies, the therapy involves changing the contingencies so that the positive behavior is rewarded and the negative behavior is not. The therapist's job, in large part, is to treat the parents to become effective behavior therapists themselves. The parents should, of course, start paying attention to the child when she is behaving normally. If the tantrums persist, they should try to reinforce the child for lessening their intensity. If the child is throwing a tantrum to which the parents must pay attention, they should wait for a momentary lull in the tantrum before attending, to try to reward the lessening intensity and gradually shape the tantrums to be less severe. Best of all would be to entirely ignore the tantrums, if possible, to try to extinguish them.

***The AB design.*** In behavior therapy, as in all therapies, research as to the effectiveness of the therapy should be incorporated into the treatment whenever possible. This seems like a fairly simple matter: measure the frequency of behavior that needs to be changed, and then institute the therapy and see if the behavior does change. We can call this an *AB* design, where *A* represents the baseline condition before therapy is applied, and *B* represents the condition after the therapy (the independent variable) is introduced. This design is used in much medical, educational, and other applied research, where a therapy or training procedure is instituted to determine its effects on the problem of interest. However, the *AB* design (Campbell and Stanley, 1966) is quite poor and should be avoided. The reason is that whatever changes occur while the treatment is being applied during the *B* phase may be caused by any number of other factors that may be confounded with the factor of interest. The treatment might produce the change in behavior, but so might any number of other sources that the experimenter has failed to control and may not even be aware of. Remember, confounding occurs when a second variable is inadvertently varied with the primary factor of interest, the therapy in this case. It is thus of utmost importance to carefully control the secondary variables to ensure the primary one is producing the observed effect. This cannot be done in the *AB* design, since the therapist-experimenter may not even be aware of the other factors.

The usual solution to this problem is to compare two groups to which subjects have been randomly assigned. One, the experimental, receives the treatment and the other, the control, does not. Then if the experimental condition improves with therapy, say, and the control does not, we may conclude that it was the treatment and not some extraneous factor that produced the result

Let's take a practical example of the *AB* design. If one were to ask a therapist how she knows her therapy works, she may well reply, "Because I have seen it help people." This is reasoning employing an implicit *AB* design—the therapist sees patients when they are at rock bottom and, a great percentage of the time, patients improve (figure 9–1). But did therapy really help, or would the patients have improved anyway? In 1952 H. J. Eysenck created a brouhaha in the therapeutic world when he reviewed twenty-four articles comparing traditional psychoanalytic therapy to two control situations. When patients underwent psychoanalysis, an average of 44 percent improved, the typical *AB* result of improvement relative to baseline. But 64 percent of patients treated by other

FIGURE 9–1.

Drawing by C. Schulz. Copyright © 1965 United Features Syndicate, Inc. Used by permission.

Evaluating therapy can be a tricky business.

techniques improved, and about the same percentage of patients only given custodial care or treated by general practitioners improved! So, sure enough, psychotherapy "improved" patients when observed in the *AB* design, but compared to appropriate control groups it actually seemed to hurt. Eysenck's conclusions have sparked a long debate, and it seems likely from more recent evidence that the results of psychotherapy are beneficial. In a carefully reasoned review of work in this area, Bergin (1971, p. 263) concludes that psychotherapy has "an average effect that is moderately positive." In order to determine this, though, we must use appropriate control groups and not simply an *AB* design.

The studies just discussed are based simply on a global measure of "improvement" under some conditions and are often not particularly analytical. A number of psychological disturbances are lumped together, and such research is not too specific about a particular problem. In the case of therapy on an individual, such as the case of the little girl we discussed, there is no potential control group, and only one subject in the experimental "group." The usual comparison between control and experimental conditions depends on having a large number of subjects to assign randomly among conditions, to introduce experimental control and eliminate the possibility of confounding. Thus such designs are called *large* n *designs* (*n* being the designation for number of subjects). Large *n* designs are inappropriate for most sorts of clinical research because the problems being dealt with are to some degree unique, such as the case of the child throwing temper tantrums. It is too much to ask that large numbers of such children be found, randomly assigned to an experimental (treatment) or control condition, and then compared in outcome. It may also be unethical to withhold treatment from the control group. Rather than attempt to employ the traditional large *n* designs in such research, special techniques known as *small* n *research designs* have been developed.

***Small* n *designs.*** Large *n* research designs have become the norm in psychological research because of the powerful statistical techniques developed in the early part of this century and now routinely applied in psychological research (see appendix A). Most psychologists have accepted these methods and the brand of research that they promote, namely large *n* designs. There have been two primary areas within experimental psychology that have successfully resisted the trend to this type of research. One is psychophysics (see chapter 5), and the other is the experimental analysis of behavior in terms of operant conditioning fathered by B. F. Skinner. Research in both these traditions is based on the intensive analysis of very few subjects rather than a few observations of behavior in a great many subjects. Small *n* designs are, then, within-subjects designs where the subjects serve in each condition. The logic developed for the study of operant conditioning by Skinner and others is especially amenable to the clinical applications of behavior modification, since such applications are based, in large part, on operant analyses of behavior.

Skinner has argued for years against the traditional large *n* designs called for by sophisticated statistical techniques. In a paper called "The Flight from the Laboratory" he argues that the use of statistics is one of several factors that has made experimental research less attractive to many students, or as he puts it, less reinforcing. "What statisticians call experimental design (I have pointed out elsewhere that this means design which yields data to which the methods of statistics are appropriate) usually generates a much more intimate acquaintance with a calculating machine than with a behaving organism" (Skinner, 1963, p. 328). Today we might replace "calculating machine" with "computer program," but the point remains the same.

The logic of small *n* design in operant-conditioning research has been most carefully presented in Sidman's (1960) book, *Tactics of Scientific Research.* The experimental control usually achieved in traditional research with large numbers of subjects randomly assigned to conditions is achieved in small *n* research by very carefully controlling the experimental setting and by taking numerous and continuous measures of the dependent variable. One powerful design commonly used in this research is the *ABA design,* or *reversal design* (Wolf and Risley, 1971).

***The ABA or reversal design.*** The *AB* design, as we have already discussed, involves measuring the dependent variable of interest to establish a baseline in the *A* phase before the intervening variable or treatment is applied in the *B* phase. The baseline period should be extended, of course, until the frequency of occurrence of the dependent variable becomes stable; otherwise it would be difficult to know what to make of changes observed when the treatment variable is applied. If there is a change in the dependent variable when the treatment is administered in the *B* phase, we cannot conclusively establish that it was caused by the treatment variable, because of a lack of control comparisons. The change in the dependent variable might have occurred anyway, without the treatment variable being applied, because of variation in some uncontrolled secondary variable that might have been unobserved by the experimenter. The second *A* phase in the *ABA* design serves to rule out this possibility by returning the conditions of the experiment to their original, baseline level with the independent variable no longer applied. If behavior in the second *A* phase returns to its baseline level, then we can conclude that it was the independent variable that effected the change during the *B* phase. The only time this generalization would not apply is when a secondary variable not detected by the experimenter happened to be perfectly correlated with the independent variable of primary interest. Such situations are unlikely.

In our previous example of the child throwing tantrums, the therapist would instruct the parents to get a baseline measure on the number of crying episodes, tantrums, and head beatings when they reacted just as they normally would. Then the therapist would instruct them to alter their behavior by rewarding the child with attention when she engaged in good behavior and by trying to extinguish the tantrums and other behavior by ignoring them altogether. If this produced a change in the frequency of the tantrums over a period of several weeks, then the therapist might ask the parents to reinstitute their old pattern of behavior just to ensure that it was their attention to the child at inappropriate moments that was really controlling the child's behavior and not something else. (If the therapist were not interested in research, of course, he or she might just leave well enough alone after the successful *B* phase.) If the original treatment produced no effect on the dependent variable, the frequency of tantrums, it would be necessary to try something else. The techniques of behavior modification based on operant analysis have met with great success in the treatment of certain sorts of psychological problems. Here we consider an example.

***Conditioning of crying.*** In an interesting study, Hart and co-workers (1964) investigated the excessive crying of a four-year-old nursery-school pupil, Bill, who otherwise seemed quite healthy and normal. The crying often came in response to mild frustrations that other children dealt with in more effective ways. Rather than attribute his crying to internal variables such as fear, lack of confidence, or regression to behavior of an earlier age, the investigators looked to the social learning environment to see what reinforcement contingencies might be producing such behavior. They decided, with reasoning similar to that already discussed in the case of our hypothetical little girl, that adult attention was the reinforcer for Bill's crying behavior. Hart and colleagues set about testing this supposition with an *ABA* (actually *ABAB*) design.

First it was necessary to gain a good measure of the dependent variable, crying. The teacher carried a pocket counter and depressed the lever every time there was a crying episode. "A crying episode was defined as a cry (a) loud enough to be heard at least 50 feet away and (b) of 5 seconds or more duration." At the end of each nursery-school day the total number of crying episodes was recorded. We could, perhaps, quibble some with this operational definition of a crying episode (did the teacher go 50 feet away each time to listen?), but let us assume it is valid and reliable.

During the initial baseline of *A* phase, Bill was treated as he normally was, with attention being given by the teacher to his crying. During the ten days of the first baseline period, the number of crying episodes was between 5 and 10 a day, as shown in the left-most panel of figure 9–2, where the frequency of crying episodes on the ordinate is plotted against days on the abscissa. For the next ten days (the first *B* phase) the teacher attempted to extinguish the crying episodes by ignoring them, while rewarding Bill with attention every time he responded to minor calamities (such as falls or pushes) in a more appropriate way. As can be seen in figure 9–2, the number of crying episodes dropped precipitously so that there were between 0 and 2 during the last six days of the first *B* phase. This completes the *AB* phase of the design, and once again we cannot be certain that the reinforcement contingencies were responsible for Bill's improved behavior. Perhaps he was getting along better with his classmates, or his parents were treating him better at home. Either of these things (or others) could have improved his disposition.

FIGURE 9–2.

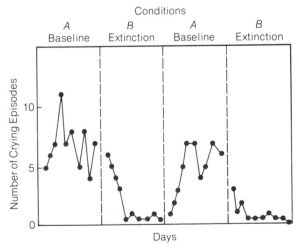

The number of crying episodes exhibited by Bill, a nursery school student, during the four phases of an *ABAB* design initiated to control his problem crying (from Wolf and Risley, 1969, p. 316).

In order to gain better evidence that it was actually the reinforcement contingencies that changed Bill's behavior, the investigators returned to the baseline where Bill was reinforced for crying. At first he was rewarded with attention for approximations to crying (whimpering and sulking) and after crying had been established again, it was maintained with attention to each crying episode. As the third panel in figure 9–2 shows, it took only four days to reestablish crying, leading to the conclusion that the reinforcement contingencies and not any number of other factors were responsible for the termination of crying in the first *B* phase. Finally, since this was a therapeutic situation, the investigators instituted a second *B* phase similar to the first, where Bill's crying was once again extinguished.

Notice that in this investigation no inferential statistics were employed to justify the conclusions drawn. Rather, with good control of the independent variable and repeated measures on the dependent variable, the differences between conditions in this experiment were striking enough to decrease the need for inferential statistics. Use of *ABA* small *n* designs can allow powerful experimental inferences.

---

**Topic:** Field Research

**Illustration:** Verbal Conditioning

**9.2**

**EXPERIMENTAL
TOPICS AND
RESEARCH
ILLUSTRATIONS**

---

In adult humans, verbal behavior is of overwhelming importance. In therapy, especially the more traditional therapies, verbal communication is of paramount importance. When disturbed patients make remarks about how depressed they are, how they feel neglected and alone, or how they are contemplating suicide, the sympathetic therapist is likely to express concern and interest in what they say. On the other hand, when topics discussed are not so dire, the therapist may feel that things are going relatively smoothly for the patients and may not express the same concern for or interest in them. To the extent that the therapist's concern and attention function as a reinforcer for patients, the therapist's actions may be reinforcing the patients' negative statements about themselves, while positive statements are allowed to extinguish. The same could be true for all sorts of other disturbed behavior, such as hallucinations, paranoia, delusions of grandeur, and so forth. When patients exhibit these behaviors, either in private therapy or on the ward of a mental institution, they receive attention. But when they are behaving more normally, the attention of the therapist or attendant may not be forthcoming or may be directed toward more pressing problems exhibited by others. This seems a likely scenario for the development of some psychological problems, though probably not all. No wonder therapy is sometimes harmful; the well meaning therapist may be making problems worse by paying attention to them.

In the preceding paragraph we have been glibly assuming that verbal behavior—language—is subject to the same learning principles of reinforcement, extinction, et cetera, as other sorts of behavior. This is by no means universally accepted as a generalization by psychologists, many of whom (especially psycholinguists) believe that principles derived from animal-learning studies will not suffice to account for the tremendously complex process involved in learning a language. In fact, a very convincing case has been made that the learning principles derived from animal studies cannot provide a complete explanation of language learning. Even if true, however, this does not necessarily imply that language use is not subject to operant conditioning. In this section and the next, we consider research on this topic since it has implications for therapy and serves to illustrate two important issues in experimentation: *field research* and *experimenter-bias effects*.

In one well-known study of this topic, Greenspoon (1955) asked subjects (college students) to simply say as many words as they could think of, as long as they were not numbers and not contained in sentences and phrases. They were just to spew out words. For one group of subjects the experimenter said "mmm-hmmm," indicating approval, whenever the subject said a plural noun, and nothing after the other responses. Another group of subjects heard "huh-uh" (a sign of disapproval) after plural nouns, whereas a control group heard neither but was asked to simply produce words. The results showed that subjects who were reinforced with "mmm-hmmm" after plural nouns produced more plural nouns than did the control group, despite the fact that the control subjects produced more responses overall. However, the subjects who were told "huh-uh" after each plural response produced fewer of these responses than did control subjects. Thus there seems to be clear evidence of conditioning of verbal responses.

Critics of the concept of *verbal conditioning* have argued that experiments such as Greenspoon's are flawed because of the problem of awareness on the part of the subjects (for example, Spielberger and DeNike, 1966). Subjects might become aware of what is expected of them in the experiment and simply produce or not produce plural nouns as required. So what looks like automatic conditioning might be mediated by subjects' consciously picking up the rules of the game in the experiment. In recent research with humans, where the purpose of the experiment is hidden from the subject, the role of subjects' expectations has come under increased scrutiny, especially in the realm of social psychological research (see chapter 13). Orne (1969) has pointed out that subjects are not passive participants in psychological experiments, but are actively trying to figure out what is going on and, likely as not, trying to be helpful. To the extent that cues or demand characteristics in the experimental situation help determine the subjects' behavior, the research may be flawed because it is not examining the behavior of interest, but what subjects expect.

The concept of *demand characteristics* is dealt with more fully in chapter 13, but we can see how it may operate in verbal-conditioning research. In Greenspoon's experiment, subjects might well have wondered why they were being asked to spew out words for 50 minutes, with the experimenter occasionally saying "mmm-hmmm" or "huh-uh" in the experimental conditions. Naturally they were trying to figure out what was going on, especially since Greenspoon did not present them with a plausible cover story for the experiment. It may well be that some of the subjects became aware of the experiment's purpose and tried to respond appropriately. Thus the "conditioning" may have been mediated by awareness on the part of subjects. In fact, Greenspoon checked for this and eliminated subjects who were able to verbalize the contingencies in their condition after the experiment, but still found conditioning in the other "unaware" subjects. Critics, nonetheless, have argued that others may have been shown to be aware, too, with more careful probing.

One way of overcoming the demand characteristics of laboratory situations is to perform research "in the field," that is, in a natural environment. Then all the problems of subject expectancies do not arise, since subjects never realize they are in an experiment at all. (Of course, other problems of an ethical nature arise, see chapter 14.) Verplanck (1955) reported an interesting field experiment concerned with conditioning of conversation. The experiment was performed by seventeen Harvard undergraduates enrolled in Verplanck's course in the Psychology of Learning. They were to engage people in conversation for thirty minutes and attempt to condition statements of opinion, such as those beginning with I think, I believe, it seems to me, I feel, and so on. The twenty-four subjects in the experiment were mostly friends and roommates, but also included a date, an uncle, and a total stranger. The conversations were held in dorms, homes, over the telephone, and in a hospital ward, among other places. The experimenters were instructed to talk as little as possible, just enough to keep the conversation going and administer the conditions. The subjects, of course, were completely unsuspecting and thus unaware that an attempt was being made to condition their conversations.

The five experimental conditions are represented in table 9–1. In four of the conditions, the first ten minutes were devoted to obtaining a baseline measure of the number of opinion statements given, or the operant level of opinion statements. During the next ten minutes in these four conditions, subjects were reinforced for opinion statements in one of two ways. In the Agreement conditions the experimenter said "That's right," "I agree," or smiled and nodded so as not to interrupt the conversation. In the Paraphrase

TABLE 9–1        The Five Conditions in Verplanck's Experiment and the Number of Subjects in Each (*n*).

| *n* | First 10 Minutes | Second 10 Minutes | Third 10 Minutes |
|---|---|---|---|
| 5 | 0—Measure operant level | A—Reinforce each opinion-statement by agreement | D—Extinguish by disagreeing with each opinion-statement |
| 2 | 0—Measure operant level | A—Reinforce each opinion-statement by agreement | E—Extinguish by failing to respond to any statement of S (silence) |
| 6 | 0—Measure operant level | P—Reinforce each opinion-statement by paraphrase | D—Extinguish by disagreeing with each opinion-statement |
| 4 | 0—Measure operant level | P—Reinforce each opinion-statement by paraphrase | E—Extinguish by failing to respond to any statement of S (silence) |
| 7 | $A_1$—Reinforce each opinion-statement by agreement | E—Extinguish by failing to respond to any statement of S (silence) | $A_2$—Reinforce each opinion-statement by agreement |

conditions the experimenter rewarded the subjects for opinion statements whenever possible by paraphrasing their remarks. There were also two different conditions for these four groups during extinction, either silence with regard to opinion statements or active disagreement. The fifth condition was a control of sorts, to see whether the change in the frequency of opinion statements could be caused by the passage of time. Subjects in this condition were reinforced for statements of opinion during the first and last ten-minute periods, with an extinction period in the middle. Conditions can be labeled *OAD, OPE,* and so on, according to the initials in table 9–1. The table also presents the number of subjects in each condition.

The experimenters doodled with paper and pencil while in conversation with the subjects, and surreptitiously recorded both the total number of statements and the number of opinion statements subjects made during each one-minute period. It was thus necessary that a clock be nearby. It appears that the undergraduate experimenters in this situation must have made superhuman efforts to keep track of everything. They were counting responses (two types); watching the clock; keeping the conversation going while adding little to it in terms of content; agreeing, paraphrasing; and disagreeing at the right times; and all the while trying to act naturally. It rather boggles the imagination, but Verplanck (1955) reported few problems. More on this later.

The results supported the idea that conditioning of conversation can occur without awareness. Subjects who heard either agreement with, or paraphase of, their opinion statements increased the

frequency of such statements, whereas those who heard silence
and disagreement decreased their frequency. Cumulative performance for subjects in the first four conditions in table 9–1 is presented at the top of figure 9–3, both for all statements and for
opinion statements during each of the ten-minute periods. Notice
that the rate of producing opinion statements, represented by the
triangles, was greater during the conditioning phase than the operant baseline phase, but then decreased again during the final ten
minutes, the extinction phase. Similarly, for the control subjects
(Group $A_1EA_2$), whose cumulative records are shown at the bottom
of the figure, there was greater responding with opinion statements
during the conditioning and reconditioning phases (the first and
third ten-minute periods) than during the ten-minute extinction
period in between.

Verplanck argued that his experiment strengthened the supposition that the concepts of operant-behavior theory could be

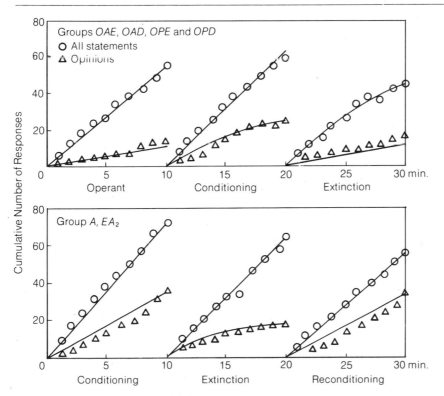

FIGURE 9–3.

Cumulative frequency curves of opinion statements (triangles) and all statements (circles)
for each ten-minute period of the experiment. Cumulative frequency is represented
in medians. In the top graphs, notice that more opinion statements are produced during
the conditioning period (in the middle) than during the baseline (operant) period
or the extinction period. Similarly, in the bottom graphs more opinion statements were
emitted during the conditioning and reconditioning periods than during the extinction
period on the middle (from Verplanck, 1955, Figure 1).

applied to more complex behavior, and that the conditioning of conversation could have useful clinical purposes. His experiment serves as an interesting extension of laboratory research into the field, where the problems of demand characteristics and subjects' awareness of the contingencies in the experiment were minimized.

## 9.3
## EXPERIMENTAL TOPICS AND RESEARCH ILLUSTRATIONS

**Topic:** Experimenter Effects

**Illustration:** Verbal Conditioning

Verplanck's (1955) results are quite dramatic since at the time this was one of the few attempts to condition human verbal behavior in a "free operant" situation. Verplanck had obtained conditioning in all twenty-four subjects, which is rather remarkable, since included were a number of different settings, experimenters, topics of conversation, and relationships between subjects and experimenters. One explanation of these remarkable results—or most any remarkable results—is that the seventeen undergraduate experimenters faked them since they pretty much knew what was expected. Verplanck considered this possibility, but ruled it out, because he knew the students well and trusted them. But in a later replication attempt, experimenter bias was shown to be a serious problem.

Two types of experimenter bias can be identified. One type is simply the conscious faking of data on the part of an investigator who simply lies about what has been found and presents fabricated results. This seems quite unlikely to be a problem very often, even with the publish-or-perish strain in academia. A more subtle form of this problem, and the one we shall consider here, may be more common. Most researchers depend on graduate students, research technicians, or perhaps even undergraduate students (as did Verplanck) to conduct experiments. There are probably eminent animal-learning psychologists who have not seen a white rat in years, and human experimental psychologists who have not tested a subject since graduate school. They depend on the reliability of their research associates to produce accurate results, and it may be that overzealous research aides "help out" occasionally by faking the results to agree better with what their mentor might want. It is, of course, impossible to know how frequently this problem occurs in psychology or any other science. The researcher can only encourage subordinates to be completely honest and, obviously, not penalize them in any way if results happen not to favor his or her pet theory.

The second general type of experimenter-bias effect is the unconscious influence of the experimenter on the results obtained.

Unlike the faking problem, which is conscious, this problem is unconscious—even the experimenters do not know they are being fooled. The way instructions are read by experimenters may even influence the outcome of an experiment. (This is why you should tape record your instructions to subjects if possible, or at least read from a written sheet without ad-libbing.) Such effects could have occurred in Verplanck's experiment as well as in many others. For example, what was judged as a statement of opinion by Verplanck's seventeen experimenters was left pretty much up to them, within some loose guidelines. It may be that the experimenters inadvertently used less rigid criteria for counting a statement an opinion statement during the conditioning period than during the baseline or extinction periods, thus unconsciously biasing the results in favor of the conditioning hypothesis.

Rosenthal (1966) has written an interesting book on experimenter-bias effects, emphasizing their importance. To be sure, some famous scientific bloopers have been committed because of conscious or unconscious bias, but we regard bias effects as minor pests rather than dread killers of the research enterprise. If an experimental result is important, it will be replicated numerous times in the course of further research on the topic. Thus faked data will be discovered sooner or later, and, in the long run, the truth will come out.

Consider a replication attempt of Verplanck's experiment by Azrin and co-workers (1961). In their first experiment, the investigators employed graduate students rather than undergraduates as experimenters. Most had extensive work in psychology behind them and all had studied and been tested on principles of conditioning and Verplanck's original study. The procedure the experimenters were to use was rehearsed in detail in class. An *ABA* design was used; half the experimenters reinforced opinion statements for ten minutes, then allowed them to extinguish for ten minutes, and then reinforced them again for ten minutes. The other half of the experimenters had a ten-minute session of reinforcement sandwiched between two extinction periods. The results were very similar to Verplanck's, with fourteen of fifteen students finding a higher frequency of opinion statements occurring during the conditioning periods. No difficulties were noted by the fifteen graduate-student experimenters. However, a sixteenth student reported that he could not do the experiment as instructed even after six attempts. He said he could not maintain the conversation without participating, and had a great deal of difficulty categorizing and counting opinion and nonopinion statements while simultaneously keeping track of the time with his watch. When this student discussed his problems in class, eight others volunteered the information that they had had similar difficulties and had to deviate seriously from the prescribed procedure in order to complete the experiment. Other problems besides those already stated were that subjects walked out during extinction (who wants to talk with someone who doesn't speak or move his or her head for ten minutes?), or subjects were aware of the experimenter recording their responses, or the experimenter lost track of the time. Also, in one tape-recorded session the investigators found extremely poor agreement among listeners as to what were opinion statements and whether or not there was conditioning. The technical difficulties of the experiment seemed overwhelming, but why was there such agreement on the results?

In the second experiment, Azrin and co-workers again replicated Verplanck's basic conditioning results with undergraduate subjects who reported no problems with the procedure, which was puzzling. This time the experimenters employed another *ABA* design, where the two *A* periods involved reinforcement of opinion statements with agreement and the *B* phase involved extinction of opinion statements with disagreement. Then in a third series of class experiments, the authors tested the possibility that experimenter bias was at work. Undergraduates who had not read Verplanck's study but who had been exposed to the topics of reinforcement and extinction performed an initial experiment where opinion statements were reinforced with agreement and extinction was accomplished by maintaining silence. Once again, conditioning of conversation was found; 44 of 47 students reported a greater frequency of opinion statements during reinforcement than extinction. No surprises here.

But now comes the clincher. About a month later the investigators tried to replicate the conditioning experiment in the same way it had been done by the second class, that is, a ten-minute period of agreement, a ten-minute period of disagreement, and another ten-minute period of agreement. Verplanck had shown that disagreement and silence both produced extinction, and the second class used by Azrin and co-workers had also found extinction with disagreement. However, the third class was led to expect *greater* rather than less responding with opinion statements during the ten-minute period of disagreement. The class had been studying emotion and were told that agreement produced catharsis (release) of emotion but that disagreement did not, so that during the disagreement period the subjects should emit more emotionally charged opinion statements. The results are presented in figure 9–4, where the mean number of opinion statements is plotted against time for both the second class, which was expecting extinction of opinion statements during the period of disagreement, and the third class, which expected facilitation. The results are in perfect accord with the experimenters' expectations: the second class found extinction whereas the third found catharsis. Since the manner of disagreeing was supposedly the same in both cases, it appears that experimenter bias produced the differences between the classes in outcome of the experiment.

Do you want more evidence on this point? One student in the class also happened to be a lab assistant in the psychology department. He was enlisted to discuss the experiment with a number

FIGURE 9–4

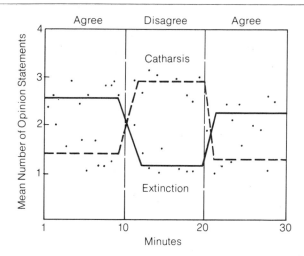

The mean number of opinion statements produced by subjects when tested by experimenters in the second and third classes in the Azrin et al. (1961) study. The results show the effect of the expectations of experimenters on the results obtained. One group of experimenters (the dotted line) was told that disagreement was expected to produce an increase in opinion statements because of catharsis. The other group of experimenters (solid line) was told that disagreement—the same procedure—would produce a decrease of opinion.

of his classmates, by saying "I'm having trouble with my experiment; can you tell me how you did yours?" Of the nineteen students he questioned twelve admitted that they faked part or all of the data, while five more deviated greatly from the procedure they were supposed to use. Only two subjects reported having conducted the experiment correctly. The authors note that the phenomenon of conditioning of opinion statements in casual conversations seems open to "serious question."

The conclusion to be drawn from the Azrin study is not that verbal conditioning does not occur, nor even that Verplanck failed to find it. Perhaps he did; experimenter bias may not have been a problem in his study and there is, at any rate, no way to know more than twenty years later. The conclusion that the Azrin group made is simply that greater experimental control is needed in the area. It is worth quoting part of their conclusion at some length, since it illustrates the basic tradeoff often found in debates about laboratory versus field research.

These findings have implications for the conduct of research in operant conditioning. Operant conditioning procedures have generally been characterized by a high degree of control. In order to avoid unreliability, the response is usually defined very simply and precisely. In order to ensure proper programming of the procedure, automatic apparatus is used. Printed records of the responses are also obtained by automatic means to eliminate bias from the [experimenter's] expectations. These and other precautions have been used, not because of any inherent fascination with "artificial" situations or with complex equipment, but because empirical situations have demanded such control. The importance of extending the procedures of operant conditioning to "real-life" situations should not be allowed to override the elementary considerations of experimental control. . . . In the absence of such objectivity, the results of studies in verbal conditioning may be more a reflection of the experimenter's expectations and theories than the subject's behavior.

In the years since the early reports discussed here, research on verbal conditioning has been dominated by the issue of whether such conditioning can occur in the laboratory in experiments such as Greenspoon's (1955) without awareness on the part of subjects. Short shrift has been given to the interesting field setting introduced by Verplanck, where this issue barely arises (see Spielberger and DeNike, 1966). Somewhat more recent evidence from a provocative study by Konečni and Slamecka (1972) supports the notion that verbal (but nonoperant) conditioning can be effected without awareness.

Awareness or no, verbal-conditioning procedures are being exploited in clinical situations. In one deservedly famous study by Isaacs, Thomas, and Goldiamond (1960), operant-conditioning procedures were utilized to reinstate verbal behavior in two psychotic adults (classified as schizophrenics) who had been completely mute for fourteen and nineteen years!

The issues of demand characteristics and experimenter bias in research are difficult ones to overcome completely. Azrin's study (just discussed) used one strategy. If a researcher suspects that experimenter bias (either deliberate or unconscious) from research assistants produced some effect, then the researcher can conduct replication studies with new assistants. Some assistants should be told to expect one outcome of the experiment; others, to expect a different outcome. If experimenters with different expectancies report different patterns of results, then the researcher would conclude that experimenter bias was probably at work in producing the original observations. On the other hand, if all experimenters obtain the same pattern of results when using the same procedures, despite their different expectations, then the researcher could breathe a sigh of relief and assume that experimenter bias did not affect the original results. Unfortunately, although this strategy is an excellent one for evaluating the possibility of experimenter bias, it is rarely used because it is expensive and difficult to implement in most situations.

Other strategies that deal with experimenter bias and demand characteristics are available. Briefly, one is for the experimenter who is conducting research to be uninformed about the specific hypothesis being tested and the expected outcomes of the experiment. (Of course, the experimenter is likely to imagine hypotheses and outcomes even if not specifically told.) Or, the experimenter may be kept "blind" with respect to conditions. In this case, one researcher administers the independent variable randomly to the subjects, and then a second experimenter tests the subjects to see whether the variable had any effect. The second experimenter does not know which of the subjects had actually received the experimental manipulation and which had not (hence being blind to conditions). In this way the experimenter has no knowledge of the subjects' conditions and thus cannot bias results one way or the other, whether consciously or unconsciously. Another strategy involves the use of a *double-blind design*, where neither the experimenter nor the subjects know in what condition the subjects serve. The reason for keeping the subjects blind with respect to conditions is so their expectations cannot affect the results. Thus the double-blind procedure avoids or minimizes to a large extent the problems of both demand characteristics and experimenter bias. This design is commonly used in medical research when new treatments or drugs are being evaluated. We will discuss such procedures in more detail in chapter 13.

---

**Problem:** Can psychologists improve toilet training in children?

**FROM PROBLEM TO EXPERIMENT: THE NUTS AND BOLTS**

---

As has already been discussed in this chapter, principles of learning and psychology have been applied to numerous problems. Behavioral techniques are even making inroads into relatively common problems faced by each of us, such as how to break a bad habit or to shape ourselves to study more effectively. We now turn to consider one of the most common, yet urgent, problems faced by all new parents.

**Problem:** What is the best way to toilet train a child?

As is always the case with problems, they must be made more specific before an experimenter can decide on independent, dependent, and control variables. The dependent variable seems fairly obvious. It is easy to measure the number of times children void and/or defecate in the toilet versus other places, such as their underpants or the floor. Even so, we still need a criterion to determine when learning has progressed sufficiently so that we can end the experiment. Such a criterion can reference the correct behavior (for example, voiding and/or defecating in the toilet for four consecutive times) or the behavior we wish to eliminate (for example, no voiding and/or defecating in underpants and not more than two near-misses on the floor in an eight-hour period). These two criteria are closely related, since a correct response (using the toilet) precludes an error. We will somewhat arbitrarily decide on a criterion of four consecutive correct responses; that is, the child must use the toilet for four urinations and/or bowel movements with no intervening accidents or errors. The "best way" of toilet training, then, is the one that produces four consecutive correct responses in the shortest time period. Note that this operational definition of the best way is also to some degree arbitrary. For example, some parents might prefer a method that produced four correct responses with the least amount of parental effort instead of in the shortest time period. But since this latter definition might imply that a child would not be trained at all, we will stick with our first definition.

**Hypothesis:** *Combining verbal praise for correct responses with verbal punishment for accidents is more effective than only verbal praise.*

Our independent variable is the kind of verbal statements made by the parent during toilet training. Since using verbal punishment occurs in one of the two conditions of interest, we must first decide whether or not to use the same children in both conditions. Technically, this means picking either a within-subjects design or a between-subjects design. Selecting a within-subjects design (same child) is impractical here since once the child is toilet trained with one kind of verbal statement, the other kind could not be tested until effects of the first training were extinguished. This would probably not be tolerated by the parent, and even if it were ethical, we still could not be sure that extinction was complete. So we need two different groups of children (a between-subjects design). One group gets only verbal praise from the parent and the other gets both verbal praise and verbal punishment.

In order to perform this study, the experimenter will have to secure the active cooperation of parents. This presents a sampling problem. Since parents who refuse permission cannot have their children tested, we cannot be sure that the sample of those children whose parents gave permission is truly representative of all children. Another problem concerns the age of the children. A random sample would encounter difficulties with older children since some of them would already be toilet trained, and hence, could not be used in the study. The experimenter would probably have to match the two groups for age, and this might interfere with randomization of other, perhaps related, characteristics of the sample. The best sampling strategy would be to use a *stratified sampling technique.* All available children would first be classified by age and then sampling would occur randomly within each classification.

Although it is difficult to control any variables in a home, as opposed to a laboratory environment, some attempts can be made. For example, the diet and amount of water consumed by children in both groups should be roughly equated. A thirsty child who has just finished a bowl of salty popcorn will drink more water and hence be more likely to urinate shortly thereafter. If more thirsty children were present in one group, results could be confounded. Another control variable would be the amount of rest the child had before the experiment. Young children especially tend to get irritable and cranky when they are tired, and this could interfere with the experiment.

**Hypothesis:** *Practice (pretraining) in walking to the potty chair and undressing will facilitate toilet training.*

The dependent and control variables are the same as just discussed. Again two groups of children would be required. The experimental group would receive practice in walking to the potty chair, and removing their underwear, pants, or dress. Again some criterion would be needed to determine how much practice should be given. This could either be an amount of time (say, half an hour) or until the child can successfully perform these acts on verbal command of the parent. The control group would begin toilet training immediately, without such practice. We would conclude that pretraining was useful if the time required for pretraining plus toilet training for the experimental group were less than the total time required by the control group.

These two hypotheses are intended to illustrate experimental design rather than how to toilet train a child—that is, they are not necessarily correct. Indeed, a total training program for children based on learning theory would combine many different strategies. If you are interested in such a toilet-training program, we recommend the book, *Toilet Training in Less Than a Day* by Nathan Azrin and Richard Foxx. This training plan was developed from a set of procedures originally devised to teach mentally retarded children and is based on contemporary findings in learning and conditioning. It is an excellent example of how principles of experimental psychology can be applied to solve an important problem outside the laboratory.

**SUMMARY**

**1.** In many applied settings, including clinical settings where behavior modification is employed, the traditional large *n* research methodology of psychological research is inappropriate. Often, there is only one subject, so experimental control cannot be obtained by randomly assigning subjects to experimental and control groups, and then holding other factors constant while the independent variable is manipulated. Thus, it is necessary to use procedures developed especially for use with small numbers of subjects.

**2.** In many applied settings, an *AB* design is used. In this technique, a baseline is established (the *A* phase) and then some treatment is imposed (the *B* phase). Researchers often conclude that the changes in behavior that occur in the *B* phase are produced by the treatment. However, the *AB* design is faulty, because other variables may be correlated with the treatment (such as practice or fatigue effects), and they may cause the observed change, rather than the independent variable (the treatment).

**3.** One powerful technique is the *ABA* design where, after a baseline on the behavior of interest is established (the initial *A* phase), the independent variable is introduced during the *B* phase and its effect (if any) on the dependent measure is observed. Another *A* phase is then instituted where the independent variable is removed in order to determine whether any changes observed during the *B* phase were caused by the independent variable or other possible confounding factors.

**4.** Experiments in applied settings are often conducted in the field rather than in controlled laboratory situations. Field research is also done in cases where demand characteristics of a laboratory setting may serve to invalidate the conclusions sought from the investigation. Verplanck's experiment was discussed as an interesting attempt to establish verbal conditioning in a setting where the problem of awareness on the part of subjects was unlikely to arise, since subjects did not even know they were part of an experiment.

**5.** The danger in field research is that it may not be possible to establish enough experimental control to draw firm inferences from an experiment. A replication of Verplanck's experiments indicated that there may have been several problems of experimental control, but most important, the replication found massive experimenter-bias effects.

**6.** Experimenter bias refers to the conscious or unconscious effect of the experimenter on the outcome of the experiment. One way to determine whether this bias is a factor in establishing some effect is to have experimenters expect different outcomes throughout several replications of the experiment. If two experimenters who each expect a different outcome find exactly the same pattern of results when they conduct the experiment independently, then we can be confident that experimenter bias is not at work in producing the particular effect. However, it may be impractical or impossible to institute such safeguards. In such cases, it is best not to tell the person who is conducting the experiment the hypothesis being tested. If this is not possible, attempts should be made to make the experimenter blind to the condition in which each subject is tested.

**KEY TERMS**

**ABA** design
**AB** design
**"blind" experimenter**
**confounding**
**demand characteristics**
**double-blind design**
**experimenter bias**

**field research**
**large *n* design**
**reversal design**
**small *n* design**
**stratified sampling**
**verbal conditioning**

**1.** What factors might lead researchers to bias (unconsciously) their research to favor the hypothesis they are testing?

**2.** How does the *ABA* or reversal design permit inferences about causation? Why is it better than a simple *AB* design?

**3.** Imagine that you have developed a program for trying to improve a friend's study habits. Outline a research program that could be used even with only one subject, to see whether your program would work. (Hint: the Psychology in Action section may provide for some general ideas.)

**4.** Discuss some of the difficulties inherent in field research. Can you think of methods to combat these problems?

**5.** Research on verbal conditioning in natural field settings was discussed in the chapter, along with problems that have plagued experiments in this area. Try to create a general design and procedure for studying this problem, one that would successfully overcome past problems, yet would still be feasible experimentally.

# Psychology in Action

## Can You Put Yourself on a Better Schedule of Reinforcement?

All of us have habits we would like to break, or other habits we would like to develop. Smoking, drinking, nail-biting, watching too much TV, and not studying enough are some of the bad habits that college students often say they would like to alter. Failure to control these behaviors is often blamed on laziness, a defective personality, and so forth. However, a behavioral analysis of such problems suggests a simple alternative to these interpretations: bad habits are being reinforced, and to change them it is necessary to alter the schedule of reinforcement by which one lives. If all these bad habits are learned, then they can be altered by learning, too. The general aim is to alter the reinforcements in one's life so that they occur after desirable behavior and not after undesirable behavior.

Suppose you are in danger of flunking out of school because you study too little and, being addicted to the movies, attend them too much. You know you have a problem, but are stuck in a rut and don't know how to get out. What can you do to modify your behavior? The first step is to set a goal for yourself. It is not enough to say you want to study more, but to have a concrete, measurable goal. Let us say you decide you want to study six hours a day outside of class. After setting the goal, your second step would be to institute some means of carefully monitoring your study behavior. How much do you already study, on the average? You should carry a special notebook and record each studying episode each day and total them at the end of the day. You can also then get a weekly average. Let us imagine at the end of a week you discover that you are averaging fifty-nine minutes a day studying; obviously a long way from your target of six hours a day.

The next step is to set yourself a realistic goal in your first attempt. It might be too much of a shock to your system to go directly from one hour to six hours a day of studying; worse, you might give up the attempt early on, deciding it is impossible. So let us assume that you decide to increase your studying to two hours a day at first. But how? You should analyze the situation and see what activities currently prevent you from studying. The main deterrent is your going to the movies, but surely other activities also intrude. You might set up an activity schedule to monitor your behavior as shown in table 9–2.

You should then try to change your environment so that it is more conducive to study. Try to avoid those friends who might encourage you to go the movies. Don't avoid them entirely, of course, but plan to spend more time at the place where you study. Analyze your study area—are there many distractions? (These might include roommates, magazines, radios, and televisions.) If there are lots of distractions, abandon your room as a place of study and find a quiet hideaway where only you and your books will be present. Studies have shown that if you can associate a particular place exclusively with study behavior and then force yourself to go to this place, you can increase studying dramatically. Finally—and this is one of the most important steps—you must figure out a reward for yourself for successfully studying the allotted amount of time. For example, you could promise yourself that once you have studied two hours each day during the first week, you can

Activity Schedule

TABLE 9–2

| Time | Monday | Tuesday | Wednesday | Thursday | Friday | Saturday | Sunday |
|------|--------|---------|-----------|----------|--------|----------|--------|
| 7:00 | | | | | | | |
| 8:00 | | | | | | | |
| 9:00 | | | | | | | |
| 10:00 | | | | | | | |
| 11:00 | | | | | | | |
| 12:00 | | | | | | | |
| 1:00 | | | | | | | |
| 2:00 | | | | | | | |
| 3:00 | | | | | | | |
| 4:00 | | | | | | | |
| 5:00 | | | | | | | |
| 6:00 | | | | | | | |
| 7:00 | | | | | | | |
| 8:00 | | | | | | | |
| 9:00 | | | | | | | |
| 10:00 | | | | | | | |
| 11:00 | | | | | | | |

then go to the movies with your friends. Thus one of the main reinforcers in your life—going to the movies—is now made contingent on other behavior. In essence, you are reinforcing yourself for studying.

During the next week try studying three hours a day, continuing to carefully monitor your time and study habits. In each successive week, increase your amount of study per day, until you reach your goal in a few weeks. Technically, you are *shaping* study behavior in yourself by reinforcing successive approximations to the target behavior, just as animals are taught complicated tricks by being reinforced for gradual approximations to them. If you can keep the reinforcement contingencies in place, you will have dramatically changed your behavior.

The case we have used here may not apply directly to your situation, but in all likelihood you have habits you would like to break or change. You can do so by applying the rules specified here—setting a concrete target goal and gradually altering your behavior to approximate that goal by reinforcing yourself for each step taken. R. D. Williams and J. D. Long have written a book, *Toward a Self-Managed Life Style*, that explores the possibility of changing many areas of one's life by effectively reinforcing positive behavior and not rewarding negative behavior. Besides methods for improving study habits, they discuss behavioral self-management programs for losing weight, increasing exercise, managing one's time, controlling smoking and drinking, and becoming more assertive.

# CHAPTER **10** ═══════════════

## Preview

This chapter deals with research techniques psychologists use to study remembering and forgetting. The three methodological issues discussed are important to memory research as well as to research on most other topics. One issue is that of scale attenuation in the dependent variable, or the problem of interpreting results where performance is nearly perfect or nearly absent altogether in some conditions. A second crucial issue is the generality of results: will the conclusion drawn from one experiment generalize to another in which there are different subjects or a different way of manipulating the independent variable? This topic is closely related to the third issue, interaction effects in multifactor experiments, which has already been briefly discussed in chapters 3 and 7.

## Chapter Outline

**Ebbinghaus's Contribution**
**Introducing the Variables in Memory Research**
**Experimental Topics and Research Illustrations**
    Scale Attenuation: Modality Differences
    Generality of Results: Modality Differences
    Interaction Effects: Methods of Testing

**From Problem to Experiment: The Nuts and Bolts**
    Is Reading Better than Listening?
**Summary**
**Key Terms**
**Discussion Questions**
**Psychology in Action**
    What Is the Best Way to Remember a Telephone Number?

# REMEMBERING
# AND FORGETTING

*The whole of science is nothing more than refinement of everyday thinking.*

A. Einstein

What experiences can you recall from your year in the eight grade? Think of them for a moment. You learned many facts there; lots of things happened to you. Probably you will never recall even a small fraction of the facts you learned or experiences you had then. What has happened to these memories? Are they lost forever? Or are the memories still stored somewhere but never actively recalled, since you never have an appropriate situation to bring them to mind? There are some things you will never forget, even if you want to, but others you cannot recall no matter how urgent the need. If a budding romance had a catastrophic ending, this memory from your days in the eighth grade may stick with you long after other events have been relegated to the dim recesses of the past. Why?

The humorist Robert Benchley, in an essay called "What College Did to Me," attempted to recall the things he had learned in college years before and to classify these by the year in which they were learned. There were thirty-nine items in the list, which decreased from twelve things he remembered from his freshman year to only eight things recalled from his senior year. A selective sampling from Benchley's list appears in table 10–1. It is selective only with regard to the number of pieces of information included, so that it does give a fair representation of the depth and range of the lasting knowledge acquired in college. You should, of course, be happy

---

TABLE 10–1          Selected Items Robert Benchley Recalled from His Years in College

---

*Things I Learned—Freshman Year*
1. Charlemagne either died or was born or did something with the Holy Roman Empire in 800.
2. By placing a paper bag inside another paper bag you can carry home a milkshake in it.
3. There is a double *l* in the middle of "parallel."
4. French nouns ending in "aison" are feminine.
5. Almost everything you need to know about a subject is in the encyclopedia.
6. A tasty sandwich can be made by spreading peanut butter on raisin bread.
7. The chances are against filling an inside straight.
8. There is a law in economics called *The Law of Diminishing Returns*, which means after a certain margin is reached returns begin to diminish. This may not be correctly stated, but there *is* a law by that name.

*Sophomore Year*
1. A good imitation of measles rash can be effected by stabbing the forearm with a stiff whiskbroom.
2. Queen Elizabeth was not above suspicion.
3. You can sleep undetected in a lecture course by resting the head on the hand as if shading the eyes.
4. The ancient Phoenicians were really Jews, and got as far north as England where they operated tin mines.
5. You can get dressed much quicker in the morning if the night before when you are going to bed you take off your trousers and underdrawers at once, leaving the latter inside the former.

*Junior Year*
1. Emerson left his pastorate because he had some argument about communion.
2. Pushing your arms back as far as they will go fifty times each day increases your chest measurement.
3. Marcus Aurelius had a son who turned out to be a bad boy.
4. Eight hours of sleep are not necessary.
5. Heraclitus believed fire was the basis of all life.
6. The chances are you will never fill an inside straight.

*Senior Year*
1. There is as yet no law determining what constitutes trespass in an airplane.
2. Six hours of sleep are not necessary.
3. Bicarbonate of soda taken before retiring makes you feel better the next day.
4. May is the shortest month of the year.

---

and proud to know that you too may soon have a college degree, a certificate that ensures you know certain basic facts like these.

Is this all Benchley really remembers from his college days? If you made a list from your days in the eighth grade, it would probably be similarly brief. This leads to an interesting question: How can we study memories that cannot be recalled? If a person cannot recall an experience, can we assume that the memory trace representing that experience has vanished?

## EBBINGHAUS'S CONTRIBUTION—WHEN MEMORY WAS YOUNG

The experimental investigation of human memory was begun by a German psychologist, Hermann Ebbinghaus (figure 10–1). Ebbinghaus was a true scientific pioneer. He believed, unlike his famous contemporary, Wilhelm Wundt (see appendix B), that experimental psychology could be developed to study the higher mental processes and not just the organs of sense. His main achievement was demonstrating how empirical research could be done to answer interesting questions about the topic of memory. This re-

FIGURE 10–1.
Hermann Ebbinghaus
began the experimental
study of verbal learning
and memory. (the
Bettmann Archive)

search was published in 1885 in a book still in press today, *Memory: A Contribution to Experimental Psychology*. One of the first questions Ebbinghaus faced was the one we have just been considering, how to measure memory. Ebbinghaus served as the only subject in all his experiments and the materials he invented to be memorized are called *nonsense syllables*. He used meaningless syllables which contained a vowel sandwiched between two consonants (and therefore called *CVC* syllables) such as *ZOK, VAP*, and so on. By using these syllables he hoped to minimize the influence of linguistic associations that would have been present had he used words, sentences, or (as he sometimes did) passages of poetry as materials to be remembered.

Ebbinghaus selected these syllables at random from a master set of 2,300 and placed them into lists that varied in length. If the list contained say, thirty nonsense syllables, Ebbinghaus would read the syllables out loud to himself at a uniform rate and, immediately afterward, cover up the list and then try to repeat it back to himself or write it down. Obviously on the first trial this feat was impossible, but he could measure the number of syllables he was able to recall correctly. Then he would read the list aloud a second time, attempt recall, and so on. One measure that Ebbinghaus used of the difficulty of recalling a list is the number of such study/test trials (or the amount of time) needed for one perfect recitation of the list. This is called a *trials of criterion* measure of memory and it was widely used in memory research for years, though it is rare now.

Suppose Ebbinghaus wanted to test his memory for a list a month after learning it. He might, as an initial cue, provide himself with the first nonsense syllable in the list. But suppose this did not help him recall the list and that, try as he might, he could recall nothing further? Does this mean the series that he memorized a month before left no lasting impression? How could we ever know? Ebbinghaus invented an ingenious method of answering this question. In measuring memory for a series of nonsense syllables, Ebbinghaus attempted to *relearn* the series, just as he had in the first place, by repeatedly reading it aloud and then attempting to recite it or write it. Once again he could measure the number of trials (or amount of time) necessary to learn the list. The memory for the list at the time of relearning could be measured by the *savings* in terms of the fewer number of trials or less time needed to relearn the list, and this measure of memory would be obtainable even when a person thought that he or she remembered nothing of the material (since nothing could be recalled before relearning). Ebbinghaus found that even when he could recall none of the nonsense syllables in a list, he often still exhibited a considerable savings in the number of trials or amount of time it took him to relearn the list, indicating that memory for the list could exist without active recall.

One of Ebbinghaus's best-known findings is presented in figure 10–2. The graph shows the relation between the amount of savings and the time since original learning, or how forgetting is related to time. As you can see, Ebbinghaus found that forgetting is rapid soon after learning, but then slows. The savings method is still used today to ask important questions about memory (e.g., Nelson, Fehling, and Moore-Glascock, 1979).

Even though Robert Benchley may have exhibited poor recall for information he learned in college, presumably, if he had been required to retake his courses, he would, like Ebbinghaus, have exhibited considerable savings. (He tells us that these courses included such gems as Early Renaissance Etchers, the Social Life of

FIGURE 10–2.

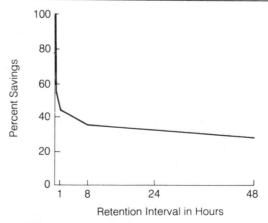

The forgetting curve. Ebbinghaus measured the savings in relearning a list of nonsense syllables after various periods of time had elapsed since original learning. Notice that forgetting is rapid at first and then levels off.

Minor Sixteenth-Century Poets, and the History of Lace Making.) Perhaps you may recall little of your geometry course in high school (or chapter 2 of this book, for that matter), but presumably you would find the course much easier were you to take it again.

Ebbinghaus's work in memory was truly original. But besides his seminal memory research, his other achievements include an interesting discussion of the problem of experimenter bias, production of one of psychology's earliest mathematical models, one of the earliest examples of explicit hypothesis testing, and an advanced (for the time) discussion of statistical problems in research. He also wrote an interesting psychology text and designed an early intelligence test.

## INTRODUCING THE VARIABLES IN MEMORY RESEARCH

### Dependent Variables

Remembering may be measured in numerous ways, but usually involve either *recall* or *recognition*. In recall tests, reproduction of material is required, whereas in recognition tests, material is presented to people and they are required to judge whether or not they have seen it previously. Three popular recall tests are *serial recall*, *free recall*, and *paired-associate recall*. In serial recall, people are required to recall information in the serial order it was presented, whereas in free recall, the order of recall is irrelevant. In paired-associate recall, people are presented with pairs of items, such as *igloo-saloon*, and at recall they are given one member of the pair (igloo, referred to as the stimulus) and are asked to produce the other member (saloon, the response). Recognition tests are generally of two types. In *yes/no tests* people are given the original material they studied, such as words, mixed in with a number of new but generally similar words. Subjects respond yes or no to each word depending on whether they believe it was in the list. *Forced-choice recognition tests* are multiple-choice tests. Several alternatives are presented, only one of which is correct, and the subject in the experiment is forced to choose the correct alternative. Forced-choice tests are preferred to yes/no tests because correcting for guessing is less of a problem.

Recall and recognition tests are not dichotomous; rather they may be viewed as lying on a continuum, with the dimension being the amount of information given about the material, or the power of the retrieval cues presented. If *GRA* is presented as a cue for the word *GRAPH*, which appeared in the list, is this a test of recall or recognition?

In each case the dependent measure in tests of recall and recognition is the number or proportion of items correctly recalled or recognized in different conditions, or the number of errors, which amounts to the same thing. Sometimes a derivative measure is used, such as $d'$ from the theory of signal detection (see chapter 6). Recently, investigators concerned with recognition have used reaction time as a dependent measure, as discussed in chapter 7.

### Independent Variables.

Many types of variables are manipulated in experiments on human memory. One of the

*(Continued on next page)*

most popular variables historically has been the nature of the material presented for memory. It can be letters, digits, nonsense syllables, words, phrases, sentences, paragraphs, or long passages of prose text, and the characteristics of each of these types of material can also be varied. For example, words that refer to concrete objects (cigar, rhinoceros) are better recalled than abstract words (beauty, dread), when other relevant factors such as word length are held constant (Paivio, 1969). Three other important independent variables will be considered in the experiments discussed in this chapter. One is quite obvious: the retention interval between presentation of material and test. How fast does forgetting occur? What are its mechanisms? Another variable attracting much recent attention is modality of presentation. Is information better remembered if it comes in through the ears or the eyes, or is there no difference? A final variable under consideration is the nature of the memory test given to people. For example, do recall tests show results different from recognition tests? This is just a sample of variables that are investigated in memory studies.

**Control Variables**

Memory experiments are typically quite well controlled. Important variables that are usually held constant across conditions are the amount of material presented and the rate of presentation, though of course these can be interesting variables in their own right. The modality of presentation is another factor that must not vary, unless it is a variable of major interest. If some characteristic of the material is being varied, then it is necessary to hold constant other factors. If a researcher is interested in varying the concreteness or abstractness of words, then other characteristics, such as word length and frequency of occurrence, must be held constant across the different conditions.

---

**10.1**

**EXPERIMENTAL TOPICS AND RESEARCH ILLUSTRATIONS**

**Topic:** Scale Attenuation

**Illustration:** Modality Differences

The first topic we are considering here is important, but is often overlooked in psychological research. The general problem is how to interpret performance on some dependent variable in an experiment when performance is either very nearly perfect (near the "ceiling" of the scale) or very nearly lacking altogether (near the "floor"). These effects are called *scale-attenuation effects* (or, more commonly, ceiling and floor effects) and, as usual, we shall embed our discussion in the context of an actual research problem.

One subject in memory research that has recently attracted a great deal of attention is that of modality differences. Do we remember information better if it comes through our eyes or through our ears? Or is there no difference? Is information better remembered if it is presented to both the ears and the eyes simultaneously than if it is presented to only one or the other? These questions are not only of theoretical importance but are also of practical import. When you look up a phone number and need to remember it while you cross the room to the telephone, is it sufficient to simply read the number silently to yourself as you usually do, or would you be better off to also read the number aloud so that information enters both your ears and your eyes?

***The eyes have it: Scarborough's experiment.*** One attempt to answer these questions was reported by Scarborough (1972). He used a short-term memory task called the *Brown-Peterson technique* after its inventors (Brown, 1958; Peterson and Peterson, 1959). Here, people are presented with information to remember for a short period of time and then are distracted from rehearsing (repeating it to themselves) by being required to perform some other task until they are later asked to recall the information. Typically, subjects are given a single *CCC* trigram (three consonants, for example, *NRF*), and are required to count backward by threes from a three-digit number (464, 461, 458, et cetera) for varying periods of time (the retention interval) up to about thirty seconds before attempting recall. Try it yourself. Three letters and a three-digit number will appear after the next sentence. Read the letters and the number out loud, look away and then count backward by threes from the number for about thirty seconds before you try to recall the letters.

XGR 679

How did you do? Chances are you recalled the trigram perfectly. People almost always do on the first trial in experiments using this task. However, recall drops off when multiple trials are used with a different trigram on each trial, so that after four or five trials, subjects are typically recalling trigrams correctly only 50 percent of the time with an eighteen-second retention interval (see figure 10–3). This phenomenon is named *proactive interference*, since the early trials in this task interfere with recall on later trials.

In Scarborough's (1972) experiment, all subjects received thirty-six consonant trigrams presented for .7 second in the Brown-Peterson technique. There were three groups of six subjects; the method in which the trigrams were presented differed for each group. One group of subjects *saw* the trigrams (Visual Only condition), one group *heard* the trigrams (Auditory Only), and a third group both saw and heard the trigrams (Visual + Auditory). Presentation time was carefully controlled by having the trigrams presented over a tape recorder or a tachistoscope, a device for quickly exposing and removing visual information. One second after presentation of the trigram, subjects heard a three-digit number, except in one condition where subjects were requested to recall

FIGURE 10–3.

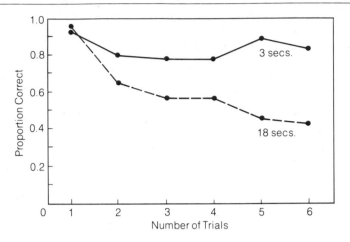

Retention of a stimulus trigram as a function of the number of trials (1-6) and the retention
interval on each trial (3 or 18 seconds). On the first trial there is very little forgetting
of the trigram, even with an 18 second retention interval. However, after a number of trials,
recall becomes poorer due to the prior tests, especially with the 18 seconds retention
interval (Keppel & Underwood, 1962).

the trigram immediately (the zero-second retention-interval condition). Subjects in each condition were required to retain the
letters during retention intervals of 0, 3, 6, 9, 12, or 18 seconds.
Once the three-digit number was presented, subjects were required
to count backward by threes aloud at the rate of one count per
second in time with a metronome. At the end of the retention
interval the metronome stopped and two green lights came on,
signaling the ten-second recall period. So each trial consisted of a
warning signal (two yellow lights and a tone) indicating that the
trigram was about to be displayed, presentation of the trigram,
presentation of the three-digit number (with one exception just
noted), the retention interval during which the subjects counted
backward by threes, and finally the recall period. A typical trial is
exemplified in figure 10–4. This procedure was repeated thirty-six
times (six trials at each of the six retention intervals, in a counterbalanced order) with different trigrams. In summary, three between-subjects conditions (Visual Only, Auditory Only, Visual +
Auditory) were combined with six within-subjects conditions (retention intervals of 0, 3, 6, 9, 12, or 18 seconds) in the experiment.

    The results of Scarborough's experiment are reproduced in fig-
ure 10–5, where the percentage of times a trigram was correctly
reported is plotted as a function of retention interval. It is quite
apparent from this figure, and the statistics that Scarborough reports back this up, that subjects who received only visual presentation of the trigrams generally recalled them a greater percentage
of the time than did subjects who received only auditory presentation. Furthermore, receiving information in both modalities si-

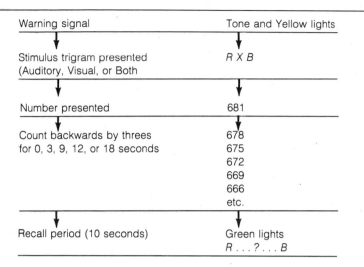

FIGURE 10–4.

| Warning signal | Tone and Yellow lights |
|---|---|
| Stimulus trigram presented (Auditory, Visual, or Both | R X B |
| Number presented | 681 |
| Count backwards by threes for 0, 3, 9, 12, or 18 seconds | 678 675 672 669 666 etc. |
| Recall period (10 seconds) | Green lights R . . . ? . . . B |

Schematic overview of a typical trial in the Brown-Peterson short term memory procedure as used in Scarborough's experiment.

multaneously did not produce any better recall than presenting the information only visually; the percentage correct at each retention interval is roughly the same for Visual Only and Visual + Auditory subjects. So far so good. But what else can we conclude

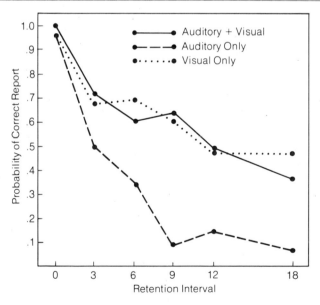

FIGURE 10–5.

The probability of correctly recalling a stimulus trigram as a function of the three presentation conditions and the duration of the counting task. Notice that (a) visual presentation is generally superior to auditory presentation, and (b) simultaneous auditory and visual presentation is no better than only visual presentation (Scarborough, 1972).

from figure 10–5? In particular, can we conclude anything about the rates of forgetting for information that is presented auditorily and visually? Is the rate of forgetting the same or different in the two cases?

Scarborough was quite careful on this score. Although the Auditory Only and Visual Only functions appear to diverge increasingly as the retention interval becomes longer, he did not draw the conclusion that the rate of forgetting is greater for information presented through the ears than through the eyes. However, consider what Massaro (1975) has to say about this experiment in his textbook:

> The figure shows that the curves intercept the $Y$ ordinate at roughly the same point and diverge significantly. The intercept value at zero sec. provides a measure of the original perception and storage of the stimuli, since it measures how much information the subject has immediately after the presentation of the stimuli, when no forgetting has taken place. The rate of forgetting can be determined from the slopes of the forgetting functions. According to this analysis, Figure [10–5] shows that the items presented auditorily are forgotten much faster than the items presented visually. (Massaro, 1975, pp. 530–531)

Unfortunately, this conclusion must be called into question. The reason is that performance at the zero-second retention interval is very nearly perfect in all conditions. When performance is perfect it is impossible to tell whether there are any "real" differences among conditions because of scale attenuation, in this case a ceiling effect. If the scale of the dependent measure were really "long" enough, it might show differences between auditory and visual presentation even at the zero-second retention interval. So Massaro's conclusion that the rate of forgetting is greater for auditory than for visual presentation cannot be accepted on the basis of the argument we just quoted, because the assumption of equivalent performance at the zero-second retention interval may not be correct.

*Fat people on the ceiling.* All this may be a bit confusing at first, so let's take a clearer case and demonstrate the same thing. Suppose two obese men decided to make a bet as to who could lose the greatest amount of weight in a certain amount of time. One man looked much heavier than the other, but neither was sure what he actually weighed, since they both made a point of avoiding scales. The scale they decided to use for the bet was a common bathroom scale which runs from 0 to 300 pounds. On the day they were to begin their weight-loss programs, each man weighed himself while the other watched and, to their great surprise, both men weighed in at exactly the same value, 300 pounds. So despite their different sizes, the two men decided that they were beginning their bet at equal weights.

The problem again is one of ceiling effects in the scale of measurement. The weight range of the bathroom scale simply did not go high enough to record the actual weight of these men. Let us imagine that one actually weighed 300 and the other 350, if their weights had been taken by a scale with a greater range. After six months of their weight-loss program, let us further suppose, both men had actually lost 100 pounds. They both reweighed themselves at this point and discovered that one now weighed 200 pounds and the other 250. Since they believed that they both had started from the same weight (300), they reached the erroneous conclusion that the person who presently weighed 200 had won the bet (see figure 10–6).

The problem here is really the same as that in interpreting the results of Scarborough's experiment as evidence that information presented auditorily is forgotten at a greater rate than information presented visually. There is no better way for us to know the rate of forgetting in the two conditions of interest in that experiment than there is for the two men to know the rate of weight loss in judging who won their bet. In neither case can we assume equivalent initial scores before the measurement of loss begins.

FIGURE 10–6.

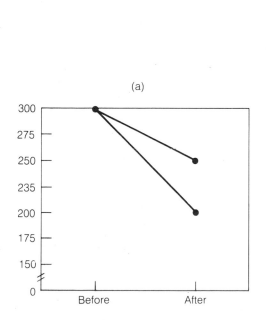

(a)

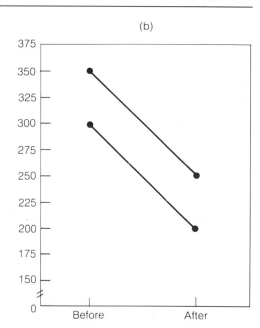

(b)

The left panel (a) illustrates the situation as the fat men believed it to be—they started at the same weight and one lost twice as much as the other. The right panel (b) reveals the actual case, with the ceiling effect in the scale of measurement removed. In fact, both men lost 100 pounds. Scale attentuation (ceiling and floor effects) can hide actual differences that may exist between conditions in an experiment.

One way to avoid this problem in Scarborough's experiment would be to ignore the data points at the zero-second retention interval and ask whether the rate of forgetting is greater between 3 and 18 seconds for auditory than for visual presentation. This could be done by computing an interaction between presentation and retention interval over the range of 3 to 18 seconds; but by simply inspecting figure 10–5, you can get some idea as to whether the Auditory Only and Visual Only points are diverging increasingly. They are between 3 and 9 seconds, but after that the difference between them remains constant. However, this lack of an increasingly larger difference over the last three points may be caused by a floor effect in the Auditory Only condition, since performance is so poor, especially on the last point (only 7 or 8 percent correct). One must be very careful in interpreting data when there are ceiling or floor effects present. A prudent investigator would hesitate to draw any conclusion from the data in figure 10–5 about rates of forgetting, which is just what Scarborough did. But we should also note that over the retention intervals where there are neither ceiling nor floor effects (3, 6, and 9 seconds), there seems to be greater forgetting with auditory than with visual presentation, in agreement with Massaro's conclusion quoted earlier.

How can problems of ceiling and floor effects be avoided in psychological research? Unfortunately, no hard and fast rule can be given. Researchers usually try to design their experiments such that they avoid extremes in performance, and then they often test their intuitions about performance on the task by testing small groups of pilot subjects. If these subjects perform near the ceiling or floor of the scale, then it will often be necessary to revise the experimental task. For example, if performance in a memory experiment is too good, the amount of material being given can be increased so as to lower performance. Similarly, if the task is so hard that people hardly remember anything, the task can be made easier by reducing the amount of material, presenting it more slowly, and so on. The prudent investigator will usually take the effort to test pilot subjects before launching into an experiment that may turn out later to have been flawed by ceiling or floor effects. The testing of pilot subjects also permits the researcher to learn about other problems in the design or procedure of the experiment.

## 10.2
### EXPERIMENTAL TOPICS AND RESEARCH ILLUSTRATIONS

**Topic:** Generality of Results

**Illustration:** Modality Differences

We mentioned in chapter 3 that there are many ways to test a hypothesis, and that single experiments that test a hypothesis, although informative to a certain extent, need to be viewed against a background of other experiments designed to test the same hypothesis in other ways. Ideally, researchers would like experiments that test a particular hypothesis in a variety of situations to converge on one conclusion. Unfortunately, this is often not the case. The issue is one of *generality of results:* often the conclusion drawn from one experimental situation does not generalize to other situations. This is frustrating, but inevitable. It is also important. We should always ask these questions after some experiment has shown an effect of some independent variable on some dependent variable: To what subject populations does this effect generalize? (Just because an effect holds for rats does not necessarily mean that it will hold for people; see chapter 14.) Under what settings, either experimental or extraexperimental, does this conclusion hold? Will the conclusion hold when the independent and dependent variables are operationalized or defined in a slightly different way than in the original experiment? The question of generality crops up, of course, in all types of research. If huge doses of some drug produce cancer in laboratory mice, should this drug be banned from human consumption, even when the dosage level is much smaller and the organism entirely different?

We will concentrate here on a problem involving generality of results that does not involve different subject populations (the problem of *subject representativeness*), but rather involves different experimental settings with the same population, and very similar independent and dependent variables. This is the problem of *variable representativeness*. Let us return to the question of modality differences in memory. Is information better remembered if it is presented to the ears or to the eyes? Scarborough's (1972) experiment was designed to answer this question and the answer was straightforward: although we could draw no conclusions about the *rate* of forgetting, memory *overall* was better when information was presented visually than auditorily and, furthermore, presenting information simultaneously in both modalities was no better than presenting it only visually. There is one major problem with this conclusion: almost every other experiment comparing modality of presentation has reached exactly the opposite conclusion! In a review of numerous experiments Penney (1975, p. 68) concluded: "For short-term memory, auditory presentation is consistently superior to visual presentation, with the difference restricted to recently presented items." Before considering why Scarborough's experiment is an exception to this generalization, let us look briefly at some of the evidence.

A typical experiment is that of Crowder (1970, Exp. I), where subjects were visually presented with lists of nine digits (0–9) randomly ordered, and were asked to recall them in the serial order in which they were presented from left to right on their answer sheets. This is a serial-recall task and is essentially the same task a person is faced with when trying to recall a telephone number. It is necessary to recall both the appropriate items and their correct order in the series. There were three conditions. In the Visual Only condition, subjects were instructed to read each digit to themselves as it appeared on the screen. In the other two conditions, subjects heard the digits in addition to seeing them. In the Visual + Auditory–Repeat condition, subjects were told to repeat each digit out loud as it appeared on the screen. In the Visual + Auditory–Listen condition the subjects heard the experimenter reading the digits as they appeared on the screen. So in all conditions, subjects received visual input. In one auditory condition, subjects vocalized the digits themselves, while in the other they simply listened to them.

The results of Crowder's experiment are presented in figure 10–7. Notice that Crowder plots errors against the serial position of the item in the list, so that high scores indicate poor performance. First notice that performance is best (there are fewest errors) at the beginning and end of the lists. This is a very general characteristic of memory studies; whenever performance is plotted against input position of the material, it is almost always best at the ends of the list. Good performance at the beginning of a list is referred to as a *primacy effect* and good performance at the end of a list is referred to as a *recency effect*. The primary interest of Crowder's experiment was how modality of presentation affected recall. Overall, subjects committed more errors in the Visual Only condition, when there was only visual input, than in the other two conditions where visual presentation was accompanied by auditory presentation. As you can see from figure 10–7, the benefit of auditory presentation was owing entirely to performance at the end of the list, that is, to improved recall of digits in the last three input

FIGURE 10–7.

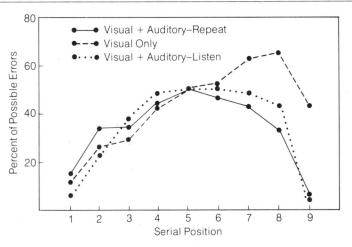

The relation between serial position and percent of errors for different modalities. When information is heard, there are many fewer errors at the end of the series than when it is only seen, but it does not much matter whether a person actually reads the series aloud (Visual + Auditory–Repeat) or only hears it read by someone else (Visual + Auditory–Listen) (Crowder, 1970).

positions. The recency effect was much stronger with auditory than with visual presentation; for visual presentation the recency effect was reduced to the last serial position. There is very little difference between the two Visual + Auditory conditions in Crowder's experiment, which agrees with the findings from numerous other experiments. The only general effect is that repeating often hurts performance near the beginning of the list (reduces the primacy effect), as compared with listening.

In Crowder's experiment, recall was better for the last few items in a list with visual plus auditory presentation, as compared with visual presentation alone. In other experiments where visual presentation is compared with auditory-only presentation, the conclusion is the same: things are better remembered, at least over short time periods, if they come in through the ears rather than through the eyes. And often the effects are more pronounced (than in Crowder's experiment) when slightly different methods are used. For example, Murdock and Walker (1969) presented twenty word lists at the rate of two words per second either visually or auditorily and asked subjects to recall the words in any order (free recall). Their results are presented in figure 10–8, where probability of recall is plotted against input position. Once again auditory presentation enhanced the recency effect; recall was better with auditory presentation for the last six serial positions. (Notice that there was a slight, and puzzling, reversal of this effect at the pri-

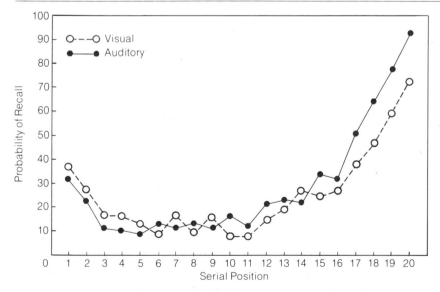

FIGURE 10–8.

Probability of correct recall as a function of serial position for visual and auditory presentation. Auditory presentation is superior to visual presentation at the end of the list, and there is a reversal of this relationship at the beginning of the list (Murdock and Walker, 1969).

macy portion of the serial-position curve.) Once again, the general finding that has been reported from numerous experiments such as these is that auditory presentation leads to superior recall of recently presented material relative to visual presentation. (See Crowder, 1976, for a discussion of theories of this modality effect.)

Let us return to our initial question. Why did Scarborough (1972) find that visual presentation was superior to auditory presentation in the Brown-Peterson task? One possibility is that there was simply something wrong with his experiment. Perhaps an unintentional confounding of some sort led him to an erroneous conclusion. For example, maybe subjects in the Visual Only condition were simply better than those in the other conditions, because subject assignment was not random. This sort of thing is the first possibility that should be checked whenever a finding is anomalous in some way. But it seems very unlikely in this case that there was any simple confounding. The experiment was carefully done, the differences were rather large and statistically reliable. We have to search harder for an answer.

One very likely possibility is the nature of the distractor activity that Scarborough used between presentation and recall, that is, counting backward from the three-digit number out loud. If we assume that there are separate auditory and visual short-term memory systems, it could be that the auditory nature of the counting task in Scarborough's experiment produced greater interference for items presented auditorily than for those presented visually. Since this is interference occurring after presentation of the material to be remembered, it is called *retroactive interference*.

Evidence for this retroactive-interference interpretation of why Scarborough did not find the usual modality effect comes from a study by Hopkins, Edwards, and Cook (1973). They showed that when words were presented auditorily in a short-term memory task, they were better remembered when the interpolated task was visual rather than auditory. However, when the words were presented visually, the converse was found—a visual interpolated task damaged recall more than an auditory task did. Similar results have been reported by Elliot and Strawhorn (1976). Such results argue for the existence of separate visual and auditory short-term memory codes, and help explain why Scarborough did not find the usual advantage of auditory to visual presentation in a short-term memory task.

Whenever an experimental result does not generalize, noting this fact is only the first step. The real problem is in finding out why. Scientists often tend to disbelieve or ignore exceptions to firmly held beliefs, at least until the exception has been replicated enough times to be made salient. It is always uncomfortable to have to change one's mind about strongly held beliefs, but one way science sometimes progresses by leaps is when an empirical exception to a widely accepted theory becomes understood. Often understanding the exception causes us to throw out or greatly modify our theory. So failures of generalization are not necessarily to be lamented; they can be great opportunities.

---

**Topic:** Interaction Effects

**Illustration:** Methods of Testing

**10.2**
EXPERIMENTAL
TOPICS AND
RESEARCH
ILLUSTRATIONS

---

The term *interaction effect* is a statistical term that arises from the use of analysis of variance in evaluating multifactor experiments. Interaction effects are more commonly referred to as *interactions* and have been discussed previously in chapters 3 and 7. (The analysis of variance is described in the appendix.) However, because the concept of interactions is so important, we consider it again in somewhat more detail. Also, we have discovered that it is a concept that is somewhat bothersome to students, so repeated treatments should provide a better grasp of the topic.

Multifactor experiments, you will recall, are those in which two or more independent variables are manipulated at the same time. An interaction effect occurs when the effect of one independent variable changes depending on the level of the other independent variable. The outcome of the experiment by Hopkins and co-workers described just above exemplifies an interaction, though we did not use this word to describe the result. They found that the effects of one variable (auditory verus visual presentation) differed, depending on the value of another variable (auditory versus visual interpolated task). Auditory presentation produced better recall than visual presentation with a visual interpolated task, and conversely.

Let us consider a different problem to illustrate the various types of interactions that may occur in an experiment. As mentioned earlier, the two main ways of testing memory are recall tests and recognition tests. In the former, material that was studied must be reproduced, whereas in the latter the studied material must be distinguished from similar material that was not studied. In classroom situations this distinction corresponds most closely to that between essay tests (where material must be reproduced) and multiple-choice tests (where correct answers must be distinguished from similar distractors or "lures"). A question of considerable theoretical and practical importance is whether tests of recall and recognition are affected in the same way by independent variables.

One independent variable that has been studied is *test expectancy*, or what type of test people expect to receive. As teachers (and former students), we have noticed that students always want to know what type of test they will be given in courses. Will it be an essay test? A multiple choice test? Some combination of questions? Presumably, students study differently depending on the type of test they are to receive. Many report that they study longer and harder when faced with an essay test rather than a multiple-choice test.

A number of experiments have asked the question as to how memory changes as a function of test expectancy. Do people study harder if they know they will be given an essay test? Do they remember more? Does this depend on the type of test they actually receive? Does it depend on the type of material tested? In a typical experiment designed to answer these questions, four groups of subjects are tested. Two are led to expect they will be given a test of recall after studying some material; two others are led to expect a recognition test. Then one group of each pair is given the type of test they expected, while the other group is given the opposite type of test. This experiment then uses a 2 × 2 factorial design, since two expectancies are created as one variable (a recall or recognition expectancy) and the two types of test given constitute the other variable (a recall or recognition test). All combinations of the two variables are given, so the four groups in the experiment could be called Expect Recall–Recall Test Given; Expect Recall–Recognition Test Given; Expect Recognition–Recall Test Given; Expect Recognition–Recognition Test Given.

What outcomes might occur in the experiment just described? Hypothetical memory data are presented in table 10–2 for four possible outcomes of the experiment. In the first case, recognition tests are superior to recall tests, but the variable of test expectancy has no (or very little) effect. Assuming that the superiority of recognition to recall is statistically reliable, the researcher would conclude that there is a *main effect* of type of test. So main effects are generalizations; they tell us that at each level of one variable (test expectancy:recall or recognition), the same effect was observed (recognition was superior to recall). There is the potential for another main effect in a two-factor experiment, as would occur, for example, if people expecting recall performed better on both types of test than those expecting recognition. We might also want to discover whether this generalization holds up over other types of variables, such as the type of material that people studied.

The other three hypothetical cases in table 10–2 illustrate the concept of interaction. In these situations no simple generaliza-

| TABLE 10–2 | Four hypothetical outcomes of an experiment examining how test expectancy affects test performance. (RCL stands for recall, RGN for recognition.) |
|---|---|

| Case 1 | | | Case 2 | | | Case 3 | | | Case 4 | | |
|---|---|---|---|---|---|---|---|---|---|---|---|
| | Test | | | Test | | | Test | | | Test | |
| | RGN | RCL | | RGN | RCL | | RGN | RCL | | RGN | RCL |
| RCL | 68 | 32 | RCL | 90 | 10 | RCL | 30 | 70 | RCL | 65 | 35 |
| Expect | | | Exp. | | | Exp. | | | Exp. | | |
| RGN | 70 | 30 | RGN | 48 | 52 | RGN | 70 | 30 | RGN | 95 | 5 |

tions can be made about the relative advantages of recognition to recall tests, or vice versa, since the conclusion in each instance depends on what type of test was expected. *In general, two variables are said to interact when the effect of one variable changes at different levels of the other variable.* Consider case 2 in table 10–2. Here there is no simple answer as to how varying test expectancy affects the results (or how varying type of test affects the outcome). In these hypothetical data, a recall expectancy leads to better performance on a recognition test than a recognition expectancy; however, on a recall test the effect of expectancy is reversed. Another way of looking at these results in case 2 is that performance on recall and recognition tests is about equivalent when people expect a recognition test, but differs when people expect a recall test. In sum, from the hypothetical data in case 2 we can draw no general conclusion about the effect of either variable. When asked what effect test expectancy has, a researcher looking at these data would have to answer that "it depends on the type of test people are given."

The same is true in the third hypothetical set of data, which illustrates another type of interaction. Here people expecting a recall test perform better on a recall test than on a recognition test, but those expecting a recognition test do better on the recognition test than on the recall test. When the effect of one variable (test expectancy) completely reverses depending on the manipulation of a second variable (type of test), researchers refer to this effect as a *cross-over interaction.* To see why this is so, look at the graph of case 3 in figure 10–9. The lines connecting the points cross. The graph of case 1 shows what one main effect with no interaction looks like, two parallel lines. Case-2 and case-3 graphs illustrate strong interactions.

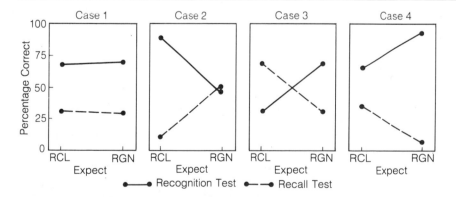

FIGURE 10–9.

Graphical representation of the hypothetical data in Table 1-2. Case 1 illustrates a main effect with no interaction between the two variables. Cases 2 and 3 illustrate interactions. The interaction in Case 3 is called a crossover interaction. In Case 4 there is both a main effect and an interaction.

Other patterns of outcome are possible, such as seen in case 4 of table 10–2 and figure 10–9. Here, both a main effect and an interaction exist. Subjects performed better on recognition tests than on recall tests (the main effect), but how great the recognition advantage was depended on what type of test people expected. Recognition performance was somewhat better than recall performance when people expected a recall test, but was very much better when a recognition test was expected.

Multifactor experiments are extremely useful and much preferable to single-factor experiments for the very reason that they help us answer the question of generality. As we discussed in the previous section of this chapter, one thing we very much want to know about the effect of some independent variable on a dependent variable is the conditions under which it holds. By independently varying a second (or even a third) variable in the same experiment, we can gain at least a partial answer to this question.

We have considered cases in which two factors are manipulated simultaneously. However, it is possible to extend this logic and design experiments that involve simultaneous manipulation of three, four, or even more variables. (In practice, researchers hardly ever design experiments with more than four independent variables of interest.) When the nature of an interaction effect between two variables changes depending on the level of some third variable, the interaction is referred to as a *higher-order interaction*, since it involves several variables. For example, suppose an investigator designs an experiment in which test expectancy and type of test are manipulated, as in our example, but now type of material is also manipulated. People in one condition receive words that occur with high frequency in English (*chair, horse*), whereas people in the other condition receive words that are also familiar English words, but that occur much less frequently (*leopard, bureau*). If the researcher finds the pattern represented in case 3 of table 10–2 and figure 10–9 with high-frequency words, but the pattern seen in case 4 with low-frequency words, this pattern exemplifies a higher-order interaction. Manipulation of a third variable (word frequency) changes the nature of the interaction between the other two variables.

Let us consider an actual experiment that examined these questions. Balota and Neely (1980) manipulated three independent variables in a memory experiment: (1) test expectancy—whether people were led to expect a recall or recognition test on the material presented; (2) the type of test given—recall or recognition; and (3) the type of material given—high-frequency (common) words or low-frequency (rare) words. Different groups of subjects were led to believe that they would be given recall and recognition tests, and different groups were also given various types of memory tests. Thus both test expectancy and type of test were varied *between-subjects*, since four different groups of subjects received all the combinations of test expectancy and type of test (Expect Recall–

Recall Test; Expect Recall–Recognition Test; Expect Recognition–Recall Test; Expect Recognition–Recognition Test). The third factor, word frequency, was varied *within-subjects*: each person in the four groups studied 50 high-frequency words and 50 low-frequency words. Since the experimental design involved manipulation of both a between-subjects factor and a within-subjects factor, it is referred to as *mixed design*. In sum, then, Balota and Neely employed a $2 \times 2 \times 2$ mixed design where the factors were test expectancy (expect recall or recognition), word frequency (high- or low-frequency words), and type of test given (recall or recognition). (Actually, their experiment was even slightly more complicated than this.)

Balota and Neely's results are shown in table 10–3 and graphically presented in figure 10–10. Several main effects and interactions were obtained. Consider first the effects of test expectancy. In three out of four comparisons, subjects expecting recall performed better than those expecting recognition, which led to a reliable main effect for the test-expectancy variable. However, test expectancy interacted with the type of material. Notice that when high-frequency words were used, the advantage of people expecting recall over those expecting recognition was 7 percent when tested by recall and 10 percent when tested by recognition. However, when low-frequency words were used, the advantage of a recall expectancy was slight (3 percent) on a recall test, and vanished altogether on a recognition test. Thus there was a main effect of test expectancy, but it interacted with type of material and type of test.

Several other results emerge from Balota and Neely's experiment. First, performance on a recognition test was generally much better than on a recall test, but this also interacted with another variable, word frequency. The advantage of recognition to recall was greater with low-frequency words than with high-frequency words (see figure 10–10). The effect of word frequency is interesting in its own right. High-frequency words are generally better recalled than low-frequency words, 21.5 percent to 16.5 percent (when results are combined across the expectancy variable). However, on a recognition test this relation completely reverses: low-frequency

The results of Balota and Neely's experiment. Numbers indicate the proportion of words recalled or recognized. (RCL stands for recall, RGN for recognition)

TABLE 10–3

| Expectancy | | High-Frequency Words Test | | | Low-Frequency Words Test | |
| --- | --- | --- | --- | --- | --- | --- |
| | | RCL | RGN | | RCL | RGN |
| | RCL | .25 | .55 | RCL | .18 | .71 |
| | RGN | .18 | .45 | RGN | .15 | .71 |

FIGURE 10–10.

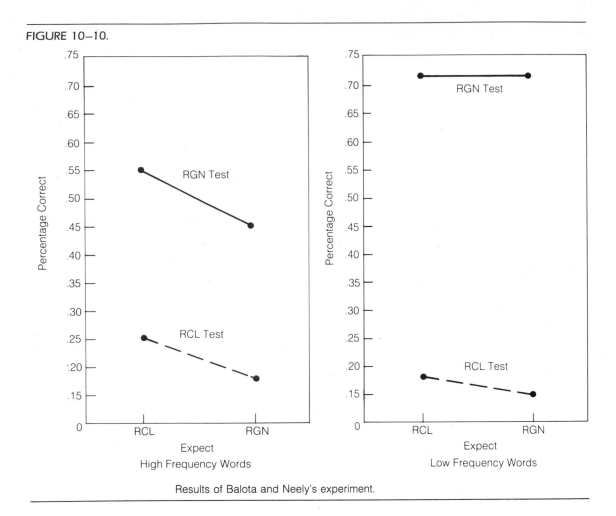

Results of Balota and Neely's experiment.

words were recognized on average 71 percent of the time, whereas high-frequency words were recognized only 50 percent of the time.

Consideration of Balota and Neely's experiments reveals the advantages and complexities of multifactor designs. The advantage is that with manipulation of several factors in one experiment, researchers can simultaneously examine the influence of the variables on one another. Rather than performing separate experiments to ask how test expectancy is affected by using different types of test and various types of material, investigators can examine all these factors in the context of one experiment. However, as you will also appreciate, the results revealed in multifactor experiments can be difficult to understand and interpret, since the discovery of interactions means that no simple generalizations are possible. For example, if someone were to ask the seemingly simple question of whether high-frequency (common) words are better remembered than low-frequency (rare) words, there is no correspondingly simple answer. From the Balota and Neely experiment and many others we can say that if a recall test is given, high-frequency words are better remembered than low-frequency words; however , if a recognition test is given, the exact opposite conclusion is obtained. Obviously, if a researcher were to ask which type of material were better remembered, and used only a recall test or only a recognition test, only half of the picture would emerge. Using both types of test in a factorial design with word frequency allows the more complicated truth of the situation to be discovered. And, of course, even this more complicated picture of the effects of word frequency and type of test may need to be qualified if there is an interaction with yet a third variable (such as what type of test people expect to receive). Only multifactor experiments with their potential for revealing such complex interactions permit researchers to gain a more complete understanding of a phenomenon. Thus, over the decades, researchers in psychology have tended to use more complex designs for their experiments as their knowledge has increased.

The topic of interactions is also related to the first problem considered in the chapter, that of scale attenuation. Often ceiling and floor effects make the interpretation of interactions hazardous. Look back at the results of Scarborough's experiment shown in figure 10–5. An interaction is pictured there between modality of presentation and retention interval. Modality of presentation has an effect, but only at the longer retention intervals. But we decided that this interaction could not be meaningfully interpreted, since it might have been produced by a ceiling effect at the zero-second retention interval. So now we can state as a general rule that (at best) extreme caution should be used in interpreting interactions where performance on the dependent variable is at either the floor or the ceiling at some level of one of the independent variables.

The psychological issue we have addressed in this section—the effect of test expectancy on performance—is a potentially important one for educational practice. Balota and Neely's study as well as many others show that people expecting a recall test often perform better on a memory test than do those expecting a recognition test. Since students in many university courses, especially large introductory courses, are tested almost exclusively by multiple-choice tests, it is reasonable to ask whether they are learning as much as they would be if they were given essay (recall) tests. This question returns us to the problem of generality of results—does the laboratory research generalize to the normal educational setting? It is difficult to answer with certainty, but it seems likely that students in normal classroom settings do learn less when expecting a multiple-choice test than when expecting an essay test. Schmidt (1983) conducted a well-controlled experiment on the effects of test expectancy on two types of prose material (one of which resembled normal text material), and found that people expecting a recall test performed better than those expecting a recognition test on both essay and multiple-choice tests. Also, it can even be argued that the laboratory situation *underestimates* the difference in learning and memory induced by differences in test expectancy. The reason is that in natural settings people expecting essay tests may study longer than those expecting multiple-choice tests, whereas in laboratory experiments this study-time variable is well controlled. As mentioned earlier, surveys have shown that students report studying longer when they expect an essay test rather than a multiple-choice test (see Schmidt, 1983). Thus, in actual practice the advantage of a recall expectancy to a recognition expectancy in promoting learning may be even greater than the laboratory research would lead us to believe.

---

**FROM PROBLEM TO EXPERIMENT: THE NUTS AND BOLTS**

**Problem:** Is Reading Better than Listening?

---

We have discussed the problem of modality differences in memory tasks that involve a simple string of stimuli, such as a series of digits. A question of more general interest is whether there are differences in the comprehension and memory of information that is read opposed to that which is heard. If the same information were presented by a lecturer or were read in a book, which would be more effective? Reading might allow us to go quickly over material we understand well and allow us to tarry over difficult ideas. But while reading we may be more apt to just glide our eyes over the page and daydream; a lecturer moving about and talking might better capture our attention.

**Problem:** Is reading better than listening?

Numerous hypotheses can be formed and operationally defined in different ways to answer this question. One such hypothesis will be considered here.

**Hypothesis:** Subjects who read a long passage of material will be better able to answer multiple-choice questions about the material than will subjects who listen to another person reading the material.

Even though this hypothesis is fairly specific, there are still a great number of matters open to interpretation in actually performing the experiment. The variables need to be given operational definitions. How long is a "long passage?" What should be the subject matter of the passage? Should we use more than one passage? How should the passage to be read be presented? How long should the presentation take? Who should read the passage, or should we vary that? What kinds of questions should we ask on the multiple-choice (forced-choice recognition) test? Should we use a between-subjects or within-subjects design? These are only some of the questions that must be answered in translating the hypothesis into an actual experiment, and how we decide these matters may affect the outcome of the experiment.

Let us consider the last question first. Should we use each subject in both the reading and listening conditions, or should we use different groups of subjects in the two conditions? In general, it is best to use the same subjects in each condition, since in that case we do not have to worry about differences between conditions being caused by differences between subjects in the two conditions. As long as we counterbalance the conditions for practice effects by testing half the subjects in the Read condition before the Listen condition, and the other half in the reverse order, there is nothing to prevent us from using the advantageous within-subjects design.

This decision helps determine the answer to another question. Since we are using each subject in two different conditions, we should obviously use at least two passages of test material, one for one condition and one for the other. We might even use more passages, since we would like to have some confidence that our results generalize to other reading material besides the particular passages used in the experiment. This issue of the generality of results over materials is an important one, especially since it is widely overlooked in certain types of research with the result that statistical tests are often misapplied (see Clark, 1973).

What kinds of passages should be used? Presumably, material that is relatively unfamiliar to the subjects would be the best choice, since we want to test knowledge they gain during the reading of the passage and not that which they acquired before the experiment. If subjects could answer all the questions on the multiple-choice test before coming into the experiment, there would be no chance for our independent variable (reading versus listening to the passage) to exert any influence over our dependent variable (recognition), since we would have a ceiling effect in the recognition test (close to 100 percent performance). In attempting to avoid familiar materials, researchers investigating memory for "naturalistic" prose passages have often chosen passages that contain so many words and concepts foreign to the subjects that we might wonder how "natural" these bizarre stories are. We would probably be better off using passages with mostly familiar words, but new information. Passages might be taken from parts of articles from *Scientific American*, or other magazines at a similar level of difficulty.

How long should the passage be? This is closely tied in with how long the presentation should take. Suppose we decide that the recognition tests should take about seven minutes in each case. We might then want to limit time of presentation of each passage to fifteen minutes in order to make the experiment last only an hour.

(There should be about fifteen minutes for instructions, handing out and picking up tests, and explaining the experiment when it is finished.)

Perhaps the trickiest aspect of designing this experiment is deciding exactly how the passages are to be presented during the fifteen minutes in each case. Suppose we pick passages that take fifteen minutes to read out loud in the Listen condition. In the condition where subjects read the passage should we also simply allow them fifteen minutes to read it? Then they could quite likely have more actual presentation time, since most people can read silently faster than they can read aloud. Thus subjects who read the passage could spend more time on the difficult material. Do we want to try to eliminate this in some way, for example, by instructing subjects to read the passage once straight through? Or do we want to leave it in as one of the natural differences between reading and listening that we are trying to investigate? If we somehow removed or minimized regression (reading back over the material) in the Read condition and then found listening to be better than reading, we may be open to the criticism that our conclusion holds only in artificial laboratory situations and not in the "real world." So, to maximize the possibility for generalizable results, let us allow subjects in the Read condition fifteen minutes to read the material, at the same time as is allowed for oral presentation, and see what differences occur. If reading is superior to listening (or vice versa) we would have to do further research to see exactly what aspects of the process are important.

The same problem arises with oral presentation of the passage. Should we vary who reads it? The sex of the person? The attractiveness? Should it be read in a monotone or with zest and enthusiasm as a lecturer might really try to do? Let us decide for one person to read it with normal intonation as much as possible, and not in a monotone.

Designing the multiple-choice test is also important, especially with regard to making it neither too hard nor too easy, to avoid ceiling and floor effects. Should the test tap only surface-level questions (was _____ discussed in the third paragraph?), or more meaningful questions about the text? Or should we vary this? We could probably agree to use meaningful questions. Or why not use a recall test in the first place? (Because it is more difficult to derive quantitative measures of recall of prose, though, of course, it is possible.)

There are even more choices and difficulties than we have discussed here, even though we have only a 2 × 2 within-subjects design with two types of presentation (read versus listen) and two passages, a variable (passage) we are not primarily interested in. Since it is obvious that we could have operationalized the basic conditions differently and used a different dependent variable, it would be important to consider results of the present experiment against a background of other experiments where the variables are operationalized differently. A series of such converging experiments is necessary if we are to gain some idea as to the generality or limitation of any particular experimental result.

This area of research examining modality differences in long-term retention of prose materials has received surprisingly little attention. However, two relevant references are King (1968) and Kintsch and Kozminsky (1977).

**SUMMARY**

**1.** Ebbinghaus was the first psychologist to study learning and memory systematically. He solved the problem of how to study weak memories by relearning material and measuring the savings in the number of relearning trials compared with those needed for original learning. Although savings methods are still used today, most researchers measure memory in other ways, typically with some variation of recall (production) and recognition (discrimination of studied from nonstudied material) tests.

**2.** Scale attenuation in psychological research refers to situations where a measurement scale is too restricted to measure differences between conditions that may actually exist. When performance is nearly perfect, the problem is referred to as a ceiling effect, since performance is bumping into the top or roof of the scale. When performance is nearly absent altogether, the problem is referred to as a floor effect.

**3.** It is an error to assume that performance in two conditions is equivalent when it is at the ceiling or floor of a measurement scale. Although subjects in two conditions may score equivalently on the dependent variable (approximately 0 percent or 100 percent), there may not be a true difference between conditions, because the measurement scale of the variable may be too restricted (too "short") to show the real difference. Recall the case of the two men weighing themselves on a bathroom scale that only registers up to 300 pounds. The examples in this chapter illustrated ceiling effects, but floor effects are as common and as important. If the mean recall in a memory experiment involving two- and three-year-old children is 2 percent for each age group, are we justified in concluding that memory capacity is the same for both groups of children? Similarly, there can be errors in interpreting interactions when performance in some conditions is constrained by ceiling and floor effects.

**4.** The modality effect in memory experiments refers to the fact that auditory presentation typically produces better performance than visual presentation in recall of the last few items from a list. However, some experiments have revealed a reverse modality effect—better performance in visual than in auditory conditions. This raises the issue of generality of results, or the range of situations over which some experimental finding will hold. It is impossible to determine a generality of results a priori; rather, the necessary research in other situations must be conducted.

**5.** When some result does not generalize from one situation to another, further research is called for to determine the reasons. In the case of exceptions to the modality effect, one reason that visual presentation sometimes leads to better performance than auditory presentation has to do with the type of activity intervening between presentation and recall. If an auditory task intervenes between presentation and recall, it may create more retroactive interference for material presented auditorily than visually, and thus eliminate the usual modality effect.

**6.** Researchers are interested in whether a particular result will generalize across several dimensions: subject populations, materials, situations, dependent measures, and so on. Multifactor experiments, or those in which more than one variable is manipulated simultaneously, are extremely important in determining generality of results. Such experiments tell us whether the effect of an independent variable on a dependent variable is the same or different when other variables are manipulated at the same time.

**7.** When the effect of an independent variable is the same at all levels of the second independent variable, this is referred to as a main effect. Two independent variables are said to interact when the effect of an independent variable on the dependent variable is different at different levels of a second independent variable. Main effects can be thought of as allowing generalizations to be made across other conditions, because the independent variable has the same effect at all levels of the other independent variable. Interactions indicate that simple generalizations about an independent variable are not safe; the effect of this independent variable depends on the level of the second independent variable in the multifactor experiment.

**8.** Recall and recognition are affected in a similar manner by many independent variables, so we can draw general conclusions about the effect of these variables on memory performance. However, other variables, such as type of material and whether people are expecting recall or recognition tests, may affect recognition and recall tests differently. Thus these variables are said to interact with recall and recognition.

**KEY TERMS**

Brown-Peterson technique
ceiling effect
cross-over interaction
floor effect
forced choice recognition test
free recall

primacy effect
proactive interference
recall
recency effect
recognition
retroactive interference

generality of results

higher order interaction

interaction

main effect

mixed design

modality effect

nonsense syllable

paired-associate learning

savings method

scale attenuation

serial recall

stimulus suffix effect

subject representativeness

test expectancy

variable representativeness

yes/no recognition test

**DISCUSSION QUESTIONS**

**1.** Identify two situations, besides those presented in the chapter, where ceiling and floor effects would probably make interpreting experimental observations difficult. How could problems caused by these effects be overcome in the experiments?

**2.** Researchers often lament the discovery that some result does not generalize to a new setting. Discuss why failures of generalization can often lead to progress in understanding a phenomenon. Can you think of discoveries in science sparked by an anomalous result when past knowledge failed to generalize to a new situation?

**3.** What are the advantages of multifactor experiments that make them so popular among researchers, despite their complexity? Discuss the relation of multifactor experiments to the problem of generality of results.

**4.** Consider a three-factor experiment in which people are required to recall lists of ten words presented one at a time after a twenty-second delay filled with a distractor task. The variables are modality of presentation (visual or auditory), modality of distractor task (visual or auditory), and serial position (1 through 10). Draw four graphs modeled after figure 10–8, showing (1) a main effect of modality of presentation, no effect of distractor modality, and an interaction between modality of presentation and serial position; (2) a main effect of modality of presentation, a main effect of distractor modality, and no effect of serial position and no interaction of any of the variables; and (3) no main effect of presentation or distractor modality, but an interaction between these factors and serial position such that the variables have their effect on the last few serial positions. Note: For each pattern, you could draw several different graphs. Draw the one you consider most plausible given the constraints described in the item. Which of these hypothetical patterns would most likely occur in an actual experiment?

# Psychology in Action

## What Is the Best Way to Remember a Telephone Number?

Looking up and dialing a telephone number exemplifies serial recall, since we must look up the number and then dial (or push the buttons) in the proper order. Examining the results of Crowder's (1970) experiment (see figure 10–7), we can say that in general it is better if we read the number aloud instead of silently. The extra auditory information reduces errors at the end of the series. However, from other experiments reviewed in the chapter, we also know that an auditory task given after the list but before recall reduces the advantage of auditory relative to visual presentation. So it is a good idea to avoid any extra auditory information after reading a telephone number aloud; certainly we should not say anything else on the way to the telephone.

A number of researchers have shown that adding an extra auditory item at the end of a series reduces recall of the last few items (the recency effect) as compared with adding a nonverbal item, or adding no extra item at all. The effect is referred to as the *stimulus-suffix effect*, and the extra spoken item is called the stimulus suffix. Since the interference occurs only with a spoken item, it seems the suffix displaces the auditory information that aids recall. The effect occurs even when people know that the suffix is coming and try to ignore it (Crowder, 1976).

The stimulus-suffix effect can be easily demonstrated with only a few subjects. First make twenty combinations of the digits 0 to 9 randomly ordered (example: 749150638). Tell each subject who participates in your experiment to number from 1 to 20 in a column on a sheet of paper and then to draw nine blanks beside each number. The subjects will write down in these spaces the digits they recall in each series. Tell each person that the task will be one of listening to a series of nine digits and then recalling them in order. (We will call each series a list.) After reading each of ten lists, say the word *recall* as a signal to the person to begin recalling the digits; and after reading each of the other ten lists, tap your knuckles on the table to signal recall. (Tell your subjects to expect these signals.) For the first person you test, say *recall* after you read the even-numbered lists, and tap your knuckles after you read the odd-numbered lists. You should do the reverse for the second person tested. (This procedure serves to counterbalance the independent variable—the event that occurs after the list—across the particular lists, so that some lists are not assigned only to one condition and other lists to the other condition.) You could probably begin to get reasonably stable results even if you tested only six subjects or so.

In scoring the results, compare the digits a person recalled with those which actually appeared in the list, and count up the number of errors made. You could then plot serial-position curves such as those in figures 10–5 and 10–7. Do this separately for lists followed by *recall* and those followed by the tap on the table. You will probably find that there is not much difference in error rates over the first five or six positions in the list, but that many more errors will occur on the last three items when the word *recall* followed that list than when the nonverbal sound did. This stimulus-suffix effect is quite robust and occurs with other sorts of material and different recall conditions (see Roediger and Crowder, 1976). You could even find it if you used real telephone numbers, as long as you presented the digits fast enough to insure that performance was not perfect (that there was no ceiling effect). For a theory of why the stimulus-suffix effect occurs, see Crowder (1978).

# CHAPTER 11 ═══════════

**Preview**

Research on complex topics, such as thinking and problem solving, presents difficult problems to the experimenter. One such problem is the reliability or repeatability of research: If an experiment is done again with slight modifications, will the same results be obtained? This question is pertinent to all research, but occurs more frequently with complex topics because of inherent variability of observations caused by individual differences among people. Because of such variability, it is necessary to introduce a great deal of experimental control in the study of these topics. Another consideration is the accuracy of people's own reports of their cognitive processes in thinking. Although verbal reports may sometimes aid description of a phenomenon, they may sometimes lead a researcher astray, too.

**Chapter Outline**

# THINKING AND PROBLEM SOLVING

Life does not consist mainly—or even largely—of facts
and happenings. It consists mainly of the storm of thoughts
that is forever blowing through one's head.

Mark Twain

In case you do not have any problems at the moment, let us give
you one. Read the following problem carefully and examine its
representation in figure 11–1. Give the problem some careful thought
before you continue reading the text.

> Two train stations are 100 miles apart. At 2 P.M. one Saturday afternoon
> the two trains start toward each other, one from each station. One train
> travels at 60 miles per hour, the other at 40 miles per hour. Just as the
> trains pull out of their stations, a bird springs into the air in front of
> the first train and flies ahead to the front of the second train. When the
> bird reaches the second train it turns back without losing any speed
> and flies directly toward the first train. The bird continues to fly back
> and forth between the trains at a rate of 80 miles per hour. How many
> miles will the bird have flown before the trains meet?

Were you able to solve the problem? Most people have a great deal
of difficulty with it, but some people solve it almost immediately.
They must be very good mathematicians, you might be thinking.
Not at all.

Let us consider how most people try to solve this problem. Because
of the way it is stated and the way the picture in figure 11–1 is
drawn, most people begin worrying immediately about how long
it will take the bird to go from the first to the second train, how

FIGURE 11–1.

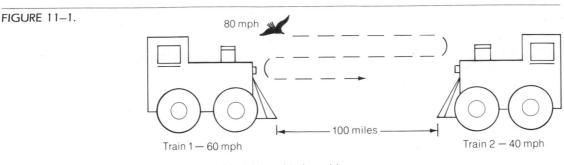

80 mph

100 miles

Train 1 — 60 mph                    Train 2 — 40 mph

An illustration of the bird-and-train problem.

far the second train will have moved by the time the bird arrives, then how long it will take the bird to trek back to the first train and how far that train will have moved, and so on. The general strategy is to try to figure out how long it will take the bird to make each trip between the trains, then add these times together to find out how many miles the bird will fly before the trains meet. This is a quite reasonable strategy and it will give you the answer, provided you have plenty of time, a good calculator, and knowledge of advanced calculus.

Since it is quite likely that you do not have one or more of these three resources, you might need to find a simpler solution. *Thought* can be defined as "the achievement of a new representation through the performance of mental operations" (Posner, 1973, p. 147), so we can say that thought is necessary in order to find a simpler solution to the bird-and-train problem. To solve the problem, you must reconceptualize it. In fact, after you make an appropriate reconceptualization, the solution to the problem is simple. What you need to focus on is how long the trains will be traveling before they meet. Since one is traveling at 60 miles per hour and the other at 40 miles per hour and they are 100 miles apart, they will meet in an hour. Once you think of recasting the problem in this way and using one other piece of information, the solution is obvious. Since the trains will meet in an hour and the bird is flying at 80 miles per hour, the bird will have flown 80 miles before the trains meet. Not much time is needed, nor is a calculator, nor higher mathematics. Just thought.

*Just* thought? Simple enough to say, but the process is very complicated. What happens mentally while a person is trying to discover a solution to the problem? How does a person go about discovering a simpler solution to the problem, or thinking? Can we find general psychological laws of thought? How can we even study this hidden process? These are among the difficult questions that we will be considering in this chapter.

The experimental topics covered in this chapter include the issue of *reliability of results* (or replicability), the problem of *extraneous variables* and *experimental control*, and the use of *phenomenological reports* in psychological research. The first concern is the reliability of results—if we were to perform an experiment a second time, how would we be likely to reach the same conclusion as in the first experiment? This problem exists in all research, but, for reasons to be discussed later, may be heightened in research on thinking and other complex processes. Second, the topic of problem solving and thought is so complicated that great ingenuity is needed to perform interesting and useful experiments in this area. How can we gain control over some independent variable while controlling the extraneous variables, since there are so many that might influence the thought process? The final issue is one of subjective report and its value in psychological research. In an area such as problem solving and thinking, people are quite willing, usually, to tell how they think they set about solving a problem. Are we to accept their reports as useful evidence on the nature of the processes involved?

Historically there have been two primary approaches to the study of problem solving that have different emphases. Both have been very influential with respect to the study of thinking and the study of learning.

**TWO APPROACHES TO THINKING**

### Thorndike's Trial-and-Error Learning

In some interesting early experiments Thorndike (1898) studied problem solving in cats. He placed them in specially constructed puzzle boxes with food placed outside. The cats' problem was how to escape from the box and obtain the food. In some cases the appropriate solution was simply clawing down a rope, but sometimes there were as many as three different solutions the cat could use. Thorndike observed the cats' performance on successive trials in the puzzle box and measured the amount of time it took them to escape on each trial. On the first trial the cat would try a variety of strategies in attempting to escape the box and would strike out in an undirected manner at nearby objects. Eventually the cat would claw at the rope that released it from the cage. It apparently learned by trial and error, for its success in escaping from the box seemed completely accidental, at least at first. On successive occasions, though, the cats began to escape from the box more quickly and systematically each time. Nonetheless, the guiding principle which seemed to govern the cats' solution attempts was one of trial-and-error learning.

In his analysis of trial-and-error learning, Thorndike was particularly concerned with success. It seemed obvious that the success of a correct movement caused it to be impressed or learned. The effect of the movement was to lead to success which "stamps in" the movement, as Thorndike put it. These early experiments led to the *law of effect* and the concept of reinforcement (see chapter 8). The historical impact of this research has been much greater in the field of animal learning, where its importance is overwhelming, than in research concerned with thinking and problem solving. The emphasis in research on human thinking and problem solving has been much more on higher-level cognitive processes, in the tradition to be discussed next. Nonetheless, there have been attempts to analyze human thought processes in terms of trial-and-error learning, or operant conditioning (see Skinner, 1957, chapter 19).

### Insight In Köhler's Chimpanzees

Wolfgang Köhler, a German psychologist, visited the island of Tenerife during 1913 in order to study anthropoid apes. Soon afterward, World War I broke out and Köhler was forced to remain on Tenerife. While there, he conducted research on the problem-solving capacities of chimpanzees. Many of the problems he used could not be solved in a simple, direct way, as could Thorndike's puzzle-box problem in which the cat merely had to claw at a rope. Instead, solutions required a more roundabout approach. Köhler discussed his research in a book published in German in 1921 and translated into English as *The Mentality of Apes* (1927).

In one problem, Köhler dangled a banana out of reach of the chimpanzees. It was too far above them for them to reach it, even with the aid of a stick placed within their enclosure. A more indirect solution to the problem was required. Köhler describes in detail attempts of the chimps to obtain the banana. Usually they would first try out various direct strategies of obtaining it, like reaching and poking at it with the stick. Failing with these methods, they would then seem to engage in various random acts or often apparently give up on the problem altogether. Somewhat later, however, the chimp would suddenly implement the appropriate solution to the problem. The solution in this case was to stack some crates (that were in the enclosure) on top of one another and then climb up them to reach the banana (figure 11–2).

Köhler emphasized the importance of *insight* in solving the problem. After a period of random activity or no activity at all, the chimp (presumably) suddenly conceived of the boxes as related to the problem. Once this insight was achieved, implementing the solution was quite simple.

Köhler's approach to problem solving emphasized its structured, planned, and conceptual nature rather than its trial-and-error aspect. Köhler was a member of the Gestalt school of psychology (see appendix B), which in general was opposed to the

FIGURE 11-2.
One of Köhler's
chimpanzees stacking
boxes on top of each
other to reach the
bananas. (From Köhler,
1927, Plate V)

more elementary type of analysis of behaviorism that grew, in part, from work such as Thorndike's. Both behavioristic and Gestalt approaches have been tremendously influential in psychology. However, current research and theory concerning the psychology of thinking and problem solving probably reflect the Gestalt influence to a greater extent.

## INTRODUCING THE VARIABLES IN THINKING AND PROBLEM SOLVING

### Dependent variables

There are three primary ways to measure the process of problem solving. Let us assume that we either do or do not present an illustration along with the train-and-bird problem. One group of subjects attempts to solve it with figure 11–1 present, and one group attempts to solve it without the illustration. What do we measure? The first and most obvious thing to measure is the number or proportion of subjects in the two conditions that are able to solve the problem within a time limit (say, forty-five minutes). But most problems chosen for study are likely to be fairly easy, or at least solvable within the time limit. What if everyone in both groups solves the problem? Then it is impossible to tell whether the independent variable had any effect, because of a ceiling effect in performance (see chapter 10). It is, of course, improper to conclude that the variable had no effect just because the percentage of people solving the problem is equivalent, since the problem was too easy

(continued on next page)

to reveal any possible differences. What we can do is look at a second measure of performance in solving the problem—latency, or the time taken to solve the problem. Even though all subjects in both groups solved the problem, they might have taken different amounts of time to do this in the different conditions. So although there may be no differences in percentages of people solving the problem, measurement of the time taken to solve the problem may prove a more sensitive index of problem difficulty in the two conditions (picture versus no picture). In fact, even if there were no ceiling effect, but the percentages of people solving the problem were still equivalent at (say) 60 percent, differences in performance might still be revealed by latencies. Therefore we can say that latencies are likely to be a more sensitive dependent variable than percentage correct, since this measure is more likely to indicate an effect of the independent variable in most situations. (It would be very unusual to find the reverse, an effect on percentage correct, but not on latency.) Of course, we would normally expect a high negative correlation between percentage correct and latency, such that in conditions where fewer subjects are able to solve a problem, they also take longer to do so.

A third measure that can be used in some problem-solving situations where more than one solution is possible is the quality of the solution. It must be possible to rank the solutions on an ordinal scale; in other words, it must be possible to order them from best to worst. Then even if percentage correct and latency measures indicate no difference between subjects solving problems under two conditions, subjects in one condition may still achieve more satisfactory solutions than subjects in another condition. One might want to use all three measures of problem solution as converging operations of some problem-solving construct, but there may well be no straightforward relationship among them. For example, subjects in one condition may take much longer to solve a particular problem than subjects in another condition, and perhaps a smaller percentage of subjects will solve the problem in the first condition, but the solutions the subjects achieve in this condition might be superior to those in the other. In other words, variation in the independent variable might allow subjects in one condition to frequently produce a poor solution in a relatively short period of time, as opposed to subjects in another condition who may less frequently produce a better solution, and take a longer time doing so. So there may be no simple relation between measures. This problem is a variant of the speed-accuracy tradeoff problem discussed under reaction-time measures in chapter 7.

## Independent variables

The primary independent variable in the study of problem solving is the manner in which the problem is presented. This can be varied in several different ways. Let us consider the problem concerning how long it takes the bird to fly between the two trains before the trains meet, which was presented at the beginning of the chapter. One thing we could vary is the order and prominence of the information needed to solve the problem. The critical fact that the bird was flying at 80 miles per hour is buried in the description of the problem. If it were made more prominent, subjects might hit the idea of using this fact earlier in their attempts to restructure the problem. A second factor that might be varied is the amount of irrelevant information presented. For example, the information that the trains began at 2 P.M. on a Saturday is completely irrelevant to solving the problem, and should be ignored.

It may well be that the more irrelevant information presented along with the few relevant facts, the longer it will take to solve the problem. Whether or not an illustration is presented and the nature of the illustration could also be varied. Presenting or not presenting an illustration with the problem may aid or hinder its solution, depending on the nature of the problem. Other sorts of psycholinguistic variables could be studied too, such as whether active or passive sentences are used in describing the problem. Besides those dealing with how the problem is presented, other variables of interest might be whether there is time pressure (or some other sort of stress) that people are working under when attempting to solve the problem, whether the magnitude of a reward offered affects the solution, or whether there are individual differences among classes of people (for example, high versus low I.Q.) solving the problem.

## Control Variables

Experiments concerned with problem solving and thinking are often more complicated than others in human experimental psychology, and thus this area, along with others such as social and environmental psychology that deal with complex processes, requires a great deal of care to produce experimental control. Since it is usual in this field to use between-subjects designs (independent groups of subjects are assigned to different conditions), care must be taken to ensure that subjects in the different conditions are statistically equivalent, either by randomly assigning them to conditions or by matching them on some dimension such as I.Q. Similarly, one must make certain that all other extraneous variables (such as the way the problem is stated or how it is presented) are held constant.

---

**11.1**

**Topic:** Replication and Reliability

**Illustration:** Analogical Reasoning

EXPERIMENTAL
TOPICS AND
RESEARCH
ILLUSTRATIONS

The basic issue with regard to reliability of experimental results is simply this: If an experiment were repeated, would the results be the same as those found the first time? Obviously this is a crucial topic in psychological research, for an experimental outcome is worthless if we cannot have reasonable certainty that the results from it are reliable.

The key to ensuring reliability of our observations is the number of observations we make. The greater the number of observations, the more confident we can be that our sample statistics approximate the true population parameter values. If we take a random sample of persons in the United States and ask them survey questions (for example, about their preference in an upcoming presidential election), we can be more confident that the results accurately represent the population if the sample consists of 100,000 people rather than only 100.

The thing to keep in mind, then, is that our confidence in the reliability of a particular result increases with the number of observations on which the result is based. So, in general, we should attempt to maximize the number of observations in the conditions of our experiments. This not only increases our confidence in the reliability of the result, but it also increases the *power* of the statistical tests we employ, or the ability of the test to allow rejection of the null hypothesis if it is in fact false.

*Reliability* involves not only sample size and statistics, but also different types of experimental replicability. In general, in the study of more complex processes, there should probably be greater concern with reliability of results than in the study of simpler processes. One reason is that in research concerned with complex processes, it is often necessary to use between-subjects designs, or designs in which a different group of subjects serves in each experimental condition, because of the carry-over effects that would occur from within-subjects designs (see chapter 8). The use of between-subjects designs rather than within-subjects designs tends to increase variability of observations, since differences among individual subjects are not as well controlled. But there is another effect as well. Typically, for very good practical reasons, it is difficult to obtain many observations per condition in the study of complex processes with between-subjects designs. This is because it is often necessary to test subjects individually, which takes a great amount of time. In experiments on complex processes such as problem solving, it might take an hour to test an individual subject. Thus even if there were only four conditions in the experiment and we wanted only twenty-five observations in each condition, that would still amount to up to a hundred hours of testing subjects. Because of these practical considerations, then, we often find very few observations per experimental condition in the study of complex processes, even though this means we will have less confidence in the reliability of the results, and our statistical tests will have less power.

***Analogical reasoning.*** We will illustrate some further points about reliability of research by discussing problem solving by analogy. When people comprehend some point by analogy, they understand one thing in terms of another. If you were told in high-school physics that the structure of the atom was similar in some ways to the organization of the solar system, or in chemistry that molecules of gas bumped off one another like billiard balls on a pool table, or in psychology that human memory could be compared to a giant library or dictionary, your teacher was employing analogical reasoning. She or he was trying to get you to understand something unfamiliar in terms of something you already understood. Psychologists interested in thinking have long recognized the importance of analogies in thinking and making discoveries. The art of discovery often lies in perceiving a resemblance between two items in different domains of knowledge (Hadamard, 1945). For example, William Harvey in the seventeenth century developed a hydraulic model of blood circulation after he conceived of the heart as a pump.

The study of reasoning by analogy is, of course, quite difficult. Problem solving, thinking, and discovery are topics that have long resisted understanding by psychologists. However, in the last twenty years or so, some real gains have been made in this area on numerous fronts (Mayer, 1983). Here we consider examples from experiments by Gick and Holyoak (1980, 1983) to illustrate how interesting research can be done on these topics and to show the importance of determining reliability of experimental phenomena.

Gick and Holyoak were interested in the effects of analogical reasoning on problem solving. Before discussing this research, let us give you the problem they used and let you mull it over before reading on. It is called the radiation problem, and was first used by Duncker in 1945. It can be stated as follows:

Suppose you are a doctor faced with a patient who has a malignant tumor in his stomach. It is impossible to operate on the tumor, but unless the tumor is destroyed the patient will die. There is a kind of ray that can be used to destroy the tumor. If the rays reach the tumor all at once at a sufficiently high intensity, the tumor will be destroyed. Unfortunately, at this intensity the healthy tissue that the rays pass through on the way to the tumor will also be destroyed. At lower intensities the rays are harmless to healthy tissue, but they will not affect the tumor either. What type of procedure might be used to destroy the tumor with the rays, and at the same time avoid destroying the healthy tissue? (Gick and Holyoak, 1980, pp. 307–308)

Shut your book and think about how to solve this problem before you read on. Do not read ahead until you have thought of at least one solution to the problem.

How did you do? Many students have difficulty solving the problem, given all the constraints placed on them. Many "solutions" depend on advanced technology, such as immunizing the healthy tissue with some drug and then passing the ray through it to the cancerous tumor. A more practical solution is to operate on the patient, and insert a tube into the affected area or otherwise expose the tumor, so that the radiation can be directly applied to the diseased organ. However, perhaps the most creative and effective solution to the problem would be to aim several weak rays at the tumor from different directions so that they converge on it. Each of the rays would be weak enough not to hurt the tissue through which it passes, but the strength of all the rays when they converge would be sufficient to destroy the tumor. This solution is generated by very few students; in the original studies of this problem by Duncker (1945), only two out of forty-five subjects (4 percent) came up with this solution.

Gick and Holyoak (1980, 1983) were interested in seeing whether they could get more people to solve this problem by giving them an analogous problem and solution before the radiation problem. The idea is that people will abstract the guiding principle from the first problem and then be able to apply it to the second. With this in mind, Gick and Holyoak developed other "analog stories" that embodied the same principle as that which applied to the most effective solution to the radiation problem. In one story, called The Commander, the leader of a tank corps needed to mount an attack on an enemy headquarters. By attacking with many tanks he had a good chance of winning, but he had to attack across narrow, rickety bridges that would permit only a few tanks to pass. An assault with such a small force across one bridge would be easily repulsed. In order to achieve victory the tank commander hit on the plan of sending a few tanks to each of the small bridges that circled the headquarters. All the tanks were then able to attack across the bridges at once and overtake the enemy headquarters.

The similarity between the tank-attack problem and the radiation problem should be apparent. In both cases it is necessary for the problem solver to forgo a direct attack on the headquarters (or cancerous tumor) and disperse forces (or radiation) for a simultaneous converging attack from different directions. But would subjects in an experiment use the principles derived from reading a story like The Commander to solve the radiation problem? Gick and Holyoak (1980) performed a series of experiments in which subjects attempted to solve the radiation problem either after reading a story similar to The Commander, or with no story (or an irrelevant story). They found in several experiments that subjects who were given no story or an irrelevant story before the radiation problem solved the problem with the most effective solution only about 10 percent of the time. However, when subjects were given an analog story before the radiation problem, about 75 percent of the people solved it within the time limit. Since this result was obtained in several experiments, the basic phenomenon was replicated several times. Obviously, people can profit from analogy in solving problems.

The results of one of their experiments led Gick and Holyoak (1980) to consider more closely the processes involved in reasoning by analogy. In Experiment 4 of their series, they gave all subjects both the analog story to read and then the radiation problem to solve. However, in the Hint condition of Experiment 4 subjects were told, after they read the story but before they got the radiation problem, to use the story as a hint on how to solve the problem. (This instruction had also been included in all of Gick and Holyoak's prior experiments in the series.) For subjects in the No-Hint condition, no mention was made about the relation between the story they had just read and the problem-solving task ahead. The results revealed that the hint was indeed a critical component to solving the problem by analogy. When the hint was given, 92 percent of the subjects solved the problem, but when the hint was not given, only 20 percent of them solved it. The results seem to show that it is not enough to have been exposed to the analogy; one must be led to make active use of it during the attempt to solve the later problem. (The higher percentage of students solving the problem in Experiment 4 relative to earlier experiments—92% to about 75%—was likely due to somewhat different stories being used across experiments.)

This fact may not seem surprising: telling people to use a source of knowledge does indeed lead them to do so. But what is surprising is how few subjects (20 percent) came upon the solution spontaneously, without the hint. The first question we ask ourselves about a surprising discovery in any experimental field is: is it real? This brings us back to the question of reliability—if the experiment were repeated, would the same result be obtained? One way to answer this question is to compute inferential statistics, the logic of which is described in appendix A. Briefly, inferential statistics are used to determine whether a difference obtained between conditions is due to operation of the independent variable or due to chance factors. If the difference between the conditions is great enough so that it would occur by chance in fewer than one case in twenty, then the researcher rejects the possibility that chance factors produced the result, and instead accepts the result as evidence for operation of the independent variable, in this case the presence or absence of the hint. In fact, Gick and Holyoak (1980) performed the appropriate inferential statistics and concluded that the difference in the percentage of solutions between the two groups was not a result of chance factors but was caused by the presence or absence of the hint. Thus we can conclude on the basis of such a test that the difference is *statistically reliable.*

Statistical reliability is a necessary condition for taking seriously an experimental result, but many researchers prefer to see an experimenter also establish *experimental reliability.* If the experiment is repeated under essentially the same conditions, will the results be the same as they were before? An adage among researchers is that "one replication is worth a thousand *t*-tests." (The *t*-test is a well-known statistical test used to evaluate the statistical reliability between two conditions.) The gist of the adage is that many researchers are more convinced by repetitions of the experiment than by inferential statistics applied to the original outcome. Although an outcome may be deemed statistically reliable, the possibility remains that it could have occurred by chance (statistical reliability still allows a 5% error rate) or because of some unintentional confounding or error on the part of the experimenter. For example, perhaps data were recorded in error or (assuming a between-subjects design) smarter subjects happened to be assigned to one condition rather than another. Although these possibilities might seem unlikely, they do sometimes occur. In some experiments subjects are randomly assigned to conditions and then, prior to the main experiment, the various groups are given the same task to determine whether the groups are actually equivalent (on the average) in ability. Occasionally control tests of this sort turn up differences on the pretest, before the independent variable has been introduced (see, for example, Tulving and Pearlstone, 1966). Since such problems can occur even in well-controlled research, researchers encourage experimental replication of research even when inferential statistics indicate that some effect is reliable.

There are three types of experimental replication: *direct replication, systematic replication,* and *conceptual replication.* Direct replication, as the name implies, is the attempt to repeat the experiment as closely as is practical with as few changes as possible in the original method. If Gick and Holyoak (1980) had attempted to repeat their fourth experiment as precisely as possible with the exception of testing new groups of subjects randomly assigned to conditions, this would have constituted a direct replication of their experiment.

A more interesting type of replication is systematic replication. In systematic replications the experimenter attempts to vary factors believed to be irrelevant to the experimental outcome. If the phenomenon is not illusory, it will survive these changes. if it does not, then the researcher has discovered important boundary conditions on the phenomenon being studied. Actually, Experiment 4 of the Gick and Holyoak series might itself be considered a systematic replication that led to important new information. In their first three experiments, Gick and Holyoak had compared conditions in which subjects solved the radiation problem either after studying a story that embodied an analogous solution (the experimental condition) or after studying one that did not (the control condition). As previously discussed, they found that a greater percentage of subjects solved the radiation problem with the "convergence solution" (aiming the rays from various sides) when tested in the experimental condition then when tested in the control condition. They replicated this observation several times. However, in each of the first three experiments, subjects in the experimental condition were told that they should use the story in attempting to solve the problem. In Experiment 4 Gick and Holyoak attempted to repeat the experiment but vary this one (seemingly small) feature, which thus allows the experiment to be considered a systematic replication. They discovered that this hint was actually a critical part of the experimental manipulation; simply having subjects study the story and they try to solve the radiation problem without the specific hint produced a much lower percentage of subjects solving the problem then when they were instructed to use the hint.

In a conceptual replication, one attempts to replicate a phenomenon, but in a radically different way from the original experiment. In later experiments Gick and Holyoak (1983) attempted to determine conditions that would promote positive transfer of analog stories to problem solutions, in follow-ups of the experiments already described. In three experiments with the radiation problem and another problem, Gick and Holyoak had subjects process the analog story in different ways (the experimental conditions), to see whether the amount of positive transfer could be increased in the case where the analogy was simply presented by itself with no special instructions (the control condition). They found that the amount of positive transfer (indexed by a greater percentage of subjects solving the problem in the experimental conditions) did not vary when (1) subjects were told to summarize stories rather than study them for a test of recall (Experiment 1), or (2) subjects were given or not given a verbal principle along with the story that captured the essence of the strategy (Experiment 2), or (3) subjects were given diagrams along with the story (Experiment 3).

Gick and Holyoak (1983) did manage to uncover conditions that produced positive transfer of the story analogs to solving the radiation problem. When subjects studied two analogs and then described their similarities (before being given the problem), greater positive transfer occurred than when subjects studied only one analog. Gick and Holyoak argued that subjects who processed two analogs and thought about their similarities could generate a better underlying idea (or schema, in their terms) which could then be spontaneously applied to solving new problems.

Although the experiments reported by Gick and Holyoak (1983) are not direct or systematic replications of their earlier experiment indicating that subjects had difficulty spontaneously using analogies to solve problems, they converge on the same conclusion that it is difficult to improve reasoning from analogies. Thus these later experiments may be considered conceptual replications in the sense that they reproduce the essence of the phenomenon of the difficulty of reasoning from analogies without overt direction to do so, even though the experimental techniques are not exact replicas of those used in the original experiment.

The problem of replicability is interwoven with the topic of generality of results. In the case of systematic and conceptual replications, a researcher is not repeating an experiment exactly, but is really asking whether the phenomenon of interest generalizes in one way or another. In systematic replications the variables manipulated (and across which generality is sought) are typically not dramatically different from those of the original experiment, whereas in conceptual replications the differences in procedure are usually much greater. In a certain sense, it is best if the researcher eventually finds conditions under which the phenomenon *cannot* be replicated. If a researcher cannot find variables that control the presence or absence of the phenomenon, then an understanding of the topic will be hampered. Performing systematic and conceptual replications should permit a researcher to delineate the *boundary conditions* of a phenomenon, or the conditions outside of which the phenomenon does not hold. When the variables that control a phenomenon can be discovered, the reseracher can construct a better theory about it, for the relevant factors are known.

## 11.2

**EXPERIMENTAL TOPICS AND RESEARCH ILLUSTRATIONS**

**Topic:** Experimental Control

**Illustration:** Functional Fixity

The topic of experimental control runs throughout this book, as it should, since it is crucial to all types of experimental research. The purpose of any experiment is to observe the effect of manipulation of certain variables—the independent variables—on the measurement of dependent variables. In order for a conclusion about the effect of an independent variable on a dependent variable to be sound, it is necessary that we gain a sufficient amount of experimental control over the situation to ensure that no other factor varies with the independent variable. In this book, these other variables are usually called control variables, although they are also referred to as extraneous variables or even nuisance variables. If an extraneous variable is allowed to vary at the same time as the independent variable of interest, we cannot know whether the effect on the dependent variable is caused by variation in the independent variable, the extraneous variable, or both operating together. In such cases we say that the two variables are confounded.

In the study of complex processes there are often greater problems of experimental control than in other types of research. In the study of topics such as problem solving there is frequently a great deal of variation in the measures taken on the dependent variable. We have already discussed some of the reasons for this. Since it is necessary to use between-subjects designs in much of this research, individual differences among subjects contribute greatly to the uncontrolled variation, or "error variance." Also, it may not be possible to tightly control all the nuisance variables that may affect a situation. Instead, they may be left to vary in an unsystematic way, since unsystematic variation will not affect one experimental condition more than another. Still, these randomly varying factors may serve to increase the variability of measurements. Because of the effect of these variations on the dependent variable, it may be more difficult to detect reliable effect of the independent variable. One other reason for experimental control, then, is to reduce these extraneous sources of variation on the dependent variables. But given that they do occur and may be more serious in the study of problem solving and other complex processes, it becomes necessary to increase the number of observations in experimental conditions to get reliable results. But, for practical reasons we have already discussed, this is not always possible. Therefore employing as much experimental control of extraneous variables as can be mustered in these situations becomes even more important and desirable.

If discussion of all these considerations makes solid research on interesting, complex processes seem practically impossible, that has not been our intent. However, it is necessary to keep firmly in mind the difficulties one encounters in such research. Some experimental psychologists view research in these complex areas as relatively "sloppy," since it often lacks tight experimental control and employs relatively few observations in experimental conditions, which leads to the possibility of unreliable results. It is as though some researchers in this area believe that the greater difficulty in studying complex psychological processes somehow justifies lesser, rather than greater, experimental control. It is quite obvious that the problems inherent in studying complex processes can be overcome, because we have instances of exemplary research in this area.

A good example is the research on the issue of *functional fixity* in problem solving. This work was begun in an important series of studies by Karl Duncker (1945, pp. 85–101). The general idea behind the concept is that if an object has recently been used in one particular way in a given situation, its use in a second, different, way to solve a problem is likely to be overlooked. Duncker invented a number of problems which he used to test this general idea, but we will focus on only one, the well-known "box" problem.

***Duncker's box problem.*** In the box problem, subjects were told that their task was to affix three small candles on a door at eye level. The material they were to use was placed on a table. Among other objects were several crucial ones: some tacks, matches, three small pasteboard boxes about the size of a matchbox, and, of course, the candles. The appropriate solution to the problem was to tack the boxes to the wall and use them as platforms on which the candles could be attached with some melted wax. In the control condition the boxes were empty, but in the functional-fixity condition the boxes were filled with the needed material. There were several candles in one, tacks in a second, and matches in a third. Thus in the latter condition the function of the box as a container was to be "fixed" in the subjects' minds. This should have been less the case in the control condition since the boxes were not used as containers. Duncker also employed a third condition which we will refer to as the neutral-use condition. Here the boxes were also used as containers, but they contained neutral objects (such as buttons) not needed as parts of the solution.

A between-subjects design was necessary in this experiment, since once subjects had been exposed to the problem, they could not, for obvious reasons, be tested again in a different condition. In this particular experiment Duncker employed only seven subjects in each condition. The results for the three conditions are reported in Figure 11–3 as the percentage of subjects solving the

FIGURE 11–3.

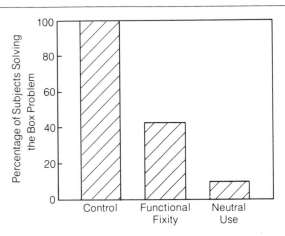

Percentage of subjects solving Duncker's box problem in three different experimental conditions. When subjects were given the boxes which contained material (the functional fixity and neutral use conditions), a smaller percentage was able to solve the problem than when the boxes were given to them empty (control). Presumably, in the former cases the function of the box was "fixed" as a container and thus subjects did not as readily think of the boxes as potential platforms for the candles.

problem in each condition. All seven subjects in the control condition solved the problem, but only 43 percent of the subjects in the functional-fixity condition (3 out of 7) were able to do so. In the neutral-use condition, only one subject (14 percent) was able to solve the problem. Of course these differences among conditions were not evaluated statistically, but the difference between the control and functional-fixity conditions was replicated with four other problems. The difference between the functional-fixity and neutral-use conditions was replicated with two independent groups solving one other problem. The functional-fixity effect has since been replicated a number of times, so we can be assured it is reliable, despite the small number of subjects used in the original studies.

*Adamson's replication.* A study by Adamson (1952) is interesting in this regard. He sought to replicate Duncker's original experiment by comparing subjects in the functional-fixity and control conditions on the solution to three problems. These included the box problem we have already discussed, as well as two others referred to as the paper-clip problem and the gimlet problem. (The exact nature of these problems need not concern us.) In each situation the comparison was between subjects who had previous experience with an object and who thus should think of the function of the object as fixed, and control subjects for whom this was not the case. Adamson was primarily concerned about how few subjects were used in Duncker's original experiment, so he used between 26 and 29 subjects in each of his six separate conditions (3 problems × 2 experimental conditions). The dependent measures he used were the percentage of subjects who were able to solve the problem in the twenty-minute period, and the amount of time it took successful subjects to solve the problem.

The results are quite instructive. When Adamson used Duncker's dependent measure of percentage of subjects who were able to solve the problem, he was able to replicate the functional-fixity effect in only the box problem. A full 86 percent of the control subjects, but only 41 percent of the subjects in the functional-fixity condition, were able to solve the box problem. Performance on the other two problems was impossible to interpret because of ceiling effects in both conditions. That is, almost all subjects in both conditions solved the problem, so performance did not differ; for both problems it approached 100 percent in each condition. This problem with results was discussed in the "Introducing the Variables" section in this chapter (see also chapter 10); once again, we are not justified in concluding that there was no difference between the two conditions under these circumstances. The conclusion, rather, is that the dependent variable was not sufficiently sensitive to allow detection of any possible differences between conditions.

Fortunately, Adamson also used a second dependent measure, the latency to solve the problem. The results, in terms of mean time to solution for subjects in the two conditions, are presented in figure 11–4 for both the gimlet and the paper-clip problems. Only data concerning subjects who actually solved the problems are included. Although almost all subjects were able to solve the problems, the amount of time it took to do so varied greatly in the two conditions, as is apparent from figure 11–4. In each case, subjects in the control condition solved the problem much faster than subjects in the experimental (functional-fixity) condition. Thus, having the function of the objects fixed by the way the problem was presented slowed, but did not prevent, solution to the problem. The important point is that functional fixity was demonstrated in all three of Adamson's problems, but in two of them it was necessary to use a latency measure that was more sensitive than simply the percentage of subjects solving the problem.

Why was Adamson unable to replicate Duncker's results with the gimlet and paper-clip prlblems, when the percentage of subjects solving the problem was the dependent measure? Adamson suggests that he simply may have had more able subjects, which is certainly a possibility. But another real possibility is that Adamson allowed twenty minutes for his subjects to solve the problem, whereas Duncker seems to have allowed much less time, though it varied somewhat from individual to individual, depending on the progress of each toward a solution.

The Adamson study is an excellent example of a systematic, well-controlled, replication that served to clean up an original demonstration of an interesting phenomenon. Such replications are

FIGURE 11–4.

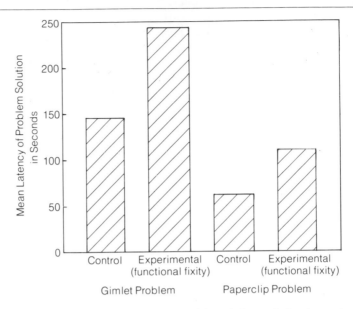

Time taken to solve the gimlet and paperclip problems in the control and experimental (functional fixity) conditions of Adamson's (1952) experiment. It took subjects in the functional fixity condition longer to solve the problems than the controls.

thus quite valuable, especially since they often lead to new knowledge on the generality of the phenomenon in question. However, after a novel phenomenon has been replicated once or twice in independent laboratories, further research effort directed at simple replications is to be discouraged. (The chances are excellent that journal editors would not see fit to publish further studies of direct or even systematic replications at this point.) The research effort must turn to developing an understanding of the factors that influence the phenomenon and developing a theory or model of the psychological processes involved.

In the area of functional fixity, Glucksberg and his associates have provided systematic research on the effect of verbalization and labeling on functional fixity (Glucksberg and Weisberg, 1966; Glucksberg and Danks, 1967, 1968). For example, it has been found that when objects in the candle problem are given verbal labels (candle, tacks, box, matches) when shown to the subjects, the problem is solved by more subjects than when no labels are given. The trick is to have the subjects think of the box not merely as a container of tacks, but as a separate object capable of being used to solve the problem. Labeling the objects aids this process. As Glucksberg has pointed out, "It is not the way the world *is* that influences what we do as much as it is *how we represent* that word symbolically" (1966, p. 26, italics are Glucksberg's).

**Topic:** Phenomenological Reports

**Illustration:** Overconfidence in Judgments

---

Early in the history of experimental psychology there was an emphasis on the use of introspective reports as a method for discovering the structure of the mind. As is discussed in appendix B, introspection was not a casual, moody, reflection on the contents of the mind during some experience or other, but a rigorous, methodical technique of describing experience. Its basic problem was one of reliability—investigators who used introspection in different psychology laboratories often arrived at different conclusions about the structure of the mind. The method would probably have fallen into disuse for this reason alone, but its departure from psychology was hastened by Watson's (1913) attack on the entire enterprise of structural psychology and by the subsequent rise of behaviorism. Since introspection has a technical meaning in the vocabulary of structural psychology, we will use the term *phenomenological report* to refer to the use of verbal reports by subjects in psychological experiments (see chapter 6 also).

Despite the success of behaviorism in sweeping away the structural approach, the use of phenomenological report has kept its place with psychology. In fact, use of verbal report is quite in accord with the scientific rules of behaviorists, since verbal reports are, of course, overt behavior. In fact, Watson, the founder of behaviorism, states this quite clearly in a section called "The Behaviorist's Platform" in *Behaviorism:*

> The behaviorist asks: Why don't we make what we can *observe* the real field of psychology? Let us limit ourselves to things that can be observed, and formulate laws concerning only those things. Now what can we observe? We can observe *behavior—what the organism does or says.* And let us point out at once: that *saying* is doing—that is, *behaving.* Speaking overtly or to ourselves (thinking) is just as objective a type of behavior as baseball. (1925, p. 6, italics are Watson's)

The use of verbal report, then, was endorsed by the founder of behaviorism. But as Spence (1948) pointed out, the use of verbal report is very different for structuralist and behaviorist psychologists. For the former, introspective reports are facts or data about internal mental events which are thought to directly mirror these events. For behaviorists, on the other hand, verbal reports are simply one other type of behavior that may be worth studying as a dependent variable. It is to be considered no more nor less worthwhile or "real" a priori than any other type of response or dependent variable. If one wants to use verbal reports as evidence for some particular mental construct, it is to be considered as only one of several needed converging operations. Phenomenological reports are, of course, more likely to be useful in certain areas of psychology than others. Research on thinking is one area where extensive use is made of verbal reports.

One critical component in thinking is the ability to evaluate one's knowledge. A number of experiments have explored the feeling-of-knowing phenomenon, first studied systematically by Hart (1965). A representative experiment is one by Freedman and Landauer (1966). Subjects were given a long series of general-knowledge questions (What is the capitol of Ecuador? Who was the fifth president of the United States?) and asked to provide answers. For each question for which subjects could not provide an answer, they were asked to rate on a four-point scale how confident they were they they could recognize the answer if it was presented with similar alternatives. The four judgments were "definitely know" the answer, "probably know" it, "probably don't know" it, and "definitely don't know" it. After making these feeling-of-knowing judgments, subjects were given the questions again and asked to pick the correct answer from among six alternatives.

The subjects recognized 73 percent of the items that they judged they would definitely know, 61 percent they had said they would probably know, and 51 percent and 35 percent of the answers to questions they thought they either probably or definitely did not know. The fact that the ratings are generally correlated with later recognition performance may be taken as an indication that people's subjective feelings of what they know (following a failure of recall) are fairly accurate. Other experiments have revealed a similar feeling-of-knowing effect (for example, Schacter, 1983). However, one other interesting feature of the data is that even when people were convinced they knew the answer to a question, they were able to respond correctly only 73 percent of the time. Obviously, the ability to monitor the state of one's knowledge is rather imperfect. Often we seem overly confident that we know something when in fact we do not.

Other studies using slightly different techniques have shown that people have this tendency to be overly confident of their knowledge. One technique is to ask people to answer questions with two alternative answers and then ask them to rate the probability of their having answered them correctly. Suppose you were given the following item: "Bile pigments accumulate as a result of a condition known as (a) jaundice (b) gangrene." After choosing the answer you believe to be correct, you would then be asked to estimate the probability from .50 to 1.00 that you are in fact correct. (Since there are two alternatives, .50 is chance.) Lichtenstein and Fischhoff (1977) reported that although there was a general correlation between judgments of confidence and accuracy, subjects were generally much more confident than warranted by their knowledge. For example, for items that subjects estimated they would answer correctly 80 percent of the time, the actual accuracy was only .70. This overconfidence does not seem to result from subjects' not taking the task very seriously, for other studies have reported the same tendency even when subjects are given elaborate instructions emphasizing accuracy and when they are given the opportunity to bet on their answers with the possibility of losing money as a result (Fischhoff, Slovic, and Lichtenstein, 1977).

These studies show that although verbal reports of our factual knowledge are generally correlated with that knowledge, they are by no means perfect reflections of what we know. This points out a shortcoming of retrospective verbal reports of cognitive processes. The vagaries of memory may produce an inaccurate or biased judgment of what we thought while performing some act. Many factors—motivational, emotional, social—may lessen the accuracy of verbal reports. Indeed, researchers in some areas have long been leery of accepting verbal reports at face value.

Nisbett and Wilson (1977) reviewed many experiments that related individuals' verbal reports to their behavior in experimental situations, and reached the rather startling conclusion that "there may be little or no direct introspective awareness to higher order cognitive processes" (p. 231). They used many lines of evidence to draw this conclusion, but one general type involves experiments comparing performance of people in between-subjects designs. Some experimental variable is manipulated and shown to have a strong influence on behavior; later, subjects in the different groups are asked why they responded the way they did. If subjects are consciously aware of the forces guiding their behavior, they should report the influence of the independent variable as a critical determinant of their performance. In many cases reviewed by Nisbett and Wilson, subjects could not do this and, in addition, often denied that the independent variable could have affected them, even when the experimenter suggested it as a possibility.

Research on bystander intervention also illustrates this phenomenon (see chapters 3 and 13). The question asked in this research is: under what conditions will an individual help another person who is in distress? In experimental studies by social psychologists, an "emergency" is standardized and subjects are exposed to it under varying experimenter conditions. The primary dependent measures are the percentage of subjects helping the victim in each condition and the speed with which they help. One of the most startling effects in such studies is seen when the experimenter varies the number of other people present in the emergency situation. As the number of other people increases, the subject becomes less likely to help the victim.

Many hypotheses have been put forth to account for this fact, but the interesting point for present purposes involves the responses that subjects give when asked about their behavior in the situation. Latané and Darley, who were responsible for the early work in this area, systematically asked their subjects whether they thought the presence of other people had influenced their behavior in the situation.

> We asked this question every way we know how: subtly, directly, tactfully, bluntly. Always we got the same answer. Subjects persistently claimed that their behavior was not influenced by the other people present. This denial occurred in the face of results showing that the presence of others did inhibit helping. (Latané and Darley, 1970, p. 241)

Nisbett and Wilson (1977) used such reports as the basis for their claim that people have no direct introspective access to the cognitive processes that mediate behavior. A corollary of this position would seem to be that phenomenological reports are generally inaccurate as descriptions of cognitive events. (Nisbett and Wilson argue that even when such reports are accurate, they may be based on general knowledge and not on some special self-knowledge.) Others argue that Nisbett and Wilson's position is too extreme (see Ericsson and Simon, 1979; Smith and Miller, 1978). They maintain that under many conditions people can be shown to have generally accurate access to their mental states. After all, the feeling-of-knowing studies discussed earlier showed that subjects are generally accurate in judging whether they know information, even when they cannot recall it. Many of the studies described by Nisbett and Wilson had features such as between-subjects designs and reports from subjects after the task was completed. Subjects likely would show better awareness if they participate in experiments that use within-subjects designs, since they would be exposed to the full range of the independent variable. Similarly, if subjects were asked to make reports during the actual performance of a task (for example, by reporting out loud to the experimenter), reports might be more accurate. Using retrospective reports rather than ones taken "on-line" makes subjects rely on fallible memory; perhaps they knew what they were doing at the time they were doing it, but then forgot (or distorted) their reasons later.

Where do all these considerations leave us in evaluating the use of phenomenological reports as a research tool? Although the issue is complex, we can venture a few summary statements. First, it is probably unwise in many instances to place too much emphasis on verbal reports, for example, by using them as the sole dependent measure in an experiment. Some psychologists have suggested that for experiments that might be impractical or unethical to conduct, researchers should describe the procedure and various conditions to subjects and have subjects say how they would react (for example, Brown, 1962; Kelman, 1966). However, the assumption that one's predictions while role playing always (or even usually) accurately reflect how one will behave when placed in an actual situation, seems risky. Second, verbal reports may very well be useful in some situations, but a researcher will have to analyze each situation carefully to determine the potential for error in using verbal reports. Most researchers consider phenomenological reports as useful extra sources of information in experiments, but not as the primary dependent variable of interest. However, Ericsson and Simon (1979) detail conditions under which they believe verbal reports can serve as primary data. Finally, we believe that verbal reports can serve as interesting dependent measures, whether or not such reports accurately reflect cognitive states of the individual. Even if Nisbett and Wilson are correct in asserting that people have little or no accurate introspective awareness of the causes of their behavior, studying people's beliefs and reports about those causes would be of interest in itself.

---

**Problem:** Incubation in Problem Solving

**FROM PROBLEM TO EXPERIMENT: THE NUTS AND BOLTS**

Many writers on the subject of thinking and problem solving have described a rather mysterious process that seems to aid in solving problems. Consider the following account of the French mathematician, Henri Poincaré. (The mathematical terms in the quote should not dismay you; just examine the passage for the psychological principle involved).

> Just at this time I left Caen, where I was then living, to go on a geologic excursion under the auspices of the school of mines. The changes of travel made me forget my mathematical work. Having reached Coutances, we entered an omnibus to go some place or other. At the moment when I put my foot on the step the idea came to me, without anything in my former thoughts seeming to have paved the way for it, that the transformations I had used to define the Fuchsian functions were identical with those of non-Euclidean geometry. I did not verify the idea; I should not have the time, as, upon taking my seat in the omnibus, I went on with a conversation already commenced, but I felt a prefect certainty. On my return to Caen, for conscience' sake I verified the result at my leisure.
>
> Then I turned my attention to the study of some arithmetical questions apparently without much success and without a suspicion of my connection with my preceding researchers. Disgusted with my failure, I went to spend a few days at the seaside, and thought of something else. One morning, walking on the bluff, the idea came to me, with just the same characteristics of brevity, suddenness, and immediate certainty, that the arithmetic transformations of indeterminate ternary quadratic forms were identical with those of non-Euclidean geometry.
> . . .
> I shall limit myself to this single example; it is useless to multiply them. In regard to my other researches I would have to say analogous things. . . .

Most striking at first is this appearance of sudden illumination, a manifest sign of long, unconscious prior work. The role of this unconscious work in mathematical invention appears to me incontestable. (Poincaré, 1929, p. 388)

There are many reports of similar experiences from writers, mathematicians, and scientists. Koestler (1964) cited several examples where a problem is solved in a sudden flash of illumination after all progress on it had ceased and in fact the solver had turned to other matters. (Recall the similar appearance in Köhler's chimps.) But what are we to make of these reports? How are they to be evaluated? Can we accept them as useful evidence on the nature of thought? If so, then apparently the search for problem solutions can proceed without conscious attention; the mind may inexorably grind away at solving a problem without any conscious direction on the part of its owner.

Experimental psychologists are unlikely to be convinced by these reports that such a process is central to thought rather than representing a more or less rare and curious accident. Instead, they are likely to consider such reports as hypotheses in need of experimental tests. On the basis of his own intuitions, Poincaré outlined four stages in the thought process. First is *preparation*, during which a person becomes immersed in trying to solve a problem and learns the numerous relevant facts and considerations. Second is *incubation*, during which a person turns to other matters after failing to solve the problem. The problem is said to incubate, much as eggs do while a hen sits on them. Next comes the stage of *illumination* (which Köhler calls *insight*), when the idea is hatched. Finally comes the stage of *verification*, when the solution to the problem must be carefully checked. These stages were identified on the basis of intuition and have thus been given only loose verbal definitions.

Although Poincaré collected many instances that seemed to confirm his theory of problem solving—and in particular the incubation process—as we all know, an example or two can be found to support almost any idea or theory, no matter how silly. And surely we can find many counterexamples where problems are solved without incubation and sudden illumination. Instead of providing anecdotes, we must subject the concept of incubation to experimental test.

**Problem:** Can we find evidence for the concept of incubation?

At present this concept is rather fuzzy and we need to provide it with a more precise operational definition so we will know exactly what we are looking for. Let us examine a definition by Posner (1973). "*Incubation* refers to an increase in the likelihood of successfully solving a problem that results from placing a delay between the period of intense work which initiates the problem solution and another period of conscious effort which finalizes the solution" (Posner, 1973, p. 171). This is somewhat precise, but a number of points still must be specified. In fact, it is a rather curious operational definition, since we do not even know if the defined phenomenon exists at this point! What we have done, really, is to suggest a hypothetical operational definition that can serve as the hypothesis of an experiment in search of the concept.

**Hypothesis:** Subjects who are allowed a break between two periods of work on solving a problem will be more likely to eventually find a solution (or find one faster) than will subjects not provided a break.

Further, the longer the break, the more likely that the subjects will find the solution (and find it faster), at least up to some limit.

There remain, as always, a host of considerations to which we must turn our attention. How long should we allow subjects to solve the problem? Two 15-minute periods, or a total of 30 minutes, might be appropriate. The primary independent variable is the delay that is to be introduced between the two periods of work on the problem. At a minimum, we would want three independent conditions, so appropriate delays might be 0, 15, or 30 minutes in between the two work periods. (Of course more conditions with a wider range of delay intervals might be appropriate, too.) The experiment should probably employ a between-subjects design, since the amount of time required for subjects to serve in all three conditions would be prohibitive. The number of subjects to serve in each condition would depend on the available resources, but should be as great as possible A minimum of 20 may be sufficient, but the power of statistical tests based on this small a sample would not be great. It would be much better to have 75 or 100 subjects per condition. Since groups of subjects could be tested rather than individuals, the amount of effort in testing 300 subjects would not be prohibitive, if this many people were available. The length of the entire procedure would vary from perhaps 45 minutes in the zero-delay condition to 75 minutes in the 30-minute delay condition.

Another important consideration is the type of problem to be used. It would probably be best to test subjects in the three conditions on more than one problem to ensure that the phenomenon, if found at all, is not specific to only one problem. If 75 subjects were used in each condition, 25 could be tested on each of three problems. It would be necessary to pretest the problems on subjects similar to those to be used in the experiment, to ensure that (1) very few subjects can solve the problems in 15 minutes, or before the independent variable is introduced; and (2) around half (at least) can solve the problem in 30 minutes with no delay. The latter requirement is to guard against floor effects, or performance too poor to allow manipulation of the independent variable to reveal any effect. A sample problem might be the following:

A man had four chains, each three links long. He wanted to join the four chains into a single closed chain. Having a link opened cost 2 cents and having a link closed cost 3 cents. The man had his chains joined into a closed chain for 15 cents. How did he do it?

Another consideration is what subjects should be doing during the delay intervals. Obviously they should not simply be allowed to sit there and mull over the problem, since then they are essentially not given a delay at all. Subjects should be occupied with mental arithmetic problems or the like, and it might even be wise to lead them to believe, at the beginning of the break, that they are going on to a new phase of the experiment and will not be returning to the problem they had failed to solve. This would ensure that subjects would not be trying to devote some attention to the problem while working on the filler activity.

The primary dependent measures would be the percentage of subjects in each condition who solved the problem and the amount of time it took them to do so. If the problems were selected carefully enough so that there were several solutions, the quality of solutions might also be evaluated. Even if the problems did not have this feature, subjects could be asked at the end of the second 15-minute period to write out how they were attempting to solve the problem, and the quality of these attempts could be evaluated to see whether the different conditions affected the quality of the terminal-solution attempts. The evaluations, of course, should be made by someone who does not know the conditions of the subjects (that is, someone who is blind with respect to conditions).

These are the essentials, then, for an experiment on incubation. Thet predictions are that subjects who experience a delay between the two 15-minute periods of working on the problem will solve the problem more often (and will do so faster) than subjects who work on the problem continually for 30 minutes. Also, subjects who have a 30-minute break should achieve a solution (and do so faster) more often than those who have the shorter, 15-minute, break.

Experiments such as this can make real contributions to the understanding of incubation. Perhaps the best evidence for incubation comes from a doctoral dissertation by Silveira (1971), which is a somewhat more complicated version of the type of experiment we have just outlined here. It is discussed briefly in Posner's book (1973, pp. 169–175). However, a similar experiment by Olton and Johnson (1976) failed to find any evidence for incubation.

If the phenomenon of incubation has been established experimentally, this is only the beginning of our attempts to understand it. What factors influence incubation. What kind of psychological theory could explain it? Saying that it is caused by "unconscious thought processes" is as bad as saying nothing at all. Actually, it might even be worse, since it gives the illusion of providing an explanation when, in fact, it does nothing of the kind. Can you think of explicit, testable hypotheses that could account for incubation? This is the path we must take to even begin to understand the phenomenon.

**1.** Studies of complex psychological processes, such as thinking and problem solving, have special problems in terms of reliability of results and experimental control. One main problem concerns the relatively great variability that is liable to occur in observations under different experimental conditions. The individual differences that people exhibit in performing a complex task, such as solving a problem, are apt to be much greater than in performing simpler tasks.

**2.** In complex experiments it is often necessary to use between-subjects designs where an independent group of subjects serves in each experimental condition, so less control is possible over variance introduced by differences between subjects than in within-subjects designs. A partial solution to these problems is to obtain as many observations per condition as possible to produce stable results, and to control as tightly as possible all extraneous variables, so they will not increase the variability within conditions.

**3.** Reliability of results from a single experiment can be assessed through the logic of statistical inference by employing appropriate statistical tests. Such tests allow us to assess how likely it is that the effect of some experimental variable is actually caused by the operation of that variable and not random (chance) factors.

**4.** Experimental reliability, which is preferred to statistical reliability by many psychologists, refers to actual replicability of experiments. Three types are identified. In direct replications the attempt is to repeat the experiment as exactly as possible, to see whether the same results will be obtained a second time. Systematic replications involve changing variables not thought to be critical to the phenomenon under consideration, to make sure it survives such changes. Conceptual replications attempt to demonstrate the phenomenon with a wholly new paradigm or set of experimental conditions.

**5.** Systematic and conceptual replications are also concerned with generality of results. Do results of an experiment generalize across the rather slight changes in procedure in systematic replications, and the greater changes in procedure in conceptual replications? Often advances in understanding a phenomenon are enhanced when researchers are able to find conditions under which the phenomenon does not replicate. When such boundary conditions are established and the researcher understands what factors control the presence or absence of the phenomenon, better theories can be constructed.

**SUMMARY**

**6.** Phenomenological reports are verbal reports about people's awareness of their cognitive processes. They are sometimes used in the study of thinking, but caution must be exercised in their use. In some instances people are overly confident in judgments of their knowledge. In experiments on various complex judgments, people provided erroneous subjective impressions regarding the influence of particular variables which were shown to actually control their behavior. Phenomenological reports are sometimes useful in psychological research, but the trust that can be put in them will likely vary with the topic being studied.

## KEY TERMS

| | |
|---|---|
| analogy | incubation |
| boundary conditions | insight |
| ceiling effect | latency |
| conceptual replication | law of effect |
| direct replication | phenomenological report |
| experimental control | reliability |
| experimental reliability | statistical reliability |
| extraneous variables | systematic replication |
| feeling-of-knowing | thought |
| functional fixity | verbal report |

## DISCUSSION QUESTIONS

**1.** A researcher in the biology department of your university has just demonstrated extrasensory perception (ESP) in rats. The rats were placed in a maze where they had to choose between two possible runways, one of which led to food. The rats could not see or smell the food at the place in the maze where they had to make their decision, and the runway in which the experimenter put the food varied randomly from trial to trial. Over a series of fifty trials, the researcher found that there were two rats out of one hundred tested that seemed to perform better than on the basis of chance. One picked the correct runway 64 percent of the time; the other picked it 66 percent of the time (with chance being 50 percent). Which of the two following tests would be more convincing to you as confirmation of these rats having ESP?—(a) the researcher performs statistical tests showing that the two rats had indeed performed better than chance in making their choices; or (b) a different researcher tests the two rats on several hundred more trials, and does succeed in replicating the first researcher's findings. Defend your choice. If you were the second researcher, what safeguards would you introduce into the experiment to insure that the rats were not using sensory cues to solve the problem (assuming the rats again performed above chance).

**2.** After seeing the results of the first experiment (namely, two out of a hundred rats apparently scored better than chance on the test of extrasensory perception), we ask the experimenter how many of the rats scored *below* chance by 10 percent or more. The researcher reports that three did, and says he is fascinated by this new discovery which seems to indicate that some rats have "negative extrasensory perception." What do you, as a dispassionate observer, conclude about these claims?

**3.** Distinguish among direct replications, systematic replications, and conceptual replications. Should the three types be considered as qualitatively different, or do they lie on a continuum? If they lie on a continuum, what dimension underlies it?

**4.** The reward system in science discourages replications of other people's work. Researchers are rewarded much more for novel contributions than for "merely repeating" the work of others. Some have argued that this reward system tends to create fragmentation and disarray in many areas of psychology, because people are rewarded for going their own way and (sometimes) ignoring progress in other closely related areas. Thus basic phenomena will often be unreplicated. Do you think replication should be more strongly encouraged? If so, how?

**5.** Many psychological journals are encouraging researchers to report a series of experiments about some phenomenon, rather than a single experiment. Do you think this is a good idea? If so, why? What dangers might be inherent in requiring that research reports contain numerous experiments?

**6.** Verbal reports are likely to be more useful in some areas of psychology than in others. For each of the following topics, discuss the pros and cons of using verbal reports. In those cases which you think verbal reports cannot be used, suggest better methods: (a) studying strategies by which people remember their childhood experiences when asked to do so; (b) studying sexual behavior of college students; (c) studying people's mental processes that occur when they decide to buy one product rather than another; (d) studying the reasons that one person likes another; and (e) studying what factors affect visual illusions.

# Psychology in Action

## Studying Mental Blocks

*Folk* is pronounced *foke,* with the *l* being silent.
*Polk* is pronounced *poke,* again with the *l* being silent.
How is the name of the white part of an egg pronounced?

If you just produced the word *yolk* to answer the question, this section is for you. *Yolk* is an erroneous answer; the white part of an egg is the *albumen.* The yolk, as you probably know, is the yellow part. The sentences prior to the question featured words that rhyme with *yolk* and therefore primed you for the word *yolk.* When you were asked the question about eggs, *yolk* readily tumbled into your mind as the answer to the question. If you had not been primed with the two sentences, you probably would not have responded *yolk.* The recent experience of reading the sentences blocked you from giving the correct answer.

Here are two more examples, although now you may be more wary:

Pronounce the word produced by the letters *T-O-P-S.* What does a car do at a green light?

Say *tin* out loud ten times. What is an aluminum can made of?

Although you may have answered the questions correctly, if you try them on a friend we think you will find them effective in producing the erroneous answers *stop* and *tin.* You should probably ask the questions aloud, rather than having your friend read them.

Such blocks in memory retrieval may play a part in limiting creative thinking (Roediger and Neely, 1982). When people try to solve a problem and fail, they often say that their "minds are in a rut." Usually they mean that when they attempt to solve the problem they are blocked from retrieving a new solution by repeatedly thinking of all the erroneous solutions that have previously been tried. What is needed for creative thinking, according to many writers (de Bono, 1971; Adams, 1974), is a method of overcoming mental blocks and hence creating more effective solutions.

Mental blocks have been studied in some detail by psychologists. Functional fixity, discussed earlier, is one example. When an object is used in one particular way so its function is fixed in one's mind, different uses of the object will be less apparent. Another example comes from work pioneered by Luchins (1942) on the effects of mental set in problem solving. You can gain some insight into the problem of mental blocks and mental set by repeating Luchins's basic experiment. Luchins gave subjects water-jar problems; he told them to imagine that they were given three containers that contained water and that they should use the water in these containers to obtain a fourth amount of water. So, if people were given containers holding 21, 127, and 3 units of water, and were told to obtain 100, they would subtract 21 units from the largest container and then 3 units twice, and end up with 100 units ($127 - 21 - 3 - 3 = 100$). Luchins told his subjects to use the smallest number of steps possible. Try your hand at solving the eight problems in table 11–1, writing your solutions in the answer column provided.

These are eight problems that Luchins used in his original experiments. Of critical interest is how you (and Luchins's subjects) solved the last two problems. For Problem 7 most subjects obtained 20 units of water by using $49 - 23 - 3 - 3$, which works fine. Similarly, for Problem 8 they used $39 - 15 - 3 - 3$, which also works. Are these the solutions you used? The difficulty is that neither solution satisfies the requirement of being the most efficient. If you examine each problem, you will discover a solution that takes fewer steps, for example, $15 + 3$ in Problem 8.

Luchins concluded that his results showed the often inhibiting effect of set on solving problems. In solving problems 2 through 6, people could use only one formula to find their solution, which can be denoted as $B - A - 2C$, where $A$, $B$, and $C$ represent the three jars. Thus subjects built up a set way of solving the problem and when the problem was changed so that the old solution was no

---

Given the following empty jars as measures                                                                      TABLE 11–1

| Problem | A | B | C | The Required Fourth Amount of Water | Answer |
|---------|-----|-----|-----|-----------------|--------|
| 1 | 29 | 3 | | 20 | |
| 2 | 21 | 127 | 3 | 100 | |
| 3 | 14 | 163 | 25 | 99 | |
| 4 | 18 | 43 | 10 | 5 | |
| 5 | 9 | 42 | 6 | 21 | |
| 6 | 20 | 59 | 4 | 31 | |
| 7 | 23 | 49 | 3 | 20 | |
| 8 | 15 | 39 | 3 | 18 | |

longer the most efficient, the subjects were blinded to it and clung to solving the problem the old way. The principle is the same as in the earlier examples of blocks in memory retrieval. Priming people with information sometimes causes them to respond inappropriately.

You can study the effects of set on problem solving by testing subjects on the water-jar problem, using the eight problems above. The problems shown in table 11–1 should be given in the same order to a random half of subjects assigned to the set, or experimental, group. The subjects in the control group should be given Problems 7 and 8 (from table 11–1) only after receiving six other problems with solutions not based on one set formula. The best procedure would be to test subjects individually and present the problems one at a time. Record the answer to each problem and (using a stop watch or simply a watch measuring seconds) record the amount of time the subject takes to obtain it.

The critical dependent measures of interest are the accuracy and speed with which people can answer problems 7 and 8. Luchins reported that about 80 percent of the subjects in the experimental condition, solved these problems using the longer solution (based on the $B - A - 2C$ formula), whereas no subjects in the control group used the long solution. Thus this is a strong example of negative transfer in problem solving from establishment of a set.

Many words of advice have been given as to overcoming mental blocks and problem-solving sets through the use of various techniques. Unfortunately, little experimental evidence is available evaluating the effectiveness of these techniques, which are supposed to foster creativity. We will leave you with another problem to solve.

Without lifting the pencil from the paper, draw four straight lines that will connect all nine dots:

Many people think this problem is unsolvable because they automatically place constraints (a set, a block) on the way they conceive of the problem. There is a solution that, once you see it, is as easy as the solution to the bird-and-train problem at the beginning of the chapter. If you solve this problem, try a harder version: Connect all nine dots with only three straight lines, again without lifting your pencil from the paper. Good luck! (If you become hopelessly stuck, your instructor can help.)

# CHAPTER 12

**Preview**

This chapter is concerned with individual differences in behavior, the unique characteristics among people that make life so interesting. These differences may complicate the search for general laws of behavior, for often people will behave differently when placed in the same situation. In this chapter we discuss reliability of measurement of individual characteristics, or how stable such qualities remain over time. We also discuss how psychological concepts are defined, or the use of operational definitions. Finally, we talk about a pesky but rather obscure problem that afflicts certain types of research when people are tested repeatedly. This problem is known as the regression artifact.

**Chapter Outline**

# INDIVIDUAL DIFFERENCES AND DEVELOPMENT

Don't let us forget that the causes of human actions are usually immeasurably more complex and varied than our subsequent explanations of them.

Dostoevsky

*Manfred rolled over once, rubbed the sleep from his eyes, and tried to remember. It was Thursday, his day to register for classes for the new term. His clock radio was playing Bach, one of the Brandenburgs, but he couldn't quite think which one. Anyway it was one of his favorite pieces to wake up to. Manfred dragged himself from the bed, unplugged his pocket GIPSY from the clock radio, showered, dressed, and hurried to breakfast. The GIPSY ordered him French toast, sausage, juice, six ounces of coffee, and a vitamin.*

*After breakfast Manfred headed for registration at the gym. That was the most convenient place to dispense paper and pay fees, although the real work was done at Central Computing by the central GIPSY. Some of the more ancient profs still talked about the old days, before General Individual PSYchometers were even thought of, when students chose their own classes, selected their own meals, even made their own dates. Weird, thought Manfred. No wonder students in those days used to get drunk, run naked, drop out, and who knows what else. He had studied all that in a social history course the GIPSY had signed him up for during his freshman year. He still wasn't sure why he had needed to know that stuff, but GIPSY knew best. That was the amazing thing about the GIPSY; she always knew what was just right for everyone. The information sheet which had come with his personal*

*GIPSY had said that she monitored his bio-circuitry via her micro-sensors and decided what it was that he most needed or wanted at that moment. This morning, she had already decided when he should be wakened, to what music, and what he should have for breakfast.*

This tale is a piece of science fiction about a time in the future when the psychological study of individual differences has made great progress. Regardless of Manfred's enthusiasm for his GIPSY, we do not propose that General Individual Psychometers should be carried by everyone, like so many pocket calculators, even if this were technically possible. Yet it should be obvious that to some extent what we are, do, say, buy, want, like, think, and perceive is unique. When does it become important to consider these unique aspects of people, and how can they be determined? Recall Manfred and his GIPSY: When there was a choice among several alternative courses of action (for example, what time to get up, what courses to take), Manfred assumed that one would be more desirable than another. It is important to study individual differences when a decision must be made among alternative courses of action, and when we think that particular characteristics of the individual(s) involved will affect that course of action.

The study of individual differences began because of important practical decisions that had to be made about people. It is a topic that has been relatively ignored by experimental psychologists, who are interested in finding general laws and explanations for behavior. Thus they tend to treat all people (or even all organisms) as behaving according to the same laws, and they regard the great individual differences that are found among people in performing almost any task as an unfortunate and pesky fact. Individual differences are thought of as a nuisance, as increasing the "error variance" of experimental operations (see appendix A), but rarely as an interesting and important fact in their own right. Investigation of individual differences is really just getting under way by psychologists who employ experimental methods, though it has long been a topic of concern for psychologists with more practical and applied interests.

The experimental investigation of individual differences illustrates the need for *reliability* of measures of individual characteristics. If individuals' decisions concerning future action are to be based on their particular mental abilities, interests, and ways of responding to events, then measures of these must yield similar results on different test occasions. In addition, the characteristics in which a psychologist is interested need to be defined in a way that can be communicated to others. It would be unreasonable to expect consistent measures of intelligence if everyone who measured it used a different definition of intelligence. The most useful kind of definition, because it is the most easily communicated, describes a procedure for measuring the characteristic of interest. Such procedures are called *operational definitions*, and are a necessary component of all research. When people are separated into classes on the basis of thc operational definitions and then these classes of people are studied in experimental settings, they are referred to as *subject variables*. Examples of subject variables are age, intelligence, sex, degree of neuroticism, or any characteristic of people that can be specified in a precise manner. Age is a subject variable of particular interest to developmental psychologists, who study changes in behavior across the life span. Later in the chapter, we consider problems associated with studying age-related changes.

Once an investigator has operationally defined an individual characteristic and found the measure to be reliable, she or he may then wish to change that characteristic through some type of learning experience. One of the hazards in interpreting such a change is known as *regression to the mean*, which may lead an investigator to believe a change has been produced when in fact it has not, or vice versa. In this chapter we will discuss reliability, operational definitions, subject variables, and regression, in the context of research on individual differences and development.

A general issue in science, and particularly in the psychology of individual differences, concerns the best method for deriving predictions of future events. Two methods of approaching the problem of prediction are the analytical and the empirical. Analytical approaches attempt to predict events on the basis of a theoretical understanding or model of the causes of those events. Empirical approaches attempt to achieve predictive power not by specifying a causal model, but by carefully observing the events that tend to accompany those events they wish to predict. Thus, the appearance of large cumulus clouds could lead one to predict rain if one understands that such clouds contain moisture and knows that the conditions are right for condensing that moisture into drops heavy enough to be pulled to earth by gravity (an analytical approach to meteorology). The same clouds could lead one to predict the same thing if one observes that rain often falls when large cumulus clouds are present in the sky (an empirical approach to meteorology).

## ANALYTICAL VERSUS FMPIRICAL APPROACHES TO INTELLIGENCE

### The Empirical Approach to Intelligence

The empirical method aims to achieve the greatest degree of predictive precision possible by any means available. This usually involves a search for any measure or combination of measures that will predict the events in question. The traditional I.Q. test given to groups of school children is an example of this approach to prediction. In 1904 the French government commissioned Alfred Binet and Theodore Simon to devise tests that would determine which children could profit from an education and which could not. Thus the original basis for intelligence tests, and the one still used today, is how well the tests can predict performance in school. Binet and Simon employed tests of memory, comprehension, attention, and the like, but the logic is the same for all tasks. If children's success in school were most highly correlated with the number of birthday candles they could blow out and how well they liked spinach on a 1 to 7 scale, then these measures would *operationally define* intelligence—the ability to succeed in school. Children would be assigned to fast or slow classes, and directed toward trade schools or colleges, on the basis of these measures. If you were to object to the proposition that these measures reflect intelligence, the test designers would probably reply, "Call it whatever you like, but what it does is accurately predict success in school."

It must be remembered that intelligence tests were first devised to solve a specific problem in prediction. School administrators wanted to know which children would profit most from what sorts of education. These tests have become highly popular because they accomplish what they set out to do—in fact, correlations between I.Q. and measures of academic success generally run in the neighborhood of + .60. In addition, the tests may have considerable *face validity*—that is, they may seem to measure something we would be willing to call intelligence. This would be the case if success in school were better predicted by test items that appeared to measure mental ability than by tests that measured candle-blowing prowess and taste for spinach. Knowing what works in science can often lead to a better understanding of why and how something works. For this reason, empirical solutions to specific problems often precede theoretical and analytical understanding of those problems.

### The Analytical Approach to Intelligence

An analytical procedure for measuring intelligence involves a theoretical analysis of what produces the effects we attribute to intelligence. If productive thinking and successful problem solving are thought to result from high intelligence, then the processes involved in these mental activities constitute intelligence. Once we have analyzed the components of the concept, we can proceed to measure them. Sir Francis Galton, in nineteenth-century England, proposed that the ability to form mental images and the ability to respond quickly to a stimulus should be components of intelligence. When he compared these abilities in scientists and statesmen with those of common workers, he was surprised to find no differences. Thus, he concluded, these abilities do not contribute heavily to intelligence, even though certain theories of his day held that they were important in thinking and problem solving.

Contemporary researchers have had better success in breaking down intelligence into its mental components. The information-processing approach to mental performance (see chapter 7) has produced measures that offer some promise as predictors of academic success (Hunt and Lansman, 1975). These include measures of the speed and capacity of various memory systems, for example. However, we are still some distance from being able to predict scholastic performance as well with these techniques as with the empiricists' I.Q. tests. Researchers pursue the analytical approach because it offers understanding and flexibility in addition to predictive power. Knowing what specific skill or capacity a child is lacking could allow for remediation through special training, or compensation through special learning aids.

### Theoretical and Empirical Approaches

We have discussed the distinction between theoretical and empirical approaches with regard to intelligence, but the same two approaches can be applied to all areas where individual differences are a concern. Personality tests have been devised to attempt to categorize people on the basis of different personality traits—aggressive versus friendly, depressed versus not depressed, and so on. Is it better to construct first a model of personality and test it to gain some theoretical understanding of the underlying processes? Or is it better simply to try to construct a test of some sort and then give it to people already classified as depressed or not by some other method, and then see which items on the test discriminate between the two types of people? The same issue crops up in the study of individual differences in personnel, such as the development of tests designed to fit people to appropriate jobs.

Analytical (theoretical) and empirical approaches to individual-difference research should be seen as complementary rather than antagonistic. Each approach is able to improve its methods by the other's advances. A theoretical understanding of depression can be furthered by examining the items that distinguish depressed and nondepressed patients. Similarly, better test items can be constructed when the empiricist has some notion of how depressed and nondepressed patients differ in their underlying mental structures and processes.

---

## INTRODUCING THE VARIABLES IN INDIVIDUAL DIFFERENCE RESEARCH

We will consider here just one type of individual difference, intelligence.

### Dependent Variables

The dependent variables in the study of intelligence are the *measures* of intelligence used by each experimenter. Since notions of what intelligence really is differ widely among experimenters, it is difficult to devise a single measure that woud be acceptable to all. Empirical approaches are generally based on the observation that, as

*(Continued on next page)*

*Variables—continued*

children grow older, they are able to perform more complicated and more difficult tasks. For individuals of any given age, an average level of performance on certain tasks can be determined by testing a large and representative sample. The particular tasks or test items will be selected on the basis of their correlations with objective criteria of success in school, such as grades and reading level, and possibly also with subjective criteria, such as teacher ratings (see figure 12–1). At any particular age level there will be some average number of items that children can pass. If a seven-year-old child can pass the same number of items as the average nine-year-old, we would say that this child has a "mental age" of nine. The Intelligence Quotient, or I.Q., is defined as mental age divided by chronological age × 100, or (in this case) 9/7 × 100 = 129. By definition, a score of 100 means that an individual scored the average for others his or her age, and every 15-point variation from this average represents one standard deviation (see appendix A) from this mean.

A purely analytic intelligence test, and none is currently in general use, would contain many subtests designed to measure specific properties of a person's information-processing system. Examples of these properties might be short-term memory capacity and scanning rate, long-term memory organization and access time, maximum information-transmission rates in various types of tasks, and ability to allocate attention. Performance on these tasks could be compared to normative performance, as with empirical tests. A combined score computed from all the separate task results may possibly be used as a predictor of scholastic performance.

## Independent Variables

Studies of human intelligence are often aimed at determining the relative importance of genetic, as opposed to environmental, factors in producing intelligence. One of the techniques employed in this research has been to examine monozygotic (identical) twins, dizygotic (fraternal) twins, other siblings, and unrelated children who are reared in the same household or in different households. Genetic similarity varies in these studies as follows: identical twins (of course) have the same genetic inheritance, fraternal twins and other siblings are genetically similar to a lesser degree than

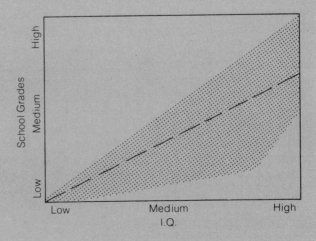

FIGURE 12–1.
An idealized representation of the relationship between grades and I.Q. The shaded area indicates the distribution of grades while the dashed line indicates the average (from Herrnstein, 1973, p. 114).

identical twins, and unrelated children have the least degree of genetic similarity. Environmental similarity varies in that children reared in the same household have more similar experiences than children reared in separate households.

A number of objections to the definition of environmental similarity can be raised. In the first place, it seems unreasonable to assume that all pairs of children in the same household have equally similar experiences. Twins, and particularly identical twins, are often treated more alike than other pairs of children, if for no other reason than that they are at the same age when various family events occur. Also, foster children and natural children may be treated somewhat differently even when they are of the same age. A second objection is based on the fact that foster children enter the family at later ages than natural children, even if by only a few weeks or months. Although this difference may appear trivial when intelligence is measured at ages of ten to fifteen years or more, many studies have shown that early experiences are quite important in the development of intelligence. A third objection is based on the potential influence of experiences that occur even earlier than those of the first few weeks in the home, namely those which occur in the prenatal environment. As with genetic inheritance, these prenatal experiences will generally be most similar for twins, less similar for siblings, and least similar for unrelated children. Similarity of prenatal and early postnatal experience may thus be correlated with genetic similarity, making it risky to intepret correlations of one or the other with measured intelligence.

## Control Variables

In studies of intelligence it is difficult to define an exhaustive set of control variables. The single most important factor to control, however, is generally thought to be specific learning that could affect test performance. If certain individuals have learned answers to a number of the test questions, rather than having to "reason out" the answers, they will appear more intelligent than other individuals who have not previously learned these particular facts, words, or relations. Although many items have been deleted from modern intelligence tests in order to make them more "culture-fair," or less influenced by particular learning experiences, it is impossible to eliminate all the effects of learning, language usage, motivation, cultural knowledge, testing experience, and other factors that are known to affect intelligence measures. This is not a problem if intelligence is interpreted simply as probability of success in school, since these other factors no doubt influence school performance. But if intelligence is interpreted as "mental capacity" or some such construct, the effects of these extraneous variables must be minimized.

---

**Topic:** Reliability of Measures

**Illustrations:** Intelligence and Developmental Research Designs

---

When psychologists speak of reliability, they are referring to the consistency of their measures of some quantity. You might suppose that several attempts to measure the same thing would all yield the same numbers, unless of course someone made an error. In fact, there is nearly always some variability in a group of measures, and the amount of variability determines the reliability of the measuring instrument and procedure. The "error" to which psychologists refer is not meant to imply that anyone goofed, but merely that certain unavoidable factors caused unpredictable variability in the data. Psychologists try to reduce this variability, hence increasing the reliability of their measures, by taking their measures under the same conditions on successive occasions.

If identical conditions could be assured, then variability in measurement would have to be caused by a real change in the measured quantity. If your height is measured on two occasions with the results 5'8" and 5'10", is this variability owing to error or to a real change in your height? The answer could be either, or both. But the more similar the conditions—shoes worn, posture—the less likely you would be to attribute the difference to error. Also, the closer the two measures were in time, the less likely you would be to attribute the difference to a real change in stature. You have some notion of how quickly stature can change, or of the stability of one's true stature.

Intelligence is more difficult to measure than stature, however, and it is more difficult to develop a notion of its stability. Does intelligence vary at all or does it remain fixed throughout life? If it changes markedly, can it do so within a week, a month, a year, or ten years? If it changes, can we determine those factors which produce the change? These are questions that psychologists would like to answer, and the answers require measurement of intelligence. But the alert reader will realize that we have now reasoned ourselves into a logical circle. Let's go around again, and try to get out. Several measures of the same quantity will not, in general, exactly agree. This variability may be a result of error, or real change in the measured quantity. We cannot tell, without some additional assumptions, how much error there is in our measurement. Thus how can we ask if I.Q. changes? A useful assumption—one that allows the logical circle to be broken—is that the measured quantity is stable over relatively short periods of time. (If a researcher measures your intelligence in the morning and then again in the afternoon, any change can be assumed to be caused by measurement error rather than a real change in intelligence.) With this assumption, a psychologist can estimate measurement error and attempt to improve and specify the reliability of the measuring instrument. Then questions concerning the stability of the underlying quantity, in this case intelligence, can be answered.

We will first review some of the techniques that test developers use to assess the reliability of their measures. Then we will review a study that attempted to determine the stability of intelligence over many years.

*Test reliability.* We noted previously that the concept of intelligence is not well defined theoretically. Some theorists postulate a number of separate mental abilities, perhaps more than a hundred (Guilford, 1967). Others believe that there is one primary mental ability and that although other more specific abilities may be isolated, they are less important. This primary ability has been described as "a capacity for abstract reasoning and problem solving" (Jensen, 1969, p. 19). In order to test for this ability, we assemble collections of problems or tasks and present them to individuals to solve, generally within a specified time period. The score that an individual achieves is then compared with scores obtained by others. Before placing much confidence in an individual's score, however, we need to know how reliable it is. Would the individual achieve about the same score if we were to test him or her again the next day, or a week later? Because we do not believe that the underlying ability changes appreciably during so short a time, we attribute a large change in scores to measurement error, indicating unreliability in our test. This procedure of giving the same test twice in succession over a short time interval is used to determine what is called the *test-retest reliability* of a measure. It is generally expressed as a correlation between first and second scores obtained from a large sample of subjects.

A slightly different procedure can be employed to avoid problems such as specific practice effects. This technique involves giving alternate or *parallel forms* of the test on the two testing occasions. Again, if correlations between first and second scores are high, they indicate reliability of the tests. Also, the equivalence of the two forms of the test can be determined in this way.

A third procedure can be used to evaluate reliability with a single test presentation. This is known as the *split-half technique* and involves dividing the test items into two arbitrary groups and correlating the scores obtained in the two halves of the test. If these correlations are high, the test reliability is confirmed. In addition, the equivalence of the test items is established.

*Stability of intelligence measures.* Modern intelligence tests are usually found to yield quite high test-retest reliabilities (correlations of about .95). If we accept these tests as reliable, we can then proceed to ask how stable measured intelligence remains over an individual's lifetime. A number of longitudinal studies have been initiated to examine this question, and reports are published every ten years or so to bring the results up to date. One report (Kangas and Bradway, 1971) includes data on a group of subjects tested with the Stanford-Binet I.Q. test in 1931, at a mean age of a little over four years, and then tested again in 1941, 1956, and 1969. The original sample consisted of San Francisco Bay area chidren who were part of a nationwide standardization population for a revision of the Stanford-Binet scale. Scores were obtained on two alternate forms of the test. In 1941, 138 of these subjects were retested with the same form of the test, and in 1956, 111 received the Wechsler Adult Intelligence Scale and the Stanford-Binet test. In 1969, 48 individuals agreed to be retested yet again.

Before we examine the results of this study, we should recall that these results will be descriptive of the population of subjects from which the data were gathered. They will also, one hopes, be representative of data from similar subjects. They may or may not be representative of subjects who differ in important respects from the subjects in this study.

Kangas and Bradway provided data to show that the 48 subjects tested in 1969 did not differ from the larger group of 111 subjects tested in 1956. They provided means and standard deviations for both chronological age and I.Q. as assessed by the Stanford-Binet test at each age, and found no differences between the two samples.

The authors reported correlations between scores obtained at each pair of test administrations, with scores from the parallel forms administered in 1931 averaged. The tests used at each age were the Stanford-Binet (S-B) intelligence tests and, for the 1956 and 1969 tests only, the Wechsler Adult Intelligence Scale (WAIS). The results are presented in table 12–1. Notice that the WAIS has

TABLE 12–1

Correlations between I.Q. test scores at four administrations from 1931–1969.

| Test | 1941 (N = 100[a]) S-B (Form L) | 1956 (N = 109–111[a]) S-B (Form L) | WAIS Full | WAIS Verbal | WAIS Performance | 1969 (N = 48) S-B (Form L-M) | WAIS Full | WAIS Verbal | WAIS Performance |
|---|---|---|---|---|---|---|---|---|---|
| 1931 S-B (Forms L & M) | .65 | .59 | .64 | .60 | .54 | .41 | .39 | .28 | .29 |
| 1941 S-B (Form L) | | .85 | .80 | .81 | .51 | .68 | .53 | .57 | .18 |
| 1956 S-B (Form L) | | | .83 | .89 | .46 | .77 | .58 | .68 | .14 |
| 1956 WAIS | | | | | | | | | |
| Full | | | | .87 | .84 | .72 | .73 | .69 | .41 |
| Verbal | | | | | .59 | .73 | .63 | .70 | .20 |
| Performance | | | | | | .36 | .67 | .47 | .57 |
| 1969 S-B (Form L-M) | | | | | | | .77 | .86 | .36 |
| 1969 WAIS | | | | | | | | | |
| Full | | | | | | | | .87 | .74 |
| Verbal | | | | | | | | | .38 |

Note—S-B is the Stanford-Binet test, given at all ages, and WAIS is the Wechsler Adult Intelligence Scale, given in 1956 and 1969. All correlations are significant beyond the .01 level. (From Kangas and Bradway, 1971, table 2. The 1931–1956 portion of the table is reprinted from an article by Katherine P. Bradway and Clare C. Thompson published in the February 1962 *Journal of Educational Psychology*. Copyrighted by the American Psychological Association, Inc. 1962).

[a]Because of incomplete data for two of the subjects, the number of total subjects on which any one correlation is based varies from 109 to 111.

a verbal component and a performance component, which together give the full I.Q. As you look from left to right across the table you see that correlations between successive testings decrease with the amount of time between testings. The drop is especially pronounced when preschool I.Q., taken when the children's mean age was 4.1, was correlated with the other scores (the top row of the table). The correlations were much higher when adult I.Q.'s were correlated. However, all the correlations in table 12–1 are statistically significant, indicating that I.Q. tested when children are about four years old predicts to some extent (a correlation of .41) how well they will do much later at age 41.6. (We should also note that intelligence tests given to four-year olds are quite different from those given to older children, which may help account for the low correlations.)

The increase in correlation between the 1969 I.Q. and previous I.Q.s as the subjects' ages increase is reflected as one looks from the top of the table to the bottom. Notice that the correlations are higher when S-B I.Q.s are correlated with each other rather than with WAIS I.Q.s, and vice versa. Since the Stanford-Binet test is verbal, it does not correlate too highly with the performance part of the WAIS. The results presented in table 12–1 indicate that I.Q. is fairly stable across thirty-seven years for this sample.

Another interesting finding of the Kangas and Bradway study is that I.Q. increased at each testing age from 4.1 to 41.6. This increase was examined separately for males and for females (twenty-four of each), and these groups were further separated into high, medium, and low I.Q. groups by taking the top eight, middle eight, and bottom eight subjects of each sex. The results are presented in figure 12–2, where gains in Stanford-Binet I.Q. are plotted for the high and low I.Q. men and women. As already mentioned, continual gains in I.Q. were recorded for all groups, including the medium I.Q. groups which are not shown. But one group seemed to gain much less than the others, the high-I.Q. group of women. Presumably this result is not caused by a ceiling effect (see chapter 10), because the high-I.Q. men show a substantial increase. (However, we do not know whether the high-I.Q. men and women were equivalent initially.) It is interesting to speculate as to whether this result is owing to factors operating in our culture that may keep bright women from reaching their full intellectual potential.

Although this study cannot be considered conclusive in itself, it is in general agreement with others in showing that measured intelligence does remain *relatively* stable over a large portion of one's life, from early childhood to middle age.

***Age as a variable.*** In the Kangas and Bradway study the primary variable of interest was age. As discussed previously, age is a subject variable. Subject variables, by definition, cannot be experimentally manipulated. Instead, a researcher can only select instances that satisfy different categories, and study those. Thus,

FIGURE 12–2.

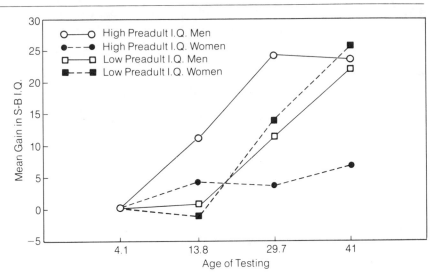

Mean gains in Stanford-Binet I.Q. at successive mean ages for men and women of differing pre-adult I.Q. levels (from Kangas and Bradway, 1970, Figure 1).

research with subject variables is largely correlational in nature; researchers can identify dependent variables that change with variations in a subject variable, but it is difficult to pin causation on the subject variable and not on some possibly confounded factor that varies with the subject variable. However, with age as a subject variable there are several important types of research design that can make causative statements more certain.

The most typical experimental design in which age is varied is called a *cross-sectional design*. In this design, a researcher takes a cross-section of the population and tests them in the experiment or procedure of interest. If a researcher were interested in how I.Q. varied with age, she or he might test people who are 5, 10, 15, 20, 25, 30, 35, 40, 45, 50, 55, 60, 65, 70, and 75. If 25 people were tested at each age, then 375 people would need to be tested. In fact, this is a quite common research design, although the large number of ages sampled is atypical. This design for developmental research has been faulted on important grounds. It has been argued that many other factors are likely to be confounded with age in this sort of design. For example, people who are 25 in 1984 are likely to differ from people who are 65 and 75 on a number of important dimensions: the older subjects will have been raised differently, educated differently, more likely to have immigrated to the United States, more likely to have served in the armed forces, and so on. Another crucial difference in many studies of intellectual performance is that older people are likely to have had fewer years of formal education than younger people. Thus, if in using a cross-sectional research design researchers discover differences among people of different ages, they will have difficulty showing that age is responsible for the difference rather than any number of confounded factors.

Many cross-sectional studies of intelligence have been conducted that show a common pattern of performance: intelligence (as measured on a standard test) increases steadily to the early twenties, then drops gradually until about age sixty, and then declines more quickly thereafter. The conclusion, then, is a rather gloomy one, since many researchers inferred that intelligence leveled off or even dropped after people turned twenty. However, in retrospect and with evidence from other studies, it seems that a more likely conclusion is that cross-sectional studies of intelligence are flawed by all the factors just mentioned, particularly differences in education over the decades. In fact, as we have just seen, when Kangas and Bradway used a different research design to ask the question of how age affects intelligence, they concluded that intelligence continually *increased* across the ages in the study.

Kangas and Bradway used a *longitudinal* design. In these designs the same group of subjects is tested repeatedly over time. In this way all the confoundings inherent in the cross-sectional design are avoided. Thus, a researcher may be more confident in some cases that age rather than confounded subject variables is responsible for whatever changes are observed in performance. However, the longitudinal design is not without problems, either. Imagine that a researcher in 1950 were interested in how age affected people's attitudes toward war and whether the United States should have a strong military capability. If people were measured in 1950, their attitudes might generally be quite favorable, since the United States had recently experienced the success of World War II. However, if these people were tested twenty years later, at the height of the unpopular Vietnam War, their attitudes might have been much less favorable. Obviously, a researcher would be rash to conclude that people's attitudes toward war and defense grow less favorable as the people age. In general, longitudinal designs will not lead to sound conclusions about how age alters behavior when experiential changes during the period between tests may have produced the change.

Given these problems of cross-sectional and longitudinal designs, how can psychologists perform sound research on developmental differences? In fact, many of the developmental studies on which psychologists depend have employed cross-sectional and longitudinal studies (with the former predominating). However, Schaie (1977) advocated other research designs that allow more unambiguous assessments of age changes in performance. One of these, the *cross-sequential design*, is illustrated in figure 12–3, which shows how people born in four successive years (1960 through 1963) might be tested later in four successive years (1979 to 1982). Each column of the figure represents a cross-sectional design, since people of different ages are being tested in one year. Similarly, each

FIGURE 12–3.

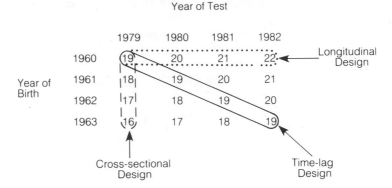

The cross-sequential research design for investigating developmental differences. People born in 1960–1963 are tested repeatedly in 1979–1982. The number in each cell is the age of the person when tested.

row represents a longitudinal design, since people of the same age are tested repeatedly as they age. In addition, a third type of design is shown in the diagonal in the figure. This is the *time-lag design*, which aims at determining the effects of time of testing while holding age constant. Notice that age at testing is held constant at nineteen in the time-lag design, so that any changes observed may be attributed to the changing eras in which people are tested. In the entire cross-sequential design, if both the longitudinal and cross-sectional components show some dependent variable changing with age, and the time-lag component shows no change with time of testing while holding age constant, then a researcher may safely attribute the observed changes to age itself and not some confounded factor.

As you might guess, few researchers are able to routinely obtain the resources to perform research using cross-sequential designs, since such designs involve testing people from several different age groups over a number of years. However, whenever it is possible to use such designs in developmental research they should be attempted. Cross-sequential designs embed both cross-sectional and longitudinal designs within them and potentially permit less ambiguous interpretations of the effects of age changes on behavior.

## 12.2
### EXPERIMENTAL TOPICS AND RESEARCH ILLUSTRATIONS

**Topic:** Operational Definitions

**Illustration:** Obesity and Eating

In scientific endeavors it is important to define precisely the terms we use. Otherwise results will seem not to agree when in fact there may have been no reason to expect them to. Suppose two investigators were interested in the effects of hunger on some aspect of performance. Both set out to manipulate hunger, the independent variable, to see how it affected the behavior in question. When the results were in, though, it turned out that they were not in agreement. One investigator found that hunger increased the behavior, whereas the other found that hunger decreased it. What is the matter here? Obviously we cannot have a science that is worth anything when problems such as this occur.

In cases like this, it is always wise to look at definitions—what did the investigators mean by "hunger?" Let us suppose that they defined it in two different ways. One investigator defined it as the number of hours that an animal had been deprived of food before being tested in the experiment, whereas the other defined it as keeping an animal at a certain percentage of its normal body weight. When hunger was defined as hours of food deprivation, increases in hunger (more hours of food deprivation) enhanced behavior. But when hunger was defined as the percentage of body weight, greater amounts of hunger (smaller percentage of body weight) decreased behavior. This might have been because the very hungry animals were simply too weak to perform. Thus, when the two experiments are carefully compared, there is good reason the results did not agree; hunger was defined in different ways in the two cases.

In chapter 5 we said that an *operational definition* is one in which a term is defined by the procedures (operations) used to measure it. Both definitions of hunger just discussed are legitimate operational definitions. Both define hunger in terms of experimental operations. One specifies hunger in terms of hours of food deprivation, the other in terms of percentage of normal body weight. In both cases we would be willing to describe the animal under study as hungry, but there is an obvious difference between the cases. (In fact, unlike the hypothetical example just discussed, the two definitions of hunger usually lead to the same results.) Early in the history of psychology there were many disputes that seemed to hinge on the meaning of terms. The problem was often one of definition of terms. Two experimenters might often be using the same term, but defining it in different ways.

Such terminological disputes are minimized in psychological research today by the use of operational definitions. Psychological constructs must be defined in terms of experimental operations that are used to study them. If you want to study and theorize about ego strength, you must be prepared to define it specifically with the operations used to study it. This greatly aids communication and understanding. Now the rest of us will know what you are talking about.

In practice, psychologists usually try to define a construct in several different ways. If different ways of defining a construct all lead to the same conclusion, then we can have more confidence in its validity; the different operations all seem to converge on the same construct. The logic of using converging operations to define psychological constructs was introduced by Garner, Hake, and Ericksen (1956) and is discussed elsewhere in this book (chapters 6 and 14).

In this section we discuss the work initiated by Schachter and his colleagues on the topic of obesity and individual differences in eating behavior. Why are some of us fat and some of us skinny? Why do some of us eat far too much while others are able to eat sensibly and remain trim? Traditional explanations of obesity and overeating are often given in terms of a lack of willpower, or a need to eat to reduce anxiety, or a reflection of dependency in childhood, and so forth. Schachter (1968) proposed a different explanation of overeating and obesity and backed this view with experimental evidence. He proposed that obese individuals were more sensitive to external, food-related, cues and tended to ignore the internal cues that govern food intake in normal people. Fat people tend to eat whether or not their internal physiological state indicates they should be hungry, as long as there are food-related cues in their environment.

In one experiment to test this idea, Nisbett (1968) varied the number of external cues that encouraged eating to see if they had a differential effect on underweight, normal, and obese people. Let us consider carefully how he operationalized these concepts in his experiment. Nisbett wanted to use three groups of people in the experiment: underweight, normal, and overweight. Obviously one cannot simply wait for people to show up for the experiment and then classify them subjectively. Instead, operational definitions of these categories must be provided. To define the three groups Nisbett, like others doing research in this area, used the Metropolitan Life Insurance Company statistics on the mean weight of people of different heights. He defined underweight as 20 to 7 percent below the mean weight for a given height, normal as 1 percent below to 9 percent above the mean weight, and overweight as 15 to 48 percent above the mean weight. In all cases the mean weight for a particular person was specified on the basis of his or her height.

Other researchers have used slightly different definitions of these groups. One operational definition that might be used is to define people 15 percent below the mean weight as underweight and 15 percent above the mean weight as overweight, although this is more stringent than the definitions typically used. The mean weights for men and women of different heights, and the weights of people who would be defined as underweight and overweight by this definition, are presented in table 12–2. Examine it so that you can get some idea as to the weights of people used in these studies (and so you can see where you fit in). These weights are only for people in the 20–24 age range. Nisbett's subjects were college students, as are most of the subjects in obesity research done by psychologists. You should keep in mind that the weights in table 12–2 are mean weights and not necessarily desirable weights for each height.

Why pick plus and minus 15 percent of the mean weight for the operational definitions of overweight and underweight? Why not

Mean weights of men and women aged 20–24 (in indoor clothing). Also included are the weights of people classified as underweight or overweight in obesity research (15% above or below normal). (From the Metropolitan Life Insurance Company *Statistical Bulletin*, 1959)

TABLE 12–2

| | Men | | | | Women | | |
|---|---|---|---|---|---|---|---|
| Height | Mean Weight | Under-weight | Over-weight | Height | Mean Weight | Under-weight | Over-weight |
| 5'2" | 128 | <109 | >147 | 4'10" | 102 | <87 | >117 |
| 3" | 132 | <112 | >152 | 11" | 105 | <89 | >121 |
| 4" | 136 | <116 | >156 | 5'0" | 108 | <92 | >124 |
| 5" | 139 | <118 | >160 | 1" | 112 | <95 | >129 |
| 6" | 142 | <121 | >163 | 2" | 115 | <98 | >132 |
| 7" | 145 | <123 | >167 | 3" | 118 | <100 | >136 |
| 8" | 149 | <127 | >171 | 4" | 121 | <103 | >139 |
| 9" | 153 | <130 | >176 | 5" | 125 | <106 | >144 |
| 10" | 157 | <133 | >181 | 6" | 129 | <110 | >148 |
| 11" | 161 | <137 | >185 | 7" | 132 | <112 | >152 |
| 6'0" | 166 | <141 | >191 | 8" | 136 | <116 | >156 |
| 1" | 170 | <145 | >196 | 9" | 140 | <119 | >161 |
| 2" | 174 | <148 | >200 | 10" | 144 | <122 | >166 |
| 3" | 178 | <151 | >205 | 11" | 149 | <127 | >171 |
| 4" | 181 | <154 | >208 | 6'0" | 154 | <131 | >177 |

$\pm 10$ percent, or $\pm 25$ percent, or any other number? There can be no explicit reason the first time it is tried. Weight, like many other characteristics on which individuals vary, is a continuous dimension, so cutoff points for classifications are arbitrary to some degree. The only justification can be made after the fact. If experimental results indicate differences in behavior between the groups of subjects, then the operational definition really discriminated among people. If no differences in behavior are discovered, either the operational definition is faulty (perhaps more extreme groups of subjects should have been selected), or the hypotheses under test are incorrect. As usual, null results are not very informative for there may be a number of reasons for failing to find some effect.

Many of the individual differences studied by psychologists are continuous in nature, and thus the classification into discrete groupings is somewhat arbitrary. Other continuous individual differences are intelligence, anxiety, length of institutionalization, degree of neuroticism, and so forth. The criteria for determining these qualities vary along a dimension (such as a score on a psychological test) in a gradual manner and generally are normally distributed (see appendix A). Other dimensions, though, may vary in a discrete manner. A person either has the quality or does not. Examples of this sort of variable are sex and color-blindness. A person is either male or female or color-blind or not. In these cases there are natural classifications, and arbitrary cutoffs along a single dimension need not be made.

Returning to Nisbett's (1968) study, we will next consider how he operationally defined and manipulated the number of external food cues that were presented to subjects. The external cues were specified very simply as food (in particular, sandwiches) placed before the subject. The number of cues was varied by varying the number of sandwiches. Subjects were told that they were participating in an experiment to measure certain physiological variables and were asked not to eat after 9 A.M. before appearing at an afternoon experimental session. After the phsyiological variables were measured and subjects were disengaged from the electrodes, the subjects were led into another room to fill out some questionnaires. The experimenter said casually, "Since you skipped lunch for the experiment, we'd like to give you lunch now. You can fill out the questionnaire as you eat. There are dozens more sandwiches in the refrigerator, by the way. Have as many as you want." The subjects were then left alone in the room with a bottle of soda and one or three sandwiches wrapped in wax paper on the table. Conditions were arranged such that subjects did not suspect that the experimenter was at all interested in how many sandwiches were eaten, though in fact this was the main dependent variable.

The results of Nisbett's study are presented in figure 12–4, where the number of sandwiches eaten is presented as a function of the weight of the subjects (underweight, normal, and overweight) for both the one- and three-sandwich condition. As can be seen in the figure, overweight subjects ate more sandwiches in the three-sandwich condition than in the one-sandwich condition, but the other

FIGURE 12–4.

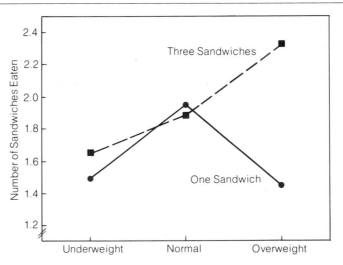

The number of sndwiches eaten by underweight, normal, and overweight subjects in Nisbett's experiment. Overweight subjects ate 57% more sandwiches when three sandwiches were placed on the table than when only one sandwich was, while normal and underweight subjects did not differ in the number of sandwiches they ate as a function of this variable. Overweight subjects are more sensitive to external, food-related cues (drawn from the data in Table 1, Nisbett, 1968).

subjects (underweight and normal) were unaffected by this manipulation. They ate about the same number of sandwiches in both cases. It should be remembered that all subjects were given access to all the food they wanted; the only difference was whether one or three sandwiches were placed before them on the table. The overweight subjects, then, were much more responsive to the external food-related cues than were the normal or underweight subjects, in agreement with Schachter's (1968) hypothesis.

When *subject variables* are studied, as discussed earlier, special care must be used, since it is impossible to assign subjects randomly to the different conditions. Rather, subjects must be assigned to the conditions because of their special characteristics. However, if we then find differences between conditions on the basis of the subject variable, can we conclude that it produced or caused the effect on the dependent variable? The answer is *no*, because there may have been some other characteristic of the subjects that varied with the one of interest, and that actually produced the effect. Some other variable may be confounded with the one of interest. In Nisbett's (1968) experiment, it may be premature to conclude that weight of the subjects caused the differences in terms of the number of sandwiches eaten. The skinny, normal, and chubby subjects could have varied on other characteristics, too, in a systematic way, such as anxiety level, intelligence, or willpower.

When subject variables are studied, one way to help rule out the possibility that it is some confounded factor that actually produced the results is to predict an interaction. Consider again Nisbett's results. Suppose that he had found that fat people ate more than the others (or less than the others) consistently in both the one- and three-sandwich conditions. If this had been the case, no one would have been particularly interested in the results. Of course fat people eat a lot. That's why they are fat. But Nisbett predicted that overweight people would respond *differently* to variation in the number of external food cues, and they did. In the one-sandwich condition the overweight subjects actually ate *less* than normal subjects, but in the three-sandwich condition they ate far more. Thus Nisbett found the predicted and interesting interaction between weight and the amount of food eaten.

In research on individual differences it is generally best to test hypotheses predicting interactions instead of simple main effects. Rather than simply predict that one group will behave differently from another, you should predict under what conditions the groups will fare better and under what conditions they will fare worse. This is so for two reasons. First, there is always the danger that you are predicting something you already know on the basis of the definition of the types of people. If you predict that fat people will eat more than thin, or that high-I.Q. people will perform verbal tasks better than low-I.Q. people, you are not exactly going to startle the world if your results conform to your predictions. This is because you are simply capitalizing on the definition of the type of people in the two cases, especially that of I.Q. By definition, high I.Q. people do better than low-I.Q. people on verbal tasks (that is how they were defined as high-I.Q. people). Of real interest would be to find tasks where this is not the case. This would be similar to Nisbett's finding conditions where the overweight subjects ate less than the normals.

The other reason it is better to predict interactions when a subject variable is studied is that this makes it less likely that some confounded variable is actually responsible for the effect. Nisbett predicted that overweight subjects would be more sensitive to food-related cues than normals, and the interaction he found supported this hypothesis. It may seem unlikely that any variable possibly correlated with weight (intelligence, anxiety, willpower, et cetera) could have produced the same pattern of results. Why should the same interaction occur in these other cases? But even when a predicted interaction is found when a subject variable is under investigation, the possibility cannot be entirely ruled out that some confounded factor produced the effect. One can never be certain with subject variables, since other relevant characteristics have not been held constant. In fact, there is more recent evidence that it is not obesity in itself that makes overweight people more responsive to food-related cues than normal or underweight people.

The norms of our society have the effect of making life unpleasant for overweight people. Thus overweight people are almost always on a diet, whereas normal-weight people are less likely to diet and underweight people usually are not worrying about watching their weight. Nisbett (1972) proposed that all organisms have a physiologically appropriate level of weight, which he calls a *set point*, that differs among individuals and may be quite unrelated to what society judges as normal weight. Overweight people may simply have a much higher set point than other people. Because it is desirable in our society to be thin, overweight people may constantly be on a diet, trying to lose weight. Those who are dieting may be below their set point and thus hungry. The reason, then, that overweight people may be so sensitive to external food-related cues is that they are hungry! It may seem paradoxical that overweight people could be hungry, but it is not, if the concept of people having different set points is accepted.

The upshot is that it may not be the fact that subjects were overweight that led them to be so sensitive to food cues, as in Nisbett's (1968) and numerous other experiments, but the fact that these people were dieting and hungry. Dieting and hunger might have been confounded with weight in these studies, and this may by the factor that produced the results. Herman and Polivy (1975) and Hibscher and Herman (1977) tested this line of reasoning in situations where obese and normal subjects were found to differ. They studied normal and overweight subjects who either restrain their eating behavior (diet) or eat pretty much what they want to. They found that it is restraint and not obesity that determines the behavior of individuals in certain eating situations. Both obese and normal-weight dieters seem not to be as responsive to those internal factors which normally tend to govern eating.

In one experiment, Hibscher and Herman (1977) had their subjects either drink two milkshakes or not drink anything before taking a "taste test" where the real interest was in seeing how much people would eat while tasting the food (ice cream). Having people drink two milkshakes operationally defines a *preload* variable, so half the subjects were given a preload and half were not. The subjects were defined as either underweight, normal, or overweight in the manner we have previously discussed. In addition, they were classified as restrained or unrestrained according to whether or not they reported on a questionnaire that they were dieting.

Previous experiments had found that when normal subjects are given a preload, they tend to reduce their eating during a taste test, but that obese subjects eat about as much regardless of whether they have had a preload. This agrees with the idea that overweight people are not sensitive to internal physiological factors whereas normal people are. Is it weight itself that determines this effect, or is it dieting that reduces the weight of the fat people below their set point? Hibscher and Herman's (1977) results are presented in figure 12–5, where it can be seen that unrestrained subjects decreased the amount of ice cream consumed in the taste test when given a preload, but that restrained subjects actually ate *more* ice cream after having two milkshakes than after having none. This and other results indicate that it is restraint or dieting that leads to the differential effects of preload and not simply weight. One

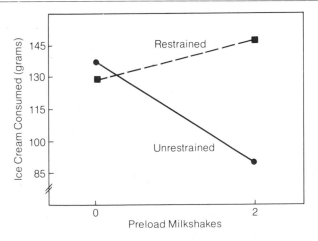

FIGURE 12–5.

The amount of ice cream eaten by restrained (dieting) and unrestrained subjects after either 0 or 2 preload milkshakes. Unrestrained subjects eat less after a preload, but restrained subjects actually eat more ice cream after they have had two milkshakes than after none (from Hibscher & Herman, 1977, Figure 1).

reason the restrained subjects might actually eat more after a pre-load is that since they have already blown their diet for the day by drinking the milkshakes, they feel they may as well go ahead and eat a lot. Fat people on diets are notorious for going on eating binges that eventually bring up their weight. If it is true that in-dividuals simply differ in their physiological set points, overweight dieters may be fighting a losing battle (Nisbett, 1972).

It is too early to say whether the restrained-unrestrained di-mension is responsible for all the effects that previously have been attributed to weight. The general point is that in research with subject variables, we must always carefully examine the situation to determine whether it is the particular subject variable rather than one of its correlates that is producing an experimental effect. We can never be certain as to cause and effect with subject vari-ables, since there is always the possibility of confounding. Perhaps it is not restraint that produces the effect of preload in the Hibscher and Herman (1977) study, but some other variable correlated with dieting (say, anxiety).

## 12.3
## EXPERIMENTAL TOPICS AND RESEARCH ILLUSTRATIONS

**Topic:** Regression Artifacts

**Illustration:** Educational Assessment

An issue related to the study of intelligence and individual differ-ences revolves around attempts by psychologists and educators to improve the performance of individuals, and the importance of evaluating such attempts. As you might suspect, accurate mea-surement lies at the heart of assessing change. Whenever there is measurement error, there is also the possibility of wrongly con-cluding that some sort of change has occurred or has failed to occur. Although this statement may appear less than profound to you, a number of psychological studies have been faulted for failing to take adequate account of its truth.

Certain designs or procedures for gathering data are particularly susceptible to bias caused by measurement error. Those designs, remember, are termed *quasi-experimental*, because subjects are not assigned to treatment and control groups on a random basis (Campbell and Stanley, 1966). Subjects in these groups may be matched on a number of factors by a researcher, but it is difficult to insure that important differences between the groups did not exist prior to the start of the treatment. This problem is amplified when the experimental (treatment) group and control (no treat-ment) group are not matched prior to the study on the variable they will be tested on at the end of the study. For example, a group of children from one neighborhood might be selected as an exper-imental group, to test a new training course for teaching running.

A second group of children might be chosen from the same neighborhood to serve as a control group. Following six weeks of training by the experimental group, both groups might be tested for running speed. This would be a quasi-experimental design because the children were not randomly assigned to one of the two groups. Even if the experimenter reported that the two groups had been of the same average height, weight, and age, we would not know for certain that the average running speed of the two groups had been the same prior to the treatment. In fact, even if control subjects had been picked to match the running speeds of the experimental group, we could not be sure that group differences following training were owing to the effects of training. This is because the possibility would remain that the two groups had been sampled from populations that differed prior to the study. When population differences exist, there is the possibility of being misled by what are known as *regression artifacts,* or experimental effects produced by "statistical regression" rather than by experimental manipulations. You will remember that we talked briefly about regression artifacts in chapter 2.

Perhaps an example will help here. Suppose that you are an *A* student, and that your neighbor is a *C* student, although you both have similar backgrounds. On one particular assignment you both receive a *B*. In an effort to improve, your neighbor decides to attend a series of help sessions. Your instructor decides to evaluate the effectiveness of the help sessions by comparing the future grades of help-session students with future grades of non-help-session students who are similar in background and received the same grades on the previous assignment. You are selected as the matched student to be compared with your friend. On the next assignment, you receive an *A*−, and your friend receives a *C*+. Should the instructor conclude that help sessions are harmful because your friend went from a *B* to a *C*+, while you went from a *B* to an *A*−? Probably not, since both of you merely regressed toward your mean grades. The effect seen in this little study is probably not a true treatment effect, but rather a regression artifact caused by the fact that you and your friend were not truly equivalent students. The help session may even have benefited your friend since her or his grade was higher than the usual grade of *C*. If *B* students on the first assignment had been randomly assigned to help-session or non-help-session groups, and then compared on grades on the second assignment, accurate assessment of the effect of help sessions on students' grades could have been obtained.

The reason for the phenomenon of regression to the mean is that all psychological measures are subject to a certain amount of unreliability. With any measure that is not perfectly reliable, the group of subjects obtaining the highest scores contains not only those who really belong in the highest category, but also others who were placed in this category due to chance errors of measurement. On a retest these chance measurement errors will not necessarily occur in the same direction. Thus the scores of the highest group will tend to average lower on a retest. Similarly, a group selected for poor performance on an original test will tend to average higher on a retest. The Psychology in Action section at the end of this chapter is intended to give you a better understanding of this point through a simple demonstration of regression to the mean.

The importance of regression artifacts such as this in quasi-experimental studies of compensatory education has been the subject of much debate. One influential study of the effects of the Head Start program of the 1960s (Cicirelli et al., 1969) received particular attention. In this study, called the Westinghouse-Ohio study, children completing their Head Start experience were randomly selected for evaluation. A control population of children from the same area, who had been eligible for the program but had not attended, was then defined. Control children were selected at random to be matched with experimental children on the basis of sex, racial-ethnic group membership, and kindergarten attendance. After the final selection of experimental and control subjects was made, additional measures of socioeconomic status, demographic status, and attitude were compiled and compared for the two groups. Differences were reported to be slight. Measures of experimental (Head Start) and control (no Head Start) children's academic achievement and potential were then computed and compared. The general conclusion from this large study was that Head Start was not effective in removing the effects of poverty and social disadvantage.

Other psychologists (Campbell and Erlebacher, 1970a) were quick to criticize this study on several grounds. First, it was pointed out that the results of the study were undoubtedly caused partially by regression artifacts. Worse, the magnitude of the artifacts could not be estimated, casting doubt over the entire set of findings.

The basic problem is one of matching (see chapter 2 for a similar example). Circirelli and co-workers laudably tried to match a sample of disadvantaged children who had been in the Head Start program with others from the same area who had not been in the program. Later differences between the two groups should be due to the program. Right? Not necessarily. It's right only if the two samples came from the same underlying population distributions, which is unlikely.

What is more likely is that the two populations differ, with the disadvantaged "treatment" children coming from a population that is poorer in ability than the "control" children. The "treatment" children are usually preselected to be from a disadvantaged background (which is why they are included in the program), whereas the "controls" who are not in the program are likely to be from a different population that is greater in ability. The basic problem is that subjects are not randomly assigned to conditions, so the researchers must try to match control subjects with experimental subjects. In order to match two samples from these different populations, the experimenters will have to select children *above* the population mean for the disadvantaged treatment group and *below* the mean for the control group. But when this is done the dreaded regression artifact will always be introduced. When each group is retested, the performance of individuals will tend to regress to the mean of the group; in other words, the disadvantaged group will tend to perform worse in this example, and the control group will tend to perform better.

This regression to the mean will happen in the absence of any treatment being given to either group, and despite matching. The effect is the same as that in the previous example of the grades of the superior student increasing to $A-$ from $B$ and the other's decreasing from $B$ to $C+$ when the two students were erroneously "matched" as $B$ students. Since we already expect a difference between the groups (favoring the control) in this situation, because of regression to the mean, how we do evaluate the outcome of our study? Cicirelli and co-workers found no difference between the groups. Since we might expect the treatment (Head Start) group to actually be worse owing to regression artifacts, does this mean the group actually improved owing to Head Start?

It is impossible to answer this question, because in the Westinghouse-Ohio evaluation of Head Start the direction or magnitude of regression artifacts could not be assessed. In the preceding paragraph, we made reasonable suppositions concerning regression artifacts in this type of study. But the conclusion that Head Start had no effect cannot be drawn from the Westinghouse-Ohio study. More properly, no conclusion can be drawn on the basis of that study, since it is not known how regression artifacts affected the results.

In general, then, regression artifacts of a difficult-to-estimate magnitude are highly probable in this type of study, and this fact is acknowledged by all. Why, then, would such studies be conducted, particularly when very important political, economic, and social decisions might be based on their results? This question was raised by Campbell and Erlebacher (1970a, b) and Cicirelli and his supporters (Cicirelli, 1970; Evans and Schiller, 1970). Their answers were quite different, and represent the type of issue that frequently confronts scientists, but that science can never resolve. Campbell and Erlebacher proposed that bad information was worse than no information at all; that if properly controlled experiments could not be performed, then no data should be gathered. On the other side of the issue, Evans and Schiller replied, "This position fails to understand that every program *will* be evaluated by the most arbitrary, anecdotal, partisan and subjective means" (p. 220). Campbell and Erlebacher concurred, but stated that "we judge it fundamentally misleading to lend the prestige of science to any report in a situation where no scientific evaluation is possible" (1970b, p. 224). As a final solution they proposed that a commission "composed of experts who are not yet partisans in this controversy" be convened to decide the matter.

This issue may not be decidable on strictly rational grounds, but we can all agree that a research study should be conducted according to the best scientific procedures available. How could the Westinghouse-Ohio study have been done appropriately? The best way would have been to randomly assign participants to either the no-treatment or treatment (Head Start) conditions. There is no substitute for random assignment in eliminating confounding factors. But it seems unfair to give half the children who seek the help of a remedial program no training whatsoever. Of course there is no guarantee at the outset that the program will do them any good; that is what the study is intended to discover. The same issue occurs in medical research when a control group with a disease is given a placebo rather than a treatment drug. The argument could be made in both cases that in the long run more people will be aided by careful research into the effectiveness of treatments than may be harmed because treatment is withheld.

There are other solutions besides random assignment. One would be to randomly assign all the children to different groups and put them in different programs, to pit the effectiveness of the programs against one another. The only difficulty here would be if the training programs turn out to be equally effective. Then one could not know if any of them is better than no program at all.

**FROM PROBLEM TO EXPERIMENT: THE NUTS AND BOLTS**

**Problem:** Why Are Overweight People More Sensitive to Food Cues?

Research by Schachter and his colleagues (for example, Schachter, Goldman, and Gordon, 1968) has shown that obese subjects do not reduce their food intake when given a preload, whereas normal subjects do. Thus the eating behavior of the obese seems not to be governed by internal physiological factors as does that of normal subjects. As we have seen, this conclusion was modified by the research of Hibscher and Herman (1977), who found that it was dietary restraint and not weight that was related to the effects of the preload manipulation. Unrestrained (nondieting) subjects ate less after a preload, but dieting subjects did not. Apparently the reason Schachter and others had found that obese subjects were unaffected by a preload is that most obese subjects were dieters.

It has also been learned that obese subjects are more affected than normals by external, food-related cues. Thus far there has been no research to see whether dietary restraint and not weight actually lies behind this effect, too. This is the hypothesis to be examined here.

**Problem:** Are overweight people more sensitive to food cues because they are usually dieting and are therefore more hungry than normal people?

**Hypothesis:** People who restrain their diets will be more sensitive to manipulation of the number of food-related cues than will people who do not, and the weight of the people will be unrelated to this variable.

One experimental design to test this hypothesis calls for four groups of subjects: Overweight-Restrained, Overweight-Unrestrained, Normal-Restrained, and Normal-Unrestrained. It would be best to obtain twenty subjects in each of these categories for use in the experiment. Half would be in a condition with few external food-related cues and half would be in a condition with more cues. The dependent measure would be how much the people ate in the situation.

In order to obtain subjects for the experiment, we need to have a very large group of people fill out a questionnaire. Two items included should be height and weight. Then overweight and normal people can be determined by consulting figure 12–2. Normal-weight subjects might be operationally defined as 90–110 percent of the mean weight for a given height, while overweight subjects would be defined as greater than 15 percent overweight for a particular height. A Restraint Questionnaire has been designed by Herman and Polivy (1975) to distinguish Restrained from Unrestrained individuals. It appears in table 12–3. There are eleven questions, and subjects are given a certain number of points depending on how they answer each question. Determining the cutoff points for Restrained versus Unrestrained would depend on the characteristics of the particular sample tested. It may be quite difficult to find Overweight-Unrestrained subjects because overweight subjects are almost always concerned with their diet. Finding appropriate groups of subjects would be one of the most difficult problems in performing this experiment.

Assuming that appropriate groups can be found, we should test subjects individually. They should be told not to eat before they come to the experiment. If they are scheduled in the morning they should miss breakfast; if in the afternoon, they should skip lunch. The experimental conditions must be designed such that subjects do not know that the real interest is in how much food they will eat. One plausible story might be that they are in the experimental group of an experiment to see how mild hunger affects learning and memory, and that they will be asked to memorize some lists. Three lists of common English words are read and the subjects are given three minutes to recall each list. (The lists might be forty words long, with a word read to the subjects every two seconds.) After the subjects recall the third list, they are told that since they were asked to skip a meal, they will be provided with food. The experimenter then takes them to another room where there are

| TABLE 12–3 | The Restraint Questionnaire developed by Herman and Polivy. The first 6 questions are concerned with diet and weight history, the last 5 with how concerned individuals are with food and eating. As indicated, individuals receive various numbers of points depending on their answers. The scores for the questions should be summed, providing a total score. Since restraint is a continuous dimension, it is necessary to make a decision as to where the cutoff point should be. Herman and Polivy used the median-split technique. That is, they determined the median of their sample on the Restraint Questionnaire (17) and operationally defined people who scored above 17 as Restrained and those who scored below 17 as Unrestrained. (From Herman and Polivy, 1975, p. 669) |
|---|---|

### RESTRAINT QUESTIONNAIRE

*Diet and Weight History*

1. How many pounds over your desired weight were you at your maximum weight? (score: 1 point/5 pounds)
2. How often are you dieting?—rarely, sometimes, usually, always. (score: 1–4)
3. Which best describes your behavior after you have eaten a "not allowed" food while on your diet?—return to diet; stop eating for an extended period of time in order to compensate; continue on a splurge, eating other "not allowed" foods. (score 0–2)
4. What is the maximum amount of weight that you have ever lost within 1 month? (score: 1 point/5 pounds)
5. What is your maximum weight gain within a week? (score: 1 point/3 pounds)
6. In a typical week, how much does your weight fluctuate (maximum-minimum)? (score: 1 point/3 pounds)

*Concern with Food and Eating*

7. Would a weight fluctuation of 5 pounds affect the way you live your life?—not at all, slightly, moderately, very much. (score: 0–3)
8. Do you eat sensibly before others and make up for it alone?—never, rarely, often, always. (score: 0–3)
9. Do you give too much time and thought to food?—never, rarely, often, always. (score: 0–3)
10. Do you have feelings of guilt after overeating?—never, rarely, often, always. (score 0–3)
11. How conscious are you of what you are eating?—not at all, slightly, moderately, extremely. (score: 0–3)

either one or three sandwiches with a glass of milk on a table. The number of sandwiches defines the number of food-related cues. As in Nisbett's (1968) experiment, the subjects are told that there are many more sandwiches in the refrigerator (and there should be). The experimenter leaves the room at this point so that the subjects do not feel uncomfortable about eating as much as they want. The experimenter should be blind with respect to whether the subject is Restrained or Unrestrained. After the subject finishes eating, the experimenter carefully explains to the subject the true purpose of the experiment and why it was necessary to use a mild deception. Finally, the experimenter counts the number of sandwiches the subject ate, which is the dependent variable.

It is predicted that Restrained subjects will eat more sandwiches than Unrestrained subjects in the condition where there are more food-related cues (three sandwiches) than they will in the condition where there are fewer (one sandwich). In other words, there should be an interaction between the manipulation of food-related cues and whether subjects are restrained or not restrained. On the other hand, weight (normal or overweight) is predicted to have no effect.

It should be remembered that even if the results come out as predicted, we could not strictly conclude that restraint causes people to be more responsive to food-related cues. Restraint, like weight, is a subject variable and thus could be confounded with other qualities that may actually be responsible for the relationship. Hibscher and Herman (1977) suggest that stress from dieting or some other factor may be responsible for the relationship they found between restraint and the effect of a preload manipulation.

**1.** The two general approaches to the study of individual differences are the empirical and analytical. Empirical approaches are based on finding correlates of the individual difference in question, such as intelligence tests designed to predict school grades. Empirical approaches generally provide the most predictive power and are useful for this reason. In addition, a good empirical relationship may offer clues to understand the underlying mechanisms of interest. Analytical theories of individual differences attempt to provide explanations for the differences in behavior by pointing to differences in underlying psychological processes. Such theories may allow greater flexibility in generalizing results to new situations.

**2.** Reliability of measuring instruments and devices is crucial to all scientific investigation, including the study of individual differences. Devising reliable measures of complicated mental abilities such as intelligence is difficult, but if reliable measures are derived they can be used to investigate such interesting questions as the stability of the quantity measured over long periods of time.

**3.** The most common design used in developmental research is the cross-sectional design in which people of different ages (a cross-section of the population) are tested. Unfortunately, any differences found may be owing to factors confounded with age, such as differences in education or other particular life experiences. In the longitudinal design the same group of people is tested repeatedly as they age, thus eliminating much of the confounding that occurs in the cross-sectional approach. Unfortunately, in some cases the longitudinal design can also be misleading, when the observed changes are not owing to age *per se*, but to life experiences that just happen to be correlated with age. The cross-sequential design embeds multiple cross-sectional and longitudinal designs within it, and permits evaluation of variation caused by changing times or eras (rather than age), through examination of the time-lag design built into it. In the time-lag design people of the same age are examined over different eras, thus revealing the effect of era rather than age. The cross-sequential design allows stronger inferences to be made about the effects of age unconfounded with other fac-

**SUMMARY**

tors, but unfortunately such designs are difficult to implement in practice. Most developmental research still relies on the cross-sectional approach, with attempts made to match people on other factors such as socioeconomic status.

**4.** Operational definitions of psychological constructs involve specifying the construct in terms of the experimental operations used to study it. In Nisbett's (1968) study of the relation of external, food-related cues to amount eaten by people of different weights, the number of food-related cues was operationally defined as the number of sandwiches placed on the table before the people; and underweight, normal, and overweight were defined in terms of percentage above or below a certain weight for a particular height.

**5.** When individual differences such as intelligence, weight, or age are examined in experiments, they are referred to as subject variables. By their nature, subject variables preclude random assignment of subjects to conditions, so one must avoid concluding that experimental effects are produced by subject variables, because some confounded factor may have produced the effect. For example, there is some evidence that it is not the fact of their weight that makes fat people generally unresponsive to internal cues regarding food intake, but the fact that they usually restrain their food intake.

**6.** In studies where subjects in two groups (a treatment and a control) are matched on some criteria rather than being randomly assigned to the two groups, there is a great likelihood that statistical regression will affect the results and conclusions drawn. When extreme groups of subjects are selected (extreme on one dimension), their scores upon retesting will tend toward the mean of the group. This occurs despite matching on other criteria. This can materially affect the outcome of a study because we expect the scores of the groups to change even without any intervening treatment. Therefore it becomes difficult or impossible to evaluate the effect of the treatment in studies employing such ex post facto quasi-experimental designs. The only sure way to avoid the problem is to randomly assign subjects to conditions in the first place.

**KEY TERMS**

analytical approach
chronological age
cross-sectional design
cross-sequential design
empirical approach
face validity
intelligence
longitudinal design
mental age
operational definition
parallel forms of a test

preload
quasi-experimental
regression artifact
regression to the mean
reliability
set point
split-half reliability
subject variables
test-retest reliability
time-lag design

**1.** Often psychological tests are constructed to measure some psychological construct, such as intelligence, depression, or dietary restraint. One prime requirement is for such tests to be reliable. What is reliability? Discuss three different ways of assessing reliability in a psychological test.

**2.** Discuss reasons why operational definitions are necessary in psychology. Provide two operational definitions for each of the following constructs: (a) thirst, (b) intelligence, (c) memory capacity, (d) sexual satisfaction, and (e) fear of snakes. Does it worry you that there can be more than one definition of the "same" construct?

**3.** Discuss the advantages and disadvantages of each of the following research designs for developmental research: (a) cross-sectional, (b) longitudinal, and (c) cross-sequential.

**4.** A psychotherapist is interested in evaluating the effectiveness of the new therapy she has invented. It is called Pet Therapy and involves convincing depressed people to keep a dog as a pet, with the hope being that by caring for the dog the person will cheer up. In order to evaluate the therapy, the therapist gives each of her patients a dog from the Humane Society to care for. She measures depression using a paper and pencil test (which has been shown to be reliable) a week before they get the pets and then two months later. She discovers that patients are much less depressed when assessed the second time, and thus concludes that Pet Therapy is a success. Discuss several things wrong with this piece of research and the conclusion drawn from it. How are regression artifacts likely to have played a part? How could the research be done better?

**5.** Discuss the following statement: "All experiments involving subject variables are quasi-experiments; the results obtained are always correlational in nature and possibly contaminated by confoundings." Is this statement true? Can you think of exceptions to it? In trying to do so, make a list of all the subject variables you can think of that might be of interest to psychologists.

# Psychology in Action

## A Demonstration of Regression Artifacts

A serious problem in many areas of research is known as statistical regression to the mean, or the regression artifact. You can best appreciate this phenomenon by allowing yourself to become a victim of it. Try the following experiment, proceeding through the steps as given:

**1.** Roll 6 dice on a table in front of you.

**2.** Place the 3 dice showing the lowest numbers on the left, and the 3 dice showing the highest numbers on the right. In case of ties, randomly assign the dice to the two groups.

**3.** Compute and record the mean number-per-die for each group of three dice.

**4.** Raise both hands over your head and loudly proclaim, "Improve, in the name of Science."

**5.** Roll the three low-scoring dice and compute a new mean number-per-die for the low group.

**6.** Roll the three high-scoring dice and compute a new mean number-per-die for the high group.

**7.** Compare the pre- and post-treatment scores for both groups. Combine your data with those of your classmates if possible.

On the average, this procedure will produce an increase in the performance of the low group, and a decrease in the performance of the high group. You might be tempted to conclude that invoking the name of Science has a beneficial effect on underachieving dice, and that overachieving dice require more individualized attention to maintain their outstanding performance. Such conclusions, however, fail to consider the effects of regression, which reflect the tendency for many types of measures to yield values close to their mean. You know that the roll of a fair die can yield values from 1 to 6, but that the average value from many rolls will be about 3.5. The likelihood of the average of three dice being close to 3.5 is higher than the likelihood of this average being close to 1 or 6. Thus, when you select three dice that give you a low average and roll them again, they will tend to yield a higher average value (a value closer to the mean of 3.5). In the same way, the three dice in the high group should yield a lower value when rolled again.

In determining the effects of experimental treatments, you must subtract the regression effect from the total observed change. In the dice experiment, for example, control groups of dice that showed the same values on the first roll but received no "treatment" should be rolled again. Only if the change from pre-test to post-test is significantly larger in the experimental group than in the control group can an effect caused by the treatment or independent variable be concluded. Studies that fail to control for regression, including many involving educational enrichment and psychotherapy, are difficult or impossible to evaluate.

# CHAPTER **13**

## Preview

*Social psychology* is devoted to the study of the effects of other people on the behavior of the individual. Since many of the topics studied involve complex social situations, the problem of gaining tight experimental control is in many cases a real one. We illustrate the pitfalls of experimentally studying a complex behavior by considering Milgram's behavioral studies of obedience. Another issue that concerns social psychologists is the influence of the experimenter's presence and instructions on the behavior of the subjects in the experiment. Demand characteristics and experimenter bias are discussed in terms of the social psychology of a hypnosis experiment. One way to try to overcome some problems associated with studying people in a laboratory setting is to study behavior in more natural settings, or "in the field." However, such field research has its own difficulties, which are discussed in the context of *bystander-intervention* research (when will people help in a crisis?)

## Chapter Outline

# SOCIAL INFLUENCE

*We know more about the atom than ourselves, and the consequences are everywhere to be seen.*

Carl Kaysen

The behavior of every human is determined by a web of complex social and cultural influences. Many of the acts we perform every day are determined by the culture and society into which we are born and raised. Our experience is limited by our culture so that we are exposed to only a very small set of potential actions humans might perform. Most people in our society will never speak Hottentot, sail outrigger canoes, or hunt wildebeest, for the very good reason that these activities are not part of our culture. In each society the individual's behavior to a large extent conforms to that of his or her "significant others," that is, family, peers, teachers, and so on.

The psychological study of how society affects the individual is part of the field of social psychology. This is a large subject and a tremendous variety of research topics falls under the general rubric of social psychology. Among other things, it is concerned with how people are influenced to change their attitudes and beliefs, how they form impressions of other people, why they like one another, the roots of aggression and violence, and the conditions determining altruism and helping. The list could easily be doubled. But with few exceptions, the topics studied by social psychologists have to do with the impact of society (other people) on the behavior of the individual.

**363**

Social psychologists generally are concerned with less global sorts of social influence than the influence of our entire cultural system on behavior. For example, a more direct form of social influence has to do with compliance or *obedience* to authority. How might one person or a group of people in authority induce others to follow commands, especially when those commands may be to perform antisocial or immoral acts? The most ghastly case of this in the twentieth century occurred in Nazi Germany, where a small cadre of fanatic Nazis instituted a program for the systematic murder of a large portion of the German populace and that of the countries it had conquered. The people who developed this plan were by far too few in number to implement it, so it was necessary for them to elicit the direct obedience of a large number of German citizens to carry out the murder of about six million Jews and five million others. They also had to receive the tacit acceptance of the bulk of the German population. Presumably this heinous program was carried out by many otherwise normal people.

Much more recently, the issue of the unthinking obedience to authority has been brought to public attention by other tragic events. In 1978 the Reverend Jim Jones, founder of Jonestown, Guyana, ordered hundreds of his followers to commit suicide by drinking poison. They obeyed. A dozen years earlier the issue of blind obedience was raised by the My Lai massacre during the Vietnam War. A portion of an interview between one of the participants and CBS reporter Mike Wallace went as follows:

*Q.* How many people did you round up?
*A.* Well, there was about forty, fifty people that we gathered in the center of the village. And we placed them in there, and it was like a little island, right there in the center of the village, I'd say . . . And . . .
*Q.* What kind of people—men, women, children?
*A.* Men, women, children.
*Q.* Babies?
*A.* Babies. And we huddled them up. We made them squat down and Lieutenant Calley came over and said, "You know what to do with them don't you?" And I said yes. So I took it for granted that he just wanted us to watch them. And he left, and came back about ten or fifteen minutes later and said, "How come you ain't killed them yet?" And I told him that I didn't think you wanted us to kill them, that you just wanted us to guard them. He said, "No, I want them dead." So.—
. . .
*Q.* And you killed how many? At that time?
*A.* Well, I fired them automatic, so you can't—You just spray the area on them and so you can't know how many you killed 'cause they were going fast. So I might have killed ten or fifteen of them.
*Q.* Men, women, and children?
*A.* Men, women, and children.
*Q.* And babies?
*A.* And babies . . .
*Q.* Why did you do it?

*A.* Why did I do it? Because I felt like I was ordered to do it, and it seemed like that, at the time I felt like I was doing the right thing, because, like I said, I lost buddies . . .

*Q.* What did these civilians—particularly the women and children, the old men—what did they do? What did they say to you?

*A.* They weren't much saying to them. They (were) just being pushed and they were doing what they was told to do.

*Q.* They weren't begging, or saying, "no . . . no," or . . .

*A.* Right. They were begging and saying, "no, no." And the mothers was hugging their children, and . . . but they kept right on firing. Well, we kept right on firing. They was waving their arms and begging. (*New York Times*, Nov. 25, 1969)

Why do otherwise normal people perform such terrible acts when ordered to? Stated differently, what are the social psychological forces that operate in determining obedience to authority? Later we shall discuss research that explores this issue.

THE ORIGINS
OF SOCIAL
PSYCHOLOGY

The enterprise of scientific psychology is only about a hundred years old, and the application of scientific method to the study of the interesting and complex phenomena of social psychology is even younger. The first two texts on social psychology appeared in 1908; one was written by William McDougall, a psychologist, and the other was written by E. A. Ross, a sociologist. In both books, the treatment of social psychology is very different from the approach used today. However, McDougall's book had a great impact in the field of psychology as a whole because he argued strongly that social behavior is largely determined by a variety of instincts that are inborn and relatively unaffected by either the history of a particular person or her or his present social situation. This view was thoroughly discredited and, even though the concept of instinct has made something of a comeback in psychology (Mason and Lott, 1976), no one today believes that it can explain complex human social behavior in the way McDougall tried to apply it.

Social psychology became established as an independent field of empirical study during the 1920s and 1930s. Many significant advances were made during this time, including the excellent early work of Muzafer Sherif (1935) on *social norms* (the generalized rules of conduct that tell us how we ought to behave), and the surprisingly powerful impact these rules have on our behavior. Sherif examined the influence of social norms and their development through studying a perceptual illusion, the autokinetic phenomenon. When a person is placed in a room that is completely dark, and a single spot of light is shown on one of the walls, the light appears to move. This movement occurs despite the fact that the light is actually stationary. The light seems to "move itself," thus giving rise to the name of the phenomenon.

Sherif was interested in how other people's judgments would affect those of a person perceiving the light. Would other people's judgments produce social norms that would affect the perception of an individual in this situation? What he discovered from a number of experiments was that a person's judgments of how the spot of light moved were greatly influenced by reports of other participants. If the experimenter (or another subject) led a subject to expect the light to move in a wide arc, then the subject would usually report that in fact it did seem to move in a wide arc. These experiments indicated that a person's perceptions could be manipulated by social influence in a dramatic way, and that this process could be studied experimentally. Thus Sherif's experiments helped provide the impetus for an experimental social psychology.

In Sherif's experiments, subjects were in a quite ambiguous situation. Perhaps they were easily influenced by others because they were so unsure of their own perceptions. Could we still find evidence for such great effects of social influence on perception and behavior if we made the situation less ambiguous? Solomon Asch (1951, 1956, 1958) asked this interesting question in his landmark experiments on conformity. Asch (1956, p. 2) remarked on the importance of the problem as follows: "Granting the great power of groups, may we simply conclude that they can induce persons to shift their decisions and convictions in almost any desired direction, that they can prompt us to call true what we yesterday deemed false, that they can make us invest the identical action with the aura of rightness or the stigma of grotesqueness and malice?" The answer to this question provided by his experiments was a qualified yes, which has led many social psychologists to become interested in the topic of *conformity*.

The basic procedure Asch used is as follows. A group of students were gathered into a room to take part in what was described as a study of visual discrimination. They were shown a single line and then three comparison lines and their task was to say which of the three comparison lines matched the standard. An example appears in figure 13–1. There were seven people in the group in one experiment, but there was only one real subject. The other six were confederates of the experimenter, or assistants. The situation was arranged so that the real subject always responded with his or her answer next to last, after five other "subjects" had already given their judgments. Everyone gave their answers out loud so that the rest of the group knew each person's response.

There were eighteen trials, and in each case one comparison line was equal to that of the standard. The confederates were instructed to give the correct answer on six of the trials, but to give a consistently wrong answer on twelve trials. The question of interest was whether or not the real subject in the procedure would conform to the group judgment and go against his or her own perception. A very large percentage of the subjects (about 70 percent—see table

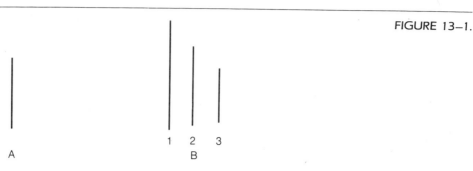

FIGURE 13–1.

Subjects in the perceptual discrimination task used by Asch were asked to decide which of the comparison lines (*B*) was the same length as that of the standard (*A*). How do you think you would respond if five people before you all said that comparison line 3 was the correct answer?

13–1) did conform to the erroneous judgments of the group on one or more of the twelve trials. A control group was also used in which the confederates never made an error; under these conditions only 5 percent of the real subjects made an error.

These experiments indicate that group judgments can have much power over the individual. However, later research uncovered many factors that can lessen the influence of the group. For example, if just one confederate responding before the subject does not go along with the group but answers correctly, then the subject will usually fail to follow the lead of the majority, too, and respond with the correct answer.

The distribution of conforming responses in the original Asch study. Of 50 subjects, 37 conformed by picking the same (incorrect) line that the confederates did on one or more trials. (From Wrightsman and Deaux, 1981)

TABLE 13–1

| Number of Conforming Responses | Number of True Subjects Who Gave This Number of Conforming Responses |
|---|---|
| 0 | 13 |
| 1 | 4 |
| 2 | 5 |
| 3 | 6 |
| 4 | 3 |
| 5 | 4 |
| 6 | 1 |
| 7 | 2 |
| 8 | 5 |
| 9 | 3 |
| 10 | 3 |
| 11 | 1 |
| 12 | 0 |
| Total 78 | 50 subjects |
| Mean 3.84 | |

At about the same time Sherif was writing about social norms, Kurt Lewin was also writing extensively about social psychology. Lewin provided a theoretical account of social behavior, known as field theory, as well as some interesting experiments. He was also quite concerned with applying the knowledge social psychologists were gathering to the solution of social problems. He helped found the Research Center for Group Dynamics (now at the University of Michigan) for the study of such topics as leadership and group productivity. He also played a major role in establishing "sensitivity training" and the T-group as a method of coping with complex human relationships.

Today social psychology is one of the fastest-growing subdisciplines within psychology. Social psychologists employ experimental methods in attempting to understand many issues that are of interest to most individuals, such as aggression, attraction, and altruism and helping. But because most people are interested in social psychology and have probably given some thought to the topics it includes, they sometimes tend to regard its phenomena and theories as mere common sense. Worse yet, some people even believe this area is one that should not be approached in a scientific way with the logic of experimental method. Lewin argued against this sort of reasoning some years ago:

> For thousands of years man's everyday experience with falling objects did not suffice to bring him to a correct theory of gravity. A sequence of very unusual, man-made experiences, so-called experiments, which grew out of the systematic search for the truth were necessary to bring about a change from less adequate to more adequate concepts. To assume that first-hand experience in the social world would automatically lead to the formation of correct concepts or to the creation of adequate stereotypes seems therefore unjustifiable. (1948, pp. 60–61)

## INTRODUCING THE VARIABLES IN SOCIAL PSYCHOLOGY

### Dependent Variables

The dependent variable in social psychological research is often a measure of preference (or liking, or belief, et cetera) obtained by having subjects fill out a questionnaire after experiencing some experimental treatment. For example, subjects might be asked to judge on a seven-point scale how much they liked or disliked the other subjects in the experiment, or how much they agree with the position that abortion is murder. These measures would usually be taken only after an experimental treatment was designed to influence the judgments in some way. Although much useful information has been gained through the questionnaire technique, social psychologists are increasingly turning to techniques by which overt behavior, rather than covert preference, is measured. Though rating scales remain an important dependent measure in social psychological research, many experimenters try to also include behavioral measurement. Instead of asking a person how much animosity he or she feels toward another subject in an aggression experiment, the experimenter might set up the situation so that the subject has an opportunity to deliver mild electric shocks to the other subject, in the guise of a learning experiment. Thus, aggression can be measured in terms of how many shocks are delivered. (Actually, the confederate would receive no shocks.) Similarly, rather than ask a male subject how attracted he is to a female confederate in the experiment, the experimenter might measure how much he talks to her, smiles at her, or whether or not he asks her out. These are behavioral measures of aggression and attraction. Generally, the more converging measures we can obtain of the same hypothetical entity (aggression, attraction, and so on) that agree, the more faith we can place in the relationship discovered in the experiment.

## Independent Variables

Independent variables in social psychology experiments usually are charcteristics of a social situation or of the people in a situation that can be manipulated. In an experiment on attitude change, the persuasiveness of a message might be varied by manipulating the number of arguments used in supoort of the position being argued (for example, that abortion is murder). In an experiment testing the hypothesis that aggression increases as the temperature rises, the experimenter might vary the temperature of the room in which a possibly aggressive activity occurs between a subject and a confederate. In an experiment on conformity, an investigator might vary the number of people who disagree with some judgment that a subject has made, to see whether the subject will be more likely to change his or her mind. Variables concerning the characteristics of the subjects in the experiment, such as sex and race, also can be manipulated. Are people more likely to help (or aggress against, or like, or agree with) people of their own sex or race?

## Control Variables

The introduction of experimental control in social psychological research is quite tricky, since the situations dealt with are usually complex. It is often very difficult to vary one or several factors while keeping all others constant, the prerequisite for providing firm inferences on the relationship of independent and dependent variables in experiments. The next section deals with this issue.

---

**Topic:** Experimental Control

**Illustration:** Obedience to Authority

**13.1**
**EXPERIMENTAL
TOPICS AND
RESEARCH
ILLUSTRATIONS**

---

Psychologists perform experiments to discover the causes of behavior. First, the investigator selects a problem of interest: Why does some behavior occur? Second, a hypothesis is suggested that provides a tentative understanding of the behavior. Usually the hypothesis will specify factors that cause or determine the behavior. The researcher will then try to create experimental conditions to test the hypothesis. If one factor has been pinpointed by the hypothesis as the alleged cause of the behavior, will the behavior in fact be affected when the factor is manipulated in a systematic way? In the experiment, the factor that is manipulated is called the independent variable, and the behavior measured is called the dependent variable. *Experimental control* has to do with the researcher gaining control over other factors in the situation so that he or she can be certain that the change in behavior is caused by the independent variable and not some other factor. The more complex the behavior of interest, the harder it is to gain control over all other relevant aspects of the situation.

*Experimental error* occurs when a change in the dependent variable—the behavior of interest—is produced by some factor other than the independent variable. Experimental control attempts to minimize or eliminate experimental error. One main source of experimental error is *confounding*, which occurs when a second variable is unintentionally varied along with the independent variable of interest. When this happens, the researcher cannot be certain whether the independent variable or the second, confounded, variable produced the change in the dependent variable.

There are several ways of reducing experimental error caused by confounding. The most direct is to control all other variables of interest, so that only the independent variable is manipulated. The other factors that are kept constant are referred to as *control variables*, as we have discussed previously (see chapter 3).

Sometimes it is not possible to rigidly control a variable across all conditions of an experiment, so other techniques must be used. This problem occurs, for example, when a between-subjects experimental design is used. If there are two conditions, an experimental and a control condition, which differ in the manipulation of the independent variable, a researcher does not want to have any second variable on which the two groups also differ. However, in a between-subjects design, there is at least one other difference in conditions, which is built in—different groups of subjects are tested in the two conditions.

When it is not possible to control a variable, as with subjects in a between-subjects design, the experimenter randomizes the variable to discount its influence. Thus, if a between-subjects design, is used, the researcher randomly assigns subjects to conditions. (The assignment is based on some scheme that guarantees true randomization, such as the random-numbers table, described at the end of the book (table F). As subjects arrive for the experiment, the researcher could use the numbers in the table's rows to assign subjects to the conditions. If there are two conditions, odd numbers would indicate subjects in one condition, and even numbers would represent those in the other condition.)

*Randomization* guarantees that even though the variable cannot be controlled, its influence will not affect the outcome of the experiment by being confounded with the independent variable. Although different subjects are assigned to the two conditions, the researcher can rest assured that on average the subjects in the two conditions are equal in all important respects. Thus if there is a statistically reliable difference in behavior between the two conditions, it could be safely attributed to the operation of the independent variable and not to the fact that there were different subjects in the two conditions.

In social psychological research, investigators are interested in situations that are generally more complex than those considered thus far in the book. That is, in social situations there are many variables besides the independent variable which must be controlled or randomized before the researcher can be certain that any change in a dependent variable is caused by the independent variable.

How do we go about studying a complex social phenomenon in a controlled setting? Consider, for example, the problem of obedience to authority discussed at the beginning of this chapter. Obviously, there are a great number of factors to consider. And how do we measure obedience? Obedience is an important topic that should be considered carefully and thoroughly understood. But how can we bring such a complex pehnomenon into a controlled setting in order to study the critical factors underlying it, while holding the others constant?

Stanley Milgram answered this question in a fascinating series of experiments which culminated in a book on the topic (Milgram, 1974). We will consider these experiments as a case history of bringing a complicated social psychological topic into the lab for close scrutiny. The original experiments (Milgram, 1963, 1964a, 1965) all used a common methodology to establish obedience to authority in a controlled experimental setting. In the first study Milgram (1963) used male subjects who responded to advertisements to participate, for pay, in a study of memory and learning at Yale University. When a subject appeared at the laboratory, he met another subject (actually a confederate of the experimenter) who was a 47-year-old accountant specially trained for his role. The confederate appeared rather mild-mannered and likable (figure 13–2). Subjects were told that very little was known about the effects of punishment on memory and that one of them was to be the teacher and one the learner in a scientific study of this topic. The subjects drew slips of paper from a hat to determine who was to appear in which role, but in actuality the drawing was rigged so that the naïve subject was always the teacher and the confederate was always the learner. The experimenter was played by a rather severe 31-year-old biology teacher who wore a white lab coat. The learner was strapped into an electric chair to prevent

**FIGURE 13–2.**
The learner (or victim) in Milgram's original study on obedience to authority. Would you risk seriously harming this man in an experiment if someone told you to? Milgram's findings suggest that you would. (Milgram, 1974, p. 17)

excessive movement, and electrodes were placed on his wrists with paste "to avoid blisters and burns." In response to a question by the learner the experimenter said, "Although the shocks can be extremely painful, they cause no permanent tissue damage" (Milgram, 1963, p. 373).

The teacher-subjects were required to read a paired-associate list to the learners (see chapter 10) and then later to test them on the list by presenting a stimulus and four alternatives, one of which was correct. The learner-confederate was required to pick the correct response from among the four alternatives and say it aloud. If he made an error, the teacher-subject was instructed to give him an electric shock by pressing a switch on an imposing shock-generator. Although the confederate actually received no shocks, the subject had been given a mild sample shock at the beginning of the experiment to convince him that the generator was real. During the course of the experiment, subjects were required to increase the amount of shock every time the learner made an error, and the primary dependent measure was the amount of electric shock the naïve subject was willing to give. The shock generator consisted of thirty lever switches clearly labeled as proceeding from 15 to 450 volts (see figure 13–3). There were seven switches (in each of four groups), and they were given the following verbal descriptions (from left to right): Slight Shock, Moderate Shock, Strong Shock, Very Strong Shock, Intense Shock, Extreme-Intensity Shock, and

FIGURE 13–3.
The shock-generator that
subjects were required to
use in Milgram's
experiments. (Milgram,
1974, p. 25)

Danger: Severe Shock. Two other switches at the far right were marked XXX.

From the beginning, the learner-confederate made errors and thus the subject-teacher was supposed to administer ever-increasing electric shocks. In the original study the confederate was out of sight of the subject, but he could be heard. His responses were standardized on tape. "Starting with 75 volts the learner begins to grunt and moan. At 150 volts he demands to be let out of the experiment. At 180 volts he cries out that he can no longer stand the pain. At 300 volts he refuses to provide any more answers. . . . The experimenter (then) instructs the naive subject to treat the absence of an answer as equivalent to a wrong answer, and to follow the usual shock procedure" (Milgram, 1965, p. 61).

All subjects who participated in this procedure appeared very nervous and upset and frequently asked the experimenter what they should do next. Whenever subjects seemed unwilling to continue the experimenter had a series of statements (which accelerated to commands) the subject was to obey. The first was rather gentle: "Please go on." Next was "The experiment requires that you continue," which progressed to "It is absolutely essential that you continue." Finally the experimenter said "You have no other choice. You *must* go on."

This is the basic procedure by which Milgram hoped to study obedience in a controlled setting. Let us ask ourselves one interesting question before considering the results: Does this setting appear to capture the essential components of obedience as it naturally occurs? Although in this experiment one person gives another commands that have a socially undesirable consequence (harming another person), as could occur in a natural setting, one element lacking in Milgram's situation that typically exists in similar real-world situations is the power of the person who is commanding (the experimenter, in this case) to harm the subject if the subject fails to obey orders. The subject could always simply get up and walk out of the experiment, never to see the experimenter again. So when considering Milgram's results, we should bear in mind that a powerful source of obedience in the real world was lacking in this situation.

Nonetheless, Milgram's (1963) results are truly remarkable. Of the 40 subjects originally tested in this situation, 26 (65 percent) "went all the way" and gave the confederate the full series of shocks, whereas the other 14 broke off the experiment by refusing to continue at or after the 300-volt level. The results are portrayed in figure 13–4. The subjects here were not impassive, cruel torturers. They were (just like you and me) normal people who felt a great deal of conflict in this situation. One chapter of Milgram's (1974) book contains transcripts which show that many subjects felt anguish but nonetheless continued under the directions of the experimenter. Most were sweating profusely and many were trembling. Another symptom of their discomfort was the occurrence of nervous laughter which became uncontrollable in several subjects. One viewer of the experiment commented:

> I observed a mature and initially poised businessman enter the laboratory smiling and confident. Within 20 minutes he was reduced to a nervous, stuttering wreck, who was rapidly approaching a point of nervous collapse. He constantly pulled on his earlobe and twisted his hands. At one point he pushed his fist into his forehead and muttered:

**FIGURE 13–4.**

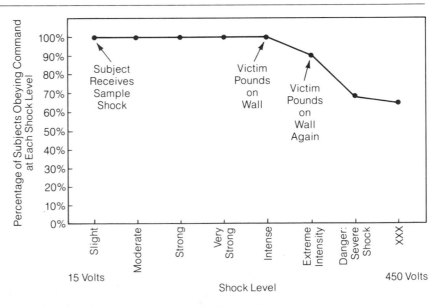

Percentage of subjects who obeyed commands to continue shocking the victim at various levels of shock intensity. Even when the victim reacted as if in pain and stopped responding to the memory task, almost two-thirds of the subjects obeyed the experimenter and administered shocks at the level of "danger" and beyond (from Baron & Byrne, 1977, p. 292).

"Oh God, let's stop it." And yet he continued to respond to every word of the experimenter, and obeyed to the end. (Milgram, 1963, p. 377)

*Conditions encouraging obedience.* You might have noticed something lacking in the description of Milgram's study, something crucial to an experiment. There was no variation of an independent variable in the experiment, and thus no information was gained about the conditions that enhance or diminish obedience to authority in this situation. Although Milgram employed a controlled setting to produce laboratory obedience, his first study is better referred to as a demonstration rather than an experiment since there was no manipulation of an independent variable. Milgram, of course, realized this and made no claims to the contrary. In the original report he outlined areas where systematic variations in the procedure might lead to useful new information about conditions necessary for obedience, and he provided some of these variations in later experiments.

One factor that could have encouraged obedience in the original study was its setting; it was conducted at Yale University, an institution presumably held in high regard by the subject (at least before the experiment). Perhaps the general Yale aura helped foster obedience, since presumably this well-known institution would not allow its premises to be used for shady purposes. Milgram (1965) reported a later study similar to the original in most details except that it was done in an old office building in a rather sleazy part of Bridgeport, Connecticut, under the auspices of Research Associates of Brideport, a fictitious company. Although compliance was somewhat reduced in the Bridgeport study (48 percent delivered the maximum shock versus 65 percent in the original Yale sample), the difference was apparently not significant and Milgram concluded that Yale's reputation was not responsible for the original high level of compliance. Since this conclusion is based on a failure to reject the null hypothesis, it is suspect (see chapter 3), especially since there was a rather large absolute difference between the two studies (17 percent). But it does seem safe to conclude that the Yale setting was not the critical factor in producing obedience.

It is of interest to ask what conclusions Milgram could have reached from this study if there had been a significant reduction in obedience in Bridgeport relative to the original Yale study. Could he have concluded that it was the nature of the setting (Yale versus a dilapidated office building) that produced the results? The answer is *no*, or at least *not strictly*, since many other conditions varied between the two situations besides the setting (for example, the city and the time of year). Thus at least several variables were potentially confounded. It may have been that the different settings produced the result, since the experimenter and the confederates were the same in the two studies. But, in general, conclusions drawn from a comparison of conditions across different experiments is hazardous, since one can never be certain that all other conditions were held constant and that no confounding occurred. What could Milgram have concluded if the Bridgeport volunteers responding to his advertisement had turned out to differ in occupation or socioeconomic status from the Yale sample? Very little indeed. (In fact, the two samples did not differ in any obvious way.)

In more tightly controlled experiments, other variables have been found to have a great effect on obedience. When other people serve in the experiment as subjects who are supposed to provide shocks (though they are actually confederates), their behavior markedly affects that of the naïve subject. In one case Milgram (1965) had the two confederates refuse to continue at predetermined levels of shock. The results are portrayed in figure 13–5, which indicates that the naïve subjects were much better able to refuse to continue when others did. On the other hand, in another experiment when there were two conforming peers who encouraged the subject to increase the shock level, subjects administered much greater shock than when they determined the shock level themselves (Milgram, 1964a).

Another interesting manipulation Milgram (1965) tried was to vary the closeness of the victim so that in one condition the subject could only hear the victim moan and complain, in another condition he was in the same room so he could also see the victim, and in yet another condition the subject was actually instructed to force the learner's arm down onto the metal shock plate on each

**FIGURE 13–5.**

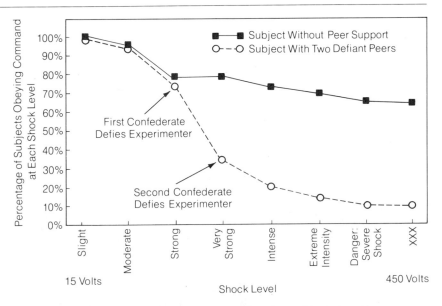

Group pressure as an influence in defying authority. When subjects do not have peer support, 65 percent continue to obey the experimenter's commands to give stronger and stronger shocks throughout the experiment. When subjects are with peers who defy the experimenter, only 10 percent continue to obey the experimenter's commands (from Baron & Byrne, 1977, p. 297).

trial (figure 13–6). Although obedience decreased with closeness of the victim, from 74% to 40% to 30% obeying the experimenter's instructions to the end in the different conditions, it is still remarkable that almost one-third of the subjects continued to give the shocks even when they had to hold down the person's hand.

Milgram's research on obedience allows us to see how an interesting and complicated problem concerning social influence can be investigated in the relatively controlled setting of the social psychology laboratory. Although not all aspects of obedience are transported into the lab (for example, the person issuing commands had no real power over the subject), the situation was still compelling enough to produce a dramatically high level of compliance.

Before leaving this topic we should briefly mention three more issues. Many people who encounter Milgram's research say "I wouldn't do that." The point is that, given the appropriate setting, you probably would. Yale college students were tested in the original situation and their results were no different from those of the "real people" in the New Haven community. Perhaps after reading this you would not participate in a situation exactly like Milgram's, but you would probably do similar things without giving them much thought.

A second aspect of Milgram's studies that often provokes comment is whether or not it was (and is) ethical to put subjects through this procedure, since their cooperation is obtained under false pretenses and the procedure is quite stressful. These issues have been debated by Baumrind (1964) and Milgram (1964b) at some length, so we will simply refer the interested reader to these articles and Appendix I of Milgram's (1974) book for comment on the ethical

FIGURE 13–6.
An obedient subject shocking a subject while forcing his arm onto the metal plate. (Milgram, 1974, p. 37)

issues involved in this research. (We consider the problem of ethics in Chapter 14.)

Finally, as Milgram points out repeatedly in his writing, obedience in itself is not necessarily bad. In fact, if almost all of us did not obey the numerous laws and persons in authority in our society, life would be all but unthinkable. It is only when one is asked to obey commands that produce harm that the issue arises.

## 13.2

### EXPERIMENTAL TOPICS AND RESEARCH ILLUSTRATIONS

**Topic:** Demand Characteristics and Experimenter Bias

**Illustration:** Hypnosis

Psychological experiments typically employ as much experimental control as can be mustered by the prudent investigator. This section is concerned with two sources of bias that even the most conscientious researcher may well overlook: bias introduced by the experimenters and by the subjects themselves. The problem of *experimenter bias* is potentially prevalent in all sciences. The most blatant form of bias is the deliberate faking of data. The social pressures that exist to be productive, to publish many articles, and to find spectacular results so as to receive more money from granting agencies have led some investigators to fake results. Broad and Wade (1982) consider a number of documented cases of such fraud and discuss the problem at length. Unfortunately, nothing much can be done by scientists to reduce this sort of fraud, except to be vigilant and to punish offenders whenever they are caught. Such frauds may be uncovered when other researchers try to replicate and confirm the work.

Experimenter bias refers not only to the conscious cases of fraud, but also to the much more subtle influences that experimenters may unknowingly exert on the outcome of their research. That such effects do occur has been established by much research as well as by anecdotal observations. In chapter 9 we considered a case of experimenter bias in a series of experiments concerned with the operant conditioning of conversation, where subjects who expected one result found it and subjects who expected the opposite result also found it (Azrin et al., 1961). In this case it is unclear whether the experimenter effects were caused by blatant faking of data or the more subtle sort of experimenter bias that we are considering here. This more covert form of bias may be inadvertently introduced in a number of ways. The experimenter may interact with the subjects in the different conditions in slightly different ways; the tone of voice and emphasis may change when the instructions are read, and, similarly, facial cues, gestures, and so forth may differ. The experimenter may not even be aware of such effects, but expectations of the way the subjects should behave in the different conditions may change her or his behavior very slightly to help produce the expected effect.

Rosenthal (1966, 1969) reviewed work (much of it his own) on the influence of experimenter expectancies and discussed various solutions to the problem. One of the most effective solutions is for the experimenter to keep himself or herself insulated in some way from knowing either the hypotheses being considered or the particular conditions of the subject being tested. In such a case, the experimenter is said to be blind with respect to conditions. Unfortunately, it is difficult or impractical to satisfy this condition in much research because the experimenter must administer the conditions.

The problem of experimenter bias, although potentially dangerous, may not be as serious as is sometimes assumed. Barber and Silver (1968) exhaustively analyzed the research on experimenter expectancy effects and argue that there is still not enough evidence to conclude that such effects are proven phenomena. Regardless of the validity of this claim, other factors make us believe that the importance of experimenter effects is often exaggerated. We have emphasized repeatedly throughout this book that the results of any individual experiment need to be viewed in the context of other, similar experiments before one can make a generalization. If a particular experimental result is considered important, one can rest assured that much future research will be directed toward discovering the conditions under which it holds, explicating the mechanisms involved, and so on. In the course of such research there will be many occasions for the basic phenomenon to be replicated by experimenters with many different views on the subject, some hoping to find it, some hoping not to. If the phenomenon is replicated by all, then we can assume that it is not produced by experimenter bias; if not, we can suspect experimenter bias of being responsible for part of the difficulty. The important point is that experimenter bias, or even the blatant dishonesty of an isolated investigator, will be discovered in the normal course of scientific inquiry. Such effects should still be guarded against with all possible caution, of course. It is simply that in the long run, effects of experimenter bias will likely be winnowed out in the scientific process.

A potentially more powerful source of bias, which is unique to psychology, has to do with the subject and what she or he expects will occur in a psychological experiment. Martin Orne (1962, 1969) pioneered in making psychologists aware of this problem. He pointed out that subjects entering an experiment have some general notions of what to expect and are probably trying to figure out the specific purpose of the experiment. They are likely to believe that reasonable care will be taken for their well-being and that whatever the experimenter asks them to do will serve a useful purpose. They will also want to know this purpose and seek clues in the experimental situation. Because many psychological experiments, especially ones in social psychology like Milgram's obedience studies, would provide uninteresting results if the true purpose of the study were known (everyone would soon refuse to obey the experimenter), elaborate deceptions are often involved to mask the true purposes of the experiment. But, as Orne points out, these might sometimes be rather transparent. At any rate, the general problem exists as to how the subject's expectations affect or determine her or his behavior in an experiment. As Orne notes:

> Insofar as the subject cares about the outcome, his perception of his role and of the hypothesis being tested will become a significant determinant of his behavior. The cues which govern his behavior—which communicate what is expected of him and what the experimenter hopes to find—can therefore be crucial variables. Some time ago I proposed that these cues be called "demand characteristics of an experiment."
> ... They include the scuttlebutt about the experiment, its setting, implicit and explicit instructions, the person of the experimenter, subtle cues provided by him, and, of particular importance, the experimental procedure. (Orne, 1969, p. 146).

If results of an experiment are produced by *demand characteristics* of the experimental situation, they will not generalize to other situations. It is well known that people's awareness of being part of an experiment will greatly affect their behavior. In Psychology in Action at the end of the chapter, we suggest an exercise you can carry out to demonstrate this point.

In all laboratory experiments subjects realize that they are being observed and that their behavior is being carefully monitored. The subjects' expectations of how they are supposed to behave may greatly determine their performance in the experiment. Another phenomenon of this sort is well known to medical researchers and is called the *placebo effect*. This refers to the fact that when patients in medical research are given a chemically inert substance and told that it is medicine that should help them, they often show an improvement in the illness or find relief from their pain. Thus when a drug is evaluated in medical research it is not enough to compare a group of patients who receive the drug with a group who do not, because the patients who receive the drug may improve simply because of the placebo effect. Instead, the drug group is also compared to a placebo group, so that the effect of the drug can be measured in relation to the placebo effect. Usually the doctors administering the drugs are also blind to the condition of the patients, so that their expectations of improvement cannot affect the results.

In one line of laboratory research Orne (1962) sought to find a task that was so meaningless and boring that normal subjects would refuse to perform it. He was interested in finding such a task because he then wanted to see whether or not subjects under the influence of hypnosis would perform the task when instructed to do so. One experiment involved giving subjects two thousand sheets filled with rows of random digits. The subjects were instructed to add together the many pairs of digits in each row on all the sheets. Clearly it was an impossible task, so Orne assumed that the control subjects would quickly realize this and refuse to go on. But instead the subjects, who were deprived of their watches, kept at the task for hours on end with little decrement in performance (figure 13–7). Subjects in a later study (that aimed at making the task even more onerous and meaningless) were told that after each sheet was completed they were to pick up a card and follow the direction written on it. Each card instructed the subject to tear up the sheet of paper into a minimum of thirty-two pieces and continue on to the next sheet. Still subjects persisted for hours. When questioned, they explained their behavior by saying that since they were in an experiment, they figured there must be a good reason for the request (an endurance test or the like).

FIGURE 13–7.

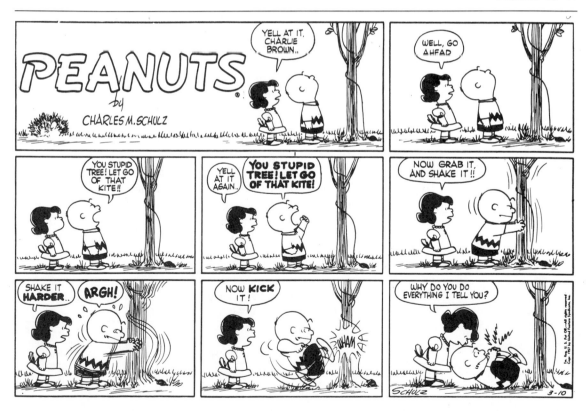

Drawing by Charles Schulz; © 1957 United Features Syndicate, Inc.

Most people will resist the suggestions of another person more than our gullible friend Charlie Brown, but when placed in an experiment most of us become like him. Orne might well have asked his subjects the same question Lucy asked in the cartoon.

Investigators have asked subjects under hypnosis to do all sorts of things, often with notable success. One apparently well-established finding is that subjects under hypnosis can be led to perform various antisocial and destructive acts, such as throwing acid in someone's face and handling venomous snakes (Rowland, 1939; Young, 1952). Orne and Evans (1965) suspected that this behavior might have been owing more to the demand characteristics of the situation than to the effects of hypnosis. They asked subjects to perform a series of dangerous acts, such as grasping a venomous snake, taking a coin from fuming acid, and throwing nitric acid in the experimenter's face. There were several treatment conditions: (1) subjects who were under deep hypnosis, (2) subjects who were told to simulate or pretend that they were under hypnosis, (3) awake control subjects who were not asked to simulate hypnosis, but who were pressed by the experimenter to comply with the requests, (4) awake control subjects who were not pressed to comply, and (5) people who were asked to perform the tasks without being made part of an experiment. The experimenter in this study was blind to the conditions of the subjects, so as not to affect their behavior. The results are summarized in Table 13–2. As would be expected, people not in the experimental setting refused to carry out the antisocial tasks, but as other investigators had reported, a high percentage of hypnotized subjects did carry out the tasks as instructed. However, *all* simulating control subjects also performed the tasks and even the nonsimulating controls performed them to a large extent if they were pressed to comply, which demonstrates the power of the experimental situation.

The conclusion to be drawn is that hypnosis is not necessarily responsible for subjects performing the antisocial acts. Rather, demand characteristics of the experimental situation, including the setting, the instructions, and the way subjects think they are supposed to behave while under hypnosis, are sufficient to produce the antisocial acts. Perhaps people can be induced to perform antisocial acts under deep hypnosis, but studies currently available

| TABLE 13–3 | Percentage of subjects who performed dangerous tasks in response to requests by the experimenter. (Adapted from Orne and Evans, 1965) | | |
|---|---|---|---|
| Subject Group | Grasp Venomous Snake | Take Coin from Acid | Throw Acid at Experimenter |
| Real hypnosis | 83 | 83 | 83 |
| Simulating hypnosis | 100 | 100 | 100 |
| Waking control— press to comply | 50 | 83 | 83 |
| Waking control— without press to comply | 50 | 17 | 17 |
| Nonexperimental | 0 | 0 | 0 |

do not offer reliable evidence to support the idea that hypnosis is responsible for the behavior.

The use of *simulating control subjects,* as in the Orne and Evans experiment, is one way of attacking the problem of demand characteristics. The logic is essentially the same as that for using a placebo condition in medical research. The demand characteristics of the situation are assumed to be the same for subjects in both the experimental condition and the simulating control condition. If the experimental manipulation (say, hypnosis) is truly effective, then the behavior of the experimental subjects should differ reliably from that of the simulating controls.

The problem of demand characteristics is a thorny one, especially in social psychological research. As Orne (1969, p. 156) points out, these concerns are less important in those experimental studies which do not involve deception and which encourage subjects to respond as accurately as possible. But in studies where optimal performance may not be encouraged for various reasons and where deception is often involved, results may be contaminated by demand characteristics. In the hypnosis study, subjects in all experimental conditions said they performed the acts because they were in an experiment and felt assured, despite rather convincing pretenses to the contrary, that the experimenter had taken precautions against harming them and himself. (They were correct.) Interestingly, Orne and Holland (1968) argued that Milgram's results on obedience may have largely been produced by similar demand characteristics in the experimental situation. Subjects might have seen through Milgram's deceptions and, at any rate, assumed that no one would really be harmed in the experiment, since the experimenter himself never became concerned. Milgram (1972) replied, and criticized their argument on various grounds. He argued that if his subjects were just doing what they thought the experimenter expected of them and were not really concerned about the safety of the person they were shocking, they would not have shown signs of nervousness and conflict, such as perspiration, trembling, and uncontrollable laughter.

---

**Topic:** Field Research

**Illustration:** Bystander Intervention

**13.3**

**EXPERIMENTAL TOPICS AND RESEARCH ILLUSTRATIONS**

---

The problems of demand characteristics in laboratory settings, along with other factors, have caused many social psychologists to turn to *field research* in recent years. Rather than attempting to bring some phenomenon into the laboratory for study in a controlled setting, the researcher instead attempts to introduce enough control into a setting (in the "field") to allow inferences to be made about how variations in an independent variable affect a dependent variable. In such cases there is no problem of generalizing to the real world, since the experiment is conducted in the real world to begin with. However, in some ways field research in social psychology is even more difficult to conceive and carry out than laboratory research. We shall discuss some of these problems before examining a field study.

The crux of experimental method in laboratory research is to abstract relevant variables from complex situations in nature and then reproduce parts of these situations, so that by varying different factors we may determine their contribution to the behavior of interest. By bringing the phenomenon into the laboratory we gain control over the situation. The main problems in field research have to do with this issue of control. How can we gain control over and manipulate the independent variable in a field setting? Presuming we can do this, how do we then simultaneously go about controlling or randomizing all the other factors which are likely to be varying willy-nilly in complex situations? And what do we measure, anyway, in a naturally occurring setting? What should our dependent variable be? There are all sorts of things we could measure, but how directly related are they to the phenomenon of interest? These are very difficult questions, the answers will depend to a great extent on the problem investigated and the ingenuity of the individual researchers in providing control in a complex situation.

The issue of specifying dependent variables was treated systematically by Webb, Campbell, Schwartz, and Sechrest in a book called *Unobtrusive Measures: Nonreactive Research in the Social Sciences* (1966). The authors were concerned with the problem of people's behavior changing when they know they are being observed or studied. They discussed a number of "unobtrusive" measures which can be taken on behavior without the subject's knowledge, and which are thus suitable for use in field research in psychology and other social sciences. Although their book contains many clever and ingenious suggestions, most of the unobtrusive measures they described have little bearing on many psychological problems under active investigation by psychologists. The primary problem in obtaining a good dependent measure, or providing a good operational definition of whatever underlying construct one is trying to measure, is ensuring that a plausible link exists between the construct and what is measured. This is a problem in all research, as is that of finding converging operations on a construct, but in field research these problems are magnified. The dependent measure seems often only tangentially related to the underlying construct, as when, say, a standard mortality ratio is used as an index of social pathology (see chapter 14).

Another problem in field research is the question of ethics. Can we justify involving people in research in the name of science when they do not volunteer and are in fact unsuspecting? Should we allow ourselves to manipulate our fellow citizens (via the independent variable) and then record their reactions (the dependent variables)? This is especially a problem when the manipulation involves inducing stress or embarrassment or some other undesirable state. In the lab, psychologists can (and are required to) debrief participants after the experiment and tell them why they were placed in this uncomfortable situation, but in the field this is usually not done, since the participants are not even aware that they are being manipulated and observed by psychologists. Psychologists have decided, not without a certain amount of self-interest, that field research is allowable as long as no great stress or harm is occasioned on the "subjects." Whether or not citizens themselves will agree with this judgment when (if) the legitimacy of field research ever becomes an issue is another matter. Certainly we do not tolerate manipulation and eavesdropping by government agencies, and it seems unlikely that the public at large will find psychologists' scientific motives any more pure. The issue has not yet arisen to a great extent, but when it does, it may spell the death knell for field research.

Before discussing a field study concerned with bystander intervention, let us examine how social psychologists became interested in this topic. Consider the following actual incidents.

> Kitty Genovese is set upon by a maniac as she returns home from work at 3 A.M. Thirty-eight of her neighbors in Kew Gardens come to their windows when she cries out in terror; none come to her assistance even though her stalker takes over half an hour to murder her. No one even so much as calls the police. She dies.
>
> Andrew Mormille is stabbed in the stomach as he rides the A train home in Manhattan. Eleven other riders watch the 17-year-old boy as he bleeds to death; none come to his assistance even though his attackers have left the car. He dies.
>
> An 18-year-old switchboard operator, alone in her office in the Bronx, is raped and beaten. Escaping momentarily, she runs naked and bleeding to the street, screaming for help. A crowd of 40 passersby gathers and watches as, in broad daylight, the rapist tries to drag her back upstairs; no one interferes. Finally, two policemen happen by and arrest her assailant.

These vignettes are taken verbatim from a fascinating book by Bibb Latané and John Darley called *The Unresponsive Bystander: Why Doesn't He Help?* (1970, pp. 1–2), in which they describe their research in trying to answer this question. Although there are potentially many reasons the bystander may not help in such crisis situations, one that cropped up early in this research had to do with the number of bystanders. The more people who observe a crisis and who are potential helpers, the *less* likely is any one bystander to help the victim. In one laboratory experiment (Darley and Latané, 1968) subjects were led to believe that they were participating (via an intercom system) in a discussion on personal problems in college life, with either one, two, or five other students. The experimenter left the scene after the subject had been given instructions. The discussion began with the students introducing themselves, but suddenly one of the students started to act, in a very convincing way, as though he were undergoing an epileptic seizure. (Actually only one subject participated at a time; the other voices heard were recorded.) The interest was in seeing how the subjects would behave when they thought there were zero, one, or four other bystanders. The results are shown in table 13–3, where it can be seen that the percentage of subjects trying to help the stranger decreased as the number of other bystanders increased. Even when subjects did respond to the emergency, they were slower when they thought others were also present in the situation. There is apparently a "diffusion of responsibility," so that the more people present, the less any individual feels responsible to intervene (and the more people there are to potentially witness one's making a fool of oneself). A student in a class with a hundred other students feels less responsible for answering an instructor's question than a student in a class with five others.

An interesting field study on bystander intervention was conducted on a New York City subway by Piliavin, Rodin, and Piliavin (1969). (We discussed another bystander intervention study by these researchers in chapter 3). They picked an express run that lasted 7.5 minutes between two stations, and produced an emergency, in order to observe who responded and how fast. Four teams of students conducted the experiment, which involved the collapse of one person on the train (the victim) about seventy seconds after it left the station. The independent variables were the race of the victim and whether or not the victim appeared to be ill (he carried a cane) or drunk (he carried a liquor bottle wrapped in a brown paper bag and also smelled of liquor). Two other experimenters served as observers and recorded the dependent measures, which were whether or not help was offered and the time that elapsed before help was offered. In addition, they recorded the race of the helper, the number of helpers, and the number and racial composition of the group of bystanders or observers.

TABLE 13–3      Both the percentage of people who help a person having an epileptic seizure and the speed with which they respond are affected by the number of others in the situation. As the number increases, fewer individuals try to help and more time passes before help is given. (Darley and Latané, 1968)

| Number of Bystanders | Percentage of Subjects Trying to Help Stranger | Number of Seconds Elapsing before Subject Tries to Help |
|---|---|---|
| 1 | 85 | 52 |
| 2 | 62 | 93 |
| 5 | 31 | 166 |

Some of the predictions were that people would be more likely to help a person of their own race than of another race, that help would more likely be given when the victim was perceived as ill rather than drunk, and that the tendency to help would decrease with the number of observers. Interestingly, these predictions (which seem to accord with common sense) were only partially verified. There was a clear tendency for help to be offered more readily to ill than drunk victims (on 95 percent of the trials for the ill victim versus 50 percent for the drunk victim). But in both of these conditions, the number of observers did not in any way affect the likelihood that help would be offered, or the speed with which it was offered. Also, the race of the ill victim did not affect whether one or the other race helped. However, when the victim was drunk, people of the same race helped the victim more than did people of a different race.

Let us consider again the diffusion-of-responsibility theory. This hypothesis was developed by Darley and Latané when they analyzed factors that might have influenced bystanders who failed to respond to crises in natural settings. They tested this idea in a laboratory situation by systematically varying the number of bystanders, and found support for it. But then when the idea was tested in the natural circumstances of the field (where the phenomenon was first noticed), no evidence was found for it! Presumably the results differed not because of any great difference between field and laboratory research, but because of other subtle factors that influence helping in such complex situations.

One other lesson to be drawn from bystander-intervention studies is that the responses of others greatly determine what we perceive as the social reality of a situation. If forty other people stand around watching a murder, you and I will, too. Such behavior is seen as appropriate, since everyone else is doing it. Why risk our necks, when all these others could help? Where are the police when you need them? Research has shown that if people are made to feel responsible for a crisis or see someone else intervene, they are more likely to intervene (Moriarity, 1975). These facts may help explain why Milgram's subjects did not intervene to help the victim: the only other person in the situation (the experimenter) remained cool and unconcerned; also, the subject was told that the experimenter was responsible if anything happened to the victim.

The field experiments concerned with bystander intervention serve as a good example of well-conducted field research. Although it is not possible to control variables as tightly as could be done in a laboratory setting, the independent variables can be manipulated without being confounded with other variables. This is achieved by randomizing over the other variables. For example, on each train run in the Piliavin, Rodin, and Piliavin study, the condition of the experiment was randomly determined. Thus other variables—such as the particular people riding on the trains—were randomized across the conditions and could not affect the conclusions drawn from the study. However, we can ask if there was an ethical problem in conducting this research, since the "subjects" did not know they were in the experiment. Suppose one of the bystanders had fainted (or had had a heart attack) while observing the crisis that was staged repeatedly in the course of the experiment? Would the knowledge gained from the experiment be worth the ordeal of the subjects? This issue confronts anyone who chooses to investigate problems through field research.

---

| FROM PROBLEM TO EXPERIMENT: THE NUTS AND BOLTS | **Problem:** Does Heat Cause Aggression? |
|---|---|

It has often been noted that in hot weather people tend to become irritable. There is some correlational evidence that aggression tends to increase in hot weather—for example, riots tend to occur mostly in the summer and seem to be related to the temperature preceding and during the riot.

**Problem:** *Is there a direct causal link between temperature and aggression, or is this correlation merely induced by other factors?*

Hot weather may drive people outdoors to seek relief, and the presence of all these people on the streets may lead to the rioting.

**Hypothesis:** *As temperature increases, so will the tendency to aggress.*

Specification of the independent variable here is mercifully simple, for once. One needs only to find a room where the temperature can be accurately controlled, and to select appropriate temperature values. Reasonable values might be 60, 75, and 95 degrees Fahrenheit to correspond to cool, comfortable, and hot conditions. (Good air conditioning and electric heaters might be needed.) Subjects should be exposed to the appropriate temperature for a period of time before given an opportunity to aggress. One strategy would be to have them fill out long questionnaires for twenty minutes before the rest of the experiment began.

How then does one go about measuring aggression? One must obviously set up some sort of potentially aggressive situation and operationalize the concept of aggression for this situation. There are doubtless many ways this could be done, but social psychologists have produced a standard procedure to study aggression that is similar to Milgram's, but that was developed independently. It involves using an apparatus known as the Buss "aggression machine" (Buss, 1961), which consists of a fake shock generator with which one subject in the experiment is supposed to shock another subject (actually a confederate) when the latter makes errors in a learning task. The subjects in this situation are allowed to choose both the level of shock (typically there are buttons on the machine representing a variety of levels) and the duration of the shock on each trial when an error occurs. The material to be learned is presented to the confederate-learner who makes a predetermined number of errors during the course of the experiment. The subjects are required to shock the confederate after each trial, but in contrast to Milgram's procedures, they are not forced to inflict stronger punishment on the victim. Aggression can be measured by at least two operations, the intensity of the shocks the subject gives the confederate and the duration of the shocks. An additional dependent measure might be a self-report measure after the experiment is completed on how angry and irritable the subject feels. The subject is convinced of the reality of the situation by being given a shock or two from the generator.

After the experiment is over, the subjects must be carefully debriefed, as in all laboratory psychology experiments. The nature of the deception must be explained to them—why it was necessary, what the true purpose of the experiment was, and, perhaps, what the results thus far seem to indicate. The subjects must be told that they actually did not harm the confederates and they should not be allowed to depart until all their questions and anxieties are alleviated as much as possible. The general maxim one should follow when testing human subjects is that they should leave the experiment no worse off than when they arrived, and preferably somewhat richer in knowledge. The experiment should be a learning experience.

With specification of the independent and dependent variables the hypothesis has now become: As ambient temperature increases from 60°, to 75°, to 95° Fahrenheit, subjects given an opportunity to aggress via the Buss aggression machine will provide both more intense and longer shocks to the confederate, and will in addition report more anger on a self-report (questionnaire) measure after the experiment. How do you think such an experiment would come out? Common sense and anecdotal observations seem to indicate that we become irritable with increases in temperature and will thus aggress more. But in an experiment similar to the one outlined here, Baron (1972) found that subjects tested in hot rooms actually provided shocks that were *weaker* and of shorter duration than subjects in comfortably cool rooms. As Baron notes, this finding may be a result of the rather artificial nature of the laboratory situation he used. Subjects in the hot conditions may have simply been eager to get out of the uncomfortable situation, and since they might have assumed that the confederate was suffering similarly, they might have gone easy on him in terms of shock. How could the same hypothesis be tested in a field study, or in a different experimental situation where these artificial conditions are not present?

**SUMMARY**

**1.** Social psychological research is in many ways more difficult to perform than other types of research discussed in this book, because the situations examined are often quite complex, with many variables affecting behavior. Thus introducing experimental control into the situation so that sound inferences can be made about the effects of different experimental treatments on the dependent variable often requires great effort.

**2.** Experimental control combats the problem of experimental error, or any variation in the dependent variable that is not caused by the independent variable. Such extraneous factors should be controlled as much as possible by equating them across conditions. If control is not possible, then these factors should be randomly distributed over conditions.

**3.** The expectations of both the experimenter and the subjects can create problems in social psychological (and other) research. The experimenter may subtly bias results in several ways, for example, by treating subjects slightly differently in the different conditions. A solution to this problem is for the experimenter to be blind with respect to the subject's condition at the time of test, but often this is not feasible since the experimenter must provide the experimental manipulation in some way. Experimenter-bias effects are likely to be discovered in the normal course of scientific research.

**4.** The problem of subjects' behavior being shaped by the demand characteristics of the experimental setting is potentially more dangerous than experimenter bias, because demand characteristics are likely to be common across experiments in different laboratories. Demand characteristics include subjects' expectations of how they should perform in the experiment. Orne developed some ingenious techniques for evaluating the effect of demand characteristics. He used quasi-control groups such as simulating subjects, which often enable investigators to assess whether demand characteristics affected a particular experiment, but not what the outcome of the experiment would have been had the demand characteristics been removed.

**5.** One way to avoid the problem of demand characteristics is to conduct an experiment "in the field," or in a natural setting. Demand characteristics are then excluded, since the subjects are not even aware that they are in an experiment. Many social psychologists are turning to field research since generality of results is no longer a problem, as it is in laboratory research. However, severe problems are involved with field research, too. It is often difficult to effectively manipulate an independent variable while controlling extraneous "nuisance" variables, and it is also difficult to know what to measure, since participants do not even know they are in an experiment and cannot be asked to perform some task, or rate how they feel, et cetera. Even if these problems are overcome, we are left with an important ethical problem, even harder to solve, as to whether psychologists are justified in experimenting on un-suspecting members of society.

| | |
|---|---|
| **bystander intervention** | **field research** |
| **conformity** | **obedience** |
| **confounding** | **placebo effect** |
| **demand characteristics** | **randomization** |
| **experimental control** | **simulating control subjects** |
| **experimental error** | **social norms** |
| **experimenter bias** | **social psychology** |

**1.** Why is experimental control often more difficult to achieve in social psychology experiments than in other sorts of research? To illustrate, make a list of variables that would have to be controlled (or randomized) in a typical bystander-intervention study that is done (a) in a laboratory situation, or (b) in a field experiment.

**2.** Evaluate the following statement: "If an extraneous variable is in danger of being confounded with the independent variable of interest in an experiment, it is better to randomize the influence of the variable across conditions than to control it so that it cannot vary between conditions." Explain why you think this statement is true or false.

**3.** Do you think that the deliberate faking of results is a threat to the cumulative progress of science over long periods of time? How might the short-term effects of deliberate fraud differ from the long-term effects?

**4.** Discuss the problem of unintentional experimenter bias and the problem of demand characteristics of the experimental situation. How can the influence of these problems be minimized in experimental situations? Are these problems equally likely to occur in all types of research?

**5.** Discuss the advantages and disadvantages of field research. Would you mind being the unwitting subject in an experiment on bystander intervention if you later found out that your reactions in the situation had been recorded?

**6.** Make a list of topics that you think (a) could best be studied in laboratory experiments, and (b) could best be studied in field experiments. Explain why you chose the topics you did in each case.

# Psychology in Action

## The Power of Being in an Experiment

People's knowledge that they are participating in an experiment often strongly affects their behavior. People do things when they are in an experiment that they would not do under other circumstances. You can demonstrate this by performing a simple experiment with your friends. Make a list of ten friends and randomly assign them to one of two conditions, either the experimental condition or the control condition. The independent variable for the two groups is the statement you make at the beginning of the experiment. Say to the experimental subjects, "I would like you to do some things for me as part of a psychology experiment for one of my courses." Say to the control group, "I would like you to do me a favor." Then tell each friend that you have a request; you would like the person to do five jumping jacks, six sit-ups, four push-ups, and to make a paper airplane as fast as possible.

Of course, the small number of subjects in the experiment makes it difficult for you to draw any strong conclusions. But you will probably discover that the friends who are asked to help you out with a psychology experiment are likely to be much more cooperative. They probably will do more of the activities, do them faster, and ask fewer questions. People in the control group will probably think you have been studying too hard.

The point of this demonstration is to show that psychology experiments do not just provide neutral surveys of behavior; they also can create the behaviors that are studied. When people know they are being observed in an experiment, they may react differently. Thus the psychologist is in danger of studying behavior produced in the laboratory that may bear little relation to behavior occurring in the outside world. The cues in the experiment that guide subjects' behavior in this way are called demand characteristics.

# CHAPTER 14

## Preview

This chapter examines three issues that confront environmental psychologists. *Generalization of results* refers to the ability to extrapolate from one experimental situation to other environments. *Converging operations* strengthen theoretical concepts by approaching the same concept from several angles. *Ethical issues,* while always an important consideration in research, become even more complex in the study of environmental psychology.

## Chapter Outline

# ENVIRONMENTAL PSYCHOLOGY

*Science is built up with facts, as a house is with stones. But a collection of facts is no more a science than a heap of stones is a house.*

J. H. Poincaré

The most important problem in this chapter is *generalization of results*. One study of noise (Cohen, Glass, and Singer, 1973) showed that children who lived on lower floors of an apartment building that was built directly over a busy freeway were poorer readers than those children living higher up, where the noise of passing traffic was less intense. As a result of this study, the building occupants demanded that a roof be built over the freeway (figure 14–1). Investigators must be able to show—as did Cohen and his colleagues—that the conclusions drawn from their data can be meaningfully generalized.

A second problem that environmental psychologists share with other social scientists involves *converging operations*. In order to establish that a theory or model of behavior is correct, we must approach it from several angles. An example that will be discussed in some detail later on is the topic of personal space. How do psychologists know there is such a thing as a space bubble that we carry around? We cannot see the bubble, or smell it, or feel it. The bubble is a theoretical construct, since it is not directly observable. Thus we must aim for converging operations to prove that certain behavior is affected by personal space.

A third problem, one that is perhaps more severe for environmental and social psychologists, involves *ethical issues* in research. The scientist has a responsibility to ensure that individuals are not harmed in the search for knowledge. Often, however, some degree of risk is involved. How, then, can the psychologist ensure that research complies with established ethical principles?

FIGURE 14–1.
These apartments are built over the approach to the George Washington Bridge in New York City. Highway noise is a severe problem for the residents,

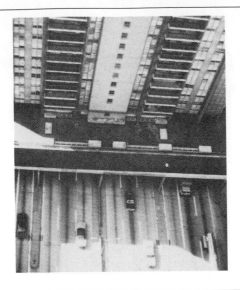

## IS SCIENCE THE ONLY PATH TO TRUTH?

Our society has placed a high value on science and technology. The landing of astronauts on the moon symbolizes the power and prestige of American science. Many citizens believe that our high standard of living, directly attributable to technological devices like automobiles, televisions, and computers, will continue to increase as science advances. Hence the quest for scientific knowledge is justified on the practical grounds that science creates better lives for people, as well as on the philosophical grounds that science, rather than art, religion, literature, and so on, offers the best chance for finding truth (figure 14–2).

Psychology has yet to achieve the stunning successes of older sciences like physics and chemistry. Therefore, it is more difficult to justify the scientific benefits of psychology on purely practical grounds. Indeed, some people claim that our understanding of physical processes such as nuclear energy has so far outstripped our understanding of human processes that we have become captives of our science rather than beneficiaries. As pollution, crowding, and related environmental problems decrease the quality of life, the importance of social science becomes more and more obvious. Environmental psychology deals with issues that directly affect our everyday lives.

Since physical scientists have built up impressive accomplishments, both theoretically and practically, it seems reasonable for

FIGURE 14–2.

Drawing by C. Schulz. Copyright © 1967 United Features Syndicate, Inc. Used by permission.

Although science is not the only path to knowledge, it is one of the most effective methods available.

social scientists to emulate their more established colleagues. Virtually all social scientists believe that powerful truths can and will be discovered by applying the scientific methods used by physical scientists. Science will grant us a better theoretical understanding of the nature of human activity and this will eventually lead to a technology capable of improving the quality of life.

Not all scientists are aware of the limitations of science, despite brief exposure to these points as part of their education. The practicing scientist may eventually discard assorted philosophical points as being of only limited value in his daily work (Medawar, 1969, chapter 1). Nevertheless, it is appropriate to present the other side of the coin and to discuss these limitations. Science focuses on only certain questions and ignores other issues. It would be extremely difficult to answer the question "Does God exist?" scientifically, so most scientists are content to pursue other matters. Similarly, psychologists tend to concentrate on the study of behavior rather than on other kinds of human experience. Aldous Huxley commented on this aspect of science:

Pragmatically [scientists] are justified in acting in this odd and extremely arbitrary way; for by concentrating exclusively on the measurable aspects of such elements of experience as can be explained in terms of a causal system they have been able to achieve a great and increasing control over the energies of nature. But power is not the same thing as insight and, as a representation of reality, the scientific picture of the world is inadequate for the simple reason that science does not even profess to deal with experience as a whole but only with certain aspects of it in certain contexts. All this is quite clearly understood by the more philosophically minded men of science. But some scientists . . . tend to accept the world picture implicit in the theories of science as a complete and exhaustive account of reality; they tend to regard those aspects of experience which scientists leave out of account, *because they are incompetent to deal with them*, as being somehow less real than the aspects which science has arbitrarily chosen to abstract from out of the infinitely rich totality of given facts. (Huxley, 1946, pp. 35–36, emphasis added)

Weizenbaum (1976) makes this same point using an anecdote about a drunkard looking for lost keys. The drunkard, kneeling under a lamppost, is approached by a policeman. The drunkard explains he is looking for his keys that he lost somewhere over there in the darkness. When the policeman asks why he isn't looking over there, the drunkard replies that the light is better here under the lamppost. Science is somewhat like the drunkard, since it looks where its tools provide the best illumination.

Environmental psychology is particularly hard pressed when this criticism of science is applied. The real world, as distinct from the somewhat artificial world of the carefully controlled laboratory studies of the experimental psychologist, is chock-full of problems outside the circle of light given off by a lamppost. Psychologists know that scientific progress comes about, slowly but surely, by staying within the rays of the lamppost until a new break-through yields a more powerful lamp. But this traditional approach offers small hope for the rapid solution of pressing environmental problems. If environmental psychologists move slowly and traditionally, they are open to the criticism that their research is irrelevant to the needs of society. This is a serious charge, since ultimately society (you and I) pays the price for this research through federal research grants and such. On the other hand, the unwary psychologist who immediately rushes in to solve the ills of society runs a high risk of obtaining results that may later prove to be inadequate. And if public policy is formulated on the basis of such incomplete research (or no research at all), the price to society may be quite high (see figure 14–3).

### Discovering the Truth about City Life

All of us, whether we dwell in large metropolitan areas or in rural communities, have an opinion about the quality of urban life. For some, the city represents the height of culture and achievement. For others, the city is a cesspool of violence, pollution, and noise. How can we discover the truth about city life?

One of the most insightful views of city life can be found in a fascinating book, *Death and Life of Great American Cities*, by Jane Jacobs (1961). As one example of her insight, we will briefly discuss Jacobs's views on the functions of the sidewalk. For most of us the sidewalk exists to get us from one place to another. Most of us, including psychologists, have not given much thought to the psy-

FIGURE 14–3.
Demolition of part of the Pruitt-Igoe housing project in St. Louis. These buildings, although physically sound were rendered unfit for occupation because of vandalism. Since then, research conducted by environmental social scientists has revealed how to prevent such tragedies.

chological functions of the common sidewalk. Jacobs shows that the sidewalk makes a great contribution to social interaction within the city. Owners of small shops that line local streets—tailors, drugstores, candy stores—provide a multitude of social services for the neighborhood street users. These services go beyond the nature of each individual business. Thus, a tailor might keep an eye out for children running into the street and warn their parents, the candy store owner might let children use his toilet facilities so they won't have to run upstairs, the delicatessen owner might receive mail for a customer who is out of town for a few days. Each such service by itself is small. But when added together, they form the basis for positive feelings about a neighborhood as a good place to live.

Anyone who has lived on such an old-fashioned city street intuitively accepts the truth of Jacobs's statements. Yet there is nothing scientific about the way Jacobs collected her "data." No systematic attempts were made to manipulate independent variables and record dependent variables; no replications were conducted; no control variables enter her descriptions of behavior. Although no scientist would reject her conclusions outright, few would accept them. Most scientists would claim that an adequate test of her suggestions or "hypotheses" has yet to be accomplished. Until the formal procedures required by science are duly performed, Jacobs's conclusions cannot be sanctified as scientific truth, but only regarded as interesting possibilities.

The problem takes us back to our example of the lamppost. Jacobs is operating outside of the light. This makes scientists reluctant to accept her truths. Yet to many people her conclusions seem obviously correct. Why is the scientific method any better than astute observation? The answer to this important question was given in chapter 1, where we discussed the fixation of belief. You will recall that the great advantage of the scientific method was that it was self-correcting. If a different observer reached different conclusions about the functions and value of sidewalks, how could you decide which view was correct? So far we do not have a better way than science to decide such issues. Science as a method of fixing beliefs is much like democracy as described by Winston Churchill: "Democracy is the worst system of government except for all the others." Accepting the scientific method does not imply that any other method of arriving at truth—like Jacobs's observations of city life—is necessarily invalid. Indeed, psychological research has confirmed many of Jacobs's suggestions (Baron, Byrne, and Kantowitz, 1977, chapter 15). There most certainly is more than one path to truth. But when we must agree on some particular truth over which there is some dispute, then the scientific method, with all its limitations, offers the best long-term solution.

## INTRODUCING THE VARIABLES IN ENVIRONMENTAL PSYCHOLOGY

### Dependent Variables

Environmental psychologists often record feelings and emotion in addition to observable behavior. Such internal states are inferred from rating scales. Thus a study on crowding might ask persons to rate things, such as their opinion of the other people involved in the study, the pleasantness of the experience, the perceived size of the room. It is important to realize that merely labeling a scale with some descriptive title does not guarantee that the scale measures that, and only that, particular facet of human experience. A rating question like the following.

In terms of physical attractiveness my partner was

| Extremely good looking | | | | A real dog |
|---|---|---|---|---|
| 1 | 2 | 3 | 4 | 5 |

where the rater must circle a number from 1 to 5, could well be influenced by nonphysical behavioral characteristics. A partner who was helpful and cooperative might be judged more physically attractive than the same partner (in a different experimental condition) who was insulting and rude.

### Independent Variables

Studies of crowding manipulate *density*, which is most often defined as the number of people per unit area—for example, six people in ten square meters (or feet). Since we can count the number of people and can measure area, density so defined satisfies our requirements for a clear operational definition. Since density has two components, we can manipulate it in two ways. First, we can hold the number of people constant and vary the size of the room that contains them. Second, we can hold room size constant and vary the number of people in the room. Although these two kinds of density manipulation may at first appear equivalent, it turns out they have different effects on behavior and feelings (for example, see Marshall and Heslin, 1975). So the usual operational definition, although precise and clear, is inadequate, because it confounds two separate variables: number of people and amount of space. For example, if density is manipulated by increasing the number of people and holding room size constant, we don't know if observable differences are best attributed to density effects or to effects of number of people. The issue is further complicated by the fact that psychological density often is not the same as physical density. The feeling of being crowded depends not only on physical density but also on social context (Rapoport, 1975). A crowded discotheque has far more pleasant associations than an equally crowded subway car.

Another set of independent variables studied by environmental psychologists falls into the category of stressors—those agents which produce stressful situations. Loud noise, high temperatures, and air pollution are examples of this kind of independent variable.

## Control Variables

Studies in environmental psychology often lack the elegant control variables found in more rigorous areas of experimental psychology. Although gross physical features of the environment, such as room temperature, are controlled, more finely grained variables, for example, the relative position of participants (side by side or face to face), are often neglected. This defect is particularly evident in field studies which by their very nature do not offer the experimenter much control over the situation. Environmental psychologists who conduct field studies are aware of this problem, but feel that the greater reality of the field situation as opposed to the more artificial laboratory setting is ample recompense.

---

**Topic:** Generalization of Results

**Illustration:** Crowding

**14.1
EXPERIMENTAL
TOPICS AND
RESEARCH
ILLUSTRATIONS**

No experiment is an end in itself. Experiments are steps along the way to the psychologists's ultimate goal of predicting and explaining behavior. Unless results of past experiments can be applied to new situations, the experiments are of little value. Thus, models explaining the flow of electricity are not designed to deal only with the small number of electrons that have been studied in the laboratory, but also with the electrons living in the wall sockets of your house.

An important criterion for judging the utility of an experiment is its *representativeness.* Experiments that are representative allow us to extend their findings to more general situations. When it was discovered that cigarette tars caused cancer in laboratory beagles, many cigarette smokers felt that such research only demonstrated that dogs shouldn't smoke. In short, they doubted the representativeness of the findings and did not believe that the results could be generalized to humans. However, later studies confirmed these earlier findings and now the Surgeon General is so convinced of the dangers of cigarette smoking that all cigarette packages must be labeled with a warning to the user.

The preceding cigarette-beagle experiment is one example of the problem of generalizing results from one sample to a different sample or to a different population. We shall term this *sample generalization*. It occurs in many forms. The most studied human organism is the college student taking Introductory Psychology who, as part of the educational process, is often required to participate in several experiments. Let's pretend that we have just completed a study about different methods of improving reading speed and comprehension, using a small sample of Purdue students enrolled in Introductory Psychology. If such a study yields appropriate results, it could have important implications for education. But first, before these implications can be made, several questions about sample generalization need to be answered. First, are these results typical or representative of all Purdue students taking Introductory Psychology? If our sample consisted of only male subjects, clearly the answer is no. Even if our sampling procedure enabled us to answer yes to this first question, we are not yet out of the woods. Are these results representative of Purdue undergraduates in general? Again, if our sample consisted only of Purdue freshmen, we cannot be sure that Purdue seniors would yield the same results. And even if our results generalized to all Purdue undergraduates, it would probably not be worthwhile to institute a drastic change in reading methodology unless it could be demonstrated that college students across the country could benefit. Even then we might ask if high-school and grade-school students could use this new reading method. Clearly, a single experiment will seldom generalize to every population of interest.

Similar problems about generalization of independent and dependent variables also exist. Environmental stress can be induced by such diverse means as increasing temperature, increasing noise level, and depriving a person of sleep the night before the experiment. To the extent that our concern is with environmental stress in general, rather than specific effects of noise, temperature, and sleep deprivation, we must ensure that these different manipulations of related independent variables allow us to make representative statements about stress. We shall term this *variable representativeness*. Let's say we are concerned with the effects of temperature on urban riots: Does the long, hot summer lead to aggression? When this is studied in the laboratory (Baron and Bell, 1976), we find that high temperatures do not necessarily lead to increased aggression. But before we can reject this explanation of summertime urban problems and advance to other hypotheses (for example, more young people are idling in the streets during the summer months), we must ensure that independent and dependent measures generalize from the laboratory to the urban scene. Most of us would be willing to accept the assertion that a temperature of 95°F in the laboratory is equivalent to the same temperature in the city street. But this equivalence is less clear when we consider common laboratory measures of aggression. The most widely used technique calls for the subject to administer an electric shock to a confederate, as described in the Nuts and Bolts section of chapter 13 (see figure 14–4). (In reality, no shock is delivered, but the experimenter hopes that the subject thinks he or she is controlling an electric shock.) Higher shock intensities and longer shock durations are interpreted as evidence for greater aggression. Is the aggression involved in pushing a button the same aggression involved in hurling a brick through a storefront window, or sniping at police and firemen with a rifle (figure 14–5)? Although the ultimate effect—harming someone else—appears to be the same in aggression inside and outside the laboratory, civil disorder may add another dimension to aggression. Establishing a physical analogy in the laboratory—as when rats are trained to "hoard" money— does not necessarily imply a psychological identity. Indeed, it is this considerable difficulty in establishing variable representa-

FIGURE 14–4.
A typical shock machine used in laboratory studies of aggression. The buttons control the (hypothetical) shock intensity. (©1983 Text-Eye)

FIGURE 14–5.
Aggression in a
nonlaboratory situation.
Do you think this is the
same kind of aggression
tested in figure 14–4?

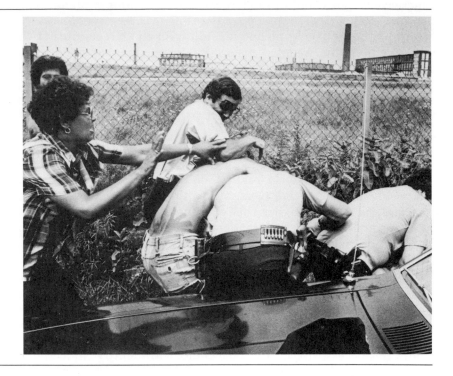

tiveness that has turned many environmental psychologists away
from laboratory studies and toward field studies despite the fact
that there is considerably less experimental control.

In this section we will discuss four studies on crowding and
carefully examine how their results might be generalized. The first
study used animal subjects, whereas the rest used humans. The
three human studies differ in that one is based on demographic
data correlated by sociologists, one uses field-study techniques with
experimental control instead of post hoc statistical control, and
one is a laboratory experiment.

***Crowding in animals: Toocloseforcomfort.*** A long series of studies
conducted by John Calhoun (1962, 1966, 1971) at the National
Institute of Mental Health produced some astonishing findings about
the long-term effects of crowding in rats. Calhoun placed his rats
in a "rat universe" (see figure 14–6) with four compartments. Since
the end compartments were not connected, the density of rats was
much higher in the middle two pens. This overcrowding caused
several pathological types of behavior to develop. The mortality
rate for infant rats was as high as 96 percent in the middle pens.
Female rats were unable to build proper nests and often dropped
infant rats. These infants died where they were dropped and often
were eaten by adult rats. The high mortality rates had the greatest
implications for the rat universe. There was also odd sexual be-

The rat universe studied by Calhoun. Note that the pens are not all joined together by ramps, so that two of them become deadends. *(Scientific American)*

FIGURE 14—6.

havior exhibited by male rats. The strangest rats were called "probers" by Calhoun. Instead of engaging in normal rat courtship, these probers would pursue female rats into their burrow, where they would eat dead infant rats. Probers were also homosexual and hyperactive. Thus the independent variable (high density) caused strange maternal and sexual behaviors (dependent variables) to evolve.

These results are frightening, to say the least and, if generalized to human crowding, strongly imply that overcrowding will eventually destroy society as we know it today. But before we forsake our high-rise apartments for the wide-open spaces, let us first examine some studies conducted with humans.

***Crowding in humans: A correlational demographic study.*** Calhoun's studies with rats imply that high density causes pathological behavior. Since it would be highly unethical for an investigator to crowd people for long periods of time in the way Calhoun crowded rats, a direct experimental test analogous to Calhoun's experiments is impossible. However, there are parts of our big cities where society has created high densities, and it is certainly ethical to observe the effects of these densities in the real world. The advantage of studying such real-life situations is that there is less difficulty in generalizing results, for example, from one city to another, than from a laboratory to a city. The disadvantage is that there is virtually no experimental control over the independent variable and possible extraneous variables. One solution often used when experimental control is not feasible is after-the-fact statistical control. This is the approach taken by sociologists Galle, Gove, and McPherson (1972), who studied crowding and social pathology in the city of Chicago.

These sociologists found five types of *social pathology* for which data were available. Their first index was the standard mortality ratio, which is the age-adjusted death rate of a specific community expressed as a ratio of the death rate for the entire Chicago population. Their second index of social pathology was general fertility rate, defined as the number of births in a specific community per 1,000 women between the ages of 15 and 44 in the same community. These two indices are essentially biological and are quite similar to those studied by Calhoun.

The remaining three indices of social pathology were public-assistance rate, defined as number of persons under 18 years of age receiving public-assistance payments; juvenile delinquency rate, defined as the number of males appearing before family court; and last, an age-adjusted rate of admissions to mental hospitals. In order to determine if these five social pathologies are more frequent in high-density areas, the investigators had to operationally define density. They first used only one measure of *density:* number of persons per acre.

The statistical technique used by Galle and co-workers was correlation. You will recall from our discussion of correlation in chapter 2 that it is often difficult to reach conclusions about causation with only correlational data. Thus we must be extra careful in interpreting the demographic data of this study. Their results are shown in figure 14–7. Correlations ranged from +.28 to +.49. Although this at first appears to support a relationship between density and social pathology, we know that other factors might account for the relationship—that is, a third "unknown" factor might correlate highly with both density and social pathology, and thus be responsible for the correlations in figure 14–7. What kinds of unknown factors might operate in urban areas? Two factors that come immediately to mind are social class and ethnicity (percentages of blacks, Puerto Ricans, and foreign-born in the community). The investigators developed two crude indices for social class and ethnicity and then used the statistical technique of partial

FIGURE 14—7.

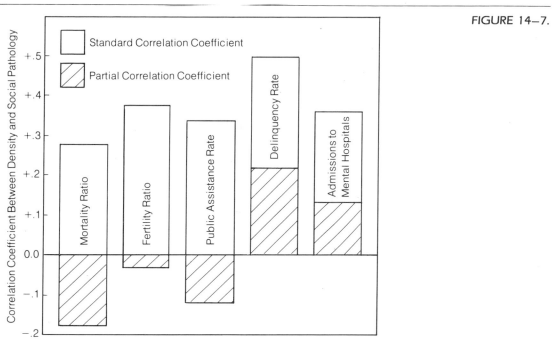

The relationship between density and social pathology when density is defined as number of people per acre (adapted from Galle et al., 1972).

correlation to introduce after-the-fact control. The partial-correlation technique allows us to remove the influence of these factors from our overall correlation coefficient. These data are also shown in figure 16–7. It is clear that with this statistical control, correlation coefficients drop dramatically. In fact the partial correlation coefficients shown do not differ significantly from zero. This means that there is no relationship between density and social pathology once social class and ethnicity are (statistically) controlled.

Although these data fail to support any relationship between density and social pathology, Galle and co-workers were not ready to throw in the towel. They decided that their measure of *density*, number of people per acre, was inadequate. Too many other components of population density could be combined to yield equivalent numbers of people per acre. So they broke number-of-people-per-acre into four smaller density components: number of persons per room, number of rooms per housing unit, number of housing units per structure, and number of residential structures per acre. Then they recalculated their correlation coefficients. (Since these new correlations are based on four measures of density instead of a single measure, technically they are called multiple-correlation coefficients. The technique of multiple correlation allows us to combine several measures into a single multiple-correlation coefficient.) These results, shown in figure 14–8, now show a corre-

FIGURE 14–8.

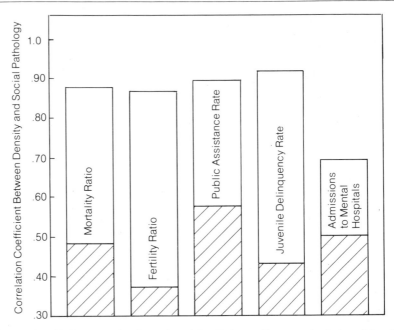

The relationship between density and social pathology with a complex index of density. Unlike the preceding figure, partial correlation coefficients (shaded bars) are all statistically reliable (adapted from Galle et al., 1972).

lational relationship between density and social pathology, even when effects of social class and ethnicity are removed statistically by using partial-correlation coefficients. So Galle, and co-workers concluded that Calhoun's results were directly generalizable to humans living in Chicago.

This conclusion, although reasonable given their data, must be accepted with caution. The possibility remains that some unknown variable in addition to social class and ethnicity should have been partialled out as well. This is the basic difficulty with correlational studies: one can never reach conclusions about causation. Although we can state that high density and social pathology are related, we cannot state that social pathology is a result of high density. Even the statistical control introduced by the method of partial-correlation coefficients is not without its problems. (The major difficulty arises when the extraneous variables to be partialled out are themselves correlated. If this is the case, portions of the variance may be removed more than once, especially if several extraneous variables have been considered. This artifact will cause an inflated partial-correlation coefficient, yielding misleading results.)

***Crowding in humans: A field study in a railroad station.*** Only a study that manipulates independent variables permits statements about causation. Saegert, Mackintosh, and West (1975) took their subjects to Manhattan's Pennsylvania Railroad Station to test effects of crowding on performance and affect (feelings). Density, the most important independent variable, was manipulated by choosing the time at which the station was visited: either 10–11:30 A.M. or 5–6 P.M. at the height of rush hour. This manipulation confounds time of day with density, but the experimenters felt that time of day would not have any significant effects on the tasks. However, this assumption was not tested empirically. The experimenters were careful to make some population counts to ensure that the number of persons actually present was within the desired ranges.

The subjects were given a list of forty-two tasks that they were to perform inside the station, things like looking up a telephone number, finding the ticket counter, buying something at the newsstand, and so forth. They were given thirty minutes to complete as many tasks as they could; this was one dependent variable. Then subjects filled out a Mood Adjective Checklist. This is a rating scheme that permits people to describe their feelings.

The main finding was that "crowding did seem to interfere somewhat with tasks requiring knowledge and manipulation of the environment," since in the high-density condition subjects completed about 25 tasks versus about 29 for the low-density condition. Statistically, however, this effect was significant only at the .10 level, which means it could have occurred by chance in one experiment out of ten. The conclusion drawn by Saegert and co-workers is not very representative. The tasks required subjects to walk back and forth through the crowds in the railroad station. Even if no cognitive demands had been made, that is, if subjects had merely been asked to walk back and forth as many times as possible, we would expect crowds to have slowed them down. It is harder to move around in a dense crowd than in an empty station. Hence, it does not seem reasonable to generalize these results, as do the authors, to mean that cognitive functioning is impaired in crowded situations. However, the rating scales confirmed that subjects felt more anxious and more skeptical in the crowded condition. Since the checklist has eleven scales, it is not surprising that some of them showed an effect of density. This shotgun approach is typical of many studies in social and environmental psychology, where large numbers of rating scales are routinely administered in the hopes that some of them will yield significant results. Although it is quite reasonable that subjects felt more anxious in the crowded condition where they were bumped and shoved, the authors do not interpret the finding of greater feelings of skepticism.

When this study is compared to the Galle demographic study, one conclusion is obvious. Although studies that manipulate independent variables should generally be preferred to studies that only correlate variables, this does not necessarily mean that any experimental study is automatically superior to any correlational study. Good research, even of the correlational variety, is always preferable to poor research, even of the experimental variety.

*Crowding in humans: A laboratory study.* We noted earlier that density can be manipulated in two ways. A study conducted by Marshall and Heslin (1975) used both techniques in a combination of two amounts of space (4 versus 18 square feet per person) and two group sizes (4 versus 16 persons). This means that a total of four experimental treatments were administered: 4 people in a 16-square-foot space, 4 people in a 69-square-foot space, 16 people in a 69-square-foot space, and 16 people in a 288-square-foot space. Additional independent variables were the sex of the people (a common independent variable in social and environmental psychology, since it is easy to manipulate) and the group composition (all same sex or half males and half females). The investigators were interested in how these different groups would feel about each other, so several rating scales were used to measure things like interpersonal attraction, liking for the group as a whole, and feelings in general. These ratings were the dependent variables. Control variables were physical characteristics of the two rooms, such as wall color, carpeting, and ceiling height, which remained constant over all experimental treatments.

The subjects were asked to perform different kinds of problem-solving tasks together. The experimenters were not particularly interested in how well problems were solved, but used these tasks as a pretext to get the members of the groups involved with one another. This type of "cover" task is fairly common in social and environmental psychology.

Results of this study were complicated, with many interactions between independent variables. Only some of the findings will be discussed here. Figure 14–9 shows that feelings toward the group have no simple relation with group size. Females like large groups more than small groups only if the group was of mixed sex. If the group was all female, females preferred the small group. Males,

FIGURE 14–9.

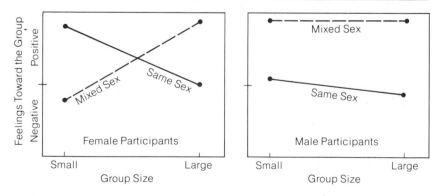

Feelings about the group according to the sex of participant, group size, and group composition. The effects of group size are quite different for male and female participants (adapted from Marshall & Heslin, 1975).

however, although preferring mixed sex groups, didn't care too much about group size.

Females showed similar results for feelings about individuals in the group as a function of amount of space (figure 14–10). Crowded groups were preferred if they were of mixed sex but not if they were all female. Males generally preferred crowded groups regardless of sexual composition.

Note how much more complicated it is to generalize these laboratory results. Effects of crowding depend on not only your sex, but the sex of the other people in your group. This kind of detail, typical of experimental studies, is missing in the other studies of human crowding we have examined. Although you might be tempted to draw the conclusion that you should avoid laboratory studies if you want life to be simple, a better way of regarding these results is to realize that the complexities of life can be studied most precisely in highly controlled laboratory situations.

***Comparison of Crowding Studies.*** We have examined effects of crowding on four studies: an animal study, a correlational demographic study, a field study, and a laboratory experiment. The kinds of generalizations we could draw from each study differed substantially. You are probably wondering which study is the best. There is no straightforward answer to this question, and psychologists do not agree on which is best, although experimental psychologists tend to prefer laboratory studies. The purpose of this section is to acquaint you with the difficulties in generalizing results of any study, regardless of type. By now you may feel that these difficulties are so great that it hardly seems worthwhile to do research at all. But this conclusion is unduly pessimistic. Although it is difficult to generalize from any single study, a set of studies may indeed lead us to representative conclusions. This is

FIGURE 14–10.

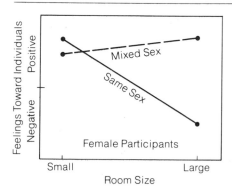 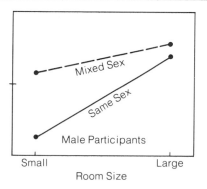

Feelings towards individuals in the group according to room size, sex of participants, and group composition. As in the previous figure, males and females differ in the effect of size (adapted from Marshall & Heslin, 1975).

especially true when researchers design the studies to come together, by approaching the same problem from related, but not
identical, viewpoints. The next section on converging operations
explains this more fully.

## 14.2

### EXPERIMENTAL TOPICS AND RESEARCH ILLUSTRATIONS

**Topic:** Converging Operations

**Illustration:** Personal Space

An excellent way to increase the representativeness and generality
of a scientific concept is to perform more than one experiment
relating to that concept. This gives the concept more than one leg
to stand on, so that it is not totally dependent on any single experimental procedure. You will remember from chapter 6 that we
call this technique of using slightly different types of experiments
to jointly support a single concept *converging operations* (Garner,
Hake, and Eriksen, 1956; Garner, 1974).

How might we define converging operations for the concept
"success?" One way to define a successful person, at least in American society, is by a high income. So anyone earning more than
$50,000 a year could be called successful. Another attribute of suc-
cess might be to have a charming family. Still another characteristic of success might be to have respect in the community. Each
of these characteristics of success is independent in the sense that
their definitions are unrelated. Yet it is quite likely that a successful
person has all three attributes. These characteristics all converge
to define the common concept "success."

Now that you have the general idea of converging operations,
we will illustrate two experimental procedures that converge on
the common concept of *personal space*. This concept implies that
you are surrounded by an invisible bubble designed to protect you
from a wide variety of social encroachments. How do psychologists
know that such a bubble exists? Since it cannot be directly sensed
by vision, smell, touch, et cetera, the concept must be indirectly
evaluated. The two experiments to be discussed demonstrate that
there is a personal-space bubble; they use two different kinds of
spatial invasion, and yield similar results.

***Personal space: Help, there's someone in my bubble!*** It is ironic
that the personal-space bubble that helps you maintain privacy is
best studied by invasions that violate the privacy it affords. A
simple experiment conducted by psychiatrist August Kinzel (1970)
shows one operation that defines personal space. Kinzel was interested in the personal-space bubbles surrounding violent and
nonviolent prisoners. Thus one independent variable—more precisely a subject variable (see chapter 2), since it was not manip-

ulated—in his study was classification of prisoners as violent (having inflicted physical injury on another person) or not. Each prisoner stood in the center of an empty room that was 20 feet wide and 20 feet long. The experimenter then approached from one of eight directions (the second independent variable) until the prisoner said "stop" because the experimenter was too close. The dependent variable was the distance between prisoner and experimenter when the prisoner said "stop." If there is no personal-space bubble, the experimenter should be able to walk right up to the prisoner (distance = 0). Control variables were the room itself and the experimenter, who was the same person throughout the experiment. Results of this experiment are shown in figure 14–11. It is clear that violent prisoners have larger personal-space bubbles than nonviolent prisoners.

This experiment may not have entirely convinced you that there really is a personal-space bubble. A concept based on only one experiment is just a restatement of that particular experimental finding. In Kinzel's experiment you may feel that there is something strange about a person walking right up to you without saying anything. Certainly if this happened to you on the street you would think it unusual, to say the least. The next experiment avoids this potential difficulty.

***Personal space: Oops, pardon my bubble.*** In order to avoid actively invading someone's personal-space bubble, Barefoot, Hoople, and McClay (1972) gave subjects the opportunity to invade the experimenter's bubble. The experimenter sat near a water fountain

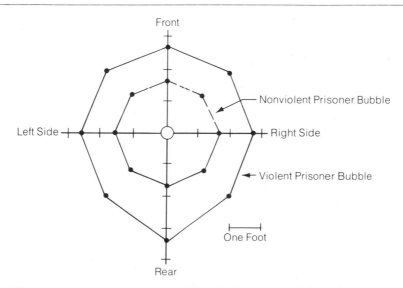

FIGURE 14–11.

Looking down on the personal space bubble of violent and nonviolent prisoners (after Kinzel, 1970).

and pretended to read a book. Anyone getting a drink of water had to invade the experimenter's personal space. The independent variable was the distance between the experimenter and the water fountain. This could be either one foot, five feet, or ten feet. This last distance is large enough so that it exceeds the bounds of the experimenter's personal space and thus is a control condition. A confederate kept track of the number of persons passing by the fountain in each of the three experimental conditions. The dependent variable was the percentage of passersby who drank from the fountain. When the experimenter was one foot away, only 10 percent drank; five feet away, 18 percent drank. Finally, at a distance of ten feet, 22 percent drank from the fountain.

These results agree with those of the active-invasion paradigm used by Kinzel. The single concept of a personal-space bubble explains findings of both experiments. Hence, the experiments provide converging operations supporting the personal-space concept.

## 14–3
## EXPERIMENTAL TOPICS AND RESEARCH ILLUSTRATIONS

**Topic:** Ethical Issues

**Illustrations:** Deception and Concealment

Psychologists are extremely concerned with the ethics of research with human participants. Although some of this concern is pragmatic, caused by fear of restriction of research funds and loss of access to subject populations, most psychologists are ethical persons who have no desire to inflict harm on anyone. The mad researcher, who will do anything to obtain data, is largely a myth.

Since it is difficult for an experimenter to be completely impartial and objective in judging the ethical issue concerning his or her own research, most universities and research institutions have peer committees that judge whether the proposed research is ethical. Indeed all federally funded research must be approved by such a committe before any funding is granted. These committees are guided by several principles advocated by the American Psychological Association (1973). One important principle is the right of *informed consent*. This means that every potential participant in an experiment is given both an explanation of all salient features of the research before the experiment is conducted and the opportunity to decline to participate in the research. Thus the experimenter has a clear ethical obligation to inform participants of any possible harmful effects of the experiment. For example, if all environmental psychology experiment calls for loud noises as stressors, participants must be told this in advance so that anyone with a history of sensitivity to sound, resulting perhaps from a childhood illness, can decline to participate. (Even with informed consent, no ethical researcher would use extremely loud sounds that might cause permanent hearing loss.)

It is extremely difficult for many proposed studies in environmental psychology to comply with the principle of informed consent. There are many situations where, if people knew they were being observed, they might not behave normally. In such cases the researcher would like to conceal the fact that an experiment is under way, only informing or debriefing participants after the study has ended. Clearly, this procedure violates the principle of informed consent, since the person has never been informed nor given consent, and such research could be banned outright. However, many psychologists feel that such a severe restriction would seriously impair their ability to design studies aimed at understanding human behavior in real-life environments, that is it would greatly reduce the ability to generalize research. They argue that the potential worth of the research must be balanced against the potential harm to participants.

Imagine you are serving on an ethics committee and decide whether or not you would allow the following examples of proposed research:

**1.** An environmental psychologist sits in a crowded library and keeps detailed records of seating patterns.

**2.** An environmental psychologist takes videotapes of seating patterns in library. These tapes are maintained indefinitely and library patrons do not know they have been filmed.

**3.** An experimental psychologist tells students that he is interested in their reading comprehension when in reality he is recording the speed of their responses rather than their comprehension.

**4.** A social psychologist is studying bystander intervention in a liquor store. Permission has been obtained from the store manager. In clear view of a patron, an experimenter "steals" a bottle of liquor. A second experimenter approaches the patron and asks, "Did you see him steal that bottle?"

**5.** A social psychologist connects surface electrodes to male participants, with their prior approval. These participants are told that the electrodes are connected to a meter in front of them that measures sexual arousal. In reality, the meter is controlled by the experimenter. Participants are then shown slides of nude males and females. The meter gives high readings for pictures of males, leading the participants to believe they have latent homosexual tendencies.

There are no absolutes in ethics, and we cannot state that some of these examples are clearly ethical and others are clearly not. However, informal discussions with our colleagues reveal that only number 1 was unequivocally considered ethical. Since the psychologist is merely observing and does not know the people (they are represented only by symbols on the data sheet), informed consent was not deemed necessary. Any individual, psychologist or not, could easily observe these same people in the library. The potential harm to participants is negligible.

You may be astonished that objections were raised to every other example. Number 2 was thought to invade personal privacy since the tapes were not erased after data had been abstracted. Number 3 would be acceptable only if the experimenter carefully debriefed participants by explaining the nature and reasons for this minor deception. Number 4 was actually performed; a patron denied seeing the theft and then called the police as soon as she left the store. The investigator had to go down to the police station to bail out the experimenters. Number 5 was considered unethical, even with debriefing. It is not clear that the potential psychological harm of the participant's thinking he had hidden homosexual tendencies could be removed by even immediate debriefing, especially if the person did indeed have latent homosexual tendencies that until the experiment had been successfully supressed.

These examples should show that there is no clear answer as to what is ethical. The responsibility rests on the experimenter and the review committees. Although deception and concealment may be justified in limited instances, great caution is demanded in such experiments.

## FROM PROBLEM TO EXPERIMENT: THE NUTS AND BOLTS

**Problem:** Is Exposure to Noise Bad For You?

An issue that concerns environmental psychologists and citizens alike is the psychological effect of noise on humans. Airports, factories, and city streets expose citizens to long-term noisy environments. How might we evaluate possible effects of such exposure to noise?

**Problem:** Does noise cause psychological harm?

As always, several hypotheses can be derived from this vague problem. First, we will try a laboratory approach by formulating a hypothesis that can be tested under highly controlled circumstances.

**Hypothesis:** Exposure to loud (110 dB SPL) continuous white noise will cause decreases in the number and accuracy of arithmetic problems that can be performed in 25 minutes.

How did we arrive at some of the variables specified in the hypothesis? The independent variable, noise intensity, (set at 110 dB, roughly as loud as a riveter) is close to the limit for safe exposure to 25 minutes of noise. Any louder noise might be harmful and any softer noise might not yield experimental effects, that is, if no effects of noise on performance were obtained with noise much less than 110 dB, we might be tempted to conclude that our noise just wasn't loud enough. White noise (which is roughly similar to the sound you hear when your radio is tuned between stations) contains all frequencies of sound and is a convenient noise source often used in the laboratory.

Why 25-minutes exposure to the noise? Since we expect to use college students as participants, we know that they find it most convenient if an experiment takes roughly one hour—that is about the same time as a class. Since our hypothesis implies a no-noise control condition, we have divided our hour experiment into two 25-minute segments, one with noise and one without. This leaves 10 minutes for instructions and debriefing.

Our dependent variable is performance on an arithmetic task. This task was chosen because it is a simple task that college students are familiar with, so that no training is needed during the experiment. Performance—number of correct and number of incorrect problems—is easy to measure. Since there may be practice or fatigue effects, we will also be careful to counterbalance our experiment by having half the participants start in the quiet condition and half start in the noise condition. Since all participants complete all conditions, this is a within-subjects experimental design, offering greater experimental precision than a between-subjects design. In a within-subjects design, each person is compared to herself or himself so that differences among people do not increase the error in an experiment. However, if we are concerned that performance following noise might be different from performance following quiet, that is, that noise effects might linger on even after the noise is no longer physically present, a better experimental design would be to use separate groups of participants for each 25-minute segment, giving us a between-subjects design.

Although our experiment is well controlled, we have several problems when we attempt to generalize results. If no effects of noise were obtained (if arithmetic performance was the same for noise and quiet segments), it could be argued that a 25-minute sample of life is far too short to tell us about a worker who has been exposed to 90-dB noise eight hours a day for many years. On the other hand, if effects of noise were obtained (if arithmetic performance was worse in noise segments), it could still be argued that eventually a worker adapts to noisy environments, so that if we had tested participants for several days or weeks, our initial effect might have disappeared. We will now formulate another hypothesis so that results can be more easily generalized.

**Hypothesis:** *Residents of a noisy city street will (a) move more frequently and (b) score lower on a rating scale for residential satisfaction than residents of a quiet street.*

Since this hypothesis deals with the long-term effects of permanent residence, it avoids the problems of generalization seen in the preceding experiment. However, this hypothesis is not nearly so precise as the other hypothesis. Sound levels for noisy and quiet streets are not specified in advance, but have to be measured during the experiment. The experimenter has to decide whether to measure sound levels only at certain times, for example, during rush hours or to take a 24-hour average. The independent variable is not completely under the experimenter's control. Furthermore, it may be confounded with things like income and status, since persons with lower socioeconomic status are more likely to reside on noisier streets.

The dependent variables are not entirely satisfactory either. Even if residents desire to move more often from noisy streets, economic factors may prohibit them from accomplishing this. On the other hand, the turnover in an area is an objective number that can be reliably measured. The second dependent variable depends to a great extent on the validity of the rating scale used to assess residential satisfaction. The experimenter will attempt to find a scale that has already been used in several studies and previously validated. If the experimenter is forced to construct a scale, then the scale must first be validated—a time-consuming and difficult process. Thus, the price of the greater ease of generalization in this study is a considerable loss of experimenter control.

When we compare both studies as solutions to the problem posed at the start of this section, it is clear that neither is perfect. This is always true with research. No single experiment can answer a question. The scientist is forced to focus on a more specific hypothesis, thus answering only a small part of the problem. This is a major source of frustration for all psychologists, since no general answers are possible until many tiny pieces, each corresponding to a specific hypothesis, are put together. An environmental psychologist could easily spend an entire career trying to answer the problem of noise and its psychological effects. For more information about the psychology of noise, see Kantowitz and Sorkin (1983), chapter 16.

**SUMMARY**

1. Science is not the only path to truth, and only certain portions of human experience are presently open to scientific analysis. However, the scientific method is self-correcting, whereas other methods of fixing belief are not. So science is preferable wherever its tools are appropriate.

2. Experiments are steps along the way to the psychologist's ultimate goal of predicting and explaining behavior. This goal can be most rapidly achieved by having experiments that are *representative* and that can be *generalized* to related situations. Two types

of representativeness are *sample generalization* and *variable repre-sentativeness*. Four studies of crowding were discussed, and the kinds of generalizations we could draw from each differed sub-stantially.

**3.** The generality of a concept can be considerably bolstered through the use of *converging operations*. Two different experimental pro-cedures that converged on the concept of personal space illustrated converging operations.

**4.** Psychologists are extremely concerned with the ethical aspects of participation in research. The right of *informed consent* cannot always be granted in research. In such cases the potential harm to participants must be balanced against the potential worth of the research. Experiments involving deception and concealment must be conducted only with great caution, if all all.

| | | |
|---|---|---|
| converging operations | personal space | **KEY TERMS** |
| crowding | representativeness | |
| deception | sample generalization | |
| density | social pathology | |
| ethical issues | variable representativeness | |
| generalization of results | | |
| informed consent | | |

**1.** A priest, a rabbi, and a scientist were walking along the beach, discussing whether or not it was possible to walk on water. As an empirical test, the priest and the rabbi waded into the ocean while the scientist watched in amazement from the beach. Soon the priest was up to his chin while the rabbi was dry from his knees up. "How are you managing to stay dry?", asked the priest. "Easy," replied the rabbi, "I walk on the rocks." What did the two clerics say about empiricism to the scientist when they returned to the beach, and what was his reply?

**DISCUSSION QUESTIONS**

**2.** Select two areas where science is *not* the appropriate path to truth. Discuss why the tools of science are irrelevant or inappli-cable in these two fields. Will it be possible for science to handle these areas in the distant future?

**3.** Rush to the library and read the latest issues of *Environment and Behavior,* and *Human Factors.* These are two journals that specialize in applied research. Discuss whether the articles you read can be more readily generalized than articles published in the *Journal of Experimental Psychology.*

**4.** Design an experiment that provides a converging operation (other than those discussed in the chapter) for the concept of personal space. Find two reasons why your proposed experiment should not be conducted.

**5.** Make up a short list of unethical experiments you would like to do. Visit faculty members who specialize in the research areas of your experiments and ask them if they would be willing to supervise the experiments. How many faculty members tell you that they refuse because your experiment is unethical? Is this assignment ethical?

# Psychology in Action

## Mapping Personal Space

This exercise allows you to replicate the Kinzel (1970) and the Barefoot, Hoople, and McClay (1972) studies discussed in the text. If you are really ambitious, go to the library and obtain the original articles. You then can go ahead and plan your replication, without needing to read any further. If you can't get to the library (or if the articles can't be found there), read on.

Stand in the middle of a room. Have a friend approach you from about fifteen feet away. (This actually works better if a stranger approaches you. But if you are not sure how to obtain a friendly stranger, go ahead with one of your friends.) Say "stop" when you start to feel uncomfortable, and then note the distance between you. Repeat this operation several times from different starting directions. Then draw your bubble on graph paper.

There are several variations you can try with this technique. One is to have people draw their space bubbles by imagining that someone is approaching them. Then verify their drawing with an empirical test. You can also try this with a person of the opposite sex. Do men and women have different-sized bubbles? (In general, women have larger bubbles. But this also depends on whether both people are of the same sex. See Baron, Byrne, and Kantowitz, 1980, for more information.)

You can also do this experiment by hanging around a water fountain. Vary the distance between you and the fountain. Have a colleague count the number of people passing by, while you keep track of how many people actually drink from the fountain. (Hint: For the condition where you sit adjacent to the fountain, you will keep drier if you sit on the side of the fountain away from the spray direction.)

# APPENDIX  A

**Chapter Outline**

# STATISTICAL REASONING: AN INTRODUCTION

*Statistical thinking will one day be as necessary for efficient citizenship as the ability to read and write.*

H. G. WELLS

Many psychology students are frightened by statistics. It seems to them a hopeless jumble of complicated jargon having little to do with the interesting aspects of psychology. The purpose of this appendix is to give you some idea as to why an understanding of statistics is actually crucial to the conduct and interpretation of psychological research. We will also give some attention to how statistical reasoning is used in psychological research, even though we can hardly hope to turn you into an expert statistician from reading this one section. This appendix will serve as a review for those of you who have already taken statistics. Students new to statistics may need to read the chapter several times very carefully, since there will be quite a bit of new information. You should probably be aware by now that if you were to complete graduate work for the Ph.D. in psychology, you would probably be required to take a minimum of three courses in statistics.

Many aspects of the world we live in can be treated in terms of probabilities. We do not always know with complete certainty that events will occur given prior conditions, but only that they will happen some proportion of the time, or with a certain probability. A common example is that of weather forecasting. Meteorologists say there is an 80% chance of rain or a 20% chance of snow, given certain prior conditions. Even when the prior conditions are known, it is impossible to predict perfectly the future weather. Much of human behavior is probabilistic in the same sense. Statistics are useful in helping psychologists estimate the probability of whether or not differences in groups of observations between two conditions have been produced by random, or chance, factors. The branch of statistics used for this purpose is **inferential statistics**. The other primary type of statistics, which helps psychologists summarize or describe observations, is **descriptive statistics**. First we shall examine descriptive statistics and then turn to inferential statistics.

## DESCRIPTIVE STATISTICS: TELLING IT LIKE IT IS

Psychologists typically conduct experiments in their quest for an understanding of behavior. Usually there are at least two conditions, an experimental and a control, which differ in the presence or absence of an independent variable. Measures are taken of the dependent variable in each condition. Numbers are produced. What are we to do with them? First, we need to systematize and organize them. We do not have to look at the whole array of numbers produced by subjects in the different conditions of the experiment, instead, we can look at a briefer version. Descriptive statistics provide this systematizing and summarizing function. The two main types of measures of **central tendency** and measures of **dispersion**.

Let us take a hypothetical experimental situation. A drug company has sponsored a test of the effects of LSD on behavior of rats, so we decide for starters to see how the drug affects the rats' running speed. Forty food-deprived rats have been trained to run a straight-alley maze for a food reward. We randomly assign them to two groups. To one group we administer LSD by injection and observe the effect on the speed with which they run the alley for food 30 minutes after the injection. The other group is tested in a similar manner 30 minutes after receiving an injection of an inert substance. The following are the running times for the 20 control subjects in seconds: 13, 11, 14, 18, 12, 14, 10, 13, 13, 16, 15, 9, 12, 20, 11, 13, 12, 17, 15, and 14. The running times for the subjects receiving the LSD injections are 17, 15, 16, 20, 14, 19, 14, 13, 18, 18, 26, 17, 19, 13, 16, 22, 18, 16, 18, and 9. Now that we have the running times, what do we do with them? One thing we might want is some sort of graphical representation of the numbers, as in the two **histograms** in figure A–1. Here the running speeds in seconds appear along the abscissa ($X$ axis) and the frequency with which each speed occurred in the two conditions is displayed along the ordinate ($Y$ axis). Running times for the control subjects are in the top histogram, and those for the experimental subjects are represented in the bottom one. Another way to represent the same information is a **frequency polygon**. Its construction is equivalent to that of the histogram; you can visualize this type of graph by connecting the midpoints of the bars in the histogram. Examples

FIGURE A–1.

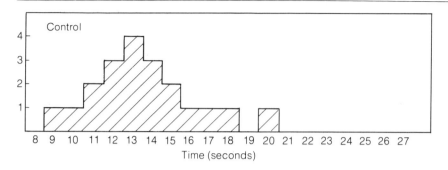

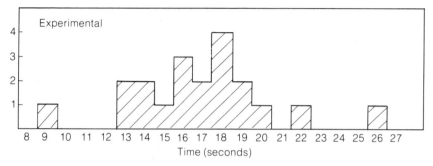

Histograms representing scores for 20 subjects in the control and experimental conditions of the hypothetical LSD experiment.

of frequency polygons appear later in the appendix (in figure A–2). Notice that in both conditions in figure A–1, the greatest number of scores occurs in the middle and they tend to tail off toward the ends. This is more obvious for the control than for the experimental subjects. Also, the times for the experimental group tend to be greater than those for the control group. Both the histogram and frequency polygon are types of **frequency distributions**. They help systematize the data somewhat, but there are more efficient summary descriptions.

## Central Tendency

The most common summary description of data is some measure of central tendency which, as the term implies, indicates the center of the distribution of scores. By far the most typical measure of central tendency in psychological research is the **arithmetic mean**. The mean $(\bar{X})$ is simply the sum of all the scores $(\Sigma X)$ divided by the number of scores $(n)$, or $\bar{X} = \Sigma X/n$. It is what most people think of as the average of a set of numbers, although the term *average* technically applies to any measure of central tendency. The sums of the running times for the experimental and control conditions of our hypothetical experiment were 338 and 272 seconds, respectively. Since there were 20 observations in each condition, the means are 16.9 seconds for the experimental condition and 13.6 for the control.

The mean is the most useful measure of central tendency, and almost all inferential statistics, which we come to later, are based on it. Therefore this statistic is used whenever possible. However, two other measures of central tendency are sometimes used. The second most common measure is the **median**; it is the score above which half of the distribution lies and below which the other half lies. The median, then, is the midpoint of the distribution. When there is an odd number of scores in the distribution, such as 27, the median is the 14th score from the bottom or top since that score divides the distribution into two groups of 13 scores. When the number of scores (n) is an even number, the median is the arithmetic mean of the two middle scores, if the scores are not tied. So the median of the scores 66, 70, 72, 76, 80, and 96 is (72 + 76)/2, or 74. When, as often happens, the two middle scores are tied, as in the distribution of scores from the hypothetical LSD experiment, the convention is to designate the median as the appropriate proportion of the distance between the *limits* of the particular score, where the limits are a half score above and below the tied score. This will be clearer with an example. Consider the distributions of scores from our experiment. If you arrange the 20 control running times from lowest to highest you will discover that the 8th, 9th, 10th, and 11th scores are all 13. Under such conditions the 10th score is considered the median and it is considered to lie three-quarters of the distance between the limits of 12.5 and 13.5. So the median would be 12.5 + .75, or 13.25, for the control subjects. By the same reasoning (and you should try it yourself), we find that the median for the experimental subjects is 17.

Why is the median used? The primary reason is that it has the (desirable) property of being insensitive to extreme scores. In the distribution of scores of 66, 70, 72, 76, 80, and 96, the median of the distribution would remain exactly the same if the lowest score were 1 rather than 66 or the highest score were 1,223 rather than 96. The mean, on the other hand, would differ widely with these other scores. Often this benefit can be extremely useful in summarizing data from the real world. In our LSD experiment, suppose that one of the rats given LSD had stopped halfway down the alley to examine a particularly interesting feature of the runway before continuing on its way to the goal box. Thus its time to complete the runway was 45 minutes or 2,700 seconds. If this score replaced the 26-second score in the original distribution, the mean would go from 16.9 seconds to 150.6, or from 3.30 seconds greater than the control mean to 137.0 seconds greater. This is only because of one very deviant score, so in such cases researchers frequently use the median score rather than the mean to represent the central tendency. Using the mean seems to given an unrepresentative estimate of central tendency because of the great influence of the one score. However, using the median often limits severely any statistical tests that can be applied to the data.

The final measure of central tendency, almost never reported in psychological research, is the **mode**, or the most frequent score in the distribution. In the distribution of control scores in our experiment, it is 13, and in the distribution of experimental scores, it is 18.

## Measures of Dispersion

Measures of central tendency indicate the center of the scores, whereas measures of dispersion indicate how the scores are spread out about the center. The simplest measure of dispersion is the **range**, which is the difference between the highest and lowest score in the distribution. For the control rats in the LSD experiment the range is 11 (20 − 9), and for the experimental rats it is 17 (26 − 9). Since the range only indicates the extreme scores, it it is rarely used.

The most useful measures of dispersion are the **standard deviation** and the **variance** of a distribution. The standard deviation is most useful as a descriptive statistic, whereas the variance of a distribution is used in inferential statistics. As we shall see, the two are closely related.

In deciding on a measure of dispersion, we want to provide a number that reflects the amount of spread that the scores exhibit around some central-tendency measure, usually the mean. One such measure that would be appropriate is the **mean deviation**. This is calculated by taking the difference between the mean and every score in a distribution, summing these differences, and then dividing by the number of scores. However, it is actually necessary to take the mean absolute difference (that is, to ignore the sign of the difference or whether the score was greater or less than the mean). The reason is that the sum of the deviations of scores about the mean is always zero, a defining characteristic of the mean (see table A–1). Thus the mean deviation must be the *absolute* mean deviation. The mean deviations for our hypothetical experimental conditions in the LSD experiment are calculated in table A–1. The symbol | | indicates the absolute value of a number, so |−6| = 6.

The absolute mean deviation of a set of scores is an adequate measure of dispersion and is based on the same logic involved in finding the mean of a distribution. However, the standard deviation and variance are preferred to the mean deviation because they have mathematical properties that make them much more useful in more advanced statistical computations. The logic behind their calculation is quite similar to that of the mean deviation, which is why we have considered the mean deviation here. In calculating the mean deviation we had to take the absolute value of the difference of each score from the mean so that these differences would

| TABLE A–1 | Calculation of the mean deviations and absolute mean deviations from two sets of scores. Notice that the sum of the deviations (differences) in calculating the mean deviation is zero, which is why it is necessary to use the absolute mean deviation. |
| --- | --- |

| Control group | | | Experimental group | | |
| --- | --- | --- | --- | --- | --- |
| $X$ | $(X - \overline{X})$ | $\lvert X - \overline{X} \rvert$ | $X$ | $(X - \overline{X})$ | $\lvert X - \overline{X} \rvert$ |
| 9 | −4.60 | 4.60 | 9 | −7.90 | 7.90 |
| 10 | −3.60 | 3.60 | 13 | −3.90 | 3.90 |
| 11 | −2.60 | 2.60 | 13 | −3.90 | 3.90 |
| 11 | −2.60 | 2.60 | 14 | −2.90 | 2.90 |
| 12 | −1.60 | 1.60 | 14 | −2.90 | 2.90 |
| 12 | −1.60 | 1.60 | 15 | −1.90 | 1.90 |
| 12 | −1.60 | 1.60 | 16 | − .90 | .90 |
| 13 | − .60 | .60 | 16 | − .90 | .90 |
| 13 | − .60 | .60 | 16 | − .90 | .90 |
| 13 | − .60 | .60 | 17 | + .10 | .10 |
| 13 | − .60 | .60 | 17 | + .10 | .10 |
| 14 | + .40 | .40 | 18 | +1.10 | .10 |
| 14 | + .40 | .40 | 18 | +1.10 | 1.10 |
| 14 | + .40 | .40 | 18 | +1.10 | 1.10 |
| 15 | +1.40 | 1.40 | 18 | +1.10 | 1.10 |
| 15 | +1.40 | 1.40 | 19 | +2.10 | 2.10 |
| 16 | +2.40 | 2.40 | 19 | +2.10 | 2.10 |
| 17 | +3.40 | 3.40 | 20 | +3.10 | 3.10 |
| 18 | +4.40 | 4.40 | 22 | +5.10 | 5.10 |
| 20 | +6.40 | 6.40 | 26 | +9.10 | 9.10 |

$\Sigma X = 272$    Total = 0.00    Total = 41.20      $\Sigma X = 338$    Total − 0.00    Total = 52.20

$\overline{X} = 13.60$                             $\overline{X} = 16.90$

Absolute mean deviation $= \dfrac{41.20}{20} = 2.06$    Absolute mean deviation $= \dfrac{52.20}{20} = 2.61$

not add up to zero. Instead of taking the absolute difference, we could have gotten rid of the troublesome negative numbers by squaring the differences. This is exactly what is done in calculating the variance and standard deviation of a distribution.

The **variance** of a distribution is defined as **the sum of the squared deviations from the mean, divided by the number of scores**. Or, in other words, each score is taken, subtracted from the mean, and squared; then all these values are summed and divided by the number of scores. The formula for the variance is

$$s^2 = \frac{\Sigma(X - \overline{X})^2}{n} \tag{A–1}$$

where $s^2$ represents the variance, $X$ the individual scores, $\overline{X}$ the mean, and $n$ the number of scores or observations. The **standard deviation** is simply **the square root of the variance**, and is therefore represented by $s$. So

$$s = \sqrt{\frac{\Sigma(X - \overline{X})^2}{n}}. \tag{A–2}$$

Calculation of the standard deviations for the control and experimental conditions from the LSD experiment by the mean-deviation method is illustrated in table A–2.

The formulas for the variance and standard deviation of a distribution given in equations A–1 and A–2 are rather cumbersome, and in practice, the equivalent computational formulas are used. The standard-deviation computational formula is

$$ s = \sqrt{\frac{\Sigma X^2}{n} - \overline{X}^2} \qquad\qquad \textbf{(A–3)} $$

where $\Sigma X^2$ is the sum of the squares of all the scores, $\overline{X}$ is the mean of the distribution, and $n$ is the number of scores, Similarly, the computational formula for variance is

$$ s^2 = \frac{\Sigma X^2}{n} - \overline{X}^2. \qquad\qquad \textbf{(A–4)} $$

Calculation of the standard deviation, s, for the control and experimental conditions by the mean-deviation method.

TABLE A–2

| Control group | | | Experimental group | | |
|---|---|---|---|---|---|
| $X$ | $(X - \overline{X})$ | $(X - \overline{X})^2$ | $X$ | $(X - \overline{X})$ | $(X - \overline{X})^2$ |
| 9 | −4.60 | 21.16 | 9 | −7.90 | 62.41 |
| 10 | −3.60 | 12.96 | 13 | −3.90 | 15.21 |
| 11 | −2.60 | 6.76 | 13 | −3.90 | 15.21 |
| 11 | −2.60 | 6.76 | 14 | −2.90 | 8.41 |
| 12 | −1.60 | 2.56 | 14 | −2.90 | 8.41 |
| 12 | −1.60 | 2.56 | 15 | −1.90 | 3.61 |
| 12 | −1.60 | 2.56 | 16 | − .90 | .81 |
| 13 | − .60 | .36 | 16 | − .90 | .81 |
| 13 | − .60 | .36 | 16 | − .90 | .81 |
| 13 | − .60 | .36 | 17 | + .10 | .01 |
| 13 | − .60 | .36 | 17 | + .10 | .01 |
| 14 | + .40 | .16 | 18 | +1.10 | 1.21 |
| 14 | + .40 | .16 | 18 | +1.10 | 1.21 |
| 14 | + .40 | .16 | 18 | +1.10 | 1.21 |
| 15 | +1.40 | 1.96 | 18 | +1.10 | 1.21 |
| 15 | +1.40 | 1.96 | 19 | +2.10 | 4.41 |
| 16 | +2.40 | 5.76 | 19 | +2.10 | 4.41 |
| 17 | +3.40 | 11.56 | 20 | +3.10 | 9.61 |
| 18 | +4.40 | 19.36 | 22 | +5.10 | 26.01 |
| 20 | +6.40 | 40.96 | 26 | +9.10 | 82.81 |

$\Sigma X = 272$   Total $= 0.00$   $\Sigma(X - \overline{X})^2 = 138.80$      $\Sigma X = 338$   Total $= 0.00$   $\Sigma(X - \overline{X})^2 = 247.80$

$\overline{X} = 13.60$                                  $\overline{X} = 16.90$

$$ s = \sqrt{\frac{\Sigma(X - \overline{X})^2}{n}} \qquad\qquad s = \sqrt{\frac{\Sigma(X - \overline{X})^2}{n}} $$

$$ s = \sqrt{\frac{138.80}{20}} \qquad\qquad s = \sqrt{\frac{247.80}{20}} $$

$$ s = 2.63 \qquad\qquad s = 3.52 $$

The standard deviations for the experimental and control scores are calculated with the computational formula in table A–3. Notice that the value in each case is the same as when the definitional formula is used.

In describing an array of data, psychologists typically present two descriptive statistics, the mean and the standard deviation. Although there are other measures of central tendency and dispersion, these are most useful for descriptive purposes. Variance is used extensively, as we shall see, in inferential statistics.

### The Normal Curve

The graphs of the scores of the hypothetical LSD experiment in figure A–1 show that the scores pile up in the middle but tail off

---

TABLE A–3　Calculation of the standard deviation, s, for the control and experimental conditions by using the computational formula (also called the raw-score method). Notice that the same values are obtained as when the definitional formula is used (see table A–2), but that the calculations are much easier to perform.

| $X$ | $X^2$ | $X$ | $X^2$ |
|---|---|---|---|
| 9 | 81 | 9 | 81 |
| 10 | 100 | 13 | 169 |
| 11 | 121 | 13 | 169 |
| 11 | 121 | 14 | 196 |
| 12 | 144 | 14 | 196 |
| 12 | 144 | 15 | 225 |
| 12 | 144 | 16 | 256 |
| 13 | 169 | 16 | 256 |
| 13 | 169 | 16 | 256 |
| 13 | 169 | 17 | 289 |
| 13 | 169 | 17 | 289 |
| 14 | 196 | 18 | 324 |
| 14 | 196 | 18 | 324 |
| 14 | 196 | 18 | 324 |
| 15 | 225 | 18 | 324 |
| 15 | 225 | 19 | 361 |
| 16 | 256 | 19 | 361 |
| 17 | 289 | 20 | 400 |
| 18 | 324 | 22 | 484 |
| 20 | 400 | 26 | 676 |
| $\Sigma X = 272$ | $\Sigma X^2 = 3838$ | $\Sigma X = 338$ | $\Sigma X^2 = 5960$ |

$$\bar{X} = 13.60 \qquad\qquad \bar{X} = 16.90$$

$$\bar{X}^2 = 184.96 \qquad\qquad \bar{X}^2 = 285.61$$

$$s = \sqrt{\frac{\Sigma X^2}{n} - \bar{X}^2} \qquad\qquad s = \sqrt{\frac{\Sigma X^2}{n} - \bar{X}^2}$$

$$s = \sqrt{\frac{3838}{20} - 184.96} \qquad\qquad s = \sqrt{\frac{5960}{20} - 285.61}$$

$$s = 2.63 \qquad\qquad s = 3.52$$

toward the extremes (tails) of the distribution of scores. Although these numbers were hypothetical, this sort of distribution has a property that occurs for most measures of behavior: that is, for most phenomena that are measured, scores cluster in the center of the distribution. This configuration is called the **normal curve**, an example of which is presented in figure A–2 (the curve labeled *B*). When put on a graph, psychological data typically are most numerous in the middle of the set of scores; they decline in frequency with distance from the middle in a roughly symmetrical way. A score ten points below the center of the distribution occurs about as frequently as a score ten points above the center.

The three curves shown in figure A–2 are all symmetrical. In such distributions of scores the mean, median, and mode of the distribution all fall at the same point or score. Curves with the same mean, median, and mode may differ in their variability, as do the curves in figure A–2. The tall, thin curve labeled *A* would have a smaller standard deviation than the other two. Similarly, the broad, flat curve (*C*) would have a greater standard deviation than the other two.

The normal curve has a very useful property. It turns out that a specific proportion of scores falls under each part of the normal curve. This feature is illustrated in figure A–3. Notice that on each side of the normal curve in figure A–3 there is a point where the curve slightly reverses its direction, it starts bending outward more. This is called the **inflection point**. The inflection point in the curve is always one standard deviation from the mean. In fact, the normal

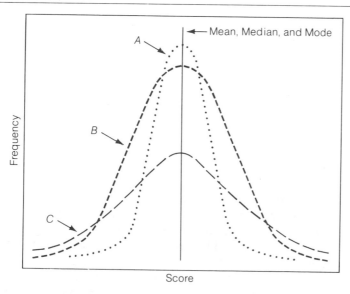

FIGURE A–2.

Three examples of the normal curve that differ in variability. *C* has the greatest variability and *A* the least. The normal curve is a symmetrical distribution in which the mean, median, and mode all have the same value.

FIGURE A–3.

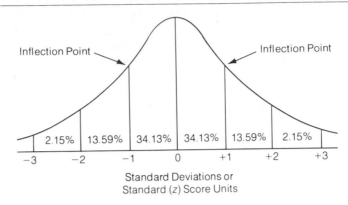

Proportions of scores in specific areas under the normal curve. The inflection points are one standard deviation from the mean.

curve has the useful property that specific proportions of the distribution of scores it represents are contained within specific areas of the curve itself. About 68% of all scores are contained within one standard deviation of the mean (34% on each side). Similarly, almost 96% of the scores are contained within two standard deviations of the mean, and 99.74% of the scores are within three standard deviations. The percentage in each area is shown in figure A–3.

This property of normal curves is extremely useful because if we know an individual's score and the mean and the standard deviation in the distribution of scores, we also know the person's relative rank. For example, most I.Q. tests are devised so that the population mean is 100 and the standard deviation is 15. If a person has an IQ. of 115, we know that he or she scored higher than 84% of all people on the test (50% of the people below the mean and 34% above). Similarly, a person with an I.Q. of 130 scored higher than almost 98% of all people, and a person with an I.Q. of 145 scored higher than 99.87% of the population.

Most distributions of scores in psychological data are, or at least are assumed to be, normal. (Often with small samples, as in our hypothetical data in figure A–1, it is difficult to tell whether the distribution is normal.) It is common to compare scores across normal distributions with different means and variances in terms of **standard scores** or **z scores**. This is simply the difference between an individual score and the mean expressed in units of standard deviations. So an I.Q. of 115 translates to a z score of 1.00, that is, $[115 - 100]/15$, and an I.Q. of 78 translates to a z score of $-1.47$, that is, $[78 - 100]/15$. Standard scores are useful since they allow comparison of the relative ranks of scores for a person across distributions in which the means and standard deviations vary greatly. Grades in courses should be calculated in terms of z scores if the means and standard deviations of the scores vary widely from one test to the next. Thus a person's eventual rank in the class is calculated more faithfully by finding the mean of the $z$ scores than the mean of the raw scores of the tests.

When it is said that data in some experiment or other are **normally distributed** it means that, if they are graphed, they will tend to form a normal distribution. Thus *normal*, as it is used in psychological research, usually refers to a type of distribution and not a value judgment as to the goodness or badness of the scores. There are various sorts of distributions besides normal ones, of course, but we cannot tarry here to consider some of the other more prevalent types.

Descriptive statistics are concerned with describing or summarizing data. The results from our hypothetical experiment can be summarized by saying that the control group's mean running time was 13.6 seconds, with a standard deviation of 2.63, whereas the experimental subjects injected with LSD had a mean of 16.9 seconds and a standard deviation of 3.52. The experimental rats ran more slowly than the controls; the difference between the means was 3.3 seconds. But should we take this difference seriously? Perhaps it is owing merely to chance factors, such as measurement error or a few rats in the control group having a particularly good day and thus feeling like running a bit faster. How can we judge the likelihood that the difference between the two conditions is "real" or reliable, that it is not a fluke? How large must the difference be for us to conclude that it is unlikely to have occurred merely by chance alone? Inferential statistics are used to answer this question.

In actual practice the procedure is not too complicated. We choose an appropriate statistical test for the experimental situation, perform a few straightforward computations on a calculator (or computer), and then we consult a special table. The table informs us of the probability that the difference we found between our conditions is a result of random factors. If is sufficiently unlikely to have occurred by chance, we conclude that the difference is statistically significant, or reliable. But although the actual computational procedures followed are often quite simple, the logic behind them needs to be understood so you will appreciate how statistical inferences are made.

## INFERENTIAL STATISTICS

### Sampling

A **population** is a complete set of measurements (or individuals or objects) having some common observable characteristic. Examples of populations are all U.S. citizens of voting age, or all albino rats that have had injections of LSD, or all people asked to remember a list of fifty words. These are all populations we might be interested in for one reason or another, but of course it is impossible to study the entire population in any of these cases. If we could measure the entire population of rats for running speed after either an injection of LSD or an injection of a chemically inert substance, then we would better know what the effects of LSD were, since we would have measured the entire population. (Any difference could still, of course, be attributable to measurement error.) But since it is almost always impractical to measure an entire population, we must *sample* from it. A **sample** is a subset of a population, and it is what we are almost always examining when we compare experimental conditions. We make statistical inferences, then, when we draw a conclusion that is based on only a sample of observations about an entire population. We really want to know about the effects of LSD and the inert substance on rats in general, but we hope to draw this conclusion from a sample of, say, twenty rats in each condition.

Samples should always be as **representative** as possible of the population under study. One way of accomplishing this is **random sampling**, where members are picked from the population by some completely arbitrary means. (Random sampling is often carried out by using a random-numbers table, such as the one in table F on page 502.) Technically, we can only **generalize** to the population from which we have sampled, although if taken literally this would make experimental research hardly worth doing. If we received fifty rats from a supply house for our hypothetical experiment, and we selected a sample of forty and randomly assigned them to the two conditions of the experiment, then would our conclusions be true only of the population of fifty rats? Well, perhaps technically, but no one would care about the result if this were so, and no one would have wasted the time doing the experiment. We would at least want to assume that the results are characteristic of that strain of rats, and we would hope that these results also generalize to other species, including humans. The problem is the same in experimental psychological research with humans. Suppose you are a researcher at the University of Toronto interested in studying some aspect of social behavior. You ready your experiment, which has three conditions, and you plan to use students from introductory psychology courses as subjects, a common practice. You put up a sign-up sheet, randomly assign those who signed up to the three experimental conditions when they arrive at the experiment, and collect your data. To whom do your conclusions generalize? To introductory psychology students at the University of Toronto who volunteered for your experiment? If so, who cares what you found? In practice, psychologists assume that their results generalize more widely than the limited population from which they sampled for their experiment. We consider the problem of generality of results and the basis of this assumption more fully in chapters 10 and 14.

---

**Box A–1** Statistical Notation

Characteristics of a population of scores are called **parameters**, whereas characteristics of a sample of scores drawn from a larger population are **statistics**. The mean of an entire population of scores is a parameter, and the mean of a sample is a statistic. So that these distinctions are maintained, different symbols are used for population parameters and sample statistics. Some of the most frequent symbols are listed here. Some have been explained, the others will be discussed in the next few pages.

$N$ = number of scores in a population

$n$ = number of scores in a sample

$\mu$ = population mean ($\mu$ is pronounced mu)

$\overline{X}$ = sample mean

$\sigma^2$ = population variance ($\sigma$ is pronounced sigma)

$s^2$ = sample variance $\dfrac{\Sigma(X - \overline{X})^2}{n}$

$\hat{s}^2$ = unbiased estimate of population variance $\dfrac{\Sigma(X - \overline{X})^2}{n - 1}$

$\sigma$ = population standard deviation

$s$ = sample standard deviation

$\hat{s}$ = sample standard deviation based on the unbiased variance estimate

$\sigma_{\overline{x}}$ = standard error of the mean, $\dfrac{\sigma}{\sqrt{N}}$

$s_x$ = estimated standard error of the mean, $\dfrac{s}{\sqrt{n}}$ or $\dfrac{s}{\sqrt{n - 1}}$

---

***The distribution of sample means.*** One way we could ask about the reliability of our hypothetical experiment would be to perform it repeatedly with new groups of rats. Of course it would be very unlikely for us to get exactly the same mean running times for the experimental and control conditions in these replications. The means in seconds for the experimental and control conditions in four replications might be 17.9 and 12.5, 16.0 and 13.4, 16.6 and 14.5, and 15.4 and 15.1. Since the experimental rats that receive the LSD always run more slowly than the control rats that do not, this would increase our confidence in the original finding, although the difference is rather small in the last replication. If we repeated the experiment like this and plotted the distribution of the sample means obtained in the two conditions, these distributions would tend to be normal. Thus they would have all the characteristics of the normal distribution, such as a certain proportion of the scores falling under a certain part of the curve. We could also find the difference between the two means in each experiment and plot the distribution of the differences between the sample means. These differences would also be normally distributed.

To give you a better idea of the concept of the **distribution of sample means**, let us borrow an example from a class demonstration by Horowitz (1975, pp. 179–182). Horowitz manufactured a population of 1,000 normally distributed scores so that the mean and standard deviation of the entire population would be known. This is almost never the case in actual research situations, of course. His 1,000 scores ranged from 0 to 100 and had a mean of 50 and a standard deviation of 15.8. The scores were listed on 1,000 slips of paper and placed in a container. Horowitz had 96 students take samples of 10 slips from the container and calculate the mean. On each draw from the container, a slip was taken out, its number was noted, and then the slip was replaced. The slips were then mixed up somewhat in the container, and another slip was drawn, and so on. After each student calculated the mean of the 10 scores in her or his sample, Horowitz collected all 96 and plotted the distribution of sample means, which is represented in table A–4. The intervals between which means might fall are on the left and the number of means falling within each interval is on the right. Notice that the distribution is almost perfectly symmetrical, with almost as many scores in any interval a certain distance below the true mean of the population (50) as above it. Also, the mean of the 96 sample means (49.99) is quite close to the actual mean of the population (50). But the main thing you should notice in table A–4 is the great variability among the sample means. Although each sample of 10 was presumably random and not biased in any way, one sample had a mean of 37.8 while another had a mean of

TABLE A–4          The distribution of sample means for the 96 samples taken by students in Horowitz's class. Each sample mean was based on 10 observations. (After Horowitz, 1974, table 8.1)

| Interval | Frequency | |
|---|---|---|
| 62.0–63.9 | 1 | |
| 60.0–61.9 | 1 | |
| 58.0–59.9 | 3 | |
| 56.0–57.9 | 7 | |
| 54.0–55.9 | 9 | |
| 52.0–53.9 | 12 | |
| 50.0–51.9 | 15 | Mean of sample means = 49.99 |
| 48.0–49.9 | 15 | Standard deviation (s) of |
| 46.0–47.9 | 13 | sample means = 5.01 |
| 44.0–45.9 | 9 | |
| 42.0–43.9 | 6 | |
| 40.0–41.9 | 3 | |
| 38.0–39.9 | 1 | |
| 36.0–37.9 | 1 | |
| | 96 samples | |

62.3. Obviously these are very disparate means, even though they were sampled from the same population. If you were doing an experiment and found two very different sample means, and you were trying to decide whether they came from the same underlying distribution or two different distributions, you might think that such a large difference would indicate that they came from different distributions. In other words, you would think that the experimental treatment produced scores reliably different (from a different distribution) than the control scores. Usually this is a good rule—the larger the difference between means in the conditions, the more likely the means are to be reliably different—but as we have seen here, even random sampling from a known distribution can produce sample means that differ greatly from each other and from the true population mean, which is known in this case. This is a lesson that should be kept in mind while pondering small differences between means. Is the 3.3-second difference between experimental and control means in our hypothetical LSD experiment really reliable?

**The standard error of the mean.** The **standard error of the mean** is the standard deviation of a distribution of sample means. In the data in table A–4, it is 5.01. The standard error of the mean gives us some idea as to the amount of variability in the distribution of sample means, or how likely it is that the value of any particular sample mean is in error. Large standard errors indicate great variability, whereas small ones tell us that any particular sample mean is likely to be quite close to the actual population mean. Thus the standard error of the mean is a very useful number.

You might be wondering why we bother to tell you about the standard error of the mean if in order to calculate it you must repeat an experiment numerous times to get the distribution of sample means and then calculate its standard deviation. Fortunately, you don't. The formula for finding the standard error of the mean (represented by $\sigma_{\bar{x}}$) is simply the standard deviation of the population ($\sigma$) divided by the square root of the number of observations ($\sqrt{n}$). Or

$$\sigma_{\bar{x}} = \frac{\sigma}{\sqrt{n}} \qquad \textbf{(A–5)}$$

Now, if you are still with us you might well be thinking, "Terrific. What good does this do me since the standard deviation of the population, the numerator in equation A–5, is never known?" That has occurred to statisticians, too, so they have devised a method for estimating the standard deviation of the population from the standard deviation of a sample. If you look back at equation A–2, where the formula for the standard deviation of a sample ($s$) appears, and simply replace the $n$ in the denominator by $n - 1$, then you have the formula for getting an unbiased estimate of $\sigma$, the standard deviation of the population. The equation for finding the standard error of distribution of sample means (called the standard error of the mean or $s_{\bar{x}}$) is

$$\text{Estimated } \sigma_{\bar{x}} = s_{\bar{x}} = \frac{s}{\sqrt{n-1}} \qquad \textbf{(A–6)}$$

Obviously we want the standard error of the mean to be as small as possible, since it represents the error we have in assuming that our sample mean represents the population mean. Equations A–5 and A–6 tell us how to do this: Increase the size of the sample, $n$, which increases the denominator in the equations. The greater is $n$, the sample size, the smaller will be the standard error of the mean, $s_{\bar{x}}$. This should be no surprise. If the population involves 1,000 scores, the sample mean should be closer to the population mean if there are 500 observations in the sample rather than only 10.

Horowitz drove this point home to the 96 students in his class by having them repeat the exercise of drawing slips from the population of 1,000 scores and calculating the mean again, but this time he had them sample 50 slips rather than only 10. The resulting distribution of sample means is in table A–5. This time, with larger samples, there is much less variability in the sample means the students obtained. They are much closer to the actual population mean of 50. The standard deviation of the distribution of sample means, or the standard error of the mean, is 2.23, as opposed to 5.01 when the sample size was only 10. If $n = 100$ in a sample

---

**Table A–5**

The distribution of sample means for the 96 samples taken by students when sample size ($n$) = 50. The distribution is again normal, as in table A–4, but when each sample is based on a larger sample size, as it is here, the variability of the distribution (represented by the standard error of the mean) is much smaller. (After Horowitz, 1974, table 8.2)

| Interval | Frequency | |
|---|---|---|
| 55.0–55.9 | 1 | |
| 54.0–54.9 | 3 | |
| 53.0–53.9 | 5 | |
| 52.0–52.9 | 9 | |
| 51.0–51.9 | 13 | |
| 50.0–50.9 | 17 | |
| 49.0–49.9 | 16 | Mean of sample means = 49.95 |
| 48.0–48.9 | 14 | Standard deviation ($s$) of sample means = 2.23 |
| 47.0–47.9 | 9 | |
| 46.0–46.9 | 6 | |
| 45.0–45.9 | 2 | |
| 44.0–44.9 | 1 | |
| | 96 samples | |

from the 1,000 scores, the standard error of the mean would be 1.59; with a sample of 500 it would be .71; and with 1,000 scores in a sample it would be only .50. (These were calculated from equation A–5 since the standard deviation, $\sigma$, is known for the entire population.) The reason we might not get the population mean even with a sample of 1,000 is that the sampling was done with **replacement**; that is, after a slip was drawn it was returned to the container and thus it might have been drawn more than once while some slips were never drawn.

The lesson to be learned is that we should always try to maximize the number of observations—the sample size—in experimental conditions so that the statistics obtained will be as close as possible to the population parameters.

### Testing Hypotheses

Scientists set up experiments to test hypotheses. The conventional statistical logic for testing hypotheses runs something like this. An experimenter arranges conditions, such as the experimental (LSD) and control (placebo) in our experiment with rats, in order to test an **experimental hypothesis**. The experimental hypothesis in this case is that LSD will have some effect on running speed. This is tested by pitting it against the **null hypothesis**, which maintains that the two conditions do not differ in their effects on running speed. Stated another way, the experimental hypothesis is that the samples of running speeds come from two different underlying populations (that is, populations with different distributions), whereas the null hypothesis is that the two samples come from the same distribution.

A critical assumption is that it is impossible to prove the alternative hypothesis conclusively, since there is always some chance that the two samples came from the same population no matter how different they appear. What inferential statistics allow us to do, though, is to determine how confident we can be in rejecting the null hypothesis. The alternative hypothesis is thus tested indirectly; if we can be quite confident in rejecting the null hypothesis, then we assume that the alternative hypothesis is correct, and that there is a real difference between scores in the different conditions. Statisticians have agreed, by convention, that if calculations from a statistical test show that there is less than a .05 probability (a 5 percent chance) that the null hypothesis is correct, we can reject it and accept the alternative hypothesis.

We will describe the concept of probability briefly in this context. Consider the following problem: What is the probability that if we randomly draw a card from a deck of 52 cards, that it will be a spade? Since there are 13 spades in a deck, the probability of drawing a spade is 13 divided by 52, or $\frac{1}{4} = .25$. In general, if there are $r$ ways that an event can occur and a total of $N$ possibilities, then the probability of the event is $r/N$. What is the probability that a fair coin will come up heads when flipped? There are two ways a coin can come up, so $N = 2$. One of them is heads, so $r = 1$. So the probability of heads is ½, or .50.

Now we can more precisely describe what the conventional level of .05 for statistical significance means. If the null hypothesis were actually true, a researcher would obtain such a large difference between conditions less than 5 times in 100. If the chances are this slight in making an error by rejecting the null hypothesis, then it is deemed safe to do so and to opt for the alternative hypothesis. The .05 criterion is referred to as the .05 level of confidence, since a mistake will be made only 5 times in 100. When the null hypothesis is rejected, researchers conclude that the results are reliably different or statistically significant. In other words, the researchers can be quite confident that the difference obtained between the conditions is trustworthy and that if the experiment were repeated the same outcome would result.

The logic of pitting an experimental hypothesis against the null hypothesis has come under attack in recent years for several reasons. Some argue that it gives a misleading idea as to how scientists operate. For one thing, not many researchers wander about the world losing any sleep over or investing any thought into the null hypothesis. In general, experiments are set up to test our theories, and what is of primary concern is how the results of the experiments can be interpreted or accounted for in light of our theories. Of special interest is the case where important experimental results seem irreconcilable with the major theories of a phenomenon. So experiments are important because of what they tell us about our theories and ideas—this is why we designed them in the first place— and not about whether or not the null hypothesis is rejected. But the null-hypothesis testing logic is widely used as an introduction, however oversimplified, of the way scientific inference proceeds. Thus we present it here. Do not be misled, though, into thinking that psychologists spend their days dreaming up experimental hypotheses to pit against the null hypothesis. This is so in part, but the processes of scientific inference are fortunately much more varied and complicated than the logic of using the null hypothesis would lead us to believe.

***Testing hypotheses: Parameters known.*** The logic of testing hypotheses against the null hypothesis can be aptly illustrated in cases where the parameters of a population are known and we wish to determine whether a particular sample comes from the population. Such cases are quite unusual in actual research, of course, since population parameters are rarely known.

Suppose you were interested in whether the members of your experimental psychology class were reliably above the national mean in intelligence as measured by I.Q. tests (or reliably below, as the case may be). We know the population parameters in this case; the mean is 100 and the standard deviation is 15. You could test your class easily enough by giving them the short form of some intelligence test, such as the Wechsler Adult Intelligence Scale developed for group testing. Suppose you randomly sampled 25 people from your class of 100 and found the mean I.Q. of the sample to be 108 with a standard deviation of 5.

How do we go about testing the experimental hypothesis that the class is reliably brighter than the population as a whole? First let us consider the hypotheses. The experimental hypothesis is that the students are brighter than people in the nation as a whole, or that the I.Q. scores of the students sampled come from a different population than randomly selected people. It is not exactly an exciting hypothesis, one in the vanguard of psychological research, but it will do for our purposes. The null hypothesis is, of course, that there is no reliable difference between our sample and the national mean, or that the students in the class are a sample from the same national population. If the null hypothesis were actually the case, the difference between the sample mean of 108 and the population parameter mean ($\mu$) of 100 would be due to random factors. And certainly this is not implausible, because we have seen from our discussion of the sample distribution of means how much a sample mean can differ from a population parameter, even when the sample is selected in an unbiased manner. Remember Horowitz's classroom demonstration, the results of which are portrayed in tables A–4 and A–5.

The normal curve, the distribution of sample means, and $z$ scores can be used to help us determine how likely it is that the null hypothesis is false. When unbiased samples are taken from a larger population, the means of these samples are normally distributed. With normal distributions we can specify what proportion of the distribution falls under each part of the curve, as seen in figure A–3. Finally, also remember that $z$ scores are the calculation of any score in a normal distribution in terms of standard deviation units from the mean.

All this is by way of review. Now how does this help us? What we do in testing the hypothesis that the sample is actually from a population with a mean I.Q. greater than the population at large is to treat the sample mean as an individual score (in terms of our earlier discussion) and calculate a $z$ score on the basis of the deviation of the sample mean from the population mean. In our case we know the population mean is 100 and the class mean of the randomly selected students is 108. In order to calculate the $z$ score we also need to know the standard error of the mean, the standard deviation of the distribution of sample means. So the equation for the $z$ score here is

$$z = \frac{\bar{x} - \mu}{\sigma_{\bar{x}}} \qquad\qquad \textbf{(A–7)}$$

The standard error of the mean ($\sigma_{\bar{x}}$) is found by dividing the standard deviation of the population, $\sigma$ (which we know in the case of I.Q. scores is 15) by $\sqrt{n}$, which is the sample size of the class, or $\sqrt{25}$. (This reasoning follows from equation A–5.) The $\sigma$, is thus $15/\sqrt{25}$, or 3. Therefore $z$ is 108-100/3, or 2.67.

What can we conclude from obtaining a $z$ score of 2.67? This value allows us to reject the null hypothesis with reasonable confidence and conclude in favor of the alternative hypothesis, that the class is actually superior to the population at large in terms of I.Q. We establish this by asking the question: How likely is a $z$ score of 2.67 to occur when a sample mean is drawn from a larger population, when the mean of the population is actually 100? The answer is that it will occur only .0038 of the time, or 38 times in 10,000. (We will come to how this was calculated in the next paragraph.) The custom in rejecting the null hypothesis is that if it could occur only 1 time in 20 by chance, we would reject it, so the difference in the class sample mean is **reliably different** or significantly different from the mean of the population.

To explain how this rather remarkable conclusion is reached we need to refer again to the special property of the normal curve, which is that a certain proportion of cases fall under each part of the curve. Figure A–3 showed that a $z$ score of $\pm 2.00$ is high improbable. Greater scores in either direction occur only 2.15% of the time. In other words, the probability of such an occurrence is .0215. This is also below the 5% or .05 level of significance or level of confidence, so any mean score two or more standard deviations from the population mean is considered, using the logic we have outlined here, reliably (significantly) different from the population mean. In fact, the critical $z$ value for rejecting the null hypothesis at the .05 level of confidence is $\pm 1.96$. At the end of the appendix section, in Statistical Table A, are presented (1) $z$ scores from zero to four, with (2) the amount of area between the mean and $z$ and (3) most important, the amount of area beyond $z$. The amount of area beyond $z$ is the probability of finding a score that distant from the mean on the basis of chance alone. Once again, when this probability falls below .05 as it does with $z$ scores of $\pm 1.96$ (or more), we reject the null hypothesis. Notice that with a $z$ of 2.67, as in our I.Q. example, the probability of such a rare occurrence is only .0038.

The statistical problem we have just considered—comparing a sample mean to a population parameter to see whether the sample came from that population—is rather artificial, since population parameters are rarely known. But this example does exhibit characteristics of most common statistical tests. In all tests, some computations are performed on the data or raw scores gathered from an experiment, a value is found as in the $z$ score just calculated, and then this value is compared with a distribution of values so that we can determine the likelihood that such a value could be obtained if the null hypothesis were in fact true. This distribution tells us, then, with what probability our result can be attributed to random variation. If the probability is less than five cases in 100 ($p < .05$), then by convention we say the null hypothesis can be rejected. This probability is sometimes called the **alpha ($\alpha$) level** and, as mentioned, some psychologists prefer values of .01 or even .001 (1 in 100 or 1,000, respectively) so that they can be more certain that the rejection of the null hypothesis is made correctly.

Our $z$-score test can also serve to very briefly introduce you to some other important statistical concepts. First, let us consider two types of errors that can be made by applying statistical tests to experimental data, according to the null-hypothesis testing logic. Some dullard named them type I and type II errors so that students could henceforth confuse them whenever possible. A **type-I error** is rejection of the null hypothesis when it is actually true, and the probability that this error is being made is indexed by the alpha level. If the alpha level is $p = .05$, then we shall mistakenly reject the null hypothesis in 5 cases in 100. This illustrates the probabilistic nature of inferential statistics; we are not absolutely certain that a null hypothesis can be rejected—only reasonably certain. Thus the lower $\alpha$ level or $p$ level we employ in determining statistical significance, the less chance we have of making a type-I error. However, this increases the probability of a **type-II error**, which occurs when we *fail* to reject the null hypothesis when it is actually *false*. Thus by setting $\alpha$ levels at different points we systematically decrease and increase the two types of errors. They trade off against one another.

Scientists are generally conservative in such matters, so the $\alpha$ level is usually kept fairly small, such as .05 or .01 (rather than, say, .10 or .15). Thus we minimize the error of rejecting the null hypothesis when it is true, or claiming a difference in our results when it is not there. As a consequence, though, we increase the probability of type-II errors. A *conservative* statistical test minimizes type-I errors, whereas more *liberal* statistical tests increase the probability of type-I error but decrease that of a type-II error.

Unfortunately we can never know for sure in our experimental situations whether we are committing type-I or type-II errors. We find this out primarily by experimental replications of our results. However, we can also find this out by calculating the **power of a statistical test**. The power of a statistical test is the probability of rejecting the null hypothesis when it is actually false, so obviously we always want to maximize the power of our statistical tests. This is not the place to describe how the power of tests is calculated, but we can note the two main factors that influence power. Look back to the $z$-score formula in equation A–7. Whatever would make the $z$ score larger would increase the power of the statistical test, or the likelihood of rejecting the null hypothesis. The value $\mu$, the population mean, is fixed. Thus only two changes in the values of equation A–7 can affect $z$. One is the difference between the sample mean and the population mean ($\overline{x} - \mu$) and the other is $n$, the size of the sample. If the discrepancy between $\mu$ and $\bar{x}$ is increased (or in other cases if the difference between sample means in an experimental comparison is increased), the probability of rejecting the null hypothesis is also increased.

But there is nothing we can do about the size of the difference between means; it is fixed. What we can do to increase the power of our statistical tests is to increase the sample size. The reason for this, in brief, is that with larger samples we can be more confident that our sample means represent the mean of the populations from which they are drawn, and thus we can be more confident that any difference between a sample mean and a population mean (or between two sample means) is reliable. Sample size can have a great effect on the power of a test, as shown in table A–6. Presented there are the $z$ scores and $p$ values for our difference between a sample mean of 108 I.Q. points and the population mean of 100 as the sample size varies. Obviously as the sample size varies, so will our conclusion as to whether the sample came from a national population or a more restricted, high-I.Q., population. If we assume that the null hypothesis is actually false here, then by increasing sample size we decrease the probability of a type-II error, or increase the power of the test we are using.

One final issue to be considered is specification of **directionality** of statistical tests. According to conventional logic involved in testing an alternative hypothesis against the null hypothesis, the al-

---

Table A–6

How varying sample size ($n$) affects the power of a statistical test, or how likely it is that the null hypothesis can be rejected when the test is used. The example is from the $z$ score (calculated in the text) on a mean sample I.Q. of 108 where

$$z = \frac{\bar{X} - \mu}{\sigma_{\bar{x}}}.$$

If the mean difference remains the same but $n$ increases, $z$ increases because

$$\sigma_{\bar{x}} = \frac{\sigma}{\sqrt{n}}.$$

| $n$ | $\bar{X} - \mu$ | $\sigma_{\bar{x}}$ | $z$ | $p$† |
|---|---|---|---|---|
| 2 | 8 | 13.14 | .61 | .2709 |
| 5 | 8 | 6.70 | 1.19 | .1170 |
| 7 | 8 | 5.67 | 1.41 | .0793 |
| 10 | 8 | 4.74 | 1.69 | .0455* |
| 12 | 8 | 4.33 | 1.85 | .0322* |
| 15 | 8 | 3.88 | 2.06 | .0197* |
| 17 | 8 | 3.64 | 2.20 | .0139* |
| 20 | 8 | 3.35 | 2.38 | .0087* |
| 25 | 8 | 3.00 | 2.67 | .0038* |
| 50 | 8 | 2.12 | 3.77 | .0001* |
| 75 | 8 | 1.73 | 4.62 | <.00003* |
| 100 | 8 | 1.50 | 5.33 | <.00003* |

\* All these values meet the conventional level of statistical significance, $p < .05$ (one-tailed);

† $p$ values are one-tailed.

ternative hypothesis may be **directional** or **nondirectional**. If there are an experimental and a control group in an experiment, a nondirectional alternative hypothesis would simply be that the two groups would differ in performance on the dependent variable. But a directional hypothesis would state in addition the predicted direction of the difference; for example, the experimental group might be predicted to do better than the control.

This distinction is important, because if the alternative hypothesis is directional, a **one-tailed** (or **one-sided**) **statistical test** is used, but if the alternative hypothesis is nondirectional, a **two-tailed** (**two-sided**) **test** is used. One versus two "tails" refers to whether in looking up a $p$ level associated with some determined value of the statistical test (say, $z = 1.69$), we consider one or both tails of the distribution (see figure A–4).

This should be clearer with reference to our earlier example. We took a sample ($n = 25$) of students, determined that the mean I.Q. of the sample was 108, and calculated a $z = +2.67$ in testing to see whether this was different from the mean population I.Q. of 100. If we had no prior expectation of how the sample I.Q. should deviate from the normal population—if we thought it could be either greater or lower—this would have been a nondirectional hypothesis. In fact we did expect the sample I.Q. to be greater than 100, so we were testing a directional hypothesis and thus used a

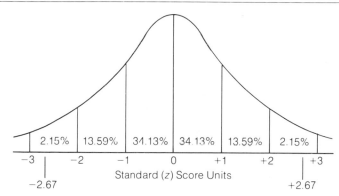

This is the standard normal distribution which was presented in Figure A-4. There are two sides or tails to the distribution, positive and negative. If an experimenter simply asserts that there should be a difference between an experimental and control condition but does not specify the direction of the difference, this is called a nondirectional hypothesis. If a $z = 2.67$ is found, it is necessary to look up the probability that this will occur in both the positive and negative tails of the distribution and add the two, since the experimenter did not specify whether the difference should be positive or negative. When the experimenter has specified the direction of difference, one need only look up the probability in one tail. Since the distribution is symmetrical, the probability that the null hypothesis can be rejected is half as great with a one-tailed as with a two-tailed test. The less certain one is about the outcome of an experiment, the greater the difference between conditions must be for it to be decided that it is not due to chance.

one-tailed test. This means we looked up the resulting $z$ score in only one tail of the normal distribution, that greater than zero. A $z = +2.67$ leads to a one-tailed $p$ value of .0038. If the hypothesis were nondirectional, then we have no a priori right to expect the resultant $z$ score to be greater instead of less than zero. The $z$ could fall in the positive or negative tail. Since the difference could have occurred in either direction, we use a two-tailed test. In practice, since the two tails of the distribution are symmetrical, we simply double the $p$ level for the one-tailed test. In our example, if the hypothesis had been nondirectional, $p$ would equal $2 \times .0038$, or .0076, still well below .05.

Two-tailed tests are more conservative and less powerful than one-tailed tests—it is harder to reject the null hypothesis. If we are uncertain about the outcome of an experiment, we need a greater value of the statistic to allow us to declare a difference. In practice, most investigators prefer to use the more conservative two-tailed test with suffficient power ensured by fairly large sample sizes.

### Tests for Differences between Two Groups

There is a bewildering variety of statistical tests for almost every purpose. At present we are interested in discussing tests that assess the reliability of a difference between two groups or conditions. How do we pick an appropriate test from all those available? There is no hard and fast rule. Tests vary in the assumptions they make, their power, and the types of situation for which they are appropriate. Perhaps the most popular test for the difference between two means in psychological research is the $t$ test. Since the $t$ test provides the same estimate of reliability as does the simple analysis of variance (to be discussed soon), we will concentrate on two other tests, the **Mann-Whitney $U$ test** and the **Wilcoxon signed-ranks test**. These tests also are useful in introducing yet another type of statistical test.

The Mann-Whitney and Wilcoxon tests are **nonparametric tests** as opposed to **parametric tests**. Parametric statistical tests are those which make assumptions about the underlying population parameters of the samples on which the tests are performed. Common assumptions of parametric tests are that the variances of the underlying populations being compared are equivalent and that the underlying distributions are normal. If these assumptions are not met, then the test may be inappropriate. But how can we ever know whether the assumptions underlying the test are met, since we do not know the population parameters? Usually we cannot, except by estimating population parameters from sample statistics. However, if we turn to nonparametric statistics the problem does not arise, because these tests make no assumptions about the underlying population parameters. Since the parameters cannot be known anyway, this provides an important reason for using nonparametric tests. Another reason is that these tests generally are very easy to calculate and can often even be done by hand. However, nonparametric tests are usually less powerful than parametric tests employed in the same situation; that is, they are less likely to provide a rejection of the null hypothesis.

The Mann-Whitney $U$ test is used when we wish to compare two samples and decide whether they come from the same or different underlying populations. It is used when the two samples are composed of different subjects, or in **between-subjects designs**. The underlying rationale for the Mann-Whitney test will not be discussed here. In general, the logic is the same as in other statistical tests in which a value is computed from the test and compared with a distribution of values in order to determine whether or not the null hypothesis should be rejected. The way in which the Mann-Whitney test is applied to actual data is outlined in Box A–2 where the reliability of the difference between the two samples in our hypothetical LSD experiment is tested.

The Wilcoxon signed-ranks test is also used in testing for the difference between two samples, but in this case the design must be a **related measures design**. In other words, either the same subjects must serve in both the experimental and control groups (a within-subjects design) or the subjects must be matched in some way. Of course precautions must be taken in within-subjects designs to ensure that some variable such as practice or fatigue is not confounded with the variable of interest (see chapter 3). But as long as the experiment has been done well, the Wilcoxon signed-ranks test is an appropriate tool for analysis of the results.

Before considering the signed-ranks test, we will examine its simpler cousin, the **sign test**, which is also appropriate in the same situations. The sign test is the essence of simplicity. Suppose we have 26 subjects serving in both conditions of an experiment in which we are predicting that when subjects are in the experimental condition they will do better than when they are in the control condition. Now suppose that 19 subjects actually do better in the experimental condition than in the control, while the reverse is true for the other 7. Is this difference reliable? The sign test allows us to answer this question without our needing more information about what the actual scores were. In terms of the null hypothesis we might expect 13 subjects to perform better in the experimental condition and 13 in the control. The sign test allows us to compute the exact probability that the null hypothesis is false when there are 19 cases in the predicted direction but also 7 reversals or exceptions. It turns out that the null hypothesis can be rejected in this case with a .014 confidence level (one-tailed). With a nondirectional prediction, $p$ equals .028 (two-tailed). Once again we cannot delve into the details of how this is computed, but in Statistical Table C we present the $\alpha$ levels (one-tailed) for cases of sample sizes from 3 to 42 when there are $x$ number of exceptions to the predicted hypothesis. So, for example, when there are 16 subjects

**Box A–2** Calculation of a Mann-Whitney $U$ Test on Hypothetical Experimental Data from Figure A–1.

*Step 1*. Rank all the numbers for *both* groups together, beginning with the smallest number. Assign it the lowest rank.

| Control (Placebo) | | Experimental (LSD) | |
|---|---|---|---|
| Latency (sec.) | Rank | Latency (sec.) | Rank |
| 9 | 1.5 | 9 | 1.5 |
| 10 | 3 | 13 | 11.5 |
| 11 | 4.5 | 13 | 11.5 |
| 11 | 4.5 | 14 | 17 |
| 12 | 7 | 14 | 17 |
| 12 | 7 | 15 | 21 |
| 12 | 7 | 16 | 24.5 |
| 13 | 11.5 | 16 | 24.5 |
| 13 | 11.5 | 16 | 24.5 |
| 13 | 11.5 | 17 | 28 |
| 13 | 11.5 | 17 | 28 |
| 14 | 17 | 18 | 32 |
| 14 | 17 | 18 | 32 |
| 14 | 17 | 18 | 32 |
| 15 | 21 | 18 | 32 |
| 15 | 21 | 19 | 35.5 |
| 16 | 24.5 | 19 | 35.5 |
| 17 | 28 | 20 | 37.5 |
| 18 | 32 | 22 | 39 |
| 20 | 37.5 | 26 | 40 |
| | $\Sigma$rank$_1$ 295.5 | | $\Sigma$rank$_2$ 524.5 |

*Note*: When scores are tied, assign the mean value of the tied ranks to each. Thus for both 9-second times in this example, the rank 1.5 is assigned (the mean of 1 and 2).

*Step 2*. The equations for finding $U$ and $U'$ are as follows, where $n_1$ is the size of the smaller sample, $n_2$ is the size of the larger sample, $\Sigma R_1$ is the sum of the ranks of the smaller sample, and $\Sigma R_2$ is the sum of the ranks of the larger sample. Obviously the subscripts are important only if the sample sizes are unequal, which is not the case here.

in the experiment (remember, in both conditions) and 13 show the predicted pattern of results while 3 exhibit reversals, we can reject the null hypothesis at the .011 level of confidence (one-tailed).

The sign test uses very little of the information from an experiment, just whether the subjects performed better or worse in one condition than in another. For the sign test it does not matter whether the difference in performance is great or small; the direction of the difference is all that matters. The sign test therefore wastes much of the information gathered in an experiment and is not a very powerful statistical test. The Wilcoxon signed-ranks test is like the sign test in that it is used in situations where the same (or matched) subjects are employed in two conditions and the di-

$$U = n_1n_2 + \frac{n_1(n_1 + 1)}{2} - \Sigma R_1$$

**(A–8)**
$$U = (20)(20) + \frac{(20)(21)}{2} - 295.5$$

$$U = 400 + 210 - 295.5$$

$$U = 314.5$$

$$U' = n_1n_2 + \frac{n_2(n_2 + 1)}{2} - \Sigma R_2$$

**(A–9)**
$$U' = (20)(20) + \frac{(20)(21)}{2} - 524.5$$

$$U' = 85.5$$

Actually it is only necessary to compute either $U$ or $U'$, because the other can be found according to the equations

$$U = n_1n_2 - U'$$
$$\text{or}$$
$$U' = n_1n_2 - U.$$

*Step 3.* Take $U$ or $U'$, whichever value is *smaller*, and look in Statistical Table B to see whether the difference between the two groups is reliable. The values in Statistical Table B are recorded according to different sample sizes. In this case both sample sizes are 20, so the critical value from the table is 88. In order for the difference between the two groups to be judged reliable, the $U$ or $U'$ from the experiment must be *less than* the appropriate value in Table B. Since 85.5 is less than 88, we can conclude that the difference between the two groups is reliable at the .001 level of confidence.

*Note:* Statistical Table B is only appropriate for situations when the sizes of the two samples are between 8 and 21. For other cases, you should consult an advanced text.

rection of the difference is taken into account. However, in the Wilcoxon signed-ranks test the size of the difference is taken into account, too. For this reason it is also called the **sized sign test**. An example of how the Wilcoxon signed-ranks test is used is in Box A–3.

## The Analysis of Variance

Most psychological research has progressed beyond the stage where there are only two conditions, an experimental and a control, that are compared to one another. Rather than varying only the pres-

> **Box A–3** Calculation of the Wilcoxon Signed-Ranks Test
>
> Imagine an experiment testing whether or not Professor Humboldt von Widget's memory course, "How to Constipate Your Mind by Remembering Everything," really works. First, a group of thirty subjects is presented with fifty words to be remembered. Then the subjects are randomly separated into two groups, and a check indicates that the groups do not differ reliably in the mean number of words recalled. The experimental group is given Professor von Widget's three-week course whereas the control group is not. Then all thirty subjects are tested again on another fifty-word list. The controls show no improvement from one list to another. The question we ask here is whether or not the experimental subjects' memories were reliably improved. (Note: We could—and should—also compare the experimental subjects' performance on the second test with that of the controls. The Mann-Whitney test is appropriate for this comparison. Do you know why?) We employ the Wilcoxon signed-ranks test to assess whether the experimental subjects improved reliably from the first test to the second.
>
> *Step 1.* Place the data in a table (such as the one presented on the facing page) where both scores for each subject (before and after the memory course) are paired together. Find and record the difference between the pairs.
>
> *Step 2.* Rank the values of the differences according to size, beginning with the smallest. *Ignore the sign.* Use the absolute values of the numbers. For tied ranks, assign each the mean value of the ranks. (See the right-hand column of the table here.)
>
> *Step 3.* Add the ranks for all the difference values that are negative (5.5 + 2.5 + 8.5 + 5.5 = 22.0) and positive (14 + 15 + 2.5 + 8.5 + 8.5 + 2.5 + 13 + 2.5 + 11.5 + 8.5 + 11.5 = 98.0). These are the signed-rank values.
>
> *Step 4.* Take the signed-rank value that is smallest (22 in this case) and go to Statistical Table D. Look up the number of pairs of observations (listed as *n* on the left). There are 15 in this case. Then look at the number under the desired level of significance. Since the direction of the outcome was predicted in this case (we expected the memory course to

ence or absence of some independent variable, researchers often systematically vary the magnitude of the independent variable. In our example of the effects of LSD on running speed of rats, it may be quite useful to vary the amount of LSD administered to the rats. Perhaps effects are different at low dosages than at high ones. We could not determine this from the two-group design where one group received LSD in some amount and the other did not. In order to evaluate the results of such an experiment with multiple groups, we must employ the **analysis of variance**, in particular **simple**

| | Mean number of words recalled | | | |
|---|---|---|---|---|
| Subject | Before | After | Difference | Rank |
| 1 | 11 | 17 | +6 | 14 |
| 2 | 18 | 16 | −2 | 5.5 |
| 3 | 9 | 21 | +12 | 15 |
| 4 | 15 | 16 | +1 | 2.5 |
| 5 | 14 | 17 | +3 | 8.5 |
| 6 | 12 | 15 | +3 | 8.5 |
| 7 | 17 | 16 | −1 | 2.5 |
| 8 | 16 | 17 | +1 | 2.5 |
| 9 | 15 | 20 | +5 | 13 |
| 10 | 19 | 16 | −3 | 8.5 |
| 11 | 12 | 13 | +1 | 2.5 |
| 12 | 16 | 14 | −2 | 5.5 |
| 13 | 10 | 14 | +4 | 11.5 |
| 14 | 17 | 20 | +3 | 8.5 |
| 15 | 6 | 10 | +4 | 11.5 |
| | $\bar{x} = 13.80$ | $\bar{x} = 16.07$ | | |

help rather than hurt recall of words), let us choose the value under the .025 level of significance for a one-tailed test. This value is 25. If the smaller of the two values from the experiment is *below* the appropriate value in the table, then the result is reliable. Since 22 is below 25, we can conclude that Professor von Widget's course really did help memory for words.

*Note*: Remember that the controls showed no improvement in performance from one test to the other. This is a crucial bit of information, for otherwise we could not rule out two plausible competing hypotheses. One is that the improvement on the second list was simply owing to practice on the first, and the other is that the second list was easier than the first. Actually, if Professor von Widget's course were as effective as numerous memory courses currently on the market, results from an actual experiment would show (and have shown) more spectacular improvement than the hypothetical results here. Memory-improvement courses, all of which embody the same few principles, really work for objective materials such as word lists.

**analysis of variance**. Simple analysis of variance is used in situations where one factor or independent variable (such as amount of LSD) is varied systematically. Thus it is also called one-factor analysis of variance. Often researchers are interested in more complex situations. They may be interested in varying two or more factors simultaneously. In such two-factor or multifactor experimental designs, the analysis of variance is also appropriate, but it is more complicated. In this section we introduce you to the logic of simple and two-factor analysis of variance (abbreviated AN-

OVA). However, in our examples and discussion, we stick to the case of between-subjects experimental designs. Calculations for within-subjects designs are different.

At the heart of the analysis-of-variance procedure is a comparison of variance estimates. We have already discussed the concept of variance and its estimation from one particular sample of observations. You should refer back to the section on measures of dispersion if the concept of variance is hazy to you at this point. Recall that the equation for the unbiased estimate of the population variance is

$$\hat{s}^2 = \frac{\Sigma(\overline{x} - x)^2}{n - 1} \tag{A-10}$$

and that when the deviation of scores from the mean is large, the variance will be great. Similarly, when the deviations from the mean are small, the variance will be small.

In the analysis of variance, two independent estimates of variance are obtained. One is based on the variability *between* the different experimental groups—how much the means of the different groups vary from one another. Actually the variance is computed as to how much the individual group means differ from the overall mean of all scores in the experiment. The greater the difference among the means of the groups, the greater will be the between-groups variance.

The other estimate of variance is the **within-groups variance**. This is the concept that we have already discussed previously in considering estimates of variance from individual samples, but now we are concerned with finding an estimate of within-groups variance that is representative of all the individual groups, so we take the mean of the variances of these groups. The within-groups variance gives us an estimate of how much subjects in the groups differ from one another (or the mean of the group). In short, two variance estimates are obtained, one for the variance within groups and one for the variance between groups. Now what good does this do?

The basic logic of testing to see whether or not the scores of the different groups or conditions are reliably different is as follows. The null hypothesis is that all the subjects in the various conditions are drawn from the same underlying population; the experimental variable has no effect. If the null hypothesis is true and all the scores in the different groups come from the same population, then the between-groups variance should be the same as the within-groups variance. The means from the different groups should vary from one another no more nor less than do the scores within the groups. In order for us to be able to reject the null hypothesis, then, the means of the different groups must vary from one another more than the scores vary within the groups. The greater the variance (differences) between the groups of the experiment, the more likely the independent variable is to have had an effect, especially if the within-groups variance is low.

The person who originated this logic was the eminent British statistician R. A. Fisher, and the test is referred to as an **F-test** in his honor. The $F$-test is simply a ratio of the between-groups variance estimate to the within-groups variance estimate, so

$$F = \frac{\text{between-groups variance}}{\text{within-groups variance}} \qquad \textbf{(A–11)}$$

According to the logic we have just outlined, the $F$-ratio under the null hypothesis should be 1.00, because the between-groups variance should be the same as the within-groups variance. The greater the between-groups variance than the within-groups variance, and consequently the greater the $F$-ratio is than 1.00, the more confident we can be in rejecting the null hypothesis. Exactly how much greater the $F$-ratio must be than 1.00 depends on the **degrees of freedom** in the experiment, or how free the measures are to vary. This depends both on the number of groups or conditions in the experiment and on the number of observations in each group. The greater the number of degrees of freedom, the smaller need be the value of the $F$-ratio to be judged a reliable effect, as you can see from examining Statistical Table E. You should follow the computational example in Box A–4 carefully to gain a feel for the analysis of variance.

If the simple analysis of variance indicates that there is reliable variation among the conditions of an experiment, this still does not tell us all we would like to know. In particular, it is still of great interest to know which of the individual conditions vary among themselves. This is especially important in cases where independent-variable manipulation is qualitative in nature. **Quantitative** variation of an independent variable refers to the case where the quantity of an independent variable is manipulated (for example, amount of LSD), whereas **qualitative** variation is the case of conditions that vary but not in some easily specified quantitative manner. An example of qualitative variation is an instructional manipulation where the different conditions vary in the instructions that are given at the beginning of the experiment. In such cases it is not enough simply to say that the conditions vary reliably from one another. It is of interest to know which particular conditions differ. To answer this question, we need to perform tests after the simple analysis of variance. In these follow-up tests, the conditions of the experiment are taken two at a time and compared so we can see which pairs are reliably different. There is a great variety of statistical tests that can be used for this purpose. We could perform analyses of variance on groups taken as pairs, which is equivalent to performing $t$ tests, but usually other tests are performed. These include the Newman-Keuls test, the Scheffé test, Duncan's multiple-range test, Tukey's HSD (Honestly Significant

---

**Box A–4** Computing Simple Analysis of Variance

---

Imagine that you have just performed an experiment testing the effects of LSD on the running speeds of rats, but that there were three levels of LSD administered, rather than only two as in our earlier example. Ten rats received no LSD, ten others received a small amount, and yet a third group of ten received a great amount. Thus the experiment employs a between-subjects design where amount of LSD (none, small, large) is the independent variable and running time is the dependent variable. First calculate the sum of the scores ($\Sigma X$) and the sum of the squared values of the scores ($\Sigma X^2$).

Amount of LSD

|  | None | Small | Large |
|---|---|---|---|
|  | 13 | 17 | 26 |
|  | 11 | 15 | 20 |
|  | 14 | 16 | 29 |
|  | 18 | 20 | 31 |
|  | 12 | 13 | 17 |
|  | 14 | 19 | 25 |
|  | 10 | 18 | 26 |
|  | 13 | 17 | 23 |
|  | 16 | 19 | 25 |
|  | 12 | 21 | 27 |
| $\Sigma X$ | 133 | 175 | 249 |
| $\overline{X}$ | 13.30 | 17.50 | 24.90 |
| $\Sigma X^2$ | 1819 | 3115 | 6351 |

A basic quantity in calculation of analysis of variance is the **sum of squares**, which is an abbreviated form for the term **sum of squared deviations from the mean**. If you look back to equation A–1, which defines the variance of a sample, you will see that the sum of squares is the numerator. There are actually three sums of squares of interest. First is the total sum of squares ($SS_{total}$), which is defined as the sum of the squared deviations of the individual scores from the grand mean or the mean of all the scores in all groups in the experiment. Second is the sum of squares between groups ($SS_{between}$), which is the sum of the squared deviations of the group means from the grand mean. Third, the sum of squares within groups ($SS_{within}$) is the mean of the sum of the squared deviations of the individual scores within groups or conditions from the group means. It turns out that $SS_{total} = SS_{between} + SS_{within}$, so that in practice only two sums of squares need be calculated; the third can be found by subtraction.

These sums of squares could be calculated by taking the deviations from the appropriate means, squaring them and then finding the sum, but such a method would take much time and labor. Fortunately there are computational formulas which allow the calculations to be done more easily, especially if the values of $\Sigma X$ and $\Sigma X^2$ have been found for each group, as in the present data. The formula for finding the total sum of squares is

$$SS_{total} = \Sigma\Sigma X^2 - \frac{T^2}{N} \qquad \text{(A--12)}$$

where $\Sigma\Sigma X^2$ means that each score within each group is squared ($X^2$) and all these squared values are added together, so $\Sigma X^2$. There are two separate summation signs, one for summing the squared values within groups and one for then summing these $\Sigma X^2$ across the different groups. The $T$ is for the total of all scores and $N$ here is the total number of scores in the experiment. So $SS_{total}$ in our example is calculated in the following way:

$$SS_{total} = \Sigma\Sigma X^2 - \frac{T^2}{N}$$

$$SS_{total} = 1819 + 3115 + 6351 - \frac{(133 + 175 + 249)^2}{30}$$

$$SS_{total} = 11,285 - \frac{310,249}{30}$$

$$SS_{total} = 11,285 - 10,341.63$$

$$SS_{total} = 943.37$$

The between-groups sum of squares is calculated with the following formula:

$$SS_{between} = \Sigma\frac{(\Sigma X)^2}{n} - \frac{T^2}{N} \qquad \text{(A--13)}$$

The first part of the formula means that the sum of the values for each group is squared and then divided by the number of observations on which it is based or $(\Sigma X)^2/n$; then these values are summed across groups, so $\Sigma(\Sigma X)^2/n$]. The second part of the formula is the same as for the $SS_{total}$:

$$SS_{between} = \Sigma\frac{(\Sigma X)^2}{n} - \frac{T^2}{N}$$

$$SS_{between} = \frac{17,689}{10} + \frac{30,625}{10} + \frac{62,001}{10} - 10,341.63$$

$$SS_{between} = 11,031.50 - 10,341.63$$

$$SS_{between} = 689.87$$

The sum of squares within groups can be found by subtracting $SS_{between}$ from $SS_{total}$, so $SS_{within} = 943.37 - 689.87 = 253.50$. But as a check it is also worthwhile to compute it directly. This is done by computing an $SS_{total}$ as in equation A--12 for each group and summing all these sums of squares for the individual groups. Unless you have made an error, this quantity should equal $SS_{within}$ obtained by subtraction.

(Continued on next page)

After we have obtained the various sums of squares, it is convenient to construct an analysis-of-variance table such as the one that follows. In the far left column appears the source of variance, or source. Keep in mind that there are two primary sources of variance we are interested in comparing—between-groups and within-groups.

In the next column are the number of degrees of freedom ($df$). These can be thought of as the number of scores that are free to vary, given that the total is fixed. For the degrees of freedom between-groups, if the overall total is fixed, all groups are free to vary except one. So the between-groups $df$ is the number of groups minus one. In our example, then, it is $3 - 1 = 2$. The within-groups $df$ is equal to the total number of scores minus the number of groups, because there is one score in each group that cannot vary if the group total is fixed. So within-groups $df$ is $30 - 3 = 27$. The total $df$ = between-groups $df$ + within-groups $df$.

The third column is for the sum of squares ($SS$), which have already been calculated. The fourth column is for the mean squares ($MS$), which are found by dividing the $SS$ for each row by the $df$. Each mean square is an estimate of the population variance if the null hypothesis is true. But if the independent variable had an effect, the between-groups mean square should be larger than the within-groups mean square.

As already discussed in the text, these two values are compared by computing an $F$ ratio, which is found by dividing the $MS_{between}$ by the $MS_{within}$. Once the $F$ value is calculated, it is necessary to determine whether or not the value reaches an acceptable level of statistical significance. By looking in Statistical Table E, we can see that for 2 and 26 degrees of freedom (the closest we can get to 2 and 27), an $F$ value of 9.12 is needed for the .001 level of significance. Our $F$ value surpasses 9.12, so we can conclude that the groups varied reliably in running speed because of variation in the independent variable, amount of LSD injected.

| Source | df | SS | MS | F | p |
|--------|-----|--------|--------|-------|-------|
| Between-groups | 2 | 689.87 | 344.94 | 36.73 | <.001 |
| Within-groups | 27 | 253.50 | 9.39 | | |
| Total | 29 | 943.37 | | | |

*Note*: If you compute analyses of variance yourself with the aid of a calculator you must guard against errors. If you ever come up with a negative sum of squares within-groups (by subtracting $SS_{between}$ from $SS_{total}$), you will know you made an error. You cannot have a negative sum of squares. You should compute $SS_{within}$ both by subtraction and directly, anyway, as a check. One common error is to confuse $\Sigma X^2$ (square each number and then sum the squares) with $(\Sigma X)^2$, which is the square of the total ($\Sigma X$) of the scores.

Differences) test, and Dunnett's test. These vary in their assumptions and their power. You should consult statistical texts when you need to use a follow-up test.

***Multifactor analysis of variance.*** A frustrating aspect to the study of behavior is that there are hardly ever any simple or one-factor explanations. Even the simplest behaviors studied in laboratory situations turn out to be affected by multiple factors. In order to discover these multiple determinants of behavior and how they interact, we must perform experiments in which more than one factor is varied simultaneously. The appropriate procedure for analyzing results of such experiments is **multifactor analysis of variance**. This may involve analysis of experiments where any number of factors is concerned, but in practice it is rare to find more than four variables of interest manipulated simultaneously. When there are two factors, the analysis is referred to as two-way ANOVA; where there are three factors, it is a three-way ANOVA; and so on.

The importance of such complex designs involving more than one factor is that they allow us to assess how different factors may interact to produce an experimental result. Recall that an interaction occurs when the effect of one experimental variable is affected by the level of the other experimental variable (see chapter 3). If we performed a 2 × 2 experiment (this refers to two different factors with two different levels of each factor) on interpersonal attraction involving sex of the subject (male versus female) and sex of the experimental confederate whom the subject was to evaluate, we might discover an interaction effect. If how close the subject stands to the confederate were one of the dependent variables, then we might find that male subjects tend to stand closer to female confederates and female subjects stand closer to male confederates. This is an example of an interaction. There is no simple generalization as to how close male or female subjects will stand to a confederate in an experiment; it depends on the sex of the confederate.

When performing a complex analysis of variance we find out the separate effects of each factor in the experiment (called **main effects**), and also how the variables affect one another (called **interaction effects**, or simply interactions). If women tend to stand closer to the confederate than do men regardless of the sex of the confederate, this would be a main effect of sex of subject on interpersonal distance. And, again, an interaction would be the different effect of sex of subject depending on sex of the confederate.

Unfortunately we cannot devote space here to explaining completely how these complex analyses of variance are performed. Briefly, the $SS_{between}$ is found as it was in the simple or one-way analysis of variance, but here it is further decomposed into the main effects of the independent variables and there interactions. Then mean squares are computed on the basis of these sums of

squares by dividing by the appropriate number of degrees of freedom, and $F$-ratios are obtained as before. An example appears in
Box A–5.

The analysis of variance is a parametric statistical test and thus
assumptions are built into the test about the population parameters underlying the samples. The two most important assumptions
in the type of analysis of variance we are considering (the fixed-
effects model) are that the observations in each condition are normally distributed and that the within-groups variances of the different conditions are equivalent. This latter assumption is called
the **homogeneity of variance** assumption. It is assumed that manipulation of the independent variables should affect the variance
between groups, but not the variance within groups. In practice,
investigators do not worry much about these assumptions. The
reason is that statisticians have shown that the analysis of variance
is a **robust** statistical test, or one in which violations of its assumptions are unlikely to lead to erroneous conclusions. Most investigators do not even check for violations of the assumptions,
but even if they do and they find that the assumptions are violated,
the best solution is simply to employ a more conservative level of
confidence (say, .01 instead of .05). The fact that a manipulation
influenced the variance of the different experimental conditions
may be quite interesting in its own right because it indicates that
the subjects in the condition with the high variance were differentially influenced by the treatment. Understanding this fact may
be a clue to understanding behavior in the situation.

## MISUSES OF STATISTICS

Statistics are used so often that it seems possible to bolster any
argument with them. They are employed by politicians, econo-
mists, advertisers, psychologists, and many others to support various views, so it is little wonder that people have gained the impression that statistics can be bent to any purpose. But an old adage
has it that "Statistics don't lie, statisticians do." Actually, there is
probably little to fear from statisticians themselves, because their
sophistication permits them to differentiate a true argument based
on statistics from a false one. Nonetheless, statistics can be misused
to create a false impression. You should be aware of some common
misuses so that you will not be misled by them.

### Use of Small or Biased Samples

Many television commercials implicitly mislead us with small and/
or biased samples. Viewers see a woman who is asked to test two
brands of detergent on her family's greasy and grass-stained clothes.
She is pitting her usual product, BAF, against new Super Crud
Remover (SCR). BAF goes into one washer, Super Crud Remover
goes into the other, and later the woman is shown exclaiming over

**Box A–5** Calculation of a 2 × 2 ANOVA on the Data from a Memory Experiment

In this experiment there were forty subjects. They were divided up into four groups of ten, each group representing a different condition. Two groups were given high-imagery words to learn, or words that refer to concrete objects that are easily visualized (for example, elephant, chair, automobile). The other two groups received low-imagery words, or ones that are abstract and hard to form images of (such as beauty, democracy, truth). The two groups that received each type of word differed in the learning instructions they were given. One group of subjects in each of the two imagery conditions was told to repeat each word until they saw the next word appear on the screen. These subjects were in the Rote Rehearsal condition. Subjects in the Elaborative Rehearsal condition were instructed to create mental images or meaningful associations between the words as they were learning them. Thus the experiment represents a 2 × 2 factorial design, with one factor being the type of material studied (high- or low-imagery words) and the other being the instructions subjects were given (rote- or elaborative-rehearsal instructions). The design is between-subjects, since a different group of subjects participated in each of the four conditions. The number of words recalled by each subject appears in the following table. Then the steps involved in the analysis of variance, which allow us to appropriately analyze the results of the experiment, are outlined.

| | High-Imagery Words | | Low-Imagery Words | |
|---|---|---|---|---|
| | Rote Rehearsal | Elaborative Rehearsal | Rote Rehearsal | Elaborative Rehearsal |
| | 5 | 8 | 4 | 7 |
| | 7 | 8 | 1 | 6 |
| | 6 | 9 | 5 | 3 |
| | 4 | 7 | 6 | 3 |
| | 4 | 10 | 4 | 5 |
| | 9 | 10 | 3 | 6 |
| | 7 | 8 | 4 | 2 |
| | 5 | 9 | 4 | 4 |
| | 5 | 8 | 5 | 5 |
| | 6 | 9 | 3 | 4 |
| $\Sigma X =$ | 58 | 86 | 39 | 45 |
| $\overline{X} =$ | 5.8 | 8.6 | 3.9 | 4.5 |
| $\Sigma X^2 =$ | 358 | 748 | 169 | 225 |

$\Sigma\Sigma X^2 = (358 + \ldots + 225) = 1500 \qquad \Sigma\Sigma X = 228$

*Step 1.* Square the grand sum ($\Sigma\Sigma X = 228$) and divide by the total number of scores (40). $(\Sigma\Sigma X)^2/N = (228)^2/40 = 1299.6$. This is the correction term.

*Step 2.* SS Total $= \Sigma\Sigma X^2 - (\Sigma\Sigma X)^2/N$. Subtract the results of Step 1 from 1500. *SS* Total $= 200.4$.

(Continued on next page)

*Step 3.* SS Imagery. Get the sum of all scores in each imagery condition, square each sum, then divide each sum by the number of scores yielding each sum, add the two quotients, and then subtract the results of Step 1 from the last sum.

$$SS \text{ Imagery} = (58 + 86)^2/20 + (39 + 45)^2/20 - \text{Step 1}$$

$$= \frac{144^2 + 84^2}{20} - 1299.6$$

$$= 1389.6 - 1299.6$$

$$= 90$$

*Step 4.* SS Rehearsal. This is calculated in the same manner as Step 3, except you base your calculations on the grand sum of each type of rehearsal.

$$SS \text{ Rehearsal} = \frac{(86 + 45)^2 + (58 + 39)^2}{20} - \text{Step 1}$$

$$= 1328.5 - 1299.6$$

$$= 28.9$$

*Step 5.* SS Rehearsal X Imagery. Square each group sum and add the squares. Then divide each sum by the number of scores in each sum. From the last result, subtract the SS Imagery (Step 3), SS Rehearsal (Step 4), and Step 1.

$$SSI \text{ X R} = \frac{58^2 + 86^2 + 39^2 + 45^2}{10} - \text{Step 1} - \text{Step 3}$$

$$- \text{Step 4}$$

$$= 14306/10 - 1299.6 - 90 - 28.9$$

$$= 12.1$$

*Step 6.* SS Error. Subtract each of your treatments SS from SS Total.

$$SS \text{ Error} = 200.4 - 90 - 28.9 - 12.1$$

$$= 69.4$$

*Step 7.* Determining degrees of freedom.

$df$ Total = the number of measures less one (40 − 1) = 39
$df$ Imagery = number of levels of Imagery less one (2 − 1) = 1
$df$ Rehearsal = number of levels of Rehearsal less one (2 − 1) = 1
$df$ I X R = $df$ Imagery X $df$ Rehearsal (1 X 1) = 1
$df$ Error = $df$ Total − $df$ Imagery − $df$ Rehearsal − $df$ I X R (39 − 1 − 1 −1) = 36

*Step 8.* Summary table. Calculate mean squares (*MS*) by dividing *SS* by the number of *df*. Then calculate the *F* ratios by dividing the treatment *MS* by the *MS* Error.

| Source | SS | df | MS | F | p |
|---|---|---|---|---|---|
| | | *Summary Table of a 2 × 2 ANOVA* | | | |
| Imagery | 90. | 1 | 90. | 46.6 | <.05 |
| Rehearsal | 28.9 | 1 | 28.9 | 15.0 | <.05 |
| Imagery X Rehearsal | 12.1 | 1 | 12.1 | 6.3 | <.05 |
| Error | 69.4 | 36 | 1.9 | | |

*Step 9.* To determine the significance of the F ratio, enter Statistical Table E with the *df* for the numerator (in this case it is always 1), and with the *df* for the denominator (*df* Error), which is 36, for any effect you are interested in.

We can conclude that the type of words and type of rehearsal both influenced recall. But we should note that the effects of word type were dependent on the type of rehearsal (that is, we obtained an interaction). Elaborative rehearsal produced better recall than rote rehearsal, but the effect was larger on high-imagery words than on low-imagery words.

the better job that SCR did. Announcer: "Are you convinced?" Woman: "Why, yes. I will always use Super Crud Remover from now on. It really gets the crud off my clothes." Even making the unlikely assumption that the whole demonstration was not rigged, observers should know better than to be convinced by such a small sample (one case). If the "experiment" were repeated honestly with a hundred women, would all of them pick Super Crud Remover? The advertiser tries to leave us with the impression that because this one woman prefers the product, everyone (the population) will. But we should be careful about assuming something to be true of the population at large from a sample of one.

Another problem is that a sample of individuals surveyed for such an ad might be deliberately biased. Advertisers are always surveying groups that are likely to be predisposed in their favor anyway, such as people who already own the product. Advertisers ask consumers, "How well do you like your Bass-o-matic?" and then show a small sample of interviews that went well from the manufacturer's point of view. It would be more convincing to sample people who had never used the product and to test the product against its main rivals. Since more advertising claims on television must now be based on facts, this type of commercial is becoming more widely used. In one interesting ad, owners of one type of luxury car are asked to test it against a competitor. Here is a case in which the sample tested is expected to be biased *against* the new product and for their old product, so if a preference is found for the new product it seems to argue much more strongly for the new product.

Whenever you hear about preferences that people have exhibited, you should ask two questions about the sample: (1) How large was it? (2) How were people chosen to be in it?

***The exaggerated graph.*** A common way to show or hide differences in graphs is to exaggerate the results being plotted. This involves changing the scale on the graph to show off a difference, or (more rarely) to hide a difference. Suppose that the numer of murders in a city increased from 72 to 80 to 91 over three years. The next year the mayor is running for reelection and is eager to show that the city has been safe for the last three years under her administration. So her campaign workers draw up the graph shown in the top of figure A–5. By making the scale on the *y* axis very long, they create the impression that the murder rate is fairly steady. In the same year the city police are arguing that they need higher staffing levels. They want to show how the city is becoming more unsafe, so they depict the murder rate as increasing steeply by changing the scale, as in the bottom graph of figure A–5.

The facts are shown accurately in both groups. However, the top graph gives the impression that the murder rate is increasing very gradually, hardly worth worrying about. (Hasn't the mayor done a good job leading the city?) The bottom graph, on the other hand, creates the impression that the murder rate is increasing dramatically. (Don't we need more police?)

These graphing techniques are common. In fact, there are exaggerated scales used in some of the graphs in this book to show

FIGURE A–5.

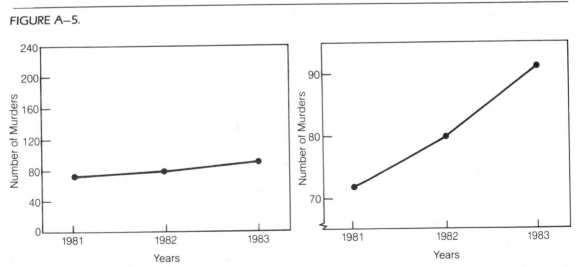

Variation in scales. The graph at the left seems to show the murder rate increasing only slightly, whereas the one at the right shows the rate going up dramatically. Yet both graphs actually show the murder rate accurately—the difference is in the scale on the *y* axis. It is important to examine a graph carefully and note the scale of measurement, since scale changes can make small differences look large and vice versa.

patterns of results more clearly. You should always look carefully to see what the scale is in a graph. With experimental data it is more important to determine whether a difference is statistically reliable than to determine whether the difference appears "large" when graphed.

### Absent or Inappropriate Comparisons

A common ploy used in advertising is to say that some product has *x* percent more of something good or *y* percent less of something bad. "Buy the new Thunderbolt since it gives 27 percent better gas mileage." This sounds convincing until you stop to ask yourself, "27 percent better than what?" A missing comparison here makes the statistic completely meaningless. Perhaps the Thunderbolt gets 27 percent better mileage than a two-ton tank, which is hardly an argument for buying it.

Even when a specific comparison is made, it is often still inappropriate. The claim is often made in advertising that a product is better than last year's model. "Buy the new, improved, Thunderbolt. It gets 27 percent better mileage than last year's model." Of course, it could still be a real dog, even if it's better than last year's dog. What the consumer would really like is a comparison of the mileage efficiency of the new Thunderbolt with other new cars in roughly the same class, as is now provided by government testing.

Another problem in making comparisons is that often there is no information on the reliability of differences. In one commercial, two cars of the same make and year were filled with one gallon of gas, and test driven at a constant speed around a track. The difference in the test was the type of gasoline used. One car stopped before the other, and the viewers were supposed to conclude that the sponsor's gasoline was superior to the other brand. But only after a long series of comparisons could a researcher statistically test for a reliable difference between the two types of gas. This is the same problem as occurs in the case of BAF versus Super Crud Remover; the sample of observations is too small.

In general, watch to make sure that in statements involving a comparison, the object of comparison is described and is appropriate. There should also be some statement about whether or not any differences are statistically reliable.

### The Gambler's Fallacy

Statistical tests are based on probability theory, the theory of expectations about the likelihood of random events. It is interesting to note that people's perceptions of the randomness of events do not agree in some important respects with ideas from probability theory. People often draw conclusions that seem irrational when judged by the logic of probability theory. There is much interesting research on this phenomenon (for example, Tversky and Kahneman, 1971, 1974). Here we will examine one of the most common mistakes in judgments of probability.

Imagine a person flipping a coin 1,000 times. If it is a fair coin, it should come up heads about 500 times and tails about 500 times. The probability of it coming up heads over a large number of trials is 0.50, but of course even a fair coin will probably not come up heads exactly 500 times in 1,000 flips—it might come up 490 or 505. Yet the result is fairly close. Let us now take the case of a person betting on whether the coin will come up heads or tails. If the situation is truly random, a gambler has a probability of 0.50 of winning on any particular trial. Imagine that on five trials in a row the gambler bets $5 that the coin will come up heads and each time it comes up tails. Of course, the fact that the coin comes up tails five times in a row is ususual, and the chances of such an event are quite low (.03). The gambler notes this odd occurrence and, on the next bet, he doubles his bet to $10 and again bets on heads. Now he is more certain that the coin will come up heads.

The logic the gambler uses is as follows. "The coin is a fair coin. On the average it will come up heads half the time and tails half the time. The coin has just come up tails five times in a row. Therefore, it is due to come up heads to even things up, because on the average it will come up heads half the time. So I should bet on heads, and even increase my bet." More generally, the logic is: "If the game is truly random and I am losing, then I should keep playing because my luck is bound to change for the better." This kind of logic keeps gambling casinos at Las Vegas and Atlantic City humming, and wipes out fortunes from otherwise intelligent people.

The fallacy of the argument is in applying the laws of probability—such as a fair coin coming up heads half the time—that hold only over tremendously large numbers of events. The laws cannot be applied to small runs. What the gambler overlooks is that the flips of the coin are independent events; what happened on previous flips does not influence what happens next. If the coin came up tails five times in a row, this does not increase the probability of heads on the next throw. It is still 0.50. The coin does not have a memory for previous trials, as the gambler seems to assume implicitly. The gambler should not feel any more certain on the sixth trial than he or she did on the first five. The probability of heads showing has not changed.

In some sense the gambler's mistake is natural. There is a ring of truth to the argument, and it is based on true laws of probability. Over a very large series of throws, a fair coin will come up heads 50 percent of the time. The error comes in applying to a small series what is true over a very large series of events. The laws do not apply to small series of random events as well. With, say,

10,000,000 coin flips, heads will come up almost exactly 50 percent of the time. But if a gambler takes a small series of the larger number, say five flips, heads could come up either zero or five times with a probability of 0.06. These outcomes (all heads or all tails) are not terribly likely, but they are not vanishingly small, either.

**1.** Understanding some elementary principles about statistics is crucial to the conduct of psychological research. There are two branches of statistics, descriptive and inferential.

**2.** Descriptive statistics are used to summarize and organize raw data. There are graphical methods for doing this, such as histograms and frequency polygons. However, the primary summary measures are those of central tendency of a distribution and dispersion of a distribution.

**3.** The primary measure of central tendency is the mean of the distribution, or what is usually called the average of the scores. The median (the middlemost score) is sometimes used, especially for distributions with extreme scores, whereas the mode (the most frequent score) is rarely used. The primary measures of dispersion are the standard deviation and variance. The standard deviation is used more often in descriptive statistics, and the variance is used primarily in inferential statistics. Most distributions in psychology are assume to be normal, which means that the mean, median, and mode all fall in the same place; that the distribution is symmetrical; and that a certain proportion of scores fall under each part of the normal curve.

**4.** Inferential statistics allow us to make inferences about the reliability of differences among conditions. We want to infer from a sample of scores what the case is for the populations involved. A great variety of tests are used in inferential statistics. A similar logic is applied in all. An alternative hypothesis is tested against the null hypothesis, which holds that there are no differences among groups in the experiment. Computations are performed that give rise to a value. This value is then compared to a distribution of values in a table that informs us as to what level of confidence we can have in rejecting the null hypothesis.

**5.** We use a $z$-score test for comparing a sample to a known population, to see whether the sample came from the same population. To determine whether two groups, an experimental and a control, differ from one another we use the Mann-Whitney $U$ test, which applies when two independent groups of subjects are employed; and the sign test and Wilcoxon signed-ranks test, which apply when the measures in the two conditions are related (either by using a within-subjects design or by matching subjects). These last two tests are nonparametric statistical tests since they do not make any assumptions about the population parameters underlying the sample observations that are actually used.

**6.** The analysis of variance is the important statistical procedure used in making comparisons among more than two groups. The simple analysis of variance is used in testing for reliability when one independent variable is manipulated. More complicated multifactor analyses are used when two or more independent variables are manipulated simultaneously. These multifactor designs are especially important in that they allow us to assess the interaction of factors that determine behavior.

**7.** Mark Twain wrote that "There are three kinds of lies—lies, damned lies, and statistics." Some ways in which statistics can be misused include drawing conclusions from small or biased samples; exaggerating the scales on graphs for effect; making inappropriate comparisons; and assuming that the laws of probability which hold for huge samples of observations can be generalized to small samples (as in the gambler's fallacy). Statistics themselves do not lie, but they can be used to give misleading impressions.

**KEY TERMS**

alpha level
analysis of variance
between-groups variance
biased sample
central tendency
degrees of freedom
descriptive statistics
directional test
dispersion
distribution of sample means
experimental hypothesis
*F*-test
frequency distribution
frequency polygon
gambler's fallacy
histogram
homogeneity of variance
inferential statistics
inflection point
interaction effect
level of confidence (or level of significance)
main effect
Mann-Whitney *U* test
mean
median
mode
multifactor analysis of variance

nondirectional test
nonparametric tests
normal curve
null hypothesis
one-tailed test
parameters
parametric tests
population
power of a statistical test
random sample
range
reliability
robust tests
sample
sign test
simple (one factor) analysis of variance
standard deviation
standard error of the mean
statistics
two-tailed test
type-I error
type-II error
variance
Wilcoxon signed-ranks test
within-groups variance
*z* score (or standard score)

# APPENDIX B

**Chapter Outline**

# Experimental Psychology: A Historical Sketch

*Psychology has a long past, but only a short history.*

Hermann Ebbinghaus

Curiosity and wonder are the prime motivations for science, and there are few topics that people have been more interested in than the workings of their own minds. Much of the writings of the great philosophers, from Aristotle's time to the present, have been concerned with what can be called psychological problems. How do we perceive and know the external world? How do we learn about it and remember what we learn? How do we use this information to build up concepts of the world and solve the problems that the world presents us? What are the roots of abnormal behavior? Are there laws that govern social and political behavior? Is there a meaning to dreams?

Although such topics have been discussed for centuries, the methods of science were not applied to the study of the human mind and behavior until three or four hundred years after they found a solid place in physics. (Thus Ebbinghaus's quote.) In fact, psychology today is to be compared, perhaps, with sixteenth-century physics. As many of the students of psychology realize (to their dismay), we still have much to learn about many important areas of human behavior.

This appendix is intended to provide a brief and very rough sketch of the intellectual history of psychology. Full histories are to be found in Boring (1950), the classic in the field, and in a more recent and readable work by Schultz (1981).

**ORIGINS OF EXPERIMENTAL PSYCHOLOGY: PHILOSOPHY AND PHYSIOLOGY**

An important issue in the history of philosophy is the mind-body problem. Are the mind and body essentially the same or different in nature? A once-popular position on this issue, which probably greatly retarded the development of a scientific psychology is that the mind and body are separate entities and do not interact. According to this theory, often called **dualism**, the body is governed by physical laws, as are inanimate objects, but the mind is not governed by laws since it possesses free will. Thus it makes no sense to apply scientific methods in an attempt to discover laws of mental life, if one is a dualist and believes that such laws do not exist.

The influential philosophical writings of René Descartes (1596–1650) helped weaken the belief that the body and mind do not interact. Previously it had been argued that though the mind could control the body, there was little influence in the opposite direction. Descartes advanced the idea of mutual interaction—the body could affect the mind and the mind could affect the body. Although the dualist position remained, and the mind was still regarded as immortal and as possessing free will and a soul, the body could be studied as a mechanical system by rational, scientific means. And since animals were regarded as not possessing souls, they too could be studied by the methods applied to the inanimate objects of physical science.

Over the years the idea became more prevalent that even the human mind could be treated as something that could be profitably studied to discover mental laws. The writings of the British empiricist philosophers (Locke, Berkeley, Hume, Hartley) emphasized the mechanical nature of mental phenomena and discussed the "laws" of association in thought and the physical basis of the perception of the external world. The idea was beginning to take hold that for purposes of scientific study the mind could be treated as a machine.

The British philosophers also emphasized the importance of learning in our understanding of the world. Descartes had argued that some ideas are innate, or develop without information from the external world impinging on the senses. Kant expanded on this position and aspects of it were later incorporated into the Gestalt school of psychology. The British empiricists received their name by rejecting this idea. John Locke wrote in *An Essay concerning Human Understanding*:

> Let us suppose the mind to be, as we say, white paper, void of all characters, without any ideas:—How comes it to be furnished? Whence comes it by that vast store which the busy and boundless fancy of man has painted on it with an almost endless variety? Whence has it all the *materials* of reason and knowledge? To this I answer, in one word, from EXPERIENCE. In that all our knowledge is founded. (Book II, chapter I).

Philosophers were preparing the way for a scientific psychology by treating the mind as subject to natural laws, but their method of study was simply one of anecdote and reflection. No matter how brilliant, these methods were likely to advance our knowledge little past the careful reflections of Plato and Aristotle centuries before. What was needed was application of the experimental methods and logic of science to the study of the mind and behavior. As Boring observed, "The application of the experimental method to the problem of mind is the great outstanding event to which no other is comparable." This method came to psychology by way of physiology.

German physiologists in the middle of the nineteenth century were interested in what is today considered sensory physiology, the physiology of the organs of sense and the transmission of information from these organs to the brain via the nervous system. A number of the topics investigated began to deal with the perceptual process more than its physiology. Many of the German physiologists hoped that physiology could be reduced ultimately to physics, and, as they became interested in the physiology of the human nervous system, they were coming dangerously close to treating the mind as a physical machine. The Berlin Physical Society was formed in the 1840s with an overriding commitment to the belief that ultimately all phenomena could be explained in terms of physics. Four of these radical young scientists, all in their twenties, signed in blood (so the story goes) an oath stating their belief that all forces in the human organism were chemical and physical ones.

### The Contribution of Helmholtz

One of these young scientists was Hermann von Helmholtz (1821–1894). He was primarily a physicist and physiologist and was not concerned with establishing psychology as an independent discipline, but his research is given much credit in having had this effect. His work in vision and audition was overwhelmingly important, but what we should emphasize here is his role in conducting what may be considered transition experiments between physiology and experimental psychology.

One famous case was his use of what is now known as a **reaction-time experiment** to study the speed of neural impulses. Johannes Müller, a famous German physiologist, had argued that transmission of nervous impulses was instantaneous, or perhaps approached the speed of light. If you pinch your hand, do you notice any time elapse between the time you see yourself do the pinching and the time you feel the pinch? Probably not. At any rate, Müller also stated that we could probably never calculate the speed of nervous impulses. Only a few years later Helmholtz (in 1851) measured the speed experimentally. The basic idea was ingeniously simple: Stimulate a nerve at two different distances from the brain and measure the difference in time it takes for the organism to respond to the stimulation. If one knows the distance between the two points of stimulation and this difference in time, then one can calculate the rate of the nervous impulse, since rate equals distance divided by time. Helmholtz stimulated blindfolded people on either the shoulder or the ankle and measured how fast they could react with their hand (by pushing a lever) in each case. Since he could measure approximately how much further the impulse would have to travel to the brain from the ankle than from the shoulder, he was able to estimate the speed of nervous impulses at the relatively slow rate of 50 meters per second—not even the speed of sound, much less that of light! Helmholtz's most careful experimental work on this issue was with frogs (where of course the technique, but not the logic, was different), and the estimates were not too different. In fact, the estimates have more or less withstood the test of time, though we know today that speed of the nervous impulse depends on the diameter of the nerves involved.

An interesting footnote is that Helmholtz so despaired of the great variability (or differences among the reaction times) he found among subjects and even with the same subject on different trials, that he gave up altogether on this line of research (Schultz, 1975, p. 43). Many psychologists since Helmholtz have also lamented the variability one finds in psychological research, although most have not given it up for this reason. Much of this book is concerned with the problem of variability in measures of animal or human, behavior, and how to overcome this problem.

## Early Scientific Psychology

Scientific psychology had its birth and early life in Germany. In this section we will mention the contributions of four early pioneers: Weber, Fechner, Wundt, and Ebbinghaus.

### Ernst Weber

Ernst Weber (1795–1878) was an anatomist and physiologist at Leipzig whose research centered on cutaneous sensation, or the sense of touch. His most important contribution to psychology grew out of some experiments he did on whether active engagement of one's muscles mattered in one's judging the weights of objects. He had people compare two weights, one of which was called a standard. In one case, blindfolded subjects first picked up a standard weight and then a comparison weight, and indicated to the experimenter whether the two were the same or different. In another case, the subjects were passive and simply had the weights placed in their hands successively, and they then made their decision.

Weber discovered that judgments were more accurate when subjects actively engaged their muscles, but more important, he noted something interesting in subjects' abilities to detect a difference between the standard and comparison weights. The greater the weight of the standard, the greater must be the difference between the standard and comparison weight before the difference could be noticed by the subjects. When the standard weight was small, only a small difference between the standard and comparison was necessary for subjects to detect a difference. But when the weight was large, the difference necessary for detection (called the **just-noticeable difference** or **jnd**) was correspondingly larger. Weber further discovered that for any of the senses, the ratio of the amount of difference necessary to produce a **jnd** to the standard was a constant. Thus not only does the amount of difference necessary to produce a **jnd** increase with the size of the standard, it does so in a quite systematic way. This fact has come to be known as **Weber's law**.

### Gustav Fechner

Weber thought that his finding was an interesting and useful generalization, but was by no means staggered by its importance. Gustav Fechner (1801–1887) was. Fechner was bizarre, in many ways, but his importance to psychology was great. He was trained as a physicist, but also made contributions to philosophy, religion, aesthetics, and psychology. At times he was something of a madman in his personal life. Among numerous other academic ventures he wrote one book on life after death and another (antedating a recent revival of interest in this topic) which argues that plants have a "mental life." In the 1830s his interests turned to the psychological topics of color vision and afterimages. He badly injured his eyes while staring at the sun through colored lenses and this, with his severe depression and strain from overwork, combined to force him into retirement in 1839.

Fechner recovered, however, to the lasting benefit of psychology. In 1850 he was worrying about the fundamental problem of whether there were laws that governed the translation of physical energy into its psychological or mental representation. He began searching for laws that would relate the intensity of physical stimuli to the subjective impression of these stimuli. While grappling with this problem, he came upon Weber's work and greatly celebrated the principle Weber discovered, naming it Weber's law. Fechner refined it somewhat and, as we discuss in chapter 5, this extension is called **Fechner's law.** To Fechner this was fulfillment of his hope that exact quantitative relationships exist between the physical and mental worlds. Thus Fechner founded the important discipline of **psychophysics,** which we consider in chapter 5.

### Wilhelm Wundt

Perhaps the first person to consider himself primarily a psychologist, at least late in his career, was Wilhelm Wundt (1832–1920). Trained in physiology and medicine (by Helmholtz, among others) he gradually became interested in psychology. In 1873 his *Principles of Physiological Psychology* was published, which the eminent historian Boring called the most important book in the history of experimental psychology. In it he systematically reviewed everything known about psychology at the time and also presented his system of psychology, which later came to be called the **structural school** of psychology. The book went through six editions and helped lay the groundwork for a systematic psychology. Wundt's contributions were primarily in organizing psychology and helping to establish it as an independent discipline, more than in making important scientific discoveries. Wundt trained many people who were later to make important contributions in their own right. He also is given credit for establishing the first laboratory of experimental psychology in 1879 at Leipzig and for establishing the first psychology journal.

Although Wundt was instrumental in establishing experimental psychology as a separate discipline, he did not believe that the higher mental processes such as memory, thought, and creativity could ever be studied experimentally. Experimental method, he claimed, could only be applied to the study of sensation and perception. He thought that the higher mental processes should be studied through the examination of the works of civilization over the centuries in various cultures, or through cultural history or cultural anthropology. Wundt contributed ten volumes of research to this pursuit.

### Hermann Ebbinghaus

In the same year (1879) that Wundt was establishing his laboratory, work was being done to discredit his belief about the extreme limits of experimental method in psychology. In this year Hermann Ebbinghaus (1850–1909) initiated his pioneering experiments on human learning and memory which culminated in his important book, *On Memory*, in 1885. This text showed that interesting experimental work could be done on more complex psychological topics such as memory. His investigations spawned the critical area of inquiry concerning human learning and memory, and are considered more fully in chapter 10.

## SCHOOLS OF PSYCHOLOGY

It is customary to divide psychology into a number of schools for the years 1890 to 1940 or so, though this does some damage to certain trends in psychology that resist being neatly fit into these pigeonholes. Nonetheless, we shall briefly describe here some of the main features of the schools of **structuralism, functionalism, behaviorism**, and **Gestalt psychology**.

### Structuralism:
### The Structure of Mental Life

Wundt was the originator of the structural school of psychology, although the school is also closely associated with the name of Edward Bradford Titchener (1867–1927). Titchener was one of Wundt's students who brought this view to the United States and advanced it from his lab at Cornell University. Though these men differed on some particulars, we can treat their views together.

As its name implies, structural psychology was primarily concerned with uncovering the structure of the mind. According to the structuralists, the three primary questions for psychology were: (1) What are the elements of experience?; (2) How are they combined?; and (3) Why? What is the cause? The basic elements of experience were considered to be **sensations:** sights, sounds, tastes, smells, and so forth. The other two elements of experience were **images** or **ideas**, which represented experiences not actually present; and **affections**, which were emotional reactions such as hate, joy, and love. Each element of experience could also be evaluated as to its attributes of duration, intensity, quality, and clearness.

The work of structural psychology was to break down complex mental experiences into their components. Thus it was elementaristic, since it sought the basic elements of mental experience. Elementary sensations and images were thought to be compounded through principles of association to become complex mental events. The method of decomposing these mental events was **introspection.** Introspection for structural psychologists did not refer to casual reflection, or even critical reflection, but rather to a specific, technical method of viewing experience. To naïve observers (that is, all of us) consciousness seems to be all of one piece, or a stream, as William James described it. Trained introspectionists were weaned from this view. They were to report the conscious contents of an experience instead of the focal object under consideration. A trained introspectionist would not report seeing a table in the environment, but rather would report seeing a particular spatial pattern, color, brightness, and so on. In other words, introspectionists were trained to see the elements of the experience of seeing a table. If one naïvely reported seeing a table, this was considered a case of committing the **stimulus error.**

Introspection was a rigorous and difficult method which people outside the structural camp felt to be sterile. It was also unreliable; introspectionists in different laboratories were not able to agree on the contents of the same experience. Titchener believed that the structural program set the pattern for the way psychology should develop, and what remained was simply to fill in the details. He railed against the newer trends in psychology, trends that eventually pushed the structural school from the scene after 1920. None theless, Wundt and Titchener trained many psychologists who were later to become prominent, and structuralism served an important function, since the other schools were, in part, a reaction against it.

### Functionalism: The Uses of Mind

Just as the structuralists were concerned with the structure of mental life, the functionalists were concerned with the functions of mental processes and structures. During the late 1800s, Darwin's theory of evolution swept through intellectual circles in both England and the United States. Thus it was quite natural that people began asking about the adaptive significance of psychological processes. What is the function of psychological processes? What differences do they make?

John Dewey (1859–1952) initiated functionalism at the University of Chicago after his arrival in 1894. Arriving at about the same time were George Herbert Mead, James Rowland Angell, and A. W. Moore. Dewey was greatly influenced by Darwin's concept of natural selection. In 1896 he published a paper called "The Reflex Arc Concept in Psychology," where he criticized the trend toward elementarism in psychology, which is the breaking down of psychological processes into their supposed elementary parts. Interestingly, he did not attack Titchener in the paper, but was more concerned with other issues. He argued that psychological processes were continuous, ongoing events and that psychologists should be careful to remember that distinctions they introduced to study the process were to some extent artificial and not part of the act itself. Dewey emphasized studying behavior in its natural context to determine its functions.

The functionalist school was more vague and amorphous than Titchener's tight little band of structuralists. The functionalists had little use for introspection, thought it was impossible to study mental processes devoid of their context and function, and were much more prone to endorse practical or applied programs in psychology. Yet the functionalists had no specific program for psychology as did Titchener, and the closest they ever came to providing a manifesto was Angell's presidential address to the American Psychological Association (1907). Besides emphasizing applied activities such as mental tests and education (the field to which Dewey migrated), functionalism helped introduce the study of lower organisms into psychology. This naturally followed from its emphasis on evolution and the developmental function of psychological processes.

Functionalism spread from Chicago in numerous directions, especially to Columbia University. Its position, never too systematic or dogmatic, was simply absorbed by psychology at large. And while functionalism was enjoying its heyday at the University of

Chicago, a young psychologist named John Watson received his degree there in 1903.

## Behaviorism: A Mind-less Psychology

In 1913 John Watson published a paper called "Psychology as the Behaviorist Views It," and there began the behaviorist revolution in psychology. Watson's ideas about what was later to be called behaviorism had begun to take shape during his days at the University of Chicago, but were not fully developed until some years later when he was teaching at Johns Hopkins University. In his 1913 paper Watson sharply attacked structural psychology and introspectionism with its emphasis on consciousness and mental contents. Watson argued that we should sweep away all this nonsense, which could not even be reproduced from one lab to another, and study something that all reasonable people could agree on: behavior. He endorsed a statement by Pillsbury that "psychology is the science of behavior" and continued:

> I believe we can write a psychology, define it as Pillsbury, and never go back upon our definition: never use the terms consciousness, mental states, mind, content, introspectively verifiable, imagery, and the like. It can be done in terms of stimulus and response, in terms of habit formation, habit integration, and the like. Furthermore, I believe it is really worth while to make this attempt now. (1913, pp. 166–167).

Watson's clear, concise statement of the position of behaviorism was quite influential. For many psychologists it justified throwing out a lot of the murky nonsense that had occupied the field for so long. Watson's flair for straightforward, interesting writing was evident also in his other work, among which is his notable book *Psychology from the Standpoint of a Behaviorist* (1919).

The behaviorists were intent on establishing psychology as a natural science, a status they felt it lacked in 1913. Its subject matter was to be behavior. There was no need to become engaged in complicated arguments about terms such as consciousness, imageless thought, and apperception, whose meanings were unclear. Watson and the other behaviorists attacked both structuralism and functionalism on the grounds of vagueness. The behaviorists did not say that consciousness, imagery, et cetera did not exist; they just maintained that such terms were not useful scientific constructs.

Behaviorists considered that most important behaviors were learned, so the study of learning became the central focus of interest. The pioneering studies of Pavlov and Thorndike, reviewed in chapters 8 and 11, indicated the possibility of an objective psychology of learning, and the focus of behavioral psychology has been on learning ever since.

The issues of behaviorism brought on a revolution within psychology, a revolution that is still with us. Much of the behaviorist point of view has by now been absorbed into the mainstream of psychology, though there are still debates over many particulars. There is, indeed, no one position that today can be called behaviorism, except for the general one that endorses the study of behavior as the appropriate subject matter of psychology. (Presumably all experimental psychologists subscribe to this view today, since all are observing behavior.) Rather, there are a number of different behaviorist positions identified with a number of different people. Some of Watson's most prominent successors in the behaviorist line are E. B. Holt, Karl Lashley, E. C. Tolman, E. R. Guthrie, Clark Hull, Kenneth Spence, and B. F. Skinner. These psychologists all have considered themselves behaviorists, though they have differed widely on a number of issues regarding how psychology should be approached. For example, Lashley and Hull were quite concerned with the physiological bases of behavior, whereas Skinner has shunned such inquiries. Critics these days who argue against behaviorism usually are arguing against the position of B. F. Skinner, who has attracted much attention as a radical behaviorist for the extremity of some of the views. But, of course, Skinner's position is not to be identified as the only form of behaviorism in psychology, since there are numerous other behaviorist positions.

It is popular to say these days that behaviorism is on the decline. Mental constructs (such as attention) have been reintroduced in psychology, even in the study of animal behavior. But these mental constructs are closely tied to observable responses. (We discuss in chapters 6 and 14 how to find evidence for unobservable psychological constructs.) Behaviorism has had a wide impact on all areas of experimental psychology, and thrives today in many forms.

### Gestalt Psychology: Perception of the Whole

Functionalism and behaviorism developed in the United States partly as a reaction to structuralism. Another revolt against structuralism developed on its home ground, in Germany. The structural view of perception can be characterized as a brick-and-motar view: sensations (the bricks) are held together by associations (the mortar). Gestalt psychologists argued against this elementaristic position and claimed that perception of objects was of wholes, not complicated sums of parts. People perceive the world in unitary wholes, in terms of Gestalt psychology.

Max Wertheimer (1880–1943) and the other Gestalt psychologists produced many demonstrations of the unity of the perceptual process that seemed incompatible with the structuralist position. One of these was the phenomenon of **shape constancy.** If you stand in front of a book on a table, a rectangular image may be produced on your retina, but if you move sideways several feet in one direction or the other, the retinal image may become trapezoidal. Despite this change in the retinal sensations, you perceive the book as being the same and having the same shape in both cases. The shape remains constant. There are similar constancies of size and brightness, as well as numerous other perceptual phenomena demonstrating the same point. Perception appears to have qualities of wholeness independent of the changing sensations projected on the receptors.

Gestalt psychology began, as did behaviorism, as a successful protest against structural psychology, but soon found itself competing with behaviorism. The Gestaltists found the same unsatisfactory elementarism in the behaviorists' descriptions of behavior as they had in the structuralists', but now the elements were stimuli and responses. The behaviorists in turn found the Gestaltists' constructs every bit as fuzzy and ill-defined as they had the structuralists' and functionalists'. In addition, the Gestaltists were often content to make some point or other through simple demonstrations, without devising clear theories and testing them experimentally. To some extent Gestaltists and behaviorists were investigating different areas, with the Gestaltists concerned primarily with perception and the behaviorists with learning. But the later Gestalt psychologists, the most notable of whom were Kurt Koffka and Wolfgang Köhler, began applying Gestalt constructs to other areas of psychology, such as the study of learning, memory, and problem solving. Thus behaviorists and Gestaltists often have come into conflict, with the experimental battles usually ending in draws. It may well be that Gestalt theorists were describing behavior at a more general level than behaviorists, and that their seemingly disparate accounts of the same psychological phenomena might not be as incompatible as they seemed at the time.

Gestalt psychology has not been as integrated into the mainstream of psychology as have functionalism and behaviorism, but its influence in certain areas of psychology has been overwhelming. This is certainly true of modern cognitive psychology, especially in the areas of perception and problem solving and thought.

## SOME MODERN TRENDS

The era of schools of psychology declined around 1940 or so, and this way of strictly dividing the field of psychology is no longer profitable. The influence of the schools lives on in contemporary research, but the organization of the field lies along different lines. Very little has been written about the history of psychology since 1940, as there are few unifying themes yet apparent. We will sketch here some modern trends, however.

### World War II and the Extension of Psychology

During World War II, psychologists were employed in such diverse occupations as studying public opinion and propaganda, aiding race relations in the armed services, training animals to aid in combat situations, designing cockpits of complicated aircraft, constructing tests for personnel selection, and dealing with clinical problems of battle fatigue, depression, and so forth. Psychologists were forced from their scholastic retreats and encouraged to apply their knowledge to the numerous problems at hand. In many cases this contact with real-world problems allowed them to see the inadequacy of their concepts and provided them the opportunity to develop new and better ideas. Thus the war had a healthy influence on many areas of psychology.

Another trend occurring at about the same time was the extension of experimental method to problem areas to which it had not previously been applied. Experimental social psychology and experimental child psychology received considerable attention during the 1930s and 1940s.

### Specialization

Perhaps the most notable recent trend in psychology is specialization. The schools of psychology tended to be all-encompassing; they had something to say about every phase of what they considered psychology. For example, behaviorists did not just concern themselves with learning, though this was their primary interest, but also applied their concepts to the areas of thought, language, and child development. Now psychologists no longer identify themselves by schools, but by areas of interest. Most psychology departments are organized along these lines, as are chapters 5–14 of this book.

Psychologists may be social psychologists, or animal-learning psychologists, or developmental psychologists, or cognitive psychologists (sensation, perception, memory, language, thinking, information processing, et cetera), or personality psychologists, and so forth. Or psychologists may specialize in psychobiology, clinical psychology, or organizational or industrial psychology. And all these areas have subareas, such as those just listed for cognitive psychology. Workers within these fields are often quite likely to know little about the other areas. This trend toward specialization is often decried as unfortunate, but there seems little alternative. Such specialization is simply the mark of a maturing science, for there seems little possibility for a psychologist to be knowledgeable in all the areas of psychology today.

Experimental psychology is one of the forty divisions of the American Psychological Association. However, many psychologists belonging to most of the other areas employ experimental method in their work. (On the other hand, members of some fields may oppose the use of experimental method in psychology.) The listing in table B–1 gives you some idea of the great diversity and specialization found among present-day psychologists.

| APA Division Number | APA Division Name |
|---|---|
| | **The Divisions of the American Psychological Association** |
| 1. | Division of General Psychology |
| 2. | Division on the Teaching of Psychology |
| 3. | Division of Experimental Psychology |
| 5. | Division on Evaluation and Measurement |
| 6. | Division on Physiological and Comparative Psychology |
| 7. | Division on Developmental Psychology |
| 8. | The Society of Personality and Social Psychology—A Division of the APA |
| 9. | The Society for the Psychological Study of Social Issues— A Division of the APA |
| 10. | Division of Psychology and the Arts |
| 12. | Division of Clinical Psychology |
| 13. | Division of Consulting Psychology |
| 14. | The Society for Industrial and Organizational Psychology, Inc.—A Division of the APA |
| 15. | Division of Educational Psychology |
| 16. | Division of School Psychology |
| 17. | Division of Counseling Psychology |
| 18. | Division of Psychologists in Public Service |
| 19. | Division of Military Psychology |
| 20. | Division of Adult Development and Aging |
| 21. | The Society of Engineering Psychologists  A Division of the APA |
| 22. | Division of Rehabilitation Psychology |
| 23. | Division of Consumer Psychology |
| 24. | Division of Theoretical and Philosophical Psychology |
| 25. | Division for the Experimental Analysis of Behavior |
| 26. | Division of the History of Psychology |
| 27. | Division of Community Psychology |
| 28. | Division of Psychopharmacology |
| 29. | Division of Psychotherapy |
| 30. | Division of Psychological Hypnosis |
| 31. | Division of State Psychological Association Affairs |
| 32. | Division of Humanistic Psychology |
| 33. | Division on Mental Retardation |
| 34. | Division of Population and Environmental Psychology |
| 35. | Division of Psychology of Women |
| 36. | Psychologists Interested in Religious Issues (PIRI)—A Division of the APA |
| 37. | Division of Child, Youth, and Family Services |
| 38. | Division on Health Psychology |
| 39. | Division on Psychoanalysis |
| 40. | Division of Clinical Neuropsychology |
| 41. | Division of Psychology and Law |
| 42. | Division of Psychologists in Independent Practice |

TABLE B–1

Note: There are no division numbers 4 or 11.

## Outside Influences

A final trend worth noting is that a number of outside influences have affected the development of experimental psychology since World War II. One pervasive influence is the use and study of psychoanalytic concepts in experimental inquiry, especially between 1935 and 1950. Freud's rich and interesting ideas were put to experimental test under controlled conditions and were often found to have considerable power. Dollard and Miller, in their book *Personality and Psychotherapy* (1950), recast psychoanalytic concepts into the terms of contemporary learning and conditioning. Thus specific learning mechanisms for psychoanalytic constructs were spelled out.

Another important influence was *information theory*, which was borrowed from engineering in the late 1940s and which has had a pervasive influence from the 1950s to the present. Information theory allowed a quantification of concepts previously measured poorly, if at all. The early proponents of information theory hoped that it would overcome many of the traditional problems in psychology, or at least let them be recast in a more manageable way. Though the early hopes of many of these psychologists were not entirely borne out, information theory has served many useful purposes, and it is now common for psychologists conceptualizing human cognitive processes to do so in terms of information flow through the system.

A final important influence from outside psychology has been the computer. It has served all areas of psychology as a tremendously useful tool for data analysis, for it has alleviated many boring calculational chores that previously were done by hand or with the aid of only a calculator. Some areas of psychology have benefited greatly from the use of minicomputers, which are capable of testing subjects with little on-the-spot aid from the human experimenter (once the computer has been appropriately programmed, of course). Finally, in the study of some psychological problems, computer programs have served as a theoretical model of how the human mind might operate.

## SUMMARY

**1.** Scientific psychology dates from a century ago, give or take a decade. The roots of psychology are in the questions asked by philosophers for thousands of years. The original techniques for studying psychology experimentally were devised by physicists and physiologists who became interested in psychological topics, particularly those concerned with reception of stimuli by the senses.

**2.** Four early pioneers of psychology were Helmholtz, Weber, Fechner, and Ebbinghaus. In an early reaction-time experiment, Helmholtz measured the speed of the nervous impulse, thus showing how experimental techniques could provide information about psychological topics.

**3.** Weber examined how much a stimulus had to change in order for an observer to notice the difference. He discovered that the amount of change needed for a just-noticeable difference was a constant proportion of the magnitude of the standard stimulus, a fact that became known as Weber's law. Fechner continued Weber's work and coined the term psychophysics for the field, which was concerned with how changes in the physical world are related to a person's perception of the changes.

**4.** Ebbinghaus performed the first systematic experiments on memory. His research methods and findings had tremendous impact on the field, because they showed that even higher mental processes could be studied experimentally.

**5.** A number of different schools of psychology came into being between 1890 and 1940. Four primary ones were structuralism, functionalism, behaviorism, and Gestalt. A summary of their primary characteristics is presented here in table B–2. The influence of the schools lives on today, but contemporary psychology is divided along lines of various subject matters of interest to researchers. As psychology has matured, the focus of most psychologists has become increasingly specialized.

Summary of Five Primary Schools of Psychology TABLE B–2

| School | Subject Matter | Research Goals | Research Methods |
|---|---|---|---|
| Structuralism | Conscious experience | To break down conscious experience into its basic components: sensations, images, affections | Analytic introspection |
| Functionalism | The function of mental processes and how they help people adapt | To study mental processes in their natural contexts; to discover what effects they have | Objective measures; informal observation and introspection |
| Behaviorism | Behavior: how it is changed under different conditions, with emphasis on learning | Description, explanation, prediction, and control of behavior | Objective measures of behavior; formal experiments |
| Gestalt Psychology | Subjective experience, with emphasis on perception, memory, and thinking | To understand the phenomena of conscious experience in terms of the whole experience (not to break down experience into arbitrary categories) | Subjective reports; some behavioral measures; demonstrations |

**KEY TERMS**

| | |
|---|---|
| behaviorism | psychophysics |
| dualism | radical behaviorism |
| Fechner's law | reaction-time experiment |
| functionalism | shape constancy |
| Gestalt psychology | stimulus error |
| introspection | structuralism |
| just noticeable difference (j. n. d.) | Weber's law |

# STATISTICAL TABLES

---

**Proportions of Area Under the Normal Curve**

*Column A* gives the positive z score.

*Column B* gives the area between the mean and z. Since the curve is symmetrical, areas for negative z scores are the same as for positive ones.

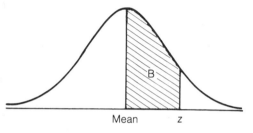

*Column C* gives the area which is beyond z.

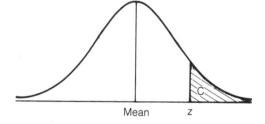

*How to Use Table A:* The values in Table A represent the proportion of areas in the standard normal curve, which has a mean of 0, a standard deviation of 1.00, and a total area equal to 1.00. To use Table A the raw score must first be transformed into a z score. Column A represents this z score, Column B represents the distance between the mean of the standard normal distribution (0) and the z score, and Column C represents the proportion of area beyond a given z.

---

| (A) z | (B) area between mean and z | (C) area beyond z | (A) z | (B) area between mean and z | (C) area beyond z | (A) z | (B) area between mean and z | (C) area beyond z |
|---|---|---|---|---|---|---|---|---|
| 0.00 | .0000 | .5000 | 0.05 | .0199 | .4801 | 0.10 | .0398 | .4602 |
| 0.01 | .0040 | .4960 | 0.06 | .0239 | .4761 | 0.11 | .0438 | .4562 |
| 0.02 | .0080 | .4920 | 0.07 | .0279 | .4721 | 0.12 | .0478 | .4522 |
| 0.03 | .0120 | .4880 | 0.08 | .0319 | .4681 | 0.13 | .0517 | .4483 |
| 0.04 | .0160 | .4840 | 0.09 | .0359 | .4641 | 0.14 | .0557 | .4443 |

**Table A** *(Continued)*

| (A) z | (B) area between mean and z | (C) area beyond z | (A) z | (B) area between mean and z | (C) area beyond z | (A) z | (B) area between mean and z | (C) area beyond z |
|---|---|---|---|---|---|---|---|---|
| 0.15 | .0596 | .4404 | 0.60 | .2257 | .2743 | 1.05 | .3531 | .1469 |
| 0.16 | .0636 | .4364 | 0.61 | .2291 | .2709 | 1.06 | .3554 | .1446 |
| 0.17 | .0675 | .4325 | 0.62 | .2324 | .2676 | 1.07 | .3577 | .1423 |
| 0.18 | .0714 | .4286 | 0.63 | .2357 | .2643 | 1.08 | .3599 | .1401 |
| 0.19 | .0753 | .4247 | 0.64 | .2389 | .2611 | 1.09 | .3621 | .1379 |
| 0.20 | .0793 | .4207 | 0.65 | .2422 | .2578 | 1.10 | .3643 | .1357 |
| 0.21 | .0832 | .4168 | 0.66 | .2454 | .2546 | 1.11 | .3665 | .1335 |
| 0.22 | .0871 | .4129 | 0.67 | .2486 | .2514 | 1.12 | .3686 | .1314 |
| 0.23 | .0910 | .4090 | 0.68 | .2517 | .2483 | 1.13 | .3708 | .1292 |
| 0.24 | .0948 | .4052 | 0.69 | .2549 | .2451 | 1.14 | .3729 | .1271 |
| 0.25 | .0987 | .4013 | 0.70 | .2580 | .2420 | 1.15 | .3749 | .1251 |
| 0.26 | .1026 | .3974 | 0.71 | .2611 | .2389 | 1.16 | .3770 | .1230 |
| 0.27 | .1064 | .3936 | 0.72 | .2642 | .2358 | 1.17 | .3790 | .1210 |
| 0.28 | .1103 | .3897 | 0.73 | .2673 | .2327 | 1.18 | .3810 | .1190 |
| 0.29 | .1141 | .3859 | 0.74 | .2704 | .2296 | 1.19 | .3830 | .1170 |
| 0.30 | .1179 | .3821 | 0.75 | .2734 | .2266 | 1.20 | .3849 | .1151 |
| 0.31 | .1217 | .3783 | 0.76 | .2764 | .2236 | 1.21 | .3869 | .1131 |
| 0.32 | .1255 | .3745 | 0.77 | .2794 | .2206 | 1.22 | .3888 | .1112 |
| 0.33 | .1293 | .3707 | 0.78 | .2823 | .2177 | 1.23 | .3907 | .1093 |
| 0.34 | .1331 | .3669 | 0.79 | .2852 | .2148 | 1.24 | .3925 | .1075 |
| 0.35 | .1368 | .3632 | 0.80 | .2881 | .2119 | 1.25 | .3944 | .1056 |
| 0.36 | .1406 | .3594 | 0.81 | .2910 | .2090 | 1.26 | .3962 | .1038 |
| 0.37 | .1443 | .3557 | 0.82 | .2939 | .2061 | 1.27 | .3980 | .1020 |
| 0.38 | .1480 | .3520 | 0.83 | .2967 | .2033 | 1.28 | .3997 | .1003 |
| 0.39 | .1517 | .3483 | 0.84 | .2995 | .2005 | 1.29 | .4015 | .0985 |
| 0.40 | .1554 | .3446 | 0.85 | .3023 | .1977 | 1.30 | .4032 | .0968 |
| 0.41 | .1591 | .3409 | 0.86 | .3051 | .1949 | 1.31 | .4049 | .0951 |
| 0.42 | .1628 | .3372 | 0.87 | .3078 | .1922 | 1.32 | .4066 | .0934 |
| 0.43 | .1664 | .3336 | 0.88 | .3106 | .1894 | 1.33 | .4082 | .0918 |
| 0.44 | .1700 | .3300 | 0.89 | .3133 | .1867 | 1.34 | .4099 | .0901 |
| 0.45 | .1736 | .3264 | 0.90 | .3159 | .1841 | 1.35 | .4115 | .0885 |
| 0.46 | .1772 | .3228 | 0.91 | .3186 | .1814 | 1.36 | .4131 | .0869 |
| 0.47 | .1808 | .3192 | 0.92 | .3212 | .1788 | 1.37 | .4147 | .0853 |
| 0.48 | .1844 | .3156 | 0.93 | .3238 | .1762 | 1.38 | .4162 | .0838 |
| 0.49 | .1879 | .3121 | 0.94 | .3264 | .1736 | 1.39 | .4177 | .0823 |
| 0.50 | .1915 | .3085 | 0.95 | .3289 | .1711 | 1.40 | .4192 | .0808 |
| 0.51 | .1950 | .3050 | 0.96 | .3315 | .1685 | 1.41 | .4207 | .0793 |
| 0.52 | .1985 | .3015 | 0.97 | .3340 | .1660 | 1.42 | .4222 | .0778 |
| 0.53 | .2019 | .2981 | 0.98 | .3365 | .1635 | 1.43 | .4236 | .0764 |
| 0.54 | .2054 | .2946 | 0.99 | .3389 | .1611 | 1.44 | .4251 | .0749 |
| 0.55 | .2088 | .2912 | 1.00 | .3413 | .1587 | 1.45 | .4265 | .0735 |
| 0.56 | .2123 | .2877 | 1.01 | .3438 | .1562 | 1.46 | .4279 | .0721 |
| 0.57 | .2157 | .2843 | 1.02 | .3461 | .1539 | 1.47 | .4292 | .0708 |
| 0.58 | .2190 | .2810 | 1.03 | .3485 | .1515 | 1.48 | .4306 | .0694 |
| 0.59 | .2224 | .2776 | 1.04 | .3508 | .1492 | 1.49 | .4319 | .0681 |

Table A (Continued)

| (A) z | (B) area between mean and z | (C) area beyond z | (A) z | (B) area between mean and z | (C) area beyond z | (A) z | (B) area between mean and z | (C) area beyond z |
|---|---|---|---|---|---|---|---|---|
| 1.50 | .4332 | .0668 | 1.95 | .4744 | .0256 | 2.40 | .4918 | .0082 |
| 1.51 | .4345 | .0655 | 1.96 | .4750 | .0250 | 2.41 | .4920 | .0080 |
| 1.52 | .4357 | .0643 | 1.97 | .4756 | .0244 | 2.42 | .4922 | .0078 |
| 1.53 | .4370 | .0630 | 1.98 | .4761 | .0239 | 2.43 | .4925 | .0075 |
| 1.54 | .4382 | .0618 | 1.99 | .4767 | .0233 | 2.44 | .4927 | .0073 |
| 1.55 | .4394 | .0606 | 2.00 | .4772 | .0228 | 2.45 | .4929 | .0071 |
| 1.56 | .4406 | .0594 | 2.01 | .4778 | .0222 | 2.46 | .4931 | .0069 |
| 1.57 | .4418 | .0582 | 2.02 | .4783 | .0217 | 2.47 | .4932 | .0068 |
| 1.58 | .4429 | .0571 | 2.03 | .4788 | .0212 | 2.48 | .4934 | .0066 |
| 1.59 | .4441 | .0559 | 2.04 | .4793 | .0207 | 2.49 | .4936 | .0064 |
| 1.60 | .4452 | .0548 | 2.05 | .4798 | .0202 | 2.50 | .4938 | .0062 |
| 1.61 | .4463 | .0537 | 2.06 | .4803 | .0197 | 2.51 | .4940 | .0060 |
| 1.62 | .4474 | .0526 | 2.07 | .4808 | .0192 | 2.52 | .4941 | .0059 |
| 1.63 | .4484 | .0516 | 2.08 | .4812 | .0188 | 2.53 | .4943 | .0057 |
| 1.64 | .4495 | .0505 | 2.09 | .4817 | .0183 | 2.54 | .4945 | .0055 |
| 1.65 | .4505 | .0495 | 2.10 | .4821 | .0179 | 2.55 | .4946 | .0054 |
| 1.66 | .4515 | .0485 | 2.11 | .4826 | .0174 | 2.56 | .4948 | .0052 |
| 1.67 | .4525 | .0475 | 2.12 | .4830 | .0170 | 2.57 | .4949 | .0051 |
| 1.08 | .4535 | .0465 | 2.13 | .4834 | .0166 | 2.58 | .4951 | .0049 |
| 1.69 | .4545 | .0455 | 2.14 | .4838 | .0162 | 2.59 | .4952 | .0048 |
| 1.70 | .4554 | .0446 | 2.15 | .4842 | .0158 | 2.60 | .4953 | .0047 |
| 1.71 | .4564 | .0436 | 2.16 | .4846 | .0154 | 2.61 | .4955 | .0045 |
| 1.72 | .4573 | .0427 | 2.17 | .4850 | .0150 | 2.62 | .4956 | .0044 |
| 1.73 | .4582 | .0418 | 2.18 | .4854 | .0146 | 2.63 | .4957 | .0043 |
| 1.74 | .4591 | .0409 | 2.19 | .4857 | .0143 | 2.64 | .4959 | .0041 |
| 1.75 | .4599 | .0401 | 2.20 | .4861 | .0139 | 2.65 | .4960 | .0040 |
| 1.76 | .4608 | .0392 | 2.21 | .4864 | .0136 | 2.66 | .4961 | .0039 |
| 1.77 | .4616 | .0384 | 2.22 | .4868 | .0132 | 2.67 | .4962 | .0038 |
| 1.78 | .4625 | .0375 | 2.23 | .4871 | .0129 | 2.68 | .4963 | .0037 |
| 1.79 | .4633 | .0367 | 2.24 | .4875 | .0125 | 2.69 | .4964 | .0036 |
| 1.80 | .4641 | .0359 | 2.25 | .4878 | .0122 | 2.70 | .4965 | .0035 |
| 1.81 | .4649 | .0351 | 2.26 | .4881 | .0119 | 2.71 | .4966 | .0034 |
| 1.82 | .4656 | .0344 | 2.27 | .4884 | .0116 | 2.72 | .4967 | .0033 |
| 1.83 | .4664 | .0336 | 2.28 | .4887 | .0113 | 2.73 | .4968 | .0032 |
| 1.84 | .4671 | .0329 | 2.29 | .4890 | .0110 | 2.74 | .4969 | .0031 |
| 1.85 | .4678 | .0322 | 2.30 | .4893 | .0107 | 2.75 | .4970 | .0030 |
| 1.86 | .4686 | .0314 | 2.31 | .4896 | .0104 | 2.76 | .4971 | .0029 |
| 1.87 | .4693 | .0307 | 2.32 | .4898 | .0102 | 2.77 | .4972 | .0028 |
| 1.88 | .4699 | .0301 | 2.33 | .4901 | .0099 | 2.78 | .4973 | .0027 |
| 1.89 | .4706 | .0294 | 2.34 | .4904 | .0096 | 2.79 | .4974 | .0026 |
| 1.90 | .4713 | .0287 | 2.35 | .4906 | .0094 | 2.80 | .4974 | .0026 |
| 1.91 | .4719 | .0281 | 2.36 | .4909 | .0091 | 2.81 | .4975 | .0025 |
| 1.92 | .4726 | .0274 | 2.37 | .4911 | .0089 | 2.82 | .4976 | .0024 |
| 1.93 | .4732 | .0268 | 2.38 | .4913 | .0087 | 2.83 | .4977 | .0023 |
| 1.94 | .4738 | .0262 | 2.39 | .4916 | .0084 | 2.84 | .4977 | .0023 |

**Table A** *(Continued)*

| (A) z | (B) area between mean and z | (C) area beyond z | (A) z | (B) area between mean and z | (C) area beyond z | (A) z | (B) area between mean and z | (C) area beyond z |
|---|---|---|---|---|---|---|---|---|
| 2.85 | .4978 | .0022 | 3.05 | .4989 | .0011 | 3.25 | .4994 | .0006 |
| 2.86 | .4979 | .0021 | 3.06 | .4989 | .0011 | 3.30 | .4995 | .0005 |
| 2.87 | .4979 | .0021 | 3.07 | .4989 | .0011 | 3.35 | .4996 | .0004 |
| 2.88 | .4980 | .0020 | 3.08 | .4990 | .0010 | 3.40 | .4997 | .0003 |
| 2.89 | .4981 | .0019 | 3.09 | .4990 | .0010 | 3.45 | .4997 | .0003 |
| 2.90 | .4981 | .0019 | 3.10 | .4990 | .0010 | 3.50 | .4998 | .0002 |
| 2.91 | .4982 | .0018 | 3.11 | .4991 | .0009 | 3.60 | .4998 | .0002 |
| 2.92 | .4982 | .0018 | 3.12 | .4991 | .0009 | 3.70 | .4999 | .0001 |
| 2.93 | .4983 | .0017 | 3.13 | .4991 | .0009 | 3.80 | .4999 | .0001 |
| 2.94 | .4984 | .0016 | 3.14 | .4992 | .0008 | 3.90 | .49995 | .00005 |
| 2.95 | .4984 | .0016 | 3.15 | .4992 | .0008 | 4.00 | .49997 | .00003 |
| 2.96 | .4985 | .0015 | 3.16 | .4992 | .0008 | | | |
| 2.97 | .4985 | .0015 | 3.17 | .4992 | .0008 | | | |
| 2.98 | .4986 | .0014 | 3.18 | .4993 | .0007 | | | |
| 2.99 | .4986 | .0014 | 3.19 | .4993 | .0007 | | | |
| 3.00 | .4987 | .0013 | 3.20 | .4993 | .0007 | | | |
| 3.01 | .4987 | .0013 | 3.21 | .4993 | .0007 | | | |
| 3.02 | .4987 | .0013 | 3.22 | .4994 | .0006 | | | |
| 3.03 | .4988 | .0012 | 3.23 | .4994 | .0006 | | | |
| 3.04 | .4988 | .0012 | 3.24 | .4994 | .0006 | | | |

## Critical Values of the *U* Statistic of the Mann-Whitney Test

To use these tables, first decide what level of significance you want with either a one- or two-tailed test. For example, if you want p = .05, two-tailed, use *(c)*. Then locate the number of cases or measures (n) in both groups in the particular subtable you have chosen. The U value you have calculated must be *less* than that at the appropriate place in the table. For example, if you had 18 subjects in each group of an experiment, and calculated U = 90, then you could conclude that the null hypothesis can be rejected because the critical U value with groups of these sizes is 99 (see subtable c).

*(a)* Critical Values of *U* for a One-Tailed Test at .001 or for a Two-Tailed Test at .002

| $n_1$ \ $n_2$ | 9 | 10 | 11 | 12 | 13 | 14 | 15 | 16 | 17 | 18 | 19 | 20 |
|---|---|---|---|---|---|---|---|---|---|---|---|---|
| 1 | | | | | | | | | | | | |
| 2 | | | | | | | | | | | | |
| 3 | | | | | | | | | 0 | 0 | 0 | 0 |
| 4 | | 0 | 0 | 0 | 1 | 1 | 1 | 2 | 2 | 3 | 3 | 3 |
| 5 | 1 | 1 | 2 | 2 | 3 | 3 | 4 | 5 | 5 | 6 | 7 | 7 |
| 6 | 2 | 3 | 4 | 4 | 5 | 6 | 7 | 8 | 9 | 10 | 11 | 12 |
| 7 | 3 | 5 | 6 | 7 | 8 | 9 | 10 | 11 | 13 | 14 | 15 | 16 |
| 8 | 5 | 6 | 8 | 9 | 11 | 12 | 14 | 15 | 17 | 18 | 20 | 21 |
| 9 | 7 | 8 | 10 | 12 | 14 | 15 | 17 | 19 | 21 | 23 | 25 | 26 |
| 10 | 8 | 10 | 12 | 14 | 17 | 19 | 21 | 23 | 25 | 27 | 29 | 32 |
| 11 | 10 | 12 | 15 | 17 | 20 | 22 | 24 | 27 | 29 | 32 | 34 | 37 |
| 12 | 12 | 14 | 17 | 20 | 23 | 25 | 28 | 31 | 34 | 37 | 40 | 42 |
| 13 | 14 | 17 | 20 | 23 | 26 | 29 | 32 | 35 | 38 | 42 | 45 | 48 |
| 14 | 15 | 19 | 22 | 25 | 29 | 32 | 36 | 39 | 43 | 46 | 50 | 54 |
| 15 | 17 | 21 | 24 | 28 | 32 | 36 | 40 | 43 | 47 | 51 | 55 | 59 |
| 16 | 19 | 23 | 27 | 31 | 35 | 39 | 43 | 48 | 52 | 56 | 60 | 65 |
| 17 | 21 | 25 | 29 | 34 | 38 | 43 | 47 | 52 | 57 | 61 | 66 | 70 |
| 18 | 23 | 27 | 32 | 37 | 42 | 46 | 51 | 56 | 61 | 66 | 71 | 76 |
| 19 | 25 | 29 | 34 | 40 | 45 | 50 | 55 | 60 | 66 | 71 | 77 | 82 |
| 20 | 26 | 32 | 37 | 42 | 48 | 54 | 59 | 65 | 70 | 76 | 82 | 88 |

SOURCE: Adapted from Tables 1, 3, 5, and 7 of D. Aube, "Extended Tables for the Mann-Whitney Statistic," *Bulletin of the Institute of Educational Research at Indiana University*, 1953, 1, No. 2. From S. Siegel, *Nonparametric Statistics for the Behavior Sciences*. New York: McGraw-Hill Book Company, 1956. Reprinted by permission of the Institute of Educational Research and McGraw-Hill Book Company.

**Table B** *(Continued)*

*(b)* Critical Values of $U$ for a One-Tailed Test at .01 or for a Two-Tailed Test at .02

| $n_1$ \ $n_2$ | 9 | 10 | 11 | 12 | 13 | 14 | 15 | 16 | 17 | 18 | 19 | 20 |
|---|---|---|---|---|---|---|---|---|---|---|---|---|
| 1 | | | | | | | | | | | | |
| 2 | | | | | 0 | 0 | 0 | 0 | 0 | 0 | 1 | 1 |
| 3 | 1 | 1 | 1 | 2 | 2 | 2 | 3 | 3 | 4 | 4 | 4 | 5 |
| 4 | 3 | 3 | 4 | 5 | 5 | 6 | 7 | 7 | 8 | 9 | 9 | 10 |
| 5 | 5 | 6 | 7 | 8 | 9 | 10 | 11 | 12 | 13 | 14 | 15 | 16 |
| 6 | 7 | 8 | 9 | 11 | 12 | 13 | 15 | 16 | 18 | 19 | 20 | 22 |
| 7 | 9 | 11 | 12 | 14 | 16 | 17 | 19 | 21 | 23 | 24 | 26 | 28 |
| 8 | 11 | 13 | 15 | 17 | 20 | 22 | 24 | 26 | 28 | 30 | 32 | 34 |
| 9 | 14 | 16 | 18 | 21 | 23 | 26 | 28 | 31 | 33 | 36 | 38 | 40 |
| 10 | 16 | 19 | 22 | 24 | 27 | 30 | 33 | 36 | 38 | 41 | 44 | 47 |
| 11 | 18 | 22 | 25 | 28 | 31 | 34 | 37 | 41 | 44 | 47 | 50 | 53 |
| 12 | 21 | 24 | 28 | 31 | 35 | 38 | 42 | 46 | 49 | 53 | 56 | 60 |
| 13 | 23 | 27 | 31 | 35 | 39 | 43 | 47 | 51 | 55 | 59 | 63 | 67 |
| 14 | 26 | 30 | 34 | 38 | 43 | 47 | 51 | 56 | 60 | 65 | 69 | 73 |
| 15 | 28 | 33 | 37 | 42 | 47 | 51 | 56 | 61 | 66 | 70 | 75 | 80 |
| 16 | 31 | 36 | 41 | 46 | 51 | 56 | 61 | 66 | 71 | 76 | 82 | 87 |
| 17 | 33 | 38 | 44 | 49 | 55 | 60 | 66 | 71 | 77 | 82 | 88 | 93 |
| 18 | 36 | 41 | 47 | 53 | 59 | 65 | 70 | 76 | 82 | 88 | 94 | 100 |
| 19 | 38 | 44 | 50 | 56 | 63 | 69 | 75 | 82 | 88 | 94 | 101 | 107 |
| 20 | 40 | 47 | 53 | 60 | 67 | 73 | 80 | 87 | 93 | 100 | 107 | 114 |

*(c)* Critical Values of $U$ for a One-Tailed Test at .025 or for a Two-Tailed Test at .05

| $n_1$ \ $n_2$ | 9 | 10 | 11 | 12 | 13 | 14 | 15 | 16 | 17 | 18 | 19 | 20 |
|---|---|---|---|---|---|---|---|---|---|---|---|---|
| 1 | | | | | | | | | | | | |
| 2 | 0 | 0 | 1 | 1 | 1 | 1 | 1 | 1 | 2 | 2 | 2 | 2 |
| 3 | 2 | 3 | 3 | 4 | 4 | 5 | 5 | 6 | 6 | 7 | 7 | 8 |
| 4 | 4 | 5 | 6 | 7 | 8 | 9 | 10 | 11 | 11 | 12 | 13 | 13 |
| 5 | 7 | 8 | 9 | 11 | 12 | 13 | 14 | 15 | 17 | 18 | 19 | 20 |
| 6 | 10 | 11 | 13 | 14 | 16 | 17 | 19 | 21 | 22 | 24 | 25 | 27 |
| 7 | 12 | 14 | 16 | 18 | 20 | 22 | 24 | 26 | 28 | 30 | 32 | 34 |
| 8 | 15 | 17 | 19 | 22 | 24 | 26 | 29 | 31 | 34 | 36 | 38 | 41 |
| 9 | 17 | 20 | 23 | 26 | 28 | 31 | 34 | 37 | 39 | 42 | 45 | 48 |
| 10 | 20 | 23 | 26 | 29 | 33 | 36 | 39 | 42 | 45 | 48 | 52 | 55 |
| 11 | 23 | 26 | 30 | 33 | 37 | 40 | 44 | 47 | 51 | 55 | 58 | 62 |
| 12 | 26 | 29 | 33 | 37 | 41 | 45 | 49 | 53 | 57 | 61 | 65 | 69 |
| 13 | 28 | 33 | 37 | 41 | 45 | 50 | 54 | 59 | 63 | 67 | 72 | 76 |
| 14 | 31 | 36 | 40 | 45 | 50 | 55 | 59 | 64 | 67 | 74 | 78 | 83 |
| 15 | 34 | 39 | 44 | 49 | 54 | 59 | 64 | 70 | 75 | 80 | 85 | 90 |
| 16 | 37 | 42 | 47 | 53 | 59 | 64 | 70 | 75 | 81 | 86 | 92 | 98 |
| 17 | 39 | 45 | 51 | 57 | 63 | 67 | 75 | 81 | 87 | 93 | 99 | 105 |
| 18 | 42 | 48 | 55 | 61 | 67 | 74 | 80 | 86 | 93 | 99 | 106 | 112 |
| 19 | 45 | 52 | 58 | 65 | 72 | 78 | 85 | 92 | 99 | 106 | 113 | 119 |
| 20 | 48 | 55 | 62 | 69 | 76 | 83 | 90 | 98 | 105 | 112 | 119 | 127 |

*(d)* Critical Values of *U* for a One-Tailed Test at .05 or for a Two-Tailed Test at .10

**Table B** *(Continued)*

| $n_1$ \ $n_2$ | 9 | 10 | 11 | 12 | 13 | 14 | 15 | 16 | 17 | 18 | 19 | 20 |
|---|---|---|---|---|---|---|---|---|---|---|---|---|
| 1 | | | | | | | | | | | 0 | 0 |
| 2 | 1 | 1 | 1 | 2 | 2 | 2 | 3 | 3 | 3 | 4 | 4 | 4 |
| 3 | 3 | 4 | 5 | 5 | 6 | 7 | 7 | 8 | 9 | 9 | 10 | 11 |
| 4 | 6 | 7 | 8 | 9 | 10 | 11 | 12 | 14 | 15 | 16 | 17 | 18 |
| 5 | 9 | 11 | 12 | 13 | 15 | 16 | 18 | 19 | 20 | 22 | 23 | 25 |
| 6 | 12 | 14 | 16 | 17 | 19 | 21 | 23 | 25 | 26 | 28 | 30 | 32 |
| 7 | 15 | 17 | 19 | 21 | 24 | 26 | 28 | 30 | 33 | 35 | 37 | 39 |
| 8 | 18 | 20 | 23 | 26 | 28 | 31 | 33 | 36 | 39 | 41 | 44 | 47 |
| 9 | 21 | 24 | 27 | 30 | 33 | 36 | 39 | 42 | 45 | 48 | 51 | 54 |
| 10 | 24 | 27 | 31 | 34 | 37 | 41 | 44 | 48 | 51 | 55 | 58 | 62 |
| 11 | 27 | 31 | 34 | 38 | 42 | 46 | 50 | 54 | 57 | 61 | 65 | 69 |
| 12 | 30 | 34 | 38 | 42 | 47 | 51 | 55 | 60 | 64 | 68 | 72 | 77 |
| 13 | 33 | 37 | 42 | 47 | 51 | 56 | 61 | 65 | 70 | 75 | 80 | 84 |
| 14 | 36 | 41 | 46 | 51 | 56 | 61 | 66 | 71 | 77 | 82 | 87 | 92 |
| 15 | 39 | 44 | 50 | 55 | 61 | 66 | 72 | 77 | 83 | 88 | 94 | 100 |
| 16 | 42 | 48 | 54 | 60 | 65 | 71 | 77 | 83 | 89 | 95 | 101 | 107 |
| 17 | 45 | 51 | 57 | 64 | 70 | 77 | 83 | 89 | 96 | 102 | 109 | 115 |
| 18 | 48 | 55 | 61 | 68 | 75 | 82 | 88 | 95 | 102 | 109 | 116 | 123 |
| 19 | 51 | 58 | 65 | 72 | 80 | 87 | 94 | 101 | 109 | 116 | 123 | 130 |
| 20 | 54 | 62 | 69 | 77 | 84 | 92 | 100 | 107 | 115 | 123 | 130 | 138 |

**Table C**

## Distribution for the Sign Test

Alpha levels of the sign test for pairs of observations ranging from 3 to 41. x denotes the number of exceptions (the number of times the difference between conditions is in the unexpected direction), while the p level indicates the probability that that number of exceptions could occur by chance. If there are 28 paired observations and 20 are ordered in the expected direction, while only 8 are exceptions, the probability that this could occur by chance is .018.

| x | p | x | p | x | p | x | p | x | p | x | p |
|---|---|---|---|---|---|---|---|---|---|---|---|
| **n = 3** | | **n = 12** | | **n = 19** | | **n = 25** | | **n = 31** | | **n = 37** | |
| 0 | .125 | 1 | .003 | 3 | .002 | 5 | .002 | 7 | .002 | 10 | .004 |
| **n = 4** | | 2 | .019 | 4 | .010 | 6 | .007 | 8 | .005 | 11 | .010 |
| 0 | .062 | 3 | .073 | 5 | .032 | 7 | .022 | 9 | .015 | 12 | .024 |
| 1 | .312 | 4 | .194 | 6 | .084 | 8 | .051 | 10 | .035 | 13 | .049 |
| **n = 5** | | **n = 13** | | 7 | .180 | 9 | .115 | 11 | .075 | 14 | .094 |
| 0 | .031 | 1 | .002 | **n = 20** | | 10 | .212 | 12 | .141 | 15 | .162 |
| 1 | .188 | 2 | .011 | 3 | .001 | **n = 26** | | **n = 32** | | **n = 38** | |
| **n = 6** | | 3 | .016 | 4 | .006 | 6 | .005 | 8 | .004 | 10 | .003 |
| 0 | .016 | 4 | .133 | 5 | .021 | 7 | .014 | 9 | .010 | 11 | .007 |
| 1 | .109 | **n = 14** | | 6 | .058 | 8 | .038 | 10 | .025 | 12 | .017 |
| 2 | .344 | 1 | .001 | 7 | .132 | 9 | .084 | 11 | .055 | 13 | .036 |
| **n = 7** | | 2 | .006 | **n = 21** | | 10 | .163 | 12 | .108 | 14 | .072 |
| 0 | .008 | 3 | .029 | 4 | .004 | **n = 27** | | 13 | .189 | 15 | .128 |
| 1 | .062 | 4 | .090 | 5 | .013 | 6 | .003 | **n = 33** | | **n = 39** | |
| 2 | .227 | 5 | .212 | 6 | .039 | 7 | .010 | 8 | .002 | 11 | .005 |
| **n = 8** | | **n = 15** | | 7 | .095 | 8 | .026 | 9 | .007 | 12 | .012 |
| 0 | .004 | 1 | .000 | 8 | .192 | 9 | .061 | 10 | .018 | 13 | .027 |
| 1 | .035 | 2 | .004 | **n = 22** | | 10 | .124 | 11 | .040 | 14 | .054 |
| 2 | .145 | 3 | .018 | 4 | .002 | 11 | .221 | 12 | .081 | 15 | .100 |
| **n = 9** | | 4 | .059 | 5 | .008 | **n = 28** | | 13 | .148 | 16 | .168 |
| 0 | .002 | 5 | .151 | 6 | .026 | 6 | .002 | **n = 34** | | **n = 40** | |
| 1 | .020 | **n = 16** | | 7 | .067 | 7 | .006 | 9 | .005 | 11 | .003 |
| 2 | .090 | 2 | .002 | 8 | .143 | 8 | .018 | 10 | .012 | 12 | .008 |
| 3 | .254 | 3 | .011 | **n = 23** | | 9 | .044 | 11 | .029 | 13 | .019 |
| **n = 10** | | 4 | .038 | 4 | .001 | 10 | .092 | 12 | .061 | 14 | .040 |
| 0 | .001 | 5 | .105 | 5 | .005 | 11 | .172 | 13 | .115 | 15 | .077 |
| 1 | .011 | 6 | .227 | 6 | .017 | **n = 29** | | 14 | .196 | 16 | .134 |
| 2 | .055 | **n = 17** | | 7 | .047 | 7 | .004 | **n = 35** | | **n = 41** | |
| 3 | .172 | 2 | .001 | 8 | .105 | 8 | .012 | 9 | .003 | 11 | .002 |
| **n = 11** | | 3 | .006 | 9 | .202 | 9 | .031 | 10 | .008 | 12 | .006 |
| 0 | .000 | 4 | .025 | **n = 24** | | 10 | .068 | 11 | .020 | 13 | .014 |
| 1 | .006 | 5 | .072 | 5 | .008 | 11 | .132 | 12 | .045 | 14 | .030 |
| 2 | .033 | 6 | .166 | 6 | .011 | **n = 30** | | 13 | .088 | 15 | .059 |
| 3 | .113 | **n = 18** | | 7 | .032 | 7 | .003 | 14 | .155 | 16 | .106 |
| 4 | .274 | 3 | .004 | 8 | .076 | 8 | .008 | **n = 36** | | 17 | .174 |
| | | 4 | .015 | 9 | .154 | 9 | .021 | 9 | .002 | **n = 42** | |
| | | 5 | .048 | | | 10 | .049 | 10 | .006 | 12 | .004 |
| | | 6 | .119 | | | 11 | .100 | 11 | .014 | 13 | .010 |
| | | 7 | .240 | | | 12 | .181 | 12 | .033 | 14 | .022 |
| | | | | | | | | 13 | .066 | 15 | .044 |
| | | | | | | | | 14 | .121 | 16 | .082 |
| | | | | | | | | 15 | .203 | 17 | .140 |

## Critical Values of Wilcoxon's *T* Statistic for the Matched-Pairs Signed-Ranks Test

In using this table, first locate the number of *pairs* of scores in the *n* column. The critical values for several levels of significance are listed in the columns to the right. For example, if *n* were 15 and the computed value 19, it would be concluded that since 19 is less than 25, the difference between conditions is significant beyond the .02 level of significance for a two-tailed test.

| | Level of significance for one-tailed test | | |
| | .025 | .01 | .005 |
|---|---|---|---|
| | Level of significance for two-tailed test | | |
| *n* | .05 | .02 | .01 |
| 6 | 1 | — | — |
| 7 | 2 | 0 | — |
| 8 | 4 | 2 | 0 |
| 9 | 6 | 3 | 2 |
| 10 | 8 | 5 | 3 |
| 11 | 11 | 7 | 5 |
| 12 | 14 | 10 | 7 |
| 13 | 17 | 13 | 10 |
| 14 | 21 | 16 | 13 |
| 15 | 25 | 20 | 16 |
| 16 | 30 | 24 | 19 |
| 17 | 35 | 28 | 23 |
| 18 | 40 | 33 | 28 |
| 19 | 46 | 38 | 32 |
| 20 | 52 | 43 | 37 |
| 21 | 59 | 49 | 43 |
| 22 | 66 | 56 | 49 |
| 23 | 73 | 62 | 55 |
| 24 | 81 | 69 | 61 |
| 25 | 90 | 77 | 68 |

Note that *n* is the number of matched pairs.

SOURCE: Adapted from Table I of F. Wilcoxon, *Some Rapid Approximate Statistical Procedures*, (Rev. ed.) New York: American Cyanamid Company, 1964. Taken from S. Siegel, *Nonparametric Statistics for the Behavioral Sciences*. New York: McGraw-Hill Book Company, 1956. Reprinted by permission of the American Cyanamid Company and McGraw-Hill Book Company.

## Table E

### Critical Values of the *F* Distribution

Find the location appropriate values in the table by looking up the degrees of freedom in the numerator and denominator of the *F*-ratio. After you have decided on the level of significance desired, the obtained *F*-ratio must be *greater* than that in the table. For example, with $p = .05$ and 10 *df* in the numerator and 28 in the denominator, your *F* value must be greater than 2.19 to be reliable.

| df for denom. | α | 1 | 2 | 3 | 4 | 5 | 6 | 7 | 8 | 9 |
|---|---|---|---|---|---|---|---|---|---|---|
| 3 | .25 | 2.02 | 2.28 | 2.36 | 2.39 | 2.41 | 2.42 | 2.43 | 2.44 | 2.44 |
| | .10 | 5.54 | 5.46 | 5.39 | 5.34 | 5.31 | 5.28 | 5.27 | 5.25 | 5.24 |
| | .05 | 10.1 | 9.55 | 9.28 | 9.12 | 9.01 | 8.94 | 8.89 | 8.85 | 8.81 |
| | .025 | 17.4 | 16.0 | 15.4 | 15.1 | 14.9 | 14.7 | 14.6 | 14.5 | 14.5 |
| | .01 | 34.1 | 30.8 | 29.5 | 28.7 | 28.2 | 27.9 | 27.7 | 27.5 | 27.4 |
| | .001 | 167 | 148 | 141 | 137 | 135 | 133 | 132 | 131 | 130 |
| 4 | .25 | 1.81 | 2.00 | 2.05 | 2.06 | 2.07 | 2.08 | 2.08 | 2.08 | 2.08 |
| | .10 | 4.54 | 4.32 | 4.19 | 4.11 | 4.05 | 4.01 | 3.98 | 3.95 | 3.94 |
| | .05 | 7.71 | 6.94 | 6.59 | 6.39 | 6.26 | 6.16 | 6.09 | 6.04 | 6.00 |
| | .025 | 12.2 | 10.6 | 9.98 | 9.60 | 9.36 | 9.20 | 9.07 | 8.98 | 8.90 |
| | .01 | 21.2 | 18.0 | 16.7 | 16.0 | 15.5 | 15.2 | 15.0 | 14.8 | 14.7 |
| | .001 | 74.1 | 61.2 | 56.2 | 53.4 | 51.7 | 50.5 | 49.7 | 49.0 | 48.5 |
| 5 | .25 | 1.69 | 1.85 | 1.88 | 1.89 | 1.89 | 1.89 | 1.89 | 1.89 | 1.89 |
| | .10 | 4.06 | 3.78 | 3.62 | 3.52 | 3.45 | 3.40 | 3.37 | 3.34 | 3.32 |
| | .05 | 6.61 | 5.79 | 5.41 | 5.19 | 5.05 | 4.95 | 4.88 | 4.82 | 4.77 |
| | .025 | 10.0 | 8.43 | 7.76 | 7.39 | 7.15 | 6.98 | 6.85 | 6.76 | 6.68 |
| | .01 | 16.3 | 13.3 | 12.1 | 11.4 | 11.0 | 10.7 | 10.5 | 10.3 | 10.2 |
| | .001 | 47.2 | 37.1 | 33.2 | 31.1 | 29.8 | 28.8 | 28.2 | 27.6 | 27.2 |
| 6 | .25 | 1.62 | 1.76 | 1.78 | 1.79 | 1.79 | 1.78 | 1.78 | 1.78 | 1.77 |
| | .10 | 3.78 | 3.46 | 3.29 | 3.18 | 3.11 | 3.05 | 3.01 | 2.98 | 2.96 |
| | .05 | 5.99 | 5.14 | 4.76 | 4.53 | 4.39 | 4.28 | 4.21 | 4.15 | 4.10 |
| | .025 | 8.81 | 7.26 | 6.60 | 6.23 | 5.99 | 5.82 | 5.70 | 5.60 | 5.52 |
| | .01 | 13.8 | 10.9 | 9.78 | 9.15 | 8.75 | 8.47 | 8.26 | 8.10 | 7.98 |
| | .001 | 35.5 | 27.0 | 23.7 | 21.9 | 20.8 | 20.0 | 19.5 | 19.0 | 18.7 |
| 7 | .25 | 1.57 | 1.70 | 1.72 | 1.72 | 1.71 | 1.71 | 1.70 | 1.70 | 1.69 |
| | .10 | 3.59 | 3.26 | 3.07 | 2.96 | 2.88 | 2.83 | 2.78 | 2.75 | 2.72 |
| | .05 | 5.59 | 4.74 | 4.35 | 4.12 | 3.97 | 3.87 | 3.79 | 3.73 | 3.68 |
| | .025 | 8.07 | 6.54 | 5.89 | 5.52 | 5.29 | 5.12 | 4.99 | 4.90 | 4.82 |
| | .01 | 12.2 | 9.55 | 8.45 | 7.85 | 7.46 | 7.19 | 6.99 | 6.84 | 6.72 |
| | .001 | 29.2 | 21.7 | 18.8 | 17.2 | 16.2 | 15.5 | 15.0 | 14.6 | 14.3 |
| 8 | .25 | 1.54 | 1.66 | 1.67 | 1.66 | 1.66 | 1.65 | 1.64 | 1.64 | 1.63 |
| | .10 | 3.46 | 3.11 | 2.92 | 2.81 | 2.73 | 2.67 | 2.62 | 2.59 | 2.56 |
| | .05 | 5.32 | 4.46 | 4.07 | 3.84 | 3.69 | 3.58 | 3.50 | 3.44 | 3.39 |
| | .025 | 7.57 | 6.06 | 5.42 | 5.05 | 4.82 | 4.65 | 4.53 | 4.43 | 4.36 |
| | .01 | 11.3 | 8.65 | 7.59 | 7.01 | 6.63 | 6.37 | 6.18 | 6.03 | 5.91 |
| | .001 | 25.4 | 18.5 | 15.8 | 14.4 | 13.5 | 12.9 | 12.4 | 12.0 | 11.8 |
| 9 | .25 | 1.51 | 1.62 | 1.63 | 1.63 | 1.62 | 1.61 | 1.60 | 1.60 | 1.59 |
| | .10 | 3.36 | 3.01 | 2.81 | 2.69 | 2.61 | 2.55 | 2.51 | 2.47 | 2.44 |
| | .05 | 5.12 | 4.26 | 3.86 | 3.63 | 3.48 | 3.37 | 3.29 | 3.23 | 3.18 |
| | .025 | 7.21 | 5.71 | 5.08 | 4.72 | 4.48 | 4.32 | 4.20 | 4.10 | 4.03 |
| | .01 | 10.6 | 8.02 | 6.99 | 6.42 | 6.06 | 5.80 | 5.61 | 5.47 | 5.35 |
| | .001 | 22.9 | 16.4 | 13.9 | 12.6 | 11.7 | 11.1 | 10.7 | 10.4 | 10.1 |

*df for numerator*

| df for denom. | df for numerator | | | | | | | | |
|---|---|---|---|---|---|---|---|---|---|
| | 10 | 12 | 15 | 20 | 24 | 30 | 40 | 60 | ∞ |
| 3 | 2.44 | 2.45 | 2.46 | 2.46 | 2.46 | 2.47 | 2.47 | 2.47 | 2.47 |
| | 5.23 | 5.22 | 5.20 | 5.18 | 5.18 | 5.17 | 5.16 | 5.15 | 5.13 |
| | 8.79 | 8.74 | 8.70 | 8.66 | 8.64 | 8.62 | 8.59 | 8.57 | 8.53 |
| | 14.4 | 14.3 | 14.2 | 14.2 | 14.1 | 14.1 | 14.0 | 14.0 | 13.9 |
| | 27.2 | 27.0 | 26.9 | 26.7 | 26.6 | 26.5 | 26.4 | 26.3 | 26.1 |
| | 129 | 128 | 127 | 126 | 126 | 125 | 125 | 124 | 124 |
| 4 | 2.08 | 2.08 | 2.08 | 2.08 | 2.08 | 2.08 | 2.08 | 2.08 | 2.08 |
| | 3.92 | 3.90 | 3.87 | 3.84 | 3.83 | 3.82 | 3.80 | 3.79 | 3.76 |
| | 5.96 | 5.91 | 5.86 | 5.80 | 5.77 | 5.75 | 5.72 | 5.69 | 5.63 |
| | 8.84 | 8.75 | 8.66 | 8.56 | 8.51 | 8.46 | 8.41 | 8.36 | 8.26 |
| | 14.6 | 14.4 | 14.2 | 14.0 | 13.9 | 13.8 | 13.8 | 13.6 | 13.5 |
| | 48.0 | 47.4 | 46.8 | 46.1 | 45.8 | 45.4 | 45.1 | 44.8 | 44.0 |
| 5 | 1.89 | 1.89 | 1.89 | 1.88 | 1.88 | 1.88 | 1.88 | 1.87 | 1.87 |
| | 3.30 | 3.27 | 3.24 | 3.21 | 3.19 | 3.17 | 3.16 | 3.14 | 3.10 |
| | 4.74 | 4.68 | 4.62 | 4.56 | 4.53 | 4.50 | 4.46 | 4.43 | 4.36 |
| | 6.62 | 6.52 | 6.43 | 6.33 | 6.28 | 6.23 | 6.18 | 6.12 | 6.02 |
| | 10.0 | 9.89 | 9.72 | 9.55 | 9.47 | 9.38 | 9.29 | 9.20 | 9.02 |
| | 26.9 | 26.4 | 25.9 | 25.4 | 25.1 | 24.9 | 24.6 | 24.3 | 23.8 |
| 6 | 1.77 | 1.77 | 1.76 | 1.76 | 1.75 | 1.75 | 1.75 | 1.74 | 1.74 |
| | 2.94 | 2.90 | 2.87 | 2.84 | 2.82 | 2.80 | 2.78 | 2.76 | 2.72 |
| | 4.06 | 4.00 | 3.94 | 3.87 | 3.84 | 3.81 | 3.77 | 3.74 | 3.67 |
| | 5.46 | 5.37 | 5.27 | 5.17 | 5.12 | 5.07 | 5.01 | 4.96 | 4.85 |
| | 7.87 | 7.72 | 7.56 | 7.40 | 7.31 | 7.23 | 7.14 | 7.06 | 6.88 |
| | 18.4 | 18.0 | 17.6 | 17.1 | 16.9 | 16.7 | 16.4 | 16.2 | 15.8 |
| 7 | 1.69 | 1.68 | 1.68 | 1.67 | 1.67 | 1.66 | 1.66 | 1.65 | 1.65 |
| | 2.70 | 2.67 | 2.63 | 2.59 | 2.58 | 2.56 | 2.54 | 2.51 | 2.47 |
| | 3.64 | 3.57 | 3.51 | 3.44 | 3.41 | 3.38 | 3.34 | 3.30 | 3.23 |
| | 4.76 | 4.67 | 4.57 | 4.47 | 4.42 | 4.36 | 4.31 | 4.25 | 4.14 |
| | 6.82 | 6.47 | 6.31 | 6.16 | 6.07 | 5.99 | 5.91 | 5.82 | 5.65 |
| | 14.1 | 13.7 | 13.3 | 12.9 | 12.7 | 12.5 | 12.3 | 12.1 | 11.7 |
| 8 | 1.63 | 1.62 | 1.62 | 1.61 | 1.60 | 1.60 | 1.59 | 1.59 | 1.58 |
| | 2.54 | 2.50 | 2.46 | 2.42 | 2.40 | 2.38 | 2.36 | 2.34 | 2.29 |
| | 3.35 | 3.28 | 3.22 | 3.15 | 3.12 | 3.08 | 3.04 | 3.01 | 2.93 |
| | 4.30 | 4.20 | 4.10 | 4.00 | 3.95 | 3.89 | 3.84 | 3.78 | 3.67 |
| | 5.81 | 5.67 | 5.52 | 5.36 | 5.28 | 5.20 | 5.12 | 5.03 | 4.86 |
| | 11.5 | 11.2 | 10.8 | 10.5 | 10.3 | 10.1 | 9.92 | 9.73 | 9.33 |
| 9 | 1.59 | 1.58 | 1.57 | 1.56 | 1.56 | 1.55 | 1.54 | 1.54 | 1.53 |
| | 2.42 | 2.38 | 2.34 | 2.30 | 2.28 | 2.25 | 2.23 | 2.21 | 2.16 |
| | 3.14 | 3.07 | 3.01 | 2.94 | 2.90 | 2.86 | 2.83 | 2.79 | 2.71 |
| | 3.96 | 3.87 | 3.77 | 3.67 | 3.61 | 3.56 | 3.51 | 3.45 | 3.33 |
| | 5.26 | 5.11 | 4.96 | 4.81 | 4.73 | 4.65 | 4.57 | 4.48 | 4.31 |
| | 9.89 | 9.57 | 9.24 | 8.90 | 8.72 | 8.55 | 8.37 | 8.19 | 7.81 |

**Table E** *(Continued)*

| df for denom. | α | df for numerator | | | | | | | | |
|---|---|---|---|---|---|---|---|---|---|---|
| | | 1 | 2 | 3 | 4 | 5 | 6 | 7 | 8 | 9 |
| 10 | .25 | 1.49 | 1.60 | 1.60 | 1.59 | 1.59 | 1.58 | 1.57 | 1.56 | 1.56 |
| | .10 | 3.29 | 2.92 | 2.73 | 2.61 | 2.52 | 2.46 | 2.41 | 2.38 | 2.35 |
| | .05 | 4.96 | 4.10 | 3.71 | 3.48 | 3.33 | 3.22 | 3.14 | 3.07 | 3.02 |
| | .025 | 6.94 | 5.46 | 4.83 | 4.47 | 4.24 | 4.07 | 3.95 | 3.85 | 3.78 |
| | .01 | 10.0 | 7.56 | 6.55 | 5.99 | 5.64 | 5.39 | 5.20 | 5.06 | 4.94 |
| | .001 | 21.0 | 14.9 | 12.6 | 11.3 | 10.5 | 9.92 | 9.52 | 9.20 | 8.96 |
| 11 | .25 | 1.47 | 1.58 | 1.58 | 1.57 | 1.56 | 1.55 | 1.54 | 1.53 | 1.53 |
| | .10 | 3.23 | 2.86 | 2.66 | 2.54 | 2.45 | 2.39 | 2.34 | 2.30 | 2.27 |
| | .05 | 4.84 | 3.98 | 3.59 | 3.36 | 3.20 | 3.09 | 3.01 | 2.95 | 2.90 |
| | .025 | 6.72 | 5.26 | 4.63 | 4.28 | 4.04 | 3.88 | 3.76 | 3.66 | 3.59 |
| | .01 | 9.65 | 7.21 | 6.22 | 5.67 | 5.32 | 5.07 | 4.89 | 4.74 | 4.63 |
| | .001 | 19.7 | 13.8 | 11.6 | 10.4 | 9.58 | 9.05 | 8.66 | 8.35 | 8.12 |
| 12 | .25 | 1.46 | 1.56 | 1.56 | 1.55 | 1.54 | 1.53 | 1.52 | 1.51 | 1.51 |
| | .10 | 3.18 | 2.81 | 2.61 | 2.48 | 2.39 | 2.33 | 2.28 | 2.24 | 2.21 |
| | .05 | 4.75 | 3.89 | 3.49 | 3.26 | 3.11 | 3.00 | 2.91 | 2.85 | 2.80 |
| | .025 | 6.55 | 5.10 | 4.47 | 4.12 | 3.89 | 3.73 | 3.61 | 3.51 | 3.44 |
| | .01 | 9.33 | 6.93 | 5.95 | 5.41 | 5.06 | 4.82 | 4.64 | 4.50 | 4.39 |
| | .001 | 18.6 | 13.0 | 10.8 | 9.63 | 8.89 | 8.38 | 8.00 | 7.71 | 7.48 |
| 13 | .25 | 1.45 | 1.55 | 1.55 | 1.53 | 1.52 | 1.51 | 1.50 | 1.49 | 1.49 |
| | .10 | 3.14 | 2.76 | 2.56 | 2.43 | 2.35 | 2.28 | 2.23 | 2.20 | 2.16 |
| | .05 | 4.67 | 3.81 | 3.41 | 3.18 | 3.03 | 2.92 | 2.83 | 2.77 | 2.71 |
| | .025 | 6.41 | 4.97 | 4.35 | 4.00 | 3.77 | 3.60 | 3.48 | 3.39 | 3.31 |
| | .01 | 9.07 | 6.70 | 5.74 | 5.21 | 4.86 | 4.62 | 4.44 | 4.30 | 4.19 |
| | .001 | 17.8 | 12.3 | 10.2 | 9.07 | 8.35 | 7.86 | 7.49 | 7.21 | 6.98 |
| 14 | .25 | 1.44 | 1.53 | 1.53 | 1.52 | 1.51 | 1.50 | 1.49 | 1.48 | 1.47 |
| | .10 | 3.10 | 2.73 | 2.52 | 2.39 | 2.31 | 2.24 | 2.19 | 2.15 | 2.12 |
| | .05 | 4.60 | 3.74 | 3.34 | 3.11 | 2.96 | 2.85 | 2.76 | 2.70 | 2.65 |
| | .025 | 6.30 | 4.86 | 4.24 | 3.89 | 3.66 | 3.50 | 3.38 | 3.29 | 3.21 |
| | .01 | 8.86 | 6.51 | 5.56 | 5.04 | 4.69 | 4.46 | 4.28 | 4.14 | 4.03 |
| | .001 | 17.1 | 11.8 | 9.73 | 8.62 | 7.92 | 7.43 | 7.08 | 6.80 | 6.58 |
| 15 | .25 | 1.43 | 1.52 | 1.52 | 1.51 | 1.49 | 1.48 | 1.47 | 1.46 | 1.46 |
| | .10 | 3.07 | 2.70 | 2.49 | 2.36 | 2.27 | 2.21 | 2.16 | 2.12 | 2.09 |
| | .05 | 4.54 | 3.68 | 3.29 | 3.06 | 2.90 | 2.79 | 2.71 | 2.64 | 2.59 |
| | .025 | 6.20 | 4.77 | 4.15 | 3.80 | 3.58 | 3.41 | 3.29 | 3.20 | 3.12 |
| | .01 | 8.68 | 6.36 | 5.42 | 4.89 | 4.56 | 4.32 | 4.14 | 4.00 | 3.89 |
| | .001 | 16.6 | 11.3 | 9.34 | 8.25 | 7.57 | 7.09 | 6.74 | 6.47 | 6.26 |
| 16 | .25 | 1.42 | 1.51 | 1.51 | 1.50 | 1.48 | 1.47 | 1.46 | 1.45 | 1.44 |
| | .10 | 3.05 | 2.67 | 2.46 | 2.33 | 2.24 | 2.18 | 2.13 | 2.09 | 2.06 |
| | .05 | 4.49 | 3.63 | 3.24 | 3.01 | 2.85 | 2.74 | 2.66 | 2.59 | 2.54 |
| | .025 | 6.12 | 4.69 | 4.08 | 3.73 | 3.50 | 3.34 | 3.22 | 3.12 | 3.05 |
| | .01 | 8.53 | 6.23 | 5.29 | 4.77 | 4.44 | 4.20 | 4.03 | 3.89 | 3.78 |
| | .001 | 16.1 | 11.0 | 9.00 | 7.94 | 7.27 | 6.81 | 6.46 | 6.19 | 5.98 |
| 17 | .25 | 1.42 | 1.51 | 1.50 | 1.49 | 1.47 | 1.46 | 1.45 | 1.44 | 1.43 |
| | .10 | 3.03 | 2.64 | 2.44 | 2.31 | 2.22 | 2.15 | 2.10 | 2.06 | 2.03 |
| | .05 | 4.45 | 3.59 | 3.20 | 2.96 | 2.81 | 2.70 | 2.61 | 2.55 | 2.49 |
| | .025 | 6.04 | 4.62 | 4.01 | 3.66 | 3.44 | 3.28 | 3.16 | 3.06 | 2.98 |
| | .01 | 8.40 | 6.11 | 5.18 | 4.67 | 4.34 | 4.10 | 3.93 | 3.79 | 3.68 |
| | .001 | 15.7 | 10.7 | 8.73 | 7.68 | 7.02 | 6.56 | 6.22 | 5.96 | 5.75 |

| df for denom. | df for numerator | | | | | | | | |
|---|---|---|---|---|---|---|---|---|---|
| | 10 | 12 | 15 | 20 | 24 | 30 | 40 | 60 | ∞ |
| 10 | 1.55 | 1.54 | 1.53 | 1.52 | 1.52 | 1.51 | 1.51 | 1.50 | 1.48 |
| | 2.32 | 2.28 | 2.24 | 2.20 | 2.18 | 2.16 | 2.13 | 2.11 | 2.06 |
| | 2.98 | 2.91 | 2.85 | 2.77 | 2.74 | 2.70 | 2.66 | 2.62 | 2.54 |
| | 3.72 | 3.62 | 3.52 | 3.42 | 3.37 | 3.31 | 3.26 | 3.20 | 3.08 |
| | 4.85 | 4.71 | 4.56 | 4.41 | 4.33 | 4.25 | 4.17 | 4.08 | 3.91 |
| | 8.75 | 8.45 | 8.13 | 7.80 | 7.64 | 7.47 | 7.30 | 7.12 | 6.76 |
| 11 | 1.52 | 1.51 | 1.50 | 1.49 | 1.49 | 1.48 | 1.47 | 1.47 | 1.45 |
| | 2.25 | 2.21 | 2.17 | 2.12 | 2.10 | 2.08 | 2.05 | 2.03 | 1.97 |
| | 2.85 | 2.79 | 2.72 | 2.65 | 2.61 | 2.57 | 2.53 | 2.49 | 2.40 |
| | 3.53 | 3.43 | 3.33 | 3.23 | 3.17 | 3.12 | 3.06 | 3.00 | 2.88 |
| | 4.54 | 4.40 | 4.25 | 4.10 | 4.02 | 3.94 | 3.86 | 3.78 | 3.60 |
| | 7.92 | 7.63 | 7.32 | 7.01 | 6.85 | 6.68 | 6.52 | 6.35 | 6.00 |
| 12 | 1.50 | 1.49 | 1.48 | 1.47 | 1.46 | 1.45 | 1.45 | 1.44 | 1.42 |
| | 2.19 | 2.15 | 2.10 | 2.06 | 2.04 | 2.01 | 1.99 | 1.96 | 1.90 |
| | 2.75 | 2.69 | 2.62 | 2.54 | 2.51 | 2.47 | 2.43 | 2.38 | 2.30 |
| | 3.37 | 3.28 | 3.18 | 3.07 | 3.02 | 2.96 | 2.91 | 2.85 | 2.72 |
| | 4.30 | 4.16 | 4.01 | 3.86 | 3.78 | 3.70 | 3.62 | 3.54 | 3.36 |
| | 7.29 | 7.00 | 6.71 | 6.40 | 6.25 | 6.09 | 5.93 | 5.76 | 5.42 |
| 13 | 1.48 | 1.47 | 1.46 | 1.45 | 1.44 | 1.43 | 1.42 | 1.42 | 1.40 |
| | 2.14 | 2.10 | 2.05 | 2.01 | 1.98 | 1.96 | 1.93 | 1.90 | 1.85 |
| | 2.67 | 2.60 | 2.53 | 2.46 | 2.42 | 2.38 | 2.34 | 2.30 | 2.21 |
| | 3.25 | 3.15 | 3.05 | 2.95 | 2.89 | 2.84 | 2.78 | 2.72 | 2.60 |
| | 4.10 | 3.96 | 3.82 | 3.66 | 3.59 | 3.51 | 3.43 | 3.34 | 3.17 |
| | 6.80 | 6.52 | 6.23 | 5.93 | 5.78 | 5.63 | 5.47 | 5.30 | 4.97 |
| 14 | 1.46 | 1.45 | 1.44 | 1.43 | 1.42 | 1.41 | 1.41 | 1.40 | 1.38 |
| | 2.10 | 2.05 | 2.01 | 1.96 | 1.94 | 1.91 | 1.89 | 1.86 | 1.80 |
| | 2.60 | 2.53 | 2.46 | 2.39 | 2.35 | 2.31 | 2.27 | 2.22 | 2.13 |
| | 3.15 | 3.05 | 2.95 | 2.84 | 2.79 | 2.73 | 2.67 | 2.61 | 2.49 |
| | 3.94 | 3.80 | 3.66 | 3.51 | 3.43 | 3.35 | 3.27 | 3.18 | 3.00 |
| | 6.40 | 6.13 | 5.85 | 5.56 | 5.41 | 5.25 | 5.10 | 4.94 | 4.60 |
| 15 | 1.45 | 1.44 | 1.43 | 1.41 | 1.41 | 1.40 | 1.39 | 1.38 | 1.36 |
| | 2.06 | 2.02 | 1.97 | 1.92 | 1.90 | 1.87 | 1.85 | 1.82 | 1.76 |
| | 2.54 | 2.48 | 2.40 | 2.33 | 2.29 | 2.25 | 2.20 | 2.16 | 2.07 |
| | 3.06 | 2.96 | 2.86 | 2.76 | 2.70 | 2.64 | 2.59 | 2.52 | 2.40 |
| | 3.80 | 3.67 | 3.52 | 3.37 | 3.29 | 3.21 | 3.13 | 3.05 | 2.87 |
| | 6.08 | 5.81 | 5.54 | 5.25 | 5.10 | 4.95 | 4.80 | 4.64 | 4.31 |
| 16 | 1.44 | 1.43 | 1.41 | 1.40 | 1.39 | 1.38 | 1.37 | 1.36 | 1.34 |
| | 2.03 | 1.99 | 1.94 | 1.89 | 1.87 | 1.84 | 1.81 | 1.78 | 1.72 |
| | 2.49 | 2.42 | 2.35 | 2.28 | 2.24 | 2.19 | 2.15 | 2.11 | 2.01 |
| | 2.99 | 2.89 | 2.79 | 2.68 | 2.63 | 2.57 | 2.51 | 2.45 | 2.32 |
| | 3.69 | 3.55 | 3.41 | 3.26 | 3.18 | 3.10 | 3.02 | 2.93 | 2.75 |
| | 5.81 | 5.55 | 5.27 | 4.99 | 4.85 | 4.70 | 4.54 | 4.39 | 4.06 |
| 17 | 1.43 | 1.41 | 1.40 | 1.39 | 1.38 | 1.37 | 1.36 | 1.35 | 1.33 |
| | 2.00 | 1.96 | 1.91 | 1.86 | 1.84 | 1.81 | 1.78 | 1.75 | 1.69 |
| | 2.45 | 2.38 | 2.31 | 2.23 | 2.19 | 2.15 | 2.10 | 2.06 | 1.96 |
| | 2.92 | 2.82 | 2.72 | 2.62 | 2.56 | 2.50 | 2.44 | 2.38 | 2.25 |
| | 3.59 | 3.46 | 3.31 | 3.16 | 3.08 | 3.00 | 2.92 | 2.83 | 2.65 |
| | 5.58 | 5.32 | 5.05 | 4.78 | 4.63 | 4.48 | 4.33 | 4.18 | 3.85 |

**Table E** *(Continued)*

| df for denom. | α | 1 | 2 | 3 | 4 | 5 | 6 | 7 | 8 | 9 |
|---|---|---|---|---|---|---|---|---|---|---|
| | | | | | | df for numerator | | | | |
| 18 | .25 | 1.41 | 1.50 | 1.49 | 1.48 | 1.46 | 1.45 | 1.44 | 1.43 | 1.42 |
| | .10 | 3.01 | 2.62 | 2.42 | 2.29 | 2.20 | 2.13 | 2.08 | 2.04 | 2.00 |
| | .05 | 4.41 | 3.55 | 3.16 | 2.93 | 2.77 | 2.66 | 2.58 | 2.51 | 2.46 |
| | .025 | 5.98 | 4.56 | 3.95 | 3.61 | 3.38 | 3.22 | 3.10 | 3.01 | 2.93 |
| | .01 | 8.29 | 6.01 | 5.09 | 4.58 | 4.25 | 4.01 | 3.84 | 3.71 | 3.60 |
| | .001 | 15.4 | 10.4 | 8.49 | 7.46 | 6.81 | 6.35 | 6.02 | 5.76 | 5.56 |
| 19 | .25 | 1.41 | 1.49 | 1.49 | 1.47 | 1.46 | 1.44 | 1.43 | 1.42 | 1.41 |
| | .10 | 2.99 | 2.61 | 2.40 | 2.27 | 2.18 | 2.11 | 2.06 | 2.02 | 1.98 |
| | .05 | 4.38 | 3.52 | 3.13 | 2.90 | 2.74 | 2.63 | 2.54 | 2.48 | 2.42 |
| | .025 | 5.92 | 4.51 | 3.90 | 3.56 | 3.33 | 3.17 | 3.05 | 2.96 | 2.88 |
| | .01 | 8.18 | 5.93 | 5.01 | 4.50 | 4.17 | 3.94 | 3.77 | 3.63 | 3.52 |
| | .001 | 15.1 | 10.2 | 8.28 | 7.26 | 6.62 | 6.18 | 5.85 | 5.59 | 5.39 |
| 20 | .25 | 1.40 | 1.49 | 1.48 | 1.47 | 1.45 | 1.44 | 1.43 | 1.42 | 1.41 |
| | .10 | 2.97 | 2.59 | 2.38 | 2.25 | 2.16 | 2.09 | 2.04 | 2.00 | 1.96 |
| | .05 | 4.35 | 3.49 | 3.10 | 2.87 | 2.71 | 2.60 | 2.51 | 2.45 | 2.39 |
| | .025 | 5.87 | 4.46 | 3.86 | 3.51 | 3.29 | 3.13 | 3.01 | 2.91 | 2.84 |
| | .01 | 8.10 | 5.85 | 4.94 | 4.43 | 4.10 | 3.87 | 3.70 | 3.56 | 3.46 |
| | .001 | 14.8 | 9.95 | 8.10 | 7.10 | 6.46 | 6.02 | 5.69 | 5.44 | 5.24 |
| 22 | .25 | 1.40 | 1.48 | 1.47 | 1.45 | 1.44 | 1.42 | 1.41 | 1.40 | 1.39 |
| | .10 | 2.95 | 2.56 | 2.35 | 2.22 | 2.13 | 2.06 | 2.01 | 1.97 | 1.93 |
| | .05 | 4.30 | 3.44 | 3.05 | 2.82 | 2.66 | 2.55 | 2.46 | 2.40 | 2.34 |
| | .025 | 5.79 | 4.38 | 3.78 | 3.44 | 3.22 | 3.05 | 2.93 | 2.84 | 2.76 |
| | .01 | 7.95 | 5.72 | 4.82 | 4.31 | 3.99 | 3.76 | 3.59 | 3.45 | 3.35 |
| | .001 | 14.4 | 9.61 | 7.80 | 6.81 | 6.19 | 5.76 | 5.44 | 5.19 | 4.99 |
| 24 | .25 | 1.39 | 1.47 | 1.46 | 1.44 | 1.43 | 1.41 | 1.40 | 1.39 | 1.38 |
| | .10 | 2.93 | 2.54 | 2.33 | 2.19 | 2.10 | 2.04 | 1.98 | 1.94 | 1.91 |
| | .05 | 4.26 | 3.40 | 3.01 | 2.78 | 2.62 | 2.51 | 2.42 | 2.36 | 2.30 |
| | .025 | 5.72 | 4.32 | 3.72 | 3.38 | 3.15 | 2.99 | 2.87 | 2.78 | 2.70 |
| | .01 | 7.82 | 5.61 | 4.72 | 4.22 | 3.90 | 3.67 | 3.50 | 3.36 | 3.26 |
| | .001 | 14.0 | 9.34 | 7.55 | 6.59 | 5.98 | 5.55 | 5.23 | 4.99 | 4.80 |
| 26 | .25 | 1.38 | 1.46 | 1.45 | 1.44 | 1.42 | 1.41 | 1.39 | 1.38 | 1.37 |
| | .10 | 2.91 | 2.52 | 2.31 | 2.17 | 2.08 | 2.01 | 1.96 | 1.92 | 1.88 |
| | .05 | 4.23 | 3.37 | 2.98 | 2.74 | 2.59 | 2.47 | 2.39 | 2.32 | 2.27 |
| | .025 | 5.66 | 4.27 | 3.67 | 3.33 | 3.10 | 2.94 | 2.82 | 2.73 | 2.65 |
| | .01 | 7.72 | 5.53 | 4.64 | 4.14 | 3.82 | 3.59 | 3.42 | 3.29 | 3.18 |
| | .001 | 13.7 | 9.12 | 7.36 | 6.41 | 5.80 | 5.38 | 5.07 | 4.83 | 4.64 |
| 28 | .25 | 1.38 | 1.46 | 1.45 | 1.43 | 1.41 | 1.40 | 1.39 | 1.38 | 1.37 |
| | .10 | 2.89 | 2.50 | 2.29 | 2.16 | 2.06 | 2.00 | 1.94 | 1.90 | 1.87 |
| | .05 | 4.20 | 3.34 | 2.95 | 2.71 | 2.56 | 2.45 | 2.36 | 2.29 | 2.24 |
| | .025 | 5.61 | 4.22 | 3.63 | 3.29 | 3.06 | 2.90 | 2.78 | 2.69 | 2.61 |
| | .01 | 7.64 | 5.45 | 4.57 | 4.07 | 3.75 | 3.53 | 3.36 | 3.23 | 3.12 |
| | .001 | 13.5 | 8.93 | 7.19 | 6.25 | 5.66 | 5.24 | 4.93 | 4.69 | 4.50 |
| 30 | .25 | 1.38 | 1.45 | 1.44 | 1.42 | 1.41 | 1.39 | 1.38 | 1.37 | 1.36 |
| | .10 | 2.88 | 2.49 | 2.28 | 2.14 | 2.05 | 1.98 | 1.93 | 1.88 | 1.85 |
| | .05 | 4.17 | 3.32 | 2.92 | 2.69 | 2.53 | 2.42 | 2.33 | 2.27 | 2.21 |
| | .025 | 5.57 | 4.18 | 3.59 | 3.25 | 3.03 | 2.87 | 2.75 | 2.65 | 2.57 |
| | .01 | 7.56 | 5.39 | 4.51 | 4.02 | 3.70 | 3.47 | 3.30 | 3.17 | 3.07 |
| | .001 | 13.3 | 8.77 | 7.05 | 6.12 | 5.53 | 5.12 | 4.82 | 4.58 | 4.39 |

| df for denom. | df for numerator | | | | | | | | |
|---|---|---|---|---|---|---|---|---|---|
| | 10 | 12 | 15 | 20 | 24 | 30 | 40 | 60 | ∞ |
| 18 | 1.42 | 1.40 | 1.39 | 1.38 | 1.37 | 1.36 | 1.35 | 1.34 | 1.32 |
| | 1.98 | 1.93 | 1.89 | 1.84 | 1.81 | 1.78 | 1.75 | 1.72 | 1.66 |
| | 2.41 | 2.34 | 2.27 | 2.19 | 2.15 | 2.11 | 2.06 | 2.02 | 1.92 |
| | 2.87 | 2.77 | 2.67 | 2.56 | 2.50 | 2.44 | 2.38 | 2.32 | 2.19 |
| | 3.51 | 3.37 | 3.23 | 3.08 | 3.00 | 2.92 | 2.84 | 2.75 | 2.57 |
| | 5.39 | 5.13 | 4.87 | 4.59 | 4.45 | 4.30 | 4.15 | 4.00 | 3.67 |
| 19 | 1.41 | 1.40 | 1.38 | 1.37 | 1.36 | 1.35 | 1.34 | 1.33 | 1.30 |
| | 1.96 | 1.91 | 1.86 | 1.81 | 1.79 | 1.76 | 1.73 | 1.70 | 1.63 |
| | 2.38 | 2.31 | 2.23 | 2.16 | 2.11 | 2.07 | 2.03 | 1.98 | 1.88 |
| | 2.82 | 2.72 | 2.62 | 2.51 | 2.45 | 2.39 | 2.33 | 2.27 | 2.13 |
| | 3.43 | 3.30 | 3.15 | 3.00 | 2.92 | 2.84 | 2.76 | 2.67 | 2.49 |
| | 5.22 | 4.97 | 4.70 | 4.43 | 4.29 | 4.14 | 3.99 | 3.84 | 3.51 |
| 20 | 1.40 | 1.39 | 1.37 | 1.36 | 1.35 | 1.34 | 1.33 | 1.32 | 1.29 |
| | 1.94 | 1.89 | 1.84 | 1.79 | 1.77 | 1.74 | 1.71 | 1.68 | 1.61 |
| | 2.35 | 2.28 | 2.20 | 2.12 | 2.08 | 2.04 | 1.99 | 1.95 | 1.84 |
| | 2.77 | 2.68 | 2.57 | 2.46 | 2.41 | 2.35 | 2.29 | 2.22 | 2.09 |
| | 3.37 | 3.23 | 3.09 | 2.94 | 2.86 | 2.78 | 2.69 | 2.61 | 2.42 |
| | 5.08 | 4.82 | 4.56 | 4.29 | 4.15 | 4.00 | 3.86 | 3.70 | 3.38 |
| 22 | 1.39 | 1.37 | 1.36 | 1.34 | 1.33 | 1.32 | 1.31 | 1.30 | 1.28 |
| | 1.90 | 1.86 | 1.81 | 1.76 | 1.73 | 1.70 | 1.67 | 1.64 | 1.57 |
| | 2.30 | 2.23 | 2.15 | 2.07 | 2.03 | 1.98 | 1.94 | 1.89 | 1.78 |
| | 2.70 | 2.60 | 2.50 | 2.39 | 2.33 | 2.27 | 2.21 | 2.14 | 2.00 |
| | 3.26 | 3.12 | 2.98 | 2.83 | 2.75 | 2.67 | 2.58 | 2.50 | 2.31 |
| | 4.83 | 4.58 | 4.33 | 4.06 | 3.92 | 3.78 | 3.63 | 3.48 | 3.15 |
| 24 | 1.38 | 1.36 | 1.35 | 1.33 | 1.32 | 1.31 | 1.30 | 1.29 | 1.26 |
| | 1.88 | 1.83 | 1.78 | 1.73 | 1.70 | 1.67 | 1.64 | 1.61 | 1.53 |
| | 2.25 | 2.18 | 2.11 | 2.03 | 1.98 | 1.94 | 1.89 | 1.84 | 1.73 |
| | 2.64 | 2.54 | 2.44 | 2.33 | 2.27 | 2.21 | 2.15 | 2.08 | 1.94 |
| | 3.17 | 3.03 | 2.89 | 2.74 | 2.66 | 2.58 | 2.49 | 2.40 | 2.21 |
| | 4.64 | 4.39 | 4.14 | 3.87 | 3.74 | 3.59 | 3.45 | 3.29 | 2.97 |
| 26 | 1.37 | 1.35 | 1.34 | 1.32 | 1.31 | 1.30 | 1.29 | 1.28 | 1.25 |
| | 1.86 | 1.81 | 1.76 | 1.71 | 1.68 | 1.65 | 1.61 | 1.58 | 1.50 |
| | 2.22 | 2.15 | 2.07 | 1.99 | 1.95 | 1.90 | 1.85 | 1.80 | 1.69 |
| | 2.59 | 2.49 | 2.39 | 2.28 | 2.22 | 2.16 | 2.09 | 2.03 | 1.88 |
| | 3.09 | 2.96 | 2.81 | 2.66 | 2.58 | 2.50 | 2.42 | 2.33 | 2.13 |
| | 4.48 | 4.24 | 3.99 | 3.72 | 3.59 | 3.44 | 3.30 | 3.15 | 2.82 |
| 28 | 1.36 | 1.34 | 1.33 | 1.31 | 1.30 | 1.29 | 1.28 | 1.27 | 1.24 |
| | 1.84 | 1.79 | 1.74 | 1.69 | 1.66 | 1.63 | 1.59 | 1.56 | 1.48 |
| | 2.19 | 2.12 | 2.04 | 1.96 | 1.91 | 1.87 | 1.82 | 1.77 | 1.65 |
| | 2.55 | 2.45 | 2.34 | 2.23 | 2.17 | 2.11 | 2.05 | 1.98 | 1.83 |
| | 3.03 | 2.90 | 2.75 | 2.60 | 2.52 | 2.44 | 2.35 | 2.26 | 2.06 |
| | 4.35 | 4.11 | 3.86 | 3.60 | 3.46 | 3.32 | 3.18 | 3.02 | 2.69 |
| 30 | 1.35 | 1.34 | 1.32 | 1.30 | 1.29 | 1.28 | 1.27 | 1.26 | 1.23 |
| | 1.82 | 1.77 | 1.72 | 1.67 | 1.64 | 1.61 | 1.57 | 1.54 | 1.46 |
| | 2.16 | 2.09 | 2.01 | 1.93 | 1.89 | 1.84 | 1.79 | 1.74 | 1.62 |
| | 2.51 | 2.41 | 2.31 | 2.20 | 2.14 | 2.07 | 2.01 | 1.94 | 1.79 |
| | 2.98 | 2.84 | 2.70 | 2.55 | 2.47 | 2.39 | 2.30 | 2.21 | 2.01 |
| | 4.24 | 4.00 | 3.75 | 3.49 | 3.36 | 3.22 | 3.07 | 2.92 | 2.59 |

**Table E** *(Continued)*

| df for denom. | α | \multicolumn{9}{c}{df for numerator} |
|---|---|---|---|---|---|---|---|---|---|---|
| | | 1 | 2 | 3 | 4 | 5 | 6 | 7 | 8 | 9 |
| 40 | .25 | 1.36 | 1.44 | 1.42 | 1.40 | 1.39 | 1.37 | 1.36 | 1.35 | 1.34 |
| | .10 | 2.84 | 2.44 | 2.23 | 2.09 | 2.00 | 1.93 | 1.87 | 1.83 | 1.79 |
| | .05 | 4.08 | 3.23 | 2.84 | 2.61 | 2.45 | 2.34 | 2.25 | 2.18 | 2.12 |
| | .025 | 5.42 | 4.05 | 3.46 | 3.13 | 2.90 | 2.74 | 2.62 | 2.53 | 2.45 |
| | .01 | 7.31 | 5.18 | 4.31 | 3.83 | 3.51 | 3.29 | 3.12 | 2.99 | 2.89 |
| | .001 | 12.6 | 8.25 | 6.60 | 5.70 | 5.13 | 4.73 | 4.44 | 4.21 | 4.02 |
| 60 | .25 | 1.35 | 1.42 | 1.41 | 1.38 | 1.37 | 1.35 | 1.33 | 1.32 | 1.31 |
| | .10 | 2.79 | 2.39 | 2.18 | 2.04 | 1.95 | 1.87 | 1.82 | 1.77 | 1.74 |
| | .05 | 4.00 | 3.15 | 2.76 | 2.53 | 2.37 | 2.25 | 2.17 | 2.10 | 2.04 |
| | .025 | 5.29 | 3.93 | 3.34 | 3.01 | 2.79 | 2.63 | 2.51 | 2.41 | 2.33 |
| | .01 | 7.08 | 4.98 | 4.13 | 3.65 | 3.34 | 3.12 | 2.95 | 2.82 | 2.72 |
| | .001 | 12.0 | 7.76 | 6.17 | 5.31 | 4.76 | 4.37 | 4.09 | 3.87 | 3.69 |
| 120 | .25 | 1.34 | 1.40 | 1.39 | 1.37 | 1.35 | 1.33 | 1.31 | 1.30 | 1.29 |
| | .10 | 2.75 | 2.35 | 2.13 | 1.99 | 1.90 | 1.82 | 1.77 | 1.72 | 1.68 |
| | .05 | 3.92 | 3.07 | 2.68 | 2.45 | 2.29 | 2.17 | 2.09 | 2.02 | 1.96 |
| | .025 | 5.15 | 3.80 | 3.23 | 2.89 | 2.67 | 2.52 | 2.39 | 2.30 | 2.22 |
| | .01 | 6.85 | 4.79 | 3.95 | 3.48 | 3.17 | 2.96 | 2.79 | 2.66 | 2.56 |
| | .001 | 11.4 | 7.32 | 5.79 | 4.95 | 4.42 | 4.04 | 3.77 | 3.55 | 3.38 |
| ∞ | .25 | 1.32 | 1.39 | 1.37 | 1.35 | 1.33 | 1.31 | 1.29 | 1.28 | 1.27 |
| | .10 | 2.71 | 2.30 | 2.08 | 1.94 | 1.85 | 1.77 | 1.72 | 1.67 | 1.63 |
| | .05 | 3.84 | 3.00 | 2.60 | 2.37 | 2.21 | 2.10 | 2.01 | 1.94 | 1.88 |
| | .025 | 5.02 | 3.69 | 3.12 | 2.79 | 2.57 | 2.41 | 2.29 | 2.19 | 2.11 |
| | .01 | 6.63 | 4.61 | 3.78 | 3.32 | 3.02 | 2.80 | 2.64 | 2.51 | 2.41 |
| | .001 | 10.8 | .91 | 5.42 | 4.62 | 4.10 | 3.74 | 3.47 | 3.27 | 3.10 |

| df for denom. | df for numerator | | | | | | | | |
|---|---|---|---|---|---|---|---|---|---|
| | 10 | 12 | 15 | 20 | 24 | 30 | 40 | 60 | ∞ |
| 40 | 1.33 | 1.31 | 1.30 | 1.28 | 1.26 | 1.25 | 1.24 | 1.22 | 1.19 |
| | 1.76 | 1.71 | 1.66 | 1.61 | 1.57 | 1.54 | 1.51 | 1.47 | 1.38 |
| | 2.08 | 2.00 | 1.92 | 1.84 | 1.79 | 1.74 | 1.69 | 1.64 | 1.51 |
| | 2.39 | 2.29 | 2.18 | 2.07 | 2.01 | 1.94 | 1.88 | 1.80 | 1.64 |
| | 2.80 | 2.66 | 2.52 | 2.37 | 2.29 | 2.20 | 2.11 | 2.02 | 1.80 |
| | 3.87 | 3.64 | 3.40 | 3.15 | 3.01 | 2.87 | 2.73 | 2.57 | 2.23 |
| 60 | 1.30 | 1.29 | 1.27 | 1.25 | 1.24 | 1.22 | 1.21 | 1.19 | 1.15 |
| | 1.71 | 1.66 | 1.60 | 1.54 | 1.51 | 1.48 | 1.44 | 1.40 | 1.29 |
| | 1.99 | 1.92 | 1.84 | 1.75 | 1.70 | 1.65 | 1.59 | 1.53 | 1.39 |
| | 2.27 | 2.17 | 2.06 | 1.94 | 1.88 | 1.82 | 1.74 | 1.67 | 1.48 |
| | 2.63 | 2.50 | 2.35 | 2.20 | 2.12 | 2.03 | 1.94 | 1.84 | 1.60 |
| | 3.54 | 3.31 | 3.08 | 2.83 | 2.69 | 2.55 | 2.41 | 2.25 | 1.89 |
| 120 | 1.28 | 1.26 | 1.24 | 1.22 | 1.21 | 1.19 | 1.18 | 1.16 | 1.10 |
| | 1.65 | 1.60 | 1.55 | 1.48 | 1.45 | 1.41 | 1.37 | 1.32 | 1.19 |
| | 1.91 | 1.83 | 1.75 | 1.66 | 1.61 | 1.55 | 1.50 | 1.43 | 1.25 |
| | 2.16 | 2.05 | 1.94 | 1.82 | 1.76 | 1.69 | 1.61 | 1.53 | 1.31 |
| | 2.47 | 2.34 | 2.19 | 2.03 | 1.95 | 1.86 | 1.76 | 1.66 | 1.38 |
| | 3.24 | 3.02 | 2.78 | 2.53 | 2.40 | 2.26 | 2.11 | 1.95 | 1.54 |
| ∞ | 1.25 | 1.24 | 1.22 | 1.19 | 1.18 | 1.16 | 1.14 | 1.12 | 1.00 |
| | 1.60 | 1.55 | 1.49 | 1.42 | 1.38 | 1.34 | 1.30 | 1.24 | 1.00 |
| | 1.83 | 1.75 | 1.67 | 1.57 | 1.52 | 1.46 | 1.39 | 1.32 | 1.00 |
| | 2.05 | 1.94 | 1.83 | 1.71 | 1.64 | 1.57 | 1.48 | 1.39 | 1.00 |
| | 2.32 | 2.18 | 2.04 | 1.88 | 1.79 | 1.70 | 1.59 | 1.47 | 1.00 |
| | 2.96 | 2.74 | 2.51 | 2.27 | 2.13 | 1.99 | 1.84 | 1.66 | 1.00 |

**Table F**          **Random Numbers**

|     | 1 | 2 | 3 | 4 | 5 | 6 | 7 | 8 | 9 |
|-----|-----|-----|-----|-----|-----|-----|-----|-----|-----|
| 1 | 32942 | 95416 | 42339 | 59045 | 26693 | 49057 | 87496 | 20624 | 14819 |
| 2 | 07410 | 99859 | 83828 | 21409 | 29094 | 65114 | 36701 | 25762 | 12827 |
| 3 | 59981 | 68155 | 45673 | 76210 | 58219 | 45738 | 29550 | 24736 | 09574 |
| 4 | 46251 | 25437 | 69654 | 99716 | 11563 | 08803 | 86027 | 51867 | 12116 |
| 5 | 65558 | 51904 | 93123 | 27887 | 53138 | 21488 | 09095 | 78777 | 71240 |
| 6 | 99187 | 19258 | 86421 | 16401 | 19397 | 83297 | 40111 | 49326 | 81686 |
| 7 | 35641 | 00301 | 16096 | 34775 | 21562 | 97983 | 45040 | 19200 | 16383 |
| 8 | 14031 | 00936 | 81518 | 48440 | 02218 | 04756 | 19506 | 60695 | 88494 |
| 9 | 60677 | 15076 | 92554 | 26042 | 23472 | 69869 | 62877 | 19584 | 39576 |
| 10 | 66314 | 05212 | 67859 | 89356 | 20056 | 30648 | 87349 | 20389 | 53805 |
| 11 | 20416 | 87410 | 75646 | 64176 | 82752 | 63606 | 37011 | 57346 | 69512 |
| 12 | 28701 | 56992 | 70423 | 62415 | 40807 | 98086 | 58850 | 28968 | 45297 |
| 13 | 74579 | 33844 | 33426 | 07570 | 00728 | 07079 | 19322 | 56325 | 84819 |
| 14 | 62615 | 52342 | 82968 | 75540 | 80045 | 53069 | 20665 | 21282 | 07768 |
| 15 | 93945 | 06293 | 22879 | 08161 | 01442 | 75071 | 21427 | 94842 | 26210 |
| 16 | 75689 | 76131 | 96837 | 67450 | 44511 | 50424 | 82848 | 41975 | 71663 |
| 17 | 02921 | 16919 | 35424 | 93209 | 52133 | 87327 | 95897 | 65171 | 20376 |
| 18 | 14295 | 34969 | 14216 | 03191 | 61647 | 30296 | 66667 | 10101 | 63203 |
| 19 | 05303 | 91109 | 82403 | 40312 | 62191 | 67023 | 90073 | 83205 | 71344 |
| 20 | 57071 | 90357 | 12901 | 08899 | 91039 | 67251 | 28701 | 03846 | 94589 |
| 21 | 78471 | 57741 | 13599 | 84390 | 32146 | 00871 | 09354 | 22745 | 65806 |
| 22 | 89242 | 79337 | 59293 | 47481 | 07740 | 43345 | 25716 | 70020 | 54005 |
| 23 | 14955 | 59592 | 97035 | 80430 | 87220 | 06392 | 79028 | 57123 | 52872 |
| 24 | 42446 | 41880 | 37415 | 47472 | 04513 | 49494 | 08860 | 08038 | 43624 |
| 25 | 18534 | 22346 | 54556 | 17558 | 73689 | 14894 | 05030 | 19561 | 56517 |
| 26 | 39284 | 33737 | 42512 | 86411 | 23753 | 29690 | 26096 | 81361 | 93099 |
| 27 | 33922 | 37329 | 89911 | 55876 | 28379 | 81031 | 22058 | 21487 | 54613 |
| 28 | 78355 | 54013 | 50774 | 30666 | 61205 | 42574 | 47773 | 36027 | 27174 |
| 29 | 08845 | 99145 | 94316 | 88974 | 29828 | 97069 | 90327 | 61842 | 29604 |
| 30 | 01769 | 71825 | 55957 | 98271 | 02784 | 66731 | 40311 | 88495 | 18821 |
| 31 | 17639 | 38284 | 59478 | 90409 | 21997 | 56199 | 30068 | 82800 | 69692 |
| 32 | 05851 | 58653 | 99949 | 63505 | 40409 | 85551 | 90729 | 64938 | 52403 |
| 33 | 42396 | 40112 | 11469 | 03476 | 03328 | 84238 | 26570 | 51790 | 42122 |
| 34 | 13318 | 14192 | 98167 | 75631 | 74141 | 22369 | 36757 | 89117 | 54998 |
| 35 | 60571 | 54786 | 26281 | 01855 | 30706 | 66578 | 32019 | 65884 | 58485 |
| 36 | 09531 | 81853 | 59334 | 70929 | 03544 | 18510 | 89541 | 13555 | 21168 |
| 37 | 72865 | 16829 | 86542 | 00396 | 20363 | 13010 | 69645 | 49608 | 54738 |
| 38 | 56324 | 31093 | 77924 | 28622 | 83543 | 28912 | 15059 | 80192 | 83964 |
| 39 | 78192 | 21626 | 91399 | 07235 | 07104 | 73652 | 64425 | 85149 | 75409 |
| 40 | 64666 | 34767 | 97298 | 92708 | 01994 | 53188 | 78476 | 07804 | 62404 |
| 41 | 82201 | 75694 | 02808 | 65983 | 74373 | 66693 | 13094 | 74183 | 73020 |
| 42 | 15360 | 73776 | 40914 | 85190 | 54278 | 99054 | 62944 | 47351 | 89098 |
| 43 | 68142 | 67957 | 70896 | 37983 | 20487 | 95350 | 16371 | 03426 | 13895 |
| 44 | 19138 | 31200 | 30616 | 14639 | 44406 | 44236 | 57360 | 81644 | 94761 |
| 45 | 28155 | 03521 | 36415 | 78452 | 92359 | 81091 | 56513 | 88321 | 97910 |
| 46 | 87971 | 29031 | 51780 | 27376 | 81056 | 86155 | 55488 | 50590 | 74514 |
| 47 | 58147 | 68841 | 53625 | 02059 | 75223 | 16783 | 19272 | 61994 | 71090 |
| 48 | 18875 | 52809 | 70594 | 41649 | 32935 | 26430 | 82096 | 01605 | 65846 |
| 49 | 75109 | 56474 | 74111 | 31966 | 29969 | 70093 | 98901 | 84550 | 25769 |
| 50 | 35983 | 03742 | 76822 | 12073 | 59463 | 84420 | 15868 | 99505 | 11426 |

|     | 1 | 2 | 3 | 4 | 5 | 6 | 7 | 8 | 9 |
|-----|-------|-------|-------|-------|-------|-------|-------|-------|-------|
| 51  | 12651 | 61646 | 11769 | 75109 | 86996 | 97669 | 25757 | 32535 | 07122 |
| 52  | 81769 | 74436 | 02630 | 72310 | 45049 | 18029 | 07469 | 42341 | 98173 |
| 53  | 36737 | 98863 | 77240 | 76251 | 00654 | 64688 | 09343 | 70278 | 67331 |
| 54  | 82861 | 54371 | 76610 | 94934 | 72748 | 44124 | 05610 | 53750 | 95938 |
| 55  | 21325 | 15732 | 24127 | 37431 | 09723 | 63529 | 73977 | 95218 | 96074 |
| 56  | 74146 | 47887 | 62463 | 23045 | 41490 | 07954 | 22597 | 60012 | 98866 |
| 57  | 90759 | 64410 | 54179 | 66075 | 61051 | 75385 | 51378 | 08360 | 95946 |
| 58  | 55683 | 98078 | 02238 | 91540 | 21219 | 17720 | 87817 | 41705 | 95785 |
| 59  | 79686 | 17969 | 76061 | 83748 | 55920 | 83612 | 41540 | 86492 | 06447 |
| 60  | 70333 | 00201 | 86201 | 69716 | 78185 | 62154 | 77930 | 67663 | 29529 |
| 61  | 14042 | 53536 | 07779 | 04157 | 41172 | 36473 | 42123 | 43929 | 50533 |
| 62  | 59911 | 08256 | 06596 | 48416 | 69770 | 68797 | 56080 | 14223 | 59199 |
| 63  | 62368 | 62623 | 62742 | 14891 | 39247 | 52242 | 98832 | 69533 | 91174 |
| 64  | 57529 | 97751 | 54976 | 48957 | 74599 | 08759 | 78494 | 52785 | 68526 |
| 65  | 15469 | 90574 | 78033 | 66885 | 13936 | 42117 | 71831 | 22961 | 94225 |
| 66  | 18625 | 23674 | 53850 | 32827 | 81647 | 80820 | 00420 | 63555 | 74489 |
| 67  | 74626 | 68394 | 88562 | 70745 | 23701 | 45630 | 65891 | 58220 | 35442 |
| 68  | 11119 | 16519 | 27384 | 90199 | 79210 | 76965 | 99546 | 30323 | 31664 |
| 69  | 41101 | 17336 | 48951 | 53674 | 17880 | 45260 | 08575 | 49321 | 36191 |
| 70  | 32123 | 91576 | 84221 | 78902 | 82010 | 30847 | 62329 | 63898 | 23268 |
| 71  | 26091 | 68409 | 69704 | 82267 | 14751 | 13151 | 93115 | 01437 | 56945 |
| 72  | 67680 | 79790 | 48462 | 59278 | 44185 | 29616 | 76531 | 19589 | 83139 |
| 73  | 15184 | 19260 | 14073 | 07026 | 25264 | 08388 | 27182 | 22557 | 61501 |
| 74  | 58010 | 45039 | 57181 | 10238 | 36874 | 28546 | 37444 | 80824 | 63981 |
| 75  | 56425 | 53996 | 86245 | 32623 | 78858 | 08143 | 60377 | 42925 | 42815 |
| 76  | 82630 | 84066 | 13592 | 60642 | 17904 | 99718 | 63432 | 88642 | 37858 |
| 77  | 14927 | 40909 | 23900 | 48761 | 44860 | 92467 | 31742 | 87142 | 03607 |
| 78  | 23740 | 22505 | 07489 | 85986 | 74420 | 21744 | 97711 | 36648 | 35620 |
| 79  | 32990 | 97446 | 03711 | 63824 | 07953 | 85965 | 87089 | 11687 | 92414 |
| 80  | 05310 | 24058 | 91946 | 78437 | 34365 | 82469 | 12430 | 84754 | 19354 |
| 81  | 21839 | 39937 | 27534 | 88913 | 49055 | 19218 | 47712 | 67677 | 51889 |
| 82  | 08833 | 42549 | 93981 | 94051 | 28382 | 83725 | 72643 | 64233 | 97252 |
| 83  | 58336 | 11139 | 47479 | 00931 | 91560 | 95372 | 97642 | 33856 | 54825 |
| 84  | 62032 | 91144 | 75478 | 47431 | 52726 | 30289 | 42411 | 91886 | 51818 |
| 85  | 45171 | 30557 | 53116 | 04118 | 58301 | 24375 | 65609 | 85810 | 18620 |
| 86  | 91611 | 62656 | 60128 | 35609 | 63698 | 78356 | 50682 | 22505 | 01692 |
| 87  | 55472 | 63819 | 86314 | 49174 | 93582 | 73604 | 78614 | 78849 | 23096 |
| 88  | 18573 | 09729 | 74091 | 53994 | 10970 | 86557 | 65661 | 41854 | 26037 |
| 89  | 60866 | 02955 | 90288 | 82136 | 83644 | 94455 | 06560 | 78029 | 98768 |
| 90  | 45043 | 55608 | 82767 | 60890 | 74646 | 79485 | 13619 | 98868 | 40857 |
| 91  | 17831 | 09737 | 79473 | 75945 | 28394 | 79334 | 70577 | 38048 | 03607 |
| 92  | 40137 | 03981 | 07585 | 18128 | 11178 | 32601 | 27994 | 05641 | 22600 |
| 93  | 77776 | 31343 | 14576 | 97706 | 16039 | 47517 | 43300 | 59080 | 80392 |
| 94  | 69605 | 44104 | 40103 | 95635 | 05635 | 81673 | 68657 | 09559 | 23510 |
| 95  | 19916 | 52934 | 26499 | 09821 | 87331 | 80993 | 61299 | 36979 | 73599 |
| 96  | 02606 | 58552 | 07678 | 56619 | 65325 | 30705 | 99582 | 53390 | 46357 |
| 97  | 65183 | 73160 | 87131 | 35530 | 47946 | 09854 | 18080 | 02321 | 05809 |
| 98  | 10740 | 98914 | 44916 | 11322 | 89717 | 88189 | 30143 | 52687 | 19420 |
| 99  | 98642 | 89822 | 71691 | 51573 | 83666 | 61642 | 46683 | 33761 | 47542 |
| 100 | 60139 | 25601 | 93663 | 25547 | 02654 | 94829 | 48672 | 28736 | 84994 |

# REFERENCES

Adams, J. A. (1972). Research and the future of engineering psychology. *American Psychologist, 27*, 615–622.

Adams, J. L. (1974). *Conceptual blockbusting: A guide to better ideas,* San Francisco: W. II. Freeman.

Adamson, R. E. (1952). Functional fixedness as related to problem solving: A repetition of three experiments. *Journal of Experimental Psychology, 44*, 288–291.

Allport, D. A. (1968). Phenomenal simultaneity and the perceptual moment hypothesis. *British Journal of Psychology, 59*, 395–406.

American Psychological Association. (1973). *Ethical principles in the conduct of research with human participants,* Washington, DC.

Amsel, A. (1962). Frustrative nonreward in partial reinforcement and discrimination learning: Some recent history and a theoretical extension. *Psychological Review, 69*, 306–328.

Amsel, A. (1971). Partial reinforcement: Effects on vigor and persistence. In K. W. Spence and J. T. Spence (eds.), *The psychology of learning and motivation,* vol. 1 New York: Academic Press.

Angell, J. R. (1907). The province of functional psychology. *Psychological Review, 14*, 61–91.

Annett, J. (1969). *Feedback and human behaviour,* Baltimore: Penguin.

Asch, S. E. (1951). Effect of group pressure upon the modification and distortion of judgment. In H. Guetzkow (ed.), *Groups, leadership, and men.* Pittsburgh: Carnegie.

Asch, S. E. (1956). Studies of independence and conformity: I. A minority of one against a unanimous majority. *Psychological Monographs, 70, 9.* (Whole No. 416).

Asch, S. E. (1958). Effects of group pressure upon the modification and distortion of judgments. In E. E. Maccoby, T. M. Newcomb, and E. L. Hartley (eds.), *Readings in social psychology* (3rd ed.). New York: Holt, pp. 174–183.

Azrin, N., and Foxx, R. M. (1974). *Toilet training in less than a day.* New York: Simon & Schuster.

Azrin, N. H., Holz, W., Ulrich, R. E., and Goldiamond, I. (1961). The control of content of conversation through reinforcement. *Journal of the Experimental Analysis of Behavior, 4,* 25–30.

Balota, D. A., and Neely, J. H. (1980). Test-expectancy and word-frequency effects in recall and recognition. *Journal of Experimental Psychology: Human Learning and Memory, 6,* 576–587.

Barber, T. X., and Silver, M. J. (1968). Fact, fiction, and the experimenter bias effect. *Psychological Bulletin Monograph Supplement, 70* (6, pt. 2), 1–29.

Barefoot, J. C., Hoople, H., and McClay, D. (1972). Avoidance of an act which would violate personal space. *Psychonomic Science, 28,* 205–206.

Barker, R. G., and Wright, H. F. (1951). *One boy's day.* New York: Harper and Row.

Barker, R. G. (1968). *Ecological psychology.* Stanford, CA: Stanford University Press.

Baron, R. A. (1972). Aggression as a function of ambient temperature and prior anger arousal. *Journal of Personality and Social Psychology, 21,* 183–189.

Baron, R. A., and Bell, P. A. (1976). Aggression and heat: The influence of ambient temperature, negative affect, and a cooling drink on physical aggression. *Journal of Personality and Social Psychology, 33,* 245–255.

Baron, R. A., Byrne, D., and Kantowitz, B. H. (1977). *Psychology: Understanding behavior.* Philadelphia: Saunders.

Baron, R. A., and Byrne D. (1977). *Social psychology: Understanding human interaction* (2d ed.). Boston: Allyn and Bacon.

Bartley, X. (1958). *Principles of perception.* New York: Harper.

Baumrind, D. (1964). Some thoughts on ethics of research: After reading Milgram's "Behavioral study of obedience." *American Psychologist, 19,* 421–423.

Beck. S. B. (1963). Eyelid conditioning as a function of CS intensity, UCS intensity, and Manifest Anxiety Scale score. *Journal of Experimental Pschology, 66,* 429–438.

Benchley, R. W. (1937). The early worm. In R. W. Benchley, *Inside Benchley.* New York: Harper.

Bergin, A. E. (1966). Some implications of psychotherapy research for therapeutic practice. *Journal of Abnormal Psychology. 71,* 235–246.

Bergin, A. E. (1971). The evaluation of therapeutic outcomes. In A. E. Bergin and S. L. Garfield, *Handbook of psychotherapy and behavior change.* New York: Wiley.

Berkeley, G. A. (1963). *A treatise concerning the principles of human knowledge.* New York: Bobbs-Merrill, (originally published 1710).

Bevan, W. (1976). The sound of the wind that's blowing. *American Psychologist, 31*, 481–491.

Beveridge, W. I. B. (1957). *The art of scientific investigation.* New York: Random House.

Blough, D. S. (1958). A method for obtaining psychophysical thresholds from pigeons. *Journal of the Experimental Analysis of Behavior, 1*, 31–43.

Blough, D. S. (1961). Experiments in animal psychophysics. *Scientific American, 205*, 32.

Boring, E. G. (1950). *A history of experimental psychology.* New York: Appleton-Century-Crofts.

Bower, G. (1961). A contrast effect in differential conditioning. *Journal of Experimental Psychology, 62*, 196–199.

Bower, G. H. (1972). Mental imagery and associative learning. In L. Gregg (ed.), *Cognition in learning and memory.* New York; Wiley.

Bramel, D., and Friend, R. (1981). Hawthorne, the myth of the docile worker, and class bias in psychology. *American Psychologist, 36*, 867–878.

Bridgman, P. W. (1945). Some general principles of operational analysis. *Psychological Review, 52*, 246–249.

Broadbent, D. E. (1958). *Perception and communication.* London: Pergamon.

Broadbent, D. E., and Gregory, M. (1963). Division of attention and the decision theory of signal detection. *Proceedings of the Royal Society B, 158*, 222–231.

Broadbent, D. E. (1971). *Decision and stress.* New York: Academic Press.

Broad, W. and Wade, M. (1982). *Betrayer's of the truth: Fraud and deceit in the halls of science.* New York: Simon and Schuster.

Brown, J. (1958). Some tests of the decay theory of immediate memory. *Quarterly Journal of Experimental Psychology, 10*, 12–21.

Brown, R. (1962). Models of attitude change. In R. Brown, E. Galanter, E. H. Hess, and G. Mandler (eds.), *New directions in psychology*, vol. 1. New York: Holt, Rinehart, and Winston.

Buss, A. H. (1961). *The psychology of aggression.* New York: Wiley.

Calhoun, J. B. (1962). Population density and social pathology. *Scientific American, 206*, 139–148.

Calhoun, J. B. (1966). The role of space in animal sociology. *Journal of Social Issues, 22*, 46–58.

Calhoun, J. B. (1971). Space and the strategy of life. In A. H. Esser (ed.), *Environment and behavior: The use of space by animals and men.* New York: Plenum.

Campbell, D. T., and Stanley, J. C. (1966). *Experimental and quasi-experimental designs for research.* Chicago: Rand McNally.

Campbell, D. T., and Erlebacher, A. (1970)(a). How regression artifacts in quasi-experimental evaluations can mistakenly make compensatory education look harmful. In J. Helmuth (ed.), *Compensatory education: A national debate*, vol. 3, *Disadvantaged child*. New York: Brunner/Mazel.

Campbell, D. T., and Erlebacher, A. (1970)(b). Reply to the replies. In J. Helmuth (ed.), *Compensatory education: A national debate*, vol. 3, *Disadvantaged child*. New York: Brunner/Mazel.

Capaldi, E. J. (1964). Effect of N-length, number of different N-lengths, and number of reinforcements on resistance to extinction. *Journal of Experimental Psychology, 68*, 230–239.

Capaldi, E. J. (1966). Partial reinforcement: A hypothesis of sequential effects. *Psychological Review, 73*, 459–477.

Capaldi, E. J. (1971). Memory and learning: A sequential viewpoint. In W. K. Honig and P. H. R. James (eds.), *Animal memory*. New York: Academic Press.

Carter, L. F. (1941). Intensity of conditioned stimulus and rate of conditioning. *Journal of Experimental Psychology, 28*, 481–490.

Circirelli, V. et. al. (June 1969). The impact of Head Start: An evaluation of the effects of Head Start on children's cognitive and affective development. A report presented to the Office of Economic Opportunity pursuant to Contract B89–4536. Westinghouse Learning Corporation, Ohio University. (Distributed by Clearinghouse for Federal Scientific and Technical Information, U.S. Department of Commerce, National Bureau of Standards, Institute for Applied Technology, PB 184 328).

Circirelli, V. G. (1970). The relevance of the regression artifact problem to the Westinghouse-Ohio evaluation of Head Start: A reply to Campbell and Erlebacher. In J. Helmuth (ed.), *Compensatory education: A national debate*, vol. 3, *Disadvantaged child*. New York: Brunner/Mazel.

Clark, H. H. (1973). The language-as-fixed effect fallacy: A critique of language statistics in psychological research. *Journal of Verbal Learning and Verbal Behavior, 12*, 335–359.

Cohen, S., Glass, D. C., and Singer, J. E. (1973). Apartment noise, auditory discrimination and reading ability in children. *Journal of Experimental Social Psychology, 9*, 407–422.

Cook, T. D., and Campbell, D. T. (1979). *Quasi-experimentation: Design and analysis issues for field settings*. Chicago: Rand McNally.

Coren, S., and Girgus, J. S. (1978). *Seeing is deceiving: The psychology of visual illusions*. Hillsdale, NJ.: Erlbaum.

Cornsweet, T. N. (1962). The staircase method in psychophysics. *American Journal of Psychology, 75*, 485–491.

Cosgrove, M. P., Kohl, G. A., Schmidt, M. J., and Brown, D. R. (1974). Chromatic substitution with stabilized images: Evidence for chromatic-specific pattern processing in the human visual system. *Vision Research, 14*, 23–30.

Craik, F. I. M. (1977). Age differences in human memory. In J. E. Birren and W. Schaie (eds.), *Handbook of the psychology of aging*. New York: Van Nostrand Reinhold.

Crowder, R. G. (1970). The role of one's own voice in immediate memory. *Cognitive Psychology, 1*, 157–178.

Crowder, R. G. (1976). *Principles of learning and memory.* Hillsdale, NJ.: Erlbaum.

Crowder, R. G. (1978). Mechanisms of auditory backward masking in the stimulus suffix effect. *Psychological Review, 85*, 502–524.

Darley, J. M., and Latané, B. (1968). Bystander intervention in emergencies: Diffusion of responsibility. *Journal of Personality and Social Psychology, 8*, 377–383.

de Bono, E. (1971). *The use of lateral thinking.* Harmondworth, England: Penguin.

DeGreene, K. B. (1970). (ed.), *Systems psychology.* New York: McGraw-Hill.

Dewey, J. (1896). The reflex are concept in psychology. *Psychological Review, 3*, 357–370.

Doll, R. (1955). Etiology of lung cancer. *Advances in Cancer Research, 3*, 1–50.

Dollard, J., and N. E. Miller, (1950). *Personality and psychotherapy.* New York: McGraw-Hill.

Drickamer, L. C., and Vesey, S. H. (1982). *Animal behavior: Concepts, processes, and methods.* Boston: Willard Grant Press.

Duncker, K. (1945). On problem solving. *Psychological Monographs, 58(5)*, 1–112. Whole No. 270.

Ebbinghaus, H. (1913). *Memory: A contribution to experimental psychology.* New York: Columbia University Press. (Reprinted by Dover, 1964).

Egeth, H., Blecker, D. L., and Kamlet, A. S. (1969). Verbal interference in a perceptual comparison task. *Perception and Psychophysics, 6*, 355–356.

Elliot, L. A., and Strawhorn, R. J. (1976). Interference in short-term memory from vocalization: aural versus visual modality differences. *Journal of Experimental Psychology: Human Learning and Memory, 2*, 705–711.

Ericsson, K. A., and Simon, H. A. (1979). Verbal reports as data. *Psychological Review, 87*, 215–251.

Eron, L. D., Huesmann, L. R., Letkowitz, M. M., and Walder, L. O. (1972). Does television violence cause aggression? *American Psychologist, 27*, 253–263.

Evans, J. W., and Schiller, J. (1970). How preoccupation with possible regression artifacts can lead to a faulty strategy for the evaluation of social action programs: A reply to Campbell and Erlebacher. In J. Helmuth (ed.), *Compensatory education: A national debate*, vol. 3, *Disadvantaged child.* New York: Brunner/Mazel.

Eysenck, H. J. (1952). The effects of psychotherapy: An evaluation. *Journal of Consulting Psychology, 16*, 319–324.

Eysenck, H. J., and Eaves, L. J. (1981). *The cause and effects of smoking.* New York: Gage.

Festinger, L., Riecken, H. W., and Schachter, S. (1956). *When prophecy fails.* Minneapolis: University of Minnesota Press.

Festinger, L. (1957). *A theory of cognitive dissonance.* Stanford, CA: Stanford University Press.

Fischhoff, B., Slovic, P., and Lichtenstein, S. (1977). Knowing with certainty: The appropriateness of extreme confidence. *Journal of Experimental Psychology: Human Perception and Performance, 3,* 522–564.

Freedman, J. L., and Landauer, T. K. (1966). Retrieval of long-term memory: "Tip-of-the-tongue" phenomenon. *Psychonomic Science, 4,* 309–310.

Galle, O. R., Gove, W. R., and McPherson, J. M. (1972). Population density and pathology: What are the relations for man? *Science, 176,* 23–30.

Garner, W. R., Hake, H. W., and Ericksen, C. W. (1956). Operationism and the concept of perception. *Psychological Review, 63,* 149–159.

Gamer, W. R. (1974). *The processing of information and structure.* Hillsdale, NJ.: Erlbaum.

Gick, M. L., and Holyoak, K. J. (1980). Analogical problem solving. *Cognitive Psychology, 12,* 306–355.

Gick, M. L., and Holyoak, K. J. (1983). Schema induction and analogical transfer. *Cognitive Psychology, 15,* 1–38.

Glucksberg, S., and Weisberg, R. W. (1966). Verbal behavior and problem solving: Some effects of labelling in a functional fixedness problem. *Journal of Experimental Psychology, 71,* 659–664.

Glucksberg, S. (1966). *Symbolic processes.* Dubuque, Iowa: William C. Brown.

Glucksberg, S., and Danks, J. H. (1967). Functional fixedness: Stimulus equivalence mediated by semantic-acoustic similarity. *Journal of Experimental Psychology, 74,* 400–405.

Glucksberg, S., and Danks, J. H. (1968). Effects of discriminative labels and nonsense labels upon availability of novel function. *Journal of Verbal Learning and Verbal Behavior, 7,* 72–76.

Grant, D. A., and Schneider, D. E. (1948). Intensity of the conditioned stimulus and strength of conditioning: I. The conditioned eyelid response to light. *Journal of Experimental Psychology, 38,* 690–696.

Grant, D. A. (1964). Classical and operant conditioning. In A. W. Melton (ed.), *Categories of human learning.* New York: Academic Press.

Green, D. M., and Swets, J. A. (1966). *Signal detection theory and psychophysics.* New York: Wiley.

Greenspoon, J. (1955). The reinforcing effect to two spoken sounds on the frequency of two responses. *American Journal of Psychology. 68,* 409–416.

Gregory, R. L. (1970). *The intelligent eye.* New York: McGraw-Hill.

Grice, G. R. (1966). Dependence of empirical laws upon the source of experimental variation. *Psychological Bulletin, 66,* 488–498.

Grice, G. R., and Hunter, J. J. (1964). Stimulus intensity effects depend upon the type of experimental design. *Psychological Review, 71*, 247–256.

Guilford, J. P. (1967). *The nature of human intelligence.* New York: McGraw-Hill.

Hadamard, J. (1945). *The psychology of invention in the mathematical field.* Princeton, NJ.: Princeton University Press.

Hanson, N. R. (1958). *Patterns of discovery.* Cambridge: Cambridge University Press.

Hart, B. M., Allen, K. E., Buell, J. S., Harris, F. R., and Wolf, M. M. (1964). Effects of social reinforcement on operant crying. *Journal of Experimental Child Psychology, 1*, 145–153.

Hart. J. T. (1965). Memory and the feeling-of-knowing experience. *Journal of Educational Psychology, 56*, 208–216.

Herman, C. P., and Polivy, J. (1975). Anxiety, restraint, and eating behavior. *Journal of Abnormal Psychology, 84*, 666–672.

Herrnstein, R. J. (1973). *I.Q. in the meritocracy.* Boston: Little, Brown.

Hibscher, J. A., and Herman, C. P. (1977). Obesity, dieting, and the expression of "obese" characteristics. *Journal of Comparative and Physiological Psychology, 91*, 374–380.

Hopkins, R. H., Edwards, R. E., and Cook, C. L. (1973). Presentation modality, distractor modality, and proactive interference in short-term memory. *Journal of Experimental Psychology, 98*, 362–367.

Horowitz, L. M. (1974). *Elements of Statistics for Psychology and Education.* New York: McGraw-Hill.

Huesmann, L. R., Eron, L. D., Lefkowitz, M. M., and Walder, L. O. (1973). Television violence and aggression: The causal effect remains. *American Psychologist. 28*, 617–620.

Huff, D. (1954). *How to lie with statistics.* New York: Norton.

Hull, C. L. (1943). *Principles of behavior.* New York: Appleton-Century-Crofts.

Hunt, E., and Lansman, M. (1975). Cognitive theory applied to individual differences. In W. K. Estes (ed.), *Handbook of learning and cognitive processes*, vol. I. Hillsdale, NJ.: Erlbaum.

Huxley, A. (1946). *Science, liberty and peace.* New York: Harper.

Hyman, R. (1964). *The nature of psychological inquiry.* Englewood Cliffs, NJ: Prentice-Hall.

Isaacs, W., Thomas, J., and Goldiamond, I. (1960). Application of operant conditioning to reinstate verbal conditioning in psychotics. *Journal of Speech and Hearing Disorders, 25*, 8–12.

Ittelson, W., and Kilpatrick, F. (1952). Experiments in perception. *Scientific American, 185*, 50–55.

Jacobs, J. (1961). *Death and life of great American cities.* New York: Random House.

Jensen, A. R. (1969). How much can we boost I.Q. and scholastic achievement? *Harvard Educational Review, 39*, 1–123.

Jones, B. (1972). Development of cutaneous and kinesthetic local-ization by blind and sighted children. *Developmental Psychology, 6,* 349–352.

Kahneman, D. (1973). *Attention and effort.* Englewood Cliffs, NJ.: Prentice-Hall.

Kangas, J., and Bradway, K. (1971). Intelligence at middle age: A thirty-eight year follow-up. *Developmental Psychology, 5,* 333–337.

Kantowitz, B. H. (1974). Double stimulation. In B. H. Kantowitz (ed.), *Human information processing—Tutorials in performance and cognition.* Hillsdale, NJ.: Erlbaum.

Kantowitz, B. H., and Sorkin, R. D. (1983). Human factors: Un-derstanding people-system relationships. New York: John Wiley & Sons.

Kaufman, L. (1974). *Sight and mind.* New York: Oxford.

Kaufman, L. (1979). *Perception: The world transformed.* New York: Oxford.

Kelman, H. (1966). Deception in social research. *Transaction, 3,* 20–24.

Keppel, G., and Underwood, B. J. (1962). Proactive inhibition in short term retention of single items. *Journal of Verbal Learning and Verbal Behavior, 1,* 153–161.

Kerlinger, F. (1973). *Foundations of behavioral research.* New York: Basic Books.

King, D. J. (1968). Retention of connected meaningful material as a function of presentation and recall. *Journal of Experimental Psychology, 77,* 676–683.

Kintsch, W., and Kozminsky, E. (1977). Summarizing stories after reading and listening. *Journal of Educational Psychology, 69,* 491–499.

Kinzel, A. F. (1970). Body-buffer zone in violent prisoners. *The American Journal of Psychiatry, 127,* 59–64.

Knight, J. L., and Kantowitz, B. H. (1974). Speed-accuracy trade-off in double stimulation: Effects on the first reponse. *Memory and Cognition, 2,* 522–532.

Knight, J. L., and Kantowitz, B. H. (1975). Probing for semantic and acoustic instructions in dichotic messages: Effects of pre-sentation rate. Paper presented to Midwestern Psychological As-sociation, Chicago.

Koestler, A. (1964). *The act of creation.* New York: Dell.

Köhler, W. (1927). *The mentality of apes.* London: Routledge and Kegan Paul.

Konečni, J. J., and Slamecka, N. J. (1972). Awareness in verbal nonoperant conditioning: An approach through dichotic listen-ing. *Journal of Experimental Psychology, 94,* 248–254.

Krasner, L. (1962). Behavior control and social responsibility. *American Psychologist, 17,* 199–204.

Latané, B., and Darley, J. M. (1970). *The unresponsive bystander—why doesn't he help?* New York: Appleton-Century-Crofts.

Latané, B., Williams, K., and Harkins, S. (1979). Many hands make light the work: Causes and consequences of social loafing. *Journal of Personality and Social Psychology, 37*, 822–832.

Latané, B., Harkins, S. G., and Williams, K. Many hands make light the work: Social loafing as a social disease. Manuscript awarded the 1980 Socio-Psychological prize by the American Association for the Advancement of Science.

Lewin, K. (1948). *Resolving social conflicts.* New York: Harper.

Lichtenstein, S., and Fischhoff, B. (1977). Do those who know more also know more about how much they know? *Organizational Behavior and Human Performance, 20*, 159–183.

Littlepage, G. E. and Whiteside, H. D. (1976). Trick or treat: A field of study of social class differences in altruism. *Bulletin of the Psychonomic Society, 7*, 491–492.

Locke, J. (1959). *An essay concerning human understanding.* New York: Dover. First published in 1960.

London, P. (1964). *The modes and morals of psychotherapy.* New York: Holt, Rinehart & Winston.

Luchins, A. S. (1942). Mechanization in problem solving: The effect of Einstellung. *Psychological Monographs, 54(6)*, 1–95. Whole No. 248.

Maller, D., and Fenman, J. (1979). *21 days to a trained dog.* New York: Simon and Schuster.

Marriot, P. (1949). Size of working groups and output. *Occupational Psychology, 23*, 4757.

Marshall, J. E., and Heslin, R. (1975). Boys and girls together: Sexual composition and the effect of density and group size on cohesiveness. *Journal of Personality and Social Psychology, 31*, 952–961.

Marx, M. H. (1963). The general nature of theory construction. In M. H. Marx (ed.), *Theories in contemporary psychology.* New York: Macmillan.

Mason, W. A. and Lott, D. F. (1976). Ethology and comparative psychology. In M. R. Rosenweig and L. W. Porter (eds.), *Annual Review of Psychology*, vol. 26. Palo Alto, CA. Annual Reviews Inc.

Massaro, D. W. (1975). *Experimental psychology and information processing:* Chicago: Rand McNally.

Mayer, R. E. (1983). *Thinking, Problem Solving, Cognition.* New York: Freeman.

McDougall, W. (1908). *Introduction to social psychology.* London: Methuen.

Medawar, P. B. (1969). *Induction and intuition in scientific thought.* London: Methuen.

Middlemist, R. D., Knowles, E. S., and Matter, C. F. (1976). Personal space invasions in the laboratory: Suggestive evidence for arousal. *Journal of Personality and Social Psychology, 33*, 541–546.

Milgram, S. (1963). Behavioral study of obedience. *Journal of Abnormal and Social Psychology, 67*, 371–378.

Milgram, S. (1964). Group pressure and action against a person. *Journal of Abnormal and Social Psychology, 69,* 137–143.

Milgram, S. (1964). Issues in the study of obedience: A reply to Baumrind. *American Psychologist, 19,* 848–852.

Milgram, S. (1965). Some conditions of obedience and disobedience to authority. *Human Relations, 18,* 57–76.

Milgram, S. (1972). Interpreting obedience: Error and evidence; A reply to Orne and Holland. In A. G. Miller (ed.), *The social psychology of psychological research.* New York: Free Press.

Milgram, S. (1974). *Obedience to authority: An experimental view.* New York: Harper & Row.

Miller, D. B. (1977), Roles of naturalistic observation in comparative psychology. *American Psychologist, 32,* 211–219.

Mitroff, I., and Kilmann, R. H. (1975). On evaluating scientific research: The contribution of the psychology of science. *Technological Forecasting and Social Change, 8,* 163–174.

Moede, W. (1927). Die richtlinien der leistungs—Psychologie. *Industrielle Psychotechnik, 4,* 193–207.

Moriarity, T. (1975). Crime, commitment, and the responsive bystander: Two field studies. *Journal of Personality and Social Psychology, 31,* 370–376.

Morin, R. E., and Grant, D. A. (1954). Learning and performance of a key-pressing task as a function of the degree of spatial stimulus-response correspondence. *Journal of Experimental Psychology, 49,* 39–47.

Murdock, B. B., and Walker, K. D. (1969). Modality effects in free recall. *Journal of Verbal Learning and Verbal Behavior, 8,* 665.

Natsoulas, T. (1967). What are perceptual reports about? *Psychological Bulletin, 67,* 249–272.

Nelson, T. O., Fehling, M. R., and Moore-Glascock, J. (1979). The nature of semantic savings for items forgotten from long-term memory. *Journal of Experimental Psychology: General, 108,* 225–250.

Nisbett, R. E. (1968). Determinants of food intake in obesity. *Science, 159,* 1254–1255.

Nisbett, R. E. (1972). Hunger, obesity, and the ventromedial hypothalamus. *Psychological Review, 79,* 433–453.

Nisbett, R. E., and Wilson, T. D. (1977). Telling more than we can know: Verbal reports on mental processes. *Psychological Review, 84,* 231–259.

Norman, D. A. (1969). Memory while shadowing. *Quarterly Journal of Experimental Psychology, 21,* 85–94.

Notterman, J. M., and Mintz, D. E. (1965). *Dynamics of response.* New York: Wiley.

Olton, R. M., and Johnson, D. M. (1976). Mechanisms of incubation in creative problem solving. *American Journal of Psychology, 89,* 617–630.

Orne, M. T. (1962). On the social psychology of the psychological experiment: With particular reference to demand characteristics and their implications. *American Psychologist, 17,* 776–783.

Orne, M. T., and Evans, T. J. (1965). Social control in the psychological experiment: Antisocial behavior and hypnosis. *Journal of Personality and Social Psychology, 1,* 189–200.

Orne, M. T., and Holland, C. C. (1968). On the ecological validity of laboratory deceptions. *International Journal of Psychiatry, 6,* 282–293.

Orne, M. T. (1969). Demand characteristics and the concept of quasi-controls. In R. Rosnow and R. L. Rosenthal (eds.), *Artifact in behavioral research.* New York: Academic Press.

Pachella, R. G. (1974). The interpretation of reaction time in information-processing research. In B. H. Kantowitz (ed.), *Human information processing—Tutorials in performance and cognition.* Hillsdale, NJ.: Erlbaum.

Padilla, A. M. (1971). Analysis of incentive and behavioral contrast in the rat. *Journal of Comparative and Physiological Psychology, 45,* 464–470.

Paivio, A. (1969). Mental imagery in associative learning and memory. *Psychological Review, 76,* 241–263.

Parsons, H. M. (1974). What happened at Hawthorne? *Science, 183,* 922–931.

Pavlov, I. P. (1963). *Lectures on conditioned reflexes.* New York: International Publishers.

Peirce, C. S. (1877). The fixation of belief. *Popular Science Monthly.*

Penney, C. G. (1974). Order of report and interference effects in four-channel bisensory memory. *Canadian Journal of Psychology, 28,* 371–382.

Penney, C. (1975). Modality effects in short-term verbal memory. *Psychological Bulletin, 82,* 68–84.

Peterson, L. R., and Peterson, M. J. (1959). Short term retention of individual items. *Journal of Experimental Psychology, 58,* 193–198.

Pfungst, O. (1911). *Clever Hans, the horse of Mr. Von Osten: a contribution to experimental, animal, and human psychology.* (Trans. by C. L. Rahn). New York: Holt.

Piliavin, I. M., Rodin, J., and Piliavin, J. A. (1969). Good samaritanism: An underground phenomenon? *Journal of Personality and Social Psychology, 13,* 289–299.

Piliavin, I. M., Piliavin, J. A., and Rodin, J. (1975). Costs, diffusion, and the stigmatized victim. *Journal of Personality and Social Psychology, 32,* 429–438.

Poincaré, H. (1929). *The foundations of science.* New York: Science House, Inc.

Posner, M. I. (1973). *Cognition: An introduction.* Glenview, IL: Scott, Foresman.

Rapoport, A. (1975). Towards a redefinition of density. *Environment and Behavior, 7,* 133–158.

Rescorla, R. A. (1967). Pavlovian conditioning and its proper control procedures. *Psychological Review, 74,* 71–80.

Reynolds, G. S. (1975). *A primer of operant conditioning.* Glenview, IL: Scott, Foresman.

Roediger, H. L., and Crowder, R. G. (1976). Recall instructions and the suffix effect. *American Journal of Psychology, 89,* 115–125.

Roediger, H. L., and Neely, J. H. (1982). Retrieval blocks in episodic and semantic memory. *Canadian Journal of Psychology, 36,* 213–242.

Rosenthal, R., and Fode, K. (1963). The effects of experimenter bias on the performance of the albino rat. *Behavioral Science, 8,* 183–189.

Rosenthal, R. (1966). *Experimenter effects in behavioral research.* New York: Appleton-Century-Crofts.

Rosenthal, R. (1969). Interpersonal expectations: Effects of the experimenter's hypothesis. In R. Rosenthal and R. L. Rosnow (eds.), *Artifact in behavioral research.* New York: Academic Press.

Rosenthal, R. and Rosnow, R. L. (eds.), (1969). *Artifact in behavioral research.* New York: Academic Press.

Rosenthal, R. T. (1966). *Experimenter effects in behavioral research.* New York: Appleton-Century-Crofts.

Ross, E. A. (1908). *Social psychology.* New York: Macmillan.

Rowland, L. W. (1939). Will hypnotized persons try to harm themselves or others? *Journal of Abnormal and Social Psychology, 34,* 114–117.

Rozelle, R. M., and Campbell, D. T. (1969). More plausible rival hypotheses in the cross-lagged panel correlation technique. *Psychological Bulletin, 71,* 74–80.

Russell, B. (1951). *Unpopular essays.* New York: Simon & Schuster.

Ryle, G. (1949). *The concept of mind.* London: Hutchinson.

Saegert, S., Mackintosh, E., and West, S. (1975). Two studies of crowding in urban public spaces. *Environment and Behavior, 7,* 159–184.

Scarborough, D. L. (1972). Stimulus modality effects on forgetting in short term memory. *Journal of Experimental Psychology, 95,* 285–289.

Schachter, S. (1968). Obesity and eating. *Science, 161,* 751–756.

Schachter, S., Goldman, R., and Gordon, A. (1968). Effects of fear, food deprivation and obesity on eating. *Journal of Personality and Social Psychology, 10,* 91–97.

Schacter, D. L. (1983). Feeling of knowing in episodic memory. *Journal of Experimental Psychology, 9,* 39–54.

Schaie, K. W. (1977). Quasi-experimental designs in the psychology of aging. In J. E. Birren and K. N. Schail (eds.), *Handbook of psychology and aging.* New York: Van Nostrand.

Schmidt, M. J., Fulgham, D. D., and Brown, D. R. (1971). Stabilized images: The search for pattern elements. *Perception and Psychophysics, 10,* 295–299.

Schmidt, S. R. (1983). The effects of recognition and recall test expectancies on the retention of prose. *Memory and Cognition, 11,* 172–180.

Schultz, D. (1981). *A history of modern psychology*. New York: Academic Press.

Schutte, W., and Zubek, J. P. (1967). Changes in olfactory and gustatory sensitivity after prolonged visual deprivation. *Canadian Journal of Psychology, 21,* 337–345.

Scott, W. A., and Wertheimer, M. (1962). *Introduction to psychological research*. New York: Wiley.

Sidman, M. (1960). *Tactics of scientific research*. New York: Basic Books.

Seligman, M. E. P. and Maier, S. (1967). Failure to escape traumatic shock. *Journal of Experimental Psychology, 74,* 1–9.

Seligman, M. E. P. (1970). On the generality of the laws of learning. *Psychological Review, 77,* 406–418.

Sherif, M. (1935). A study of some social factors in perception. *Archives of Psychology,* No. 187.

Sidman, M. (1960). *Tactics of scientific research*. New York: Basic Books.

Silveira, T. (1971). Incubation: The effect of interruption timing and length on problem solution and quality of problem processing. Doctoral dissertation, University of Oregon.

Skinner, B. F. (1955). Freedom and the control of men. *American Scholar, 25,* 47–65.

Skinner, B. F. (1956). A case history in scientific method. *American Psychologist, 11,* 221–233.

Skinner, B. F. (1957). *Verbal behavior*. New York: Appleton-Century-Crofts.

Skinner, B. F. (1960). Pigeons in a pelican. *American Psychologist, 15,* 28–37.

Skinner, B. F. (1961). Teaching machines. *Scientific American, 205,* 90–102.

Skinner, B. F. (1963). The flight from the laboratory. In M. Marx, (ed.), *Theories in contemporary psychology*. New York: Macmillan.

Smith, E. R., and Miller, F. D. (1978). Limits on perceptions of cognitive processes: A reply to Nisbett and Wilson. *Psychological Review, 85,* 355–362.

Spence, K. W. (1948). The postulates and methods of 'behaviorism.' *Psychological Review, 55,* 67–78.

Spielberger, C. D., and DeNike, L. D. (1966). Descriptive behaviorism versus cognitive theory in verbal operant conditioning. *Psychological Review, 73,* 306–326.

Sternberg, S. (1969). Memory scanning: Mental processes revealed by reaction time experiments. *American Scientist, 57,* 421–457.

Stevens, S. S. (1961). The psychophysics of sensory functions. In W. A. Rosenblith, *Sensory communication*. Cambridge: M.I.T. Press.

Stroud, J. M. (1956). The fine structure of psychological time. In H. Quastler (ed.), *Information theory in psychology*. Glencoe, IL: Free Press.

Stroop, J. R. (1935). Studies of interference in serial verbal reactions. *Journal of Experimental Psychology, 18,* 643–662.

Suppes, P., and Zinnes, J. L. (1963). Basic measurement theory. In R. Luce, R. Brush, and E. Galanter (eds.), *Handbook of mathematical psychology*, vol. 1. New York: Wiley.

Taylor, D. A. (1976). Stage analysis of reaction time. *Psychological Bulletin, 83*, 161–191.

Theios, J. (1975). Reaction time measurements in the study of memory processes: Theory and data. In G. Bower (ed.), *The psychology of learning and motivation*, vol. 7. New York: Academic Press.

Thorndike, E. L. (1898). Animal intelligence: An experimental study of the associative processes in animals. *Psychological Review Monograph Supplement, 2.*

Tulving, E. and Pearlstone, Z. (1966). Availability versus accessibility of information in memory for words. *Journal of Verbal Learning and Verbal Behavior, 5*, 381–391.

Tversky, A., and Kahneman, D. (1971). Belief in the law of small numbers. *Psychological Bulletin, 76*, 105–110.

Tversky, A., and Kahneman, D. (1974). Judgments under uncertainty: Heuristics and biases. *Science, 185*, 1124–1131.

Underwood, B. J. (1975). Individual differences as a crucible in theory construction. *American Psychologist. 30*, 128–134.

Verplanck, W. S. (1955). The control of the content of conversation: Reinforcement of statements of opinion. *Journal of Abnormal and Social Psychology, 51*, 668–676.

Warren, R. M. (1963). Are loudness judgments based on distance estimates? *Journal of the Acoustical Society of America, 35*, 613–614.

Watson, J. B. (1913). Psychology as the behaviorist views it. *Psychological Review, 20*, 158–177.

Watson, J. B. (1919). *Psychology from the standpoint of a behaviorist.* Philadelphia: Lippincott.

Watson, J. B. (1925). *Behaviorism.* New York: Norton.

Watson, J. B., and Rayner, R. (1920). Conditioned emotional reactions. *Journal of Experimental Psychology, 3*, 1–14.

Waugh, N. C., and Norman, D. A. (1965). Primary memory. *Psychological Review, 72*, 89–104.

Webb, E. J., Campbell, D. T., Schwartz, R. D., and Sechrest, L. (1966). *Unobtrusive measures: Nonreactive research in the social sciences.* Chicago: Rand McNally.

Weizenbaum, J. (1976). Computer power and human reason. San Francisco. W. H. Freeman.

Williams, R. L. and Long, J. D. (1979). *Toward a self-managed life style* (2d ed.). Boston: Houghton-Mifflen.

Wolf, M. M., and Risley, T. R. (1971). Reinforcement: Applied research. In R. Glaser (ed.), *The nature of reinforcement.* New York: Academic Press.

Wrightsman L. S., and Deaux, K. K. (1981). *Social psychology in the 80's* (2d ed.). Monterey, CA: Brooks-Cole.

Wundt, W. (1874). *Principles of physiological psychology.* Leipzig: Engelmann.

Young, P. C. (1952). Antisocial uses of hypnosis. In L. M. LeCron (ed.), *Experimental hypnosis.* New York: Macmillan.

Zajonc, R. B. (1962). Response suppression in perceptual defense. *Journal of Experimental Psychology, 64,* 206–214.

# GLOSSARY

**Abscissa**  the horizontal axis (or x-axis) in a graph

**Analysis of variance**  a statistical test appropriate for analyzing reliability from experiments with any number of levels on one or more independent variables

**Anthropomorphizing**  attributing human characteristics or emotions, such as happiness, to animals

**Autokinetic phenomenon**  when a person is placed in a dark room and a single spot of light is shown, it appears to move

**Balanced Latin square**  counterbalancing scheme in which each condition is preceded and followed equally often by every other condition

**Behavior modification**  therapy that involves the use of operant conditioning procedures, emphasizing observation of behavior, its controlling variables, and contingent reinforcement

**Behaviorism**  school of psychology originated by John Watson that directed psychologists' attention to the study of overt behavior, not mind nor mental events

**Beta**  a statistic in signal detection theory related to the criterion adopted by the observer

**Between group variance**  a measure of the dispersion among groups in an experiment

**Between-subject design**  an experimental design in which each subject is tested under only one level of each independent variable

**Carry-over effect**  relatively permanent effect that testing subjects in one condition has on their later behavior is another condition

**Case study** intensive investigation of a particular instance, or case, of some behavior; does not allow inferences of cause and effect, but is merely descriptive

**Categorized list** words used in memory experiments that are related by being members of the same category, e.g., articles of furniture: chair, bed, sofa, table

**Ceiling effect** see scale attenuation

**Central tendancy** descriptive statistics indicating the center of a distribution of scores; see mean, median, and mode

**Classical conditioning** a basic form of learning in which stimuli initially incapable of evoking certain responses acquired the ability to do so through repeated pairing with other stimuli (unconditioned stimuli) that are able to elicit such responses

**Conceptual replication** attempt to demonstrate an experimental phenomenon with an entirely new paradigm or set of experimental conditions (see coverging operations)

**Conditioned response** (CR) the learned response to a conditioned stimulus

**Conditioned stimulus** (CS) an originally neutral stimulus that, through repeated pairings with an unconditioned stimulus, acquires the ability to elicit the response originally produced only by the unconditioned stimulus

**Confounding** simultaneous variation of a second variable with an independent variable of interest so that any effect on the dependent variable cannot be attributed with certainty to the independent variable; inherent in correlational research

**Continuous reinforcement** schedule of reinforcement in which a reward follows every time the appropriate behavior is emitted

**Control variable** a potential independent variable that is held constant in an experiment

**Converging operations** a set of related lines of investigation that all bolster a common conclusion

**Correlation** a measure of the extent to which two variables are related, not necessarily causally

**Correlation coefficient** a number that can vary from $-1.00$ to $+1.00$ and indicates the degree of relation between two variables

**Counterbalancing** refers to any technique used to vary systematically the order of conditions in an experiment to distribute the effects of time of testing (e.g., practice and fatigue) so they are not confounded with conditions

**Cross-sectional studies** taking a large sample of the population of various ages at one time and testing them (contrast with longitudinal studies)

**Crossover interaction** when the effect of one independent variable on a dependent variable reverses at different levels of a second independent variable

**d'** a statistic in signal detection theory related to the sensitivity of the observer

**Data** the scores obtained on a dependent variable

**Deduction** reasoning from the general to the particular

**Degrees of freedom** the number of values free to vary if the total number of values and their sum are fixed

**Demand characteristics** those cues available to subjects in an experiment that may enable them to determine the purpose of the experiment, or what is expected by the experimenter

**Dependent variable** the variable measured and recorded by the experimenter

**Descriptive statistics** methods of organizing and summarizing data

**Deviant case analysis** investigation of similar cases that differ in outcome in an attempt to specify the reasons for the different outcomes

**Dichotic listening** a test of attention in which two separate messages are delivered simultaneously one to each ear

**Direct replication** repeating an experiment as closely as possible to determine whether or not the same results will be obtained

**Discriminative stimulus** one that indicates whether or not a response will be reinforced

**Dispersion** the amount of spread in a distribution of scores

**Distribution** a set of values on a variable

**Dizygotic** developing from two different fertilized eggs

**Double blind** experimental technique in which neither the subject nor the experimenter knows which subjects are in which treatment conditions

**Dualism** idea that the mind and the body are separate entities

**Einstellung** see set

**Expirical** relying upon or derived from observation or experiment

**Ex post facto** literally, from after the fact; refers to conditions in an experiment that are not determined prior to the experiment, but only after some manipulation has occurred naturally

**Experiment** the systematic manipulation of some factors in the environment in order to observe the effect of this manipulation upon behavior

**Experimenter bias** the effect that an experimenter may unknowingly exert on results of an experiment, usually in a direction favoring the experimenter's hypothesis

**Experimental control** holding constant extraneous variables in an experiment so that any effect on the dependent variable can be attributed to manipulation of the independent variable

**Extinction** weakening or eliminating conditioned responses by withholding reinforcement

**Face validity** when a measuring instrument intuitively seems to measure what it is supposed to measure

**Factorial design** an experimental design in which each level of every independent variable occurs with all levels of the other independent variable

**False alarm** incorrectly reporting the presence of a signal on a trial where only noise occurred

**Field research** research conducted in natural settings where subjects typically do not know that they are in an experiment

**Floor effect** see scale attenuation

**Frequency distribution** a set of scores arranged in order along a distribution indicating the number of times each score occurs

**Functional fixedness** inability to use an object in a new context if it has already served a different function

**Functionalism** school of psychology concerned with the function of psychological processes

**Generality of results** the issue of whether or not a particular experimental result will be obtained under different circumstances, such as with a different subject population or in a different experimental setting

**Gestalt psychology** school of psychology emphasizing whole patterns as being important in perception rather than the artificial analysis of experience into parts as in structuralism

**Hawthorne effect** refers to conditions where performance in an experiment is affected by the knowledge of participants that they are in an experiment; see demand characteristics

**Heterogeneous** dissimilar; varying from others

**Higher order interaction** interaction effects involving more than two independent variables in multifactor experiments

**Histogram** a frequency distribution in which the height of bars in the graph indicates the frequency of a class of scores; also called a bar graph

**Hit** the correct detection of a signal that has been presented

**Homogeneous** similar; of the same kind as others

**Hypothesis** a testable statement that offers a predicted relationship between dependent and independent variables

**Independent variable** the variable manipulated by the experimenter

**Induction** reasoning from the particular to the general

**Inferential statistics** procedures for determining the reliability and generality of a particular experimental finding

**Instrumental conditioning** conditioning in which a subject learns to make a response that leads to a reward or prevents a punishment, in contrast to classical conditioning, no eliciting stimulus is presented

**Intelligence** mental age (as determined by a test) divided by chronological age $\times$ 100

**Interaction** an experimental result that occurs when the levels of one independent variables are differentially affected by the levels of other independent variables

**Interpolated task** one used to fill the interval between the study of material and its recall in memory experiments

**Interstimulus interval** the time between two successive stimuli, usually (but not always) measured from the onset of the first to the onset of the second

**Longitudinal studies** testing one group of people repeatedly as they age (contrast with cross-sectional studies)

**Main effect** when the effect of one independent variable is the same at all levels of another independent variable

**Matched groups design** experimental design in which subjects are matched on some variable assumed to be correlated with the dependent variable and then randomly assigned to conditions

**Mean** measure of central tendency; the sum of all the scores divided by the number of scores

**Median** measure of central tendency; the middle score of a distribution, or the one that divides a distribution in half

**Modality effect** different effects on retention often produced by visual and auditory presentation; auditory presentation usually produces better memory for the last few items in a series than does visual presentation

**Mode** measure of central tendency; the most frequent score

**Monitoring task** a form of dichotic listening where observers are not required to verbalize a message as it is presented

**Monotonic relationship** relationship between two variables in which an increase on one variable is accompanied by a consistent increase or decrease on the other variable

**Monozygotic** developing from the same fertilized cgg

**Naturalistic observation** description of naturally occurring events without intervention on the part of the investigator

**Nonreactive** term to describe observations that are not influenced by the presence of the investigator; nonreactive methods are also referred to as unobtrusive

**Normal distribution** one producing a symmetric, bell-shaped curve

**Null hypothesis** states that the independent variable will have no effect on the dependent variable

**Null result** an experimental outcome where the dependent variable was not influenced by the independent variable

**Observational methods** research techniques based on simply observing behavior without trying to manipulate it experimentally

**One-tailed test** test that places the rejection area at one end of a distribution

**Operant conditioning** see instrumental conditioning

**Operational definition** a definition of a concept in terms of the operations that must be performed to demonstrate the concept

**Ordinate** the vertical axis (or y-axis) in a graph

**Parallel forms** two alternative forms of a test

**Partial reinforcement** schedule of reinforcement in which a reward follows a desired response only on some occasions when it is emitted

**Partial reinforcement effect** the greater resistance to extinction exhibited for responses learned under partial rather than continuous schedules of reinforcement

**Pay off** the explicit monetary costs and benefits associated with making a certain type of response to a stimulus

**Personal space** the physical area surrounding a person that a person will defend

**Phenomenological report** subject's description of his or her own behavior or state of mind; also called subjective report

**Placebo effect** improvement often shown in drug effectiveness studies where patients believe they have received a drug although they actually received an inert substance

**Population** the total set of potential observations from which a sample is drawn

**Positive reinforcer** an event that serves to make a preceding response more probable

**Power (of a statistical test)** the probability of rejecting the null hypothesis in a statistical test when it is in fact false

**Primacy effect** better retention of information occurring at the beginning of a list, relative to information in the middle

**Proactive interference** forgetting produced by prior learning

**Probability** estimate of the likelihood that a particular event will occur

**Problem** a vague question that is too general to be tested without additional refinement; see Hypothesis

**Pseudoconditioning** a temporary elevation in the amplitude of the conditioned response that is not due to association between the conditioned stimulus and unconditioned stimulus

**Random groups design** when subjects are randomly assigned to conditions in a between-subjects design

**Range** descriptive measure of dispersion; the difference between the largest and smallest score in a distribution

**Reaction time** the time between the onset of a stimulus and the making of a response to that stimulus

**Reactive** term to describe observations that are influenced by (or may be, in part, a reaction to) the detected presence of the investigator

**Recall** measure of retention in which reproduction of material is required

**Recency effect** better retention of information at the end of a list, relative to information in the middle

**Recognition** measure of retention in which familiarity of information is judged

**Regression artifacts** an artifact in the measurement of change on a variable when groups of subjects who scored at the extremes on the variable are tested again; see regression to the mean

**Regression to the mean** tendency for extreme measures on some variable to be closer to the group mean when remeasured, due to unreliability of measurement

**Reliability** refers to the repeatability of an experimental result; inferential statistics provide an estimation of how likely it is that a finding is repeatable; also refers to the consistency of a test or measuring instrument determined by computing a correlation between scores obtained by subjects taking the test twice (test-retest reliability), or taking two different parallel forms of the test, or scores obtained on each half of the test (split-half reliability)

**Replication** the repetition of an earlier experiment to duplicate (and perhaps extend) its findings (also see systematic replication)

**Reproduceability** see reliability

**Respondent conditioning** see classical conditioning

**Retrieval cue** information presented at the time of a memory test to aid recall

**Retroactive interference** forgetting of material produced by learning of subsequent material

**Reversal (ABA) design** small n design in which a subject's behavior is measured under a baseline (A) condition, then an experimental treatment is applied during the B phase and any changes in behavior are observed; finally, the original baseline (A) conditions are reinstituted to ensure that the experimental treatment was responsible for any observed change during the B phase.

**ROC function** (receiver operating characteristic) a plot graphing hits against false alarms

**Sample** observations selected from a population

**Scale attenuation effects** difficulties in interpreting results when performance on the dependent variable is either nearly perfect (a ceiling effect) or nearly lacking altogether (a floor effect)

**Scatterplot** a graphical relationship indicating degree of correlation between two variables made by plotting the scores of individuals on two variables

**Serial position** order in which information appears when studied for a later memory test

**Serial position curve** graphical representation of retention as a function of the input position of the information; usually memory is better for the first items (primacy effect) and the last items (recency effect) than for those in the middle; this typical finding is referred to as the serial position effect

**Set** the effect of expectancy of cognition; for example, if the people solve problems in one particular way, they will often approach new problems in the same set way even when the original strategy is no longer effective

**Shadowing task** a form of dichotic listening where the listener is required to repeat aloud (shadow) the message presented in one ear as it occurs

**Shaping** a technique for conditioning a desired response by rewarding successive approximations to that response

**Significance level** probability that an experimental finding is due to chance, or random fluctuation, operating in the data

**Skewed distribution** a nonsymmetrical distribution

**Small n design** research design utilizing a small number of subjects

**Speed-accuracy tradeoff** in reaction time experiments, the ability of the responder to substitute changes in the percentage of correct responses for changes in speed of responding

**Split-half reliability** determining reliability of a test by dividing the test items into two arbitrary groups and correlating the scores obtained on the two halves of the test

**Split-litter technique** randomly assigning animals from the same litter to different groups; a type of matched groups design

**Standard deviation** descriptive measure of dispersion; square root of the sum of squared deviations of each score from the mean divided by the number of scores

**Standard error of the mean** the standard deviation of the distribution of sample means

**Stratified sampling techniques** subjects are placed into groups of some dimension ("stratified") and then randomly sampled from these different strata and assigned to different conditions

**Stress** a psychological state of an organism when there is a disparity between its ability to cope with demands of the environment and the level of such demands

**Structuralism** school of psychology originated by Wundt where the primary task of psychology was considered to be the analysis of the structure of conscious experience through introspection

**Subject representativeness** determination of generality of results across different subject populations

**Subject variable** some characteristics of people that can be measured or described, but cannot be varied experimentally (e.g. height, weight, sex, I.Q., etc.)

**Subjective report** see phenomenological report

**Subtractive method** a technique by Donders to estimate the amount of time required for various mental operations by subtracting one component from another

**Survey research** technique of obtaining a limited amount of information from a large number of people, usually through random sampling

**Systematic replication** repeating an experiment while varying numerous factors considered to be irrelevant to the phenomenon to see if it will survive these changes

**Test retest reliability** giving the same test twice in succession over a short interval to see if the scores are stable, or reliable; generally expressed as a correlation between scores on the tests

**Threshold** in psychophysics a hypothetical barrier that incoming stimuli must cross before they can be preceived

**Token economy** technique of positive reinforcement often employed by mental hospitals and other institutions in which patients are rewarded for socially constructive behavior by tokens, which may later be exchanged for privileges

**Truncated range** a problem in interpreting low correlations; the amount of dispersion (or range) or scores on one variable may be small, thus leading to the low correlation found

**Two-tailed test** test that places the rejection area at both ends of a distribution

**Type 1 error** probability that the null hypothesis is rejected when it is in fact true; equals the significance level

**Type 2 error** failure to reject the null hypothesis when it is in fact false

**Unconditioned response** (UCR) response made to an unconditioned stimulus

**Unconditioned stimulus** (UCS) stimulus that can elicit a response in the absence of conditioning

**Unobtrusive methods** see nonreactive

**Variable representativeness** determination of generality of results across different manipulations of an independent variable or different dependent variables

**Variance** measure of dispersion; the standard deviation squared

**Weber's law** the smallest perceptible difference (the just noticeable difference) between two stimuli (e.g., weights) can be stated as a ratio between the stimuli that is independent of their magnitude

**What if experiment** an experiment performed to see what might happen rather than to test a specific hypothesis

**Within group variance** a measure of the dispersion among subjects in the same group in an experiment

**Within-subject design** an experimental design in which each subject is tested under more than one level of the independent variable

# NAME INDEX

**531**

# SUBJECT INDEX

†